MAKING HISTORY

MAKING HISTORY

The Struggle for Gay
and Lesbian Equal Rights

1 9 4 5 – 1 9 9 0

An Oral History

ERIC MARCUS

HarperCollins*Publishers*

HarperCollins books may be purchased for educational, business, or sales promotional use. For information, please call or write: Special Markets Department, HarperCollins Publishers, Inc., 10 East 53rd Street, New York, NY 10022. Telephone: (212) 207-7528; Fax: (212) 207-7222.

FIRST EDITION

Designed by Irving Perkins Associates, Inc.

Library of Congress Cataloging-in-Publication Data
Marcus, Eric.
  Making history : the struggle for gay and lesbian equal rights, 1945–1990: an oral history/Eric Marcus.—1st ed.
     p. cm.
  Includes index.
  ISBN 0-06-016708-4 (cloth)
     1. Gay liberation movement—United States—History. 2. Gays—United States. I. Title.
HQ76.8.U5M36   1992
305.9'0664—dc20   90-56389

92 93 94 95 96 CC/RRD 10 9 8 7 6 5 4

To my mother, Cecilia Marcus, and grandmother,
May Sperling Marcus. And for Homer, again.

When the dust settles and the pages of history are written, it will not be the angry defenders of intolerance who have made the difference. That reward will go to those who dared to step outside the safety of their privacy in order to expose and rout the prevailing prejudices.

—John Shelby Spong,
Episcopal Bishop of the Diocese
of Newark, New Jersey

Contents

PART FOUR
1973–1981

PART FIVE
1981–1990

Preface and Acknowledgments

THE STRUGGLE for gay and lesbian equal rights did not begin on June 28, 1969, with a riot at New York City's Stonewall Inn. This misconception has been reflexively asserted in both the gay and mainstream press so often and for so many years that it would seem to be an unassailable fact.

Perhaps claiming the Stonewall riot as the birthplace of the struggle for gay rights is a necessary misconception. It offers the benefit of a clean starting point, an easy line of demarcation: Before Stonewall; after Stonewall. And it was an explosive and undeniably significant moment in history in which we can all take pride; gay people fought back against police repression. But there were many earlier confrontations, breakthroughs, and defining moments. By investing so much in Stonewall, we have elevated this one event to mythic status, diminishing all that came before and tying all that has happened since to a single point of origin.

In *Making History*, the Stonewall riot takes its place as part of a rich, heartbreaking, and ultimately heroic forty-five-year struggle for gay and lesbian equal rights in the United States.

I HAVE divided the story of the struggle for gay and lesbian equal rights into five parts. Part 1, covering 1945 to 1961, introduces men and women who were involved in the first gay and lesbian discussion groups and organizations in the years following World War II. They include a woman who in 1947 published the first lesbian newsletter (from her office typewriter) and a heterosexual psychologist who made the very radical claim, for 1956, that there were no discernable psychological differences between gay men and heterosexual men.

Part 2, 1961 to 1968, covers the rise of the "homophile" movement of the 1960s, which paralleled and gained inspiration from the black civil rights movement. The men and women in this section participated in some of the first public protests by gay people and were involved in a major confrontation with police at a fund-raising event in San Francisco in 1965.

Part 3, 1968 to 1973, covers the turbulent, divisive years of "gay liberation," which was strongly influenced by the rise of leftist and anti-Vietnam War activism in the late 1960s. This period was marked by a dramatic increase in the number of people and organizations involved in the gay rights struggle; a significant shift in goals and tactics; and swift, if not complete or uniform, progress toward achieving equal rights.

Part 4, 1973 to 1981, tracks both a period of significant broadening of the gay rights effort and an antigay backlash.

Part 5 begins in 1981, the year the mainstream press first published news of a perplexing disease affecting gay men in Los Angeles, New York, and San Francisco. The stories in this final section demonstrate the impact that AIDS has had on gay and lesbian rights and on the lives of gay people. They also exemplify the achievements of the gay rights effort after forty-five years.

As I started my research for *Making History*, I was struck by the fact that the gay and lesbian rights effort has been almost entirely ignored by mainstream historians, biographers, textbook writers, and encyclopedias. For example, in the most recent edition of *The Encyclopedia of American Facts and Dates*, published by Harper & Row in 1988, there is no entry related to homosexuality until 1973. That entry is about two Houston teenagers who were indicted for the homosexual abuse and murder of twenty-seven people over a three-year period. This coverage is actually an improvement over standard high school American history textbooks, like Prentice Hall's 1988 edition of *The United States: A History of the Republic*, in which gay men and lesbians are not even mentioned.

Fortunately, since the mid-1970s, a growing number of gay and lesbian historians, biographers, and journalists have begun to illuminate this dimension of American history. Their work served as the foundation for my research.

As I worked on *Making History*, I was constantly asked if I was going to include this or that well-known man or woman, usually individuals who had made important contributions to the struggle for gay rights. Almost without exception, I had to say no. The reason is simple: This is not a comprehensive history of the postwar struggle for gay and lesbian equal rights.

What I set out to do in this book is more modest. This is a selective oral history, an assortment of recollections representing a cross section of people, from high-profile leaders to little-known and largely forgotten contributors to the gay rights effort.

Early on, I was influenced by an essay on biography written by Lytton Strachey, the gay Bloomsbury writer, in the preface to his groundbreaking book *Eminent Victorians*:

It is not by the direct method of a scrupulous narration that the explorer of the past can hope to depict that singular epoch. If he is wise, he will adopt a subtler strategy. He will attack his subject in unexpected places; he will fall upon the flank, or the rear; he will shoot a sudden, revealing searchlight into obscure recesses, hitherto undivined. He will row out over that great ocean of material, and lower down into it, here and there, a little bucket, which will bring up to the light of day some characteristic specimen, from those far depths, to be examined with a careful curiosity.

Here and there I have lowered a bucket into the teeming and complex waters of the recent struggle for gay and lesbian equal rights. It is my hope that these few stories contribute to our understanding of that struggle and an appreciation of the life and times, the heroism, and the passion of the thousands of people who participated in it.

FOR THE three years I worked on this book, many people told me what a wonderful idea it was. I agree, but *Making History* wasn't my idea. Rick Kot, my editor at HarperCollins, came to me in the summer of 1988 and asked me if I would be interested in taking on the project. I was interested, and I'm grateful to Rick for his concept, encouragement, and editorial expertise during the years it took to get from idea to publication. I'm also grateful to my agent, Eric Ashworth, for helping me get from idea to signed contract. And many thanks to my editor's able assistant Sheila Gillooly.

For sharing research, background information, and contacts, I am indebted to Elver Barker, Allan Bérubé, Betty Berzon, Midge Costanza, Barbara Gittings, Jim Kepner, Morris Kight, Kay Lahusen, Phyllis Lyon, Del Martin, Craig Rodwell, Randy Shilts, Barbara Smith, Francis Smith, Manuela Soares, Tom Stoddard, Don Slater, and Randy Wicker. I am deeply indebted to historian John D'Emilio, whose landmark book, *Sexual Politics, Sexual Communities: The Making of a Homosexual Minority in the United States, 1940–1970*, was my primary resource for the thirty-year period covered in his book. And many thanks to Bill Walker and the Gay and Lesbian Historical Society of Northern California for unlimited access to the society's library.

To my Columbia School of Journalism professors Dick Blood and Judy Serrin, thank you for teaching me the importance of spelling a name right the first time and the importance of thorough reporting. I'm also grateful to Miriam Cohen, my history professor at Vassar College, for her sage advice on how to catalog and keep track of historical research.

My friends and family have graciously listened to my complaints; generously read various parts of the manuscript; and offered their comments and advice, their libraries, and even their homes. Thank you to Terry Anderson; Ellen Atkinson; Mark Burstein; David Calle; Kate Chieco; Kate Doyle; Brad Friedman; Posy Gering; Cynthia Grossman; Pat Kenealy; Steve Lawson; Hunter Madsen; Cecilia Marcus; Mynette Marcus; Armistead Maupin; Bill Megevick; Richard Moll; Ivor Muroff; Phil Roselin; Stuart Schear; Bill Smith; Rick Stryker; Howard, Peggy, Mara, Michael, and Nathaniel Swan-Levine; and Scott Terranella. A special thanks to Grandma May for the Macintosh on which I wrote this book.

Most important, my thanks to the many people who so generously gave their time to be interviewed for *Making History*. There would be no book without you.

Finally, to my beloved spouse, Barry Owen, who spent months editing the manuscript, not to mention years of soothing my angst, dispelling doubts, and allaying fears, and who never once answered, no, when I asked all too often, "Can I read this to you?" Thank you.

PART ONE
1945 – 1961

Taking Root

MORE THAN *four decades before World War II, the first organization for homosexuals was founded in Germany. The goals of the Scientific Humanitarian Committee, as the organization was called, included the abolition of Germany's antigay penal code, the promotion of public education about homosexuality, and the encouragement of homosexuals to take up the struggle for their rights. The rise of the Nazis put an end to the Scientific Humanitarian Committee and the homosexual rights movement in Germany.*

In the United States, except for a very short-lived effort in the 1920s in Chicago, the first stirrings of a sustained movement did not occur until after World War II, when homosexual men and women first met formally in Los Angeles homes to talk about their lives and their hopes.

What was it about this moment in time that made possible these meetings and the subsequent emergence of a gay rights movement? Historian Allan Bérubé, author of Coming Out Under Fire: The History of Gay Men and Women in World War Two, *attributes the "gay awakening" in part to both World War II and the Cold War, when gay people became targets of institutionalized discrimination in the military, government employment, and in urban gathering places across the country. In* Sexual Politics, Sexual Communities, *historian John D'Emilio also credits the war years, when "mobilization of American society for victory during World War II . . . uprooted tens of millions of American men and women, many of them young, and deposited them in a variety of nonfamiliar, often sex-segregated environments." World War II and its dislocations provided gay young people with unprecedented opportunities to meet one another and to discover that they were not alone. D'Emilio also credits the publication of the Kinsey reports on male and female sexual behavior, in 1948 and 1953, with permanently altering "the nature of public discussion of sexuality as well as* society's perception of its own behavior," and legitimizing "sexuality as a topic of discussion in the popular, mass circulation press." Americans first learned from the Kinsey reports that significant numbers of the nation's men and women had engaged in homosexual activity.

Following World War II, gay people in the United States first began to consider systematically the nature of homosexuality, share information about how to survive in a relentlessly hostile world, and organize secretive groups for gay men and women. At meetings of these organizations—including the Mattachine Society, the Daughters of Bilitis, and ONE, Inc.—gay people explored who and what they were; debated whether they were indeed sick, as psychiatrists claimed; sought the advice of experts; and argued among themselves what, if anything, they should—or could—do to improve their standing in American life. They also began using the courts to fight for their rights to congregate in bars without fear of arrest or police harassment and to send their magazines through the mail. When the local postmaster withheld the October 1954 issue of ONE magazine as "obscene, lewd, lascivious and filthy," the publishers, ONE, Inc., successfully fought their case all the way to the Supreme Court.

These early California-based gay organizations inspired new, usually tiny chapters in other cities around the country and even held national conventions, despite the bleak cultural and political climate. During the 1950s, gay people were linked to Communists and, like the Communists, were assumed to be subversive. They were purged from governmental jobs, hounded out of the military, and harassed at bars and other popular gathering spots as antigay campaigns swept the country.

During this era, the general public rarely had a glimpse of the homosexual subculture and nascent gay rights organizations, and then only as a result of police actions. For example, during a 1954 crackdown on gay men in Miami, local headlines screamed: "Perverts Seized in Bar Raids," "Crackdown on Deviate Nests Urged," and "Great Civilizations Plagued by Deviates." One article about the police sweeps revealed the existence in Los Angeles of a new gay organization and even a gay magazine. The article, published in the Miami Daily News, was entitled "How L.A. Handles Its 150,000 Perverts." It posed the question: "Is Greater Miami in danger of becoming a favorite gathering spot for homosexuals and sexual psychopaths?" It reported that In California "homosexuals have organized to resist interference by police. They have established their own magazine and are constantly crusading for recognition as a 'normal' group, a so-called 'third sex.' " The article went on to alert readers that the January 1954 issue of ONE magazine urged homosexuals in the Miami area to organize and sue the City of Miami Beach for their arrest in a raid "on homosexuals gathered at the 22nd Street bathing beach." It concluded with a police estimate that "between 6,000 and 8,000" homosexuals lived in the Miami *area. Without intending to, reports like this, which were not uncommon, helped spread the word to gay men and women that they were not alone and that it was possible to fight back against police repression.*

Politicians also helped raise the profile of homosexuality throughout the 1950s, particularly when they seized it as a campaign issue. For example, in San Francisco in 1959, Democratic mayoral candidate Russell Wolden charged incumbent Mayor George Christopher with making homosexuals feel so welcome in San Francisco that they moved their national organization to Christopher's "open city." To support his charge, Wolden offered as proof the fact that the number of bars, steam baths, nightclubs, theaters, and hotels catering to homosexuals in San Francisco had climbed to an "astounding" twenty-seven. ONE magazine scoffed at the claim, stating: "Such an anti-climax! When, in recent decades, have there ever been so few as 27 homosexual spots in San Francisco, or any comparable city?"

Wolden's emphasis on the specter of homosexuality in his campaign resulted in front-page press coverage, but he was uniformly criticized for raising the issue in the first place. ONE magazine reported that the San Francisco Examiner called Wolden's "smear campaign" an "unforgivable slur on San Francisco" and "explained that it's no news that homosexuals exist, but it is vicious to try to make political capital by stirring up public emotions on such a misunderstood subject." Although Wolden's use of homosexuality as a campaign issue backfired—he was trounced in the election—homosexuality has proved an effective weapon in campaigns for both local and national office right up to the present day.

Looking back to this time, when exposure of homosexuality could mean the loss of job, friends, family, and home, it seems remarkable that these first gay and lesbian organizations survived long enough to take root. But they not only survived, they established a foundation, however shaky, on which the gay rights struggle was built.

"Gay Gal"

Lisa Ben

In 1945, Lisa Ben,* a young secretary from northern California, set out for
Los Angeles to escape her overbearing parents. It was there that she first met
other women like her, and it was there that she first put her ideas about
homosexuality down on paper in her own "magazine" for lesbians, which
she produced using sheets of carbon paper on her office typewriter. Beginning
in mid-1947, Lisa produced nine editions of Vice Versa, which she distributed to her friends, who, in turn, passed them on to their friends.
Although Lisa was able to produce only ten copies of each edition, her
publication was almost certainly read by dozens, if not hundreds, before it
disappeared into history.

Lisa lives in a modest bungalow in a residential neighborhood in Bur-
bank, California. She has shoulder-length, wavy brown hair, which frames
a pretty, almost girlish, round face. Her eyes, set off by a colorful blouse and
coordinated slacks, sparkle. The small front room of her house, where she
spends most of her time, was tidy, a condition that Lisa explained was not
its usual state. An upright piano was on one wall, and a sofa on the
opposite wall. Lisa noted that she owns her home, paid for by a life's work
as a secretary.

Lisa Ben was born in 1921 and grew up in a rural northern California
town, where as a young woman of fourteen, she fell in love for the first time.

My first real lesbian love was in high school. I was very much taken
with her. She was fifteen. Of course, we did nothing below the waist,
if you'll pardon my being so frank. I loved her dearly, and we would
hug each other and that sort of thing. She was so spontaneous in her
hugs and kisses. We were so innocent about it and so joyous.

One time after she left me for another girl at high school, I was
crestfallen. My mother said to me, "You never did anything wrong
with her, did you?" I never thought that my love for this girl was
weird or strange, but when my mother asked me that, I suddenly

*Lisa Ben is a pseudonym. She chose not to use her real name because she is concerned that she
would upset elderly relatives who "might not take it well if they find out I'm gay."

realized that there was something not quite right. I immediately turned to her and said, "Well, no, Mother, what do you mean?" I was quite serious, because by *wrong* I thought she meant playing doctor when you're five or six years old or maybe stealing something or smoking cigarettes. And we hadn't done any of those things. Up until that time I would talk to my mother and say, "Oh, she's left me, and I'm so blue," but after that, I didn't mention the girl to her very much, and my mother and I just grew apart.

Later on, when I was living in the town where this girl lived, I ran into her on a rainy night. I remember I was hungry and I had holes in the bottoms of my shoes. I was walking to this man's place where I did secretarial work, and out from this hotel doorway came my friend. "Oh," she said, "How are you? I thought that was you. You know, I'm married now and you should see Junior. I have the cutest little boy." She had grabbed hold of my arm, and before I could think, I said, "Don't touch me!" I reacted that way because all through those years I had never resolved my love for her. Grabbing my arm the way she did was just like sticking me with a knife. She let go and said, "Well, if that's the way you feel about it." And I said, "I'm sorry, I didn't mean that. I'm not feeling well tonight, and I'm late to go to a job. Please excuse my saying that. I think that's very nice that you're married. Well, I've got to go now. Bye, bye." I went home and I was just crushed, although, since she was married, I wouldn't have taken her back. I didn't want her. She was tainted.

A FEW years later, in 1945, I moved down here to Los Angeles to get away from my mother, who was always coming by and going through my things. I didn't know any gay people when I moved here. As a matter of fact, I didn't even know the word *lesbian*. I knew how I felt, but I didn't know how to go about finding someone else who was like me, and there was just no way to find out in those days. Everything was pretty closed about things like that.

So it was a while before I knew other gay gals and learned from them what *gay* meant. I found out one day when I was sunning myself up on the top of the garage of the place where I had a room. Some other girls that lived in the building came up and spread out their towels and started to talk among themselves. I noticed that although there was plenty of talk, they never mentioned boys' names. I thought, *Well, gee, that's refreshing to hear some people talk who aren't always talking about their boyfriends and breakups.* I got started talking to them just out of friendliness.

* * *

I don't know what brought up the subject, but one of the girls turned to me and said, "Are you gay?" And I said, "I try to be as happy as I can under the circumstances." They all laughed. Then they said, "No, no," and told me what it meant. And I said, "Well, yes, I guess I am because I don't really go out and search for boyfriends. I don't care for that." So they said, "You must come with us to a girl's softball game." I went with them, but I didn't tell them that softball bored the tar out of me. I just don't care for sports. I know that's very funny for a lesbian to say. But it's true, I never have cared for sports. I went along to be with the crowd.

The next week or so they took me down to a gay bar called the If Club. When we all walked in there, why, someone was bringing a birthday cake to one of the booths. There were some girls sitting there, and they were all singing happy birthday. I looked around me, and tears came to my eyes—partly because of the cigarette smoke—and I thought, *How wonderful that all these girls can be together.* Of course, we called them girls at that time.

The girls could dance together there. I started dancing with one or the other of them who would come over and ask me. I never asked them. They asked me because I was obviously feminine. I had my hair long and I wore jewelry. I didn't look like a gay gal. I didn't have the close-cropped hair and the tailored look that was so prevalent in those days. I didn't do any of that jazz because I just didn't feel like it. And I was darned if I was going to do it just because everybody else did. I'm a girl and I've always been a girl. The only difference is I like girls.

So I danced quite a few dances. On the other side of this If Club was a bar, and men could come in off the street and they could sit at the bar and watch the girls dance. They were straight, as far as I knew. They would look, but they never talked to us or anything. The proprietor never let the men over where the girls were. That was forbidden.

After I got to the If Club and danced there with different people, I got invitations out to here and there, and I found out about a few more gay bars. I was always afraid that the police would come, although they didn't seem to bother the girls' clubs much. But I was afraid, and for that reason I never drank any strong liquor at any of the clubs. I would always have a Coke or a 7-Up or something like that so I'd have my wits about me if anything like that did happen. I didn't want to be so addled that they would take me off in the paddy wagon and put me in the pokey.

I was in a club down at the beach one time when the police came in. It wasn't a raid or anything; they just swaggered around. They were very unpleasant. They zeroed in on one boy in a bright red shirt. He had slightly long hair for that time. Today you wouldn't look at him twice. The police gathered around him in a circle, and I think they made him prove that he was a boy, but you couldn't see. I thought, *What a horrible thing to do to the poor fellow*. And then they came around to the tables. I was sitting with a couple of women who I didn't know too well. The policemen came over to our table. They had their notebooks out with pencils and asked us, "What are your names, please?" When they got to me I said, "My name is Wlmdom-mennn. . . ." And one of the policemen said, "What was that?" With my real name, if you slur it together you wouldn't know exactly what you said. And at that moment, the music was playing real loud. So the policeman made a pretense of taking down my name and walked off. I don't think he thought I was gay because I had on little bright red earrings and long hair and all. After that, the police left. They didn't take anyone with them. They were just intimidating people.

Well, I was frightened. I said, "I think I'll leave." The two women at the table said, "Don't leave yet. Wait a half hour because sometimes they lurk outside and then as you leave they'll take you in." So I waited for half an hour and then I got in the car and drove home. I never went back to that place again.

So I was never in a real raid, but I read about them. In those days, every once in a while there would be an article in the newspapers like, "Party of Perverts Broken Up at Such and Such," and there would be a list of names. Or else, you would hear thirdhand about a raid down at some boy's club, and they took in a certain amount of—they didn't say gay people, they would say perverts or some unpleasant name.

I didn't think I was a pervert or sick. Why would I be sick? I never ever wanted to be like everyone else and raise a family or have babies. In fact, the mere idea of having a baby in the physical sense appalled me. I would not have gone through that for anything in the world. I never was interested in that. On the other hand, I never wanted to go stomping around in boots either or be in the business world. I was a misfit all the way around I guess.

AROUND THIS time, I started writing *Vice Versa*, a magazine for gay gals. I published the first issue in June 1947. I wrote *Vice Versa* mainly to keep myself company. I called it *Vice Versa* because in those days our kind of life was considered a vice. It was the opposite of the lives that were being lived—supposedly—and understood and approved of

Lisa Ben in 1947, at the time she was working as a secretary for a Hollywood movie studio and publishing *Vice Versa*. *(Courtesy Lisa Ben)*

by society. And vice versa means the opposite. I thought it was very apropos. What else could I have called it?

I handed out the magazine for free. I never charged for it. I felt that that would be wrong. It was just some writing that I wanted to get off my chest. There was never anything in the magazine that was sexy or suggestive. I purposely kept it that way in case I got caught. They couldn't say that *Vice Versa* was dirty or naughty or against the law.

I typed the magazines at work. I had a boss who said, "You won't have a heck of a lot to do here, but I don't want you to knit or read a book. I want you always to look busy." He didn't care what I did as long as I got his work done first.

I put in five copies at a time with carbon paper, and typed it through twice and ended up with ten copies of *Vice Versa*. That's all I could manage. There were no duplicating machines in those days, and, of course, I couldn't go to a printer. I learned to be a very fast typist that way.

Then I would say to the girls as I passed the magazine out, "When you get through with this, don't throw it away, pass it on to another gay gal." We didn't use the term *lesbian* so much then. We just said *gay gal*. In that way *Vice Versa* would pass from friend to friend.

I wrote almost everything in the magazine, although once in a while I would get a contribution. I wrote book reviews, although there were very few books around at the time that said anything about lesbians. Even though it had been around since 1928, I wrote a book review on

The Well of Loneliness, Radclyffe Hall's lesbian novel. If there were any movies around that had the slightest tinge of two girls being interested in one another, I would take that story within the movie and play it up and say, "Such and such a movie has a scene in it with two young ladies and they seem to be interested in one another." And then I wrote poetry. Not a great deal of it, but a few things.

I was never afraid of being caught. That's the funny part about it. I never realized how serious it was. I blithely mailed these things out from the office with no return address, until one of my friends phoned me and said, "You know, you really shouldn't be doing that. It *is* against the law and it could land you in trouble." And I said, "Why? I don't mention the city it's from. I don't mention anybody's name. And it's not a dirty magazine by any stretch of the imagination." And she said, "Well, it would be dirty to the straight people because it's about girls, even though you have no cuss words or anything like that in it." So I decided I wouldn't mail it from the office anymore. But can you imagine the naïveté of me? Oh dear!

THERE'S AN essay I wrote for *Vice Versa* that I wanted to read to you. I haven't looked at it in a long time. It's one of my favorites, and I think it will give you some idea of the kinds of things I was thinking about back then. I'm not sure what issue it's in. Let me see. Oh, here it is, *Vice Versa*—"America's Gayest Magazine," Volume 1, Number 4, September 1947. The essay is called "Here to Stay."

Whether the unsympathetic majority approves or not, it looks as though the third sex is here to stay. With the advancement of psychiatry and related subjects, the world is becoming more and more aware that there are those in our midst who feel no attraction for the opposite sex.

It is not an uncommon sight to observe mannishly attired women or even those dressed in more feminine garb strolling along the street hand-in-hand or even arm-in-arm, in an attitude which certainly would seem to indicate far more than mere friendliness. And bright colored shirts, chain bracelets, loud socks, and ornate sandals are increasingly in evidence on many of the fellows passing by. The war had a great deal to do with influencing the male to wear jewelry, I believe, with the introduction of dog tags, identification bracelets, etc. Whether the war by automatically causing segregation of men from female company for long periods of time has influenced fellows to become more aware of their own kind is a moot question. It is interesting to note, however, that for quite some time the majority of teenage girls seem to prefer jeans and boy's shirts to neat, feminine attire. It is doubtful that this has any vast social significance, yet might not the masculine garb influence them toward adopting boyish mannerisms more than if they had adhered to typical girlish fashions?

Nightclubs featuring male and female impersonators are becoming increasingly prevalent. Even cafés and drive-ins intended for the average customer, when repeatedly patronized by inverts, tend to reflect a gay atmosphere. Such places are ever the center of attraction for a "gay crowd" and become known as a likely rendezvous in which to meet those of similar inclinations.

Books such as *Dianna* and *The Well of Loneliness* are available in inexpensive editions at book marts and even the corner drugstores. With such knowledge being disseminated through fact and fiction to the public in general, homosexuality is becoming less and less a taboo subject, and although still considered by the general public as contemptible or treated with derision, I venture to predict that there will be a time in the future when gay folk will be accepted as part of regular society.

Just as certain subjects once considered unfit for discussion now are used as themes in many of our motion pictures, I believe that the time will come when, say, Stephen Gordon will step unrestrained from the pages of Radclyffe Hall's admirable novel, *The Well of Loneliness*, onto the silver screen. And once precedent has been broken by one such motion picture, others will be sure to follow.

Perhaps even *Vice Versa* might be the forerunner of better magazines dedicated to the third sex, which in some future time might take their rightful place on the newsstands beside other publications, to be available openly and without restriction to those who wish to read them.

Currently appearing in many popular magazines are comprehensive articles on psychological differences between the two sexes, which are enlightening many women as to the unbridgeable gaps between the opposite sexes and why most of them in this rapidly changing world are unable to come to terms with each other on a mental and emotional basis.

In days gone by, when woman's domain was restricted to the fireside, marriage and a family was her only prospect, the home was the little world around which life revolved, and in which, unless wives were fortunate enough to have help, they had to perform innumerable household chores besides assuming the responsibility of bearing children. But in these days of frozen foods, motion picture palaces, compact apartments, modern innovations, and female independence, there is no reason why a woman should have to look to a man for food and shelter in return for raising his children and keeping his house in order unless she really wants to.

Today, a woman may live independently from man if she so chooses and carve out her own career. Never before have circumstances and conditions been so suitable for those of lesbian tendencies.

It surprises me now, reading this, because I haven't read it for so long. I had to stop and think, "Did I write that?" But I wrote it. I never thought of it as being bold at the time. I was just sort of fantasizing. It all has come to pass: the magazines, the movies, women that choose to live by themselves if they so wish, even if they aren't gay. Makes me feel like a fortuneteller. Yes, that's me in there. Although, I didn't sign my name to it.

I used no names in *Vice Versa* because that was back in 1947. I assured the few people who wrote articles and poems and things that I wouldn't use their names. I never used my own name in it either and never even thought of using the pseudonym "Lisa Ben" in those days. I first started using Lisa Ben in the 1950s when I wrote a story for *The Ladder*, the Daughters of Bilitis* magazine. I was a member of Daughters of Bilitis down here in L.A. Nobody used their names in that publication. So I signed my story, "Ima Spinster." I thought that was funny, but they didn't. They put up a big argument. I don't know whether they thought it was too undignified or what, but they objected strongly. If I had been as sure of myself as I am these days, I would have said, "All right, take it or leave it." But I wasn't. So I invented the name Lisa Ben. If you've ever played anagrams you know what it turns around into.

I PUBLISHED nine issues of *Vice Versa* before the job where I could do a lot of personal typing on my own came to an abrupt halt. Someone else bought the company, and almost everyone was let go—bosses, secretaries, errand boys, everybody. It was a mass exodus. Out we went. At the next job, I did not have an opportunity to do the magazine because the work load was heavier and there was no privacy. I didn't have a private office as I did in the first job. I thought, "Well I'll just have to give it up, that's all. I can't attempt to do the same here, or there would be repercussions." So the magazine folded.

I always hoped that I would stay in that one job and that I could turn out one of these a month and that I would be able to meet more and more girls this way, by handing out the magazine, and that I would become known among the group. You see, I was very lonely.

I didn't suppose anything could come of *Vice Versa* because I knew that in those days such magazines could not be sent to the printers and published. So it was just a sort of a gesture of love—of women loving women, and the whole idea of it. It was an enthusiasm that boiled over into these printed pages, and I wanted to give them to as many people

*An organization for lesbians founded in San Francisco in 1955.

as possible. It was a way of dividing myself into little bits and pieces and saying, "Here you are, take me! I love you all!"

AFTER I stopped publishing *Vice Versa*, I began writing gay parodies of popular songs and singing them in the clubs. I'll tell you how that came about. One of the clubs I went to was the Flamingo. They used to have Sunday afternoon dances there just for the gay kids.

Beverly Shaw, the well-known gay singer, used to perform there. They would put on a little show for us during the afternoon, and as evening wore on, the straight people would wander in just to see how the other half lived. The fellows would get up there on the stage and do their female-impersonation acts and they would tell the most atrocious dirty jokes, which dismayed me because I was such an idealist at the time and, in a way, such a little prude. One of them got up and made a terrible remark about Beverly Shaw and her being a butch or something. It was a very offensive joke, and all the straight people laughed at it. It burned me up that these guys would come up and tell dirty stories demeaning the gay people so that they could earn a buck by amusing these straights sitting out there.

I got disgusted so I never went back. At the time I thought, *What a stupid thing to do, to play into the hands of these outsiders by demeaning themselves in this way.* It offended me and it also made me very angry at the gay entertainers, because they weren't doing themselves any good by doing this. Sure they were making a little money, but look what they did to earn it.

That's when I started writing gay parodies of popular songs. I thought, *Well, I'm going to write some gay parodies, and they're going to be gay, but they are not going to be demeaning or filthy.* After I got two or three of them written, I went up in front of the microphone—they'd let a lot of us sing in front of the microphone in the afternoons, not in the evenings—and I sang a couple of these ditties. And boy, they went over.

My parodies were about gay life, with lyrics set to popular songs like "I'm going to sit right down and write my butch a letter and ask her won't she please turn femme for me." I didn't do a heck of a lot of singing, but once in a while if I had a new parody, I'd get up and sing it.

Some people might have thought my songs were political, but I was not politically active. Even today I'm not one to march in a parade or something. But I guess I did react to the female impersonators. I did not get up and tell them why I was writing parodies and performing them. I did not tell the gay entertainers, "You're doing yourselves a disfavor by doing such and such." I wouldn't have had the nerve to. I just presented something else instead, hoping that people would latch onto it and realize they didn't have to talk themselves down to be accepted.

I sang my songs at various clubs, but I never sang my gay parodies for straight people. I was very much what I would call a separatist. Now, the other day, somebody said a separatist is a lesbian who doesn't like gay men. Is that true? Well, that's not me. I had many gay men friends. Not boyfriends, you understand, but like brothers or cousins.

Anyway, I want to sing one of my songs for you. This song isn't a parody; it's one of my own compositions, my favorite. It's called "A Fairer Tomorrow." It echoes what I wrote in *Vice Versa*. I wrote it in the 1950s, I think.

Scattered are we over land, over sea.
How many we number will never be known.
Each one must learn from the start.
She must wear a mask on her heart.
And live in a world set apart.
A shy secret world of her own.

Here's to the days that we yearn for.
To give of our hearts as we may.
Love's always love in sincerity given, despite what the others may say.
The world cannot dare to deny us.
We've been here since centuries past.
And you can be sure our ranks will endure as long as this old world will last.

So here's to a fairer tomorrow, when we'll face the world with a smile.
The right one beside us to cherish and guide us.
This is what makes life worthwhile.
The right one beside us to cherish and guide us.
This is what makes life worthwhile.

I WAS recently asked to come up to San Francisco to do another "Evening with Lisa Ben" with my music. I'm tempted to do that, but I have to find somebody to take care of all my pussies. I have fifteen of them. I can't leave them for more than a day. That's a big question. That will give me something to do with my birthday. Usually, when my birthday comes, I go out to dinner by myself, and that's it for a celebration. Because when you get old, nobody thinks of you anymore. I don't feel particularly bad for myself. I love to go out to dinner. If I could afford to, I'd go out to dinner every night. But I can't, so I go once a year on my birthday. I choose a certain restaurant that I want to go to and then I go there and eat a good meal and enjoy it. I think if I went up to San Francisco, I'd probably enjoy my birthday a lot more. It'd be kind of fun. They want me up there, and I'm thrilled that they do. It's very flattering to me.

The Psychologist

Dr. Evelyn Hooker

PSYCHIATRISTS AND *psychologists in the postwar period, with few exceptions, believed that all homosexuals were mentally ill and that their illness was treatable: You could make a homosexual into a healthy heterosexual. Despite the near absence of dissenting opinion, some homosexuals refused to accept the prevailing dogma, but they were almost powerless to challenge it. Who would do the research and write the papers that questioned the opinions of the American Psychiatric and Psychological Associations?*

In 1945, a young gay man and his friends found an ally, Dr. Evelyn Hooker, a professor of psychology at UCLA. Through their encouragement, Dr. Hooker pursued pioneering research that led to her controversial and widely publicized conclusion that there was no inherent connection between homosexuality and psychopathology. Remarkably, until Dr. Hooker began her work, no one had scientifically tested the stated belief of the mental health profession that homosexuals were mentally ill.

When Dr. Hooker speaks, it is easy to imagine her commanding the attention of any audience, regardless of what she has to say. Now in her early eighties, she still has a powerful voice, which resonates through the double-height living room of her Santa Monica apartment. Hobbled by spinal arthritis, Dr. Hooker no longer moves with the same determination she once did. But as she took her seat in a comfortable high-backed easy chair in the living room of her book-filled apartment, cigarette in hand, speaking and gesturing emphatically, her independence of thought and strength of character were apparent.

It was during World War II, and I was teaching for the University Extension Division at UCLA and doing some research. Sammy was in one of my small introductory night classes. It became clear almost immediately that he was the most outstanding student in the class. He talked with me at intermission. He asked questions. There was just no doubt that he was *the* bright and shining star. You know, when a teacher finds a person like that, you fall for it hook, line, and sinker. Sammy would walk me downstairs after class. When he discovered that I was taking the streetcar home, to save gasoline, instead of driving, he began driving me home. Sammy had all the gasoline he wanted because he was writing million-dollar contracts between the air force and the aircraft industry in this area. He had a high school education. His father was a junk dealer.

Our friendship developed gradually, but I had an idiotic policy then. I thought instructors should not fraternize with their students. It wasn't until he had finished my course that Sammy called me and asked if he could come over. We spent the evening talking. When he left, Don, my first husband, turned to me and said, "Well, you told me everything else about him, why didn't you tell me he was queer?" I assume that's the word he used. It was the 1940s, after all. I said, "How could you possibly tell? You're crazy!" To which Don replied, "He did everything but fly out the window." Sam had a fragile build, but it wouldn't occur to you that he was gay. A thought might enter your head if you knew enough. But usually not, because he could put on a macho sort of manner. Not too exaggerated.

Sammy was very eager to get to know us. He and his lover, George, who was introduced as his cousin, invited us to dinner, and we went. George was a much older man. They wanted my approval so much that they were afraid to let me know they were gay. It was a delicious dinner.

Gradually, the fog came down and they became very good friends of ours. I liked them. They were very interesting people. I don't remember a time when Sammy or George said, "We're gay." They just gradually let down their hair. They adored Don. Don was very handsome, a marvelous talker. He was a sort of free-lance writer in Hollywood and also worked on radio and did some painting. He liked them very much. He wasn't bothered by the fact that they were gay. It wouldn't have occurred to him to be bothered by things like that because he had lived in Hollywood for a long time.

I've tried hard to remember what I knew about homosexuality before I met Sammy, George, and their friends. I didn't know much. As a matter of fact, when I was in college at the University of Colorado, *The Well of Loneliness* was circulating quietly. I remember reading it and thinking, *Oh, gee. I wouldn't like to have to live my life with all that secrecy.* It makes a lot of sense to me and has always made a lot of sense to me when gay people say, "I had to have been born this way because almost from the very beginning of my sexual consciousness I was interested in men" or "I was interested in women." I was interested in men from the time I was an adolescent, and there was never any question about that. I think that understanding, together with the rather extraordinary cross section of society into which I was introduced by Sammy, made the difference.

* * *

IN 1945, after I had known them for about a year, Sam and George invited us to join them on a Thanksgiving holiday in San Francisco. We had an absolutely marvelous time. Sammy was one of these people I described as an "If" personality. If all restraints were off, if he didn't have to behave like a businessman or a manager, then he was funny, funny, funny! He was dramatic, campy. On the first night we were there, Sammy insisted that we go to Finocchio's—to see female impersonators. My eyes were wide. I had never seen anything like that.

It was a tourist place, not a gay bar, where they did dance routines. And it was a place for transvestites and would-be transvestites. Besides the dance routines, there were two old bags from Oakland who did a lot of female patter; it was funny, funny, funny! You absolutely believed that these female impersonators were the real thing. Then all of a sudden, they took out their breasts and bounced them up and down on the stage! The whole house just came down. The part that was most impressive and most astonishing as you watched these— you can only say—beautiful women in their beautiful evening clothes was their feminine curves. Whether they were on hormones, I don't know.

After the show, we came back to the Fairmont Hotel on Nob Hill for a snack. I was unprepared for what came next. Sammy turned to me and said, "We have let you see us as we are, and now it is your scientific duty to make a study of people like us." Imagine that! This bright young man, somewhere in his early thirties, had obviously been thinking about this for a long time. And by "people like us" he meant, "We're homosexual, but we don't need psychiatrists. We don't need psychologists. We're not insane. We're not any of those things they say we are."

But I demurred. I was already teaching about eighteen hours a week and doing some animal research and God knows what else. I said, "I can't study you because you're my friends. I couldn't be objective about you." He replied that they could get me a hundred men, any number of men I wanted.

I couldn't see how I could do it. The thought of it was not in any way disturbing. It was not that. But I couldn't see how I could add anything more to what I was already doing. Sammy would not let me go. He said, "You're the person to do it. You know us. You have the training."

The purpose of the study Sammy wanted me to do was to show the world what they were really like. What he wanted countered was the kind of thing that I was teaching at the time. I taught everything in the psychology domain, including abnormal psychology and social psychology. You name it, I did it. And I probably taught the usual junk that homosexuality is psychopathological, that it's a criminal offense, and that it's a sin. I had no reason to think that these three things weren't true.

Sammy was pressing me hard, so I said I would talk to a colleague about it. I had a colleague with whom I shared an office. He was half-time, and I was part-time research. His name was Bruno Klopfer. Bruno was one of the world's greatest experts on the Rorschach test. So I went to Bruno and I told him about this suggestion. He jumped out of his chair and said, "You must do it, Eee-vah-leeeen! You must do it! Your friend is absolutely right. We don't know anything about people like him. The only ones we know about are the people who come to us as patients. And, of course, many of those who come to us are very disturbed, pathological. You must do it!" So I told Bruno I would do it. Bruno later served in my research as a judge. Unfortunately, Sammy was killed in a tragic automobile accident and never learned the outcome of what he urged me to do.

DESPITE MY decision to proceed with the study, I was so pressed in my work and my personal life that it was difficult to do the research. I started to do a sort of hand-to-mouth study. My gay friends—and their friends—all longed to be in the study, of course. And I would say, "Now, don't talk to anybody else about what you saw in the Rorschach. Don't tell them how many responses you had or what you saw." With the Rorschach, you show an individual ten different ink blots and ask him to describe what he sees. The normal number of responses might be something like fifty. Well, the first thing you know, I was getting three hundred to four hundred responses to the Rorschach test. If they are really creative, and many of these men were, then you're going to have a lot of unique responses and that, of course, is fine. But not three hundred or four hundred. They certainly were talking to their friends.

In the middle of all this, my own house of cards blew up. I had known for some time that Don, my husband, was an alcoholic. He finally decided to be divorced. He said, "It's enough that I destroy myself; I can't bear to destroy you." I wrote to my friends in the East and said, "If you hear of a job there, let me know." I'm a Hopkins Ph.D., and a lot of my psychological friends were in the East. I didn't think that I could stand staying in California. It was awful. Dreadful. And just like that, I was hired at Bryn Mawr, outside Philadelphia. It was crazy. So I just dropped the project. By then I had done maybe fifty or seventy-five interviews.

I stayed one year at Bryn Mawr. If I had stayed there, you never would have heard from me. I wouldn't have done the study without the guys in California. But after one year, I came back to my old job at UCLA. It was 1948. The housing situation was dreadful. It so happened that I met Helena, the wife of a man named Edward Hooker who. . . . Shall I make it dramatic? It was dramatic, I can tell you. They had this beautiful home in Brentwood. When I met Helena, she said, "I am leaving my husband and I'm not coming back." They lived on an acre of ground, with a big orchard in front. There was a main house and then there was a little house that Helena had been living in separately from her husband. She invited me for dinner and asked me, "Would you like me to talk my husband into renting you the house once I'm gone?" I said yes because it was perfect, only fifteen minutes from UCLA.

The fateful day arrived, and I went over for dinner, and after a bit Edward Hooker came out from the bedroom. He was deaf and wore a hearing aid. He walked over to me and said, "I'm Edward Hooker, and I think it's time we met." He knew we had something in common, that we took our Ph.D.s on the same commencement platform at Johns Hopkins University, in 1932, though we had never met until that day.

He was delighted to rent the little house to me. So Helena moved out, and I moved in. I had been told by Helena that Edward was very asocial and that I must not have any parties. One night I was coming home and I said to myself, "I don't care if he's asocial. He's always there working, working, working. And I'm going to stop and buy some food and I'm going to invite him to dinner."

I invited him to dinner. A few months later, we were having dinner again, and we were sitting in my living room, eating at the card table. I was giving him a lecture about how he had a lot to give to some woman and he ought to do something about it. He looked up at me, with his eyes twinkling, and said, "Do I have to go out and look?" I looked at him seriously and said, "Well, of course, how else do you think you're going to find someone?"

One thing led to another, of course. Edward was a distinguished professor at UCLA. He had a Guggenheim Fellowship at Cambridge, England, in 1950 to 1951. I had an appointment at the Tavistock Clinic in London, just by chance, you know. So at the end of that year, we were married in the Kensington Registry on High Street, and then returned home to California.

For the first time in my life I was really free. I was in love. I didn't have to teach eighteen hours a week. I had just heard that the National Institute of Mental Health [NIMH] had been founded, which started me thinking. I began looking through the interviews that I had done with the original group of gay men and knew I couldn't use them. First of all, they were not planned enough. And second, I didn't have anything to compare them with.

What I had learned, of course, with every step I took, was that these men represented a cross section of personality, talent, background, adjustment, and mental health. The whole kit and caboodle was there. But I had to prove it.

As I was sitting there in my study, I said to myself, "What I think I'll do is apply to NIMH. If the study section thinks this project is worth doing, I'll do it." So I wrote out an application for a grant. I said that I could get any number of gay men.

The chief of the grants division, John Eberhart, flew out and spent the day with me. He wanted to see what kind of a kook this was. "Is she crazy or can she do this?" At the end of the day he said, "We're prepared to make you this grant, but you may not get it." By this time it was 1953, the height of the McCarthy era. The concern was that if somebody were to come across my name in connection with homosexuality and come across the fact that my first husband was in the Bureau of Medical Aid to Spain in the Spanish Civil War, they would have killed the research. And here I was proposing to study normal male homosexuals in 1953? As John had said to me, "If you get the grant, you won't know why, and we won't know why." And to this day, I have no idea why I got it because several years later, I learned that McCarthy's henchmen had indeed been keeping an eye on me.

Later, once the results were known, I was often asked by gay women, "Why didn't you do for us what you did for the gay men?" First I said, "You didn't ask me, and the men did." But there's more to it than that. Suppose I had gone to NIMH in 1953 and said, "I want to do a study of lesbians." The first thing that would have happened, I am convinced, is that they would have said, "We think this bears investigation." They would have been thinking, "Perhaps she herself is a lesbian." I think that may have been one question in John Eberhart's mind when he came and spent the day with me. He knew that if I was going to go into this field, I had to be above reproach. I would have to be as pure as the driven snow.

THE REAL excitement began when NIMH gave me the grant. There was excitement about doing something you felt was going to be ground breaking, whatever it led to. It was exciting because it would have been the first time anybody ever looked at this behavior and said, "We'll use scientific tests to determine whether or not homosexuality is pathological."

When I set out to find the thirty gay men I needed for the study, I had a few rules. I wanted to be certain that they were all what Kinsey called a "five" or "six"—exclusively homosexual.* I didn't want anyone who had extended therapy or arrest records.

I found the gay men primarily through friendship networks, the Mattachine Society†—I had been invited to some of the original public meetings of the organization—and ONE, Incorporated. I interviewed them in the apartment in back of our garage. I could not have carried on my study at UCLA. No one would have participated because they would have been afraid of the stigma. Everyone knew that I was doing this research, so these men would have been identified immediately as homosexuals.

I HAD no difficulty getting these men to talk. And I had no difficulty finding many more gay men than the thirty I needed, although I only used thirty. The problem was getting the straight men. Remember, this was the early 1950s. I thought that if I went to a labor union and asked for the personnel director and told him what I was doing, he would be willing to speak individually to men he thought were thoroughgoing heterosexual men. Not a bit of it. The personnel director I went to wouldn't do it. He said, "Are you doing a Kinsey study?" I said, "No, I'm not." "Any study that involves sexuality," he said, "might boomerang, and I would lose my job."

I was just at my wit's end to find heterosexuals who were of the general educational, economic, et cetera level of my gay group. So I got heterosexuals in the most unusual ways. One day, for example, I was sitting in the study and I heard some steps coming down the driveway. I looked out, and there were blue trouser legs, four of them. I said, "Oh boy!" It turned out that they were firemen who had come by to look at our fire precautions. I went out to meet them, and as we walked toward my office, one of them said, "Oh, you're a writer?" I said, "No, not exactly. I'm a psychologist." "Oh," he said, "I have

---

*Alfred Kinsey's *Sexual Behavior in the Human Male*, published in 1948, challenged widely held beliefs concerning male sexuality. Among Kinsey's conclusions: 37 percent of American men had at least one postadolescent homosexual experience leading to orgasm, and 4 percent were exclusively homosexual throughout adulthood. Homosexuality, as evidenced by the Kinsey reports, was far more widespread than anyone had imagined. Kinsey's human sexuality scale ranges from zero to six: Zero is exclusively heterosexual; six is exclusively homosexual.
†The Mattachine Society was an organization for homosexuals founded by a small group of men in Los Angeles in 1950.

Dr. Evelyn Hooker at her home on Saltair Avenue in the mid-1950s. (© *Karl Muenzinger*)

two boys, and they're in a psychology experiment at UCLA." I asked him if he would be willing to be in a psychology experiment. He said he couldn't because of work. When I asked him about participating on his days off, he said he had to take care of his boys. So I offered to pay for a baby-sitter. Finally, he agreed to participate. That's when my husband said, "No man is safe on Saltair Avenue."

The fireman introduced me to a cop. The cop wanted to come to me because he was having marital troubles and was willing to exchange a little information for some advice. I learned all about the ins and outs of the police department downtown. In my search I also went to the maintenance department at UCLA, but instead of getting a maintenance man, I found a man who was working on his master's degree in sociology. After two years, I got my thirty and thirty.

Each of the sixty subjects was given three projective personality tests widely used at the time: the Rorschach Test, the Thematic Apperception Test, and the Make A Picture Story Test. The assumption underlying their use was that the person being tested would reveal his anxieties, fears, and fundamental personality predispositions without being fully aware that he was doing so.

The test results were then submitted to three judges, all nationally and internationally known psychological experts who did not know whether a subject was homosexual or heterosexual. The judges evaluated each test and assigned a rating of overall psychological adjustment on a scale of one—superior—to five—maladjusted. On all three tests, two-thirds of the heterosexuals *and* homosexuals were assigned a rating of three, which was average, *or better!* There was *no* inherent association between maladjustment or psychopathology and homosexuality. This finding was validated later by my own use of objective psychological tests and the reports of other psychologists.

Bruno Klopfer was one of the original judges who evaluated the responses. He was living in Carmel. When I went up there, people said, "You'll never get away with this. Your face will reveal who is and who isn't. He'll know." I said, "Oh, nonsense. He's the great Rorschach expert." I think we spent ten days just going over the materials, one after the other. It was terribly exciting to see Bruno make his decisions. It was simply that he was sure he could pick out the homosexuals from the heterosexuals, but he couldn't.

At that time, the 1950s, every clinical psychologist worth his soul would tell you that if he gave those projective tests he could tell whether a person was gay or not. I showed that they couldn't do it. I was very pleased with that. Bruno could hardly believe his eyes. He was absolutely positive that the dynamics would be such that he would know immediately who was gay and who wasn't. But he didn't know.

ONE OF the most exciting days of my life was the day I presented that paper—my study—at a meeting of the American Psychological Association in Chicago in 1956. The title of the paper was "The Adjustment of the Male Overt Homosexual." In my paper I presented the evidence that gay men can be as well adjusted as straight men and that some are even better adjusted than some straight men. In other words, so far as the evidence was concerned, there was no difference between the two groups of men in the study. There was just as much pathology in one group as in the other.

My presentation was held in one of the big ballrooms in one of the big hotels. The air was electric. We were still going strong at the end of the hour, so they moved us to another ballroom. Of course, there were some people, not too many, who were saying, "That can't be right." And they set off to prove that I was crazy. At the time, the hard-liners among the psychoanalysts, like Irving Bieber, would as soon shoot me as look at me.

I think for everybody—unless they were severely prejudiced, as lots of people were and are—what I had to say was a very exciting concept. And, of course, I made it electric. I used to have a fairly good speaking voice. A woman came up to me after I finished reading the paper and said, "If I had your voice, I'd patent it."

When I came back from Chicago, I remember a meeting at a restaurant in Hollywood. I had promised the gay men that I would let them know what the results were. Oh, they were uproarious with laughter. "This is great. We knew it all the time!" I didn't meet with the straight men. They didn't have the motivation to follow an old lady around.

In his book, *Homosexuality and American Psychiatry: The Politics of Diagnosis*, Ronald Bayer wrote about me and his reaction to my study. He described the study quite accurately and then said—I'm paraphrasing—"But in spite of the fact that she drew tentative conclusions"—which, of course, any scientific study does—"she nevertheless accepted the honors of the gay community. She was an advocate for them. . . ." There's a slight no-no in that, I think. But I don't care. As far as he's concerned, I was tainted by my association. I ought to be that perfectly impartial, objective researcher. That's why I had to use judges, so I couldn't be accused of anything.

I THINK that the net impact of my study was felt in a number of ways. My friend Ed Shneidman described it when the Clinical Division of the American Psychological Association gave me the Distinguished Contribution Award. Among the things he wrote was that I had made homosexuality a respectable field of study. That cannot be discounted. It paved the way for a lot of people who had the courage—gay and straight psychologists alike—to do research.

But what means the most to me, I think, is. . . . Excuse me while I cry. . . . If I went to a gay gathering of some kind, I was sure to have at least one person come up to me and say, "I wanted to meet you because I wanted to tell you what you saved me from." I'm thinking of a young woman who came up to me and said that when her parents discovered she was a lesbian, they put her in a psychiatric hospital. The standard procedure for treating homosexuals in that hospital was electroshock therapy. Her psychiatrist was familiar with my work, and he was able to keep them from giving it to her. She had tears streaming down her face as she told me this. I know that wherever I go, there are men and women for whom my little bit of work and my caring enough to do it has made an enormous difference in their lives.

The Organizer

Chuck Rowland

AT THE conclusion of *World War II, Chuck Rowland thought almost anything was possible. He returned to civilian life full of idealism and energy, committed to creating a new and better world. He became an organizer for the American Veterans Committee (AVC), a left-liberal World War II veterans organization that, among other radical concepts, promoted racial equality. During the late 1940s, Chuck crisscrossed the Midwest giving speeches and organizing new AVC chapters. During that time he also became a member of the Communist party.*

Chuck's idealism was rekindled in 1950, when he was introduced to a group of men who were talking about starting an organization for homosexuals. At last, here was a way Chuck could integrate his interest in social issues with his homosexuality. This new, highly secretive organization, which Chuck and the handful of founders named the Mattachine Society,* became his life.

Between 1950 and 1953, the Mattachine Society spawned dozens of discussion groups throughout southern California and a handful in the San Francisco Bay area. The discussions, which were held in private homes, were conducted in such a way that most of those attending had no idea who was in charge. The identities of the Mattachine leaders, including Chuck, were kept secret from all but a handful of Mattachine members at the top of the organization's hierarchy.

Although the Mattachine Society was not the first gay organization—a short-lived group was founded in Chicago in the 1920s and a gay veterans social group, the Veterans Benevolent Association, was organized in New York City in the 1940s—it served as a significant foundation on which the early gay rights movement could build and grow.

Born in 1917, Chuck Rowland is a gentle, boyish-looking man. He lives in a modest one-bedroom apartment one block from Grauman's Chinese Theater in Hollywood. On a wall just inside the entrance to his tidy apartment hangs a large photograph of Dr. Evelyn Hooker. As he spoke of his time in the army, his years as an organizer, and the first years of the

---

*According to historian John D'Emilio, the name *Mattachine* was taken from mysterious masked medieval figures, who, one of the organization's founders speculated, might have been homosexuals.

Mattachine Society, it quickly became clear that Chuck was recalling the most exciting period of his life.

The American Veterans Committee was a wonderful idea. We had just won the war. We had rid the world of fascism, except in Spain. We came back and were going to save the world. When you're thirty-something, you can believe those things. That's what I was dedicating my life to by joining the AVC.

The AVC was a New York outfit, and to them, there wasn't much of anything between the Hudson River and San Francisco other than Chicago. So it didn't seem unreasonable to them that I should be in charge of several states. I was made organizer for North and South Dakota, Minnesota, Kansas, Nebraska, Missouri, Iowa, and Wisconsin. A modest little territory. My job was to travel throughout this empire and organize new AVC chapters. It was a very good job. I was paid mileage and per diem. I had an incredible record. I didn't know this until later, when I found out that the New York office was absolutely dazzled. I was the only organizer in the country who was actually making his own salary from dues.

This was the Truman era. It was a wonderfully liberal period. Organizing was so easy. I was making speeches and advocating all the leftish things. We did some very daring things in the AVC. To start with, we were interracial—and I was organizing chapters in places like Missouri and southern Iowa. It was incredible. I didn't know of any other interracial organizations at that time. AVC gave an interracial dance in Chicago. That was not my territory, but I had friends there. This dance became a national news story: "Veterans organization gives interracial dance with black men and white women . . . " and all this kind of stuff. But there were no incidents. Plus, women were admitted on an equal basis. We didn't have a women's auxiliary or anything like that.

THERE WERE some Communists in the AVC, and they seemed like fine people to me. I had a dear friend, Henry, who had also started as an AVC organizer and was working with the Omaha chapter. His parents were Communists, but he thought that that was kind of old-fashioned. I loved him dearly. We never had an affair, but I think we could have very easily. We were too busy saving the world. Henry and another friend, who was my part-time assistant, and I started discussing very seriously this whole Communist business. Henry

said, "Dad seems to make more and more sense." So Henry and I
joined. That would have been in 1946.

I became head of the youth division of the Party, which was called
the American Youth for Democracy, for both Dakotas and Minnesota. I was paid a modest salary. For years it had been called the
Young Communist League; they decided it wouldn't have that onus
if they changed the name.

To most Americans, Communists were wicked, horrid people.
Even to liberals. But the so-called liberals sat around and talked about
socialized medicine, integration, and the rights of women. The Communists, on the other hand, were out there on the barricades or
picketing or closing down something—doing something about it instead of just talking.

We were more American than most Americans. The idea that we
had studied in Russia or some idiotic thing like that was ridiculous.
The Communist party was never conceived of here or in the Soviet
Union as a mass party. It was a small group that liked to "infiltrate"
other liberal organizations to try to push them a little further.

I left the Communist party in 1948, not because I was kicked out,
not because I disagreed with anything, but because I just wanted out.
Joining the Communist party is very much like joining a monastery
or becoming a priest. It is total dedication, 24-hours-a-day, 365-days-
a-year. I thought I wanted that, and I did for awhile, but I realized that
I was getting very little sex and I didn't have a lover. I decided that I
needed more out of life. I also decided that I wanted to do something—this was kind of in the back of my mind—with organizing gay
people, although I hadn't yet verbalized it at that time.

UNLIKE so many people I know who had guilt feelings about being
gay, I never had any fuckin' guilt feelings. I knew I was gay by the time
I was nine. I didn't know the word, of course. I just knew I was
different from the other boys. At ten I fell in love for the first time
with this beautiful boy. This was no puppy-love affair. I would have
killed or died for that boy. I knew it was the real thing. I knew I was
in love. And I knew, of course, that this was strange, but it was so
clear to me that I wasn't crazy. That never crossed my mind.

It also helped that around that time I came across a series of articles
on homosexuals in a magazine called *Sexology*, which I found in my
father's drugstore. His drugstore had the only newsstand in town, a
little rural village called Gary, South Dakota, population 535 at that
time. It was a totally contained community. We had doctors, lawyers,
dentists. We had a public school. We had a municipal form of gov-

ernment with a mayor. My father, being a pharmacist, was one of the leading citizens of the community.

My father didn't want to put *Sexology* out in front of the store because it was too daring. He kept it in the back. I remember very distinctly snatching a copy as soon as it came in and taking it out to the backyard of our house. I was on my stomach, in the shade, in the backyard reading the magazine. There was a whole special section on homosexuality. It explained that if one was homosexual, he shouldn't feel strange or odd, that there were millions of us, that there was nothing wrong with it. Perfectly marvelous. I've talked to others who got their lives straightened out by reading the articles that appeared in this publication.

As soon as I read that there were millions of us, I said to myself, *Well, it's perfectly obvious that what we have to do is organize.* (I was about nine years old at this time.) *We have to organize, and why don't we identify with other minorities, such as the blacks and the Jews?* I had never known a black, but I did know one Jew in our town. Obviously, it had to be an organization that worked with other minorities, so we would wield tremendous strength.

I guess I was a born organizer. That's what Dr. Evelyn Hooker said. I was part of her study of gay men. She gave me all those crazy tests. And I said, "Can you tell me anything about it?" And she said, "No, they would question my objectivity if I discussed the results with you." But, she said, "I will tell you one thing, you have an absolute genius for organization."

In the army, during the war, I knew lots of gay people. Some poor guys went through absolute purgatory. The army, by its nature, has a lot of shit connected with it. Basic training, would you believe, in northern Minnesota in midwinter? I was so proud that I survived it. But for the most part, I had a ball in the army. It was one of the happiest periods of my life. I met a lot of sweet guys, many who weren't gay and a lot who were. I made friends very easily. I would have been about twenty-eight when I was in the army. The average age was something like nineteen. I wasn't old enough to be called "Pop"—anyone who was in his thirties was automatically referred to as "Pop." I didn't plan it or anything, but I sort of found myself in a leadership role among my peers.

I met lots of wonderful people and had three marvelous gay love affairs when I was a staff sergeant. I had this lover who was a corporal. A corporal is pretty lowly in comparison with a staff sergeant. He didn't give a shit about his rank or anything. One night, we were both

Chuck Rowland with his
sister, Mildred Reinhardt, in
1943. *(Courtesy Mildred
Reinhardt)*

hot. We wanted to have sex. There were big, tall grasses out on one
side of the barracks. He said, "We can fuck right here." And I said,
"But the barracks is right over there." It was about a half a city block
away. He said, "Shit, nobody's going to see us." So he fucked me
right there in the high grasses. Of course, we both would have been
castrated and discharged if we had been found.

I worried about being caught, but I was very careful, except for one
time on a troop train. Let me tell you about it. One of the bleakest
things that can happen in the service is to get separated from your
unit. Because you know everybody, your company begins to be like
a family. To be transferred to another unit, which can happen at any
moment without any warning, is something everybody hates. This
horrible thing happened to me only once, but it was traumatic. This
would have been 1944. We were in Virginia. We knew we were being
shipped, but we didn't know where. One fine day we went to the
bulletin board, and there were the shipping orders. Everybody's name
was on it but mine. Well, obviously there had been a typo by some
clerk. So I rushed right in to the top sergeant and said, "Hey, Joe,
somebody goofed. My name is not on the shipping order." He said,

"Rowland, you're not going with the unit." And I said, "Not with the unit? Why not?" He said, "Damned if I know. You can talk to the captain if you want to, but the order is very clear. You're being shipped to Illinois." So we said our good-byes. And here I was quite literally alone at this place. Everyone had been shipped out, and I hadn't gone yet. Nobody around. Nothing to do. No place even to eat because everything was gone.

My order called for shipping out at nine o'clock at night. So with my barracks bag, feeling very sad and very alone, I got on this late-night troop train headed for Illinois. It was a huge troop train. These were old cars without heat or air-conditioning. The train was steam driven, with smoke coming in through the windows. Perfectly hideous. There were many cars on this train, but not a single seat. I went from car to car. I was traveling on military orders, so I was entitled to a seat. I was also a staff sergeant, so I sure as hell was entitled to a seat.

The conductor said nicely, "Well sir, I'm sorry, but I can give you a compartment. Would that be all right?" I had never been in a compartment before. Compartments were lavish. They accommodated about three people and had a private toilet and a sink. Unbelievable luxury for a serviceman. I had it all to myself. I said that I thought it was satisfactory. Of course, I was supplied with a fifth of whiskey. So I sat down and began drinking. And I thought, *This is awfully lonely and just plain boring. What am I doing here?* So I simply started walking along the aisles of the troop train. Now, you understand, I'd never seen the people on this train before in my entire life. I can't imagine myself doing this, but I swear I did it. I made several trips the length of this long train, walking back and forth. I finally decided that this one soldier was the cutest guy on the train, and I said to him, "Come with me for a minute." I didn't want to say anything more in front of other people.

I got him away from the others and said to him, "I've got a bottle and I've got a compartment. Would you like to join me?" A big grin spread over his face, and he said, "Hell, yes! Anything but this shithole!" So we went into our compartment and we had a drink. I don't think we had any conversation at all. We got undressed and just starting fucking. We fucked all night. Beautiful boy. Well, it was a wonderful night. Then the next morning, about nine o'clock, the conductor came in and said that there was a paying customer who had reservations for this compartment. He didn't kick me out, because the compartment was for two people, but the other guy had to go. And I eventually got to Camp Grant.

*   *   *

I DON'T think there was any thinking gay person who hadn't, at some time back in the 1920s or 1930s, said at a bar one night when feeling a little happy, "You know, we should have an organization. We should get together and have a gay organization." And usually you would be laughed out of the place. People would say, "You'll never get a bunch of faggots together, those dizzy queens. You'll never get them to do anything." But I had heard this way back, before the war, before I was politically active.

I think we started talking about a gay organization in Los Angeles in 1949, but I know the Mattachine wasn't formally organized until 1950. I don't think we had anything written down. It was just something my lover, Bob Hull, and I talked about. He had been in the Party also. Bob was a concert pianist and a chemist. He was making a living as a chemist, but what he really wanted to do was give concerts.

Bob had a music class taught by Harry Hay. One day Harry showed Bob something he had written about a gay organization. Bob brought this home and showed it to me. When I read what Harry had written, I said, "My God, I could have written this myself!" So Bob said, "You've got to meet Harry." Harry lived up in the Silverlake district on Fargo. We drove up there. Harry says I jumped out of my car waving the document saying, "I could have written this myself!" I don't think I would have approached a stranger in that way at that time, but that's the way Harry tells the story.

Harry; his lover, Rudi Gernreich;* Bob; Dale Jennings, a friend who had been involved in defending the rights of Japanese Americans during the war; and I started talking about this gay organization. We started having regular meetings. We had been saying, "We'll just have an organization." And I kept saying, "What is our theory?" Having been a Communist, you've got to work with a theory. "What is our basic principle that we are building on?" And Harry said, "We are an oppressed cultural minority." And I said, "That's exactly it!" That was the first time I know of that gays were referred to as an oppressed cultural minority. But gay people didn't want to be an oppressed cultural minority. "Why, we're just like everybody else, except what we do in bed." They wanted to be like everybody else.

But that isn't true; we're not like everybody else. I don't think or

---

*Rudi Gernreich was born in Vienna in 1922. At the time of his involvement with the Mattachine Society, he used the pseudonym R. He achieved international fame in the mid-1960s as the designer of topless bathing suits, see-through blouses, and minidresses inset with clear vinyl strips. He died in Los Angeles in 1985. In his obituary in the *New York Times*, he was described as a "quiet, cultivated man."

Chuck Rowland *(in glasses)* at a 1951 or 1952 Mattachine Society
Christmas party in Los Angeles. *From left to right:* Konrad Stevens *(back
of head)*, Dale Jennings *(in profile)*, Harry Hay, Rudy Gernreich, Stan
Witt, Bob Hull, Chuck Rowland, and Paul Bernard. *(© John Gruber)*

feel like a heterosexual. My life was not like that of a heterosexual. I
had emotional experiences that I could not have had as a heterosexual.
My whole person, my whole being, my whole character, my whole
life, differed and differs from heterosexuals, not by what I do in bed.
I believe there is a gay sensibility. When we tried to explain this to
somebody, I would say, "There is a gay culture." People would say,
"Gay culture? What do you mean? Do you actually think we're more
cultured than anybody else?" I would explain that I was using "culture" in the sociological sense, as a body of language, feelings, thinking, and experiences that we share in common. As we speak of a
Mexican culture. As we speak of an American Indian culture.

We had to say that gay culture was an emergent culture. For example, as gay people, we used certain language, certain words. The word
gay itself is a marvelous example of what I mean by gay culture. You'll
get a lot of argument about this. But I know that *gay* was being used
back in the thirties, and we didn't mean "merry" or "festive." We
meant "homosexual." This does not constitute a language in the sense
that English is a language and French is a language, but it's more
comparable to Yiddish culture. A lot of people, Jews and non-Jews,
use Yiddish words like *schlepp* and *meshuga*. These words separate
them culturally from my mother, for example, who would never have
heard of such words. A lot of people still don't agree with the gay-

culture issue. But you see the term *gay culture* all the time now. I think the leadership of the gay movement today accepts essentially what the Mattachine Society advocated.

People were horrified by what I said, and not just about gay culture. At the first constitutional convention of the Mattachine Society, which was held at a church in Los Angeles in 1953, I made a speech before about one hundred people in which I remember saying, "The time will come when we will march arm in arm, ten abreast down Hollywood Boulevard proclaiming our pride in our homosexuality." One of my friends in Mattachine said he almost had a coronary at such an outrageous thought at the time. I deliberately built this speech up to what I hoped would be a rousing climax. I got some applause, but people were more in shock than anything else. To me, it seemed perfectly reasonable.

In Mattachine, during those first years after we formed the organization, we talked about working for things like retirement homes for gay people and a home for gay street kids. We wanted to provide job placement services and legal advice. And we wanted to go further. We said, "Why can't we do the same sort of things the Jews do? If you had five hundred thousand Jews in the community, they would have several temples. They would have a symphony orchestra. They would have ballet. They would have several theaters. They would have a hospital. Why can't we do all those kinds of things?"

MATTACHINE WAS growing so fast in the first few years that it became obvious to me there was no way we could control it. It was a very tight top-down organization, where no one who attended the meetings knew who the leadership was. It was kept very secret, but it had become unmanageable. Harry Hay has never quite forgiven us for what happened next, but several of us said that it was obvious we couldn't go on like this. I said that the only thing to do was to open up Mattachine, to make it a fully democratic organization. To this end, I proposed that we call a constitutional convention.

So I wrote a constitution, which I thought was a damn good one. And then we at the highest echelon of Mattachine worked on it for weeks and months. I thought it was really a marvelous document. We thought it was so good and so workable that it never occurred to us that anybody would come up with another constitution. Or if they did, that they could get anybody to vote for it. But this group of conservative insurgents came up with this half-baked piece of shit, and it was obvious that they were going to pass it.

To most of the people who attended that convention, the only way we were ever going to get along in society was by being nice, quiet, polite little boys that our maiden aunts would have approved of. We were not going to get along in the world by going out and flaunting our homosexuality. There were people of goodwill, who would help us, but we could not do anything naughty like having picket signs or parades. Only Communists would do things like that.

And although some of us had been Communists and others had been fellow travelers, these people at the convention began calling us Communists, not because they had even the faintest shred of evidence for this accusation, but because we were saying such daring things. That's what Communists do: They create waves, they make scenes, they're unpleasant, they don't balance their coffee cups on their knees politely. Oh, fuck!

What this group of conservative people wanted was an open organization, which is what we were advocating. But because we were Communists, we couldn't be trusted. So they came up with their constitution, which was as strictly top-down in structure as Mattachine had been to begin with. I said that we couldn't live with this constitution; it was clearly unworkable. So we had a very quick meeting and we, the original leadership of Mattachine, decided that we would resign.

The people who took over Mattachine couldn't solve anything at the April convention, so they had another convention a month later. I was chosen as the delegate from a Mattachine club in the Wilshire district, but the people running Mattachine, including Hal Call, their leader, would not seat me. I said, "How can you not seat me? I've been sent here as a representative of my club." Their response was, "Because we don't seat Communists." Ridiculous!

The constitution that was ultimately passed was a piece of shit. You see, we thought we were dealing with knowledgeable people, but these people had never been in an organization. They didn't know how an organization worked. They had no concept of what a constitution should be. Ours was a few pages; theirs was like a whole manuscript. They didn't want anything to happen that wasn't known to the leadership.

Hal Call was leading this group. He was, at that time, a handsome young man. He gave a speech in which he said that in San Francisco there was a lot more understanding than there was here in L.A., and that he had connections with church groups and others who were going to help him. Of course, this rotten son of a bitch turned our sacred Mattachine into a cock suck-off club. It made me sick to my stomach when I first heard about that. And he simply used the Mattachine all these years as a device for supporting himself.

So we resigned. Mattachine, as Hal envisioned it, was unworkable. It called itself the Mattachine, but it wasn't. We said we'd try to work with some of the individual clubs, but then a lot of personal things happened. We founders of the Mattachine had given so much of ourselves, had dedicated ourselves so utterly to this organization. Mattachine was our lives, and suddenly it was gone, simply gone. And as a result, lovers began breaking up. People who had been the closest of friends were screaming and swearing at each other. Harry was so inaccessible that we thought he hated us. This guy who we had been through hell and paradise with suddenly was not available. You practically had to have an appointment to see him. Now Harry says it was because he was having terrible problems with his lover. And Rudi had pulled out altogether. Rudi never spoke to anybody again, except for Harry. Rudi went on to become rich and powerful. I think as an indirect consequence of the breakup of Mattachine, Bob Hull killed himself. I lost touch with my friends from Mattachine for years.

As I think of it, in retrospect, it was a terrible, terrible time after I left Mattachine. We should never, never have given Hal Call our name, never have let him take our name. I became absolutely suicidal. This was my life. I was prepared quite literally to devote my life to the Mattachine, and here this bright glory was all gone. It all turned to shit.

The Editor

Martin Block

FROM THE very beginning, people in gay organizations had disagreements over everything, from what a homosexual was to what approach should be taken to achieve change. Martin Block, a self-confident young man from The Bronx, had strong dissenting opinions and wasn't afraid to express them from the moment he arrived at his first Mattachine meeting in 1950.

Although he disagreed with almost everything the Mattachine founders had to say, Martin became involved with the organization during the early fifties and its spin-off magazine, ONE. Martin's devil-may-care approach to life served him well in his work on ONE, especially since the legal right to send homosexually oriented material through the mail had not been established. The use of the word homosexual in a positive context was considered by many—including the post office—to be obscene.

Born in 1919, Martin is a round man of medium height, who exudes self-confidence and has an incredible memory for detail. Martin lives on a quiet side street of West Hollywood, in a house almost bursting with furniture and knickknacks.

I arrived in Los Angeles on July 4, 1945, and spent my first night in a Turkish bath. I was so tired, all I did was sleep, which was not the usual thing you did in a Turkish bath in those days. Los Angeles was a wild city. You must remember that there were many movie stars who were gay and famous, even in 1945.

I knew the police were very active in this town, but I wasn't afraid of going to the baths. The police were very active in New York, and they didn't bother me. As a matter of fact, I had an affair with a motorcycle cop here in L.A. It started sometime early in 1948 and lasted until about 1951.

I was living in the Valley. My mother and I had bought a house. I did not have a car and did not know how to drive. One rainy day, while I was waiting for the bus, this car pulled up, and the man inside asked me if I wanted a ride. I thought a ride would be marvelous. I opened the door and sort of did a double take because the driver was a policeman. So I very carefully sat close to the door.

Martin Block in 1945, shortly after arriving in Los Angeles. *(Courtesy Martin Block)*

I wasn't frightened. I just thought I should be on my best behavior. I was amused, if anything, and a little intrigued, but I wasn't going to do anything. I remember when we came into Hollywood, he turned down one of the side streets, and I said, "Oh, you can drop me at Hollywood Boulevard." I had a bookshop at the time, and it was just about four doors from where he was going to drop me.

Later the same week, I was going home to meet my mother and I was in a great hurry. As I rushed toward the corner to catch the next trolley, I heard a horn and somebody said, "Come on in, and I'll give you a lift." It was the same cop. I said, "Oh, dear." Then I thought, *Oh, the police are out to get me.* Several people I knew had recently been arrested. Anyway, I got in the car. I said, "I'm grateful for this because I have to be home early to do something for my mother." When we got to the corner, I said, "This is where I get off." He said, "You have a little extra time. If you had taken the trolley, you'd be at least forty minutes longer. Why don't we have a drink?" He just drove on past my corner. And I thought, *Oh, dear.*

We didn't go too much farther; I don't think we went six blocks. He pulled into the grounds of a pleasant little house. The Valley didn't have any large houses, at least not where we lived at that time. He opened the door to his house, showed me inside, and the next thing I knew my tonsils were being washed. And I must say, he was very excited. I wasn't. I was still a little put off by this, but it was all right. Over the years it got to be pleasanter. Gay cops are nothing new.

* * *

I HEARD of Mattachine through Rudi Gernreich, who was a friend of mine. Rudi came to see me one day in 1950 at the bookshop and said he wanted to talk. So we went out and had a cup of coffee. Rudi and I had mutual friends. At that time he was known primarily as a dancer in the Lester Horton Modern Dance Troupe. Lester Horton was a very fine modern dancer who died much before his time.

Rudi lived with his mother and had Harry Hay as a lover. Harry was the principal founder of Mattachine. When we had our coffee, Rudi told me about this organization that was being formed, an activist organization. He said, being a little alarmed, "We have to be careful," but if I was interested, he would like to bring me to one of the meetings.

Everybody was scared. I guess people were rather psychotic about it. But because of my background, this business of being afraid of the FBI or the police was a lot of shit to me at the time, and it is now. You see, my father was a socialist, and my mother was an anarchist. When the time came for the meeting, I think Rudi drove, and we took some sort of circuitous route to avoid being followed. Everybody was very worried about Mr. Hoover's crazy FBI men. I don't think anybody was interested in following us, but Rudi was fearful. The whole group was fearful, although I think Rudi was more so than anyone else because he was an immigrant.

There was little more than a handful and a half of people at the meeting—but not two handfuls—who were sitting around. I was introduced to a few of them. First names, always. And then eventually Chuck Rowland spoke. He was the speaker for the day. The subject of his speech was, well, you wouldn't have called it gay liberation at the time, but it was on the subject of more freedom for homosexuals. Chuck gave a long speech, well organized. He's a very good speaker. He spoke for about forty or forty-five minutes. Early on I sensed that the speech was directed at me.

When he was finished, everybody looked at me as if I was expected to get up and give some sort of an answer. I said, "I have to admire the way Chuck spoke, the cogency, the specifics, the planning that has gone into his speech, and therefore it almost pains me to say that I disagree with every single word of it." This response, I think, was a little bombshell. My point of disagreement was that Chuck had described the homosexual world, the gay world as we knew it, as a parallel to the labor movement, which I thought was absolutely untrue. There was no parallel.

The labor movement grew in the face of antilabor efforts. But there was no organized antigay movement. And there was no formal gay movement. You can say of the gays as people say of the Jews, "If you meet two of them, there are three opinions." That was and, to me, still is the case.

Of course, with so many opinions, we argued. For example, anytime there was a proposal to do something public, people argued, "Well, I don't want those drag queens coming" or "I don't want that one coming" or "Isn't she outrageous with her constant swish?" I'm not saying that drag queens were not welcome. I'm saying that they were not welcome by everybody. In every gay movement, there has always been a schism. Some people don't want anyone who sticks his little pinky out, and some people don't want anyone who doesn't stick his little pinky out. None of us is without bias. And I am delighted to say that I am full of bias myself, but my bias is mostly against stupidity. I think everyone's entitled to be alive. That's my anarchist background.

I don't think gays were ready for political organizing then, and I don't think they are now. Gays were ready for some sort of an organization, but I didn't feel truthfully that they could all be organized in the way that workers were organized. I felt there would be some resistance among them because not all gays were going to be activists.

After about the fourth or fifth meeting, I was invited to become a member. I was fascinated by it. I went to meetings, and all we did was talk, talk, talk. We talked about sex and boyfriends. You couldn't believe the talk going on. Eventually we did more than talk. We started a magazine. I had two friends, one named Alvin, and Johnny Button. Johnny died a few years ago. Alvin and Johnny lived together in what was little more than a shack in West Hollywood, which was then part of the county and not a separate city. They were going to host one of the Mattachine meetings, which were held every week or every second week. At that particular meeting there were twelve to twenty people. This was just one of the evenings when we talked on general topics. And Johnny finally said, "You know, this whole thing is a lot of shit. We sit around here talking and talking. We don't *do* anything. Why don't we do something practical? Why don't we do something real? Why don't we start a journal or a magazine or something?"

It was all Johnny's doing. It was Johnny's push and excitement. We all got really worked up and planned the whole thing. We elected officers, and I was chosen editor, a position I held for a number of issues. That was the start of ONE magazine. I think we even chose the name that night. There's a quotation from Thomas Carlyle, "A mystic bond of brotherhood makes all men one."

At first, we thought if we had to, we would write articles ourselves.

We called our friends and asked them to contribute. Surprisingly enough, we got some contributions. Our basic feeling was that we would, if anything, promote ourselves as we were. We would not attempt to turn anyone in our direction. We weren't going to go out and say you should be gay, but we said, "You can be proud of being gay." You could be proud of being yourself. You could look yourself in the mirror and say, "I'm me, and isn't that nice?" That in itself was radical. Nobody put it in words, but that was the underlying thought and underlying feeling behind the magazine.

At that time, gay was something you didn't want to be. It was thought to be a disease. You didn't think that it was a disease necessarily if you were gay, but even gays differed very strongly about what being gay was. Every now and then in Mattachine, you would hear somebody say that being gay was a sickness, but more often, people were beginning to say, "This is what I am, and so what?"

To sell the magazine, we went around to the magazine stands. There were almost no bookshops. We asked the magazine stands if they would take it, and several of them said yes. Then more and more said yes. The magazine stands that we went to in Los Angeles all had gay customers. They didn't have the magazines showing male "activity" that you can buy now. But they carried the physique magazines that had photographs of men in a jock strap or posing strap. They knew they had customers for the physique magazines, so why not sell ONE magazine as well? Eventually one of the magazine-distributing companies said they would take it on. So by 1955, the peak year, we were selling thirty-four-hundred copies through subscriptions and on newsstands, primarily in the Los Angeles area, New York, and San Francisco.

All of this was not in one day's or one week's or one month's work. This was going on for months and months and months and months. It took dedicated people. I don't think I was ever really dedicated. I'm too lazy to be dedicated, but still, I worked on the magazine for three or four years.

WHEN I look back, to me it was all a charming experience. The word *charming* is somehow wrong. But I look at it as something in my youth, although I wasn't that young. But *charming* is the word I've chosen. I think that's what's wrong with so many activists: They have no sense of humor and no sense of pleasure. All these things are much better if you know you're enjoying them while you're doing them.

The great thing about my involvement in Mattachine is that I have remained friendly with those members who are still alive. Chuck

Rowland is still a very important friend to me. I still don't agree with everything he does, by the way, and I often tell him so.

These days, I'm a member of APLG, which is Asian/Pacific Lesbians and Gays. Sort of rice queens* and their rice. It was started by the Asians to bolster themselves. My lover happens to be an Asian. Since I became a member of APLG, our whole relationship, which had no big problems, has had even fewer problems. It's warmed even more. We've been together now twenty-two years, my dear. And if we haven't killed each other by now. . . .

*Non-Asian gay men who are attracted primarily to Asian men.

News Hound

Jim Kepner

DURING ITS *first years of publication, the pioneering* ONE *magazine attracted the attention of the U.S. Post Office and the FBI. The magazine also attracted the interest of Jim Kepner, a young man who worked nights at a milk-carton-manufacturing plant south of Los Angeles. Jim first learned of the magazine in 1953, through the Mattachine Society. He eventually joined ONE's small volunteer staff, working as a news writer and columnist.*

Jim Kepner doesn't know exactly when he was born because he was found on August 19, 1923, under an oleander bush in Galveston, Texas, wrapped in a Houston newspaper. He was estimated to be about seven months old. Jim grew up in Galveston and didn't learn that he was adopted until he was nineteen. He was relieved when he learned of his adoption because, "then I could believe in the theory of heredity. My adoptive parents tried hard, but they were both heavy drinkers."

Jim is now curator of the International Gay and Lesbian Archives in Hollywood, which he founded in 1972. He lives in a small, rundown cottage at the bottom of a steep hill in an outlying Los Angeles neighborhood. His front yard is filled with cactus plants, a longtime hobby. Inside, the house overflows with files, books, and personal records collected during three and a half decades of involvement with the gay rights movement. When he recalled the past, Jim pulled details from a mind that seemed to be as fact packed as his house.

I realized at a very early age that I liked men. My father took me to the beach just before my fourth birthday. Out on the beach pavilion a band was playing while fireworks were going off across the waves. I was down in the middle of the crowd, knee high to everybody around me, and my father stepped away for the third or fourth time for a double boilermaker (two shots of whisky in a can of beer), leaving me holding a post.

While my father was gone, a young man picked me up so I could see over the heads of the other people. I was in heaven. I was excited by the silky hair on his wrists and wanted to rub them, but I knew even then that you weren't supposed to do that. I also knew you weren't supposed to let strange men pick you up, but this was just so wonderful.

A YEAR later we moved to a new house. Many afternoons I looked out across the street through my white picket fence and saw blond twin brothers, a year younger than I was, holding hands like the Dutch Cleanser boys. I wanted to make it triplets.

During those first years in school, I confessed to some other boys, who I thought felt the same way I did, that I felt about guys the way everybody was supposed to feel about girls. In the fifth grade it got all over school. It got so damned uncomfortable that I had to transfer to the only other school in my part of town, a German Lutheran school.

So I knew I was different, but I didn't know it was a category, and I had no concept of it having anything to do with sex. But I had had fantasies from the time I was ten of meeting a guy named John. His family would have a fatal accident, so my family would adopt him. And then, as soon as we were brothers, my family would take off for the hills, and we would be brothers for the rest of our lives.

It wasn't until I was a year out of high school that I began to have a clearer understanding. I went out on a triple date one night. The other two guys kept joking, "We're going to go all the way tonight." My girl was eyebrowless. She was more scared than I was. We got some rum and Coke. My girl took a sip of it and apparently thought she had had it and vomited on me. So the girls left. All three of us guys relaxed. We had done our duty. We had made the attempt. And then they started talking about homosexuals.

"What are homosexuals?" I asked. They said, "Well, that's when sailors are out at sea and there aren't any broads around and they can't get their rocks off. So they piss and shit in one another's faces to get their rocks off." Well, I nearly vomited. But I knew instinctively that their definition was right, that they had defined me, even if that wasn't what I had any desire to do. By the next day I was investigating the possibility of joining the navy or the merchant marine.

I eventually confessed to them what I felt, and one of them recommended his therapist. The therapist told me that it would go away, that all guys feel like that up to the time they're twenty or twenty-one. So he suggested that I find a nice young girl and get married and have a kid. I automatically knew that that would be a shitty trick to play on the nice young girl, and it would be a hell of a trick to play on the kid, too.

Then a few days later—this was early 1942—our newspaper had a three-page ad for the Haldeman-Julius Little Blue Books. Those were enormously popular among free-thinkers of the twenties through the fifties. They were five-cent books, the size of little gospel tracts, with a cheap soft blue cover, running twenty-eight to fifty-six pages. There were short stories of H. G. Wells, plays by Shaw, books on how to build a birdhouse or a fence, secrets of infants found buried under nunneries, all sorts of antireligious tracts and socialist tracts, and other literature that I was just ready for. Among the 1,792 titles at that time was, *What Is Homosexuality?* and *Homosexuality in the Lives of the Great.* So at a nickel a piece, I ordered at least twenty of them, including those two, hoping that no one would notice where my interests were focused. I sat on the post-office box for the next two or three weeks until they arrived, to make sure my parents wouldn't get them.

What Is Homosexuality? was a standard Freudian exposition explaining that homosexuality is caused by the Oedipus complex, the fixation on the mother who is domineering and overseductive, and a distant or absent or hostile father. I sort of bought the theory.

The booklet entitled *Homosexuality in the Lives of the Great* didn't deal with theory so much, but told me that whatever my problem or condition was, it was shared with Michelangelo; Leonardo; all the old Greeks; Whitman; Wilde; Florence Nightingale; and many, many others. That was wonderful because I thought I was something sick and degrading. And to be in the company of these great people, that's an incredible standard of degradation. I thought that if this was a sickness, it was a strange kind of sickness.

A few months later my sister and I moved out to San Francisco, where I quickly discovered bookstores with lots of science fiction, which I was just going wild with, and a lot of gay books. While many critics now say that Gore Vidal wrote the first one,* I had thirty or forty of them on my shelves by the time his appeared. Several of them were more advanced than his. Vidal's book, like many of the others, was a Freudian case study of a poor unfortunate who, if only his mother hadn't really wanted a daughter and if society hadn't treated him badly, could have been a successful tennis player or pianist or whatever. That was the formula for many of them, and they ended in suicide or accidental death. There were a few that broke the mold: *His Finer Shadow* in 1934; *The Divided Path* in 1949; and *Quatrefoil* in 1950, which did end in sudden death, but none of those three were Freudian case studies.

The City and the Pillar (Dutton, 1946).

So I found a lot of literature about gays, but most of it was terribly depressing. And most of the nonfiction placed homosexuals in the category of sexual monstrosities, who were written about as if they were all lined up in pickle jars on a shelf.

IN 1943, I got into a pen-pal thing accidentally that put me in touch with what I thought was a gay organization. Someone put my name in *Weird Tales* magazine, and I received several letters from heartsick young girls in the Midwest and from one guy in Rhinelander, Wisconsin, who sent me his picture—very cute. We began the hinting process, which usually occupied two or three letters. The way you hinted was by saying that you were interested in philosophy, poetry, and biographies, but not very interested in sports, except walking and swimming. You could mention tennis or Ping-Pong or miniature golf. So then you named a few recent biographies or poets that you'd read. You didn't start with people like Wilde or Whitman, but you could include Bacon or some of the ones who were less specifically identified. And then you brought it up.

In one of his early letters, this pen pal asked if I had ever heard of the Sons of Hamidy. After another two or three letters, he described this as a secret national homosexual rights organization started in the 1880s that fell apart due to bitch fights, which is naturally what gay groups do. He said it was reorganized in 1934 and again fell apart during bitch fights and was now being reorganized with some senators and generals in leading roles. Through three or four letters I asked, "How do I join?" And he kept being vague. By this time he had been drafted and was stationed in Coolidge, Arizona, which he told me was another big center of the Sons of Hamidy, along with Rhinelander, Wisconsin. He said, "We have people out looking over San Francisco to see if it's the right sort of town."

I began receiving visits and letters from some of my pen pal's other correspondents and learned that I was national secretary of the Sons of Hamidy! Well, that was a jolt because, poor little me, I was a nobody. With all of these senators and generals, what the hell was I doing as national secretary? And how did I get to be secretary, when my pen pal hadn't even told me how to join yet? It turned out that the Sons of Hamidy was his fantasy, as far as I can tell.

WHEN I first heard about the Mattachine—in the early 1950s, when I had just moved to L.A.—I thought it might also be a fantasy because the people who ran it had allowed rumors to circulate that some very influential people were behind it. The phrase, "senators and generals," was one of the first I heard, just like the Sons of Hamidy. So I was not quick to join.

But I kept hearing about Mattachine through the grapevine all over town. Everybody was buzzing about this gay group where people discussed things and where there were social activities. I would occasionally hear where a meeting was taking place, but I didn't drive at the time, and the meetings would be in some other hilly area in another part of town. Also I had to be at work at midnight about eight or nine miles southeast of L.A.

In the meantime, some friends gave me a housewarming, which turned into a regular Thursday night and Friday night party. The Friday night party sometimes lasted until Monday morning. The place was crowded with a mixture of science-fiction fans, gays, ex-radicals, and other assorted individuals. Several times I took a few people into the other room to discuss quietly starting a gay magazine or organization. A few times I got three or four people who were interested, but when I called them the next day, they would say it was party talk. They'd tell me, "The last thing I want to do is get in a room with a bunch of screaming queens. Nobody could agree on anything." I said, "Look, you're not a screaming queen. I'm not a screaming queen. Why are you bringing that up?"

They also thought that nothing would ever change. But unlike most people—due, in part, to my Marxist and science-fiction background—I did not believe that society was static. Most gays did. If you mentioned organizing, they'd say that society hated us and always would, that you couldn't change things. Well, I knew that society was changing in many ways and needed to change in lots of other ways. I instinctively took a political approach to social problems. I always said, "Let's do something." Well, that approach was alien to most people, particularly most gays, and particularly at this time. This was an enormously conservative, conformist period, probably the most conformist period in our history, or at least in our recent history. We were coming into the McCarthy era.

Nothing came of my attempts to start a group of my own. Eventually, in 1952, I went to my first Mattachine meeting. My friend, Betty Perdue, took me. It was in someone's big house in Los Feliz. Betty was known as "Geraldine Jackson" in the movement. She wrote a poem, "Proud and Unashamed," in the first issue of ONE magazine, though she never managed to achieve that condition herself. A Lutheran minister also went with us. He was terribly nervous, nellie, and paranoid.

When we got to the house, we knocked at the door. It was almost a "Joe sent me" sort of thing. They knew Betty and the minister, so we went right in. There were about 180 people in the room, sitting everywhere. There was a circular stairway going up to a landing, and both of those were filled with people. I was quite shocked by the number of people. About 80 percent were men, 85 percent in their thirties or younger. No one was underage. That was verboten.

The announced topic was, "What do we do with these effeminate queens and these stalking butches who are giving us a bad name?" It was a lively discussion, but it seemed to me that the ones at this meeting who were most worried about the problem happened to be the effeminate queens and stalking butches.

It took me a while to speak up. I was pretty shy, but I finally blurted out this story about the first time I went to a gay bar in the late spring of 1943. It was the Black Cat bar in San Francisco. I told them how I was going to join my brothers and sisters for the first time. I was on a cloud of idealism, so high that I was walking down Montgomery Street four inches above the sidewalk. I got almost to the door of the bar. I think I even touched the door, when all of a sudden a whole bunch of San Francisco policemen went past me and burst into the bar. I didn't see them coming. By this time I had read eight or ten novels and had read several accounts of bar raids, so I knew what was happening.

Standing outside the bar, I had chivalric visions of mounting my white charger and going in to save my brothers and sisters, but instead, I hid in the doorway across the street, feeling like shit, feeling cowardly, feeling guilty.

The first view I got of my brothers and sisters was when 12 or 15 drag queens and about 12 or 15 butch numbers—men who would be called San Francisco clones today—were led out of the bar by the police. All the clones were looking guilty, and practically all the queens were struggling and sassing the cops. I felt so good when I heard one of the queens scream at the policeman who was shoving her, "Don't shove, you bastard, or I'll bite your fuckin' balls off!" That queen paid in blood. They beat her and two or three of the others. I was still hiding in the doorway, wanting to do something, wanting to shout something, but I wouldn't have known what to shout.

When I finished this story I said, "Look, the queens were the only ones who ever fought. If not for the queens, there wouldn't have been bars that the rest of us could sneak into. Because of them, we could go to the bars and be gay for one night; we could let our hair down"— figuratively. "But when we left the bars, we pinned up our hair and pretended we were like everyone else. And they didn't." When we left the bars, we were very careful not to go out at the same time any of the queens did. Some of them were real cute about tricking us and would walk out the door at the same time one of us more closety ones went out. There was a two-step that you used to do as you went out the door. You would take the minimum number of steps you had to in order to get into a position where you appeared to be passing by the bar.

I got very angry at this attack on the queens. I said, "They're our front line. And they're not the ones who cause prejudice. People are much more upset when they find out that their neighbor or friend who wasn't obvious is, in fact, gay." I think that causes a lot more prejudice than some obvious queen. People can relate to the queens in the same way they relate to Stepin Fetchit.

The format of the meeting was such that you couldn't tell who was running it. There were unofficial cochairs, but they were instructed not to act as if they were really running things, just to keep the discussion going. There were also people who made announcements of activities. "There's going to be a beach party" or "Why don't we have a beach party, and would some people like to volunteer for arrangements?" This secrecy about who really ran the discussion groups was intentional.

By the time I got to my second or third meeting, the gossip was getting around that some of the people in charge were Communists. That was very disturbing in this period of history, because almost all the people who came to the discussion groups were very conformist, and they loved nothing better than to say, "We're just like everybody else except for what we do in bed. We don't want any special rights. We don't want to rock the boat."

When I got more involved in the organization, I realized that the need for secrecy was exaggerated. This was due, in part, to the fact that Harry Hay, one of the founders, had been through the Party, which was a pretty secret organization. But Harry also had this idea that gays had been an underground society throughout history. He had developed a Masonic Lodge approach to running Mattachine. Some of the others, like Martin Block, thought all this secrecy was a lot of bullshit.

AFTER THE changeover in leadership in 1953, when Mattachine became an open, democratic organization, the society went into decline—for two reasons. First, the new leaders, who were ultraconservatives, wanted tight control of what the different chapters of the organizations did. The result was inaction—paralysis—because a chapter would decide to do something and the ultraconservatives would veto it. Second, the mystique was gone. The mystique of the original Mattachine depended on the impression that there were some big people behind the organization. That impression made it seem safe and made it seem as if there were people who would take care of things for us, so we only had to show up at meetings and discuss things like, "Should I tell my parents?" "Can you be gay and Christian?" "If we're really gay, do we have to swish?" But that wasn't the case anymore. Suddenly, we had to do something besides talk, and a lot of people weren't interested in that.

I stayed with Mattachine for a while after the changeover, but eventually I became more involved in ONE magazine, which had begun publishing in early 1953. It was not a very impressive publication, and we never sold more than a few thousand copies a month, but it was the first, and it was ours.

ONE's staff seemed a little closed at the time I tried to get involved. When I spoke to a couple of people who ran the magazine, Dorr Legg and Dale Jennings, about doing some work, I wasn't exactly snatched up. So I began coming into the office frequently and talking to Dorr about ideas for articles. I did one called "The Importance of Being Honest," which appeared in March 1954. Then I wrote an article on the British witch-hunt, which had begun in the middle of 1953. Hundreds of men were arrested on homosexual charges, including several prominent men, among them actor John Gielgud. At the same time, a similar, more limited witch-hunt began in Miami. There were other witch-hunts later in various other places, including one in South Carolina at a black college and one at the beach in Santa Monica. So I began reporting on these sorts of things. Then I started writing a regular column called "Tangents." It was concerned with gay news, censorship, conformity, civil rights, gender oddities, and other subjects that seemed to relate to our field of interest.

I got lots of complaints about the column from readers because the news was bad. Bars raided. Guys murdered by someone they had picked up or someone who saw them on the street and thought they were queer. Public officials arrested in public tearooms. I explained several times to ONE subscribers that we did not have five hundred reporters scattered around the world to provide us with independent reports. I depended on the straight press, and those were the kinds of stories they were publishing about gays. I was buying as many out-of-town newspapers as I could.

You could read most papers for a year without finding any gay news unless you learned how to read between the lines. They might not have mentioned the raid of a homosexual or queer bar, but they'd

mention a "house of ill repute." And if several men were arrested and
no women were mentioned as present, you assumed it was not a
whorehouse. In the article they might mention one man was dressed
in a "womanish" manner. When *Time* magazine mentioned the subject, they usually used words like *epicene* to describe someone. When
they reviewed—holding their noses—Tennessee Williams or Carson
McCullers, they would use the term *decadent*. You looked for those
words and then read the whole thing carefully. Then you would go
and investigate. So I would write to one of our subscribers in the place
from where the story was reported and ask, "Is this a gay story?"

I also explained to readers who complained about the negative
news, "If I should know that a gay person was made president of
General Electric, do you think I could report that?" Of course, I
couldn't. First, we didn't report that kind of thing because of the
absolute code by which it was considered unfair to bring another
person out. That was an individual decision. Second, I would not
have reported that kind of thing because we would have been sued for
slander. The person we identified as gay would have probably lost his
position anyhow. It would have hurt everybody. There was no point
to it.

I also followed conformity stories. For instance, I opened one
column with the awful line, "Elvis, the pelvis doesn't amuse me." But
I objected to what the local authorities were doing about his concerts,
raiding them or refusing permission for him to perform because of his
sexy gyrations. Of course, I had to show my superiority first. Actually
it wasn't until the fifth or sixth song I heard that I thought Elvis was
any good.

And I also reported on the slow development of long hair and the
breakaway from orthodox clothing styles. I did a story on the owner
of a Beverly Hills antique store who was arrested because he had a
statue of Michelangelo's *David* in the window. Things like that. These
were censorship questions in general. Censorship hit us extra hard
with a double standard. Anything that was heterosexual was considered obscene if it was extremely disgusting, provocative, or sexually
explicit or had an excessive use of Anglo-Saxon language or detailed
descriptions of the mechanics of sex. Anything that mentioned homosexuality was obscene simply if it did not point out how terribly,
terribly disgusting and evil homosexuality was. No detail was permitted. That was what got the magazine hooked by the post office.

The August 1953 issue, which had the phrase "homosexual marriage" on the cover, was seized by the post office—using the obscenity
hook—and released. *ONE* printed an angry article saying that *ONE*
was not grateful to the postmaster for releasing it. Some people

thought that the fact that the postmaster had released it signified that
we were okay, but that wasn't the case because the post office seized
another issue of the magazine, the October 1954 issue, which ironically happened to have a cover story on the law of mailable material.

I think the reason behind the post office's seizure of this second
issue was an article in the previous issue suggesting that everybody
knew that J. Edgar Hoover was sleeping with Clyde Tolson, his close
partner. That article attracted the interest of the FBI. Much later,
through the Freedom of Information Act, we found a note from
Hoover to Tolson, which I have a copy of somewhere in storage,
saying, "We've got to get these bastards." There was also a note to the
post office from Hoover urging them to check into ONE.

At the same time as the seizure, the FBI showed up at ONE's office
wanting to know who had written the article about Hoover. They also
came to visit me a couple of times and visited most members of the
staff. One of the FBI agents sat right there in that chair. I was nervous;
it was a tense situation. They asked me if a couple of members of the
staff were Communists, and I hooted and said that they were very
conservative. They were. I probably shouldn't have even told them
that. I did say that I had been a member of the Communist party and
that I had been kicked out for being gay. They wanted me to name
people I had known in the Party and what they did. I owed no thanks
to the Party for kicking me out, but I would not give information
about individuals who were in the Party, whom I still respected.

The case went up through the Ninth Circuit Court of Appeals, and
the courts found the magazine utterly obscene, with no redeeming
social values. But for the time being, the seizure affected only the
individual issue. We were only forbidden to mail out further copies
of that particular issue of ONE. But then several other issues were
held up for a month or two. So we began using extreme measures to
mail the magazine. Each member of the staff would take several long
drives. At each town we would go off the highway, find the mailbox,
and put in five or six copies. Nothing was on the plain brown wrapper
to identify the magazine. Just the addressee and our return address.
We mailed no more than fifteen or twenty copies in any one town.

We did this for three or four months before we discovered that the
post office knew exactly what we were doing. About five weeks after
we mailed one particular issue from towns all over southern California, I got a call from the post office to come in. The post office had
virtually all of the issues we had mailed out for that month on a
couple of flats. You see, they were inspecting each individual copy of
the magazine we sent out for anything that they could hold it for, and
some of the packages we mailed didn't have enough postage. There

were different enclosures in each issue, depending on whether someone was getting a renewal notice. So a lot of issues would be right on
the line as to whether they needed more postage, and because Dorr
Legg, who was in charge of running the magazine, was always so much
of a skinflint, he wouldn't let us use extra postage.

When I was called down by the post office, I had to weigh each
magazine and put extra postage on about one out of ten copies. After
that, we figured there was no point mailing the magazines from all
over the state, since the post office obviously had no trouble finding
each copy of the magazine we mailed, no matter where we mailed it
from.

The ONE obscenity case went all the way up to the United States
Supreme Court, which reversed the lower court's ruling, clearing the
magazine. That was in January 1958. Unfortunately, though, there
was no written opinion from the Supreme Court. But the ruling sort
of opened the floodgates to publications that discussed homosexuality. It ended the double standard over what was considered obscene,
and we were never bothered again.

The Attorney

Herb Selwyn

ATTORNEYS WERE *essential to gay organizations and individual gay people as they struggled to avoid entanglement with the police, federal agents, and the courts. At the same time, organizations and individuals had to avoid falling into the hands of unscrupulous attorneys who profited by cooperating with authorities to exploit gay people.*

Herb Selwyn wasn't that kind of lawyer. Heterosexual himself, he believed gay people deserved equal treatment under the law, despite a criminal justice system that treated them as inherent criminals. Beginning in the early 1950s, Herb represented fledgling organizations, provided critical legal advice, and assisted many individual gay clients at a time when few legitimate attorneys, gay or straight, would take them on.

Herb was born in 1925 and raised in West Hollywood. He attended UCLA before and after World War II. During the war, he served in the U.S. Army Air Corps in England, France, and Germany. After graduating from UCLA, he went to law school at the University of Southern California. He later married and had four children.

Herb Selwyn lives in a 1960s-era, ranch-style house at the end of a quiet street in an affluent Los Angeles neighborhood. He's a small man, who speaks with the steady voice of one who is confirmed in his convictions.

About three years after I opened a practice, in early 1953, my father, who was a doctor, told me about a patient of his, a woman who was a lesbian. He had mentioned to her that I was a lawyer, and she told him that she belonged to a group called the Mattachine Society. She asked if he thought I'd give a talk to their group. So my dad asked me, and I said, "Certainly." I didn't see why not. I'm a lawyer; you help people who need help. That's supposedly what a lawyer does. And people who don't have a lot of money, especially those who aren't very popular, do need help.

You see, I was not raised to despise people whose sexual interests were different, just as I didn't despise people who were black or Hispanic or had disabilities. I think most of these dislikes are taught by your family at an early age. My parents were never homophobic.

They explained to me that some people have different predilections than others. Of course, by the time I was invited to speak to the Mattachine group, I was well aware that there were gay people. Growing up, we knew that there were gay bars in the area where we lived. Two pretty good friends I played poker with I later found out were gay. I didn't know at the time, but I found out after the war.

During the war I remember a young soldier who was arrested and sentenced to a lot of years because he had had a relationship with a teenaged English boy. I told the major that I thought it was rather unjust that he get that much time because the kid was willing and that he should be sent for psychotherapy instead. The major made some nasty crack like, "Well, you guys ought to go out and psychoanalyze each other" or something like that. He knew I wasn't gay. He was just one of these guys who thought that this was beyond the pale and felt it was improper for me to take up for them. He was not a terribly enlightened individual.

I was probably not considered the most disciplined soldier in the armed forces because I always said what I thought and didn't care to whom I said it. I still don't. I've always stuck my neck out.

BEFORE I went to talk to the Mattachine group, I checked out the various sections and statutes that might affect people committing homosexual acts. Section 286 is having sexual relations with an animal, or a man having sexual relations through the anus. Section 286 also included a man having anal intercourse with a woman. And Section 288a involved oral copulation—copulating the private parts of one with the mouth of another. In those years, oral copulation was a crime punishable by up to fourteen years in prison, whether it was heterosexual or homosexual. But while both 286 and 288a could affect heterosexuals, very few heterosexuals were ever arrested under these laws. It was mainly male homosexuals. Later on I had a couple of cases involving female homosexuals, but both of those were dismissed because they were very difficult for the police to prove.

At any rate, I reviewed the laws and then I gave a talk to the Mattachine group, which was then rather small. It was at a private home, and I don't think there were more than twenty-five or thirty men and women there. In those years men and women got along pleasantly together. There weren't the schisms that developed later on.

I was very well received because, you see, at that time, there were no homosexual lawyers at all. They were all very deeply in the closet. In fact, they were in so deep that most of the people that represented gay organizations—as opposed to criminal cases—were straight. Homosexual lawyers were very reluctant to get involved because the climate at that time was very homophobic. If a gay lawyer was found out, it could hurt his practice.

After I gave that first talk, Mattachine began coming to me for legal advice. And I started representing gay clients in criminal cases. I handled the incorporation for Mattachine in 1954. I think it was the first gay organization that was incorporated. I know someone from Mattachine had once gone to another lawyer, and he wanted twenty-five thousand dollars to incorporate. I did it for free. I felt that a corporation would be a way for Mattachine to later on get a tax exemption from the IRS so that people could give donations. Unfortunately, the rich gays at that time were very deeply in the closet and weren't about to give money to a gay organization.

ONE TIME, in the mid-1950s, I advised Mattachine and other gay groups about going on a television panel. I think it was the "Paul Coates Show," here in Los Angeles. Some of the people at Mattachine were a little afraid that Coates might do something harmful to what was then an infant movement. I told Mattachine that if they wanted to do it, they should make sure they had some preapproval of what was going to be on the air. The Coates people also wanted to shoot some film of the Mattachine meetings. They wound up showing the meetings and some parties. It was rather innocuous, but for those days it was a fairly bold venture.

I wasn't on the "Paul Coates Show" panel, but I was on some shows a little later in the 1950s that involved the question of homosexuality. I recall a Judge Guerin on one particular show. There was also Dr. Frederick Hacker, a famous psychiatrist from Vienna, who did a lot of work in the field of homosexuality and psychodynamics. Dr. Hacker treated a lot of homosexuals and he was used by a lot of lawyers, including me, to make reports for the probation department for gay people who got into difficulties. There was also a private investigator on the panel.

During the show, Judge Guerin claimed that all homosexuals became such because they were seduced by sailors when they were twelve or thirteen years old. Dr. Hacker disagreed with Judge Guerin, and Judge Guerin had a stroke right on television. He hated to be disagreed with, and he had a violent temper. Probably his temper, combined with some cerebral arterial sclerosis, caused blood vessels in his brain to burst. I saw immediately what was happening and waved to the host of the show to get the camera off Judge Guerin. The poor man was taken to the hospital and died a few days later. Several members of the district attorney's office said rather gleefully, "Well, Herb, I hear you killed Judge Guerin. Good for you!" But, of course, I wasn't the one who made the fatal comment.

ONE OF the earlier criminal cases I tried involved a man who met another man in a public rest room. The two men started talking, and when they walked out, one fellow said, "Well, I'm just down from Sacramento and I'm a lather,* and I don't know anybody down here." After a little conversation, my client allegedly made a proposal to this other man, who, it turned out, was an undercover officer, who then arrested him. At the trial, my client admitted that he had lied about his identity—he wasn't a lather and he wasn't from Sacramento—but the jury acquitted him nonetheless. Either the jury believed that my client hadn't propositioned the policeman or they thought that this was no way for the police to act.

I'll never forget one case in the late fifties, in which the state tried to revoke the license of a hairdresser, a cosmetologist, for being gay. I think the hairdresser had a lewd-conduct arrest for propositioning an undercover policeman or something like that. But it was a misdemeanor, and it wasn't something that affected his work. It wasn't as if he was a crook or a person who might assault somebody. It was simply that he was a homosexual, and therefore the prosecutor believed he should be stripped of his cosmetologist's license.

When we got to court, I suggested to the administrative law judge, who I knew was a married man, that he should ask his wife how many of the male hairdressers she had gone to in her life she thought might be gay. And I jokingly asked him how all of our wives and girlfriends would look if all the gay hairdressers had their licenses removed. He chuckled at that one. The prosecutor frowned. The whole thing was very amusing, but not for the poor guy whose license was at stake because he had a nice little shop. If he had lost his license, it would have caused a great deal of harm to him and to the people who depended on him.

I DON'T think my handling these criminal cases or affiliation with gay rights groups hurt my career. Besides, I didn't care. I figured I was in there to practice law and represent people who needed me. I didn't look to see if it would further my career. Probably my affiliations with

---

*Someone who puts up lath and plaster.

the American Civil Liberties Union have caused more comment from friends, colleagues, and clients than anything I've ever done in the gay movement.

The only time anyone got upset was when I wrote a little card called "Know Your Legal Rights," which Mattachine distributed to its members and people at the gay bars. It was designed to fit in your wallet. It basically told you what your rights were in the event of an arrest. This was in the late fifties, before the police had to read you your rights. And this friend of mine, a classmate, in fact, a prosecutor who was with the city attorney's office, showed the card to me, not knowing that I had written it. He said, "Isn't this awful? Isn't it horrible?" I looked at it. I didn't tell him I wrote it. I said, "Look, are there any statements of law there that are incorrect?" He said, "No, but you're telling people they don't have to talk to the police." I said, "If these are their rights, don't you think they have the right to know them?" That guy just got peeved at me and walked away.

As far as objections from gay people because I was straight, if there were any, that wouldn't have been said to my face. There was one exception: a remark from somebody in Mattachine I didn't know who said something about Mattachine's lawyers making a lot of money off the gays. That was rather ludicrous because the fees I charged people on these criminal cases were about half what some of the gay lawyers who were willing to take these cases charged. My fees were always reasonable.

I NEVER really stopped representing gay organizations. Eventually, they just stopped calling me. They must have felt that they wanted gay lawyers representing them and later, in the 1960s, they were able to find gay lawyers who were willing to do that kind of work.

Without flattering myself, I think I can probably say that my greatest contributions were my pioneering efforts when straight lawyers weren't interested in the cause and gay lawyers were afraid to take it up. I was at least able to help Mattachine and several other early educational organizations get a start in what later became a movement that gained an enormous amount for gays.

"Gay Sexualist"
Hal Call

WHEN HAL CALL took over the Mattachine Society in 1953, he believed that the struggle for gay rights was a fight for sexual freedom. He also knew how he wanted to wage that battle—gingerly, through education, and with the help of experts and leaders in the straight world.

People have very definite opinions about Hal Call. Some consider him a hero for having been as publicly up front as he was in running the Mattachine Society at a time when many gay people, including those involved in gay organizations, hid behind drawn curtains and pseudonyms. They admire him for being a tireless advocate of gay sexual freedom in the face of brutal police repression. Others accuse him of stealing the Mattachine Society from its founders and turning it into a sex club and personal profit center.

Today, Hal's office is located above the Circle J Cinema, a gay sex club he owns and operates in the Tenderloin neighborhood in San Francisco. To get to his office, you have to walk past a sign-in window just inside the cramped entrance to the theater and step through a black curtain. A staircase to the right of the movie screen leads to the second floor and Hal's office. On one wall of the office, several television monitors are stacked to the ceiling. Three were turned on, displaying images much like the ones being shown in the theater just a floor below. Across from the monitors is a sofa and several straight-back vinyl-covered office chairs. Hundreds of videotapes line the wall behind the sofa from floor to ceiling.

Hal was seated on the sofa, casually dressed in a crisp blue-checked shirt and jeans and stylish glasses. He looked years younger than his more than seventy years. His white hair and trim white moustache, once blond, contrasted sharply with his ruddy complexion. Hal spoke with authority and a full voice, as if his audience numbered more than one. He had his video camera focused on the sofa. It was set on record.

My name is Harold L. Call, and I'm executive director of the Mattachine Society, Inc. I was born in north-central Missouri in 1917.

I've known I was a gay person ever since I was twelve turning thirteen on the farm where I grew up. I was very curious about sexual information and very much turned on to the male penis. So I broached those things to an older man. He was fourteen. He was my second cousin, and we masturbated together. We were masturbatory partners for a while there. Later I tried to get the seventeen-year-old farmhand to masturbate, to sort of show and tell. He wouldn't do it.

I went through a period in my life when I tried to change. Back when I was a sophomore at the University of Missouri, I dated a girl and I tried to get a hard-on for her, but I never was able to. Cats could swim a lot better than I could get an erection. And she was a wonderful woman. That's been the case all my life.

I was inducted into the army in 1941. If people were caught engaging in homosexual acts, some of them were shipped back to the States with less-than-honorable discharges. I thought that was a waste. I had absolutely no sexual activity in the armed forces with anyone because I knew it was a no-no. Besides, when you became a commander and an officer, you didn't carry on with troops. There were some who were carrying on, and we'd hear of it now and then, but we'd never try to investigate it. You have to consider the circumstances. You were in the South Pacific, down on Espiritu Santo. You came from a combat operation in the Marianas and were going up to a combat operation in the Ryukyus. The men had not been home or had a furlough or leave or anything like that for two or three years. Years, not months. They were under the stress of war, and they were going into combat again where a lot of them were not going to come out. So if they went up under the coco trees and sucked a little cock and jacked off together or something like that, so what? Who was harmed? Nobody. That's the way the armed forces should look at it. The armed forces could not operate without homosexuals. Never could. Never has. And never will.

After the army, I stayed in the active reserve for a few years in Missouri and finished work for my degree in journalism at the university. Later I worked for the *Kansas City Star* in the national advertising department and got sent to Chicago.

In Chicago in August 1952, I was arrested. There were four of us in a small automobile. It was a two-door, two-seater, parked at one-thirty in the morning about fifty feet from the police station in Lincoln Park. These three guys who I met at a gay bar were going to drive me home, but instead they drove to Lincoln Park and parked the car. The police were out patrolling with flashlights, and as soon as we turned the car off, they were flashing the lights on us.

The three of them thought that if they accused me of trying to do something to them, they would get off scot-free, that it would put the onus of guilt on me. But the police didn't buy it, and all four of us got busted. The attorney who we got was in with the system. At that time, in 1952, eight hundred dollars bought off the arresting officers and the judge, and it included the attorney's fee, so that one court appearance brought a dismissal.

To be accused, though, was to be guilty. At that time I was so naive that I didn't see any harm in telling my supervisor at the *Kansas City Star* what had happened. When I told him, he said, "We can't have anybody like that working for the *Kansas City Star*." I said, "That may be so, but if you fired all the homosexuals on the *Kansas City Star*, you wouldn't get the newspaper out. You couldn't even set the linotype." He didn't believe that. In my FBI file, I later found out that the FBI went back and checked up on me at the *Kansas City Star*.

I decided after my arrest that instead of going where the job took me, I was going to go where I wanted and find my own career. So my lover and I drove from Chicago to San Francisco with all of our possessions in the autumn of 1952, and I've been here since. Now, we didn't choose San Francisco because it was some kind of gay mecca. Back then, it wasn't. But from when I first saw San Francisco during World War II, I thought it was the best place to live in North America because of its beauty and location.

NOT LONG after we got to San Francisco, I heard that an organization called the Mattachine Society, out of Los Angeles, was having meetings and discussion forums in Berkeley near the University of California campus. I also heard that they were concerned with the problems of male homosexuals, particularly the legal problems. I went to my first meeting in February 1953. There were about fifteen or twenty people. A number of them were students, and some of them were people who later became well known in the beat literary period of the 1950s. We brought the idea back here. We started getting our gay friends together in San Francisco for discussions.

It was all men. And let's get something straight right here, right now. I know that women's liberation in this country has come a long way, so that everything has to be spoken of in two genders—male and female—all the time. Now in the days I'm speaking of, the early days of the gay movement, the women weren't in it. They didn't have any problems compared to what the male did. It's only since the movement got going that the women have come forward, and, honest to God, it has been an astounding revelation to me.

Back in the 1950s, the police were playing cat and mouse with the guys, not the women. The male homosexual, because he was a cock-sucker and because he played with his penis and somebody else's

penis, was a threat to the straight man. That's where the whole problem was. Females didn't count.

NOT LONG after I started going to Mattachine meetings, I got involved
in taking over the organization. I was one of the wheels that caused the
original secret Mattachine Society to become a democratic one. Because of fear, the core of the organization was secret. We didn't know
who was running Mattachine. Remember, this was the time when
Senator Joseph McCarthy in Washington, D.C., was going around
with names and addresses of people in the government, saying,
"These are homosexuals, and these are Communists." McCarthy was
spreading fear among homosexuals and all kinds of people, equating
the condition of homosexuality with Communism. Of course, Communism at that time was an ogre, a demon, that we can't even imagine
today.

We wanted to see Mattachine grow and spread, but we didn't think
that this could be done as long as Mattachine was a secret organization. But we knew that if we became a public organization, the FBI and
other government agencies would find out about us. That was okay
with us, but before we went public, we wanted to make sure that we
didn't have a person in our midst who could be revealed as a Communist and disgrace us all. We wanted to be able to stand up and say who
we were and what we were about and not be accused of these other
things. Despite the secrecy, we knew that some of the founders of the
Mattachine Society, the inner circle, had been rumored to have some
Communist leanings and maybe connections elsewhere. They had
to go.

So we sort of took the organization out of the founders' hands. We
did this at a pair of meetings in the spring of 1953 in Los Angeles. At
the second meeting, which was held in May, the founders of Mattachine gave over the Mattachine idea to those of us who wanted to
form a democratic Mattachine Society with elected officers and with
members and officers we knew.

I didn't just disagree with how the original Mattachine was run. I
also disagreed with the philosophy of the Mattachine founders. I felt
that they were sort of pie in the sky, erudite, and artistically inclined.
Take Harry Hay, the kingpin of the original founders. You could
never talk to him very long without him going way back in history to
some ancient Egyptian cult or something of that sort. He was always
making Mattachine and the homosexual of today a parallel to some
of those things he found out about in his historical research.

We saw Mattachine as a here-and-now, practical thing because we were a group of cocksuckers that the police were chasing. They were assassinating character at will and causing all kinds of mischief and expense and damage to us as individuals. We wanted to see changes brought about, changes in law, changes in public attitudes, research into the realities of sexual behavior and education. You see, I was a journalist and a public relations man and I felt that education and getting the word out was the best thing we could do, so the whole society could ultimately say, "Homosexuals are human beings in our midst. They're only different in certain ways from the rest of us. Leave them alone."

We wanted to see those goals achieved by evolutionary methods, not revolutionary methods. We were pretty pure and bland, really. By today's standards we were a bunch of limp-wrist pussyfoots. But we were out of the closet, and that was a very courageous thing in those days because there were not very many of us.

So public protests were not part of our program. Not at all. We wanted to see changes come about by holding conferences and discussions and becoming subjects for research and telling our story. We wanted to assist people in the academic and behavioral-science world in getting the truth out to people who had an influence on law and law enforcement, the courts, justice, and so on. For example, the Kinsey group in Bloomington, Indiana, was soon in contact with us, and we cooperated with their research.

WE HAD to deal in a lot of euphemisms in those days. We didn't call homosexuals, *homosexual*. We called them *sex variants*. We knew that if we were going to get along in society, we were going to have to stay in step with the existing and predominant mores and customs of our society and not stand out as sore thumbs too much because we didn't have the strength of tissue paper to defend ourselves.

Staying in step meant, by God, keeping your sex life private, very much to yourself, and between adults because we knew what society's feeling was about getting children mixed into it. And it also meant that you didn't go wearing your heart on your sleeve. We wouldn't dare hold hands on a street. And you couldn't even put your hand on another person's shoulder in a gay bar without it being "lewd conduct." We had people in drag who would come out on Halloween. They knew better, but they dared to do it. They knew the chances were good that they would be busted, and many of them were, but they dared to come out and wear furs and all that. I admire those brave people for that, but they were asking for it. Because the cops could do any damn thing they wanted. All we could do was run and hide.

Mattachine tried to help people avoid getting in trouble because if you got arrested and your name got in the paper, you would lose your job. In those days the *San Francisco Examiner* printed in bold type on the front page the names of every gay person arrested, his age, his address, his marital status, and his employment status. And, my God, when accused of lewd conduct or sucking cock, which is the filthiest thing on Earth, your name was printed in the paper and all kinds of things resulted from that—divorces, suicides, wrecked careers, and the loss of credit or rented apartments.

The cops were making arrests at the bars, so we were getting calls from a lot of the people they busted to arrange for an attorney or a bail bondsman. I remember one night, in August 1961, hell, the cops took in nearly a hundred people from the Tay-Bush Inn. Ethel Merman just missed getting busted on that night by about fifteen minutes. She was starring in *Gypsy*, which was playing down here at the Curran or Geary theater, and had gone up to the Tay-Bush with some gay friends after the show.

When I heard about that Tay-Bush Inn incident, I had to get my ass down to the old Hall of Justice. I was there all night trying to help get everyone processed. And you know, as soon as I walked down there, the people in the police department said, "Oh, there you are, Hal Call. The Mattachine's on the job, right?" Yes, we were. The cops knew there was a Mattachine Society, a group of queers that was daring to stand up and work on behalf of other queers whom the police were busting. But every arrested person had to cough up money and pay for his own bail bondsman, own attorney, and so on. The cops could get away with that in the Tay-Bush days.

When you were sitting in a gay bar, you were always in danger of being tapped on the shoulder by a cop and taken out. A fellow who was sitting in the Fez bar on Turk Street reached down to get a pack of cigarettes out of his sock, and an Alcoholic Beverage Control* agent who was there accused him of groping the man next to him at the bar and took him out for lewd conduct.

THERE WERE people in Mattachine who wanted us to challenge the laws, to write legislators, to do those sorts of things. I didn't alto-

---

*The Alcoholic Beverage Control Department was a California state agency that policed the bars in cooperation with the local police. It used arrests for lewd conduct and solicitation as a means of closing down gay bars.

gether disagree, but I knew we didn't have a handful of toilet paper to do it with. That's the thing: It was absolutely futile. We were doing a $300,000-a-year—in 1950s dollars—public relations job on $12,000 a year income with three or four people doing the work. And what we needed to do was a $3 million-a-year PR job. We were overwhelmed by what we needed to do. So we had to pick out what we could do with the resources that were available. All kinds of people in our membership, in our discussion groups, and so on were willing to tell us what we should be doing. But when you asked them to do it: "Oh, no, not me. I'm on the faculty at the college"; "I'm working for this law office"; "Oh, I couldn't dare be connected with anything like that."

Still, we were more successful than we should have been. We were almost like what Churchill said about the Royal Air Force in Britain in World War II. I never knew when so few gay people ever made an impact that spread so far and wide and made it sound like it was so vast. It wasn't; Mattachine membership has never been all that great. We never had as many as four hundred on our mailing list. We didn't have a pot to piss in, much less the window to pitch it out. But we created some little leaflets and publications, and they were distributed and had an impact. Sometimes we were covered in the press, and even bad press was good to have.

One of the biggest public relations successes came more than ten years after I took over the Mattachine, in 1964. In January of that year, people from *Life* magazine contacted us and wondered if we could help them get a photographic representation of the homosexual community in the San Francisco area. It had to be authentic news, not staged, because *Life* was a news magazine. But the identity of people in the photographs had to be protected because in those days you couldn't just go out and photograph a bunch of gays and then label them without being subject to lawsuits.

We chose two bars, and they were both reluctant. One of them was the Tool Box. We chose it because it had a particular black-and-white mural of macho, leather cowboy types. We got a number of regular customers to come in. For the photo shoot, the place was lighted by opening the door wide to allow daylight to flood in on one side. Most of the people inside were shown in silhouette. Plus, there was smoke haze in the air. One or two faces were somewhat identifiable after the picture was taken, so *Life* did an air brush job on them.

When the article came out in June, the owner of the Tool Box said, "Jesus Christ, Hal Call, we shouldn't have done that! Now the ABC is going to close my bar." I said, "Don't you worry. You've got a black-and-white double-page ad in *Life* magazine. You couldn't have bought that for seventy-five thousand dollars." This was in 1964, when ad rates were not what they are now. Anyway, he was pacified, especially when business picked up. My God, every gay that came to San Francisco wanted to see the Tool Box and see that mural! Everybody took pictures of that mural.

The other bar *Life* photographed was the Jumping Frog, a beer bar on Polk Street, just north of Broadway. The Jumping Frog was particularly popular on Sunday afternoons and evenings. Beer was twenty-five cents a glass at the time. The bar itself was in the middle of a large square room, so there was access all around it. On Saturday nights at ten or eleven o'clock, they used a sixteen-millimeter movie projector, as some of the other bars did, to show Hollywood films. At the time we made arrangements for the photographs to be taken, they were showing the Marilyn Monroe movie *Some Like It Hot*. Early in the evening we arranged for a person stationed at the door to tell everyone who came in that at eleven o'clock *Life* magazine photographers were going to take some silhouette pictures in the bar, but would not take any photographs that included direct shots of anyone's face. Those who wanted to stay could; those who didn't could step outside. That was the rule. Believe it or not, most people stayed. They didn't fly out of there in a panic. So they got pictures of the Marilyn Monroe movie on that screen with people in silhouette jammed in there watching. That was the first time a national magazine had ever treated the subject of homosexuality with any sensitivity or understanding. My photograph was in it. I was running our printing press where we were printing the Mattachine magazine. Don Slater, from Los Angeles, his photograph was also in there. He was with ONE, Incorporated, the organization that printed *ONE* magazine.* And they had some other, you might say, friendly photographs, as well as photographs of people who were very antagonistic and very antihomosexual—fag haters. They also had an article that came from the Kinsey people at the Institute for Sex Research in Bloomington, Indiana, that told how homosexuals were in our society and always had been.

By the mid-1950s Mattachine was becoming a full-time job. We had so much to do at Mattachine that we tried to raise money for a staff. We were getting many phone calls and making referrals to psychiatrists and Ph.D. psychologists. We were also talking man to man with a lot of the people who came to us with problems. We needed people

---

*By this time, ONE magazine had left the Mattachine Society and was being published by an organization in Los Angeles called ONE, Incorporated.

who knew public relations, who were articulate, and who would be there year after year. Not just volunteers who were here today, but gone the moment their gay-identity problem was resolved.

The other reason we wanted a paid staff was that those of us who had been in the Mattachine Society for a year or so wanted to keep the organization within the control of the steadfast board of directors. We didn't want it to be subject to the whim or the vote of the newest wave of members. We wanted the original group to stay in office and get paid for it. This was a bone of contention because others thought Mattachine should use all-volunteer help. Some of those who disagreed were later instrumental in founding an organization called the Society for Individual Rights (SIR) in 1964. I probably contributed to the dissension as much as anyone.

In the beginning we wanted to raise money with publications and maybe do some book publishing on a small scale. We also hoped that we would be able to get bequests from older gay people. The idea of applying for grants was so wild and far in the future that we never dreamed it.

In the mid-1950s, some of us in the Mattachine created Pan Graphic Press, our little printing company, so we could keep the physical equipment, including the printing press, out of the hands of the Mattachine membership. We didn't want the press to be subject to the whims of the membership. We knew they'd play with it, and it would be destroyed.

Among the things Pan Graphic printed was the *Mattachine Review*, Mattachine's monthly magazine, which we sent to our membership. We started publishing the *Mattachine Review* in January 1955. It was an educational and informational tool. The idea was to spread the word about what we thought was the reality of homosexual behavior.

I was the editor of the *Mattachine Review* from about the first issue. I did the writing, printing, binding, and distribution. I used pen names for some of my writing because I felt that it was too much for the editor to have his own name as the byline for one article after another. Material was so scarce in those days that we had to write a lot of the stuff ourselves.

Presumably, we were billing the Mattachine Society for printing the *Mattachine Review*, but we never, ever got paid what we should have for the work we put into it. Mattachine didn't have the revenue. So in essence, Pan Graphic Press, a private business, supported the Mattachine Society. That wasn't how everybody saw it. A lot of people had the idea we were making a lot of money through Pan Graphic

Press and that we were milking the Mattachine, but it was the other way around.

One of the things Pan Graphic printed was a bar directory. In the early 1960s I helped Bob Damron, who was a gay bar owner here, create his *Address Book*, a directory of gay bars for the nation that fit in a shirt pocket. It first came out in fifty tiny pages. It has now been around long enough to have a twenty-fifth anniversary edition.

Bob Damron's Address Book was not the first directory of gay bars. In 1954, we mimeographed a directory of gay bars on the West Coast, from San Diego to Seattle. There were about thirty-five on the list. We numbered the sheets of paper and we signed out the numbered copies for people to fold up and put in their wallets. They signed for them because we did not want the list to get into the hands of the police. It was that sensitive a matter in those days. We had only about fifty copies. That was all we dared print.

MATTACHINE NEVER functioned much as a national organization, even though we had chapters in San Francisco, Los Angeles, New York, and elsewhere. For one thing, we couldn't be a cohesive national organization with a headquarters in San Francisco because New York wouldn't cooperate. New Yorkers don't like to be the branch office of anything. So they tried to take it over, but instead New York eventually went its own way.

Mattachine was going into its eclipse by the late 1960s. In fact, it went downhill from the time the Society for Individual Rights came into being in 1964. A lot of the people who worked with Mattachine in the early days became involved in SIR because it was more strongly a membership-participation and volunteer service-type group.

For those of us who had been in Mattachine for ten or fifteen years, it had been a labor of love, and we were getting a little weary. We were ready to let some of the rest of them help carry the ball. But we didn't disappear entirely; we started showing movies in the Mattachine library over here on Ellis Street in 1970. We called the movie presentation *Cinemattachine*. It was a coined word, but it was the damndest word we ever coined because it was no good; people couldn't pronounce it. Cinemattachine was sort of a private gay sex club, where people paid a small entrance fee. They could watch erotic movies and masturbate.

We came under fire from the police for running Cinemattachine, which led us to get involved in working with the city to set up guidelines for private sex clubs that the city and the police department could accept. The sex clubs helped move a lot of that kind of activity out of the parks and bushes, the toilets of the railroad stations, and all those kinds of places where it was going on. I say: "Let them do it in private. Everyone should accept the fact that it's good for mental health."

THOSE PRESENTATIONS at the Mattachine library were done under the auspices of the Seven Committee of the Seven Society, which dated back to the late 1950s and early 1960s. This was a group within the Mattachine Society comprised of a good many of its directors at the time and two or three others. We set it up to arrange social events. So we had some overnight weekend outings in the redwoods, in Big Sur country. We had a thing or two up at somebody's ranch in the Guerneville area; sometimes we even had a few little things in some of our own apartments or facilities in the city. They were just mainly all-night fuck, suck, and circle jerks. And we often had cooked food, like beef stew or a big pot of American chili. It was, in a sense, a social-activities event under the Mattachine Society. But we didn't want it to rub off on Mattachine and besmirch our good name, so we did it under the Seven Committee of the Seven Society. After all, we were gay sexualists and we were fighting for sexual freedom, so why not have some?

My philosophy was and is, if you don't like it, look the other way—don't bother with it. People are so incensed and concerned about what homosexuals are doing. To me, that means they're god-damned jealous because they're not getting enough themselves.

These days Mattachine is still alive as a corporation, but it's in limbo. It has a board of directors, and I'm the head queen, but we don't have the strength of a powder puff.

The Teacher

Billie Tallmij

A HANDFUL of lesbian couples got together in 1955 in San Francisco and formed an organization they called the Daughters of Bilitis (DOB). The name of this new organization was inspired by the heroine of the fictional Songs of Bilitis, which was written by the late nineteenth-century author Pierre Louys, who portrayed Bilitis as a sometime lesbian and contemporary of Sappho. At the time the women first gathered, they weren't aware that the Mattachine Society had been headquartered in their city for two years.

Billie Tallmij,* who was living in Berkeley when she first heard about DOB through friends in 1956, quickly became deeply involved in the fledgling organization. As a member of DOB, Billie did everything from counseling women who had been thrown out of the military to holding "gab n' javas"—the 1950s' version of the consciousness-raising group—in her living room. DOB offered Billie the chance to provide a new generation of women with the answers she herself had so desperately sought as a young woman coming of age in the 1940s.

Now in her early sixties, Billie lives with her partner, Marsha, and their three cats—two enormous calicos and one tiny kitten—in a small house in a rough neighborhood across the bay from San Francisco. Billie and Marsha added the kitten to their family after they rescued it from almost certain death at the hands of neighborhood children who had bloodied its head.

Sitting at her dining-room table, Billie lit a cigarette before she began to explain how she came to be a veteran crusader for lesbian rights. Billie is a heavy-set woman, with short reddish blond hair. Warm and forthcoming, she laughed easily and spoke with the excitement of a pioneer.

I was seventeen, and in my first year of college in Kansas in the late 1940s, when a high school friend wrote me a letter from school and described how she had gotten involved with another girl. It blew me away. I could not accept that Joanna could have done this. So I went to my dean of women, who was marvelous, and I said, "I've got to talk to you." I said, "A friend of mine is a homosexual. I don't know what

*Billie Tallmij is a pseudonym.

it means. Tell me what it's about." So she gave me a whole bunch of books to read, including *The Well of Loneliness*.

The Well opened the door for a lot of people, including me. I read that book and found that I was coming home. I recognized myself in the characters, and I also recognized the emotions that were so beautifully written there. I was always a tomboy and I had crushes on girls. I tried things with boys, but they were simply not my cup of tea. I was uncomfortable. This was an answer that I had sought for a long time.

After reading *The Well* I decided that if this was what I was, then I needed to know what one was supposed to do in this sort of business. The problem was finding information. Beyond *The Well*, which was the Bible for me, there were certainly no books that I could have read. There was nothing that existed for a total tyro like me. The only thing that you could get was Krafft-Ebing,* which is not something to teethe your newfound identity on. The particular cases in his book were so abnormal and so beyond the pale of who I felt I was.

Of course, there was no organization to call for information, so I had to find someone to talk to who could give me the answers I needed. I had heard from other students about this big dyke on campus. I didn't even really know what *big dyke* meant, but I just knew that she was someone who I wanted to talk to. So I followed her, followed her for days. Finally, I saw her coming out of a café just off campus. She was going to her car, and I went up to her and I asked her if she was Esther. And she said, "Yes." And I said, "I want to talk to you." I'm sure I came off just that strong. She sort of looked at me and said, "Okay, get in the car."

We got in her car, and she started driving. She said, "What is it you want to talk to me about?" I said, "I just found out I'm a homosexual and I want to know what this is all about." She looked at me and she said, "What do you want to know?" I said, "I want to know how to make love to a woman. I never have and I think I'd better know." She kind of chuckled and said, "Well, the only way, really, is to show you." And I said, "No, don't show me, tell me."

We drove out to a park, and I asked her every question I could think of: What is this? What causes this? Where does it start? Why is it? How *do* you make love to a woman? What do you do? She could have blown me out of the water. She could have been brusque and bitter, but she wasn't. She was just as gentle as she could have been and answered to the best of her ability anything that I put to her. When I look back on that particular scene, I think I knew then that

---

*Richard von Krafft-Ebing was a late-nineteenth-century psychiatrist and medical writer who argued that homosexuality violated the hidden laws of nature.

everybody was asking questions like that and that somewhere, somehow, there should be people who could answer these questions as
honestly as they could.

AFTER COLLEGE, I discovered firsthand what could happen if you were
found out. I was working in the acoustics division at Boeing Aircraft
in Seattle. Boeing was one of the early companies that made rockets.
Because I handled important material, I had to have top-secret clearance, which meant I was investigated. I was followed by an FBI agent
for about three weeks before I discovered the FBI had begun the
investigation process. Naturally, I wasn't told. But I found out one
evening when the agent followed me right into a gay bar, right along
with me! The bar was on my way home from work, and I sometimes
stopped in there at about six o'clock for a Coke. I didn't go to the bar
for any long length of time except on the weekends. Shorty, my lover
at the time, and I would go there on Friday and Saturday nights.

So the agent sat down on the bar stool next to me. He was in his
late twenties. He introduced himself and said, "By the way, I'm checking on your security clearance." I said, "For what?" He said, "Your
work at Boeing." He had my name, my address, and my lover's name.
Everything! He said, "You're just lucky." And I asked, "Why?" He
said, "Because I'm gay myself, otherwise you would have been out of
your job immediately." I was flabbergasted. I couldn't believe it.

I saw him in there one other time. He told me he wasn't there on
business. We sat and chatted, and I asked him, "How do you get away
with this?" And he said, "I'm open. They know it. I'm chosen often
to do this kind of work." His immediate boss knew that he could send
this guy into a gay bar and that he wouldn't stick out like a sore
thumb. He wasn't swish or anything. He was very nice. We didn't
discuss it any further. I don't know if they knew up the ladder at the
FBI that he was gay.

The agent knew I was going to quit my job at Boeing within a few
months. Shorty and I had planned to move to California. She was
working with the telephone company at the time, and we were waiting
for her transfer down to the San Francisco area. I told him that. I
assume that's why he didn't say anything. I never did know exactly
why. It's funny, just before I quit, I finally got my top-secret clearance.

SHORTY GOT her transfer in 1951 or 1952, and we moved down to
Berkeley. We had been together as a couple for several years at this
point. I was working for a drugstore chain while taking a couple of

classes to be certified as a schoolteacher in California. That is when I found out all about blackmail.

Shorty and I had met this woman in the Bay Area whom we liked very much. I thought she was the perfect match for my friend Bonnie, who lived in Tacoma. So I started a communication between them.

Bonnie wrote to me to ask me something about her relationship with this woman I had introduced her to, and I wrote her and explained something. I don't remember exactly what. But from the letter it was obvious that I was gay and that Bonnie was, too. I hadn't heard from Bonnie for a bit, so I called her. She said, "I can't talk about it on the phone." We were very, very close. I knew something was wrong, but I didn't know what. I told her, "I'm coming up there." So I flew up over the weekend.

What happened was that Bonnie had gotten my letter and read it hurriedly and left for work. Apparently, as she went out the door, she dropped the letter. The postman picked it up. Because I had written my letter on company stationery, the postman knew my name, my address, and where I worked. He proceeded to blackmail Bonnie. He told her that if she didn't provide him with what he wanted, he would see to it that I was blown all over the map. He wanted Bonnie to submit to him. He wanted her physically.

I was livid when she told me the story. I said, "Why in the hell didn't you go to the police? Why didn't you do something?" She felt she couldn't. She said, "I want to work with this. I think it will be all right. I think I can persuade him."

I was angry, but I wasn't frightened. I should have been because at that time there was a list of about twenty-one things that you could lose your teaching certificate for. The first one was to be a card-carrying Communist, and the second was to be a homosexual. It was as bad then as it is now being charged with child molestation. The suspicion is it: You're convicted, hung, tied, and quartered. And not only would you never teach in California, you would never teach again in public schools anywhere.

So come Monday, I took my lunch hour and looked up the FBI in the phone book. I didn't know what else to do. At that time I was new at all this. I went to the FBI office, but no one was there. The FBI happened to be above the Oakland post office, so I stormed down to the postmaster and said, "I want to talk to somebody about blackmail." He said, "What do you mean?" And I said, "I want to talk to somebody about a postal carrier who is trying to blackmail me." And he said, "My God! In my jurisdiction?" And I said, "No, the guy happens to be in Tacoma."

The postmaster waltzed me over to the postal inspector. This was an education in itself because the postal inspector went all the way around the barn to ask what was in this letter. He said, "Okay, let me ask you this. Does the word *homosexual* enter the letter?" And I said, "Yes, it's there, but it's nothing that's wrong." And he said, "Let me ask you this. Could my sixteen-year-old daughter read this letter? Would I allow her to?" And I said, "Yes, and it would probably educate her, but it would not harm her." And he said, "Well, the difficulty is that nobody has ever come up with a definition of what is pornography. And as you know, it's illegal to send pornography through the mail." He said again, "Is there anything in this letter that could not be read in court?" And I said, "Yes, it could be read in court, and I wouldn't be afraid for it to be read. I would be embarrassed, perhaps, but I would not be afraid." He also asked me why Bonnie didn't go to the postal inspector in Tacoma. I explained that her father was a retired postmaster and that the postal inspector was a friend of the family. He said, "Okay, you let me handle this."

So the postal inspector in the Oakland area contacted the postal inspector in the Tacoma area, and they landed the guy right smack on his ass. The postman was confronted, and he confessed. He got three years in jail.

I was so angry about the blackmail that I never thought about the risk I was taking—certainly, it had nothing to do with guts. Anger was also the driving force at DOB. We were angry with the injustices we saw, and our anger on those issues made us totally forget any fear. This is the only thing that drove us. I know, and I know I speak for all of us who were DOB members.

In 1956 Shorty and I had already been living in Berkeley for a while when we first heard about DOB from somebody we knew. This friend had been invited to a buffet dinner at Del Martin and Phyllis Lyon's house. She ended up not going, but Shorty and I went.

Of the eight women who were the actual founders of DOB, the only ones left were Del and Phyl. The rest had lost interest, broken up, moved away, or whatever. This was Del and Phyl's last thrust to see if they could get anybody interested. Shorty and I were both so very impressed with Del and Phyl and with what they were trying to do, that we stayed late after dinner to ask questions. We sat in the kitchen and just fired questions at them like crazy. We both became very interested in DOB and moved right into the organization.

What interested us about DOB was the possibility of really helping people. My main drive was to educate the public, but foremost, to educate our girls, to give them the answers I had once needed and to give them some sense of who they were. We had to teach our people that it wasn't a crime to be a homosexual. At that point in time, people still thought it was criminal just to *be* a homosexual. What was criminal were certain kinds of sexual activity: the act of fellatio, the act of sodomy. But this activity was also illegal in most states for a husband and wife. You see, people didn't know that. That's an important distinction because when people were arrested in bar raids, they thought they were guilty for just being a homosexual. So they'd plead guilty to whatever they were charged with, pay a fine, and wind up with a record.

One of the other things we told our women was how to answer certain questions in court if they were arrested. For example, the women wanted to know, "What do you say if you're asked in court if you're homosexual?" And I told them, "I would say no." My girls would look at me and say, "Why?" I said, "Legally, I am not a homosexual. A homosexual is male. If I were asked if I were a lesbian, I would say yes." Just knowing something like that would allay a tremendous amount of fear.

We also had a speakers' bureau to educate the general public. This was a whole new frontier for DOB, as well as for the public itself. Almost no one had ever met a self-proclaimed, self-avowed homosexual face to face. When we went out to speak, parents would ask, "What do I look for in my daughter?" "What do I do if I suddenly find out my child is homosexual?" The parents would ask me, "Does your mother know?" And I said, "Yes, she does." I hadn't planned to tell her, but Mother read a letter that I had written and put away in my school annual, thinking she would never find it. But she did, and it just blew her away. She's dead now, but I always had an exceptional relationship with Mother.

I was lucky. In lots of instances, when the parents did find out, it was brutal. We had one young woman from New Orleans who tried to tell her parents. They set up a gravestone with her name on it. They declared her dead and announced her death in the newspaper in an obituary. She lived with that for the rest of her life.

THE BETTER known the Daughters became, the more letters and phone calls we got. We had people in Podunk, Iowa, writing letters that would break your heart. "Here I am. I'm the only one in the world. What do I do? How do I make contact? Where do I find people? Who can I talk to? What books can I read?" Every one of them felt like she was the only voice crying out in the wilderness.

If the Daughters did nothing else—and we did a lot else—we were able to bring some sense of solace to these women. Just knowing that we were there would sometimes keep them from cracking up or from suicide. I talked more than one person out of suicide in those early days. The women were so frightened because they didn't understand why they were so goddamned different from everybody else. You see, no one knew that women could be this way. People seemed to know that guys did this, but people knew nothing about the lesbian. In the very, very early days of the Daughters, there had been one or two studies of gay men. One of them was done by Dr. Evelyn Hooker. But Dr. Hooker wouldn't touch the Daughters with a ten-foot pole—no one had touched women. She told us she couldn't because profession-ally, she would have been dead. A woman studying gay women would be highly suspect on any information she presented—it would not have been accepted. Nonetheless, Dr. Hooker was a very close friend, and she would come to all of our meetings and conferences and panels, but she never did a study on gay women.

We thought it was very important for the women to be studied, so we banged at the door of the Kinsey Institute to try to get some kind of involvement, and we got it. They interviewed us as couples and individuals. Shorty and I were both interviewed. Many of the women volunteered. That took real courage.

Another reason the Daughters existed, one of the main reasons, was to keep our kids out of the bars, to give them an alternative place to socialize with other women, because the bars were being raided and raided and raided. There was a lot of antagonism between the so-called authorities and the gay guys and the gay women. But gay women had no one to go to for help. So we had people who had problems with the police call us from everywhere at all hours of the night.

We had a lot of kids who called us or came to us. You had to be twenty-one to be in DOB, but these were seventeen year olds. They were right on our doorstep, but we wouldn't allow them in the DOB offices—absolutely not! We couldn't touch them legally because that was one way the police could have gotten us. They would have charged us with contributing to the delinquency of a minor. They could have sent us to the state pen. So we had house parties for them, but they were not officially DOB events. And we would not let them drink. They had soda pop.

THE DAUGHTERS had been in existence for several months before anyone knew that the Mattachine Society existed. In the same city! You see, not only did the lesbian not exist—psychologically or historically or whatever—in the minds of the general public, there was also a tremendous division between gay men and women. Everybody was totally separate. There was no sense of communication because the gay male feared women, and a lesbian was a woman. And the same thing existed on the other side. But for the gay women, there wasn't just fear. There was also a lot of animosity and resentment over the fact it was the gay guys who were creating such havoc with the police—the raids, the indiscriminate sex, their bathroom habits, and everything else.

The division between the men and the women was one of the things that we in DOB tried to address. We did that first at one of our gab n' javas. I started the gab n' javas, a get-together in my home. We had coffee. I would present a particular topic and moderate it. It was all women, all ages, and all backgrounds. We had young people and we had grandmothers. We even had great-grandmothers.

So this one time we invited a couple of gay guys from the Mattachine Society to come and be in the catbird seat. It was very interesting. The poor guys—they were bombarded. There was hostility, and there was a lot of bitterness. I warned them, "You're really going to get massacred here, and don't blame me if you come out bloody and bowed."

Afterwards, there was a real breaking down of barriers between the men and the women. This was the first time that many of the gay gals had talked—literally talked—to a gay guy, and vice versa. And out of that there started to be more communication between the two groups, at least the officers. Eventually, the Daughters became more involved with the Mattachine. The Mattachine printed our newsletter, *The Ladder*, and we would coordinate on different things.

WE HAD gab n' javas on all kinds of topics. For instance, we had one on how to make a butch into a dolly—something weird like that. It was about how to accommodate to a given situation. Our goal in helping our people fit in was to allow them to live within whatever societal guidelines and framework and limitations they had to contend with and to come out of it as whole and healthy and sane as possible. You have to remember how dangerous the world was then.

I'll give you an example. When we had our first DOB national convention, which we had right here in San Francisco in 1960, one woman called us from the Los Angeles area. She had been a subscriber to *The Ladder* and a member of DOB for several years, although we had never met her. She asked, "Do we have to wear skirts?" She hadn't been in a skirt in seventeen years. And we said,

"Yes, you have to wear a skirt." So she went out and she bought one skirt. She had several different men's shirts to go with it. I didn't care about the men's shirts; nobody else did, either. But she had to wear a skirt, for her own safety. There was a law on the books that you could be arrested for impersonating a male, which included wearing fly-front jeans! We knew there would be police at our first convention and that they would scan every one of us. We wanted to protect people who came. We didn't want to put them in jeopardy.

At another gab n' java, we talked about religion. This one was over at Del and Phyl's house. We had women stacked all the way up the stairway. Many of our people said they missed going to church. And my question was, "Why can't you go to church?" The answer was that you could go as yourself and herself and himself, but not as an open gay couple. We did an informal survey among the members here in the San Francisco area and found out that most of them had stopped going to church once they found out they were gay. They said they still believed in God, but the church no longer provided a community for them. It was interesting that those with children were emphatic about their children going to church, but they themselves ceased to go.

We found that many of our people felt a real spiritual aridity, a real blankness. So, to begin a dialogue with the various churches in San Francisco, we got together with the Mattachine Society to try to organize a weekend conference, which ultimately resulted, in 1964, in the formation of an important new organization called the Council on Religion and the Homosexual.

With Mattachine, we wrote to as many ministers as we could from as many different faiths as existed. We got representatives from the Episcopalians, the Quakers, and the Baptists. We held the conference in Marin over a three-day weekend. We had about twenty guys, quite a few of whom were ministers, and seven women. The women were a minority in a minority. Del and I deliberately arranged it so all the participants were brought there and dropped off. We did it that way so no one could leave. To put it bluntly, they came to convert us, and we came to convert them.

The very first night they served us dinner, and talk about being in little groups! There were barriers of communication that could not be bridged that night. The gals sat here. The guys sat over there. And the ministers were all the way over there.

We started early the next day. One representative from each group started with an opening statement. The Episcopalian bishop spoke for the ministers. One of the guys spoke for the gay guys. And I spoke for the women. They said, "Ladies first," but I said, "No, I'm last."

I wanted to be last because I wanted to drop some real bombs, such as "Where does it say in the Bible that homosexuality is wrong? Where does it say that love is wrong between two women?" We wanted the ministers to answer our questions. We wanted to keep control of what was being discussed.

Then we broke up into small groups to discuss these various questions that I'd raised. By the time we went to lunch, people were talking everywhere. And that night, Saturday night, it was impossible to go up the stairs to your room because people were on the stairs, just talking together. One would stop, two would stop, and five and six and seven. The communication was just tremendous. It was marvelous. This was the first time that many of those ministers had met face to face with someone who said, "I'm a homosexual."

One of the things that came out of that meeting was that many of the ministers said they didn't feel qualified to talk about sexual problems, period, let alone this kind of sexual problem. Some of them couldn't talk about it. Some of them couldn't even say the words *sex* or *homosexual*. I don't know where *lesbian* came in. Remember, this was 1964.

After the weekend conference we took some of these ministers to some of the gay bars. We started with the pits—these places were toilets; they were filthy—and then we moved up to some of the better ones. Our point was, "Because you will not allow us to be open, this is where we have to meet. Would you bring your wife here? Would you want your son to go here? Do you know that your son isn't going here?" It really jarred the living hell out of a lot of them.

I WAS recently interviewed by the girls who are doing a documentary on DOB. I'm very glad they're doing it because a lot of us who were involved at the beginning are getting up there. If a history isn't done somewhere along the line, people will really not know some of the tremendous things that occurred.

We recently saw a preview of the documentary. They asked questions of those of us in the audience. This one question was, "Were you aware at that time that you were a part of the gay movement?" And my answer was, "We were so involved in what we were doing that we didn't know that there was a gay movement going on until we had enough distance to look back."

So much has changed since those days—the openness in the bars; the openness, period. Coming out of the closet. You can go into a gay bar without fear. Today—and I think this is probably one of the most important changes—lesbians can most often keep their children after a divorce.

Some things haven't changed. I'm not using my real name for this interview. If we were not living on my salary, I wouldn't care about using my real name. I would not be fired on the spot if they found out, but it would be made so difficult for me that I would have to quit. That's the usual way now because you can fight this kind of discrimination. But what you can't fight is the way they get around it and make it so god-awful that you say, "Fuck it!" and quit. And financially at this point in time, I can't. That's the only reason I'm not using my name.

I LOOK back on some of the things that we did and I think that we were certainly pioneers, with an ax in one hand and a whip in the other. But I would not call us militant, as it's defined today. Given the way the world was then, I'm sure we would have been thrown in jail if we had been.

The Outsider

Paul Phillips

By THE late 1950s, gay organizations had reached beyond San Francisco, New York, and Los Angeles to establish tiny chapters in a handful of other cities around the country, including Chicago, Philadelphia, and Denver. In one of these cities, in 1958, Paul Phillips* made his way out of isolation to his first Mattachine meeting. His involvement with Mattachine not only led him to feel better about himself, but inspired him to take risks he can hardly believe today.

Now in his mid-eighties, Paul prefers not to have his real name used or the city where he lives identified. He's concerned that word of his homosexuality would find its way to the church he attends or to the town where he grew up and that people would think badly of him and his family.

Paul lives by himself on a quiet street about fifteen minutes from downtown. When he bought his tidy one-story house in 1960, he was the first black person to live on his street. He says he had to trick the buyer into selling him the house, even though he was an attorney in a high-level government job. These days, painful arthritis keeps Paul from going far from home and from playing the organ in his living room. Music is his first love.

Paul came to the door dressed formally, in suit pants, black shoes, a white shirt, and a tie. He's a big, handsome man with a beautiful smile. Seated at his dining-room table, he talked about the past shyly and always with a mix of pain and wonderment. Even as he told stories about the risks he took back in the 1950s in attending Mattachine meetings and trying to save a young gay man from going to jail, he found it remarkable that he was describing his own life.

I was raised in a very segregated society, which always kept me aware that I was different. We lived about a mile from town. My dad was a lawyer there. His clientele was entirely white, and so was the town. There was also a little town not too far away which was a black town.

As I grew up, the pressure seemed to be directed toward me, rather than my father. If anything went wrong in the town, I was always the

*Paul Phillips is a pseudonym.

one who did it. One example that stands out in my mind happened after I graduated from college. Somebody was looking into some lady's room one night, and the whole town thought it was me who was doing it. They brought in the bloodhounds right to my folks' house.

I was shocked. I hadn't thought about the possibility of being accused because being as I was, women weren't in my program. Yet, here I was supposedly looking at these women getting ready for bed. So I did something my father asked me not to do: I asked the lady if it was a white face she saw or a black face. Dad didn't want to inject the racial issue, but this thing got serious for me. Since I was through college, I thought that if I was going to be a bit independent, now was a good time to start. So I went to her house and asked her, "Was the face you saw at the window a white or black face?" She said, "It was a white face." There's no reason anyone should take me for white, midnight or any other time of day. So I got that word out to the crowd that was following, "The lady said the face is white. It ain't mine." That broke up the crowd just as slick as a whistle.

But the pressures started before that, all through high school in the 1920s. I remember one little guy who called me a nigger, and I wasn't going to take it. He had a book in his hand, and I took it and tore out all the pages. The hell with him. He was trying to emphasize the racial thing and he didn't have a pot to. . . . You know what I mean? I try to forget that stuff. I've never carried a lot of prejudice in my own life. I hate to see other people do it. Why not live and let live? That's my theory, shucks.

GRADUALLY I began to discover that I was different, besides my color, and I thought I was the only one in the world. I remember when I first discovered that things were not right, sexually, I wanted to kill myself. I'd say this was in 1919. I was about fifteen then. I knew I didn't care anything about girls. Everybody else was chasing after girls, and I couldn't figure out why. Didn't make sense to me and still doesn't. But I just didn't want to go through life this way. I was just completely down and out. I practically gave up.

Finally, my dad came to me one day and told me what he had heard. He told me that I was not natural. Whether he heard it or just looked at me and could tell, I don't know. He never did tell me who told him.

So he said, "We'll go to the Mayo Clinic, get you examined, and see if we can find out what causes this and what to do about it." I was willing to go because I wanted to be changed. So he put Mother and me in the car, and she and I went up to the Mayo Clinic, in Rochester, Minnesota. That was back in the days when you couldn't get a place to stay or a place to eat because we were blacks. We bought crackers and baloney in the store and took them out and ate them. We got one of these ten-by-twelve tents and we stayed in the tent at night.

They had me in and out of the hospital for several days. I was terrified. They asked all kinds of questions. They determined that I was homosexual and that there was nothing they could do about it. They said that because of the final report, according to their state laws they should report me and have me incarcerated. Put me in jail! But they said that since I was a client of theirs, they would not do that, but there was nothing they could do for me. That almost put me under the ground.

So we went back home and reported to Dad. My dad was not really an educated man. He was a lawyer, but he was self-educated and he didn't know anything about gays. I might say this, that I was an adopted child. And I often used to wonder as a kid, "What will he do when he finds it out? Will he put me out? Or will he accept me?"

Dad was very understanding. When I say understanding, I don't think he actually understood, but he was willing to accept. So he finally told me, "Since they don't know what to do about it, find yourself a friend that you can trust. And bring him home. I don't want you playing around on the streets or out on the country roads because you never know who's going to step up behind you. Bring him home. What you do in your room is your business."

That helped me a lot. At least I was loved by my father. And, of course, Mother, she just idolized me, regardless. Still, I felt I was just nobody. First because I'm black, and second—and all the other numbers you can think of—because I was homosexual. Because of the opposition against the gay life, I was never proud of what I did as a gay person, as the kids say. Now how do you get around that? I haven't gotten around that yet. I suppose I'll die without getting around it.

In college I found a friend in Topeka whom I could talk to. He was a colored boy—a black boy, as they say now. He was the same way I was. He was a real good musician, and I liked to hear him play. He played for one of the churches down there. We never had any relationship between us. We were friends—that's as far as it went.

Much later on—I was already a lawyer—I found my friend. He was a country boy who didn't know what was going on in the world. He was a handsome kid—dark hair, very wavy; tall; dark complexion. And we had a time together. That was in 1935. Running around with a high school kid. Can you imagine that? He was the first lasting relationship. The others were, you know, there today and gone to-morrow. Somebody sees you with me and somebody is going to say something to you about running around with that nigger, see. So it don't happen. He don't come back anymore. He's afraid to come back.

But this country boy was as sweet as he could be. That lasted for six years, and I thought I was in heaven while he was with me. He was in high school living at home. We didn't live far apart. I still lived with my parents. He would come over, and we would go out in the garage. Winter, summer he'd be there every other night just as regular as the days come. We'd go out in the garage and sit in the car and do what we had to do. I think he was kind of afraid to come into the house. He didn't know my people too well. He had no chance to get acquainted with them. I think that made it a little uncomfortable for him because he didn't know how or what they might have to say. My parents told me to bring him in, but I couldn't get him to come in. I don't remember that he ever stayed all night with me during that time.

But then one day we came here to this city together. He had one more year in high school. We stayed together here in one of the colored hotels downtown. I was in heaven that first night we stayed together. Then we drove to another town to a rodeo. I had a Chevrolet at the time. We spent a couple of days camping out. I asked him, "Are you ready to go back home, or do you want to go farther?" And he said, "I'm with you wherever you want to go." Oh, I loved that boy.

When we quit driving, the front wheels of my car were in the Pacific Ocean in Seattle. I remember driving down to Puget Sound—drove my car just far enough to get the tires in the water. That was my first time in the Pacific. And by this time my friend was passing for colored. There wasn't any question. He had a very dark complexion. He had a head full of curls.

This first time we were in Seattle, we stayed for six weeks. The next year we went out there again, and I stayed a year with him, right by my side all the time. You know, I used to stammer very badly as a child. I didn't know what caused it. I got him, and the stammer left. I was out from under that pressure, and I had someone I could share my life with.

Then he went into the service. It was the start of the war; he was about to be drafted. One morning he said, "If I have to be drafted, I'd rather be drafted from home than from Seattle." I lost him to the military, and we haven't been together since. He left me without telling me he was going. He said he thought that that was the best way for us to part, for him to disappear. You talk about someone being devastated. That really got me; I almost lost my mind over that. I loved that boy.

One time I got a letter from him. He was a Marine in Florida. He asked me not to send him any more messages. He said, "You know I can't get out. I'm in here and I can't get out." He said he was getting all my messages, but he couldn't do anything.

I've seen him once since then. Toward the end of war, he came back to our home town to visit. But by that time he had married. Of course, I've never tried to have any communication because I didn't want to break up whatever relationship he had with his wife.

I respected his situation. He had a wife and could love her, and she could love him, Lord, power to him. But inside I was miserable. I have cried over it many, many times, but what can I do about it? There's nothing I can do. I've often wondered if he would come back or if he ever thinks of me even. As much fun as we had together, I don't know how he could forget.

AFTER THE war I came to this city. I was a lawyer and I had been admitted to the bar here. It was so much better here than where I came from that I thought I was free. Of course, there was prejudice here, but I wasn't too much bothered about that.

It was here, in the late 1950s, that I first came across Mattachine. The Mattachine Society was the first organized gay group as far as I can think of. I had a friend who worked down at the train depot. He was gay. He was going to a meeting one night and asked me if I wanted to go along. We went to somebody's home. There was a group of guys sitting there, maybe ten or twelve. I was the only black one. They weren't accustomed to having any contacts with blacks.

So I came in, and for once I found somebody else besides me that would say they were gay. I knew a few, but to have a group! I had never been in that sort of situation before. I was completely happy because I thought I would be accepted and be a part of the crowd. But the guys were not friendly. That was all right; they didn't know me. All they knew was, I was a lawyer. They were terrified of the law. "What's this guy doing here?" "Who's he going to turn in?"

I think I scared them worse than they scared me. I was concerned about my job at every meeting I ever went to because I was working in a high position in the state government. First black to work at that level. I had my office right there in the capitol building. Wasn't that a lot of nerves to go to those meetings? Crazy! Just plain crazy! As I look back now, I wouldn't do it over again. No way. I'd be afraid to. But when you're younger, you take chances. When you get older, you sit back and kind of look at things first and then see what's going to happen.

I went to Mattachine in the first place to meet somebody who was like me, somebody gay. That was my primary purpose in going. Once I found there were others besides me, I was much better able to accept myself. I was always a thorn in my own flesh because I was gay. I was my own thorn. This talking about and going over experiences together helped me to realize, well, maybe I'm not the only one. But my search for a friend didn't work out. Whether it was me or it was my job or because I was black, or what it was, I don't know, but I don't have a single friend from Mattachine with all I did. Although, I didn't really do too much because of my work. Can you imagine if someone at the newspaper found out and came out with a front-page article: "First Black in Government Office a Homosexual"? I'd almost be justified in throwing myself off the capitol building.

THERE WAS a Mattachine convention here in the late 1950s. There must have been seventy-five people from around the country. I was there for two hours one afternoon. I was very careful not to take any part in it because of my job. The press was there. I was the only black person there. You can imagine how people reacted: "Who is he, and what is he doing here?" I just slipped in and slipped out. I thought to myself after it was all over, *Why would I do a silly thing like that?* But I just wanted to know what was going on.

After that convention I did something really silly. A boy from Mattachine got himself caught with a whole lot of nude pictures. I didn't know him well; I don't even remember his name. He had a bunch of nude pictures that he'd sent for, and some way or another, he was showing them around. I kept telling him, "Don't show that stuff. You don't know who you're showing them to." Things got kind of warm for him. I guess he heard that they were after him for these pictures, and he asked me if I'd keep them for a while. And I said, "Sure, I'll keep them." He brought me a whole box.

Then one day he said, "Paul, so-and-so is coming over to see me tonight. I'd like to have my pictures back." So I got them back to him. That night the undercover man came to his house, and this boy threw the pictures out on the table for him to see, and that was the end of that. He was arrested. I thought to myself, *Suppose he had been at my house and let the man up?*

Of course, they took him down for a trial. I don't know whether he asked me or the Mattachine Society asked me. But anyhow, I knew the judge: He happened to be gay. So I went down and talked to the judge personally. As I look back now, I was plumb nuts, I can't deny it. I told him this guy was coming in and I wished he'd be as lenient on him as he could. I thought I had made arrangements with the judge, but damn it, when it came time for the trial, the judge took that day off. He didn't want anything to do with it. But I was kind of glad afterwards that I had warned him ahead of time because he and I had been good friends. Nothing between us, but just good friends. That's the only time I did something like that. I stuck my neck way out. It's a wonder somebody didn't chop it off.

The Mattachine group here fell apart not long after that. People were terrified of the police and the publicity from that arrest. That was the end of it for me. Mattachine had thought so little of me, even after I had taken such chances. Why stick my neck out for the next group?

THESE DAYS, I live here alone. Companionship would be worth a lot to me. I don't have much company. I don't know any gay people my age. Whether they're out there, I don't know.

I have a couple of acquaintances now who know I'm gay. In my church, for instance, I had a couple of young fellows just within the last three or four years who asked me, "Paul, do you know anything about the gay life?" And I said, "Why would you ask me a question like that?" They answered, "Well, I don't know for sure why, but for some reason. . . ." Both of them admitted they were gay. They had watched me for years and always felt that I might know more than I was showing on the outside. I told them I was gay. But I couldn't have done that before I went to Mattachine. Mattachine helped me to accept myself, so if somebody asks me, depending upon who it is, of course, I'll tell them, "Yes."

PART TWO
1961-1968

The Homophile Movement Emerges:
Speaking Out, Setting Goals, Making Demands

ELEVEN YEARS *after the first meeting of the Mattachine Society and six years after the first gathering of the Daughters of Bilitis, the combined national membership of Mattachine and DOB was less than four hundred. This was a phenomenal number of people, given the times, but far from a solid foundation for a mass political movement. The painful reality of 1961 was that gay men and lesbians faced a world that was just about as hostile as it had been a decade earlier. For all but a few, the dangers posed by exposure were far too great to risk association with an organization for homosexuals. But fear wasn't the only factor. As historian John D'Emilio noted in* Sexual Politics, Sexual Communities, *gay people "absorbed views of themselves as immoral, depraved, and pathological individuals. . . . Such a self-image would hardly propel men and women into a cause that required group solidarity and the affirmation of their sexuality, nor would it encourage them to entertain the idea that their efforts might create a brighter future."*

Gay men and lesbians had only to turn to the pages of Time *magazine for a taste of public opinion. In the January 21, 1966, issue of* Time, *an unsigned essay entitled, "The Homosexual in America," offered an analysis of homosexuality and a corrosive two-page perspective on the male homosexual's place in American life. Lesbians were mentioned only in passing. The essay stated, "For many a woman with a busy or absent husband, the presentable homosexual is in demand as an escort—witty, pretty, catty, and no problem to keep at arm's length. . . . The once widespread view that homosexuality is caused by heredity, or some derangement of hormones, has been generally discarded. The consensus is that it is caused psychically, through a disabling fear of the opposite sex." The essay went on to discuss the classic Freudian dominant mother–subservient father explanation for homosexuality. It noted that both male homosexuality and lesbianism were "essentially a case of arrested development, a failure of learning, a refusal to accept the full responsibilities of life. This is no more apparent than in the pathetic pseudo marriages in which many homosexuals act out conventional roles—wearing wedding rings, calling themselves 'he' and 'she.' "*

The Time essayist saved the best for the conclusion:

[Homosexuality] is a pathetic little second-rate substitute for reality, a pitiable flight from life. As such it deserves fairness, compassion, understanding and when possible, treatment. But it deserves no encouragement, no glamorization, no rationalization, no fake status as minority martyrdom, no sophistry about simple differences in taste—and above all, no pretense that it is anything but a pernicious sickness.

Opinions like these, which were given wide and continuous circulation, and fear of exposure did not prove strong enough to suppress the aspirations of some gay men and lesbians for change. Beginning in the early 1960s, as new gay organizations formed, like the boldly independent Washington, D.C., chapter of the Mattachine Society, and old organizations changed leadership, the struggle for gay dignity and equal rights began to shift direction. A new generation of believers, as well as some veterans of the movement dismissed the "sickness" label. They began actively and publicly working for equal rights and an end to governmental discrimination, rather than focusing on personal problems and soliciting morale-boosting professional opinions.

Ironically, these efforts were bolstered by the negative publicity, like the 1966 Time essay. First, the fact that homosexuality was being discussed and named was an improvement over earlier times, when virtually nothing— good or bad—appeared in print about homosexuality. Second, the Time essay, like many articles during the 1960s, referred to "deviate lobbies" that argued that homosexuality should be accepted as a fact of human existence. The Time essay named the "best known" of those lobbies, the Mattachine Society, and noted that the organization had a Washington, D.C., branch. Time inadvertently provided valuable free nationwide publicity.

Press coverage, although still scant and often negative, increased as gay organizations, following the example of the black civil rights movement, organized public demonstrations. In 1965, gay men and lesbians took to the streets in a handful of cities, including the nation's capital, where they demonstrated in front of the White House, Pentagon, and State Department to protest antigay federal policies. The marchers, who numbered no more than two dozen, carried placards that read "Governor Wallace Met with Negroes, Our Government Won't Meet With Us"; "Halt Government's

War Against Homosexuals"; and "Fifteen Million American Homosexuals Protest Federal Treatment."

The July–August 1965 issue of The Ladder, DOB's magazine, reported that the May 29 demonstration at the White House in which ten men and three women participated received significant press coverage that was "favorable or factual." According to The Ladder, the demonstration was "covered by American and foreign newspapers and press services, including AP, UPI, Reuters, French News Agency, White House Press Corps. Reports are known to have appeared in the New York Times, New York News, Washington Star, Orlando Sentinel, Chicago Sun-Times. The demonstration was filmed at length by ABC-TV and a spokesman was interviewed. The film was seen in New York, Chicago, San Francisco, Seattle, Miami, Indiana, and Texas."

The demonstrations, as well as provocative antisickness statements from "homophile" activists, were not met with uniform approval within gay and lesbian organizations. These actions inspired bitter internal debates between those who wanted to push ahead more boldly and those who accused the homophile activists of rocking the boat and drawing unnecessary public attention to the largely hidden—and relatively safe—gay and lesbian subculture. These warnings and complaints were not baseless. The FBI, as well as a number of local police departments, had taken great interest in the activities of the homophile movement. Beginning in 1953, and continuing for more than twenty years, the FBI conducted extensive surveillance of gay organizations and their leaders.

Despite the internal debates over the tactics and direction of the homophile movement, as well as divisive tensions between gay men and lesbians, organizations in a handful of major cities drew new support from mainstream clergy and politicians and were increasingly able to challenge police repression. The largest confrontation between the police and gay people during this time came on January 1, 1965, at a fund-raising ball in San Francisco, where hundreds of gay and lesbian party goers were met by a massive police presence. This event dramatically changed the course of gay rights efforts in San Francisco.

During this time, gay and lesbian organizations also discovered the value of building coalitions with other gay organizations, first through an affiliation of East Coast groups and then through a national association called the North American Conference of Homophile Organizations, or NACHO (pronounced NAY-ko). At a Chicago NACHO conference in 1968, delegates from twenty-six organizations from around the country endorsed the then-radical slogan, "Gay Is Good," in effect adopting pride as a goal in itself. The conferees also adopted a five-point Homosexual Bill of Rights, which spelled out the immediate goals of the homophile movement:

- Private consensual acts between persons over the age of consent shall not be an offense.
- Solicitation for any sexual act shall not be an offense except upon the filing of a complaint by the aggrieved party, not a police officer or agent.
- A person's sexual orientation or practice shall not be a factor in the granting or receiving of federal security clearances, visas, and the granting of citizenship.
- Service in and discharge from the armed forces and eligibility for veteran's benefits shall be without reference to homosexuality.
- A person's sexual orientation or practice shall not affect his eligibility for employment with federal, state, or local governments, or private employers.

These five points did not address all the problems faced by the nation's homosexual men and women in their daily lives. But those who attended the 1968 NACHO conference agreed that these issues were of the highest priority and began planning a course of action.

Perhaps the most mainstream public acknowledgment of the homophile movement's impact up to this point was a Wall Street Journal article on July 17, 1968: "U.S. Homosexuals Gain In Trying to Persuade Society to Accept Them." The article got it half right. By this time, many in the homophile movement had begun to abandon the gentle arts of persuasion, embracing, instead, a strategy of confrontation based on unnegotiable demands for equal rights.

The Very Mad Scientist

Frank Kameny

NEARLY ALL of the thousands of men and women who were thrown out of the military and government jobs because of their homosexuality departed quietly, hoping that their secret would not emerge again to strike them down. Frank Kameny, who was fired from the U.S. Army Map Service in 1957, was an exception.

Born in 1925, Frank Kameny grew up in New York City. In 1956, after completing his Ph.D. at Harvard University, he moved to Washington, D.C., to join the faculty at Georgetown University. At the end of the academic year, he was offered a position with the U.S. Army Map Service.

Perhaps if Frank had been able to find another job after being fired, he would have disappeared back into his career. But as a specialized astronomer, he had little idea how to locate work outside the scientific community. Within the small pre-NASA world of professional astronomers, everyone knew Frank was a homosexual.

Frank responded to his expulsion from professional life by fighting to win back his job. For three years he waged an unsuccessful one-man battle before deciding to join forces with other gay people. In November 1961, he and Jack Nichols, a native of Washington, D.C., launched the aggressive and very public Washington, D.C., Mattachine Society. No newspaper recorded the event, but every move that Frank and the society made was documented and immortalized in the files of the FBI.

Sitting behind his desk in the office of his two-story brick house on a leafy street in a comfortable Washington, D.C., neighborhood, surrounded by countless files and unidentified dust-covered piles, Frank Kameny looked more like the astronomer he studied to be than the dogged gay rights champion he's been for more than three decades. But when Frank began telling his old war stories, there was no question that here sat an old soldier who had lived much of his life on the front lines. Frank's tales of protests, court cases, FBI surveillance, and confrontations were filled with the strong emotion and intense conviction that have characterized his crusade. As he spoke, almost wild eyed, slicing through the air with his hands, one could easily imagine Frank Kameny verbally vanquishing his opponents.

While I was on assignment in Hawaii in November or December of 1957, I got a call from my supervisor in Washington, D.C., to come back at once. I told him that whatever the problem, it could wait a few days, and I returned to Washington at the end of the week. As soon as I got back, I was called in by some two-bit Civil Service Commission investigator and told, "We have information that leads us to believe that you are a homosexual. Do you have any comment?" I said, "What's the information?" They said, "We can't tell you." I said, "Well, then I can't give you an answer. You don't deserve an answer. And in any case, this is none of your business." I was not open about being gay at that time—no one was, not in 1957. But I was certainly leading a social life. I went to the gay bars many, many evenings. I've never been a covert kind of a person, and I wasn't about to be one simply because I was working for the government. I've never been one to function on the basis that Big Brother may be looking over my shoulder.

So they called me in, and ultimately it resulted in my termination. They did it the way the government does anything: They issued a letter. They said they were dismissing me for homosexuality. I was in shock.

The next two or three years were extremely difficult because I had no source of income. In fact, by 1959 I was living for about eight months on twenty cents worth of food a day, which even by 1959 prices was not terribly much. It was a great day when I could afford five cents more and put a pat of butter on my mashed potatoes.

Keep in mind I had been training all of my life for a scientific career, for this kind of occupation. I was not at all familiar with the job market. When I was thrown out, I had nowhere to go. Perhaps if this had happened five or ten years later, I would have had a professional reputation to fall back on, but in this case I didn't. For a long time I applied for jobs in astronomy, but there was nothing. Ultimately, in 1959, I got a job doing something in physics. My bachelor's degree is in physics, in the area of optics.

But meanwhile, I had decided that my dismissal amounted to a declaration of war against me by my government. First, I don't grant my government the right to declare war against me. And second, I tend not to lose my wars. So that started an eighteen-year war, which is this country's longest. It was fought by every possible means and ultimately ended on July 3, 1975, when the then-Civil Service Commission issued its surrender documents—in the form of a news release—saying, in effect, but not in these words, that the government was changing its policy to suit me. The commission said that they would no longer exclude homosexuals from government employment. But I'm jumping way ahead of myself.

What I did after I was fired was to go through such appeals procedures as there were, which took me through the lower level of the bureaucracy. Once I had exhausted the formal appeals process, I corresponded with the House and Senate Civil Service Committees, which were hardly receptive then. All along the way, they said no.

Having exhausted everything, I was put in touch with a local attorney, who had been a congressman. He was willing to take my case on a contingency-fee basis, since I had no money. He took it through the U.S. District Court and the U.S. Court of Appeals. I was turned down in the U.S. District Court, and then in 1960, the U.S. Court of Appeals turned it down. The attorney indicated that he thought my case was hopeless and therefore didn't want to pursue it further.

I wanted to continue to pursue my case to the Supreme Court. So the attorney gave me a copy of the Supreme Court rules and told me about filing *pro se*—for yourself—documents. With the Supreme Court, you have two knocks at the door. Your first effort is a knock at the door to say, "Will you let me in, or won't you?" If they say, no, that ends it. If they say, yes, then you prepare all your briefs and really go at it. The first knock is called a petition for *writ of certiorari*. So I prepared my petition. Whenever I had questions, I called up the Supreme Court or I walked over there and said, "Here's my question. Give me an answer. I need some instructions. Instruct!" Which they did very nicely. My philosophy, then as now, is that I pay for the government with my taxes; therefore they're there to serve me. I ultimately filed my own petition in January of 1961. It simply set out my case.

Preparing the petition was extremely useful because it forced me to sit down and think through and formulate my entire ideology on this whole issue. My ideology has not changed one iota in all the years. At that time, the government put its disqualification of gays under the rubric of immoral conduct, which I objected to because under our system, morality is a matter of personal opinion and individual belief on which any American citizen may hold any view he wishes and upon which the government has no power or authority to have any view at all. Besides which, in my view, homosexuality is not only *not* immoral, but is affirmatively moral. Up until that time, nobody else ever said this—as far as I know—in any kind of formal court pleading.

So I filed the petition with the Supreme Court in January, and in March the letter came. As I recall, it was on blue paper—I still have it upstairs. It was signed by Chief Justice Earl Warren, indicating that *certiorari* had been denied. That ended the formal case, but not the battle.

At that point I felt that, given the realities and problems of fighting the government on my own, the time had come to fight collectively. You see, by this time I had become radicalized. You don't hear that word much now, but it describes exactly the process I and many others have experienced. I have handled many cases over the years of people who were mild and unassertive, who just wanted to go about doing their work, and then, suddenly, they were hit hard. They were trampled upon with a hobnailed boot, and it radicalized them! And off they went marching militantly! In case after case after case!

So, in 1961, with the intention of starting a Mattachine chapter here in Washington, D.C., I contacted Curtis Dewees or Al de Dion, who together ran the New York chapter of Mattachine. At that time, they were right at the center of the deeply divisive politics, the turf wars, going on inside Mattachine, of which I knew almost nothing and cared less. Curtis and Al saw the opportunity to get a Washington Mattachine group going as a way to add to their power within the Mattachine structure. They figured that they would have no trouble controlling us and looked forward to having a flunky, which I had no intention whatsoever of being.

Meanwhile, other things were going on with Mattachine. The national structure of Mattachine collapsed in March of that year. The San Francisco Mattachine had cut loose all the other affiliates and wished them well, urging them to change their names and to keep on working. The Denver group became The Neighbors and disappeared. The New York group retained its name and incorporated as a nose-thumbing gesture to San Francisco. It became the Mattachine Society, Incorporated, of New York versus the Mattachine Society in San Francisco. It was very petty.

In any case, Curtis and Al came down here for a meeting, which has since become famous because the local vice squad sent somebody as an observer. We held the meeting at the Hay-Adams Hotel downtown on Sixteenth and H, in August 1961. The New York Mattachine had a mailing list of gay people all up and down the coast, and sent invitations to all the Washington people on their list, who included, covertly, the chief of the morals division here in Washington, who had gotten onto their mailing list. So that's why one of the chief's subordinates was present at our meeting and could validly claim that he had been invited. He was recognized immediately by one of the people at the meeting.

At that time, the police were hunting us down, harassing us, entrapping us in parks, and so on. There was a small crew of them who were known to their victims. So after we all sat down, and just before the meeting was convened, one of the men who helped me set up the meeting called me out of the room and said, "Do you know that that's Sergeant Louis Fouchette?" Fouchette was the head of the so-called perversion section. I went back in and took a look and I could see his gun holster.

After we'd gone through much of the meeting, I decided we had better do something about Fouchette. So I said, "I understand there's a representative of the Metropolitan Police Department here. Could he please identify himself and tell us why he's here?" Well, Fouchette didn't expect that at all. He sputtered and fumed and indicated, truthfully, that he had been invited and was just there to gather information. Whereupon he left. The FBI has a substantially accurate report about this meeting.

That following November, on November 15, 1961, we had our first official meeting of the Washington Mattachine. I was the organizer and founder. We did all the things that an organization does when it gets going. We took out a bank account, got a post-office box, wrote our constitution, elected our officers, set up our meeting structure, and chose a name. I opted against using the Mattachine name, but I was outvoted. I wanted something that was more explicit and expressive, but wouldn't have used the word *gay* then. While it was an in-group word, it hadn't yet gone public.

Now the movement of those days was very unassertive, apologetic, and defensive. I don't say this critically, and not necessarily derogatorily, because it was a different era. First of all, up to this time, homosexuality had never been publicly discussed. Let me give you an illustration of that. As you're aware, the question of queers in the government was very much part of the grist of the mill for McCarthy in his hearings in the early 1950s. When McCarthy was riding high, I was still in graduate school at Harvard. I read the *Boston Herald* every day. I read the *New York Times* every Sunday. I listened to the radio all the time. I read *Time* magazine weekly. Yet I did not learn until somewhere around 1958 or 1959 that homosexuality had been a theme of those hearings because it was not widely reported: the word *homosexual* was not fit to print or discuss or be heard. Virtually from one end of the decade to the other, outside the medical books, there was nothing anywhere on the subject. It was blanked out, blacked out. It wasn't there!

Because there was no publicity, there was no way of getting to people. The people in the small movement at that time were only talking to themselves. There was absolutely nothing whatsoever that anybody heard at any time, anywhere, that was other than negative!

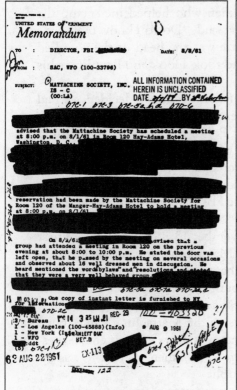
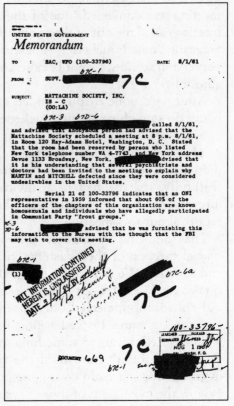

FBI documents, obtained through the Freedom of Information Act,
regarding the founding meeting of the Washington Mattachine
organization on August 1, 1961.

Nothing! We were sick; we were sinners; we were perverts. And so
the movement, predictably, in retrospect, did not take strong positions. It gave a hearing to everybody, saying, "As long as it deals with
homosexuality, all views must be heard, even those that are the most
harshly and viciously condemnatory to homosexuals. We have to
defer to the experts." My answer to that was, "*Drivel!* We are the
experts on ourselves, and we will tell the experts they have nothing to
tell us!" Giving all views a fair hearing didn't suit my personality. And
the Mattachine Society of Washington was formed around my personality.

So we at the Washington Mattachine characterized ourselves
within the movement as an activist militant organization. Those were
very dirty words in those days in the movement, such as it was. You
weren't supposed to be militant. And we were, both in our actions
and our goals. Our statement of purposes set out our goals, which

were generally to achieve equality for homosexuals and homosexuality against heterosexuals and heterosexuality. Equality was the primary theme.

ONCE WE completed our organizational chores, we started to think about how we would address the world. We realized that politics in one way was the place to go for ultimate affirmation of our rights. In those days we had fewer political avenues open to us here in Washington than any other place in the country. We had three presidentially appointed commissioners who ran the D.C. government, such as it was. We had absolutely nowhere to go at all. By default, we decided that our focus would be the federal government and the policies of the federal government with respect to gays. That focus fell into three prime areas. One, civil service employment, because gays were flatly barred from government employment. Two, security clearance, because gays couldn't get security clearance or, if found out, lost it. And three, the uniformed military, because if you were discovered to be gay, you were thrown out, almost always then with an undesirable discharge. One of our picketing slogans was, "If You Don't Want a Man, Let Him Go, But Don't Throw Him on the Human Trash Heap for the Remainder of His Life."

In the middle of 1962 we sent out a news release announcing our formation and included a copy of our statement of purposes. We sent this to the president, the vice president, all members of the Cabinet, each member of the Supreme Court, certain other selected members of the federal judiciary, every member of Congress—postage was cheap in those days—and sundry other selected federal officials. Ultimately, one congressman who was viciously opposed to us printed everything—our cover letter, our news release, and our statement of purpose—in the *Congressional Record* as an example of the horrible things going on here in Washington. Thanks to that congressman, Representative John Dowdy from eastern Texas, everybody in the world knew what we were up to. This was a welcome bounty. Later, Dowdy was convicted for taking bribes, conspiracy, and perjury.

The second thing we did was start a publication, a newsletter, to get the news across and because people liked to express themselves. We called it *The Gazette*. However, we decided that we were not going to fall into the trap of so many organizations that have publications in which the tail wags the dog. When that happens, you suddenly find you're devoting all your organizational resources to getting out your publication on time, so you don't have any time to do anything that could be reported in the publication. We decided that we would do what we needed to do first and then do the newsletter. Ultimately, it ended up coming out extremely irregularly, approximately seasonally.

We put selected people throughout the government, including the president; the Supreme Court; and J. Edgar Hoover, director of the FBI, on our *Gazette* mailing list. One day in August of 1963 or 1964, shortly after we had mailed an issue of *The Gazette*, I got a phone call. The voice at the other end of the phone said, "This is agent John A. O'Beirne of the FBI." He said that he wanted to come over and talk to me. Well, I don't allow FBI agents into my house, and I don't believe in talking to the FBI unless there's some good reason that will serve my purposes. I asked him what he wanted to talk about. He mentioned *The Gazette*.

Now, while *The Gazette* may well have published things of possible interest to the FBI from issue to issue, the one that had just come out happened to be singularly innocuous from that viewpoint. I asked agent O'Beirne if this was indeed the issue in question. He got very flustered and said, "This is *The Gazette* of the Mattachine Society of Washington. . . ." and he gave the date. Clearly he was reading from the masthead of that particular issue. It was a small mimeographed paper.

My curiosity was piqued, so I said, "I'll meet with you, but at your office, not at my house." We set up a meeting for the following day. I called up the editor of *The Gazette* and asked him if he would accompany me, and off we went to the Justice Department. (The FBI building hadn't been built yet.) With some trepidation we went into the appointed room. It was a big, carpeted room, and there at the end was agent O'Beirne and one of his colleagues.

We had a discussion, and what he told us was that he wanted to know why Mr. Hoover was receiving *The Gazette*. So we explained that we felt there was material in *The Gazette* that was of potential interest to a number of people throughout the government and therefore we had put quite a number of government officials on our mailing list. He said, "Mr. Hoover would like to be taken off your mailing list." We asked him why, and he gave us all sorts of reasons. He explained that this was a highly contentious issue and that Mr. Hoover didn't want to be associated with it, and so on.

At just that particular moment in history the FBI had been dragged kicking and screaming into the escalating civil rights battle in the South. This was a matter of some news, so I latched onto that and said, "Just as the FBI is participating in the civil rights battle down there, ours is also a civil rights issue, and we feel that we have a right as American citizens to have the full and active support of the FBI."

I indicated that it was our First Amendment right to send any material we wanted to any public official we wanted. From that point forward he went on the defensive. He said, in one phrasing or another, "Well, we recognize that you have the right to send this to Mr. Hoover if you wish, but Mr. Hoover would like to be taken off your mailing list."

Well, we debated back and forth, but ultimately we said that this matter would have to come before my executive board. We left, sort of bemused. It was rather hilarious. Here the members of the Mattachine Society were concerned that they might be on lists maintained by J. Edgar Hoover and his organization, and J. Edgar Hoover was even more concerned that he was on a list maintained by the Mattachine Society of Washington!

I brought this up at the board meeting the following week and suggested we let it ride until the next meeting. I just wanted to mull this over. Then suddenly one day I realized something. In those days, for all kinds of reasons of anonymity, *The Gazette* did not use bylines, and all the names that were on the masthead were pseudonyms. And while I did not use a pseudonym, my name didn't appear anywhere at all in that issue of *The Gazette*. Nevertheless, I was the person Mr. O'Beirne called.

The unavoidable conclusion was that the FBI was maintaining a file on the Mattachine Society of Washington. And when they got *The Gazette*, they went to the file, and there was my name. It was the only name that wasn't a pseudonym, so they could track me down. So, we sent a letter to Mr. O'Beirne saying that we would be willing to remove Mr. Hoover from our mailing list if we received written assurance from Mr. Hoover that all files on the Mattachine Society of Washington maintained by the FBI had been destroyed and would remain so. We also requested that all references to the Mattachine Society in any individual citizen's file be removed. Secondly, we asked that someone else at the FBI be designated to receive *The Gazette* in place of Mr. Hoover. And thirdly, since we knew there would be from time to time some particular item in *The Gazette* that would be of concern to Mr. Hoover, we wanted to be able to send individual issues to him without feeling that we had violated any such agreement. That was in 1963 or 1964. Mr. Hoover died in 1972, never having responded. And we never took him off our mailing list.

Years later, I saw the actual FBI files, and there was the whole thing, from the initial memorandum raising objections to being on the mailing list to a memorandum from O'Beirne narrating what had happened at that meeting. There was also a copy of our letter, and there was a memo written by O'Beirne saying, "This is obviously a contemptible"—*contemptible* is my word—"effort by these people to create publicity at the expense of the FBI. We recommend that no further communications from this organization ever be responded to by the FBI." And none ever was.

For years I had been telling people about this little episode, and as good journalists will do, they've always said, "Well fine, that's your version, but let's have something that shows that all of this isn't a figment of your imagination." And now we have the proof in the FBI documents.

FOR ABOUT three or four years, we were at the cutting edge of the movement; nobody else was doing anything. So we simply wrote our own agenda and, without any competition, went ahead and did it, whether that meant going after the Civil Service Commission or protesting publicly against the Pentagon. It was an exciting, stimulating, fascinating time, with an enormous sense of accomplishment! We had the whole world ahead of us.

Mattachine was *the* leading gay organization in the country. It set the pace, until it was supplanted in about 1965 by an organization in San Francisco, the Society for Individual Rights. Here in Washington, for a little under ten years, Mattachine was the only gay organization. At our peak, we had about one hundred members.

The Mattachine incorporation is still there. I send in the annual report every year. We're still on the D.C. government's rolls of fully registered nonprofit corporations. I still have Mattachine letterhead. You find that it's very useful now and then to have a hat to put on. When you testify, for example, at city council hearings, you get five minutes if you're a private citizen and ten minutes if you represent an organization. So out comes the Mattachine hat, and I have five more minutes to be verbose in.

OUR FIGHT with the Civil Service Commission went on and on and on, well past the lifetime of Mattachine. We created a long line of cases of people who were fired, and these successful cases, along with the general change in climate, made the Civil Service Commission's antigay policy just untenable. They finally changed it, going through the formalities in 1975. Justice triumphed. I was right, and they were wrong, and they admitted they were wrong. You have open gays all over the government now.

The battle with the military, we have largely lost for the present. The only difference nowadays is that most people who are thrown out get fully honorable discharges. In the past, they invariably got undesirable discharges. Security clearance is still a burning issue today, and I'm still handling those cases, although if they're properly handled, you can obtain or retain the clearance. But the battle with the Civil Service Commission is one book that has been closed and put on the shelf as a complete success.

AT THIS point people call me a living legend, or, humorously, the world's oldest living homosexual, or the grandfather or the great-grandfather of the gay movement, which is not technically correct.

Looking back, if anyone told me years ago that I would be a political activist, I would have thought he was insane. If anybody had ever told me as late as the 1950s, when giving a three-minute speech in a class involved two weeks of nightmares, that I would reach the point in my life where three minutes would be the first half of a good opening sentence and that without preparation or notes I could talk for two hours, I would have thought he was absolutely insane.

Ultimately, in retrospect, and except for the constant nagging problem of money for most of my adult life, my life has been more exciting and stimulating and interesting and satisfying and rewarding and fulfilling than I ever could possibly have dreamed it would be.

The Rabble Rousers

Barbara Gittings and Kay Lahusen

THE MORE *aggressive approach to securing equal rights for gay people alienated some activists and attracted others, including two women who met in 1961 at a Daughters of Bilitis picnic in Rhode Island. Barbara Gittings and Kay Lahusen, who then went by the name Kay Tobin, grew increasingly impatient with the approach taken by the organization that brought them together. By the mid-1960s, the Philadelphia couple was out on the picket line carrying placards in front of the White House and Independence Hall.*

For Barbara and Kay, the struggle for gay rights became a full-time career. Yet, because they were volunteers, they had to make many sacrifices to support their involvement on the front lines. At their home in West Philadelphia, Kay and Barbara pointed out their odds-and-ends mix of furniture and noted that they were never interested in making money. Today, as they look toward retirement, and having semiretired from the movement, Barbara works as a free-lance typist, as she has for much of her life, while Kay sells real estate.

At fifty-seven, Barbara is a tall, big-boned woman with an expressive face that's constantly animated by a ready smile. Kay, who is two years older, is short with a small frame. Like Barbara, she is strong willed and was full of passion when she spoke about her life's work. The couple's conversation was filled with the knowing looks and laughter of two people who have shared three decades and countless adventures together.

Barbara:

I carried the torch for one particular girl all through high school in Wilmington, Delaware, but it was not reciprocated. I got to see a lot of her in extracurricular activities, and we also double-dated.

The boy I was dating was one of those who had lied about his age to get into the army and fight in the war. After World War II, he came back to finish high school, so he was a couple of years older and obviously much more mature than most of the other boys. He and I gravitated to each other. I have suspicions today that he may have been gay. He didn't paw me or try to make out with me all the time. This may have been why we got along so well.

I think if I were to look at my high school records today, they would be shot through with comments from my teachers saying, "This child is homosexual," or "This child is becoming queer," or whatever words they would have used in that day. I think it must have been very obvious to them, but it wasn't obvious to me because I was still pretty naive.

A little later in my high school career, one of my teachers tried to warn me that I would have a difficult time ahead in college. I can't remember the context, but she used the word *homosexual* as a label for me. I kind of knew what it meant in a vague intellectual sense, but it didn't seem to apply to me. I didn't really put the two together until I went to college. By the way, I found out later that I had been rejected for a kind of high school honor society that I was otherwise qualified for, on the grounds of character. I think the character problem had something to do with my obvious homosexual leanings.

After I graduated from high school, I went to college at Northwestern for one year. This was in 1949. I flunked out because that was the year I put the homosexual label on myself and tried to come to terms with what it meant to be gay. I stopped going to classes and started going to the library and ended up with a lot of incompletes which turned into failures. I haven't returned to college since. But despite the fact that I failed all my classes, I learned a great deal that year. I wanted to know what my life was going to be like. I also started to try to find my people. The first place I found them was in books. Oh, I devoured everything! I looked myself up in the books on abnormal psychology. I tried to find myself in legal books. I tried to find myself in encyclopedias. I found everything I possibly could.

What I found was puzzling. It was me they were talking about, but it wasn't me at all. It was very clinical; it didn't speak of love; it didn't have very much humanity to it. They were talking about some kind of condition, an alien condition that was a departure from the norm. It was possibly treatable, but possibly not. There was something wrong with people like this—everything I read said that we were deviants. So that's what I thought about myself.

The closest I got to some sense of gay people with personalities and real lives was in Havelock Ellis's book, of all things, *Studies in the Psychology of Sex*, his famous two-volume work, which was published in the 1930s. It was full of good stuff because you could find something to identify with in most of the people Ellis wrote about, even if they sounded very peculiar.

Then I began to find the homosexual novels. That was a big improvement because the characters were much closer to real life. They had their moments of happiness, even if the endings were terrible. It made me feel better about myself. You could take a novel like the great classic, *The Well of Loneliness*, which was my first big gay novel. A tragic story—very overwritten, of course, and a very unhappy ending. But even though the heroine was a moneyed Englishwoman of good breeding, who had horses, a place in the country, and rich parents, and who lived a rich life in Paris, which was nothing like my life, I could feel what she was feeling.

I also came across odd things in the books I read. For example, I read that homosexuals could not whistle. I could whistle, so I didn't quite know what to make of that. I learned that the favorite color of homosexuals was green, and my favorite color was not green. I didn't know what to make of that either. I actually tried to mold myself according to what I thought was the role—the way—but that approach didn't last long.

Then I started finding my people. Somehow I found out about gay bars. I had left home and was living in a rooming house here in Philadelphia. I did not know where the gay bars were here, but I found out about one in New York. I don't like bars, but I went because that was the only place I knew to find other gay people.

There were two types of women in the bar: the kind who had short hair and wore men's shirts, boy's pants, and heavy shoes and the other kind, who wore skirts and high heels and stockings and had hair piled up on their heads. I'm not really the kind for skirts and high heels and hair piled up on my head. So I looked at this division and said, "Well, I must be the other kind." So that's how I dressed because I thought that's what you had to do to fit in. It was as silly as that and as simple as that. And it really meant absolutely nothing. I have really never felt any sense of butch-femme in my relationships. I played the role for a while when it seemed necessary for the social convention.

To save money on bus fare, I would hitch rides to New York with truckers. I would dress as a boy. I got away with it and was never harmed, although, there was one time here in Philadelphia when I came very close to being hurt. By this time, I had found gay bars here. I was out one night with a young gay male friend at a mixed gay bar—men and women. There were a few straight people wandering around, but they were a minority. I was dressed as a boy. I was going by the name of Sonny. The friend I was with, a schoolteacher, was nicknamed Pinky. I was drinking ice water. Pinky got friendly with a couple of uniformed guys who had come into the bar, marines, I believe. They were sitting and talking with us. When we left the bar, the four of us, out came the brass knuckles. The marines proceeded to rip up Pinky's face. They cut open his nose entirely. And they said to me, "We aren't touching you, Sonny, because you wear glasses." I thought to myself, My God, what a close call I've had.

It was terrifying, and there was not a damn thing I could do until they had finished their dirty work and left. Then I helped Pinky up and got him to a hospital. He had thirteen stitches in his nose. That was my one and only personal experience of antigay brutality. I guess in my innocence I hadn't thought people could feel and be so hateful and violent toward us. Pinky didn't want to report it to the police. He figured they wouldn't do anything about it and they might give him a hard time. He was probably right.

Kay:

Like Barbara, I had some terrific crushes in high school. I went to the Withrow High School in Cincinnati, Ohio. I also had crushes on a couple of movie stars, most especially Katharine Hepburn, who has made so many antigay remarks. But back then I kept these scrapbooks of Katherine Hepburn and all these other women. I also had a terrific crush on my English teacher. You can't hide those things—my word, at that age, you don't even think to hide them. Of course, my family was aware of what I was doing, and I remember a couple of disapproving remarks. But I had barely heard the word homosexual at that time, and I had no sense of being one myself. So I didn't realize the implications of what I was doing.

The summer after I graduated, in 1948, I met a girl who had gone to the same high school that I had. We hadn't met before. I fell in love with her. She fell in love with me. She had had a little experience, so we very quickly developed a physical relationship. For a year I thought it was the world's greatest friendship. But after a year together, I finally faced the fact that this was more than friendship. This was desire and sex and lust and love, just like straight people feel. I have to tell you, I had a breakdown over this revelation. I literally had to go to bed and lie down. I was totally weak. It was like a hammer was pounding my head. This went on for two weeks. Viral pneumonia was big then, so they thought that that was what was wrong with me.

I was raised by my grandparents in a partly Christian Science household, so they arranged for a Christian Science practitioner to come to the house and pray over me. Of course, I wasn't about to tell her what I was agonizing over. And I couldn't turn to my lover because she wasn't the strong one. So I finally brought it to a head within myself.

I just decided that I was right and the world was wrong and that there couldn't be anything wrong with this kind of love. I had a quick healing, but I had a hard time convincing my lover that there was nothing wrong with what we were doing. She felt that our love was really not right but, of course, she loved it. You know how it is, forbidden love—this is so wrong, but it feels so good.

In any case, we had a difficult relationship. She went to Ohio State, so I went there to be with her even though I was supposed to go to a small, wonderful liberal arts school. Her family didn't have the means to send her to one, so I went where she went. We were together in the dormitory. I remember those incidents where somebody opened the door when we were about to embrace and we jumped apart and wondered what they thought. There was a great deal of trying to hide it. In another case, I remember being in a roomful of people in our dormitory. We were having some sort of meeting. I looked at her across the room, and an older woman who lived in the dorm—she was about forty—caught this glance between us. And she said, "My, that's an awfully understanding look to pass between two people." I probably said something lame like, "Well, we both have a big exam in the same subject tomorrow."

My lover was this pillar-of-the-community type, the soul of rectitude. If anything went wrong in the dorm, the dorm mother turned to her for advice, little realizing that the two of us were carrying on like crazy. One time, the dorm mother caught two girls in bed together. That incident in itself was totally shocking, but what put them girls beyond the pale was that they were sort of butch-femme, which we weren't. They were even shocking to me because of that. I saw them on the bus one night holding hands and I thought, *My God, what a terrible thing to do in public*. I was against that kind of display back then. Oh, and to top it all off, one was black and the other was white! Well, they broke every rule.

When the dorm mother caught these two girls, what did she do, first thing? She turned to my lover and said, "I found these girls. What should I do? How do I handle this?" I forget what Jane* said to her, but Jane was all upset and wouldn't touch me for *two* weeks! It was totally traumatic for us. The other girls were separated. They had to have separate rooms and they were warned that they would be tossed out of the school, or out of the dorm, whatever it was, if they were found together again. Of course, we didn't go near them. God forbid—they had been tainted; their cover was blown.

We were together all through school and for another two years

*Jane is a pseudonym.

afterward. Jane had always told me that she wanted to get married and have children. She came from a Jewish family where the whole purpose in life was to get married and have children. Not only that, she wanted to be Miss Wonderful in the larger community. She wanted to be looked up to, and she couldn't be if she was a lousy lesbian. Six years we were lovers!

There are some people who are gay but don't have the strength to go against the crowd. I'm glad to say that it's not so hard to go against the crowd anymore, but back then, it was very hard. Jane finally came to the point where she said to me, "I agree with you that there isn't anything intrinsically wrong with our loving each other, but we cannot have a good life together because there's no way we can integrate ourselves into the world. We'll always be this separate little twosome off to the side without any friends."

Jane met a guy she liked and he liked her, and they got married. I had feedback that they were not all that happy. I'm told she would sit all uptight on the couch and look to him to see what she should say, what she should do, and so forth. Whereas, with me, she had been relaxed and spontaneous, laughing and dancing. With him she was a shriveled-up person looking to *this man* to tell her what to be and what to do. What a price to pay!

I never spoke to her again. Never! I tore up every photo and threw it all in the garbage. I was devastated. Jane was a very central thing in my life. I tried to find some solace in religion. I tried to find a way to love men, which didn't work because I couldn't just conjure up those feelings. So even though I had a couple of quick liaisons with men, it wasn't true to my nature. There just wasn't any real love there. I liked them. I didn't love them.

After it was over with Jane, I headed for Boston and went to work for the *Christian Science Monitor* in the reference library doing research for the writers and editors. I was there from 1956 through 1961. I couldn't find gay people in Boston. Sometimes I would see someone sitting in a restaurant who might look gay. Usually, it would be some sort of down-and-out type who also looked worn down by the world—nobody I would go up to. I did hear of a gay bar and went and looked at it, but it was on the wrong side of Beacon Hill and didn't seem like the kind of place I could relate to. I didn't feel I could find love and a quality relationship in a bar. After all, I was a churchy type. I didn't drink and do all of those things. I was fairly puritanical.

I had worked in the reference library for several years when the light bulb went on, and I said to myself, *I'm researching every other damn subject in the world for all these writers and editors, why don't I research what interests me most in this world?* So I went to the reference books and looked up homosexuality. The *Christian Science Monitor* filed homosexuality under *vice*. When you looked under the listing for *homosexuality*, it said, "See Vice." That got me! I used to argue with some of the other staff about that. Of course, I didn't say that I was gay. I pretended to argue purely as an intellectual exercise. There was hardly any material; you hardly ever even saw the word. Some British spy was found, and he was homosexual. Or an occasional shrink would say something.

I finally unburdened myself to some other human being. I went to a Christian Science practitioner and told her. Actually, I had gone to a male practitioner several years before. He had been a chaplain in the navy. I thought, *Well, he'll be worldly, and I can tell him.* I told him my story, and when I was finished he got up and closed the transom to his office and said, "I have never heard such a sordid story in my life."

For years, I didn't broach it to another church muckety-muck until I went and talked to this woman practitioner who was British. I thought, "Well, here's a woman of the world." She said to me, "Well, what of it? One of my good friends is in California, and she is homosexual." She agreed with me that the church was just very culture bound and that it had the biases of the general culture. She was very reinforcing.

In doing my research at the *Monitor*, I found a book called *Voyage from Lesbos: The Psychoanalysis of a Female Homosexual*, written by a psychiatrist named Richard Robertiello. In the book Robertiello focused on a lesbian he had treated and—he believed—cured. He was a well-known psychoanalyst at the time. So in 1961 I made an appointment with him in New York. I asked him a couple of questions about what made people gay, which I wasn't really interested in. Then I came to the real question, "How do I meet others?" So he said, "Oh, if that's what you want, that's easy." He reached over on his desk and pulled out this old copy of *The Ladder* and gave it to me. He said, "Here. This is published by the Daughters of Bilitis. They have an office here in New York. You can call them up. Here's the phone number." Well, I almost fell off the chair. I said. "That's enough," and even though I only spent ten minutes with him, I wrote him my check for twenty dollars for the full hour. I was lifted to the skies, but I was so thrown I couldn't even think of contacting DOB that minute. I had to regroup. I drove back to Boston on a cloud.

When I got back to Boston, I read my copy of *The Ladder*. I could see they were trying to improve things for lesbians and that they were providing a coffee-klatsch kind of meeting place for lesbians, as well as opportunities to meet by working in the organization. So I said to myself, *This is it! I can improve things in the world for gay people and I can meet other women. I will join this group and I will work in it until I find somebody. If I join the New York chapter and don't find anybody, I'll go to Chicago and join the Chicago chapter. If I don't find anybody there, I'll go to San Francisco. I'll do whatever it takes.* I didn't see myself going on for years not finding anybody.

So I wrote to DOB in New York, and who got my letter but Barbara. I wrote that I wanted to come to the next meeting and participate. Barbara was going on a trip to California, but she said I should come to the meeting in New York. So the day of the meeting, I got in my car and drove down to the DOB office. Well, I imagined this big place with a lot of people. When I got there, it was like this postage-stamp office that they shared with the Mattachine Society. The office could accommodate no more than ten people, but only five came: Marion Glass, Florence Conrad from California, two others, and me. I was very much in the spotlight. Here was this stranger from the *Christian Science Monitor* in Boston! I had driven all that way, and they were all wondering what the hell I was going to look like and be like. I remember I was just in a sweat, and I think my face was red. My heart was probably pounding.

While it wasn't what I expected, I was very heartened by a couple of the women there. Marion—peculiar person that she was, she blinked and winced and had nervous tics and everything—was very bright. She was a civil servant. And Florence Conrad was a teacher of economics at a junior college in California. So she was an OK type who I could relate to. Florence was heartening.

As I quickly learned, the purpose of DOB was to get gay people to jack themselves up. If you were a lesbian, you were to put on a skirt and join the human race.

Barbara:

That had nothing to do with my joining the movement. I never cottoned to that statement of purpose. Kay and I used to have some battles with the DOB bureaucracy about that.

What got me started in the movement was a book I found in 1953, which had been published two years earlier. It was called *The Homosexual in America: A Subjective Approach*, by Donald Webster Cory. The book was fascinating because, now that I look back on it, Cory's book was very much a call to arms. Cory said that we ought to be working to gain our equality and our civil rights.

Kay:

He was the first to say we were a minority.

Barbara:

That's right. He said that we were a legitimate minority like any other minority group. At that time, it was a very challenging book because it was saying, in effect, that we could stand up and do something for ourselves and change our situation. Eventually, I wrote the author through his publisher to ask for a meeting. I wanted to talk to him about finding more literature on gay people and making up a list. That was really what I was interested in. At the time I wasn't thinking about the real-life situation of gay people and what could be done about it. So I met Cory and in the course of our conversation about literature found out from him that there were organizations of homosexual people. I didn't realize there were such groups.

Cory told me about an organization called ONE, Incorporated, in Los Angeles. Lo and behold, for my next vacation I arranged to take a plane out to Los Angeles. This was in 1956. I arrived with my rucksack at the offices of ONE, Incorporated, and said, "Here I am. What can we do?" I don't think I had a crusading feeling in me; that really developed later. I was still really trying to find my people, but here was an organization engaged in doing something. They had a library, they had lectures, they published a magazine. It was all very new and very interesting. This was a subject that was still very much taboo, and just to be publishing a magazine about it was quite a breakthrough. Just to have an office at a time when I thought that we all lived underground was also a breakthrough.

At ONE, Incorporated, they told me about the Mattachine Society in San Francisco. So I hopped another plane and went up to San Francisco and talked to them, and they told me about DOB. I called and spoke to somebody from DOB, and I was so brash that in my first contact I criticized the name they had chosen. Not very nice, but I thought the name was lousy. It was unpronounceable, and it didn't mean anything unless you knew about the stories of Bilitis. Bilitis was fictional, and she was bisexual, not fully homosexual. On all these counts I thought it was a pretty poor choice.

In spite of my rudeness, they were kind enough to invite me to their meeting. Then I found myself for the first time, not in a bar, but in someone's living room in a nice setting with twelve other lesbians. It was a marvelous experience. It was a business meeting where they were planning the publication of their magazine, *The Ladder*. I just sat there reveling in the company. These were nice women—it made a big difference. But I didn't actually join DOB until two years later. So I date my earliest participation in the movement to 1958, when I was invited by Del Martin and Phyllis Lyon at DOB in San Francisco to help start a New York chapter. Even though I was living in Philadelphia, they didn't know anyone else who they thought might be interested in doing this. I guess they had sized me up as someone who would be willing to take the bit and run a little.

They were right. Look, I think I'm temperamentally a joiner and I figure if the gay movement hadn't come along, I would probably be active today in something like the wilderness conservation movement, which also interests me. But the gay movement caught me at the right time of my life, so I started putting my energy into that. I formally became a member of DOB and started going up to New York almost every weekend to help get this chapter of the national organization launched. There were other chapters: Los Angeles had one; Chicago had one. You see, it was the right time for a national organization. At the time, the tiny handful of women in any particular city wouldn't have had the courage, the means, and whatever else it might have taken to set up and form a separate organization. It was much easier to get yourself launched by becoming a chapter of an established organization. ONE, Incorporated, did not have chapters, but Mattachine and DOB did.

As far as official members were concerned, we might have had ten at the start. But a lot more turned up for the social events and the public lectures.

Kay:

I met Barbara at one of these events. It was a picnic in Rhode Island in 1961, not too long after I went to my first DOB meeting in New York.

Barbara:

The purpose of the picnic was to pull together some women to try to start a DOB chapter in the New England area. Kay was on the mailing list, and I wrote to all the women on DOB's list who were within a hundred-mile radius of Rhode Island and invited them to start a chapter up there.

Kay:

When I met Barbara at the picnic, I thought she was a very interesting person. I was quite taken with her.

Barbara:

And I was quite taken with Kay. We started jabbering away, and as I recall, after the picnic we went somewhere, and then we started long-distance courting.

Kay:

Barbara expected some mousy little old lady to turn up.

Barbara:

That's because I knew Kay worked for the *Christian Science Monitor*. My stereotypes were such that I expected this rather dour type of person. And Kay was anything but that. She was dressed in bright, cheerful colors. Red hair. Just awfully attractive.

Kay:

It was a pretty motley crew that showed up at the picnic. I don't think we even had ten people. There was Marge and her hopeless love for Jan. There was an older woman who wasn't with anyone. And I think because of her age she felt out of it. But she told Barbara that I was a "cute little package" and that she should go after me. That really ticked me off.

Barbara:

It's been a standing joke with us ever since—"cute little package."

Kay:

Frankly, in the beginning days of the movement, the people who turned up were, by and large, pretty oddball. It's only from the most oddball fringey-type gay people that we have worked our way into the mainstream of the gay minority. You see, in the early days, getting involved in the movement was such an unpopular thing to do. It was nonconformist at a time when most gay people were trying to blend in and pass. And you had to have some reason to want to crusade, in spite of whatever it might cost you. Because back then it could cost you a lot, including your job.

Barbara:

Believe it or not, there was a genuine fear that we would be raided by the police, even at our most distinguished public events where we had name people from the law and the ministry and the mental health professions. It didn't happen, but it was an ever-present fear.

Kay:

Actually, DOB didn't have big public lectures—Mattachine did. We members of DOB would go to these Mattachine events.

Barbara:

Sometimes DOB would be a cosponsor, so we'd sort of hitch with Mattachine's greater strength to get our name onto something.

Kay:

It was usually a lecture on the law and changing the law.

Barbara:

Or on changing your homosexuality.

Kay:

Or it was some psychotherapist or some shrink.

Barbara:

Usually some shrink looking for clients to cure.

Kay:

Or a gay therapist who wasn't out of the closet would present an academic paper. What did Fritz always talk about? Monkeys and things? He talked about homosexuality and animals.

Barbara:

This was an academic exercise. These lectures were really excuses to hold a function to get together and to let people come out a little bit. The content of the lecture didn't really matter that much. It's amazing to people now that we put up with some of the nonsense that was parlayed in these lectures. And yet, we had to go through that because we really needed the recognition that we got from these people who were names in law, the ministry, and the mental health professions. They had credentials and were willing to come to address a meeting of ours instead of just ignoring us entirely. That was important—just their coming and recognizing our existence gave us a boost.

We even had Albert Ellis, who was a real stinker. People like Ellis talked about homosexuality being a sickness. And they talked about a cure or moving in the direction of a cure. We'd sit there and listen and politely applaud and then go for the social hour afterward.

Kay:

Most gay people in New York who had any kind of income were going to a therapist in those days to get straightened out, and most therapists were trying to cure them. It was really something trying to get people out from under that whole therapy stuff. It was chic to be going to a therapist. Deep analysis. Find out what went wrong in your childhood and so forth. Not too many people just thought for themselves and came to the conclusion that this was all a crock of shit.

Barbara:

Besides the public events and social hours that followed, DOB had its own socials and what were called "gab n' java" sessions—literally, talk and coffee. These socials were very successful and drew large numbers of women.

Kay:

Barbara, when you say large, what do you really mean? I remember thirty to thirty-five women at a meeting.

Barbara:

Fine. That was a very large number in someone's living room, especially in a New York apartment. So I call that a big crowd.

Kay:

And then once a year we would have a covered-dish supper. It was a big deal, and we would allow the men to come to that. Some of the Mattachine men came.

Barbara:

Other than the covered-dish supper, the gab n' javas were strictly for women. There was always a topic of discussion. Sometimes there was a short presentation by somebody. It made for good fellowship. People letting their hair down and talking rather freely on all kinds of topics, like telling your parents, going to the therapist, and legal problems.

Kay:

Topics like, "Should lesbians wear skirts?"

Barbara:

Or, "Acceptance by the world at large."

Kay:

And people would talk about their therapy. Therapy was the overriding thing then. Law reform and politics were secondary.

Barbara:

By this time I was beginning to feel my crusading oats a little bit. I couldn't help it. And yet I didn't have a very clear sense of what we were doing and why we were doing it. We sort of bumbled along. I wasn't much of a leader for the New York group in the sense that I provided direction and vision. I was more of an administrator.

Kay:

You pulled it together. You built up a mailing list of over three hundred.

Barbara:

I also got out a good little newsletter. I cranked things up and got them going. But where we were going, if you had asked me, I probably wouldn't have been able to say clearly. Kay was a big help because she's got a very clear mind and some very definite ideas about the world.

Kay:

The Mattachine guys pushed things along. After all, they did a sit-in at a bar and demanded to be served, and that was very important. Randy Wicker was the first to picket.

Barbara:

He picketed the Whitehall military induction center in 1964 in lower Manhattan. Before that, at Cooper Union, when they had all of the Irving Bieber analysts on a panel talking about homosexuality as a sickness, Randy demanded equal time. He said, "Stop talking about us and let us talk for ourselves." I wasn't there, but I heard about it. This was one of the historic breakthroughs. He didn't get the equal time, but he sure got a lot of publicity.

It was beginning to filter through to me that you could do things like that. Also around that time I met Frank Kameny in Washington. He was a major influence on my thinking.

Kay:

We were taken with these challenging kinds of activities. But I think even before the surge of real activism, Barbara and I were unhappy with DOB's posture.

Barbara:

It was sort of a scolding-teacher attitude.

Kay:

It was, "Now, you lesbians had better put on a skirt and shape up and hold a job and go to work nine to five and make yourselves acceptable . . .

Barbara:

" . . . to the world and then you can expect something of the world in return." It was scolding the laggard lesbian.

Kay:

It was pointed toward the ne'er-do-wells who lolled around in gay bars all day long. Most of us were already in skirts fitting in all too tightly.

Barbara:

It seemed to me that at every national convention of DOB, Kay and I would come up with radical proposals that were always voted down. We wanted associate memberships for men. We wanted to change the name of the magazine. We wanted to change the makeup of the national board.

Kay:

The magazine was called *The Ladder* because you were supposed to climb up the ladder and into the human race on an OK basis.

Barbara:

The first six issues or so had a drawing of a ladder on the cover, literally. The ladder was in a muddy marshland with some vaguely humanoid figures down there and a ladder up into the clouds and into the sky.

Kay:

The little lesbian was beginning to climb the ladder, upgrading herself so that she would become an OK person instead of a "variant," who had a poor self-image, who didn't hold a regular job, who wasn't a participating member of society. As if there weren't thousands of lesbians who were great contributors to society.

Barbara:

What they needed was support—help to get the bigots off their backs and ways to meet other lesbians. They didn't need to be taught. But education of the "variant" was one of the big things in DOB.

Well, we were sort of itching under all of this, yet we stuck with DOB for several years, especially because it was then joining with several other gay groups in the East to form what was called ECHO— East Coast Homophile Organizations. The word *homophile* was very big in the late 1950s and early 1960s. If you wanted to be up front, the best you could do was to say *homosexual* or *homophile*. And very few used *homosexual*.

Anyway, we met Frank Kameny at one of the ECHO conferences in the early 1960s. Frank was a fantastic man. He was a big influence on me because he had such a clear and compelling vision of what the movement should be doing and what was just. He believed that we should be standing up on our hind legs and demanding our full equality and our full rights, and to hell with the sickness issue. *They* put that label on us! *They* were the ones that needed to justify it! Let *them* do their justification! We were not going to help them!

Kay:

So the burden of proof was on them. In the absence of valid evidence to the contrary, homosexuality was not a disease, impairment . . .

Barbara:

. . . malfunction, disorder of any kind. It was fully on par with heterosexuality and fully the equal of it. And when he put that forward as a credo for the movement in 1964, it was the most radical thing that had come down the pike. DOB was one of the groups that wouldn't go along with it. They said that we couldn't say that for ourselves.

Kay:

Their view was that we had better help these experts with their research studies and all that. Once the professionals said we were OK, then the world would accept it. Frank said, "This is rubbish! If we stand up and say, 'We're right,' and nobody listens, we will not have lost anything. But if somebody listens, we will have gained something."

Barbara:

Even if it's only one gay person who needs a little reinforcement, we will have gained something.

Kay:

DOB wasn't ready to go along with this stuff. For one thing it was the intellectual East versus San Francisco, where they had nice coffee-klatches and all that, right? They felt a little bit intimidated, I think, by the East.

Barbara:

And Kameny was an intellectual heavyweight who had a knack for using good, plain, strong English to package some of these ideas. This all finally came to a head around the time we were editing *The Ladder*. I was the nominal editor, and I asked Frank to write an article dismissing our participation as a movement in research by professionals on the subject of homosexuality, which is something he felt strongly about. He wrote it, we published the article in *The Ladder*, and I quickly got a response from the research director of DOB. I published that response a couple of issues later, and then I got a rebuttal from Frank. So he got the last word.

Kay:

The research director believed that nobody would listen to us if *we* said we were OK. So, therefore, only if Dr. So-and-So persisted in his study and said we were OK would we really make progress.

Barbara:

It's so strange today to realize that this was a hotly debated issue at the time, but it was. It was terrific back and forth, just the kind of intellectual exchange we wanted more of in *The Ladder*.

Kay:

Florence Conrad, from DOB in California, said, "This isn't subject matter that can be marketed like toothpaste." And Frank said, "Unfortunately, this can be marketed just like toothpaste!" Poor DOB. They had never been grabbed by the short hairs and shaken up this way in their lives, these San Francisco ladies.

Barbara:

There were more shake-ups to come.

Barbara Gittings (*foreground*) at an October 23, 1965, demonstration in front of the White House. The next woman in line is Ernestine Eckstein. Her sign reads "Denial of Equality of Opportunity is Immoral." The demonstration was staged by ECHO (East Coast Homophile Organizations) to protest the federal government's policies of "discrimination and hostility against its homosexual American Citizens." FBI documents noted that "35 individuals" picketed the White House "beginning at 2:30 P.M." The other marchers are unidentified. (© *Kay Tobin Lahusen*)

Kay:

We wrote all about the picketing in Washington in *The Ladder*.

Barbara:

That was in 1965.

Kay:

We were in Ohio because of an illness in my family when the first picketing took place. We were thrilled to hear that the ECHO affiliate organizations had picketed the Civil Service Commission in Washington. We were on the phone to Frank Kameny because we wanted to bring the latest news of the latest activism to our constituency.

Barbara:

Kay's grandfather died, and we came back in time to take part in all the summer demonstrations that year. We were at the first protest at the White House and the first one at the Pentagon.

Kay:

And the first one at Independence Hall here in Philadelphia. That was on July 4, 1965. We went back to Independence Hall every July 4, right through 1969.

Barbara:

It was thrilling. You knew you were doing something momentous. People would stare at you. They had never seen self-declared homosexuals parading with signs.

Kay:

There were fifty in the line in front of the White House.

Barbara:

Fifty? It wasn't that many. There were twenty-six.

Kay:

Well, there was a second picket that had more people. The men were in suits and ties. The women wore dresses.

Barbara:

That was one of the few things that all the groups participating in the protests agreed on at the time. We decided that we were the bearers of a message. To keep attention on the message, not on ourselves, we had to look unexceptional and blend into the landscape. So the order went out, and everybody followed it. The stirrings to disobey the dress code didn't really come up until 1969.

Kay:

Also, at the Civil Service Commission, we were picketing for employment. Frank Kameny's thought was, "If you want to be employed, look employable." At the time that meant turning out in a fairly conventional, respectable way.

Barbara:

And I think there was another element. The anti–Vietnam War protests had been mounting in size and fervor during this period. But by and large, these protesters were a really scruffy lot. The people who came out for those protests were flouting conventions—their hair, their dress, and everything was so wild as to turn off a lot of people to their message. We wanted to distance ourselves from this kind of protest and not have our message spurned because of who we were as the bearers. That's why there was this business of blending into the woodwork. Besides carrying signs, we handed out literature. We really had a great time.

Kay:

Unfortunately, we were hardly noticed by the mainstream press. You know who noticed us? This little supermarket rag. It was sort of a *National Enquirer*.

Barbara:

And they had this wonderful headline: "Homos on the March!" We bought a lot of copies of this dreadful scandal sheet because it was a good story. Their reporter really got the facts. It was a reasonably sympathetic story. It didn't picture us as strange or crazy.

Kay:

The *New York Times* wasn't paying any attention to us. How else were we to get the word out there in the world? So we were all for picketing. Again, picketing was against DOB's philosophy. They wanted to hide behind the skirts of the professionals and have the professionals say we were OK. They thought we shouldn't run out in the streets and do this kind of thing. So we put this debate in *The Ladder*. Of course, that enraged DOB, too. What was the name of that article?

Barbara:

"Picketing: The Pros and Cons." The majority of groups in the movement were finding that picketing was a really effective way of getting some mainstream publicity and feeling much better about yourself and reaching out to gay people.

Kay:

We had one of our major contributors write to us in a private letter that only dirty, unwashed rabble did this kind of thing.

Barbara:

Because of these differences and because of the sheer complications of my being on the East Coast and not meeting deadlines, in mid-1966, I was out as editor, and *The Ladder* continued without me.

Kay:

But just to put this in perspective, after we'd done our picketing and DOB had disapproved, something happened on the West Coast. I can't remember what it was, but they ran out and picketed. And that was the end of that. After giving us such a hard time, they went and picketed themselves.

Barbara:

I did not continue to be active in DOB after mid-1966. There seemed no reason. I stayed friendly with some women who were in a Philadelphia DOB, but their affiliation with DOB didn't last long. They had a bad experience that alienated them from the organization. There was a raid on a lesbian bar here in Philadelphia that really galvanized them because it was so clearly a pure exercise of police power designed to make life miserable for us, the gay people. The police went into the bar and more or less picked out women at random and put them in paddy wagons. They arrested eight women, including the hatcheck concessionaire. The women spent a night at the police station and they were outraged. They wanted to do something. They were ready for action. The obvious vehicle was the existing chapter of DOB.

But they found that they could hardly blow their noses without permission from national headquarters of DOB, which was all caught up in a big election for the board and sending out campaign literature and so forth. The women in Philadelphia, who were brainy women, finally said, "What do we need Daughters of Bilitis for? We can't move in this organization. All we get is campaign literature." So they broke off from DOB, ended the chapter, and founded a new organization for both men and women, called Homophile Action League, that was dedicated to political action.

In the movement, groups that accepted both men and women have almost always evolved from organizations started by men that have later allowed women to join. But here was an organization started solely by women that was open to both men and women from the beginning. And from the start, it always had a majority of women members. The Homophile Action League started in 1967, and, of course, I joined.

Kay:

Let me leave you with one thought. The driving force and the reason I am so passionate about this is because it's so wrong that a good gay relationship had to break up because it was felt at the time that this was no kind of life to be lived. I just want to turn that around in this world. This is what drove me then and still drives me now.

One Angry Nurse

Shirley Willer

SHIRLEY WILLER *was born on September 26, 1922, in Chicago, Illinois. Her father was a judge, a road commissioner, a lady's man, and a heavy drinker. He also beat his wife, who one day in 1931 packed Shirley and her three-year-old sister into the family car and fled. Despite the challenges of her childhood, Shirley eventually made her way to nursing school in the early 1940s.*

In 1962 Shirley celebrated her fortieth birthday by moving to New York City to join the Daughters of Bilitis. Shirley's involvement led to her election as president of the New York chapter and later as national president of DOB. Before long, however, Shirley found herself torn between allegiance to the low-profile DOB and her affinity for gay women and men who were determined to take the struggle public.

Shirley says that people have always considered her to be a "big butch" because of the way she looks. "Because of my haircut and the way I dress, frequently I'll pull into a gas station and they'll say to me, 'Yes, sir?' And I'll say, 'Don't say sir, I'm a woman.' Look, I don't feel like a big butch. I wear men's clothes because I'm too damn fat to buy women's clothes. They don't make the kind of slacks that I like to wear in a forty-eight-inch waist for women. They make them for men."

Shirley was sitting in a wheelchair behind her desk in a large, simply-furnished room at the back of her home in a working-class neighborhood of Key West, Florida. The room, which overlooks a small inlet behind the house, was filled with the delightful songs of her many pet birds. Shirley's hair is mostly gray and cut in a flattop style. She looked out from behind thick black-rimmed glasses and spoke in a deep, smoky voice. As she talked about the past, her eyes often filled with tears.

I discovered I was gay—we'll use that word, it's easier nowadays—sitting in a classroom in nursing school in Chicago, listening to a lecture on mental hygiene. The teacher described what a lesbian was, how lesbians were not attracted to men and had these violent crushes on women, and I said to myself, *Oh, gee, I'm one of those things!* You see, I thought everybody was like that. I could never quite figure out why these girls were getting all excited about going out on dates when I preferred hanging around with *them*. I was very stupid. I guess the nice word is *naive*.

After class, I went home and told my mother. As all parents do, she said, "What did I do wrong?" But my mother always trusted me a great deal, which had a lot to do with the fact that I ran the household. She had to work split shifts and weird hours all the time. It was very interesting what my mother did next. She got me a copy of the *The Well of Loneliness* to read. My mother was a very intelligent women.

When I finished reading *The Well*, I started looking up words in the dictionary and the encyclopedia. I didn't find very pleasant descriptions. *Pervert* was the most commonly used word. It was a perversion of the natural instincts of the human animal. At that time it was considered a criminal act. Just the assumption that I was gay was justification enough for one policeman to pick me up by the front of my shirt and slap me back and forth. He called me names, the same ones they use now. "You god-damned pervert. You queer. You S.O.B." I had been walking down Rush Street in Chicago trying to find a gay bar I had heard of, the Seven Seas. I had never been to a gay bar before. It was eleven o'clock at night and I had on women's slacks and a women's sport shirt—all, of course, made as tailored as possible. I liked tailored clothes. Because I was heavy, I looked much better in tailored clothes than I did in ruffles. I guess the way I was dressed and the late hour were enough evidence for the policeman to hit me.

I was so angry at the policeman I could have killed him! I wasn't frightened; I was angry! He had no right to do that to me! And that's been my attitude all my life. They have no right!

IN MANY ways, these were very sad times to be alive. There are many reasons, but let me tell you what happened to my friend Barney. I met Barney after the war at the hospital where I worked. He was a nurse. You see, when World War II ended, all the navy and army corpsmen came back and were allowed to take an examination to become registered nurses. Most of them were flaming queens. Thank goodness the hospital didn't seem to pay much attention to it. They did their jobs right, and that's all that mattered. Of course, we all met each other and became friends.

Barney and I and the other fellahs had a lot of fun together. One of the things we did was go to the annual Halloween costume balls, which were run by the Mafia. We would have them at these two huge ballrooms; one was on the north side of the city and the other on the south side. These balls were big events in Chicago, the only events where all bets were off and the police left us alone. This was the one time of year that gay people could be gay. It was the only visible sign that there were literally thousands and thousands of gay people in the city. All the women would get tuxedos and dress in our butchiest styles.

The first time I went was shortly after the fellahs got out of the service because I remember they dressed me. They put me in a tuxedo. They tied my tie. And they put makeup on me. I'd never worn makeup in my life! Almost all the fellahs wore dresses. Barney had on some huge sequined thing.

Barney worked the eleven P.M. to seven A.M. shift at the hospital because he was going to medical school during the day. He had his first class at nine o'clock, so he would go home and shower and wait for a school friend to pick him up to go to class. Well, one day Barney fell asleep while he was waiting, and by the time his friend got there, the couch and Barney were totally enveloped in flames. Barney had been smoking. Everybody smoked.

They took Barney to a Catholic hospital run by a brotherhood. He was badly burnt, but didn't receive good care because he was queer. They didn't even change his dressings! Even then we knew enough to use saltwater dressings. If you couldn't do anything else, you put dressings on and kept them saturated in salt water to keep them wet. They weren't even doing that! They just let the dressings dry, and then seepage was coming through and. . . .

I couldn't go and see Barney because I was a woman, and women weren't allowed to go into the hospital whatsoever, but the men went. So we moved heaven and earth to try to get him transferred out of there to a veterans hospital. We got him moved the day before he died. He was twenty-four. That was in 1947.

BARNEY'S DEATH probably had a great deal to do with my aggressiveness. It certainly had a lot to do with why I've spent a large percentage of my life being angry. And it wasn't just me. We were angry people. Now my memory isn't too clear on this point, but I think Barney's death was part of the reason that a group of six of us—six women—met with an attorney in Chicago to talk about starting some sort of organization. I didn't really know what I wanted this group to do, but I wanted to formalize the existence of such a group so we could begin to work toward some material result. I believe this was in the late 1940s, but it could have been in the 1950s. The attorney's name was Pearl Hart. Pearl later worked with the Chicago Mattachine group.

We asked Pearl how you went about starting a group, and she said,

"You don't. It's too dangerous." At that time, Pearl was like everyone else. She felt that people would get further by simply doing things quietly without announcing themselves, without having large formal meetings and so forth. She was a grand old lady. I never slept with her, so I can't swear to it that she was a lesbian, but she wore tweedy tailored suits.

Nothing came of that meeting, no formal organization, so my girlfriend and I did things pretty much on our own. We took in young women and sometimes young men who had been thrown out of their homes. They had no place else to go, so they came to us. As a nurse I always made better money than the average person, so I always had quite a nice home. Sometimes, though, we were a little short on space. I remember one time having three boys sleeping on the kitchen floor.

These kids weren't prepared for life. Most of them were in their late teens, really not old enough to know how to handle life, not settled into any kind of a career. We'd have them hang out at our house until we could help them find jobs that were suitable. A lot of them you had to teach how to read the want ads. Now, a majority of these kids wouldn't take jobs where they would be in danger of being fired because of being gay. They would go for the dirty jobs, the rough jobs. I remember one girl in particular, a very bright girl. The only job she could get was running an elevator because she wouldn't wear a dress. That was OK because we encouraged these kids to be themselves, to stop trying to hide it. Some of them we were able to help get scholarships for school.

We knew at that time that we couldn't do much to change the laws in Chicago, but we could give these kids a sense of self-esteem. We could show them that what we did, they could do. We could have a life, a good life, a comfortable life; earn a good living; own cars; and be citizens, with all the duties and responsibilities, as well as the benefits.

I DIDN'T hear of any gay organizations anywhere in the country until the late 1950s. By that time, I was at the University of Iowa in Iowa City trying to get my master's in nursing education. I don't remember how, but I heard that there were organizations in New York for both men and women. So, of course, I had to go to New York, which I did on a visit in 1959. Then in 1962, I packed up my things and moved there. I was forty. You know, life begins at forty.

After I got to New York, I sent a letter to the Daughters of Bilitis. Marion Glass—her pseudonym then was Meredith Grey—answered the letter and told me where their next meeting was going to be and at what time. Marion and I later became a couple.

My introduction to the Daughters was wild. I was told that the meeting was going to be at this particular lady's house and I could distinguish it by the barking dog. So I went to the address and went up the steps to the second or third floor, and sure enough there was this barking dog. I knocked at the door, and a young lady answered and said, "What do you want?" I said, "Well, there's going to be a meeting here tonight, isn't there?" She said, "Oh my God, no!" She had a sink full of dirty dishes, an accumulation of at least a week, and her house was a total disaster. And here there was going to be a meeting there that night—she had totally forgotten. So I washed dishes and helped clean her apartment. That was my introduction to the Daughters.

Marion came to the meeting, along with about twelve other members. During the meeting, they worked on revising a statement for the inside cover of *The Ladder*, the DOB magazine. The statement defined the meaning of the Daughters, where the name came from, and the dress code. We went over that statement and over it and over it and over it until I was ready to scream! It should have been a very simple statement, such as "The purpose of the Daughters of Bilitis is to affect the acceptance of the homosexual into society as any other member." That would have been my statement.

One of the first things we did when I got involved with DOB was to find an office so we would have some place to meet besides an apartment with a barking dog and dirty dishes. We found an office to rent where a guy had had a hemorrhage on the floor. Nobody had ever cleaned the room up after he left, so there was dried blood all over the floor. After work, we'd go down to the office and take a spatula and scrape away at this jazz on the floor. Luckily there was a corps of young women who were willing to do this kind of thing with me.

Publishing *The Ladder* was one of our major activities. I couldn't understand why we spent so much time trying to reach out to the lonely little lesbian out in the boondocks with this magazine. I was concerned about the lesbians here in New York. So we started having dances and discussion groups, but I have to admit I always enjoyed a meeting more than a party because you would accomplish something, even if it was only one thing. You didn't accomplish much at any of the parties except to see a bunch of women get drunk and sick. But you had to have the parties in order to have the other part.

* * *

Shirley Willer in the
mid-1960s at the beach in
Atlantic City, where she and
her lover, Marion Glass, had
gone to scout a location for a
DOB outing. (© *Lesbian
Herstory Archives/DOB
Collection*)

ALL DURING this time, through the mid-1960s, I traveled all over the
country helping to form organizations of every kind, mostly DOB
chapters. I went to Boston, Chicago, Cleveland, Philadelphia, Phoe-
nix, and someplace in Texas. All over. In whatever town I went to, I
got hold of people I knew and said that we were coming there to help
form an organization. Naturally I was expected to try and form an
organization of women, another branch of the Daughters. But once
you gave them the information, it was up to them to do as they
pleased. Usually, some kind of organization would result from my
visit.

A lot of times I had a lot of men attend these things. That happened
in Chicago once, where there were many more men at this particular
meeting than there were women. It would have been silly to try to
form a chapter of the Daughters, so we gave them all the literature
from Mattachine. I didn't care what kind of group resulted, just so
long as there was some kind of group going. That, of course, offended
a good many members of the Daughters.

I was lucky in that I found a sponsor who helped me with my travel
money; otherwise I couldn't possibly have done it. This very prominent woman was gay, but there was no way she could do the work I
was doing. She was from one of the first ten families in the country;
my family was down there around seven millionth. I was also able to
finance all the chapters of the Daughters from her. There wasn't an
operating chapter of the Daughters that didn't receive at least six
thousand dollars to put toward a building fund or toward office
expenses or toward publications. In fact, she financed the printing of

The Ladder on slick stock, and because of her we were able to get the magazine into the hands of a major distributor, who put it on newsstands all over the country. We wanted to try to see if that would work, but people were afraid to buy it from newsstands. I can't see why. It was the most boring thing I ever ran across. Cute little love stories of any kind, straight or gay, never did appeal to me. And that's what *The Ladder* was packed with.

We used some of the money to fund legal work in San Francisco and New York. You know Frank Kameny, of course—well, for at least two years we helped finance his livelihood.

I served as the conduit for the money because it was all done anonymously. It was a hell of a responsibility. The procedure was this. I would give this prominent woman a name, usually the name of a DOB member, and she would give me a cashier's check made out in that individual's name. Nobody was supposed to talk about our benefactor or what she did. And this woman will never take credit for her contribution to the movement, which amounted to more than one hundred thousand dollars. But she does have the satisfaction of being able to go down the street and see a couple of guys or a couple of girls walking hand in hand, of seeing the Mafia lose control of the gay bars, of seeing homosexuality become much more acceptable. It's the same satisfaction I have.

MANY GAY people attacked those of us involved in groups like DOB or Mattachine. They frequently challenged us for being self-appointed messiahs. They felt that we weren't speaking for them, that they weren't having any trouble, so why did we have to get out there and make waves? Well, I didn't really think they looked good in all those closets. But unfortunately, most people were content to be in their closets, and plenty of the men were content to cruise the tearooms after three A.M., hoping to hell that it wasn't a cop they were cruising.

That was a whole other controversy within DOB. A lot of the women resented working with the men because it was the men, not the women, who were cruising the tearooms and getting in trouble with the police. "Why should we fight to help the men?" I said, "What difference does it make whether they're men or women? They're homosexuals." The fact that Marion and I associated with the men and predominantly male organizations, such as Washington Mattachine, New York Mattachine, and ECHO—the East Coast Homophile Organizations—didn't go over very well with a lot of the women in DOB. The San Francisco chapter objected. The national board of directors objected. Even some of our own members in New York objected. They just felt we were putting too much time into associating with the male homosexuals and not enough trying to conform to society's regulations. We sure weren't, and we didn't intend to.

Despite the objections of a lot of women in DOB, I even supported public protests and went to them—in high heels! The picketing in Philadelphia at Independence Hall was my first time. It was July 4, 1965. I wore a skirt. They decided we would all wear skirts and heels. Now, to me, high heels are two inches. *Cuban* heels they called them then. You see, I never wore heels because as a nurse you wore flat shoes. When I wasn't working, I wore penny loafers or something like that. And here I had to put these damn heels on and carry a sign and walk around and around in a circle. We had a large selection of signs and we swapped them every now and then. Walking in those heels took all the flesh off my ankles.

We had to do the public protests because people never got the chance to see what a gay person looked like. Everybody was in the closet! Until they saw people who said publicly that they were gay, they couldn't know that we looked like every other human being— that we had faces, ears, and noses, that we dressed the same and had the same kinds of jobs. Protesting in those days was about the only way we could get out there and let the public have a look at us.

This split between those who wanted to make noise and those who wanted to do things quietly affected me very directly. During the second half of the 1960s, I was more and more at odds with the official position of DOB. What made this situation impossible was that, as president—first of the New York chapter and later of the national group—I had to represent the official conservative views of DOB. For example, I always had to differentiate when I was talking to someone that I was definitely not against demonstrations, but the Daughters was. In all my official correspondence I had to state the party line, no matter what I believed personally. It was schizophrenic. So while I went to protests like the ones in Philadelphia every year for the Fourth of July and took as many people as would go, I wasn't officially representing the views of DOB membership or the national board. I tried to change DOB, but just as the president of the United States cannot dictate, there was no way I could dictate.

By 1968, this all came to a head, and I was forced to do a very traumatic thing. It was at the NACHO meeting in Chicago—the North American Conference of Homophile Organizations—where we adopted Frank Kameny's slogan, "Gay Is Good." There were a couple of dozen organizations that were a part of NACHO by then.

Well, by the end of that conference, DOB wasn't one of them. I had to pull DOB out of NACHO because there were resolutions passed at that meeting by participating organizations that were contrary to the official interests of DOB. Ironically, I was the one who had made the motions to pass these resolutions.

From the NACHO conference, I went to the national convention of the Daughters and tried to get the bylaws changed to allow us to participate in what NACHO was doing and to give the local DOB chapters more autonomy, but I wasn't successful, so I resigned. I should have gone into the Mattachine and stayed there. DOB was hidebound; it was restricted in what it could do. This goal of integrating the lesbian into society didn't make sense, but I thought I could use DOB as a tool.

I was quite bitter in 1968. I felt that having to pull DOB out of NACHO was like being cut off at the ankles. Without DOB, there was no way I could participate in a position of authority at NACHO. I felt that I had really failed. I saw no future for DOB. For me this was like my religion. To have it explode in your face was not a successful ending to a career. I felt totally frustrated and left the movement.

The Best Kind of Friend

Nancy May

IN 1964, *a group of San Franciscans gathered in the home of a gay bar owner to form a new organization, the Society for Individual Rights—SIR. They had been frustrated by Hal Call's autocratic rule of the local Mattachine Society, as well as the financial shenanigans of the League for Civil Education, a group founded in San Francisco by Guy Strait in 1961. Nancy May, a heterosexual woman in her midtwenties, attended that meeting with her husband, Bill, and became a founding member. Within a few months, on the night of January 1, 1965, Nancy found herself face to face with a policeman at a fund-raising costume ball and at the center of a pivotal event in the gay rights effort in San Francisco.*

Today, Nancy lives with her two grown sons in Concord, California, a conservative suburban community in what San Franciscans call the East Bay. She and Bill bought their small ranch-style home in 1986. According to Nancy, "We felt that after thirty years we were probably going to spend the rest of our lives together, one way or another. He's still living in San Francisco until his job ends and these kids can find a place to live."

Nancy sat at the picnic table in her well-kept yard, dressed in slacks and a sleeveless shirt. Her dark hair was pulled back from her round face in a ponytail. She spoke with great emotion, her tears never far from the surface.

Let me explain how I got into the gay movement. I lived in San Diego and had a number of friends who were gay. This was back in 1957. One of my best friends was a bisexual woman. She was incredibly intelligent and had friends of every make and matter. We just ran around together and she took me to the first gay bars I ever went to. The gay bars were fun places and they were not threatening. You have to realize, I had been raised in a very small town, Lake Stevens, Washington. There were four hundred people there. And I was raised in the country, so I wasn't even associating with any of the four hundred. I was raised by my grandparents, and they were very protective of me. I was really isolated. When I finally got to be eighteen, I left for San Diego, got a job, and slowly evolved into my own person. By the time I was twenty-one, I had been to straight bars and I had been to gay bars. And I just preferred gay bars.

At the time, I worked as a file clerk for a collection agency. It was a nothing job. Sometimes my friends would come and pick me up for lunch. I knew my friends were gay, but I didn't think there was anything remarkable about that. And because I didn't think it was unusual or peculiar, I talked to my friends at work about it.

One day my boss called the entire company together in the lobby of the office without telling anybody why. I was sitting at the counter in the reception area. There were about thirty or thirty-five people. My boss was standing opposite the counter, so he and the counter were between me and the door. And he just started talking about how there were certain people who lived their lives in an unnatural manner. I was looking around kind of wondering, *Why did he call us together to talk about this and what has that got to do with what we do in this business?*

Then he got down to the specifics: One of his employees associated with these people who, he said, were lower than the animals, than the snakes that crawled on the earth. Then he said that anyone who associated with such people was also a lowlife. That's when I realized he was talking about me! I was almost in a state of shock. It was like I had been caught doing some unmentionable act, like I had been behind a curtain and the curtain was thrown aside, and everybody was observing me doing something I didn't want anybody to know I ever did. I didn't know what else to do, so I just got up and went to the coat closet, got my coat, and went around behind him and left.

I didn't wait for him to fire me. I walked out and I never went back. And I never saw anybody from that office again. I left there in tears and utter humiliation, determined that this would never happen again to me and, if I could prevent it, to anybody else.

As SOON as I left my office, I went to a phone booth and called Bill May. He was one of my best friends and later became my husband. I told him what had happened, and he came to get me.

I knew Bill was gay even before I met him. I had heard about his parties. The first time I saw him I thought he was the most beautiful human being I had ever seen in my life. It was at a three-day party. He was dancing with somebody else when I arrived, and I said to the person I was with, "Who in the world is that?" My friend said, "That's Bill May." The attraction at that point was so strong, even though I knew he was gay. It was almost like seeing someone I'd known all my life.

Bill drove me to the beach and got me calmed down. He said, "We were planning to move anyway, so let's do it." We had already talked about moving because there was such a gestapo atmosphere in San

Nancy May with her
husband, Bill May, in a San
Diego delicatessen in 1961.
(*Courtesy Nancy May*)

Diego at that time. The police department was on your ass for everything. So we left San Diego and came to San Francisco, where things
weren't as bad. That's not to say that San Francisco was an easy place
for gay people to live then, but it was at least a little better than San
Diego.

For the most part, gay people accepted me pretty well in San
Francisco. Sometimes I was called a "fag hag" or a "fruit fly," but I
didn't take it personally because it really had more to do with what
had happened to them than anything I could have done to them.
When I first heard the expressions, I had to get them explained to me.
A fruit fly is usually somebody who runs around with a hairdresser.
A fag hag is somebody who just hangs out with gay men. Both terms
sound real derogatory, but sometimes they were used in a real off-
hand, lighthearted, kidding kind of way.

Because I was a straight woman and older than most of my gay
friends, they told me a lot of things like, "I've got to tell my mother
I'm gay. How am I going to do it? How do you think she's going to
react to it?" There was always the risk of being disowned. That
happened a lot. It was such an atrocity that parents could be so
judgmental about their own kids, that they actually said to their
children, "Go away." The kids were so young. It's painful for me to
think about that, even today.

A lot of gay people misunderstood my presence in a particular
group or gathering. I think there are people in the gay community, not
necessarily in the gay movement, who are bitter toward straight people. From time to time, I became the focus of that bitterness. It's kind
of hard for me to talk about it. There's always that thing in the back
of my mind, *If you knew the risks I'd taken! If you only knew who you were*

talking to! But I would never say it because then it would make me fall down to their level, and I wouldn't do that. Look, there are mean people and nice people no matter where you go.

ONE EVENING after we had been in San Francisco for a while, Bill called me from a League for Civil Education meeting. The LCE was Guy Strait's gay rights group. There was some stuff going on in the LCE—money problems—and Bill said, "We're thinking of forming a new organization and wondered if you were interested." I went down to the meeting because Bill and I had been talking about the gay movement for quite some time, and I was interested in getting involved in some way. And really, there wasn't a gay movement at that time. It was just a bunch of people who thought by joining together they could get something accomplished, like stopping the police harassment, the bar closings. There was a general atmosphere of gay bashing by the cops. There was a policeman in the Haight-Ashbury who used to ferret out gay people and take them down the alley and beat them up. There was a bar on Haight Street called the Golden Cask, and the policeman liked to watch people come out of the bar and then just beat the shit out of them.

So the LCE dissolved because of financial problems, and SIR began. I was the only woman at this first meeting. There were eleven of us in all. I wanted SIR to be everything for everybody. It was to be for the grass-roots people, unlike Mattachine, which was an elite kind of thing. SIR was for the people who needed help, who needed legal and employment advice. We also wanted to have places where people could go to further their interests. For example, we had the SIR bowling league. At first we had one lane on Monday night. Within two or three years in the mid-1960s, we took over that entire bowling alley on Monday nights. The SIR bowling league stayed on at the Park Bowl for years after SIR was no longer in existence, and the last I heard, they had taken over the whole place for two nights every week.

We also wanted to create an atmosphere where people could come sort out their lives and find direction. So we had discussion groups where people could get together and talk about the gay movement and about things like dealing with parents and jobs. Our goal was to make it easier to be gay, whether that meant getting civil liberties or just helping you live your life in a more comfortable way.

I was political chair for SIR. I've always loved politics; I've always thought that getting on the inside in politics was the way to make the most changes. Our thing was to get the politicians to recognize the gay block vote. We put out the word that there were ninety thousand gay votes to be had in San Francisco, and that those people would vote as a block. We actually made it up—we felt that the situation called for strong measures. We thought it was probably true, but had no way of finding out—and they didn't have any way to find it out, either.

The first time we had a candidates' night, in the fall of 1964, people said we were crazy. And we were, because no candidates came. Some candidates sent letters, and there were a couple of fringe groupers, but there were certainly no incumbents. It was especially embarrassing because I had said that all we had to do was make sure the politicians knew there were going to be plenty of people there, and they would all come, because they needed the votes. But it didn't work. They didn't want the stigma of coming to a place where gay people gathered. And they certainly didn't want to address any gay issues.

The second candidates' night we had, in 1965, was more for local elections, and we got an incumbent member of the Board of Supervisors—that's our city council. Another politician sent a representative. They didn't jump right in feet first into this unknown area—they put out feelers. But I think we were more successful at that second candidates' night because of what had happened at the costume ball, which was put on by the Council on Religion and the Homosexual (CRH), on New Year's Day, 1965. That was a big turning point for all of us.

The CRH, was formed by a group of really liberal ministers. Cecil Williams was one of them, and so were Ted McIlvenna, Robert Cromey, and Chuck Lewis. These guys thought that there was a whole constituency that they were not ministering to—gay people. They also thought, from a civil rights perspective, that gays were not being treated very well. By 1964–65, people were starting to really think in terms of civil rights. This is before the riots and all that other stuff that came a little later. I think part of it was Martin Luther King. People, especially people in the ministry, were starting to re-examine what was going on.

With CRH, the ministers met with the gay community. They wanted to start an organization that would create an atmosphere for gay people to come back to the church. These ministers said, "But we need money to get our organization started, and we have to have clerical help, et cetera." They consulted with SIR and the Daughters of Bilitis. They gathered everybody together and asked if we would help with a fund-raising dance. So we formed committees to plan a costume ball for New Year's Day.

We were real careful to avoid selling tickets at the ball itself, so there wouldn't be accusations of solicitation. Instead, we asked for advance donations to the CRH and gave people a piece of paper to show that they had made a donation. We went through all these convoluted things, and then the ministers went to the police and told them where the dance was going to be!

The ball was held at California Hall, which at that time was kind of run down. The owner hadn't had much action there for quite a while, and I'm not real sure he knew exactly what he was getting into. When I got there the evening of the ball, the police had the whole place lit up. They were taking pictures as people got out of their cars. We had told everyone to act in a dignified manner, as though they had a perfect right to be there, and to ignore the fact that they were being photographed. And they pretty much did. They got out of limousines and walked up the stairs with their heads held high. Luckily most of them were in costume, so you couldn't tell who they were, anyhow.

It was such a big deal just to go to that ball. We were surprised that anybody showed up. When we reached "ticket" sales of 500 people, we figured 100 would show up. Probably 200 to 250 came. There were people who drove up, saw all the hassle going on in front, and turned around and left. There were kleig lights; there were movie cameras going. People knew that their pictures were being taken, and they crossed that war zone knowing there was a possibility that their bosses would get pictures of them going in there. It took a degree of bravery on their part.

I was super proud that as many people came as did. And it was like something was happening. It was like an historic event was happening. I think a lot of people there knew it was historic, partly because the church was sanctioning it. And we had been fighting with the church so bitterly—the Catholic bishop had been making some awful statements about gay people.

Anyhow, my husband was taking pictures of the police taking pictures. About an hour or so after we got there, he had used up two rolls of film, which he brought me and said, "Here, I know that nothing's going to happen to you, so take this film and do something with it." At about that time, I went up to Phyllis Lyon and Del Martin, from DOB, who were taking the donation receipts and said, "If you guys want to go in and see the show, I'll take over the table here."

People were trying to have as good a time as they could under the circumstances, but it wasn't easy, because every fifteen minutes the police would go around the perimeter of the dance floor and open up the closets where they stored all the chairs. And they would look in the closets, acting as if they had never seen a closet before. They would walk through the bar, too.

By the time I took over the ticket table from Phyllis and Del, the police had come through about eight times. The last time they had come in to inspect the premises we told them they couldn't come back anymore, that the premises were thoroughly inspected, and if they wanted to come back again they should bring the fire chief with them or a warrant.

At this point, the police had already arrested our attorneys, Evander Smith and Herb Donaldson. They just came and grabbed hold of their elbows on either side and literally carried them to the paddy wagon with their feet dangling. My feeling was that since Evander and Herb were already gone, and since they were the main troublemakers, as far as the police were concerned, they would probably leave us alone from then on. So I didn't feel I was in any great danger.

About twenty minutes after Herb and Evander were taken away, the police came back. I was at the ticket table by myself. The man who had volunteered to work at the table with me never showed up. I had just picked up a whole bunch of half-filled drinking cups and was carrying them over to the trash can, and this man stopped right in front of me. I started to go around him, and he said, "We're coming in to inspect the premises." And I said, "No, you're not. I've just about had it with you people." And he said, "Look, lady, we're coming in." He flashed his badge at me, and I said, "That doesn't make any difference to me. You don't have a warrant. You don't belong here. Now get out!"

This guy was about six-four, and weighed about two hundred fifteen pounds, and he turned around and left. I went, "Whoa!" I thought, *That was easy.* But then he came back with three uniformed policemen and said, "Put that woman under arrest." So I said to the policemen, "Can I get my coat?" And they said, "No. Take her out there." Cecil Williams, the minister from Glide Memorial Methodist Church, came up and said, "Let the poor girl get her coat. For God's sake, man, it's cold out there." All I had on was a sleeveless blouse, so Cecil just grabbed me by the elbow and started marching me away from the door in the opposite direction toward the coat room. I said to Cecil, "Tell Bill that I'm being arrested." I meant Bill May, my husband. But somebody ran off and got Bill Plath, who was also a founder of SIR. So I gave Bill Plath the film my husband had given me. All I needed was to have a bunch of film when they took me to jail.

Between the time Herb and Evander were taken away and when I got arrested, they had called this guy named Elliott Leighton, an attorney they knew. He was not gay and he was not associated in any way with this thing up until that point. But he came down there to keep an eye on things. When he saw me being hauled down the hall, he came running up behind me and started yelling at the police, "You can't take that woman! You can't take that woman! You can't come in here anymore and you can't do this and you can't do that!" The police picked him up, and off he went to the paddy wagon. At least I had some companionship.

You know, I wasn't scared. I was more angry than anything else because I really didn't think they had a right to do this. I was convinced that there was something really wrong about what they were doing. Of course, when Elliott got in the paddy wagon, he was furious. When we got down to Northern Station, they strip searched him. They didn't strip search me; I don't know why. They took Elliott's wallet, his papers on other clients, everything. He was ready to file a lawsuit within ten minutes.

Back at California Hall, Bill Plath had started making some phone calls. By the time we got to Northern Station, our bail had already been arranged. We spent maybe twenty minutes in the holding tank, but the police took fingerprints and the whole thing. I had been told repeatedly, "Don't tell them where you work." But I was still kind of naive. I was afraid that if I didn't tell them I worked someplace, they would think that I had some other business that wasn't as legitimate as working where I did. So I told them. And the next morning I read in the newspaper, "Gay Ball Raided: Teamster Secretary Arrested." There were three days of newspaper stories. I figured that surely I was going to be fired. I had only gone to work there in November, and this was January.

When I got back to work, there were no comments. I was really surprised. I walked in, sat down at my desk, and started to work. At coffee break, one of the women called me over and said, "I just want to ask you one thing." I thought, *Here we go.* She said, "Why do you think those ministers would want to associate with a bunch of queers?" I said, "Betty, you're a religious woman, aren't you?" And she said, "Well, of course." And I said, "Why would they want to associate with you? What could they possibly do for you? You're convinced that you're right all the time, anyway. They're ministering to people who they think need to be ministered to, who have troubled lives and want to be saved. Now I don't see any reason why any ministers would even want to say hello to you because you're obviously saved and you're so damned self-righteous that I can hardly believe that you can live with yourself!" I let her have it. She didn't speak to me again. But a few people did. A few people understood where I was coming from.

Even though I wasn't fired that first day, I still felt I was going to be fired for sure. This wasn't the first time I had a feeling like this.

There was always the thought in the back of your mind, *Well, this is it. I'm going to get discovered. My life's going to be destroyed.* So I waited until the end of the week, and I wasn't fired. I waited until the end of the month, and I wasn't fired. After another three weeks had gone by, I stayed late one night because I knew the personnel manager, the same guy who had hired me, was working late. When he started to leave, I called him over to my desk and asked, "Don, are they going to fire me?" And he said, "No. It was touch and go there for awhile. We had a meeting about you. I told them that what you do from nine to five is our business. What you do from five to nine is your business. But I wonder if I could ask you one favor? Please try to keep the company's name out of the paper. We get in enough trouble on our own." I still love that man. I still think he's the greatest.

People who I didn't expect to be were very supportive of me. A manager at work became one of my best friends. I didn't know at the time that she was gay; we never discussed it, and I don't know officially to this day that she is. I think she sensed that if I ever found out about her, I wouldn't pass judgment. She didn't have any friends in that office. She didn't associate with other lower-echelon people at all. I was the only person she talked to.

THE TRIAL to find out if we were guilty of obstructing a police officer in the performance of his duties at the dance at California Hall started at the beginning of March. The charge was a misdemeanor, a nothing charge. But it was an important trial. We had a packed courtroom every day—mostly gay people. The question was whether the judiciary was going to condone what the police had done.

Their case was based on the contention that we would not allow the police on the premises. The policeman that originally told me he was going to come in there, the big guy, testified that I beat on his chest with my hands to prevent him from going in. Of course, this wasn't true, because I had had all those cups in my hands. The judge asked me to walk around to the area between the table and the judge's bench and stand up in front of this guy as though I were going to beat on his chest. The policeman towered almost two feet above me. The courtroom broke into peals of laughter. Well, that was the end of that. You see, at the time I was a lot smaller than I am now. I weighed one hundred ten pounds. I'm five-two; he was six-four. Even if I had wanted to obstruct him, he could have stepped over me. People saw the difference and just laughed.

The prosecution presented its side, but before the defense even started, the judge ruled that we had not obstructed the police from

entering the premises because they were already over the threshold of
California Hall at the time the arrest took place. So the case was
thrown out on a technicality. As a result, we didn't really feel we had
proven anything, not to the extent that we wanted to. Still, the New
Year's Day ball became a sort of cause célèbre around town.

THE UPSHOT of the dance was that it brought the gay movement a big
step ahead because a lot of people decided, "What the hell, we've got
nothing to hide now." It wasn't like a throwing open of the closet
doors. But people really started examining how being in the closet was
affecting their lives. I keep using that expression, "the closet," like it
meant something at that time, but we didn't use that expression then.
What I should say is that people were willing to be more open with
their friends and neighbors.

The New Year's Day ball acted as a catalyst. It created the atmosphere for people to say, "There are people in this movement who are
willing to stand up for what they believe in. Why shouldn't I do the
same thing?" People got real stubborn. You know, when you push
people, they often get stronger in their beliefs.

SIR blossomed after the ball. We went from about three hundred
members to about one thousand. We had international standing in
the gay movement because of the news coverage from the ball. *Pravda*
said that for the United States to take away people's liberties in such
a fashion was hypocritical. We even did interviews for the BBC in
England.

I STAYED very involved with SIR for another couple of years, but as
time passed, SIR became more and more a social organization. They
held dances and a lot of drag shows. I didn't mind what they were
doing, but attention was being distracted from the gay rights efforts.
Maybe it wasn't necessary for SIR to do the movement's work anymore because by this time—the late-1960s—many other gay organizations were already taking the lead. Also, by this time I had gotten
distracted from the movement as well. My time was taken up by my
family and my son, who had some severe medical problems.

WHEN I talk about those days and how hard it was then, I can see the
changes. But some things haven't changed. In Concord right now
there's a big fervor over an antidiscrimination ordinance related to
AIDS passed by the city council. The good people of Concord signed

petitions to have that ordinance put on the ballot this coming November [1989] for a vote. They want it revoked. So really it hasn't stopped.

As a matter of fact, one of those petitioners stopped me in front of the Safeway store the other day. She said, "Would you sign my petition?" Well, I'm always interested in petitions because I really believe the people have the right to say something about how they're governed. So I took a look at it, and when she told me what it was about, I started yelling at her in her face, "How could you? How could you possibly think that it was appropriate for people to discriminate against people who are ill through no fault of their own!" I was just coming down on her, marching right up to her, chest to chest. My older son was pulling at my arm saying, "Mom, Mom, let's go do our shopping. Leave that woman alone."

The Defenders

Herbert Donaldson and Evander Smith

WHEN HERB Donaldson and Evander Smith met on a beach in San Francisco in the early 1960s, they never imagined they would share the back of a paddy wagon on New Year's night in 1965. But as the attorneys overseeing the landmark costume ball of the Council on Religion and the Homosexual (CRH), they became a natural target for a police department that was determined to disrupt this first very public event staged for the city's homosexual community.

Evander, born in 1922, is courtly and soft spoken. Herb, a San Francisco Municipal Court judge, is five years younger. Sitting at the counter in Evander's spacious San Francisco kitchen, the two old friends consumed a couple of slices of pecan pie as they conjured up images of a time both are glad has long since passed.

Herb:

Back then, in the early 1960s, I was in private practice. I was sharing space at Third and Market here in San Francisco. The Mattachine Society was nearby at Third and Mission. I was trying to build a clientele, so I got on Mattachine's referral list. Later, there was an ad in the paper announcing that a group called the League for Civil Education was having a meeting on the top floor of the library. I thought, *Well, I'll attend that meeting because that's a way of finding new clients.* Guy Strait, who ran the LCE, was lecturing to a motley bunch of people, myself included. Most of us were gay. We had all kind of zeroed in on this League for Civil Education. I talked with Guy, and before long he started sending me people who had been arrested.

San Francisco hasn't always been as kind as it is now. At that time the police were sending plainclothesmen into gay bars and parking squad cars in front to discourage people from going in. They'd make arrests in the bars. Then there was tearoom activity—people would get arrested there, too. And if you were arrested, you're name could turn up in the newspaper. I think it was before you got here, Evander, they had this raid on some gay bar, and the *Examiner*, the "family"

newspaper, published the names, occupations, and addresses of everybody who was arrested.

Evander:

The police didn't have to deal with any trials from these cases because
the clients were too embarrassed to be subjected to a jury trial, and
the attorneys were too embarrassed to defend them. So they would
either plead guilty and pay a fine or they'd waive a jury trial. When
they waived the jury trial, they would most often be convicted by the
judge, pay a fine, and be left with a police record.

Herb:

Most of the gay men who were arrested were so ridden with guilt and
so afraid of exposure that they couldn't imagine facing a jury trial. But
I encouraged my clients to demand a jury trial because you could
actually win or hang on one. Even then, the average citizen in San
Francisco wasn't nearly as bigoted as the police.

Eventually, Evander got interested and helped me in my law practice; he had another job working for a corporate legal department. At
the same time we were also attending meetings of the NAACP housing committee.

Anyhow, I was defending these oral-copulation cases in Judge
Harry Neubarth's court, the Superior Court. You see, "oral cop" was
a felony then. You could go to prison for fifteen years. So one time
I had one of these cases, and I was talking to the judge. The defendant
didn't want a jury, so we waived a jury trial. I knew he would be found
guilty and get a two-hundred-fifty-dollar fine, and that would be it. I
was in chambers talking with the judge, and as I expected, he said that
he thought he would give him the standard fine. And I said something
about, "As a gay man. . . ." He looked at me and said, "I wouldn't
voice that around too much if I were you." He didn't object, but he
just thought it wasn't prudent of me to voice it around. Remember,
this was in the middle 1960s. I didn't have anything to lose because
I just had my private practice. Nobody was going to fire me—although, when we were arrested at the CRH ball, both of us had some
concern about whether the bar would take our licenses away.

Evander:

You see, if you were queer, it was moral turpitude. Therefore, the
state bar association would not permit you to practice. And you

couldn't go to another state to practice because you would have to be approved by that state's bar association, which would conduct a search of your background. All the state bar associations belonged to the National Bar Association, so that kind of information was shared.

I had a client, a successful attorney, who was trying to come here from another state. They found out in the state where he lived that he was queer. (I'm using *queer* simply because it was the word that was in coinage at that time.) So this attorney applied to the California bar and was called in. The association said, "Look, we don't think you're worthy to be a member of the California Bar." I took an appeal on it and got it into the hearing board. That's a trial within the bar association itself.

So we went to the committee, which was a life-and-death group. As I recall, there were three members on it. If they turned thumbs down on this man, his life would have been ruined as far as the law was concerned. He made a very good witness on his own behalf, and I made, I think, a creditable presentation, arguing that this man should not be condemned. Between the two of us, we were so effective that before we could get out of the building they sent one of the members running down the hall to tell us that they were very impressed, and to get a good night's sleep because there would be no problems.

Herb:

Also, at the same time, Evander was handling bar-license revocations because the state Alcoholic Beverage Control Department, the ABC, would revoke the licenses of gay bars. Even after the California State Supreme Court said in the early fifties that you couldn't close a bar down simply because it was a gathering place for homosexuals, the ABC found other ways to take away a license.

Evander:

They'd accused men of fondling each other. The police would lie.

Herb:

They'd say there were lewd acts occurring on the premises. What would happen was, they would target a bar they wanted to close and send plainclothesmen in. I had one client who went into this bar on Polk Street near Broadway. He talked to this guy who was very handsome, and they arranged to meet the next night. So they met and then they decided to go to his place. They got out of the bar, and then the handsome plainclothes cop arrested him. The ABC used that as the basis for trying to close the bar. They said, "This is a place where lewd acts are occurring. We're not closing the bar because it's a homosexual gathering place, but we can't have places where lewd acts are being committed." Of course, every straight bar in the city was having assignations and propositions all over the place. But the police never acted against them.

Next they'd file the accusation, and the bar owner had to show cause why the bar's ABC license shouldn't be revoked. Then you'd have to schedule an administrative hearing before a hearing officer.

Evander:

The administrative officers were like sitting judges. And like Nero, who used to look to the crowd to see if he should point his thumb down or up, judges were not immune from public opinion. Even today, judges are much affected by what the community wants.

Herb:

Then there were the police. Two of them said to me, "Look, if we arrest one of your clients, all he has to do is tell us that you're his lawyer, and we'll make arrangements." They were on the take. If I accepted this arrangement, then, of course, they wouldn't take any client of mine in and book him. And they would get paid for it. It was an old shakedown routine. Mind you, we never did this.

Evander:

Other attorneys did.

Herb:

The attorney would get a fee from the client for avoiding the prosecution. And the client was so happy that he was not going to have a record that he was glad to pay. You'd say to the client, "Well this is a serious matter. If they book you, you're facing up to fifteen years in state prison." Anal copulation was life imprisonment.

My lover, Jim, before I met him, was arrested for lewd conduct in a john. That's why he could never teach. He went to this lawyer who gave him this song and dance, "Well, there's the solicitor and there's the solicitee. And if you're just the solicitee, you don't have anything to worry about." He paid a big fee to the attorney. The attorney waived the jury knowing that in a court trial Jim would be found guilty. And the judge found him guilty. Jim paid a fifty-dollar fine.

Evander:

There was this policeman from Novato who made this usual type of arrest. It had been a sucking job in a cafeteria at Fourth and Market—a felony. I represented one of the two arrested, a German who was on these friendly shores with a visa. The other one copped a plea—pleaded guilty—right off the bat. I explained to my client, "You'll get kicked out of the country if you let this thing go against you by copping. So you've got to go through a trial." I've got a lot of imagination, and I had to use it all for the next six months because he wanted it over with. He simply couldn't take it anymore.

Herb:

It gets very tense for the people who are charged with crimes. Most people facing the bar of justice, all they want to do is get it over with.

Evander:

Each time we'd go to court, every two weeks or so, he'd plead with me to get it over with. He finally gave me an ultimatum and said, "You either get rid of this case the next time we go to court, or I'm going to get another attorney."

Now the arresting cop from Novato was the most arrogant, good-looking stud you ever saw in your life. He was the only witness to the incident, so without him there would have been no case. On the Saturday night before our Monday morning court date, the cop and his wife were in the city and he ran a red light. A Greyhound bus hit their car and smeared him and his wife all over the concrete. When I read the paper the next morning, I knew that was the end of the kid's case. No witness.

So we went into court on Monday, and the case was dismissed. My client didn't know about the accident and I hadn't had a chance to tell him until after we left court. But before I could say anything, he turned to me and said, "My lover said that if I really put the screws to you I'd get results. It occurred to us over the weekend that you would probably pull some shitty thing like this because you've been sucking the money out of me for six months now and that's why you haven't done this before, isn't it?" I probably got all of six hundred dollars for that case. That was the end of it.

Herb:

The fact is, we both had very successful practices, not in terms of money, but in terms of satisfaction.

Evander:

Herb and I would have made a decent living practicing law, but not on the clients that we were willing to put our lives on the line for because they couldn't afford to pay. The gay people who were being arrested didn't have any money. Fortunately, both Herb and I have made good investments over the years that have left us financially secure.

We had a lot of fun with these cases. I would draw strings over the lines of sight to see if these policemen could see what they said they saw. I could prove that a policeman was lying by using my famous strings. I drew the string from the point at which he said he was viewing to the point where the alleged act was taking place, demonstrating that he could not have seen it. But some policemen, like the cop from Novato, were good at perjuring themselves and would laugh about it afterwards.

Herb:

Evander and I were involved with the Council on Religion and the Homosexual, the CRH, almost from the beginning.

Evander:

Through the Mattachine we met lots of ministers: Clay Caldwell, Chuck Lewis, Ted McIlvenna, Cecil Williams, Bob Cromey, and others. The ministers' consciences had become aroused.

Herb:

There was a group of us who formed CRH. And then the gay organizations—there were about a half-dozen of them, some existing only on paper—decided they were going to have a fund-raiser for the CRH, to get it started. It was going to be a Mardi Gras on the night of January 1, 1965.

Evander and I were both involved in this event. Actually, much of it was Evander. He met with the police to make sure that there wouldn't be any police interference. You see, at that time the police took a position that the only time you could dress up in drag was on Halloween. This was going to be a gala affair, where if you wanted to go in drag, you could. And it wasn't Halloween. At first the police agreed not to interfere, but later they went back on their word.

Evander:

We found out the police reneged when we got a phone call from Don Lucas and Hal Call at Mattachine. We went to see them, and they were all shook up. They said that the cops had been there and had given them an ultimatum. Hal and Don were told to get the message out to these "queer ministers," as the police referred to them—if they weren't queer themselves, they were queer lovers—that if they held the event, the police were going to get rid of all these people by arresting them. The police meant what they said. So Herbert and I took it from there.

Herb:

Then didn't you have a meeting with the ministers up at the hall?

Evander:

Oh, yes. There was a cop at the meeting who said he couldn't rest until he wiped out all the queers. He was a good Catholic. At any rate, we got the message that they were going to make wholesale arrests if the event transpired. We assured the police that it would take place nonetheless, so they prepared two hundred arrest cards with numbers, which they used to identify people when they photographed them going into the ball.

When we got to the ball, the police had every intersection blocked off at California Hall and they were diverting traffic. They had the place lit up with kleig lights. They had police on motorcycles. They also had the paddy wagons, and they were wearing helmets. They had riot gear. They would not have been any better prepared if they had gone there to face gangsters with machine guns.

Herb:

We were at the door to the hall. We were there to make sure that everything was on the up-and-up, so there couldn't be any reason to make arrests. The plainclothes police started coming in to make inspections. There was a fire inspection. There was a health inspection. I think it was about the fourth inspection when we said, "That's enough! If you want to come in, you're going to have to get a search warrant." It really was completely unplanned. We had reached a point where we didn't know what to do. We were cheek to cheek with the police. We were just standing there, and they were standing there.

Evander:

We were frightened.

Herb:

They didn't know what to do, either.

Evander:

They didn't believe that we would stand them off. The hallway in the building is about ten feet wide. And Herbert and I were standing abreast, leaning against each other in the middle of the hall. We were both so nervous that we would have fallen down if we hadn't had someone to lean on. There was enough space on either side of us to run a motorcycle through.

Herb:

They could have gone right past us. But they were afraid of us. Then all of a sudden, a whole bunch of uniformed police came in.

Evander:

With their movie cameras.

Herb:

At one point one of us asked somebody to call the mayor.

Evander:

It was you. You were the one who wanted the mayor called.

Herb Donaldson at the time
of his arrest outside
California Hall on the night
of January 1, 1965. *(Courtesy
Herbert Donaldson)*

Herb Donaldson in the back
of a police paddy wagon
following his arrest outside
California Hall on the night
of January 1, 1965. *(Courtesy
Herbert Donaldson)*

Herb:

Not that it would have done any good. He wouldn't have known what
to do. So we were still cheek to cheek with the police. Then all of a
sudden, they grabbed me, one on each side. I thought that when the
police arrested you they said, "You're under arrest."

So I said, "Am I under arrest?" What a silly question. They had
already hauled Evander out to the paddy wagon. Next, they put me
in the paddy wagon. For some reason or another, they didn't take us
away. We sat there for what seemed like a long time. During that time,
somebody contacted Elliott Leighton, an attorney we asked to be on
standby for us that evening. We had thought something might happen. So he came right down to California Hall and got arrested.

Evander:

We would have preferred that only lawyers be arrested. It would have
been a good clean issue there. But Nancy May, the dear soul . . .

Herb:

. . . she was collecting tickets. They hauled her off, too. In the meantime they had taken us up to Northern Station. They put us in jail. They still didn't know what to do with us. They let us use the telephone. I called Judge Don Constine first.

Evander:

Constine wouldn't do anything.

Herb:

So we called Judge Bernard Glickfeld.

Evander:

He's priceless—a doll in many ways.

Herb:

He ordered us released on our own recognizance. But we had to go over and be booked first. On top of everything, I had an outstanding parking ticket. The bail bondsman came and posted the bail for that.

Evander:

After we got out, Herbert said to me, "That booking officer paid you a real compliment." I thought, *Well, did he want to have a date with me?* I asked Herb, "What kind of compliment?" He said, "Well, he told me that you were the nicest American Indian he had ever met."

Herb:

Evander had given his nationality as American Indian.

Evander:

I'm American Indian. I always put that down. Some of the Indians they see in the booking process, the poor guys are drunk. It's a bad scene.

Herb:

After we were released, somebody took us back over to California Hall. The place was in chaos. For all intents and purposes, the police were just running roughshod, walking in and out across the dance floor like they had taken over the place. Some of the people were just terrified, especially the schoolteachers. And there were quite a few teachers at the ball. At that time, if a teacher was known to be homosexual, they'd move to yank their license, because, of course, he or she didn't have the proper moral standards. I remember a couple of women who were schoolteachers. They wanted to be sneaked out the back way because the police were taking pictures of people as they left. They were terrified that somehow the state Board of Education would get the pictures and move against them. Well, they didn't. The state government is as inefficient as the federal government.

Evander:

They didn't make any more arrests.

Herb:

Didn't they arrest those two guys who were standing on folding chairs?

Evander:

I don't remember what happened to them.

Herb:

We represented them, and they were convicted. Judge Leland Lazarus presided over the jury trial. Remember that? They were convicted of lewd conduct. The police had to show that all of this police action had been legitimate. So they charged these guys with fondling each other. They hadn't been fondling each other. Evander represented one, and I represented the other. When the jury came in, Judge Lazarus didn't think they were going to convict, but they did. And then he said, "They've suffered enough. I'll fine them twenty-five dollars."

Evander:

Those poor guys had on their records that they were arrested and convicted of performing a lewd act with another man.

Herb:

At that time 647a, lewd conduct, was registerable.* And they couldn't be hired by the federal government for a job.

Evander:

And if they had had a teaching credential, it would have been taken away.

Herb:

When we went home, Jim and I went to bed. He said, "I'm so proud of you." I was so touched because I was feeling kind of low. I was thinking, *There goes my legal career.*

Evander:

I got up early the next morning and went down to get the *Chronicle*. There it was in the newspaper: our names and addresses. I was just sick. I thought, *Oh shit. I've got to face it. I'm not dreaming.*

Herb:

Had you told your Jim that night?

Evander:

No, I had not told him. I let him get a good night's sleep. I took the paper up and waited until he had his first cup of coffee. Then I said, "This is something that you ought to know about." And I tell you, if he had had Herbert and me in a toilet, he would have flushed us down.

---

*When moving to a new city, a person with a lewd-conduct conviction had to register with the chief of police within thirty days of taking up residence.

Herb:

At least my Jim was at the ball, so he didn't care.

Evander:

Your Jim was always more understanding. My Jim felt that Herbert and I were never going to be appreciated. And if you live in this world expecting appreciation, you would do better to look in the dictionary for it. But there are things you do because they need to be done. But my Jim, he felt I had already paid my dues and that we should not have done it. He was furious.

Herb:

The next morning, I guess, was kind of a letdown. But then we got a call that the CRH was going to have a press conference at Glide Church. All the ministers were there, and the press conference got good coverage in the *Chronicle*.

Evander:

From that press conference my Jim could see that there were legitimate people coming out and acknowledging that you could be gay and still be respectable. You see, Jim and I are now sixty-seven. We grew up when things were different. Herbert isn't that much younger, but he's much better adjusted than I can ever be. I was raised in the South in a very repressive atmosphere. My father was a minister. I'm not the most well-adjusted gay person you'll ever meet by any circumstances. And that arrest has affected me materially. I've never been one to lead the parade. I can really be very effective in trial work and any other kind of legal work, but that experience has made a hermit out of me. I'm very insecure as a result. I have never failed to do my share of gay work and I have done a respectable amount of that, but it exacerbated my feeling of insecurity and being less worthy.

When I went to work after having been arrested, nobody would have anything to do with me, including my own secretary. I was one of two attorneys for an insurance stock-investment group. The headquarters was here in the city. If you've ever heard the expression that the picnic was a failure because this whore came, well that was the prevailing attitude. It was an all-pervasive blanket of disaster.

Everyone had seen the paper. It told that three attorneys and a housewife were arrested at a homosexual dance. It gave the whole works. The reporters were sympathetic to the Establishment; they were being instructed by the Establishment. You see, it's only been within the last few years that the local newspapers, the Establishment newspapers, have acknowledged that it's all right to be gay. Up until the AIDS epidemic, the two local newspapers would not identify a decedent as being gay.

Finally, I was given a formal letter at noon on Wednesday from the company president. He asked me not to come back until Friday. Because of the holiday weekend, I had only been back at the office a day and a half.

I was officially the secretary to this corporation and, therefore, on the management team. So I was asked to come in for a "team meeting" on Friday. I knew that it was to be a lynching just as sure as I know where I am at this moment. I knew his tactics. I also knew that the other people were beholden to him for their jobs, just as I was, because he was the president. No one was going to buck him. So I thought, *There is nothing short of an earthquake that will keep me from being fired come noon Friday. Therefore, I think I'll go out with my self-respect.*

I called Reverend Cecil Williams at Glide Church and told him what the problem was. I said, "Now I don't expect you to do anything or say anything and I don't want you to think I'm using you in a bad sense, but Cecil, I'm using you for the same purpose that some people use a rubber. I'm just going to use you for show." I told him what they were going to do. I said, "The cocksuckers are going to fire me. And I want to take you along just to show them that in addition to being a fucking queer, and having a police record, and representing other queers, that I've got niggers for friends." I said, "They're going to have a lynching, and you know about lynchings, so come and participate in mine." And he said, "You want me to pick you up, or you want to pick me up?"

We got down to the office, and they were shocked, to say the least, because this meeting was to be very clubby. Very English, if you will. The old boys' network was going to operate, and nobody was going to be embarrassed. But they saw that I had this black man with me wearing his Roman garb; he had his collar on. So they had a meeting before the meeting to decide what to do.

They asked the company's other attorney to talk to me. He had brought me over from the Bank of America; we were very close. So he came out and asked me to go over to a corner. He said, "Evander, who is that guy with you?" And I said, "Come, let me introduce you to him." And he said, "I don't want to meet him. But what is he doing here?" I said, "He's here for my moral support." And he asked,

"What do you need moral support for?" I said, "I'm fixing to get fired. They're going to cut my balls off. They're going to gut me like you do a hog." And I asked him, "That's what's going to happen, isn't it?" And he said, "Yes." And I said, "I respect your position, Art, and I would never embarrass you, but I'm going to have somebody in there with me." He said, "Well, it's not going to do you any good." I said, "It won't hurt me." And he said, "Come on." So we went in. Of course, my close friend Art never spoke to me again.

They tried to excuse the reverend. They said, "Reverend, this is a personal matter, will you please excuse us?" I said, "If he goes, I leave, too." You know, I can be very fast on my feet. I took the show away from them. Everybody was frightened. In a courtroom I'm not frightened, but I was frightened then because my economic security was at stake. It turned out that it was the greatest thing they ever did for me. I didn't look back. I was never sad about it. I went home and faced up to reality with Jim. I explained to him, "Look, for Christsakes, I'm a member of the bar. I can make a living. I didn't have a job when I was born."

I called Herbert and told him what had happened, and he said, "Why don't you come up here and join me, and we'll work it out?" Herbert took me into his office. We formed a partnership for just the two of us.

Herb:

Getting arrested was one of the peak experiences of my life. Sometimes you experience peak experiences afterward. But in this case, I knew it at the time.

Evander:

I wholeheartedly agree with that, but the arrest has left a lot of damaging marks on me. But so what? I've got physical marks that I had from my childhood playing with knives. They hurt at the time. With Herbert, it was like water off a duck's back.

Herb:

Boy, this incident galvanized the gay community into action. One of the things that was really humorous is that the police made this estimate that there were 70,000 homosexuals in the city. There weren't, but when they carry it on the wire services that there are

70,000, you've got 70,000 others out in the country who want to come and join that 70,000 here! They're still coming.

Evander:

We also made friends with straight people, who started realizing, "Sure they're queer, but they're not bad people." I honestly think that it was the match that set off the renaissance here in San Francisco, that awakened straight people to the fact that gay people maybe aren't as bad as they had thought up to that point.

Herb:

We stood up and were counted. We didn't go back into the wood-work.

Evander:

By the way, we, Herbert and I, and I guess Nancy May and Elliott, the four of us sued the city and county. Unfortunately, our attorney really didn't follow up on it.

Herb:

But the effect of the suit was very important. The police started having somebody on their police–community relations board whose job it was to be a liaison to the gay community. That was unheard of then. They knew we had a good case. We got better than our money's worth.

And at our criminal trial—the case was ultimately dismissed because we hadn't interfered with the police—we must have had twenty-five of the prominent criminal lawyers in town listed as "of counsel." The American Civil Liberties Union represented us.

Evander:

Those ministers and their wives, all dressed up in their Sunday "go to church" clothes, would come and sit in the audience at the trial. This was so important for the jury to see—to see the support.

Herb:

You know, Evander, the last time I had my annual physical, my internist, whom I've had now for about ten years, said, "I was a medical student at Vanderbilt when I heard the radio report of the dance in San Francisco. You have no idea how good that made me feel. You were part of it, and I really appreciate that." And now we have openly gay and lesbian police and a sizable number of gay deputies.

Herb:

Sometimes Evander and I and some of the old-timers will talk. The kids coming up now, they can't enjoy their freedom as we have because they take it for granted that it was always like this, that they could walk arm in arm and kiss on the street. I've represented several couples who were arrested for having a hand on the other's knee in a bar—something as innocent as that.

Evander:

The community is never going to be able to push gay people back into the closet. As conservative and as reserved as I truly am by nature, I would go out tonight and immolate myself if that would make the world acknowledge that the homosexuals are here and are not going to be put back in the closet. I would do that.

Herb:

Don't do that.

Evander:

I don't think it's necessary, Herbert. But the point is, I think that enough gay people have now accepted their responsibility that they're not going to let the kids be pushed back in the closets.

Herb:

I went on to become chief counsel at the law office of one of the poverty programs. I was there three years. Then I went into private practice briefly and then went into the coffee business with my lover,

Jim. I stayed in the coffee business and didn't do much law until Governor Jerry Brown appointed me judge. I got the call on New Year's Eve, 1982. It was a couple of minutes before midnight. Actually, I thought somebody was calling to wish me a happy new year. This woman said, "Judge Donaldson. . . ." And I said, "Well, not 'Judge Donaldson.' " And she said, "Governor Brown is on the line. He'd like to talk to you."

The governor called to offer me an appointment to the Superior Court. I told him that I appreciated it, but that I would rather be on the Municipal Court. That's where you see all the young lawyers. That's where you can help them get their trial experience. That's where you see the little guy get hauled into court. That's where you get the best opportunity to do something.

I was surprised when the governor called, but his call didn't come out of the blue. I had applied to be a judge. In 1978, a friend of mine told me the governor wanted to appoint a gay judge. At the time, my lover, Jim, was sick with a terminal disease, and I couldn't fill out the application. It was a terrible time. A year after Jim died, I got a message that the governor wanted to know if I was going to apply. But I just couldn't. Then, toward the end of Governor Brown's term, I decided to put in an application. I got a lot of help from many people, including Willie Brown, the powerful Speaker of the State Assembly. You lobby for an appointment to the bench just like you do for an election to office. People like Evander also helped. In fact, Evander wrote me a great recommendation.

Evander:

Just the truth. I said that Herbert is an exceptional person. That he's honest and will speak the truth irrespective of who it's going to hurt. And that he has a lot of discretion and is humanistically inclined.

Herb:

The governor knew I was gay. I was absolutely thrilled because the appointment was being made with everybody knowing I was up-front gay. It meant that I was being appointed for my qualifications. It was a great moment.

These were Jerry Brown's last few days in office. He wanted me to come up to Sacramento the next day. So I went. And, of course, the Capitol Building was closed tighter than a drum, so we went in through the garage.

I was sworn in eighteen years to the day I was arrested at California

Herb Donaldson being sworn in as a municipal court judge at a ceremonial swearing in on February 6, 1983, by Judge Dorothy Von Beroldingen, as Carole Migden looks on. In 1990 Carole Migden and Roberta Achtenberg became the first publicly acknowledged lesbians to be elected to the San Francisco Board of Supervisors. (© Rink Foto 1983)

Hall. It was very gratifying. When I called to tell my mother that I was being appointed, she was just so matter-of-fact. She didn't really say much about me being a judge. Unfortunately, she couldn't come up for the installation because she had just had surgery for cataracts. So I called her at the hospital after the installation. The nurse answered the phone, and I gave her my name. And I heard my mother say, "Oh, it's my son, the judge."

"Dear Abby"

Abigail Van Buren

ABIGAIL VAN BUREN *began her "Dear Abby" column in 1956. In the late 1960s she began responding to letters concerning gay issues and, ever since, has spoken positively about gay people and gay rights. She has arguably helped more gay people accept themselves and more families accept their gay children and siblings and altered public opinion more positively on this issue than anyone living today.*

Abby, whose column is now published in more than fourteen hundred newspapers nationwide and overseas, said, "I was one of the first nationally prominent persons who was not gay to come out in support of gays and lesbians. I was simply defending everyone's *right to be themselves—gay or straight! People tell me it took a lot of guts. Well, it did take nerve to speak out publicly on this issue because there were many people who thought I was wrong to stick my neck out for them. I was glad I had the platform from which to do it."*

Standing in the high-ceiling hallway of her Beverly Hills home, dressed in lavender hostess pajamas, Abby looked tiny, which, at five feet, she is. Her hair was perfectly coiffed and her complexion was flawless. Abby was as warm and gracious as one would hope of the legendary purveyor of commonsense advice. She insisted on being called "Abby."

It's as if I've always known that there was nothing wrong with gay and lesbian people, that this is a natural way of life for them. Nobody molested them, nobody talked them into anything. They were simply born that way. It's in the genes, and I don't think environment has a heck of a lot to do with it. I just knew that they deserved compassion and understanding.

I always knew gay people, even when I didn't know what homosexuality was. In junior high school there was a girl in our gym class who could outrun any boy. If I had known what a lesbian was at that time, I would have known that Mary was a lesbian. She had no interest in getting a date. For a young girl, she was very masculine. I knew she was "different," but I also knew that she was herself and that was her style. I didn't know anything about sexual behavior, but I knew that

Mary was pretty much like a guy. Also, I knew rather effeminate boys in class who were quite dainty and soft-spoken—sort of girlish. And I knew early on that this was their style, and there was nothing wrong with that either.

Of course, the boys were teased and made fun of. For someone like Mary, it was different. A woman could be athletic, and no one really paid much attention. But a guy who's a little loose in his loafers can be spotted early, and he takes a razzing. I thought it was cruel.

After I started writing my column, there was my hairdresser. I'll call him "Glen." He's been my hairdresser for twenty-nine years. Glen came from Louisville, Nebraska—a beautiful guy, a real sweetheart. He had to leave his hometown because he couldn't survive there as a gay person. So Glen came to California and took a hairdresser's course. I took him to Korea one time when I was a judge for the Miss Universe pageant. We had a ball! He and I were in a helicopter, and there were all these big macho army guys. Glen is not really "nellie," but he's not all that subtle either. Well, the helicopter tilted back, and Glen's leather purse slid across the floor. And I said, "Hey, hold it, my friend lost his purse!" The pilot just broke up.

Glen never came out to his parents. They were lovely church-going, middle-class, hard-working people. He said they would never be able to handle his being gay. He had three very macho brothers, and Glen was the youngest. His mother just adored him. Glen was her favorite, and he was a wonderful son.

IT MAY have been Dr. Franz Alexander who confirmed for me what I've always felt. I met Dr. Alexander socially, long before I became "Dear Abby," in 1945 or 1946. Franz Alexander was born in Budapest and was the head of the Chicago Institute for Psychoanalysis. He was a brilliant, charming man—I just can't say enough about him. Regarding "curing" homosexuality, he said, "There's one doctor I know who has a fifty percent 'cure' rate. He had two gay patients. One he turned 'normal' and the other he didn't. That's the fifty percent." He said, "Of course, there is no cure for homosexuality because it's not a disease."

I've met psychiatrists who say that if a patient is sufficiently motivated, he or she can change. Any therapist who would take a gay person and try to change him or her should be in jail. What the psychiatrist should do is to make the patient more comfortable with what he or she is—to be himself or herself.

Years ago, when people first wrote me about homosexuality, they'd say they felt guilty and asked, "Can I change?" Or, "What can I do to change?'' This letter I'm going to read to you is from a little later on, but it's very much like the early ones:

> Dear Abby,
> To get right to the point, I'm gay. But I don't like being gay. I want a wife, children, and a normal social life. I also have a career in banking in which further advancement is impossible if it becomes known that I'm gay. Psychiatrists and other therapists I've gone to have tried to help me adjust to my homosexuality rather than help me to change. Abby, adjusting to being homosexual is fine for those who have accepted their homosexuality, but I haven't. I know I'd be happier straight. Please help me.

He signed himself, "Unhappy in Houston." This was my reply:

> Dear Unhappy,
> Did you *choose* to be homosexual? If so, then you could choose to be straight. But if you have always had erotic feelings for men instead of women, then face it, you are homosexual and even though you may be able to change your *behavior*, you will not be able to change your *feelings*. Some therapists insist that if a homosexual is sufficiently motivated, he or she can become straight. Maybe so, but the chances are slim. Marrying and having children may make you happier, but what about the other people you involve? To thine own self be true. Only then will you find true happiness.

I've always been bold. I never fudged. I never apologized. And I tell you, the Bible thumpers have really let me have it over the years. I've had a steady stream of hate mail, more than on any other subject. Every time I say something compassionate or sympathetic about gays, I get a couple of thousand negative letters. When I make the statement, "God made gays as well as he made straights," I get Leviticus and Corinthians and all that stuff. . . . They tell me that I ought to burn in hell and that "You're wrong, wrong, wrong, and I hope that you find the truth. You should be saved." People want to show *me* the light. They think *I'm* misguided.

I just tell them that I feel God loves me, that I have already been saved, that I'm very comfortable with the way I feel, and thank you very much for your concern.

You're not going to change the minds of those people because they're fanatics. They can't help it because this is what they believe. That's okay with me, but don't tell *me* what to believe. Biblical injunctions mean nothing to me. You can find all kinds of contradictions in the Bible. You can find anything you want in the Bible, but you can't take it literally. If the Bible makes people behave better, fine. But if it makes people less understanding of their fellow man, then something is wrong. Your beliefs should make you better and should make you kinder, not more hateful. I've found a lot of anger and a lot of hate in those letters. It saddens me that people could be so unfeeling and ignorant.

Of course, the newspapers weren't always so happy with me, either, but while lots of papers complained, they never dropped me. Some papers had never published the word *homosexual* in their newspaper when I started, unless it was in the context of someone going to jail. My column was the first time these papers had ever published the word *homosexual* in another context. And to speak kindly toward a homosexual? To be understanding? I was a breakthrough.

What keeps me going, despite all the hate mail, is that I get a lot of love letters. There's a gay guy who's been writing to me from Honolulu for years and years. He came out of the closet because of me. He's an older man now, but he was a kid when he first wrote to me asking for advice about coming out. I try not to meet people to whom I've written. But one time, when I was speaking in Honolulu, he introduced himself to me. You see, after I speak I never disappear. I always go out into the audience to shake hands or sign programs. I'm always available. So I went out into the audience, and this guy came up to me and said, "I just think you're wonderful. You don't know who I am, and it doesn't make any difference. . . ." And out of his pocket he pulled a letter. My stationery has my picture with a little heart on top, so as soon as I saw that, it hit me that this was the guy who had been writing to me. And he said, "Could I just hug you?" Well, I don't hug an awful lot of strangers, but I hugged him. Oh, his heart was beating a mile a minute. When I got home, I got another letter from him, and he said that meeting me was one of the best days of his life. He felt as though I were a friend. I value that.

I'll tell you what really delights me. Many parents have written me to tell me that they now understand their gay or lesbian child because they've read in my column, "There's nothing wrong with your child. Love them, love them, love them!" That makes it so much easier for the gay child. Heretofore the parents thought, *There is something wrong with my child. How can we change him? How can we save him? Maybe we should put him into therapy.* I've told them, "You're never going to change them. You'll just make them ashamed of being who they are, that they aren't good enough. And they *are* good enough. They're as good as anybody else and they should be themselves."

I don't know why people listen to me. I guess they trust me. I have no ax to grind. I just wish the best for all people, and the gays have taken such a beating.

ONE TIME I got a letter from a woman complaining about some people who had just moved in next door. There was a guy with long hair and a couple of women with short hair. It was clear from her letter that these were gay people, and she wasn't happy about having them move into her nice neighborhood. She said, "We're disgusted with these types. What can we do to improve the neighborhood?" My answer was, "You could move!"

That got a lot of attention. Gays thought it was hilarious. But other than being entertaining, there was a good message there, which was that they have as much of a right to be there as you do.

PART THREE
1 9 6 8 – 1 9 7 3

Liberation:

Time for Revolution

THE SOCIAL and political upheavals that transformed American life in the late 1960s had a stunning impact on the struggle for gay rights. By 1968, the antiwar movement, the women's movement, the black civil rights movement, the student revolts, and the politics of the New Left had not only energized the nearly fifty gay organizations across the country, but also inspired bitter internal battles over the direction of what was then called the homophile movement. More upheaval was to come.

As gay life became more visible and gay men, women, and organizations became more vocal, police harassment and repression kept pace. Police raids of gay bars continued, and despite the volatility of the times, this traditional police action most often inspired more fear than resistance among the patrons. Consequently, New York City police were completely unprepared for the two days of violent confrontations that followed their raid of a gay bar in New York City's Greenwich Village in the early-morning hours of Saturday, June 28, 1969. While confrontations between the police and students, blacks, and antiwar protesters were common by 1969, the police never expected homosexuals to do anything but submit passively to their skull-cracking authority.

The riot at the Stonewall Inn sent shock waves through New York's small homophile circles and the wider but inchoate community of uninvolved gay men and women. The shock waves did not end at the city's boundaries. Because of New York's role as the nation's communications center, the riot at the Stonewall Inn was reported and broadcast across the nation. Although much of the news coverage was negative, the startling word of gay people fighting back inspired the formation of new, and newly radical, "gay liberation" organizations in cities large and small and on university campuses from Berkeley to Harvard.

In cities with a history of gay organizations, fearless young gay men and women who were intent on changing the world, joined the struggle. They dismissed the veterans of the homophile movement as old-fashioned "accommodationists" and swept away their organizations, as well as the national coalition they had labored to build. In cities where no organizations existed, new ones were born, often on the campuses of local universities. By the early 1970s, the number of gay and lesbian organizations soared to nearly four hundred, ranging from politically-oriented groups with names like Gay Liberation Front, to chapters of the gay Metropolitan Community Church.

In San Francisco, New York, Los Angeles, and other large cities, protests against antigay discrimination became commonplace. These protests ranged from "kiss-ins" at restaurants that refused to serve gay customers to highly publicized applications by gay and lesbian couples for marriage licenses to on-air interruptions of national news programs that gay people accused of avoiding or distorting gay issues. One protester even broke onto the set of the "CBS Evening News with Walter Cronkite" during a live broadcast and held up a sign proclaiming, "Gays Protest CBS Prejudice." Newspapers and magazines, including the Los Angeles Times and New York magazine, which refused to take ads that included the words homosexual or gay, found themselves the target of gay "zaps." Most were quickly persuaded to change their policies.

Protesters demanded that local and national politicians address the issue of gay civil rights. They were so effective that, in 1972, Democratic presidential candidates spoke favorably of supporting national legislation to protect gay people from discrimination. And two openly gay delegates addressed the Democratic National Convention in Miami.

Gay college students challenged administrators to give their new organizations the same official status, recognition, and funding accorded other student clubs and activities. Many took their schools to court when their requests were ignored or denied. Gay students also organized discussion groups, held gay dances, urged fellow gay students to come out of the closet, and lobbied for courses on gay rights issues. In a handful of college towns, university-affiliated gay liberation organizations successfully lobbied local city governments to amend existing antidiscrimination laws to include protections for homosexuals.

These were optimistic years, when young gay protesters and seasoned activists achieved many important victories. States began to decriminalize homosexual acts, federal antigay civil service regulations started to crumble, and public figures, including an increasing number of religious leaders, began offering unprecedented words of support that challenged deeply rooted antigay attitudes. But the most hopeful sign of change came in 1973, when after many years of discussion and internal debate—and three years of protests and pressure from gay activists—the American Psychiatric Association's Board of Trustees voted to remove homosexuality as a mental disorder from the Diagnostic and Statistical Manual of Mental Disorders. Gay men and women no longer had to live with the burden of the abhorrent official "sickness" label.

Despite this progress, many impediments to equal treatment remained firmly in place. Homosexual acts were still considered criminal in most states. Servicemen and women, if exposed, were routinely given immediate dishonorable discharges from the armed forces. Civilian life was often no better, since many continued to lose their jobs when their homosexuality was discovered. Gay people still struggled for the right to gather in places of their choosing and to be allowed to behave like everyone else. The courts, although at times useful allies, often ruled unfavorably in gay rights cases. And even when there were successes, the outcome could fall far short of a complete victory. In a precedent-setting California case, an acknowledged lesbian won custody of her children in divorce proceedings over the challenges of her husband of fifteen years, but only on the condition that she and her female companion live separately.

Perhaps most discouraging was the fact that public support for the gay liberation movement, even in the major cities, was, at best, feeble. Yet, although there was still much to be accomplished, there were many more reasons than ever before for the nation's gay and lesbian citizens to be optimistic that further change would swiftly follow.

The Radical Activist

Martha Shelley

IN 1968, *twenty-five-year-old Martha Shelley found herself living three different lives. One Martha Shelley worked at Barnard College as a secretary. Another Martha Shelley was president of the New York City Daughters of Bilitis (DOB). The third Martha Shelley read feminist literature and enjoyed nothing so much as sitting in a darkened movie theater, watching* 2001: A Space Odyssey *while tripping on LSD. A year later, the Stonewall Inn riot illuminated a single path that led Martha to a critical role in what became known as the gay liberation movement.*

Martha grew up in Crown Heights, Brooklyn. Long before she understood the implications of her sexual orientation, she began learning about what it meant to be different from her best friend in junior high school, who was black. Martha is white and Jewish. According to Martha, her mother worried that if she grew up with black people, she would "get used to them" and end up marrying one. "You know what?" says Martha, laughing. "She was right!"

Martha shares a home in Oakland, California, with her lover, who is black. A short, trim woman who speaks in the accent of her native New York, Martha first learned about the Mattachine Society and DOB from the "psychological tripe" she read on the subject of homosexuality.

I STARTED going to DOB in 1967. I remember walking into the place for the first time. There was this woman—she used the name Joan Kent—who was signing people up. I was going to use my real name, but she insisted that I not do that. She had been hounded by the FBI and insisted that the FBI might get a hold of the mailing list. I thought it was silly, but I chose a pseudonym, wrote it down, and then underneath put "care of" my real name.

My pseudonym was Martha Shelley. Later I made it my real name. It's now on my driver's license. My given name is Martha Altman. It just got to be too much of a hassle to have both names going at the same time. I figured that if the FBI wanted to find us, they were going to find us. And, of course, as it turned out later, they were looking. They were keeping an eye on us all the time.

DOB was located in an industrial loft in Manhattan on Twenty-Ninth Street or Thirtieth Street, somewhere around Seventh Avenue, I think. It was dark and dingy, but it was better than the bars. Everybody smoked, but it wasn't like being in a smoke-filled bar, with so much noise that you couldn't hear each other talk and where you were being hustled for drinks. We were there to talk to each other and to get to know each other as people.

In DOB, I was really able to feel good about myself for the first time as a lesbian because people who felt successful in the bars were those who were really cute according to standard definitions of cuteness in the society: blond, blue eyed, or whatever. I'm Jewish and I look it. At DOB I was able to meet people who would relate to me in terms of my personality rather than, "Here is a cute thing standing by a bar."

The women who went to DOB meetings were different ages, different sizes. I think on average there were about ten people at a meeting. Sometimes there were more. If you had a speaker or some really interesting meeting, twenty people might show. Sometimes they would come in couples—there were couples for whom this was their social life. But for the most part, people came looking for someone, and when they got involved in a couple relationship, they would drop out.

I went to DOB to meet women. I wasn't thinking about changing the world. I didn't think it was possible—until later. Now, by 1967 there already was a women's movement. I was relating to that, and it gave me a certain amount of ideology to buttress my feelings about not liking roles. By then I had read *The Feminine Mystique*. There wasn't a whole lot else out there. I'd read Simone de Beauvoir. I was starting to read whatever I could find on feminism, even if it was published half a century ago. Ideologically, I had already moved in that direction, toward a society in which your behavior isn't determined by your sex.

I had my point of view and I was pretty articulate. I didn't say it in terms of feminism, but I remember being against butch-femme roles. And I was against marriage, too. I didn't see why we should replicate the heterosexual society and try to re-create the relationships that I felt we had rebelled against. I didn't realize that *we* hadn't rebelled against them. *I* had. I was only really speaking for myself. Most of the women disagreed with me. Most of them wanted the house with the white picket fence. That wasn't my ideal. I was in my early twenties, and the idea of settling down with anybody was appalling to me. I still wanted to get out and run around.

There was this lesbian couple that had been together for twenty-five years and had a house in New Jersey together. They always headed up the meeting about how to make your lesbian marriage work. Sometimes we'd have political discussions about what we could do to influence legislation or something. I don't think it was really conceivable that we could have much influence at that time. And there was the annual Fourth of July picketing at Independence Hall in Philadelphia. I went a couple of times.

I thought it was ridiculous to have to go there in a skirt. But I did it anyway because it was something that might possibly have an effect. I remember walking around in my little white blouse and skirt and tourists standing there eating their ice cream cones and watching us like the zoo had opened.

I BECAME the treasurer of DOB for a brief period because nobody else wanted the office. Then I became president for the same reason. I was never an organizational person. I was always a loner in school. Since I was articulate, Joan Kent, who had originally signed me up at DOB, asked me to run for office. But Joan and her lover, Eleanor, still wanted to run the organization from behind the scenes. Eventually, I said, "Look, I don't want to be president. I don't want to organize. I'm good at speaking. I'll speak." So I got to be the public speaker, which meant going to abnormal psych classes.

The abnormal psych teachers knew that there would be 100 percent attendance whenever they brought in a genuine live homosexual. People are intensely curious about homosexuality, especially students. Older people—let's say, right-wing Christians—would just refuse to go to a place where there was a gay person. But their kids, if the kids have half a chance, will go out of curiosity. And in the late sixties, a gay person was a real curiosity. There weren't that many of us out in the public eye.

We were asked, in couched terms, what we did in bed. "How long do your relationships last?" "What are your relationships with your parents?" Really standard questions—they were always the same. "Did you have domineering mothers or passive fathers?" Parents had to fit the male aggressive–female passive role, otherwise the kids would be screwed up and turn out gay—that was the theory.

When I went to speak, I also did this exercise where I tore up pieces of paper and handed them out. There were usually about thirty kids in the class. I asked them to mark an X if all of their experiences had been heterosexual, Y if all their experiences had been homosexual, and an XY if they'd had both kinds of experiences. Then I told them to fold up the pieces of paper and give them back to me. Next, I opened them all and said, "Well, this class is statistically normal. One out of every ten people is gay."

There was a lot of quiet rumbling. I'm sure people went home thinking, *I wonder who? I wonder who?* Of course, I'm sure the ones in the class who *were* gay received some aid and comfort, which was my point. Basically, what I was trying to do was reach out to the gay kids and let them know, "Hey, you are not alone," and make the straight kids uncomfortable with the knowledge that among them are gay people and they don't know who's who.

AT THAT time I worked in the office of an administrator at Barnard College. She was sixty-five and was going to retire that year. She didn't know I was gay and here I was also doing work with DOB and I was making these public speeches, and not just at schools. One time a radio station called up because they were doing a story on the sexual revolution. The next morning I went into the office and I was drinking my first cup of coffee and the boss sailed in. And she said, "Guess what? This guy was here from WOR radio last night interviewing the girls at Plimpton Hall," which was the first coed dormitory at Barnard College. "And I must stay up late tonight and listen to this radio program." And I thought, *Oh shit, she's going to hear me!* They had already taped me, and I was scheduled to be part of the program that night.

I didn't know what to do. I wasn't sure whether I would still have a job the next morning or not. I called Joan Kent and told her what was going on. She said, "Why don't you call the radio show and explain what happened, and I'm sure they can remove that segment." And I said, "Well, I'll think about it." At that time in my life I was more afraid of being considered a coward than of dying, although I wasn't a fool. If somebody said, "Jump off the bridge," I wasn't going to jump off a bridge, but I had a tremendous investment in trying to prove to myself that I was a brave person.

I walked around freaked out all day. But instead of calling to have the thing taken off the air, at five o'clock, just before I left the office, I went up to my boss and said, "I'm going to be on that radio show tonight." She wanted to know why. I said, "I'm representing an organization called the Daughters of Bilitis." And she said, "What's that?" And I said, "It's a civil rights organization for lesbians." And she said, "Well, that's nice, dear. It's wonderful that you young people are taking up all these causes." She gave me the biggest wink and said, "Now help me on with my coat. I've got to go catch my bus." Not long afterwards, I found out she was living with a well-known businesswoman.

With that radio show and the other public things I did in those years, I discovered that I could take a risk and survive. I could march in Philadelphia. I could go out in the street and be gay even in a dress or a skirt without getting shot. Each victory gave me the courage for the next one.

I WAS always aware of the outsider's point of view. First, from being Jewish. Second, from having friends who were of a different race. That made it easier for me to be gay. I was used to being different. I was used to being an outsider. Being gay added one more color to the rainbow of outsider experiences. Being gay fit in with my personality of being a rebel and an outsider. I didn't even want to fit in. I remember Joan Kent from DOB had tremendous difficulty with that. She was WASP and a Republican, and it was very important for her to be a "lady" the way she defined it. And her definition was, I guess, the same as society's definition. It caused her tremendous grief that the world wouldn't accept her on her terms as a lesbian and as a Republican lady.

It was very easy for me in the late 1960s, when the gay liberation movement came along, to run around in a tie-died tank top and a pair of cutoff jeans and say, "The hell with it," and thumb my nose at the world. Gay liberation just blew away the last restraints. I felt like I didn't have to fit in anymore—at least I didn't have to pretend to fit in. There was a whole movement that was supporting my not fitting in. The civil rights movement gave me a deep underpinning. The women's movement questioned sexual roles. The yippies and the left-wing movements of the sixties questioned the politics I grew up with and the economic and social underpinnings of the whole society. Then the drugs, LSD, and writers and philosophers caused me to really question everything and to say, "The whole perception of reality I was raised with is fucked up, totally crazy, certifiably insane."

One of my friends from the Student Homophile League at Columbia University turned me on to LSD in the men's dorm of Columbia University. This was even before the Stonewall riots and gay liberation. I was having an affair with him. It wasn't a very hot sexual affair. It was just more thumbing our noses at the universe. We used to walk into these meetings arm in arm. It was a scandal. There were these seven little homosexual organizations: DOB, Student Homophile League, and I forget the others. Some of them were just two people and a mimeo machine. So it was a scandal, in a sense, but at the same time, because the two of us were so blatant and out there in public being pro gay, they certainly couldn't afford to throw us out. And it wasn't like we were sleeping only with each other.

Anyway, while I was tripping around, my friend from the Homophile League took me to see *2001*. It was a real blast of an experience. It shook a whole lot of my previous notions of reality. All of a sudden I saw the great white light. And a lot of the teachings of Eastern philosophy weren't just mumbo jumbo anymore. That pushed me a little further over the edge.

So even before Stonewall, I was going to junk the whole thing. I was planning to leave my Barnard job at the end of the semester. I was offered another job there even though I was openly gay—I guess I had done my work well. But I said, "No, thanks." I had an offer of a part-time job doing typesetting in Greenwich Village for this woman who did typesetting for the Black Panthers on the side and all kinds of radical and artistic groups. I figured I would quit my job, move down to the Village, work part time, and have the rest of the time to write and be a political activist. Here I was, the end of the semester, June 1969. And just around that time, the Stonewall riot happened. The shit hit the fan.

The night of the riot I was escorting two women from Boston around Greenwich Village, taking them on a tour of the bars. The women were going to start a DOB chapter in Boston. While we were walking around, we saw these people who looked younger than I was throwing things at cops. One of the women turned to me and said, "What's going on here?" I said, "Oh, it's a riot. These things happen in New York all the time. Let's toddle away and do something else." I took them to Joan Kent's house and then I went over to my lover's place in New Jersey. It was too late to get the last bus across the bridge. So I walked across the George Washington Bridge and hitchhiked the rest of the way at three in the morning. This was a long time ago.

The next day I had to get up and attend some DOB thing; I don't remember what. When I got there, I found out what happened at the Stonewall. From lack of sleep and exhaustion, I was sort of feverish. And I lay on my couch that evening or the next day thinking, *We've got to do something! We've got to do something! We can't just let this pass.* I went to Joan Kent and said, "We should have a march." Joan said, "Well, if the Mattachine Society agrees, we'll cosponsor it." Mattachine was already having a meeting about the riot, and all these gays showed up at the meeting to talk about what was going on.

I showed up with a proposal for a jointly sponsored march. Dick Leitsch, who was the head of Mattachine, wasn't really into it, but when he asked for a vote—"How many people are in favor of holding a march?"—every hand went up. So he said, "If people want to run a march, the march committee meets over there at the end of the meeting."

I didn't get to know Dick Leitsch very well. My strong impression was that Dick wanted only one gay organization in New York, Mattachine, with him at the head of it. So he wasn't really happy with all of these little splinter groups. I think he could accept DOB because, after all, there was no other organization for lesbians. But I think the march threatened to get out of hand. As long as there was the Mattachine Society with him at the head and being the public spokesperson, he had a pretty secure niche in the world.

So we met in one corner after the Mattachine meeting and decided to form a march committee. My assignment was to find out if we needed a police permit. I really didn't want us to need a police permit. I made phone calls and found out that we only needed a police permit if we had sound equipment. I thought, *Fine, we'll march without sound equipment and without a permit.*

We took an ad in the *Village Voice* to announce the march. We all showed up, and it was agreed that Marty Robinson would speak for the guys and I would speak for the women. So we marched around the Village and ended up at Sheridan Square across the street from the Stonewall.

I thought there were only five hundred protesters; the number changes, depending on who you talk to. I've heard people say there were as many as two thousand, but I don't know. I remember us jumping up on this little water fountain, because that was the only platform, and making our speeches. And afterwards I thought, "What else can we do?" I said, "Well, we should disperse and go home because nobody else has anything to say." I said, "Keep your ears open. There are going to be more meetings. This ain't the end of us." I wasn't going to say, "Let's leave and riot against the police station." It was sufficient that we went out there, marched around and made our little speeches, and went home.

The march committee started having meetings, and somehow we decided that we needed a name for our committee. Marty Robinson thinks I came up with the name Gay Liberation Front. I don't know who said it; I remember it coming up at the meeting, and I remember pounding my fist on the table and yelling in exultation, "That's it! That's it! We're the Gay Liberation Front!" GLF was it because it was like the National Liberation Front of North Vietnam—the Vietcong. The Vietcong were heroic in the eyes of the Left—all of these little Vietnamese peasants running around in their conical hats and black pajamas, daring to stand up to the most powerful army in the world, with all its tanks and helicopters and napalm. They were like David against Goliath, fighting for their nation and for the liberation of their people. We were all against the war, at least all of us in GLF. Most of us were young, in our twenties and thirties.

When Dick Leitsch from Mattachine heard about us, that we had a name, he was freaked out. He said, "You're not forming another group, are you?" I said, "Oh, no, no, no. We're just a committee. We just chose this name for our committee." I think in my heart I knew I was lying.

At the same time that we had this little group of about two dozen people in GLF, we heard about a group called Alternate U. Alternate U occupied a big, well-lit industrial loft. They had classes in Marxism, karate, printing and graphics, and different kinds of political theory; maybe they had classes in dance, I don't know. They weren't druggies, although we all did a little something on the side. So we went down there to talk to them. The people we met there were mostly gay people who had been involved with the political Left but were forced to stay in the closet. They were leftists who were closeted gays, just as we were gays who were closeted leftists.

Those of us in GLF who had come from Mattachine and DOB were to the left of the rest of the members of those organizations. We felt that we were being held back in our politics and our beliefs by the necessity of putting forth the aims of the organizations we belonged to, like having to wear skirts to the Fourth of July protest. In Mattachine and DOB we couldn't openly state that we were against the Vietnam War because they believed that getting mixed up in other struggles was bad strategy. They thought that fighting for gay rights was difficult enough without having to take on all these other struggles. But those of us in GLF felt that the struggles should be united: the black civil rights movement, the struggle against the Vietnam War, the women's movement, feminist politics, socialist politics. Every ethnic group had its own civil rights cause. And, of course, the gay cause.

I'm not sure how to describe this, but in a sense it was also a movement for psychic liberation, which was related to the insights we got from taking psychedelics. Taking drugs was one of our platforms. But the point wasn't taking the drugs. The point was—at least this is the way we thought at the time—to liberate our minds from the philosophical constraints, the psychological constraints, from limits on what you were allowed to think.

So we joined forces with the people at Alternate U. They offered us the use of Alternate U as a home where we could hold dances and meetings. We started a newspaper at Alternate U, which became *Come Out!* And the dances we had there were massive. I mean, these

Martha Shelley inside New York's Oscar Wilde Memorial Bookshop in Greenwich Village, 1970. The store, which opened in 1967, bills itself as the "world's first lesbian and gay liberation bookshop, featuring good gay and lesbian books, periodicals, buttons, cards, records." (© *Diana Davies*)

dances were jammed! Hundreds of people! I remember serving on security and being up most of the night because we had had threats. There were people who didn't like us having dances where we sold beers for fifty cents and sodas for a quarter when they were busy flogging beers for a couple of bucks in their damn bars. If you wanted, you could dance all night without buying a drink or paying extra to go into a special room where dancing was allowed, which is the way it was in some of the old bars, like the Sea Colony.

WE TALKED all the time about our goals at GLF. We formulated all these grand ideas, grand political platforms, that involved ending this, that, and the other kind of oppression. We took all this very seriously. We had the feeling that the revolution was right around the corner and that we were part of the vanguard. I'm smiling when I say this now because we were young and idealistic and wonderful and brave and naive. All those things, with no sense of history whatsoever. And I'm smiling because we were right. We just had the timetable wrong. I really haven't changed a lot of my views, but just developed more of a sense of history.

We thought the government was going to come down. Some of us really believed it. I was kind of skeptical, I have to tell the truth. I felt it would be just to end the system that we had because we had an unjust system. On the other hand, the idea of that much bloodshed made me real nervous, especially since I thought that some of it might wind up being mine.

Getting rid of the Pentagon, that was number one on our priority list, probably number one on a lot of people's priority lists. Getting rid of the Defense Department, including the Soviet one, was also up there. I wasn't for other people having guns and not us. But I figured, let's start with the problems in our own backyard. Legalize sex between consenting adults. Legalize drugs. Legalize abortion. Legalize prostitution. Basically, you could do what you wanted with your body as long as you didn't hurt other people. An end to poverty— that was a harder one. It's a lot easier to legalize drugs than to end poverty.

The problem was, we had all these platforms, but we never could figure out how to get from here to there. What we did do, I think we did well. We actually had protest marches, dances, and a newspaper, as well as mutual support for people who were having problems.

Things like the dances were really important because we were expressing our affection for each other and our sense of community, which you couldn't do in gay bars. The bars were for meeting people in a furtive manner. Then you'd go home together for furtive sex. The conditions were pretty oppressive—at least for the guys—because you never knew if somebody next to you was from the vice squad. I don't think the vice squad sent women around to the lesbian bars, but there was still the same oppressive feeling. The fear of being raided was really strong. Also, there was the tremendous emphasis on looks in the gay bars. I'm sure there still is. At the GLF dances the consciousness was, "We are here to give each other love and acceptance. And who we are is okay." There were circle dances—you never saw that in a gay bar. Instead of two people against the world, it was our whole community giving each other support.

Later we started having separate women's dances, and that felt pretty great because it was like the kid in the Hershey factory. We could strip down to the waist, which we sometimes did. We had dances where we were stripped to the waist, and some women just stripped to the altogether. It was primeval ritual time.

ONE TIME we had this big debate about the Panther Twenty-one, the Black Panthers who were in jail. People were raising money to get them out. I thought it was nuts. About one million dollars had to be raised to bail these people out. All of a sudden, all the other activities on the Left came to a halt as people spent all their time raising ransom money to get a handful of people out of jail. The Black Panthers were in jail for some trumped-up conspiracy charge by the federal government.

The Panthers called themselves revolutionaries. I suppose they were as much as we were. They wore black berets and black shirts and pants. They had a breakfast program for kids, run by the women, which was great, and a self-defense program, which meant that the men ran around with guns. The idea was that the police were an occupying army in the black community and that the black people had the right to defend themselves against police brutality.

We were debating whether or not to give money, because Huey Newton, the leader of the Black Panther party, and other people in the Panthers constantly used the word *faggot*. They were on a big macho trip and they were really uptight about gayness. The question was, "Why should we support the Black Panthers when they were so antigay and used that kind of rhetoric?" We realized we were a smaller group than they were, with less support in general. For example, Leonard Bernstein threw a big bash to raise money for the Panthers. You didn't see Leonard Bernstein raising money for the gay movement. And guess what Leonard Bernstein was!

We debated giving money as though we were equals with the rest of the left groups, which we weren't. And then out of all of this debate Huey Newton issued a statement, which I felt was somewhat patronizing when I read it, that homosexuals can be revolutionaries, too—something like that. You know, the great Chairman Huey Newton gives his imprimatur. Thank you, Chairman Huey.

I was against our giving money to the Panthers, not because I wanted the Panther Twenty-one to stay in jail or wanted the Panthers to be oppressed, but because I felt that we were such a small organization—we had so little money; also, I didn't feel we should try to bribe them to approve of us. Some left groups welcomed us, and some didn't; some feminist groups—the little Left splinter ones, the more radical ones—welcomed us immediately. NOW, the National Organization for Women, was really spooked by us. Different groups that were antiwar had different reactions. The traditional Left, the Communist party and the Trotskyists were the last to change.

We ended up giving the money. I thought it was dumb. It wasn't a lot, a couple of hundred dollars or maybe a thousand dollars. But it was a big chunk for us.

GLF DIDN'T last. We got involved in these endless theoretical debates about what we should do and what our relationship was to other organizations. I think we just talked ourselves to death. It got really wearing to meet and continue talking about politics and stuff. I remember all these splinter groups forming, like the Red Butterfly Cell—those were the serious Marxists who wanted to read socialism and put out position papers. GLF disintegrated into so many splinter groups that it just disappeared.

While it lasted, I was the big mouth for GLF. I don't know what motivated me to do it; I think I did it because nobody else did. When I first started doing public speaking for DOB, nobody else was doing it in the way I was. I had a funny sense of responsibility. Now there are so many people out there doing one thing or another. I no longer feel that if I don't do it, no one else will.

The Drag Queen

Rey "Sylvia Lee" Rivera

REY RIVERA *scares lots of people—straight and gay. He fulfills almost every negative gay-male stereotype. He is profoundly effeminate. He dresses in drag. He spent years selling his body on New York City's streets. And he's been involved with drugs and alcohol. If anyone is going to be pointed to as an example of why gay people should not be given equal rights, it's Rey Rivera. Given his appearance and the life he's lived, it's easy to overlook Rey's remarkable courage and the role of Rey and people like him in the struggle for gay and lesbian equal rights.*

Rey was at the Stonewall Inn when the police entered the bar at about 2:00 A.M. on Saturday, June 28, 1969. By the end of the evening, he was drawn into a movement that didn't know quite what to do with him.

Today, Rey Rivera lives with his lover of ten years in a working-class neighborhood in a small Hudson River city about an hour north of Manhattan. Standing in the light of a bare light bulb at the door to his apartment, Rey was a startling sight. He was in what he called "scare drag," or partial drag. His thick, wavy brown hair tumbled onto his shoulders. Light makeup highlighted his strong features: high cheekbones, prominent nose, and full lips. His smile revealed a large gap between his front teeth. Rey was dressed in a black halter top, tied at the waist, over a black skintight undershirt. He tucked his hot-pink spandex pants into beige knee-high boots.

The front door of the apartment led into a small kitchen. A pot of chili was cooking on the stove. A bottle of vodka on the kitchen table was well on its way to being emptied.

I was born at two-thirty in the morning on July 2, 1951, in a taxi cab in the old Lincoln Hospital parking lot in the South Bronx. I came out feet first. This old queen couldn't wait. She says, "I'm ready to hit the streets!" My grandmother always used to joke about that. I says, "Yeah, you see why I'm always standing out on the street corner?"

I didn't choose to be effeminate. It wasn't something that you just decided to do. I really believe I was born to be an effeminate child. My grandmother used to come home and find me all dressed up. My grandmother raised me because my mother died when I was three years old. She'd whip my ass, of course, for dressing up. "We don't do this. You're one of the boys. I want you to be a mechanic." And I says, "No, I want to be a hairdresser. And I want to wear these clothes."

From day one I was like this. I remember sitting down with my grandmother sewing and knitting when I was seven years old. I said, "Would you teach me?" And she'd sit there and just say, "Okay, we'll do this." After I left home she couldn't understand why I came out this way. "But don't we remember sitting down and doing everything together?" We used to sew and cook. We used to wash clothes. And she'd say, "No, you're supposed to be one of the boys." And I'd say, "No, I'm one of the girls." She couldn't stand that.

I remember in 1961, on July 2, when I turned ten years old, I had such a bad feeling about everything that was going on in my life and what my grandmother was going through—she took shit because I was an effeminate boy—that I attempted to commit suicide. I almost killed myself. I took all her pills. After I started getting the effect, I went upstairs and told my aunt, who wasn't really my aunt, and she rushed me to Bellevue Hospital.

You feel so afraid. I thought there was nobody out there. As far as I was concerned, I was the only one that was different. I just felt that I was the only gay person, the only faggot in the world, the only person that felt the way that I felt, that was attracted to men. I couldn't discuss it with my grandmother, even though she knew where I was coming from. There was nobody to talk to. I couldn't deal with school. I was a great student as far as certain things were concerned, but *we* will *not* play football. And *we* will *not* go in the locker room. We won't!

School was hard: "You fuckin' fag." When I used to go to Coney Island with Granny, I remember that as soon as that subway train would stop on Forty-Second Street, the queens would get on. And everyone would say, "Look at the *maricónes*. Look at the *maricónes*." I'd sit there and I knew I was part of them. The other kids from the neighborhood would say, "Oh, look, Rey, isn't that funny?" And I would turn my head and look at the wall and think to myself, *Why do people have to do this?*

A few months after I tried to kill myself, I left home. I was grown by then. I thought I was grown. I knew I had to leave because of life, because of what my being gay was doing to my grandmother. She came home crying one day. She says, with tears in her eyes, "They're calling you *pato*." That means "faggot" in the Spanish language. It hurt her so bad because they were doing this to me. She knew where I was coming from. She knew. But it hurt her. I didn't want her to suffer. It wasn't my suffering. I was worrying about her suffering. That's why I left. I went to Times Square. I became a streetwalker. You stand out on the street and you make money. At that age it was easy to make money.

Every dirty old man that called himself straight picked me up. I remember playing psychiatrist to a lot of them. "If my wife knew that I was laying with a man. . . ." Give me a break! I don't want to hear this. Are you paying me? Fine. Then I have to deal with it. This is when I was dressed as a boy. A year or two later I started living in drag. These people who picked me up were sick. They would say, "My wife would never appreciate the fact that I was laying with a man that dresses in women's clothes." And I said, "Just give me the money. Don't worry about it."

You can sell anything out on the streets. You can sell men, young boys, and young women. There's always a customer out there, and they are the ones that are sick. They are the ones that have the problem.

I remember going home and just scrubbing myself in a tub of hot water. "Oh, these people touched me. This sleaze." Even if they weren't old, I felt that way. They could have been young. When I was thirteen and fourteen years old, I remember sleeping with guys that were twenty and twenty-one. They were paying me. And they had their hang-ups. I'd screw them up the ass and whatnot. That's what I was getting paid for. But I'd go home and clean myself. I didn't understand then and I still don't really, why people have to go through all them problems.

I thought I had my head together because I could sit there and talk to somebody for a half an hour. If you paid me fifty dollars, oh, I'd tell you anything, honey. And if my alarm clock went off, give me some more money, or you've got to go out the door. I knew I was a whore. I was out to make money.

WHEN I was growing up, if you walked down Forty-Second Street and even looked like a faggot, you were going to jail. I went to jail a lot of times. I remember the first time I got arrested. I was walking down the street with this other queen, and she said, "We got to move it! We got to move it!" I asked, "Why?" She says, "The camarónes are coming! They're coming to get us!" I'm like, "What the fuck are you talking about?" So she explained to me that camarónes was slang for plainclothes cops. With that, I'm like, "Okay, I'll walk, I'll walk!" We did triple steps.

The police didn't get us from behind, though, they got us from the front. Then they stuck us in this hallway by one of the theaters. We were jampacked in there, like thirty queens and twenty hustlers. I always differentiated. It's not nice to differentiate like that, but the boys had their dicks hanging in their pants, and we had makeup on. We always looked like girls. Back then, when I first started out in women's clothes, it was what they call "scare drag," like I'm dressed right now. You don't have the tits on. You just have a little makeup on. You have your hair out. You got women's clothing on.

The paddy wagon pulled up to the hallway, and they took us in. I'll never forget, we're halfway up Forty-Second Street heading for Eighth Avenue, and here comes Miss Tish. I'm sure she's dead by now. She was an old drag queen, a show queen. They slammed on the brakes. They jumped out of the paddy wagon and snatched her and threw her right in, and she says, "What the fuck is going on?" She's freaking out. This queen must have been forty or fifty years old. And she was saying, "This is not happening to me." She was really freaking. She finally calmed down.

Before we got to the police station, everybody who had prior arrests and was on parole was sitting there tearing up pieces of paper. It was like a ticker-tape parade coming out of the back window of the van. I asked, "What are you all doing?" And they said, "We were in jail before, so we've got to get rid of these. These are parole cards. I'm on parole for three years." And I'm like, "Parole? What is parole?" It's funny, you know, the things that we went through.

I don't know how many times my grandmother had to come and bail me out of jail. She always came and got me. She would say, "That's my grandson. I have to take him out." She loved me very dearly.

BEFORE GAY rights, before the Stonewall riot, I was involved in the black liberation movement and the peace movement. I felt I had the time and I knew that I had to do something. Back then, my revolutionary blood was going. I did a lot of marches. I had to do something back then to show everyone that the world was changing.

I got involved with a lot of different things because I had so much anger about the world, the way it was, the way they were treating people. When the Stonewall happened, it was fabulous. Actually, it was the first time that I had been to the friggin' Stonewall. It was like a God-sent thing. I just happened to be there when it all jumped off.

The Stonewall wasn't a bar for drag queens. Everybody keeps saying it was. The drag-queen spot was a bar called the Washington Square Bar, at Third Street and Broadway. This is where I get into arguments with people. They say, "Oh, no, it was a drag-queen bar, it was a black bar." No, Washington Square Bar was the drag-queen bar.

If you were a drag queen, you could get into the Stonewall if they knew you. And only a certain number of drag queens were allowed into the Stonewall at that time. I wasn't in full drag that night anyway. I was dressed very pleasantly. When I dressed up, I always tried to pretend that I was a white woman. I always like to say that, but really I'm Puerto Rican and Venezuelan. That night I was wearing this fabulous woman's suit I had made at home. It was light beige—very summery. Bell bottoms were in style then. I had my hair out. Lots of makeup and lots of hair. I was wearing boots. I don't know why I was wearing boots.

We had just come back in from Washington, D.C., my first lover and I. At that time we were passing bad paper around and making lots of money. And I said, "Let's go to the Stonewall." So I was drinking at the bar, and the police came in to get their payoff as usual. They were the same people who always used to come into the Washington Square Bar.

I don't know if it was the customers or if it was the police, but that night everything just clicked. Everybody was like, "Why the fuck are we doing all this for? Why should we be chastised? Why do we have to pay the Mafia all this kind of money to drink in a lousy fuckin' bar? And still be harassed by the police?" It didn't make any sense. The people at them bars, especially at the Stonewall, were involved in other movements. And everybody was like, "We got to do our thing. We're gonna go for it!"

When they ushered us out, they very nicely put us out the door. Then we were standing across the street in Sheridan Square Park. But why? Everybody's looking at each other. "Why do we have to keep on putting up with this?" Suddenly, the nickels, dimes, pennies, and quarters started flying. I threw quarters and pennies and whatnot. "You already got the payoff, and here's some more!"

To be there was so beautiful. It was so exciting. I said, "Well, great, now it's my time. I'm out there being a revolutionary for everybody else, and now it's time to do my thing for my own people." It was like, "Wow, we're doing it! We're doing it! We're fucking their nerves!" The police thought that they could come in and say, "Get out," and nothing was going to happen. They could padlock the door and they knew damn well like everybody else knew that as soon as the police were gone, the Mafia would be there cutting the door. They had a new cash register. They had more money and they had more booze. This is what we learned to live with at that time. Until that day.

So we're throwing the pennies, and everything is going off really fab. The cops locked themselves in the bar. It was getting vicious. Then someone set fire to the Stonewall. The cops, they just panicked. They had no backup. They didn't expect any of this retaliation. But they should have. People were very angry for so long. How long can you live in the closet like that? I listen to the stories of my brothers and sisters who are older than I am. I could never have survived the lives that my brothers and sisters from the 1940s and 1950s did. Because I have a mouth. I would never have made it. Somebody would have killed me.

That night I got knocked around a bit by a couple of plainclothes cops. I didn't really get hurt. I was very careful that night, thank God. But I saw other people being hurt by the police. There was one drag queen, I don't know what she said, but they just beat her into a bloody pulp. There were a couple of dykes they took out and threw in a car. The dykes got out the other side. It was inhumane, senseless bullshit. They called us animals. We were the lowest scum of the Earth at that time.

EVEN THOUGH I was at the Stonewall riot, I didn't join the movement per se until February 1970. I didn't feel like I wanted to be bothered with anything organized. Then I joined the Gay Activists Alliance, GAA. That first year after Stonewall, we were petitioning for a gay rights bill for New York City, and I got arrested for petitioning on Forty-Second Street. I was asking people to sign the petition. I was dressed casually—makeup, hair, and whatnot. The cops came up to me and said, "You can't do this." I said, "My constitution says that I can do anything that I want." "No, you can't do this. Either you leave, or we're going to arrest you." I said, "Fine, arrest me." They very nicely picked me up and threw me in a police car and took me to jail.

When I got to the precinct, I called GAA to see if they could get me out of this bind. When I went in front of the judge, he looked at the two arresting officers and he's like, "Don't you realize what's going on?" I could see the look in his face. He said, "Number one, I'm letting him go." He says to the policemen, "Don't you realize what you just did? The whole country is in an uproar, and you're messing with a person who's circulating a petition?" They let me go home.

I testified for the gay rights bill at City Hall. It was hard to get up there to testify because the City Council tried to push the drag queens into the background. There was this councilman who said, "Why should I have my children being taught by them, men that dress in women's clothing?" I testified a couple of times. It was not a very agreeable experience. I am the straight person's stereotype of the gay community. They don't want their children to be exposed to someone like me. Even my own community, the gay community, doesn't want to be bothered with people like me. Nobody wanted us queens there.

When the bill was finally passed, in 1986, I was living up here, and this man came to me in a bar and kissed me. My straight friends were coming up to me and kissing me because we finally did it. That bill was mine. I worked very hard for it. The fucking community has no respect for the people that really did it, the drag queens. We did it for our own brothers and sisters. Don't keep shoving us in the fuckin' back and stabbing us in the back! You get beaten up by you own, and that hurts. We're just the low trash of life. I'm tired of being the bottom of the heap. I want to be the top of the heap.

I ALSO went to protest demonstrations, like the one in the fall of 1970, when we did a sit-in at New York University. At that time I was sleeping in the park, in Sheridan Square. I had given up my job, given up everything, for gay liberation. Bob Kohler from the Gay Liberation Front (GLF) came and says to me, "Sylvia, come on, let's go, we're having a sit-in." New York University didn't want us to have a dance there. So, okay, we won't have any dances there, but we took over the basement of the building where we would have had the dance. It was a nice sit-in for three or four days. Here again, my brothers and sisters from the gay community were not very supportive of anything that went down. They just did not react properly.

By the last day of the sit-in, when the police came to throw us out, there was nobody left in the basement except for the street people. Everybody was saying that we stayed there for the whole time because we didn't have a place to live. That wasn't true. We could have picked up a trick and stayed at a hotel. We were there for them, for myself, and for everybody else.

Out of that NYU protest, STAR was born, the Street Transvestite Action Revolutionaries. We formed STAR because my brothers and sisters kept using us when they needed us, but they weren't treating us fairly. So we wanted to be by ourselves. Myself, Marsha Johnson, Bambi Lamour, Endora, Bebe, and a few others were involved in STAR. Marsha Johnson and I fought for the liberation of our people. We did a lot back then. We had a building on Second Street, which we called STAR House. When we asked the community to help us, there was nobody to help us. We were nothing. We were nothing! We were taking care of kids that were younger than us. Marsha and I were young, and we were taking care of them. And organizations like GAA had teachers and lawyers, and all we asked was for them to help us teach our own, so we could all become a little bit better. There was nobody there to help us. They left us hanging.

There was only one person that came and helped us: Bob Kohler. Bob helped paint and put wires together. We didn't know what the fuck we were doing, but we tried. We really did. Marsha and I and a few of the other older drag queens, we took this slum building and kept it going for about a year or two. We went out and made money off the streets to keep these kids off the streets. We already went through it. We wanted to protect them, to show them that there was a better life.

Our kids came from everywhere. We had kids from Boston, California. They were good kids. I've seen a couple of them since the movement. The ones that I've seen, they've done very well. It makes you feel good.

But we just didn't have the money. The community was not going to help us. The community is always embarrassed by the drag queens because straight society says, "A faggot always dresses in drag, or he's effeminate." But you've got to be who you are. Passing for straight is like a light-skinned black woman or man passing for white. I refuse to pass. I couldn't have passed, not in this lifetime.

Except for GLF, who made us the vanguard of the revolution, everyone else left us in the dark. They pushed us aside. Actually, it was not even the men that pushed aside the drag queens. It was the gay women from this radical group. One of them was Jean O'Leary. We hated each other from day one and always will. She has her own political view. I have my political view. But do not put me down. We were all put down as human beings for being gay, but she always put down the gay male and she always put down the drag queen because she hated men. And that's not right.

Basically, a lot of the women I knew in the movement appreciated the fact that I was bold. Women like Martha Shelley, from GLF. We got along very well. But Jean O'Leary was a bitch, a bitch in plain English. She was the one who had the hatred not just toward the drag queens but toward men in general. We did a lecture together one time at Queens College, me and Jean, and I was in full fuckin' drag sitting there looking fabulous. She got very nasty as I was speaking and jumped up and says, "You are a genital male." And I'm like, "Who the fuck asked you?" I says, "We're here telling college students where we come from, and this is your attitude?" Why was she putting me down? We were supposed to be a part of each other.

*   *   *

A LOT of times I just sit here and I hurt. I hurt for the simple fact that the movement never recognized the drag queen until this year [1989], twenty years after Stonewall. It was always, "We must wear a suit and tie. We have to look part of their world. We can't be different." But the whole world is different from one another. It just so happened that for the first part of the movement, the drag queen was part of the vanguard of the revolution. We were the front liners. And we didn't take no shit from nobody back then.

I don't condemn the rest of the community for not being as bold as some of my sisters and some of my brothers. Because I do understand. You do have a family. You do have a job. And back then you did have to hide. But when you were obvious back then, the effeminate male or the butch woman, there was nothing to hold you back.

I like being myself. It's fun being Sylvia. It's fun playing the game. I've been up here in this town for a lot of years. I'm proud of what I am, and they respect me for that. We've done drag shows up here, and this whole community loves it. Curiosity will always kill the cat, so they always want to see something different. And when they see something different, they freak out.

The years that I've lived up here I feel that I've liberated a lot of people just by living here and by being myself, just by being a campy

Rey "Sylvia Lee" Rivera, in the early 1980s. *(Courtesy Rey Rivera)*

queen. Of course, when you go to a local bar, you get some strange looks, but eventually you become friends with everybody. I'm not saying that I haven't had people try to attack me, but when that happens, I have these other people who sit at the bar with me and they'll say, "You can't touch her. She is our friend. If you touch her, you've got to take on the whole bar." These are women that are jumping to back me up. "Oh, no, we do not touch her. You want to fight her, you're coming through us first."

You know, I'd still like to do a lot more for the movement, but the movement just doesn't want to deal with me.

THE PLACE where I work now, my boss knows where I'm coming from. I work with food and always wear a baseball cap because I have so much hair. I work at a home for children who come from problem homes. Actually, they're a terror.

Fearless Youth
Morty Manford

MORTY MANFORD *had little interest in politics in the late 1960s. In 1968, he was a hardworking seventeen-year-old college student at Columbia College who spent his spare time in gay bars in Greenwich Village. Marginally involved in the gay student group at Columbia, he did not become active in the movement until 1970, nearly a year after he witnessed the Stonewall Inn riot. Once he had been drawn into the gay movement, however, it became his life, inspiring youthful outrage that led him to drop out of school to join his "sisters and brothers in the struggle for gay liberation."*

Now a lawyer working for the New York State attorney general's office, Morty Manford was raised in a quiet, semisuburban neighborhood in Flushing, Queens, in the same house he now shares with his widowed mother, Jeanne. Morty is a handsome man of medium build, with short brown hair. He measured his words carefully before speaking.

Before I became involved in the gay rights movement, I first had to come out. That battle was intense. It was a personal civil war that started around the age of fifteen or sixteen. The conflict was over trying to repress my homosexuality in order to conform to society's values. I remember extremely intense mental activity all the time.

I began seeing a psychiatrist. I don't think he paid too much attention to my homosexuality. He was trying to focus on other supposedly underlying reasons for my "adolescent adjustment" problem, as he called it. Then things got worse. The sexual issue was tearing me apart.

The whole society was telling us it was horrible. A homosexual was a flaky, vacuous, bizarre person. If you wanted to insult somebody then (as now), you accused him of being a faggot. The newspapers always referred to homosexuals and perverts as if they were one and the same. The official line from psychiatrists was that homosexuals were inherently sick. Homosexual acts were illegal. People referred to homosexuality in terms of sinfulness. This attitude was pervasive.

People didn't realize the impact such positions and attitudes had on gay men and women. These attitudes affected the way you thought and lived, what you felt, and how you thought of yourself. If you were gay and you accepted those societal norms, then you were at war with yourself.

I changed psychiatrists. The new psychiatrist was a dynamic guy. I wouldn't say he was approving, and he did some things I found very objectionable, like telling my parents I was gay without getting my permission. However, in the course of our therapy, he said some fairly positive things. He told me, "It doesn't matter. I don't care if you want to fuck an animal or a woman or a man."

By then my desires were sufficiently strong that I decided I was going to do something about them. I went to Manhattan and walked and walked, hoping that somebody would come sweep me off the street and make mad, passionate love to me.

Well, it happened. I was seventeen, and this fellow was a few months older than I was. He was a beauty: blonde, with blue eyes, a boyish kind of face, and a swimmer's body. Nice smile—warm smile. And a nice person. He had this sort of colorful quality to his personality. Everything had a little flair. He had a black cape and, I think, a silver-tipped cane. He just had fun. Of course, back in the late sixties all young people were dressing with a lot of individual taste and wearing colorful clothes. It was the love generation. On the other hand, I always wore blue jeans and a flannel shirt—very plain.

We met at this public forum at the corner of Sixth Avenue and Eighth Street. It was where people would gather; all the local Greenwich Village intellectuals, or pseudo-intellectuals, would come out and debate the issues of importance. This was the summer of 1968. People literally debated the issues in the news, the civil rights struggle, the political direction of our country. This fellow started talking to me. We were talking about the world and social issues. The two of us just kept on talking. He said, "Let's walk. Let's go get a drink." We must have spent six or eight hours that night just walking and talking. He made a few vague allusions to homosexuality, to test my reaction, I guess. I didn't say too much in response.

He was staying with a homosexual man in the Bronx. It was an untenable situation, he said. And I said, "Well, if you need a place to stay for a few days, you're welcome to come and stay with me in Flushing."

First we went to his place in the Bronx. We took the subway. He got a few things. Then we came back here to my parents' house and talked all through the night. I remember the sun was up when we went to sleep.

He was working as a waiter in a restaurant in Manhattan. One evening I went to pick him up at work with the car, and he said, "A few of us from the restaurant are going over to a bar down the block to have a drink." We walked into this bar on the Upper East Side, and I was stunned because it was all men in there, and they were all dancing together. I was amazed and delighted and anxious. He danced with one of his friends and then turned to me and asked me to dance a slow dance.

It was a moment of such. . . . It was your greatest desire and your greatest fear all in one. I knew I wanted to dance with him. We danced. I think the song they were playing was "Turn Around, Look at Me." It goes something like, "There is someone walking behind you. Turn around, look at me. There is someone to love and guide you. Turn around, look at me." (I can't sing.)

We left the bar and came back here to Flushing, and the fireworks were in the sky that night. My conflict persisted in diminishing increments for a few years, but that night was a milestone.

AT THIS point I had already graduated from Bayside High School and was getting ready to start as a freshman at Columbia College in fall of 1968. That spring, before I graduated, there had been an article on the front page of the *New York Times* about the official recognition of the Student Homophile League at Columbia. I think the league was first formed on an underground basis in the fall–winter of 1966. I had already been accepted to Columbia, and I was excited that there was a gay group there.

When I started school, I called the Student Homophile League. Although you could call their office number from any phone on campus, I went off campus to a telephone booth to dial. I was still very afraid of being discovered by anybody. The group hadn't reassembled for the semester, so it took a couple of weeks before somebody got back to me. The student who called said, "I'll come visit you. We'll talk." I told him where I was. I was in the dormitory. Two of them showed up. We went off campus to a coffee shop. We sat and talked a little bit. They asked me to come to a meeting, which I did a week or so later. I wasn't terribly inspired by what I saw in the Student Homophile League, and nothing they were doing really interested me. It was a very loose affiliation at that time.

At this point I had already discovered the bars. I suppose my gay life pretty much revolved around going to the bars, even though there was always the threat of bar raids—everyone heard about them. But the only raid where I was actually inside the bar was at the Stonewall. That was in late June 1969.

The Stonewall was my favorite place. It was a dive. It was shabby,

and the glasses they served the watered-down drinks in weren't particularly clean. The place attracted a very eclectic crowd. Patrons included every type of person: some transvestites, a lot of students,
young people, older people, businessmen. It was an interesting place.
I met friends at the Stonewall regularly. There was a dance floor and
a jukebox. There was a back-room area, which in those days meant
there was another bar in back. There were tables where people sat.

The night of the raid, some men in suits and ties entered the place
and walked around a little bit. Then whispers went around that the
place was being raided. Suddenly, the lights were turned up, and
the doors were sealed, and all the patrons were held captive until the
police decided what they were going to do. I was anxious, but I wasn't
afraid. Everybody was anxious, not knowing whether we were going
to be arrested or what was going to happen.

It may have been ten or fifteen minutes later that we were all told
to leave. We had to line up, and our identification was checked before
we were freed. People who did not have identification or were under
age and all transvestites were detained. Those who didn't meet whatever standards the police had were incarcerated temporarily in the
coatroom. The coat closet. Little did the police know the ironic
symbolism of that. But they found out fast.

As people were released, they stayed outside. They didn't run
away. They waited for their friends to come out. People who were
walking up and down Christopher Street, which was a very busy
cruising area at that time, also assembled. The crowd in front of the
Stonewall grew and grew.

I stayed to watch. As some of the gays came out of the bar, they
would take a bow, and their friends would cheer. It was a colorful
scene. Tension started to grow. After everybody who was going to be
released was released, the prisoners—transvestites and bar personnel,
bartenders, and the bouncers—were herded into a paddy wagon that
was parked right on the sidewalk in front of the bar. The prisoners
were left unguarded by the local police; they simply walked out of the
paddy wagon to the cheer of the throng. There's no doubt in my mind
that those people were deliberately left unguarded. I assume there was
some sort of a relationship between the bar management and the local
police, so they really didn't want to arrest these people. But they had
to at least look like they were trying to do their jobs.

Once all of the people were out and the prisoners went on their
merry ways, the crowd stayed. I don't know how to characterize the
motives of the crowd at that point, except to say there was curiosity
and concern about what had just happened. Then some people in the
crowd started throwing pennies across the street at the front of the

Stonewall. Then someone apparently threw a rock, which broke one of the windows on the second floor. The Stonewall had a couple of great big plate-glass windows in the front. They were painted black on the inside. And there was a doorway in between them, which was the entrance. The building had a second floor, which I think was used for storage space. With the shattering of the glass of the second-floor window, the crowd collectively exclaimed, "Ooh." It was a dramatic gesture of defiance.

For me, there was a slight lancing of the festering wound of anger that had been building for so long over this kind of unfair harassment and prejudice. It wasn't my fault that many of the bars where I could meet other gay people were run by organized crime. Because of the system of official discrimination on the part of state liquor authorities and the corruption of the local police authorities, these were the only kind of bars that were permitted to serve a gay clientele. None of that was my doing.

The tension escalated. A few more rocks went flying, and then somebody from inside the bar opened the door and stuck out a gun. He yelled for people to stay back. Then he withdrew the gun, closed the door, and went back inside. Somebody took an uprooted parking meter and broke the glass in the front window and the plywood board that was behind it. Then somebody else took a garbage can, one of those wire-mesh cans, set it on fire, and threw the burning garbage into the premises. The area that was set afire was where the coatroom was.

They had a fire hose inside, and they used it. It was a small trash fire. Then they opened the front door and turned the hose on the crowd to try to keep people at a distance. That's when the riot erupted.

Apparently, a fire engine had been summoned because of the trash fire. As it came down the block, uniformed police started to arrive. They came down the street in a phalanx of blue with their riot gear on. In those days the New York City police had a guerrilla-prone cadre known as the Tactical Police Force, the TPF.

Who knows whether the violence would have escalated in the way it did if the TPF had not come in? That's what they always looked for; they wanted confrontation. Chasing after people and hitting them with their billy clubs, I think, provoked a greater response than there would have been otherwise. One way or the other, though, gay people had stood up and rebelled.

I watched. I wasn't looking for a fight. I can't claim credit for the small acts of violence that took place. I didn't break any windows. I wasn't the one who had a knife and cut the tires on the paddy wagon.

I didn't hit a cop and didn't get hit by a cop. But it was a very emotional turning point for me. It was the first time I had seen anything like that.

Once they started attacking people and forcing people onto the side streets, I tried to get out of the way. I saw people breaking windows, but I didn't stay too much longer. I returned the next night to see what was going on because the riot was continuing. For me, this festering wound, the anger from oppression and discrimination, was coming out very fast at the point of Stonewall.

Several days later I went to Philadelphia to march in the annual picket line in front of Independence Hall. It was July 4, 1969. I think I wore sunglasses. When I saw cameras, I turned my face away. I went with friends from New York, from the Stonewall. That night, back at home in Flushing, I had a personal crisis over somebody I was infatuated with and I attempted suicide. The relationship wasn't progressing as I had wanted. On some level he rejected me. I think that all of my own conflict was starting to come to the surface. Even though I had been actively gay for almost a year at this point, the struggle was still going on. I took a large quantity of pills—tranquilizers. I had gotten them from the psychiatrist.

My parents found me. In my stupor I must have gotten up and fallen and made some noise. I spent a few months in a psychiatric hospital. It was not uncommon in those days for gay people to attempt suicide. I remember many young people who I met telling me about their attempted suicides. It was not uncommon to see somebody with stitch marks on their wrists.

THE FOLLOWING March, in 1970, I was sitting with some friends having a sandwich at Mama's Chick n' Rib, a coffee shop on Greenwich Avenue popular with gay people, when a demonstration went by. Hundreds upon hundreds of people with protest signs were chanting. It was obviously a gay demonstration. I said to my friends at the table, "Let's join it." Nobody wanted to join it. I said, "I'll see you later." I wasn't going to let the parade go by.

The purpose of this march was to protest police conduct at the raid of a bar called the Snake Pit. One of the customers who was taken prisoner was an Argentine national who leapt from the second-story window of the precinct headquarters in a panicked attempt to escape deportation. He became impaled on a steel fence. The moral outrage was certainly very personal in my own heart.

At the conclusion of the march a number of people went over to the headquarters of the Gay Liberation Front at Fourteenth Street and

Sixth Avenue. I went with them. There were some speeches. I really was left uninspired by their political line. My impression was that they were talking about general revolution, which I had heard plenty of around Columbia. This talk didn't really address my subconscious, and increasingly conscious, concerns about being gay or my reasons for joining the march in the first place. They were talking about some black cause and some antiwar cause, about meetings that were coming up in the next week or so. It was just a general rallying point for the New Left. I was sympathetic to all of those things, but somehow or another I was extremely busy as a student and didn't get involved in the New Left issues. I was a hardworking student and spent virtually all my time studying. The only breaks I had from being a serious student were my journeys down to the Stonewall.

Somebody at that GLF meeting who I was talking to mentioned another group to me, the Gay Activists Alliance. When I went to GAA's next weekly meeting, the political discussion was appealing, so I joined GAA, and things started to move very fast in terms of my political education.

GAA's express purpose was gay liberation. Organizationally it was a cardinal rule that we were going to limit our agenda to gay liberation issues. We felt that by doing so we could draw together gays of all political persuasions: lesbians, gay men, gay youth, conservatives, right-wing people, left-wing people. And, in fact, this is what we did. We had a tremendous range of types and ages. And by focusing on a common agenda, gay rights and gay liberation, we avoided a lot of conflict that might have otherwise torn the group apart.

At GAA we first and foremost wanted to send a message to other lesbians and gays in the closet that there was an alternative to the homophobic message that we'd all been imbued with. Second, wherever there was antigay and antilesbian discrimination, we would oppose it. We addressed a vast range of discriminatory policies, from the policy at certain gay bars of excluding transvestites to avowed employment discrimination against gays by private industry.

We very early decided, as a strategic focus, to work for the enactment of civil rights legislation in the New York City Council. That campaign involved participation on many different levels. Some people were involved in lobbying. Our focus was highlighting, for the benefit of the gay public as well as for the heterosexual public, that there was, in fact, discrimination; that it was improper and morally objectionable; and that that's why we needed legislation. Our protests focused on discrimination in three main areas: employment, housing, and places of public accommodation.

There were bars and restaurants that had policies against admitting

gay customers. When people were ejected from the Gold Rail up at
Columbia because somebody kissed a friend hello and was judged to
be gay, we had a demonstration and a "kiss-in." We went to the bar
en masse as gays and started to kiss each other to affirm our rights. I
think this demonstration was led by the Columbia group. We had
maybe thirty or forty people at the kiss-in. We kissed and kissed until
the management agreed it would not again refuse to serve anybody
who was gay. And we left as fast as we had come in.

Once I got involved in GAA, I quickly became active in the Columbia organization. We changed the group's focus, and we changed
its name to Gay People at Columbia. We tried to make demonstrations fun and campy, and enjoyable, as well as making sure they had
a serious impact. There was a demonstration at an investigatory firm
called Fidelifacts. These were private investigators who served employers by trying to track down information on, among other things,
people's sexual lives. That information was used to fire gay employees. When asked, "How do you know somebody is homosexual?" the
guy who ran Fidelifacts said, "If it walks like a duck and talks like a
duck, then I assume it's a duck." So we rented a duck costume and
sent one person there dressed up like a duck, of course, handing out
our leaflets. And we addressed the media. We had little squeaky
rubber ducks that made a noise, a sharp piercing noise. It was a very
loud protest right on Forty-Second Street between Broadway and
Sixth Avenue, where the Fidelifacts offices were.

There was a demonstration at Park West Village, an apartment
complex up on Central Park West, because the owners had a policy
of not permitting two women or two men to rent an apartment. The
assumption was that they might be doing something in these apartments that the owners didn't approve of.

This was a very idealistic era, when young people felt they could
change the world. We truly felt we were being a part of history. We
were doing something new. We were doing something righteous. We
were part of the generation of committed youths.

IT WAS soon after I first started attending the GAA meetings that I was
arrested for the first time. I was with a friend who lived at Fifteen
Christopher Street, and we were sitting on the steps directly across
the street from his apartment. Christopher Street was the heart of gay
street life in New York City at that time. There were many bars along
the street. People would go in and out of bars, walk to a restaurant or
to another bar, or just stand and watch the street traffic. This was
1970. I was nineteen.

Some people walked hand in hand down Christopher Street. Actually, at that point, the only ones doing that were members of GAA, who held hands as much for the sheer joy of it as for the political statement. We made a point to do it, and not just on Christopher Street. We tried to emphasize the positive, the joyful aspects of being gay. A simple act like holding hands was something that most gays at the time wouldn't do in public.

So my friend and I were just sitting there on Christopher Street. The police came along and said, "Move along." And one of us, probably me, said, "Why?" And the cops just said, "Move along. You can't sit here." They didn't want to argue the point. And we said, "No." They were familiar with gay demonstrations, but I don't think they expected two kids to stand up to them. I think they threatened us, "If you don't move, you'll get arrested." We said, "All right, we're not moving." So they arrested us. They brought us to the police station. They said, "We'll give you desk-appearance tickets." And we said, "No." If we had simply accepted desk-appearance tickets, which are summonses, we would have had to come back individually in a few weeks to appear in court and face the charges. That wouldn't have made the point that we were opposing the conduct of the police. So we refused, and they locked us up for the night.

We wanted to push this to the point where they knew this was a political protest. They were harassing us because we were gay. They didn't walk through the East Village in those days, where there were a lot of young hippie-type people, and bother the ostensibly heterosexual community. They didn't walk along side streets on Manhattan's West Side and tell people they had to move. There's a lot of street life in New York in residential areas. And this area wasn't even residential. This was basically a commercial strip. We felt that we had to put an end to this police harassment.

We were allowed to make a couple of phone calls. We called Arthur Evans, the chairman of GAA's political action committee. He was also a very dear friend of mine. I knew he would do the right thing in alerting people that two of our members had been arrested. We made another call to this new candidate for Congress in the Village district, who had expressed her interest in supporting gay rights in a meeting with some representatives of GAA. So we decided to give her a call to let her know what the police were doing on the streets of Greenwich Village. I don't think I called home. It was two o'clock in the morning, and I may not have wanted to wake up my mother at that hour. But I didn't mind waking up this ambitious politician, Bella Abzug.

We stayed overnight in jail, from two o'clock until ten o'clock in the morning. A few hours in jail were insignificant. This was the fight for liberation. When we got to court in the morning, Bella Abzug had sent a lawyer to represent us. They brought us to a series of holding cells in the courthouse downtown. Ultimately, we were placed on a bench in the courtroom as our case was getting ready to be called. Then when our case was called, the two of us walked up to the table where defendants stand with our arms around each other's shoulders. The judge started screaming at us about this public display. But we wanted to make it clear to the judge that the police action was politically motivated.

The judge had the case "second called," which means "Sit down. Get your act together, and we'll call your case again in ten or twenty minutes." The attorney came over to us and said, "You can't do that here. The judge can't deal with it." He wasn't telling us there was anything wrong with what we were doing. He was a good guy. He gave us ample representation. He wanted to make some sort of a statement on our behalf, to calm down the judge. I think what he ended up saying was, "My clients meant no disrespect, but Your Honor has to understand they were arrested because they are gay" and so on and so forth.

The case was dismissed. We weren't guilty of doing anything wrong. And justice was ultimately done in the dismissal.

All of these things were firsts for all of us. Every demonstration, every issue, had this sense of "It's something new." We had brought our issue into the judiciary. We had brought the issue of our rights into the chambers of government, the legislature, and the mayor's office.

Unlike the things we did at GAA, we did this as individuals. At GAA all the protests were done as a group, usually a very loud and vocal group. I don't know that I'd call what we did gutsy, but it was the right thing to do. If we had turned and walked away when the police told us to walk away, we wouldn't have felt right about ourselves.

SOMEHOW OR another I had encounter after encounter, face to face with John Lindsay, the city's mayor. One time was on my twenty-first birthday. The mayor was speaking at New York University on the Vietnam War. The week or so preceding his speech, there had been some raids on gay bars. The police were going wild raiding the bars. Classically they did this each year as the elections started to roll around. The politicians would want to build up their statistics for the coming elections to show that the police were arresting all these perverts. Those were the sorts of things they would say in the *New York Times*. We had already reached the point where we weren't going to stand by and let this stuff happen.

I think there was a big uproar at One Sheridan Square, which was a bar. The police had physically beaten some gay people who were there. Police brutality against gays was the inspiration for the demonstration at NYU against John Lindsay. That was September 17, 1971: Constitution Day.

We had our demonstration outside. We set up our picket lines. We had scores of people. We wanted to go into the hall and protest, but people were having trouble getting inside. It was a quickly organized protest. Somehow I got inside. There I was. A thousand people sitting in the audience. And the mayor was up at the podium talking. And what was I going to do? It was just me. So naturally I did what anyone else would do. I walked onto the stage and I took the podium away from John Lindsay. I walked right up next to him and I said, so the audience could hear, "The police are brutalizing gay people three blocks away from where you're sitting." Before I could say much more, the police dragged me off the back of the stage and ejected me through an exit.

Apparently, after I left, the audience called the mayor to account for what was going on with the police bothering the gay community. This was Greenwich Village. You had a lot of progressive people who had already been exposed to two years of gay rights propaganda— actually counterpropaganda to all the heterosexual negativism. The one thing they couldn't deal with was violence going on against us. These were people who were genuinely interested in peace and the antiwar movement. Apparently John Lindsay had made the statement that he would permit me to speak. Of course, he knew darn well that the police had already thrown me out. He didn't realize that I'd be back.

I snuck back in. I can't remember how I broke through the security lines again, but I got back in and I came right down the aisle. I could see the mayor looking up from the podium at me, biting his lip and thinking, *Oh shit, here he comes again.* I walked right back up on stage and said, "I understand you said I can speak." And he said, "Yes," and yielded the podium to me.

I addressed the audience about the police brutality and the harassment we were facing. I said my piece. I thanked them and left as surreptitiously as I entered. What I did had to be done. It was simply a matter of believing that it was the right thing to do. I believed that political protest was going to bring some cure to the problems we were facing.

Another time, we held a protest at Radio City Music Hall at Rockefeller Center. This was a fund-raising event for John Lindsay's presidential campaign. It was a well-planned demonstration.

In talking about these things, I hope I'm not giving the impression that I did all these things on my own. These were all team efforts. I was active in them. I participated. I got arrested in a lot of them. But many people worked on them. The Political Action Committee of GAA did the planning for the Radio City protest. We went to Radio City weeks in advance to case the place and figure out the logistics for a demonstration. We spent hours thinking of all the possibilities and contingencies. The man was running for president. Lindsay was going to have Secret Service men with him. These guys were very touchy, so we weren't going to attempt to go near him physically.

We got about ten tickets to the event from our fifth columnists, people on the inside who had access to tickets. The audience was filled with public officials, city employees, and members of the media. A number of us had already become fairly well known to the politicians in the city because we had been lobbying at City Hall for legislation and other things. So we had to disguise ourselves. I remember a few of us put on false moustaches or sunglasses or different kinds of clothes. We had somebody who knew how to do these things, so it looked right. We infiltrated the crowd at Radio City Music Hall.

We went to our appointed locations. I think I was the first one to speak. The trigger was when John Lindsay started talking. We had decided we were not going to permit him to speak until he addressed the problems of the police department brutalizing gays on the streets. The police were going into bars and beating up people during the raids. There were also raids on the baths. The police arrested people and then they'd call up employers and say, "Your senior clerk was just arrested in a gay bar."

Anyhow, there was a group of us who were going to do things inside. There were about five hundred people from many groups demonstrating outside, but we had one of the largest groups out there. And because we were also on the inside, it became a Lindsay versus gay event.

I was up in the mezzanine, where all the media were located. I was at one end and Cora Perotta was at the other. Alan King did his routine to get the audience all giddy for John Lindsay. I went right up to the railing at the front of the mezzanine and handcuffed myself to it. As Lindsay started to speak, I made my statement: "Homosexuals need your help to end police harassment!" Then Cora stood up on her chair at the other end and started yelling. We had people down in the orchestra. Some people had little pocket alarms in case you're being raped. You're supposed to pull the pin out, throw the pin one way, and throw the alarm the other way to chase off a mugger or a rapist. We had several alarms, which created upset. We were all shouting that the police were harassing and brutalizing gays. "You've got to stop this!"

In the meantime, the police were trying to get my handcuffs off. I told them that I had thrown away the key, but I had hidden it in my vest pocket. If they hadn't come along to take off my handcuffs, I didn't want to be left there all night attached to the balcony rail.

While all this chaos was going on, one lively fellow from GAA tried to come into the mezzanine where I was located. When he got stopped, he said to the guard at the door, "Officer, I'm here to arrest that man." He meant me. So they let him in, and he went up to the front of the mezzanine. He had a raincoat on. Underneath the coat he had a couple of thousand leaflets. He then showered the orchestra seats with all these leaflets, which described the police atrocities directed at gays. All this time, while we were honking and hooting and shouting our one-liners, Alan King was trying to convince Lindsay, "Let me try talking to them." But once the place was showered with leaflets, you could see their sense of loss. They had lost this battle. They left the stage. John Lindsay was supposed to do a song and dance for the crowd. The curtain came down, and they started to show a movie that was part of the program for the evening.

I was still there when the movie began. All these police were tinkering around. They had lots of keys to handcuffs, but it took them a while to find one that fit mine. I just let them tinker. And I kept on shouting while they were tinkering.

They took us out and released us. They didn't arrest us that time. You see, at certain kinds of events we were prepared to be arrested, but we knew it would make John Lindsay look bad to arrest people who were protesting a legitimate issue. His problem was that he pretended to have values that he was not living up to. He pretended to be for these very generalized civil rights issues.

We started getting some real restraint from the police following a number of these demonstrations. There was a definite cause and effect there.

BESIDES THE protests, I was also involved in organizing. One summer in the early seventies, my friend Lou Todd and I did an organizing tour in the South. It was the same year that two other people from GAA did an organizing tour of the Midwest. We went out like Johnny Appleseeds. Lou and I covered fifteen cities in the South in

Lou's yellow Datsun. GAA paid for the gas. We were lucky if there was anybody in those towns who had heard about gay liberation.

We used our wits to meet people in the gay community. You'd meet one person and ask questions: "Where do we meet other people?" "Are there any organizations?" There rarely were. But there were bars. You'd go in. You'd find somebody who you could talk to who might have heard something, and you'd try to interest them in helping get local people to talk with us about the new gay liberation movement.

We had lots of adventures. Many stories. There were a couple of wonderful men down in New Orleans. They were lovers. They had apartments, one above the other. They gave us one of the apartments. We didn't stay in any hotels. We traveled on the hospitality of the gay community.

There was one colorful fellow in Charlotte, North Carolina. We located him because he was listed in a gay guide as some sort of gay organization. We went to the address, and it was the man's house. He was very nice, but kooky. There was no gay organization there. He had himself listed in one of those national guides so he could make pickups. People would come into town, and he'd be the first one to meet them. Of course, we didn't get into any compromising situation with this guy, but everything he did was wild and wacky. He had a get-together for us. We invited everybody from the town we could talk to. We went to the bars. We worked the crowd. "Come to Tom's house Saturday afternoon." Some people came. There was a woman there. She must have been eighty years old. She made us a great big bowl of potato salad, at least twenty pounds of potatoes. Everybody was telling us about how sixty years earlier, she had hacked her sister to death with a hatchet. Those are the sort of things you remember.

It was a different world from New York. New York was, for a gay activist, such an extreme. It was an intense, exciting place. You can't undervalue the moral support of the group—people sharing common commitments in a hostile world, a world where you were confronting prejudice. But it was so important to go into a place where nothing was happening yet. We wrote long reports every day and sent them back to the people at GAA, because the intention was to continue to support the local groups' efforts directly and indirectly, through providing money, advice, literature, or whatever. Groups emerged very fast in some of those places. Some of them even called themselves GAA.

* * *

I HAD interrupted my college education to "join the revolution, to fight with my sisters and brothers in the street." When I left Columbia, my letter to the dean said basically that. I didn't return to Columbia to finish school until the fall of 1976.

Upon returning to Columbia, I reduced my activism to doing research and writing papers. At this point I had resolved I was going to finish my education. I wanted to become a lawyer. I devoted my energies to those pursuits.

By that time, the mid-1970s, the movement had started to turn direction. The National Gay Task Force, a national gay organization founded in 1973, and the *Advocate*, a gay newspaper, had sold a lot of people on the idea of gay respectability. It was an antiactivist type of gay theology. The idea of gay respectability was all right, but being antiactivist wasn't. Their more conservative, more Establishment approach was all right. I believed then, and I believe now, that the movement needs both activists and Establishment people. The activists make it possible for the more Establishment-oriented gays to gain entrée. The activists break down barriers that it would take the more conservative types years to do, if they could do it at all.

This more conservative trend grew for many reasons: the demise of the antiwar movement; the evacuation of Richard Nixon from the White House; and the general dissipation of the Left, which had really been held together by the antiwar movement. People were becoming more self-centered. The whole national psyche was changing.

I suppose that people had become tired of all of the activism and the confrontation tactics as a means of dealing with problems. Once the war was over, national sympathy for demonstrations abated. It was getting very difficult to get large numbers of people to come out and demonstrate. In 1970 or 1971 we were having demonstrations where we got three and four hundred people to show up. By the mid-1970s, we were having trouble getting fifty people.

I saw the changes in attitude dramatically when I returned to Columbia in 1976. When I was a student there in 1969 and 1970, the classroom was an exciting place because of the students. No matter what the professors said, somebody challenged them: All authority and tradition were subject to question. In the fall of 1976, I returned to the very same school, and when professors asked a question, just one hand would pop up: mine.

IN THE early years of GAA's activism, there was an awful lot of resentment from other gays over our tactics and our openness. People thought we should not be protesting against the antigay policies of the mayor. Their arguments were not really reasoned. They just thought we were going to make things worse, that public resentment would end up being directed at gays. Our own view was that it was important to bring to the surface the deep down anger and resentment that gays had against the repressive policies of society. It was a process whereby gays started to become aware of gay rights as a political issue. And it was part of the long process of achieving positive self-identification as gays and lesbians. We didn't let the negativism of other gays bother us. I think time has proven that we did the right thing.

The Old Timers

Barbara Gittings and Kay Lahusen

BY THE time of the Stonewall riot, Barbara Gittings and Kay Lahusen had been working as a team for eight years in what was then called the homophile movement. They represented a new wave in the struggle for gay rights, a younger, more vocal generation who overcame fear of exposure to lead public demonstrations as early as 1964. They were out in the streets years before most of the gay liberationists were out of high school.

By the fall of 1969, Barbara and Kay had become symbols of the past, "Establishment accommodationists," who, according to gay liberationists, represented everything that was wrong with the movement before the Stonewall riots. But unlike many of their friends from the homophile movement, Barbara and Kay had no intention of being dismissed. Instead, they became deeply involved in the newest phase of the struggle for gay rights, including the battle to convince the American Psychiatric Association to remove homosexuality from its list of mental disorders.

Barbara and Kay were vacationing on Fire Island, a gay resort off Long Island, when they first heard about the Stonewall riot.

Kay:

We had rented a lovely house that summer, along with some other women. When we came back into the city that September, I immediately started attending the meetings of a new organization called the Gay Liberation Front [GLF]. They were huge meetings. It was the best theater in town. This was the heyday of radical chic. These people were out there in million-dollar rags, each more far out than thou in terms of their leftist ideology. They were spouting stuff I had never heard before. And here I was, this plain Jane dinosaur out of the old gay movement. They didn't know me from anybody. Barbara and I would sit there in amazement. It was a whole new lingo of oppression. "Where are your blacks? Where are your Indians? Where are your women?" Every minority was oppressed.

Barbara:

They were attacking the movement for being mostly gay white males.

Kay:

There were endless guilt trips against the gay white males. These meetings were really wild.

Barbara:

Let's face it, for a lot of people who were not ready to be so angry about everything, GLF had limited appeal.

Kay:

It was a total emotional blowout at every meeting. It was like going through a catharsis every time. It was unlike anything we had ever seen, and it just came out of the blue! I was convinced that this was a Communist or a New Left plot. I even made an effort to investigate these people for taking over our movement. I think most of them were gay, but they had been tucked away in other leftist causes and suddenly saw the gay bandwagon as the one to hop on. There were still a few of us around from the old gay movement, but suddenly we were drawn into all this radical hoopla, with all these different factions and endless blowouts.

Even though I wasn't interested in advancing some leftist ideology, I went to GLF meetings because I always cared passionately about what happened to gay people. I certainly didn't think that this ideology would save the gay minority. They were pointing to Cuba and to Russia and constantly trying to make the good case for how great it would be under socialism and how our cause was really an economic cause. That we really needed to overthrow capitalism and have a socialist regime, and blah, blah, blah.

Barbara:

Suddenly, here were all these people with absolutely no track record in the movement who were telling us, in effect, not only what we should do, but what we should think. The arrogance of it was what really upset me.

I remember a meeting I attended, along with Frank Kameny and a gay activist woman from Philadelphia, as well as a couple of others, all of whom had long track records in the movement. Would you believe, the gay liberation people called us on the carpet during the meeting and asked us to explain who we were and what we were doing at a GLF meeting? They wanted to know, "What are your credentials?" It was incredible! For once, I think even Frank was dumbfounded. As if we owed them an explanation. The meetings were advertised as being open to everyone. I think I finally said, "I'm gay. That's why I'm here." It was outrageous.

Kay:

We were easy to pick out of the crowd because we didn't have on the right radical rags. We didn't have enough money to buy what all these leftists with no jobs somehow had the money for.

Barbara:

Maybe they didn't have anything serious to talk about that night, and they decided they would just try to zap these old-timer interlopers who were coming along and spoiling their game.

Kay:

But, of course, the new wave frequently tries to put the last wave out of business. Certainly, we had our differences with Del Martin and Phyllis Lyon at DOB [Daughters of Bilitis]. We had said to them, "You're over the hill. Your thinking is out of date." So GLF did the same to us.

Barbara:

We didn't do that in a public setting.

Kay:

But we took their magazine in a totally different direction, and they weren't happy with that. We thumbed our noses at them—almost.

Barbara:

Yes, but this was a very public attempt to discredit us. Anyway, right after Stonewall, GLF was the only game in town other than the

Mattachine Society, which seemed to some people to be rather slow to respond to the riots.

Kay:

Mattachine was so stuffy, and its day was over. These organizations seem to have a built-in life expectancy.

Barbara:

Mattachine wasn't up to managing a lively response to the Stonewall riots. GLF came in to fill the void.

Kay:

GLF was here today, gone tomorrow. Even they said, "We're just here as a catalyst to push things in another direction. We'll push this into a movement of the people, and we'll all be up front." It could be said that, in a sense, they did just that.

Barbara:

They got people out to picket at the Women's House of Detention on Sixth Avenue. They got them to picket for the Black Panthers. Finally a lot of people started saying, "Who's coming out for the gay cause? What are we doing for the gay issues? I'm going out for the blacks. I'm going out for the women. But what am I doing for myself?" Out of that kind of feeling was born Gay Activists Alliance [GAA].

Kay:

I was one of the original twelve members. GAA developed because we wanted a single-issue group. We didn't want somebody telling us we had to go out and picket for all these other causes. We also wanted a structured group. GLF was always chaotic. The GLF people, of course, said they had no leaders. That was part of their thing. We didn't want chaos. We wanted a structured group. So we decided on *Robert's Rules of Order*. We decided to have officers, elections, and all those standard things. GAA was almost totally political. Politics was everything. You had to have your meetings with the police, to put the squeeze on. Organize gays as a voting block. That was GAA's big thing.

We did all sorts of public protests. We lay in wait for Mayor

Lindsay to come out from the Metropolitan Museum and then stormed up the steps and got right in front of him and asked him embarrassing things. When the U.S. ambassador to the United Nations came out of some meeting and got in his big black limousine, I remember going crazy, rocking and beating on the limousine. He didn't know what was going on. He had never been besieged by a bunch of homosexuals before. But he had said something that got us going.

Leafleting was a lot of fun. I was the first to leaflet the men's department at Bloomingdale's. I stood just outside the entrance to the men's department and handed out leaflets that explained where the various political candidates stood on gay rights. Those uptown faggots, their minds were blown. They didn't know whether to take the pamphlets or not.

We did plenty of things, and I covered it all for the GAY newspaper. I was interviewing and writing news stories and taking pictures. I would confront politicians and say, "I'm with GAY newspaper. Where do you stand on . . . ?" I would dutifully write down their answers. I would even tape their answers, so I would be dead accurate. It was a very exciting time.

Barbara:

While Kay was very involved with GAA, I became involved in the American Library Association [ALA]. I'm not a librarian, but I've always had profound respect for the literature and what it says and doesn't say about us and for how it makes us feel about ourselves and how it makes other people feel about us. From the early days, when I first tried to find out what it meant to be gay and went to the library, I've been very much addicted to books. In my youth, would you believe, I had lots of time to spare, and I spent a lot of it going around to bookstores buying gay books. There were no gay bookstores then. I went to regular used bookstores and searched for gay titles. I amassed quite a collection before I found out that there were a couple of other people in the country who had far outdone me, and I abandoned my efforts.

In 1970 I was doing a gay radio news show once a week for fifteen minutes on WBAI in New York. One day I found a little notice in our box at the station saying that a group of gays had organized within the ALA, and they were meeting in New York, and were looking for others to join them. Books! Libraries! That rang bells for me. I went to a meeting of the group, and even though I wasn't a librarian, I was welcomed.

The purpose of the group was to raise gay issues, to get gay literature into libraries and into the hands of readers, and to deal with issues of discrimination against gay people in libraries. This last point was specifically open in wording, so it could mean either gays as library workers or gays as patrons.

At this meeting I learned that they were planning a big bibliography—everything ever written about homosexuality. That, of course, was going to take some time. What they needed was a short, manageable list of the most positive materials that could be distributed at the next small midwinter conference of the ALA.

Kay:

The important point is that all the positive materials fit on one legal-size flyer.

Barbara:

Letter size. At that point, it happened that from my reading I knew as much about the existing literature as anyone else in the group, even though I was not a librarian. So I helped put together that first list. I believe it had thirty-two entries. I couldn't afford to go to that particular conference, though, which was in January in Los Angeles.

The next big meeting was to be in Dallas in 1971. This time I attended. We gave the first gay book award at that meeting. We even got some money from our parent group in the ALA, the Social Responsibilities Round Table, to pay for the author's airfare to come to Dallas to accept the award in person. The book was called *A Place For Us*, by Isabele Miller, but the author's real name is Alma Routsong. When her book was later republished by one of the major publishers, the title was changed to *Patience and Sarah*.

During the conference in Dallas, we had a talk by Michael McConnell, a gay librarian. Michael had been promised a librarian job at the University of Minnesota in 1970, but was denied the job by the Board of Regents after they found out he and his lover had applied for a marriage license. It became a major court case. We also had a pair of talks under the charming title, "Sex and the Single Cataloguer: New Thoughts on Some Unthinkable Subjects," which was about the funny subject headings that gay materials were classified under at the time. We also had an expanded edition of the gay bibliography. This time it had a big "Gay Is Good" logo at the head, and it was printed on a legal-size sheet.

Barbara Gittings *(in print dress)* kissing author Alma Routsong at the
"Hug-A-Homosexual" booth at the American Library Association annual
conference in June 1971 in Dallas, Texas. *From left to right:* Israel
Fishman, cofounder of the ALA Social Responsibilities Round Table
Task Force on Gay Liberation; unidentified Task Force member; Barbara
Gittings; and Alma Routsong, winner of the first Gay Book Award
(1971). *(© Kay Tobin Lahusen)*

Kay:

Not only did we leaflet, we plastered the bibliography in elevators and
in the elevator waiting areas. We were very aggressive with them.

Barbara:

But that's not what really made the ALA sit up and take notice. None
of these activities drew the professional interest we thought they
would. So we did something that wasn't at all connected with libraries. It really made them sit up and take notice: We had the first ever
gay kissing booth.

Kay:

In the convention hall.

Barbara:

We were one of six self-created task forces that were formed to deal with neglected issues in librarianship. Each group was given a couple of hours to have a booth in the exhibit area. We could have devoted our turn to an exhibit of gay book jackets and handed out copies of the bibliography. But we decided to bypass books and show gay love, live! So we called it, "Hug a Homosexual." We stripped the booth down to the bare curtains and put up a sign, "Men Only" at one end, and "Women Only" at the other. We stationed ourselves, all four of us, under the signs, to give free same-sex kisses and hugs. Well, let me tell you, the aisles were jammed, but nobody came into the booth.

Kay:

A *Life* magazine photographer was there.

Barbara:

Two Dallas television stations sent camera crews. The lights were on, and all these people were jammed in the aisles, craning their necks to see the action, but nobody wanted to take part. I think people were intimidated. So we did the action ourselves. We kissed and embraced each other for two hours. We handed out copies of the bibliography. We called out encouragement. We kissed and hugged each other some more. Alma Routsong, the award-winning author, was an absolute peach. She and I were on the female end. And a couple of the men were on the other end. That really put us on the map.

Kay:

So there we were on the six o'clock news. The ALA people were livid. They said, "We have all these famous authors here, and all they cover is the kissing booth!"

Barbara:

They put us on again for the eleven o'clock news and again the next morning. This was *news!* It was wonderful. Our spirits soared! The booth had an important message that was useful in any arena; that gay people were no longer willing to be subject to a double standard. We should have the same right to express our affection publicly as heterosexuals have. No more, but no less. For 1971, our kissing booth was very bold.

Kay:

It was revolutionary.

Barbara:

We thought it was marvelous. It was a thrill. And the reaction, oh, they wrote about us in the library press for the next six months! We couldn't have asked for better free publicity. So then they knew who we were.

———

Barbara:

Besides the ALA, I was also very involved, along with many other people, in efforts to get the American Psychiatric Association [APA] to drop its listing of homosexuality as a mental illness. Psychiatrists were one of the three major groups that had their hands on us. They had a kind of control over our fate, in the eyes of the public, for a long time.

Kay:

You don't realize what it was like back then. They were the experts. They said we were sick, and that's what most people believed.

Barbara:

Because gay people were considered mentally sick, people turned to psychiatrists for answers to the question of homosexuality. What causes it? What can we do about it? How can we eliminate it?

Kay:

When we were spoken of, people wanted to hear what a psychiatrist had to say. They didn't care what we said. We had to change all that.

Barbara:

Religion and law were the other two groups that had their hands on us. So besides being sick, we were sinful and criminal. But the sickness label infected everything that we said and made it difficult for us to gain any credibility for anything we said for ourselves. The sickness issue was paramount.

Kay:

It was Frank Kameny who said that we had to proclaim, in the absence of valid evidence to the contrary, that we were not sick. And the burden of proof rested on those who called us sick.

Barbara:

Well, it made great sense to us that we shouldn't wait around for the experts to declare us normal. But in the early days of the movement, many gay people believed they were sick. And even those who didn't agree still felt that we had to wait for the experts to change their minds. Frank and others started to feel that we couldn't wait.

Our confrontation with the APA began in May 1970, when a large group of feminists and a few gays invaded a behavior therapy meeting at the association's convention in San Francisco that year. I wasn't there, but from what I understand, they disrupted the meeting and said, in effect, "Stop talking *about* us and start talking *with* us! We are the people whose behavior you're trying to change. Start talking with us!" Well, a lot of psychiatrists fled the room in horror, but a lot stayed and started talking with the people who had invaded the meeting.

Now, the APA's conference managers are very smart people. They were not about to let themselves get kicked year after year by some group that wanted to invade the association's meetings to get its message across. So the very next year they invited gay people to be on a panel called, "Lifestyles of Non-Patient Homosexuals," which we informally called, "Lifestyles of Im-Patient Homsexuals." They invited six gay people to be on a panel and then to be available at small roundtables for discussions. Well, this was an important recognition that there were gays who did not come for therapy. It wasn't a huge turnout, but it was successful.

Frank Kameny and I ran an exhibit at that convention called, "Gay, Proud, and Healthy: The Homosexual Community Speaks." We had a good corner location in the exhibit area. We had pictures of loving gay couples; a rack of literature, including a story about a confrontation with an antigay psychiatrist; and the word *love* in great big red letters. I'm sure that was the first time they had seen anything like that at an APA convention. Some people came and took literature; others made very obvious detours.

During the convention, a handful of gay psychiatrists talked to us informally. It turned out that for years there had been a kind of Gay Psychiatric Association—a Gay PA—meeting during the annual APA conference, but it was a very closeted affair. At the time they talked to us, some of these gay psychiatrists were beginning to talk about being more open and doing something within the APA.

The next year Frank Kameny and I were invited by a member of the APA who was interested in the subject of homosexuality to be on a panel, along with a couple of heterosexual psychiatrists, including Dr. Judd Marmor. The panel was called "Psychiatry, Friend or Foe to Homosexuals? A Dialogue." Kay said, "Look, you have psychiatrists on the panel who are not gay. And you have gays who are not psychiatrists. What you're lacking on the panel are gay psychiatrists—people who can represent both points of view. Why don't we try to get a gay psychiatrist?" Well, the moderator was perfectly agreeable. But he needed us to find somebody. I made a number of calls, but nobody was quite yet willing to be that public. They all feared damage to their careers.

Finally, I talked with this one man who said, "I will do it provided that I am allowed to wear a wig and a mask and use a microphone that distorts my voice." And that's what he did. He was listed in the program as "Dr. Henry Anonymous," which is what he requested. He was going to talk about what it was like to have to live in the closet because of the fear of ruining his career. To back him up, I wrote to all the other gay psychiatrists I knew and said, "Please send me a few paragraphs about what it's like to be a gay psychiatrist in the association. You do not have to sign it. I will read them at the APA convention."

It went off marvelously! The house was packed. Naturally, I think the anonymous psychiatrist was the main reason the house was packed. And, let's face it, given the man's physical size, there were people who were going to recognize him in spite of the microphone and wig. But he was willing to take that chance. He made a very eloquent presentation. Then I read the statements from the other psychiatrists, and that clinched it.

Kay:

Frank Kameny was absolutely against the mask. He wanted it to be up front.

Barbara:

I know, but it went off so well that Frank had to admit afterwards that it was a great gamble. Kay took a wonderful photograph of that panel, and you can see the smile on Frank's face.

Barbara Gittings *(left)* at the May 1972 convention of the American Psychiatric Association. With Barbara *(left to right)*: Frank Kameny, "Dr. Henry Anonymous," and Dr. Judd Marmor. *(© Kay Tobin Lahusen)*

I think that panel discussion jolted enough of the gay psychiatrists who were in the audience or who heard about it to feel they really should be doing something on a more formal basis. The result was the beginnings of an official gay group in the APA. Because I encouraged them and went to their meetings and helped them along, I like to think of myself as the fairy godmother of the gay group.

All of these efforts helped move the APA along much further and much faster on the issue of removing homosexuality from the listing of mental disorders and mental illnesses.

Kay:

This was always more of a political decision than a medical decision.

Barbara:

It never was a medical decision—and that's why I think the action came so fast. After all, it was only three years from the time that feminists and gays first zapped the APA at a behavior therapy session to the time that the Board of Trustees voted in 1973 to approve removing homosexuality from the list of mental disorders. It was a political move.

When the vote came in, there was a wonderful headline in one of the Philadelphia papers, "20 Million Homosexuals Gain Instant Cure." And there was a picture of me and a little interview. It was a front-page story. I was thrilled. We were cured overnight by a stroke of the pen.

From 1967, when I made my first public lecture to a straight audience, I had to deal with people's conviction that we were sick simply because they had heard some psychiatrist say so. The APA action took an enormous burden off our backs. We could stop throwing so many resources into fighting the sickness label and begin to devote some of that energy and money to other issues.

Kay:

Even the churches deferred to the shrinks. They abdicated totally. They didn't say we were immoral; they said we were sick. Now they just say we're immoral.

Barbara:

But at least that's arguable. The problem with the sickness label is that it's supposedly scientific and is therefore not subject to dispute. You can argue with people who say you're immoral because you can say that there are so many kinds of morality. There are no absolutes. Now that people don't have the sickness label, they're coming out with more basic reasons for being against us: "I don't like you." "I don't like the way you live." "I think you're immoral." "I think you're rotten." All of that is more honest than this "you're sick" nonsense.

Barbara:

Things have changed much more than I dreamed possible! The sheer growth of the movement in size and the variety of organizations is something I wouldn't have thought possible when I first joined the movement in 1958. I'm just thrilled that we have gay marching bands, gay choruses, gay outdoor groups, the Gay Games, and gay rodeos in addition to the standard political-action groups and legislative efforts. I love this proliferation of special-interest groups because in their way, every single one of them, even if it doesn't have very high visibility, is doing its little bit to advance the cause. These groups bring gay people together who start talking about their problems and eventually start talking about how they might solve them. It was how the movement got started in the first place.

Kay:

We're not involved to the degree that we used to be because we have to think a little bit more about money, keeping the house and all of that.

Barbara:

During the fifteen years that I was running the Gay Task Force in the ALA, I spent more than 50 percent of my time answering correspondence and helping set up our programs at conventions. It was all volunteer work. I have never received a cent, except occasionally for a speaking engagement. Even then I would tell people, "If you're going to give me money, fine, but it's going back into the movement." I make my living as a free-lance clerk typist, working mainly for a small tax-accounting firm, which I've done for eight years now.

Kay:

We've never been rich. We've always scrimped along. A lot of this furniture is secondhand and thrown together higgledy-piggledy from assorted places. Now that I sell real estate, I try to get something from every house I sell.

Eighty percent of my real estate business is gay. My latest crusade is to try to organize gay realtors in this area, the Delaware Valley. I've organized a little network within my own chain, and I've been the one gay realtor in the New York Gay Pride Parade for the last three years. There are other realtors in the parade, but they march with other contingents. I'm going to try to get a group behind me this year [1990] who march as realtors. But I told Barbara recently that I feel the life going out of me. Getting the realtors organized is my last crusade.

Barbara:

You know, it's been a ball. I love being part of a special people. I think gays are a special people. However much we may now blend into the woodwork, and however desirable it may be for us to have as few barriers and obstacles as possible so that we are more like other people, we will always be a special people. There is something innately different about us. I prize it. I value it. I think in our hearts most of us do. And I think it gives us that special bond that's very enriching to me. I just don't feel that same sense of community with straight people. Oh, sure, there are straight people I like, but I can't imagine

Barbara Gittings *(left)* and Kay Lahusen at the June 1988 Gay Pride Parade in New York City. *(© Kay Tobin Lahusen)*

not being gay. What would life have been like? Dull? Dismal? Decrepit?

Kay:

Come to think of it, there is something important still to be done. The gay retirement home. We're not actively working on that, but it is a twinkle in our eye.

Barbara:

I want a place where I can sit back in the rocker and say, "Do you remember when we picketed the White House in 1965?"

The Idealist
Randy Shilts

ACROSS THE country students took a leading role in the new gay liberation movement. They were, for several reasons, in a unique position to do so. They didn't have to worry about ruined careers, at least in the short term. Often far from home, they could avoid dealing with fallout from their families. And because universities and colleges had so dramatically changed during the 1960s, most students were in no danger of being expelled, unlike generations of students who preceded them. At the University of Oregon in Eugene, young firebrand Randy Shilts took up the cause as president of the school's Gay People's Alliance. Before long, Randy discovered that despite the advantages of time and place, he would nonetheless have to pay a harsh price for his very public life as a student gay rights leader.

Randy is now an award-winning journalist at the San Francisco Chronicle. He's the author of two books: The Mayor of Castro Street, a biography of Harvey Milk, San Francisco's first openly gay city supervisor, who was assassinated in 1978; and the best-selling And The Band Played On, a chronicle of the AIDS crisis.

Seated in an easy chair in the living room of his San Francisco home, his undiscriminatingly affectionate golden retriever at his side, Randy couldn't talk fast enough to keep up with his thoughts and constantly interrupted himself to make another point.

Stonewall happened three weeks after I graduated from West Aurora Senior High School in Aurora, Illinois. I grew up never hearing anybody talk about being gay. The one time I heard the word *homosexual* before I was eighteen was from my sociology teacher, who I admired beyond all other teachers. She was so neat, and she really liked me. She said, "Maybe they're not criminals. Maybe they're just sick." Then she stopped, realizing that what she had said was hopelessly radical, and added, "Well, at least that's what some people think." I'll never forget that because I knew so well by then that I was gay, but, of course, I was very self-alienated about it. And then to hear that opinion from somebody you admired; it was the most liberal thing that I'd ever heard. So I thought, "Gee, maybe I'm only sick."

I left Aurora the minute I could. At the end of 1969, I hitchhiked to the West Coast with a woman friend, who had mentioned that there were lots of bisexuals there. That was obviously a big incentive for me to go west. I was also a hippie, so I had long hair, smoked marijuana, listened to the Moody Blues, read Hermann Hesse, and spent time staring at the three-dimensional album cover of *Their Satanic Majesties Request.* That's a Rolling Stones album. You'd get stoned, stare at the cover, tilt it from side to side, and see little pictures of the Beetles in the corners.

I wound up in Portland, Oregon, and fell into the counterculture. I was very much a hippie, but I still couldn't bring myself to come out. It was this taboo I couldn't make myself violate. I had no links to my home or family, so I was independent. But I just couldn't bring myself to do it.

I HAD to work my way through college. My parents were pretty poor. Besides, they were conservative, and we were estranged for two or three years. So I worked and went to a community college in Portland for two years. It was in my second year that I came out. This takes a little explaining. I had my last heterosexual affair with one of my professors. One reason I had an affair with her was because in every one of her classes she would bring in people from the local Gay Liberation Front [GLF] to speak. This last heterosexual affair was just a ruse so I could meet other gay people. In the end, she terminated our relationship so she could go out with a woman for a while. She left me for a woman.

As I hoped, I met one of her friends in GLF. We talked, and in just one week I was able to put the whole gay thing in perspective, to shift it from being my problem to being society's problem. I was able to adopt the political analysis that, "Gee, I'm all right, it's society that's wrong."

About a week after I met this guy and was able to talk all this out, I was scheduled to give a lecture to my cultural anthropology class. I was going to be an anthropology major then. The subject was the Yanomami tribe—fierce warriors who live in the Amazon in Brazil. At the last minute I changed the lecture topic and invited all of my friends to come to the class. Then I invited two women and this guy from GLF to join me for a panel discussion. I introduced the panel to the class and said, "We are all gay and we're going to talk about what it's like to be gay in America." That was May 19, 1972. I told everybody in my life that day, except for my parents, who I told about a year later.

Everybody was great. Everybody was real cool. I only lost one friend, who was one of the guys I had a crush on. I think he had his own closet issues that he was dealing with. But other than that, it was easy. Everybody was very accepting. I didn't have any traumas or anything.

The next fall I moved to Eugene and went to the University of Oregon. I became totally involved in the gay movement and was president of the Gay People's Alliance there—one of the oldest gay campus groups in the country. The official name was Eugene Gay People's Alliance at the University of Oregon.

We did lots of things in the Gay People's Alliance. We had rap sessions, which were crucial for me in terms of integrating a positive self-image. These sessions were like the women's consciousness-raising groups—real intensive talking. Sometimes we had speakers like Del Martin and Phyllis Lyon come up from Los Angeles and San Francisco. We also joined the antiwar marches, even though there wasn't much of a war left by then. We had meetings every Tuesday night. The first meeting of every semester would be packed with up to a hundred people (about 90 percent men) because everybody would come to see who else was gay. And then about 80 percent would disappear back into the woodwork.

The next year I was elected to a five-member student committee that gave out over a million dollars of students' incidental fees to the campus student organizations. Then I was elected chairman of the committee. My slogan was "Come Out for Shilts." It was obviously a gay thing. Straight people didn't get it.

When I was elected committee chairman, I became the number-two person in the student government after the student-body president. Because of my position I was able to give money to the Gay People's Alliance, which was the first time it got money from the student government. Then we did things like have a gay pride program with speakers. We also put on the first gay dance at the University of Oregon, a gay-straight sock hop. It was all sixties music and Motown. We allowed straight people—you know, we were very liberal.

ONCE I understood being gay in a political context, it all fell into place almost right away. When I ran for student government, I could say to myself, "I am running because I want to show that gay people can live openly, that they don't have to hide." I was very assertive about the fact that we didn't have to stay in the closet. You could be well adjusted, healthy, and out front. I made the decision in 1972 that I never wanted to live a day of my life having to hide being gay.

Everybody I knew who was gay was just like me, up front about it. But even though I was up front, it was an article of faith that you didn't hassle people who weren't. Coming out was a personal choice. You didn't force people out. You didn't hassle them if they didn't have the courage to come out. My feeling is that not coming out is an act of moral cowardice. Sure, it's a hassle, and I can understand all the reasons why you shouldn't come out, but I think it's cowardly.

At the time, I figured that once people knew you could come out of the closet, everybody would come out. It just made such perfect sense to do it. I was sure that the only reason people hadn't come out was because it hadn't crossed their minds before. This belief reflected nothing but my naïveté. I was surprised and disappointed when people didn't come out.

BY THE time I got to the University of Oregon, I was going to write great novels. But I couldn't write a simple declarative sentence because when you're an English major, they don't teach you how to write; they teach you how to read. So I took a journalism class in my fourth year of college just to learn grammar. It turned out that I was very good at it, if I do say so myself. I stayed in school an extra year and got my degree in journalism. After that first journalism class, I wouldn't take anything else. I could have graduated Phi Beta Kappa if I had taken one more science course. But I wouldn't take another science course because I was just so excited about journalism, and I was so good at it.

I got my first journalism award in November 1974—a William Randolph Hearst Award for a story about drag queens in Portland. My subject was the court system,* the Empress stuff, which originated in Portland in 1959. I always wanted to write about gay topics because I thought this was important to furthering the rights of gay people. I figured all you had to do was get the facts out about gay people, and they would speak for themselves. I still believe that, but I was never into advocacy journalism. I just feel you can put both sides out there, and the truth will win out in the end.

I received a second Hearst Foundation Award for a story about discrimination against gay people. It was a dramatic story for which I interviewed all kinds of closet cases—prominent people in Portland and Seattle, who had to conceal who they were.

I worked real hard at school and got more journalism awards than

---

*The court system got its start in 1959 when bars in Portland, Oregon, elected the city's most popular drag queen "Empress." By the time Randy wrote about the court system in the early 1970s, the coronations of the Empress and her court had become major fund-raising events in cities across the country. The money raised at these events was donated anonymously to local charities, most of which never would have accepted the money if the contributors had identified themselves.

any other person in ten years at the University of Oregon. I got tons of awards. I got great grades. And I was managing editor of the campus newspaper. I'd also been very out front about being gay. A number of people told me that it was really going to hurt my career. My teachers were concerned. Graduate student types were blunt: "You can't do this. You'll never have a career." I was real adamant that I was going to be out front. Once you come out, especially in the public way I did, you can't go back in the closet. It wasn't an option.

So in 1975, when I was about to graduate, I couldn't get a job anywhere. I sent my résumé out everywhere, and people who didn't have grades as good as mine, who didn't have my awards, who hadn't done as much on the campus newspaper, were getting job offers. But I wasn't. It was just so clear that it was discrimination. What's so unfair is that I had this incredible ambition, and I was willing to work like fucking crazy.

At the time I was trying to find work, I was selected to take part in a national writing competition. Because I had won those two awards from the Hearst Foundation, I was rated one of the top eight college journalists in the United States when I graduated. The eight of us participated in this national writing championship, and I won second place. The Hearst people brought us to San Francisco for the awards ceremony. Afterwards, I took everybody out to a real hot gay disco in North Beach. This was 1975. Everybody had a wonderful time. These were people from Indiana University, the University of North Carolina, and places like that, so for them it was real exciting. Boy, they went to a gay bar!

When the Hearst people heard about it, they freaked out. A few weeks later, they took away my award. That was devastating. And they canceled the thousand-dollar award check before I could cash it. They said they made a judging error, which to this day they maintain was the case.

I got real depressed. It was devastating because it was so unfair. I knew I was good, and I knew I'd do well in this field because I liked it so much and found it so exciting. It was also devastating because I realized then that I wasn't going to be able to get a staff job, which meant I was going to have to make it as a free-lancer. I swore when I got out of college that I'd never make a penny except through my writing. I had so many friends who had become waiters to make money until they got their first job in journalism. A year or two after they graduated, they were still waiters. So I said to myself, "Well, I'll be broke if I have to, but I will make money only by writing." That was my resolution, and I stuck to it.

I moved to Portland and free-lanced for some publications there and then for the *Advocate*, which was a gay newspaper based in Los Angeles. Also, I free-lanced for a friend from college who was a year ahead of me and was the editor of a community newspaper, a shopping advertiser. I covered the dump-commission hearings, planning-commission hearings, and things like that for thirty-five dollars a shot. I was in Portland for six months, but it wasn't working out because there just weren't enough publications to write for. Then I moved down here to San Francisco and continued writing for the *Advocate*. They wouldn't give me a job, but they more or less assured me that I'd get to do about six hundred dollars a month worth of stories. So I devoted myself to writing exclusively for the *Advocate*, and within five months, in April of 1976, I became a staff writer for them. Even though I wasn't working in the mainstream press, which is what I'd always wanted, at least I was covering stories I liked. Plus, it was a great training ground.

So here I was, writing for this publication that had all these dirty classified ads in it. I couldn't even send it to my parents because it was filled with "Gay white man wants somebody to piss on." It was so embarrassing. Occasionally, I'd send my parents stories I was proud of, but I'd always paste them onto something, so they wouldn't see the dirty ads on the other side.

Sometimes I go back and read the little diary fragments I wrote back then. What's really striking about 1976 through 1978 is the ambition and the rage. I was real ambitious. It was never a question of whether I was going to make it because I knew I was. I just worked around the clock and every day of the week. I was always free-lancing something. But there was also this anger, this rage, this horrible rage. At the beginning I was angry at this big, nebulous "them"—all the places where I couldn't get work. My anger became more specific as time went on.

I GOT my big break in February 1977. KQED, the public television station in San Francisco, had a show called "Newsroom," which was a nightly news show like "The MacNeil/Lehrer NewsHour." They wanted to start covering gay stuff. They were going to be the first because nobody covered gay stories. San Francisco's daily papers, the *Chronicle* and the *Examiner*, never covered gay stuff; neither did TV stations. It was like gay stuff didn't even exist. KQED wanted somebody who was openly gay, somebody who they could say was gay in a press release, because they knew it would be good press. And it was. After I was hired, the story went out on the Associated Press wire. The *St. Paul Pioneer Press*, which won the Pulitzer Prize for their AIDS coverage a few years back, ran an article with the headline, "Homo Hired to Be TV Reporter." I saved that clip.

So I got the job even though I had a horrible voice. I'm not really meant for TV. Well, working for KQED was just *the* thing. It was a free-lance job, but I thought I had arrived. The ratings for the show were miserable, but news junkies were into it. My first story was about Harvey Milk in February 1977. Harvey Milk was an openly gay candidate for San Francisco's Board of Supervisors. By that time I knew one thing about him: He was just going to be the best story. He was a character and he was going to win, but he also articulated a vision about gay rights. He was an idealist. He was a visionary in the true sense of the word, a human being who embodied an idea, which you don't get very often. At the same time, Castro Street* was so fucking exciting. It was just so exciting to be gay and be on Castro Street. The new way of being gay was coming from Castro Street. We were going to create a new world!

The new way of being gay was to be open, not to hide, of being powerful and asserting your power. When gangs came in to beat us up, we organized our own street patrols. We weren't going to be the sissies anymore. Being butch was the new way. It was a total recasting of what it meant to be gay in America. And we were doing it on Castro Street. Everybody else in the gay world was following us. We created it, and everybody was following us. We were the mecca. It was so heady. There was this incredible provincial egotism that came from being in San Francisco back then.

I knew this was so fucking important, but nobody was really covering this story in the mainstream press. They'd cover the news stuff, like when Harvey Milk was elected supervisor, but that was about it.

Around this time I tried to get a full-time job in mainstream print journalism. I applied to the *Chronicle* and the *Examiner,* and everywhere. Nobody would hire me. The *Chronicle* let me do free-lance stuff, but there were union rules that kept me from doing local stories. So I'd think of all kinds of creative ways to get around the guild's rules. I really wanted to write for the *Chronicle.* I really wanted to be in the mainstream and be back in print.

Then I started applying to TV stations. My voice wasn't great, but I was such a good reporter. I was better than a lot of people because I was smarter. I was a good TV journalist because I came from a print background. But I couldn't get a job. One closeted lesbian news

---

*Castro Street is the main commercial street in the predominantly gay Castro neighborhood in San Francisco. By 1977, most of the shops, bars, and restaurants on Castro were owned and operated by gay people.

director at a TV station flatly told me that she couldn't hire me because people would change stations if they saw somebody on TV who was public about being gay. I was just stunned. When I was at KQED, I never went on TV and talked about being gay. When *Newsweek* did a story on gays in San Francisco, they'd quote me and say that I was gay, but I never went on TV and said, "I'm a homosexual. I'm doing this report." I was always thoroughly professional, but that's the kind of shit I came up against.

My break in commercial television came in 1978 after Harvey Milk and Mayor George Moscone were murdered.* I was offered a job at KTVU, Channel 2, a week after the riot at City Hall. KTVU needed somebody to explain what was going on, so they let me free-lance for them. I did that for about a year, until I was in an article in a short-lived local magazine about the ten most eligible gay bachelors in San Francisco. I was number two after Armistead Maupin.† The news director saw the article, freaked out, and told my best friend at the station that it was a disaster for my career. He said that it was one thing to be gay, but that you shouldn't talk about what you want in a boyfriend. What else are you supposed to talk about when you're selected a "most eligible bachelor"? In the article I said that he'd better like rock and roll and the Rolling Stones. The news director stopped using me as a free-lancer.

This is where the big despair hit. KTVU stopped using me, and then a few months later, in August 1980, the KQED news show got canceled. That's when I wrote the book about Harvey Milk, *The Mayor of Castro Street*. I didn't have anything else to do! Nobody would hire me! By then I had been on TV three and a half years. At Channel 2 I had been nominated for a local Emmy for a story I did on the children of Nazi holocaust survivors. At least 60 percent of my work had been on nongay stuff. I did a lot on City Hall, a lot of political stories. I did lots of human-interest stories, social issues. But nobody would hire me. I couldn't get a job. By then it was just so clear. I was *so* good and *so* qualified. I was free-lancing for *California* magazine and for the *Village Voice*. I was free-lancing for major publications, but I couldn't get a staff job anywhere.

Despite the despair, I never thought about killing myself. That never crossed my mind. I was just going to have to work harder. I

---

*Harvey Milk and Mayor George Moscone were murdered at San Francisco City Hall by former city supervisor Dan White in November 1978. White was later convicted of voluntary manslaughter, which brought a maximum of seven years, eight months in prison. The announcement of the verdict sparked a riot by thousands of outraged gay San Franciscans at City Hall. The police countered with an attack on gay people on Castro Street.
†The best-selling author of a series of novels set in San Francisco.

always knew I was going to make it, even though by then I was drinking a lot. I was also a daily marijuana smoker—marijuana was my drug of choice. Nonetheless, I managed to do the Harvey Milk biography, and just a few weeks after I finished it, the city editor at the *Chronicle* hired me. He had been there maybe a year. He loved TV people and loved the show I worked for at KQED. That was in August of 1981. I was the first openly gay news reporter to be hired at a mainstream newspaper anywhere in the country. The timing was ironic because this new gay disease had been detected just weeks before.

Mother and Child

Jeanne Manford and Morty Manford

A REMARKABLE sight confronted spectators at New York City's second annual Christopher Street Liberation Day parade in June 1972. A simply dressed middle-aged woman was carrying a sign that said, "Parents of Gays: Unite in Support for Our Children." No one watching the parade had ever seen anything like it before. For most gay people, who had yet even to tell their parents they were gay, such open support was almost beyond belief.

Jeanne Manford, an elementary school teacher and mother of gay rights activist Morty Manford, didn't think she was doing anything remarkable. She loved her son and believed he deserved her full support. But the experience of the march and the constant telephone calls from gay men and women and their parents in search of help made it clear to Jeanne and her son that there was more to be done than simply show support. They decided there was also a pressing need for an organization for parents of gay children.

Jeanne and Morty live in the Flushing, Queens, home where Jeanne and her late husband, Jules, raised their two children. The house is just down the block from P.S. 32, the elementary school that she and her children attended and where Jeanne has taught for the past twenty-five years.

Now in her sixties, Jeanne Manford looks as if she stepped out of central casting for the role of an elementary school teacher. She is small, gray haired, and well groomed. Jeanne is soft spoken, even shy, but her self-effacing manner conceals a will that has served her well both in the classroom and in the gay rights movement.

Jeanne:

When Morty was around fifteen, he asked if he could go to a psychologist. I couldn't believe he had problems, because he was always a leader. He always had a lot of friends. He had parties here. He was president of his student organization in his junior high. One of his teachers told me, "Send him to the best colleges. He's going to be a senator someday." When he said he needed help, both my husband and I said, "You think so? Sure, why not?" But we didn't know why.

We later found out when the psychologist told us that Morty was gay. My initial reaction was to tell Morty that I wanted him to be happy and that whatever made him happy was fine with me. Morty was no different from the way he'd been the day before. I didn't look at him in a different light. I was very naive; I didn't understand society's condemnation.

Morty:

My father's initial reaction was to be quiet. He had a lot of thinking to do. He didn't say anything critical, but he just decided he had to think about it. I think he harbored a hope that things would change.

Within a year and a half, I became very involved in the gay liberation movement and was bringing friends home from the Gay Activists Alliance. We would sit down and talk with my parents about our civil rights demonstrations. These friends from the organization would speak with my parents, which was particularly helpful to my father. My father later commented that it was difficult for him to examine his attitudes by talking to me alone because there was a lot of emotional involvement. But as he started to speak to some of my friends, who had this heightened sense of gay consciousness, he felt he could consider the issues and the societal biases from a more detached and dispassionate view. That helped him reexamine his old attitudes.

Jeanne:

I remember one night I got a phone call from the police at 1:00 A.M. "Your son is arrested."

Morty:

I was in the police station, and the officer made the phone call. I remember that he went out of his way to say, "Your son has been arrested. And you know, he's homosexual."

Jeanne:

I think my reply was something like, "Yes, I know. Why are you bothering him? Why don't you go after criminals and stop harassing the gays?"

Morty:

I couldn't hear what my mother said, but the officer was scratching his head after he put down the phone. He had just been zapped.

Jeanne:

I worried about Morty. I knew he could be hurt physically. That was always in the back of my mind, although I tried not to think about these things. I believed Morty had a right to do what he was doing. I didn't think he did anything unlawful. I believed he was being harassed. But I worried—there was one time when Morty did get hurt. That was in April 1972. He had been at the Hilton Hotel, giving out leaflets to the Inner Circle.

Morty:

The Inner Circle was and still is an annual get-together of politicians and the political press in New York City. It's organized by the City Hall reporters. They do skits and have a big dinner and give speeches to each other.

I was handing out leaflets to protest media oppression, including an editorial that had run in the *Daily News* about a week before this dinner. The editorial commented on the refusal by the U.S. Supreme Court to consider an appeal by Mike McConnell, who was denied a job at the University of Minnesota because he was gay. McConnell had already been promised a librarian's job, but after the Board of Regents found out that he and his lover had applied for a marriage license, the job disappeared. The *Daily News* editorial was entitled, "Any Old Jobs for Homos?" The lead sentence was, "Fairies, nances, swishes, fags, lezzes, call 'em what you please." And then it went on to say some obnoxious things about gays. It was outrageous.

We went to the dinner to distribute leaflets to people in attendance, many of whom were good people who were supportive of gay rights and had welcomed our arrival. However, there were thugs in attendance who were guests at the dinner, and they proceeded to physically attack six of us. A number of us, including me, ended up hospitalized.

I was beaten up by Michael May, the president of the firemen's union. The guy was a Golden Gloves boxing champion. He punched and kicked me. I didn't have any broken bones or internal injuries, but it was a bad beating. I was on painkillers for a week. At the trial that followed, although everybody identified him as my assailant, he wasn't convicted.

Jeanne:

I had a call from the hospital. I was furious. I remember thinking, *What right have they got to assault my son and the others? Why didn't the police protect them? What kind of a police force do we have in New York?* Then I sat down and wrote a letter to the *New York Post*. This was long before Rupert Murdoch owned it. I mentioned that my son was gay and that the police stood by and watched these young gays being beaten up and did nothing. And it was printed. Then Morty called me up and said, "You can't believe how everybody's talking about your letter!" I didn't think anything of it, but I guess it was the first time a mother ever sat down and publicly said, "Yes, I have a homosexual child." I was never quiet about having a gay son. I'd tell strangers; I didn't care. I figured this was one way to educate people.

At one point, my name was in the *New York Times*. The principal of my school told me that parents were complaining because my name was on the front page of the *Times*. She asked if I would be more discreet. I said, "Look, my professional life is one thing. And my private life is another, and I'll do as I please." She never bothered me again.

Morty:

I thought my mom was terrific! On one level, her reaction and concern and involvement seemed very natural for a parent. What I thought was extraordinary was that other people weren't doing the same thing at that time. She's a unique person.

Jeanne:

My family was important. I loved Morty. I've always felt that he was a very special person. I'm very shy, by the way—I was not the type of person who belonged to organizations. I never tried to do anything. But I wasn't going to let anybody walk over Morty.

Morty:

A lot of parents who knew their children were gay felt their families were important to them. But the question is, what was there about our family? I would have to say that we were always very open thinkers, that my parents would not simply reject something out of hand. They understood, especially following discussions that we had and the discussions they had with my friends, that this was an area they really didn't understand. There was a lot of ignorance, but they were willing to consider, "What are the prejudices we were taught?" And this was the right time, too. We had all learned a great lesson from the black civil rights movement of the early sixties and from the women's movement. I think my parents agreed that demands for civil rights for blacks and women were just. This was simply bringing a new civil rights perspective into the discussion.

Jeanne:

Also I felt that the love in my own home was more important than what others thought about me. I didn't care what my neighbors said. They had their problems. If they had to talk about me, that was their problem.

The next step was that I was asked to be on a television show in Boston.

Morty:

The three of us went. This was within a week or two after my mother's letter was published in the *Post*.

Jeanne:

There was another couple on that show with a daughter who came in from California.

Morty:

Many TV programs and radio shows followed. We went out to Cincinnati. At one point my parents appeared on a TV show in New Orleans. They went to Detroit. Some shows we did together, and some they did on their own.

Jeanne:

We were in Toronto one time. Morty's father spoke on television. They already had a mother, so they didn't use me. They put his makeup on, and suddenly the stage was dark. I turned to the producer and I said, "Why is it dark? Why aren't their faces showing?" I was told to be quiet. So I sat in the audience and was very angry. I said, "Why do you have to put their faces in shadow when these people are willing to talk publicly?"

Jeanne:

Not long after Morty was beaten up, he came to me and said, "Will you march in the Gay Pride Parade with me?" I said, "I'll march if you let me carry a sign. What good does it do to have another person marching unless they know why you're marching?"

Morty:

The sign said, "Parents of Gays: Unite in Support for Our Children."

Jeanne:

My husband was a ham-radio buff at the time. The day of the march, he had his field day, so he didn't go. So Morty and I went without him. As we walked along, people on the sidewalks screamed! They yelled! They ran over and kissed me, and asked, "Will you talk to my mother?" We had so much of that. "Wow, if my mother saw me here. . . ." They just couldn't believe that a parent would do this. There were, of course, other parents there, but they weren't visible.

Morty:

When people started cheering as we were coming by, did you think it was for you at first?

Jeanne:

No, because Dr. Spock was walking in back of us. I thought they were cheering him. After all, he was well known. But more and more people crowded around me and spoke to me.

Morty:

We marched shoulder to shoulder. It was a great experience. The outpouring of emotion from our own community was overwhelming. No one else got the loud emotional cheers that she did.

Jeanne:

We learned that they were fearful of telling their parents. And many had been rejected because their parents knew. I guess they didn't feel that any parent could be supportive of a gay child.

Jeanne Manford *(carrying sign)* and her son, Morty Manford *(to her left)*, marching in New York City's Christopher Street Liberation Day parade in June 1972. Dr. Benjamin Spock is behind and to the left of Morty. *(© Les Carr)*

Morty:

We are the only minority whose parents do not share our minority status. In other words, a black child who is fighting for civil rights is going to have his parents share that issue with him. Because of the importance of family to all of us, being estranged from your parents is a very traumatic thing. Being forced to closet your life from them is very devastating. The symbolic presence that my mother provided was a sign of great hope that parents could be supportive, that the people we're closest to, whom we love the most, need not be our enemies. I think the desire on the part of gays to share their totality as people, as gays and lesbians, was very much the reason why the parents have always gotten such an overwhelming response.

Jeanne:

As Morty and I walked along during that first march, we were talking about starting some kind of organization. So many people said, "Talk to my parents." Then later there were the phone calls—all day long my phone was ringing. So that's really where it began. We decided during the march that a parents' group might be a good idea.

Each parent thinks, *I'm the only one who has a child who is homosexual*, and nobody was willing to let anyone else know about it. An organization was needed so parents could talk to each other and know that they were not the only ones. So they could get together and say, "Look, there's nothing wrong with them. It's just a different way of life."

Morty:

In addition, it would be an organization that would support the struggle for gay liberation.

Jeanne:

Actually, we envisioned the parents' group as a bridge between the gay community and the heterosexual community. My thinking was, *Someday we will fight for the rights of our children. We will become political. We will have a national organization.* I remember thinking that at the beginning. But the immediate thing was to talk to parents and help them come to terms with the fact that they had a gay child and that this was nothing to be ashamed of.

Morty:

My mother participated in a panel discussion hosted by the Homosexual Community Counseling Service. Among the other panelists was a minister from the Metropolitan Duane Methodist Church in New York City.

Jeanne:

I told him we were interested in starting a group. He said, "You can use my church."

Morty:

He was on the side of gay rights. In fact, he was, I think, separated from his wife. He had some grown children and had been involved sort of peripherally with the Mattachine Society for many years. But he didn't tell us he was gay at first. He was simply being supportive of the parents groups. He was an ally with a vested interest—the best kind.

Jeanne:

We had the first meeting at the church. I think there must have been eighteen or twenty people.

Morty:

I handled the nuts and bolts of publicizing it. I placed an advertisement in the *Village Voice*. I also coordinated everything with Barbara Love, a respected lesbian writer at that time. You may recall, she and her lover Sidney Abbott wrote a book, *Sappho Was a Right-On Woman*. In those days we were very sensitive to the need for men and women to be working together, that nothing we did should be done solely from a gay male point of view. It was very important that Barbara was one of the organizers of this effort. She was able to reach out to the lesbian community as I reached out to the gay male community in an effort to publicize this meeting. We asked everybody to let their parents know we had a place for them to come.

Jeanne:

It was a nice turnout of parents for the first meeting. Gay people also came without parents. There was a young man from Ames, Iowa, who came from a big family. His father and brothers would go hunting, but he was never interested. He had a hard time until a teacher told him to get away from there and go to the big city.

I guess I did most of the talking, with the help of my husband, who was an articulate person. He was a much better speaker than I. He was right along with me on everything.

Morty:

Let me just bring things full circle with my father. By the time of this meeting, in March 1973, my father had been fairly well educated about gay issues. He had made the comment to me, "I understand intellectually that this is a civil rights issue, that we've been imbued with prejudices. I still have a lot of those prejudices deep in my gut because after so many years it's hard to get rid of them." I, of course, realized that he was facing his own upbringing and was making a conscious effort to change. So at these meetings he understood the processes that the parents were going through in coming out of their closets, facing the values that they'd been taught by society and grappling with the emotional impact they had. Thereafter he marched in parades regularly and spoke openly and became a great supporter of the gay rights movement.

Jeanne:

During this time, I got so many calls and letters—so many. Many people who called were crying. They were upset because they had a child who was homosexual. I told them to come to a meeting and talk. At the meetings they would tell me how much I had helped them on the phone.

You know, some of the meetings made me feel pretty good. A couple would come over to me after a meeting and say, "We were on the verge of divorce, blaming each other. We feel differently now." There was one man, who was a prison warden upstate in a small town, and he started to cry because he had abused gay people and then discovered that his son was gay. He was quite upset when he realized what he had done.

Morty:

It was not so much what my mother said, but that she said it. I remember her saying many times, "There's nothing wrong with your son being gay or your daughter being lesbian. We've been taught by society that there's something wrong, but society has been wrong." People had never heard this before. To hear it from another parent, a peer, had an especially compelling effect. They expected to spend the phone conversation in tears with someone at the other end saying, "Now, now, dearie," but that's not what they got.

Jeanne:

You don't just believe everything you're told by society. Society could be wrong. I guess that was a revolutionary thing to say because they put me in the revolutionary calendar the following June.

Morty:

There was a calendar that somebody published, which I picked up over on St. Mark's Place that next year. For each month it had a picture marking some occasion. For example, for the month of Mao Zedong's birthday, there was a picture of Mao. There was a picture of Martin Luther King, Jr., during his birthday month. And for June, guess who the calendar girl was?

Jeanne:

Before Morty turned to June, I said, "This is not a true revolutionary calendar unless there is something about the gay march—about gays—for the month of June." And when I turned the page, there was my picture.

The irony, of course, is that I considered myself such a traditional person. I didn't even cross the street against the light. After all, although I didn't like McCarthy, I never considered myself a Communist, either.

Jeanne:

At some meetings we had only three or four people. It was very slow at the beginning. But we always felt that if we helped one person, it was worth the effort.

A few months after we started meeting, a woman named Sara Montgomery called me. She was seventy-five or seventy-six at that time. She told me the story of her son in California, who, because it was discovered that he was gay, had lost his job and then committed suicide with his lover. She came to a meeting and talked a great deal. Of course, she upset some people because of the story, but the gay people really loved her. For a couple of years during the marches, she was one of the guest speakers. She spoke very well, and I used to say to her, "Sara, why don't you write a book or put it on tape?" but she never wanted to do it. She's gone just over a year now. She lived to be over ninety.

I remember when Sara and I and Morty's father went to a protest in front of a hotel, where the mayor was speaking. We were in so many marches that I'm not exactly sure what this one was about. But somebody was heckling nearby, and my husband turned around and said something. At that time he had had a stroke and carried a cane. He picked up his cane and was ready to hit the heckler over the head.

Morty:

I was handing out leaflets. This man pushed my hand aside in a very rude way. He and I started to exchange words; it was a verbal confrontation. He acted like he was going to be violent. All of a sudden a few people gathered around, and I looked up over this bigot's shoulder where I saw my father's stick hovering above the guy's head waiting for him to make a move. My father thought, as the rest of us did, that this guy was on the verge of starting a fistfight with me. But it never came to that. There my father was, disabled, carrying a cane, and he was going to protect *me*. You know, the family that marches together stays together.

Jeanne:

I remember another time, at the start of the gay pride parade, when Morty and I were on Christopher Street at Sheridan Square. We were standing in the street, and a policeman came over and said to get on the sidewalk. And I automatically did. Then I saw that Morty was still standing there in the gutter, and I said to myself, *I'm a law-abiding citizen! I pay my taxes! The nerve of him!* This was going through my head. I got off the curb and stood there in the street with Morty and I stared at the policeman. I was just so angry.

Morty:

The cop turned and walked away.

———————

Jeanne:

I was very involved for many years, but since the death of my husband in 1982, I've found it difficult to travel into Manhattan, and I don't like coming home at night. I also feel there are stronger people than I, people who speak very well. At this stage I'm not needed, except if someone calls me for help.

Morty:

I think people like my mother have been particularly effective because the general public will listen to parents in a different way than they will listen to advocates who are gay. A lot of people can identify with parents. They look at me and say, "There is a gay person; I'm not like him," and therefore they don't listen to what I'm saying as readily. For that reason, parents have been able to reach a lot of people faster than we would have been able to reach on our own.

To understand how important the parents' groups were and are, you have to remember that the parents' organization began at a time when the police were still raiding bars where gays went. Gays had no job protection in virtually any city of this country. And there was still the stigma of being gay. I used to be fond of saying, "The churches say we're sinners. Psychiatrists say we're sick. Capitalists say we're subversive. And Communists say we're immoral." Many gays accepted these prejudices, if only tacitly. There was no progay propaganda; the support wasn't out there. The emergence of the parents' group at this time provided much-needed progay propaganda for both gay and lesbian people, as well as for the general public.

Today when people are facing problems because they're gay or have gay kids, they have an alternative voice to turn to. In the early seventies those voices were very few and far between. That's why the parents' group was so important. It was one of the first progay voices.

Jeanne:

Morty, do you remember one time when you told me my picture was over a bar in Brazil?

Morty:

Somebody came back from Brazil and said he was in a bar and saw a big mural on the wall, with my mother marching.

Jeanne:

And another time my niece was taking a course in college, and she turned a page in a book and said, "Oh, that's my uncle and aunt!" We never knew whether we were famous or infamous.

The Good Doctor
Judd Marmor

WHEN THE *American Psychiatric Association's Board of Trustees voted to remove homosexuality from its list of mental disorders in late 1973, many commentators, from inside and outside the profession, claimed that the American Psychiatric Association had capitulated to extreme pressure from gay activists. Certainly, many gay men and women had exerted pressure, conducted protests, and made appeals in the three years leading up to the decision. But there were also respected psychiatrists within the organization who worked over the years to effect the change.*

One of these people was Judd Marmor, a Los Angeles psychiatrist and psychoanalyst, who began moving away from the prevailing sickness theory in the 1950s. Dr. Marmor was not willing, initially, to accept fully Dr. Evelyn Hooker's 1956 assertion that homosexuality was not a mental illness. Within a few years, however, he came to believe that the psychiatric profession was mistaken in its assessment, and by the early 1970s, he had become a leading voice in the campaign to reconsider the classification.

Dr. Marmor maintains his office in Westwood, an affluent neighborhood adjacent to UCLA. A vigorous eighty, he continues to see patients and to play tennis three times a week. He's a small man, trim, completely bald, and deeply tanned. Dressed in a well-tailored suit, Dr. Marmor pointed out his many awards on one wall of his office, particularly those bestowed by gay organizations.

After the war—World War II—I saw homosexual patients who wanted to change their sexual orientation. At that time I used to try to help them change. We all used to think in those days that psychoanalysis could cure everything, from chilblains to homosexuality. But I wasn't too successful. Some were able to function bisexually, but most of them remained gay. The gay men who came to see me were mostly in the literary field or in the show business field. They were intellectual; they were bright; they did not consider it a disgrace to be analyzed. All their straight friends were being analyzed, too—it was the thing to do in the fifties. I also saw a few lesbian women, but they were married and were mostly concerned with making their marriages work.

The gay men I saw were caught up, for the most part, in the common myth that it was bad to be gay and that, if they possibly could, they ought to try to be heterosexual. This was before the gay rights movement, you understand, and before gays thought in terms of coming out and functioning on their own, openly. So, although I didn't feel it was bad to be homosexual, I was sympathetic to their wishes to try to become straight if they could.

We did a lot of talking about what it took to *make* a girl, to win a girl, to seduce a girl, to participate in a mutual seduction. And we dealt with their anxieties, if they had any. Now, many of them were capable of functioning heterosexually, but they said, "It just doesn't feel the same to me. I just don't enjoy it as much." We went through the usual thing of trying to understand why they couldn't enjoy it. In those days we still assumed all explanations lay within the family dynamics. The fear of competing with the father. The incest barrier. Castration anxiety. God, we used to work that myth of castration anxiety! Not that people don't have castration anxiety, but I understand it in very different terms now. It's a symbol, not a fact. In those days we used to think it had a literal meaning—almost. My patients understood these things, but it didn't usually change matters for them.

I very quickly realized—since I wasn't judgmental about them being gay—that if I couldn't help them achieve heterosexuality, which they assumed they wanted, then my job was to help them accept their gayness and live effectively within that scheme of things. Usually, I ended up saying, "Look, there's nothing bad about being what you are. Just live your life and don't be ashamed of it, and let's deal with whatever your problems are within the context of your gayness." So early in my practice, even in the 1950s, I was working in that manner.

THE FIRST time I heard Dr. Evelyn Hooker state that homosexuality was not an illness, I wasn't prepared to go all the way. This was in 1956, when she presented her study of gay men. I was sympathetic to what she was saying, but I wasn't totally convinced. I still had a feeling that it was a developmental deviation, but I did not think that we ought to be judgmental about homosexuals. We were also making a lot of unwarranted assumptions about the so-called homosexual personality. But I still wasn't ready to assume that there was something other than a developmental deviation involved in it.

Now, I had met Dr. Hooker before she presented her study and liked her. So when I heard her making these statements about homosexuality, I saw her not as a stranger, but as a good friend whom I admired and whose work I knew and respected. I felt that there certainly was research to be done in that area, that we were taking a lot for granted that we didn't understand.

Within a few years, I began to work on my own book, the first of two books that I did on homosexuality. I came to write the book, or to *edit* it, because the publisher of Basic Books came to me and said he would like to publish something by me. He asked, "What would you like to do it about?" And I said, "I feel that my colleagues' views about homosexuality are wrong." He said, "Great! Let's do a book on that." So I did. The book is called *Sexual Inversion*, a title I hate. My publisher insisted that I have the word sexual in it. He wouldn't let me call it just *Homosexuality*, which I wanted to—that title had been preempted by too many other books. So we called it *Sexual Inversion: The Multiple Roots of Homosexuality*.

In that book I stated that it was hard to believe that people would be homosexual in the face of the enormous social opprobrium they had to live with, unless there were powerful developmental reasons for it. At the time, I still believed that. The research hadn't yet been done on the constitutional factors—not necessarily genetic, but intra-uterine, prenatal—that might create the predisposition to homosexuality.

I pointed out, though, that the assumption that homosexuality was an illness was based on a skewed sample because psychoanalysts saw only disturbed homosexuals in their offices. I said that if we made our judgments about the mental health of heterosexuals only from the patients we saw in our office, we'd have to assume that all heterosexuals were mentally disturbed.

One of the reasons I wanted to do this book was that I was appalled by the stereotypic generalizations being made about homosexuals in the various psychoanalytic meetings I was going to. I was still a young analyst, but I'd go to meetings and I'd hear about the homosexual personality and about the fact that homosexuals were vindictive and aggressive, couldn't have decent relationships, and were not to be trusted—all terribly nasty, negative, disparaging things. I knew gay men and women. This view just didn't make sense to me. I felt we were making generalizations about people who were really very different from one another, just as heterosexuals are. That's one of the points I attacked strongly in my book, that this stereotyping of a group really concealed a discriminatory prejudice. I don't think the word *homophobia* had yet been coined.

I stated that our attitudes toward homosexuality were culturally determined and influenced, which was a big step forward in the analytic profession. It was considered a relatively revolutionary statement, coming from a member of the American Psychoanalytic Association.

I got heat from my classical analytic friends, but at meetings of the American Psychiatric Association, psychiatrists began to come up to me and say, "Look, I want to tell you how much I appreciated your book. I'm gay." Gradually, I came to know a large number—much larger than I had known before—of gay men, particularly, but also some lesbians. My knowledge and experience of homosexuality, then, was broadened by precisely the thing that I had commented on in my book: the fact that psychoanalysts didn't know enough gay people outside the treatment community who were happy with their lives, who were satisfied and well adjusted.

WE HAD some very dramatic confrontations over this issue during the early 1970s. The gay liberation movement became very vocal and very assertive and began to appear at American Psychiatric Association meetings and demanded a voice. These were the days in which homosexuality was being treated by aversive therapy, by shock therapy, and things like that. The gay people were justly very angry at that. They demanded that they be given a session in which they could present their views. At this session I spoke on a panel with a number of other people. There was the head of the lesbian movement at that time, Barbara Gittings. Frank Kameny was there. Another psychiatrist was on the panel, from Philadelphia. He wore a mask and spoke into a microphone that concealed his voice and admitted that he was gay. This was an unheard-of thing. It was a very dramatic session with this fellow speaking with a grotesque mask on. And I spoke out very strongly.

Then, a year later we had an official debate, the debate about the *Diagnostic and Statistical Manual of Mental Disorders*, which listed homosexuality as a mental illness. On the platform representing various points of view were myself, Richard Green, Robert Stoller, Charles Socarides, and Irving Bieber. This was a very, very dramatic debate, which was attended by several thousand psychiatrists at one of the conventions of the American Psychiatric Association. I think, by and large, we won the debate.

At any rate, shortly after that, the debate got into the Board of Trustees of the American Psychiatric Association. Different points of view were presented, and the board made its decision. This was all detailed in a book by Ronald Bayer, *Homosexuality and American Psychiatry: The Politics of Diagnosis*. The only thing I disagree with Bayer on is that he assumes that the attitudes of the psychiatrists were developed under pressure from the gay community. That's not entirely true. I don't in any way want to minimize the importance of the gay liberation movement, but there were people like myself and Evelyn Hooker and others who were independently developing their views about the wrongness of our attitudes toward homosexuality. I think Bayer either didn't understand that or underplayed it.

After the Board of Trustees made its decision to remove homosexuality from the list of psychiatric illnesses, Socarides, Bieber, and others were furious. They were convinced that the majority of the psychiatrists in the profession would be aghast at this decision, so they forced a vote of the general membership. The board's decision had not been made by a vote, but after considerable scientific exploration. To the dismay of Socarides and Bieber, a majority of the psychiatrists voted to support the board's decision. The vote was 58 percent to 37 percent, with 3 percent abstaining. The remaining 2 percent didn't vote.

I wasn't totally surprised by the outcome, but I was a little worried before the vote as to whether the board's decision would be supported. At the point the vote was taken, I was already a candidate for president of the American Psychiatric Association. I urged a positive vote. I won the election, too, so there may have been some connection there.

The removal of homosexuality from the list of psychiatric illnesses was very significant because it meant that people who wanted to discriminate against homosexuals could no longer say, "Look, the psychiatrists call it an illness. It's considered a sexual perversion. And we can't have people who are sick working for us. We're entitled to stop them from being schoolteachers or from hiring them."

We didn't merely remove homosexuals from the category of illness, we stated that there was no reason why, a priori, a gay man or woman could not be just as healthy, just as effective, just as law abiding, and just as capable of functioning as any heterosexual. Furthermore, we asserted that laws that discriminated against them in housing or in employment were unjustified. So it was a total statement, and I think it was a very significant move. Shortly after that, the American Psychological Association and the American Bar Association came out in support of homosexuals. It was an important step that we took.

THE GAY psychiatrists who I came to know ultimately formed a group within the American Psychiatric Association that they called the Gay PA. It was originally closeted, but it finally became what is now the

Caucus of Homosexually Identified Psychiatrists. It's an open organization with a representative in the Assembly of the American Psychiatric Association. It's a very effective representative for the gay and lesbian community. I have gone to most of their annual meetings and was honored at their last one. They are a significant part of the association, even though many psychiatrists and psychoanalysts still remain closeted.

Unfortunately, many psychiatrists still believe that homosexuality is a mental illness caused by fear of the dominant mother, competing father, et cetera. I would say that maybe a third of the psychiatrists in the United States and maybe half of the psychoanalysts, and possibly even more, still believe it is an illness. They haven't accepted the fact that it's not.

The American Psychiatric Association is not the gestapo. It can't force psychiatrists to change their minds about this issue. It has simply taken homosexuality out of its official diagnostic and statistical manual, so it's no longer listed as an illness—that's why the struggle still goes on. These psychiatrists and psychoanalysts are apt to say, "I can help you change and I will try." Particularly among the classical Freudian psychoanalysts, there is a strong feeling that this can be accomplished. Many younger analysts—more progressive ones—will examine the reasons for the person wanting to change, to see whether it's a genuine wish that has real strength and motivation behind it or whether it's a product of society's disapproval, in which case, many of them will say, "Look, *why* do you want to change?"

This issue is not totally resolved by any means, although there is, in my judgment, a constantly increasing body of information that fortifies the position that the American Psychiatric Association has taken. But I think there's a great deal of unconscious homophobia. People grow up feeling that homosexuality is something bad, something frightening, something alien. When they become professionals, they rationalize that into a need to change it, a feeling that it ought to be changed, that people ought not to be content to be homosexual. That then plays into their professional activities and theoretical perceptions.

As far as my role in this movement is concerned, I'm very proud of what I've done. I think it's one of the good things that I've done as a psychiatrist. I only regret that I didn't come to it sooner.

PART FOUR
1973–1981

Coming of Age

FROM THE vantage point of the early 1970s, it was easy to see that the struggle for gay and lesbian equal rights had evolved through three distinct periods: the development of gay and lesbian discussion groups and organizations in the years following World War II; the homophile movement of the 1960s; and the gay liberation movement, which paralleled the rise of leftist and anti–Vietnam War activism in the late 1960s.

By 1973, another shift was well under way. The confrontational, left-oriented gay liberation movement was rapidly becoming institutionalized as the gay and lesbian rights movement. Most of the gay liberation organizations that had called for radical social and political transformation in the United States passed into history within a few years of their founding. Many were torn apart by internal political battles, while others failed to maintain the interest and financial support of their members.

The street protests and "zaps" sponsored by gay liberation groups had a tremendous impact, particularly on the media and on big-city politicians, who were forced to recognize gay people as an emerging political constituency. But the youthful energy, fueled by idealism and anger, that drove many gay liberationists could not be sustained. Many participants were college students when they joined the gay liberation movement. Upon graduating, they became absorbed by other goals, including graduate school and careers. The advances they achieved removed or mitigated some of the most blatant forms of discrimination that had inspired their rage. To young gay people who were coming of age just a few years later, in the early to mid-1970s, the world was a dramatically different place from what it had been in 1968.

The lesson for both surviving and newly formed gay and lesbian organizations was that lasting change required hard work and time, primarily within traditional political and community channels. Equal rights would have to be won one on one with families—through churches; schools; the local, state, and federal governments; and when possible, in the courts. In this new era, like the era of gay liberation before it, much would still depend on the courage of individual gay men and women to go public by acknowledging their homosexuality to families, colleagues, and friends.

For the most part, gay rights organizations across the country focused on immediate issues. Their pragmatism hearkened back in many ways to the homophile movement that had been overshadowed by the radical and often uncompromising gay liberationists. These gay rights groups often concentrated on passing local gay rights legislation. In dozens of cities they succeeded in convincing elected officials to protect homosexual citizens from discrimination by adding sexual orientation or similar phrases to existing antidiscrimination laws, which often included provisions forbidding discrimination based on race, color, creed, sex, and religion. They also focused on combating police harassment, overturning state sodomy laws, providing a variety of services to local gay communities, and increasing visibility in the media.

A few activists worked to develop a national agenda and to coordinate the efforts of local organizations across the country. Their work culminated in a meeting between gay rights leaders and White House representatives in 1977 and a national march on Washington in 1979 by 75,000 to 100,000 gay rights supporters. The national agenda—promoted primarily by the New York City–based National Gay Task Force—included a range of issues, from passage of national gay rights legislation to an end to the Defense Department's official policy of discrimination against gay men and lesbians.

As the gay rights movement gained more attention locally and nationally, it also attracted strong opposition. Although city councils may have been willing to listen to the pleas of gay activists for civil rights legislation, much of the American public was at best ambivalent about the rights of gay people and at worst, vehemently opposed to them. To many, if not most Americans, homosexuals were still sick, sinful, or criminal, hardly deserving of legal protection.

The antigay backlash erupted nationally in 1977 with a campaign led by Anita Bryant, a pop singer and spokeswoman for the Florida orange-juice industry. Deeply religious, Bryant successfully campaigned for the repeal of the newly passed gay rights ordinance in Dade County, Florida. This success inspired her to lead a countrywide crusade that resulted in the swift repeal of gay rights legislation in St. Paul, Minnesota; Wichita, Kansas; and Eugene, Oregon. Bryant drew the support of conservative political and religious leaders, including the Reverend Jerry Falwell, a popular television evangelist, and was able to build her crusade on existing networks of fundamentalist churches.

Anita Bryant's success galvanized gay rights organizations, forcing them to set aside differences and work in coalitions to challenge the antigay tide, resulting in enormous public demonstrations by gay people on a scale never seen before. In June 1977, San Francisco's gay pride parade attracted more than two hundred thousand marchers. Nonetheless, most gay organizations were wholly unprepared to deal with the well-focused, well-financed Bryant-led campaign.

The national antigay campaign crested on the West Coast with battles at the ballot box in two states. In California, voters defeated the statewide antigay Briggs initiative that would have permitted local school districts to dismiss or deny employment to homosexual teachers. In Seattle, voters overwhelmingly turned back an effort to repeal the city's gay rights protections.

By the end of the 1970s, sobered and strengthened by the antigay backlash, the gay rights effort was poised for a period of steady, if not dramatic, gains in the struggle to achieve full equal rights.

The Ex-Nun

Jean O'Leary

AS MOST lesbian and gay activists concentrated their attention on local matters, Jean O'Leary, a former nun who played a central role in the turbulent and radical politics of the gay liberation era in New York City, set her sights on a national agenda. In 1974 she joined the tiny staff of the New York–based National Gay Task Force. Founded in 1973, NGTF, according to its founders, "sought to bring gay liberation into the mainstream of the American civil rights movement." Although its resources were extremely limited and its attention often failed to reach beyond its headquarter city, NGTF began serving as a national clearinghouse for information on local gay rights legislation.

Two months after she arrived at NGTF, Jean became co-executive director and quickly earned a reputation as a tireless, strong-willed organizer. Her determination and outspokenness have also earned her more than a few critics over the years. "People have criticized me all my life," says Jean. "What doesn't kill you just makes you stronger."

Everything about Jean speaks of strength: her personality, her body, her voice. Seated in the double-height living room of her spacious apartment in North Hollywood, California, looking through a pile of photographs, Jean, now in her early forties, spoke with a passion and sharp sense of humor that must have come in handy during her two decades in the rough-and-tumble world of the gay rights movement.

I found out I was gay when I was in about the third grade at Our Lady of the Elms Elementary School. I was "married" to Debbie Evans* for about two years. We were very much in love and we had a little ceremony. Everybody loved us; we were very popular. We stayed overnight at each other's houses and kissed and watched "77 Sunset Strip" together. We just had a wonderful time. But then I had to go to this coed parochial school for sixth and seventh grades.

Nobody thought I was gay—not in a million years—but I walked a pretty thin line. I'd stay overnight at people's houses or have them

*Debbie Evans is a pseudonym.

over to my house, and we'd touch and do whatever we possibly could. We said we were practicing for when we got with the boys. I would never do anything that could be construed of as, "she's gay," because I knew that would be anathema. Also, as long as I didn't do anything like that, I could deny to myself what I was. I thought homosexuality was a disease—it was a sickness; it was a perversion; it was definitely immoral. But despite what I thought about homosexuality, I loved girls, and that was very confusing.

I had a great time in high school. I went to the Magnificat School in Cleveland, an all-girls high school. I loved being around all the women. I had lots of friends and lots of fun. I was really a cutup. I was bad. I held the record for detentions. I used to do all of these little things, like setting off the fire alarm and holding dances in the auditorium during lunch. They were just little baby tricks, but it was pretty upsetting to the nuns.

At one point I wanted to run for president of my junior class, but I wasn't allowed to run because I had too many detentions. So I ran Connie Scott's campaign. I was in love with Connie during high school. I was also in love with Betty Stevens.* We had a wonderful campaign. We pasted up little rhymes on the walls everywhere. We had campaign placards. We had bands going through the cafeteria. It was really the sexiest and most visible kind of campaign the school had ever seen. I just loved it—I think I was born to do campaigns.

ALL THROUGH high school I knew that I loved women. I also knew that these feelings had better go back down where they belonged, even though nobody talked about anything like this. So I dated men. I was in a band called the Intoxicators. I played the drums and dated the lead singer. For our dates we'd do gigs. I remember we were kissing one time and starting to make out a little bit, and I said, "Woody, we can't do that anymore. It's a sin." And he said, "Look, I want to marry you. But I'll tell you what. Until we get married, when we go out, you'll sit on that side of the car, and I'll sit on this side of the car. I won't touch you." I told him I was going to the convent. He said, "We'll have twenty kids. Ten will be nuns and ten will be priests. Now isn't that better than one nun?" He was so cute. He was really darling.

I think I broke Woody's heart. What a shame that I couldn't tell him, that I couldn't be honest. I'm sure he went away in pain and

*Connie Scott and Betty Stevens are pseudonyms.

confusion, which was how I felt. That's what we all do to each other's lives because we're not able to come out.

I wasn't kidding about the convent. When I told my parents what I had decided to do, they were a little upset. They thought it was just a phase. My mother wanted to be a grandmother. I was the oldest, so her feeling was, "There goes our first shot." They eventually got used to the idea, but it was still painful. When you go away to a convent, your family can only come visit you maybe once a month. So even if it's a liberal convent, you're gone from their lives.

The convent was great. It was one of the best experiences of my life on every single level. You lived with the same people twenty-four hours a day, day in and day out. The convent was in a villa, which we were not permitted to leave, so it was really intense. We were up to all hours of the night. We would go smoke in the cafeteria and talk.

I was always in love at the convent. One of the women I got involved with, Eleanor,* was seeing this priest who was a therapist. I just knew that she had blown the whistle. I thought, *Oh, my god. It's my fault!* So I went to him and told him I was gay. I took total responsibility for what had happened because I brought Eleanor out. I brought everybody out. I had eight relationships while I was in there. God was an innocent bystander.

The priest asked me all these questions. Now I had been asked questions like these before and had learned to lie without blinking. Questions like, "Did you date boys?" "Did you do . . . ?" "Do you ever have feelings of . . . ?" But this time, with the priest, I told the truth. It was the first time that I had ever told anybody, including Eleanor, or even myself, that I thought I was gay.

The priest said, "Don't you think it's because we're in a same-sex environment, and that these feelings are natural under the circumstances and we just have to try to be celibate?" I said, "Fine." But his assessment was debilitating. Here I had finally told someone, and he glossed over the whole thing because he didn't want to hear it. He said I was a very interesting, very vivid, very open person. Then he wanted to analyze my dreams. I thought, *Oh, boy.* So I left his office.

That wasn't the first time at the convent that I encountered this attitude of evasion. One time, Eleanor and I were walking down by the lake, and we were holding hands. We probably kissed. We used to call these sorts of things "particular friendships" or "PFs." Some of the old nuns saw us and reported us to my novice mistress who called us in. The novice mistress was very sweet and said, "We don't go walking down by the lake at night." She didn't say, "You queers,

*Eleanor is a pseudonym.

get out of here!" The attitude was, "We don't acknowledge this sort of thing, so shape up."

WHEN I left the priest's office after telling him that I was gay, I didn't know what I was going to do with my life. I felt intense loneliness and emptiness and that I was not being heard. I was ready to come out, but nobody wanted to hear it. I had been saved one more time. Ha! Saved from the truth. Everybody was in collaboration. It's like a conspiracy of silence: Even when you're ready to break out of it, it's not easy. People don't want to hear it.

I stayed around at the convent for a while longer, but I eventually left and went to Cleveland State to get my degree. I still thought I was absolutely the only gay person in the world. Then, in 1969, when I was just finishing up at school, I saw a sign for a gay liberation organization meeting in the cafeteria. I thought, *Oh, my God, this is great!* I had never seen anything like that in my life. When I went to look at the sign again to find out where in the cafeteria the meeting was going to take place, the sign was gone. So I missed my first connection.

My first real connection was something of an accident. I had read an article in *Cosmopolitan* magazine by an anonymous lesbian about how all the lesbians lived in Greenwich Village. So I said to myself, *I have to figure out how to get there.* At Cleveland State I had been involved in organizational development. One of the very few places in the country with programs in this field was Yeshiva University in New York City. There was a magnificent man at Yeshiva who I wanted to study under. It turned out to be a difficult program to get into, but I got accepted. There were only two people in my class.

So I went to New York. My father drove me. I took one little suitcase and my set of drums, which I had taken with me to the convent. The plan was for me to share a studio apartment in Brooklyn Heights with a man I had met when he visited Cleveland State University. He had a book on his bookshelf called *The Gay Militants*, which I had been dying to look at. As soon as he left on a business trip, I took it off the shelf, and all these news clips about gay politics and places to meet gay people came fluttering out. This man was gay! When he got back, we started talking about all of these issues. We went to a meeting in Brooklyn Heights sponsored by the Gay Activists Alliance [GAA], which was based in Manhattan. They were starting up an affiliate group. There were two or three women and seventy-five men. I remember thinking, *Oh, my God! Look at all the gay people in one place!* My host and I also shared an interest in organizational development, so the two of us decided to use our organizational skills to become a major part of the group.

The reason I became involved was that I knew by then that I didn't want the kind of oppression I experienced to happen to anybody else. I knew it had to be eliminated. I had this calling to change the way the world reacted to gay people. And like many others, I wanted a place to meet and socialize with my peers.

Ken and I also went over to check out GAA in Manhattan. There were hundreds of gay people at this meeting, using *Robert's Rules of Order*. It was all very professional and very energetic. They were all working on the New York City gay rights bill. This was probably around 1971. That was my introduction to gay rights activism. Right away, I started to get involved with the women at GAA. At that time, the women's group was called the Subcommittee of the Human Relations Committee of GAA. It was about as low as you could get.

SEXISM BETWEEN men and women was just rampant in the early 1970s in the gay community in the larger cities, and that included the men in GAA. It was blatant. The men actually treated women like surrogate mothers, lovers, and sisters. There were few women in leadership positions, and women were consciously kept out of them. The men were listening, but they just weren't hearing what we had to say. It wasn't like they didn't know we were there. We had arguments every single day. We had debates on the floor. It was very powerful. But they held on to their stereotyped views of women. And they would make a point of crashing our women-only events.

Through a lot of internal struggle, we became the Lesbian Liberation Committee within GAA. I was the second or third chair of that committee, and during my tenure, I instigated a split from the men. I said, "Let's take a look at what's going on here and decide if we want to stay in GAA or not." What ensued was a six-month effort to achieve genuine, 100 percent consensus. This effort meant that if we got close to complete agreement one week, with just three women left to go, we'd think, *Okay, next week we'll really accomplish this.* But in the space of a week, new people would come in. So we'd have to start all over again.

I almost lost it during the process. I was trying to deal with these really hard-core holdouts who were against leaving GAA and I was negotiating with the men to make sure that we could use the Firehouse, GAA's community center, on Sundays for our film festival and Fridays for our dances. One of the holdouts was an old-time gay activist who didn't like the elements of feminism that were creeping into things, and she, as well as some of the other women, was concerned about how we would make it on our own financially. I thought we had to bite the bullet and go for it. We had to *find ourselves* as a group. Women had to be separate, to do their own thing.

You know, I really hate talking about this. I don't believe in separatism now, so for me to sit here and go back twenty years and say, "These are the reasons why women have to be separate" is very difficult. Today, when I say these things, it just sounds off the wall. But this is how it was then, and I realize that we have to go back and talk about these things so that people can learn from history. Still, I really hate doing it.

Anyway, we ended up splitting from the men by forming Lesbian Feminist Liberation, LFL. We were trying to establish our identity and, wherever we could, gain visibility. Just as gay people have had to become visible in society, lesbians had to become visible within the gay community, as well as in the larger society. Up until that time, whenever people thought about gays, they thought only about gay men.

ONE OF the things LFL objected to during this time were the transvestites. The way we saw it was, here is a man dressing up as a woman and wearing all the things that we are trying to break free of—high heels, girdles, corsets, stockings—all the things that were literally *binding* women. We found out that there were plans to have a transvestite as part of the entertainment for the 1973 gay pride rally in Washington Square following the march, and we decided to make a statement critical of transvestites. I'm sure we had protested this for weeks with the organizers and had not been heard. So we decided that we were going to stand up on the stage and tell everybody what we thought.

We stayed up the whole night before the rally and typed up this little statement. We thought it was very important. You see, we were actually creating theory at the time. What we came up with was that we weren't going to attack cross-dressing because both men and women could be thrown in jail for that. But we decided to attack men who did it for profit—professional female impersonators and prostitutes—as opposed to those who did it simply to make a statement. This is so embarrassing; I can hardly believe that we believed this.

Anyway, we decided to attack only those men who made money by dressing in women's clothes. Vito Russo, who was hosting the rally, was a very good friend of mine. We had a falling out over this issue, but he was still trying to accommodate me. So I got up on the stage in front of thousands of people and I said that we of the Lesbian Feminist Liberation protested men cross-dressing for purposes of profit and we wanted to make that statement clear. We probably had some sort of tag, like, "Here we are, Lesbian Feminist Liberation! Women come join us so you can work with all women!" That kind of wonderful thing.

There was this incredible reaction to the statement, a lot of hostility. One of the transvestites got up at the microphone and started yelling. Men and the women in the crowd started fighting with each other. I remember getting off the stage and walking through the crowd. I went over to a women's bar right around the corner to meet up with the other women. That's where we heard that Bette Midler had come down to the rally to smooth things over and sang, "You gotta be friends . . . ."

Looking back, I find this so embarrassing because my views have changed so much since then. I would never pick on a transvestite now. In the late seventies, I stayed at a hotel in Florida that was full of transvestites and transsexuals. They were wonderful, darling, lovable people who I got to know *as people.* I got to know their lives and their stories, who they were, why they were. And, you know, as you grow older, you learn more and you mellow in terms of what has to be exactly right and politically correct. Now I find that I have no patience with political correctness. But I know that I went through it, so I have to have patience with the people coming up now, who are going through the same process I went through.

I was involved in another conflict with transvestites around this time. It was very painful. We were working on getting the gay rights bill passed in New York City, trying to structure a bill that would be passable. Early on, the transvestites wanted to be included in the bill as a protected group. Politically, we had to say, "This doesn't work. We are never going to get the bill through the City Council if transvestites are included in the bill. This is not what our battle is about. It's about gay rights, not transvestite rights. We're talking about being able to love someone of your own sex, being able to have a relationship. This is not about how we dress."

So the transvestites were excluded from the bill, and they never got reinstated. It was an extremely hard thing to do; it was horrible. How could I work to exclude transvestites and at the same time criticize the feminists who were doing their best back in those days to exclude lesbians? What it came down to was pragmatism: doing what you had to do to keep the issue moving ahead on the agenda. You just had to make those hard decisions and then go with it. But it's something that

Vito Russo and Bette Midler on stage at the 1973 Gay Pride rally in Washington Square in Greenwich Village. According to Vito, who served as emcee for the event: "The rally used to be a battleground for ideas and politics. I knew that the tensions would be running high that day because a group of radical lesbians were opposed to a couple of comic drags scheduled to be a part of the entertainment program. Drag was high on their hit list. So I began working on Bette Midler weeks in advance to come and sing to sort of calm things down. Well, the lesbians heckled the drag queens throughout their numbers, and when it was over, Jean O'Leary got up and made a very angry speech in which she said that men who impersonate women for profit insult women. All hell broke loose in the audience between the men and the women, and Bette got up on stage and sang 'Friends.' She had brought Barry Manilow with her.

"Bette worked like a charm. It wasn't that the issues were forgotten, but she provided a tremendously healing presence. It was a great thing for Bette, too. She said later that it was one of the great things she did, that she felt like she was Marilyn Monroe singing in Korea." *(Courtesy Vito Russo)*

still bothers me a lot. You tried to keep your integrity as intact as you possibly could.

SERVING AS chair of Lesbian Feminist Liberation proved to be very wearing. There were all kinds of struggles, including an internal battle between the old school of thought and feminism. We were constantly arguing about how much we should be tied into the men or into the feminists. Lesbians were in the middle, between gay men and feminists. Besides, everything moved very slowly. I wanted to participate in a wider arena and have more of an impact. So I left LFL to do a little one-on-one lobbying in Albany. I drove my little green Volkswagen with one headlight up to the state capital every Tuesday to talk with legislators about laws to protect gay people. In those days, they thought that basically all a lesbian needed was . . . you know. Pretty soon we had a little caravan going up every Tuesday. There were a few liberal legislators who listened, but the others who drove up there quickly lost interest in making the trip every week. And we didn't exactly get the feeling we were making much of a difference.

IN 1974, I took a job with the National Gay Task Force. I don't remember if I approached Bruce Voeller, the executive director, or if he approached me. In two months I became co-executive director. Working with NGTF was perfect for me because I love the big picture—I've never been a detail person. And NGTF was the largest gay group in the country.

I wanted to start organizing nationally, to take the message of gay rights out of Manhattan and to the rest of the country, where they were having a much tougher time of it than in New York City, Los Angeles, or San Francisco.

We did a lot of traveling during these years. We helped people in local areas pass legislation. For example, let's say one bill passed in Miami. We would take the text of that bill and send it to Idaho, along with the text of other bills. The Idaho activists could study the options and decide which one came closest to meeting their needs and realities. We did a lot of strategizing both for passage of gay civil rights bills and for the repeal of sodomy statutes. We also did lots of community organizing, always emphasizing visibility because this was—and is—at the core of our oppression. There's no question about it: If everybody who's gay was visible, we would probably eliminate 70 percent of the oppression. Everybody already knows gay people. They just don't know that we're gay.

OF ALL the things we did while I was co-executive director at NGTF, the one that gave us the most visibility was our meeting at the White House in 1977. This meeting was a first. We even got national television coverage, which was extremely unusual in those days.

This meeting came about through Midge Costanza, who was one of nine assistants to President Carter. Midge was the first woman ever to be named a presidential assistant. I first worked with Midge on Democratic platform-committee issues long before Carter got elected. After Midge went to work for President Carter, I told her, "It's time, Midge. It's time." Those are the exact words. And she said, "Well,

I've only been here a week!" But it wasn't long before she said, "Okay, Jean, set up the meeting. Let me know when you would like to have it and who you would like to include, and we will see what we can do."

Bruce Voeller and I chose twelve issue areas that we thought would be pertinent to White House action, that they could help us with in some way or another. Then I called up twelve leaders around the country and asked them to prepare white papers on everything from immigration to civil rights. The night before the White House meeting, we all met and rehearsed how we were going to give our presentations to make sure that everybody was coordinated. This was going to be done very professionally.

The next day all of us went to the White House. None of us had been there before, so it was thrilling. I remember walking in and seeing the guards, the Oval Office, and the Roosevelt Room, where we had the meeting. We met with Midge; Marilyn Haft, who worked for Midge; and a representative of Jimmy Carter's domestic-policy staff. Jimmy Carter had gone to Camp David.

After we presented everything, we came out on the front lawn of the White House and were greeted by all three television networks. It was very exciting; this was real breaking news. I think one of the reporters asked Midge, "Did President Carter know that you were having this meeting?" And she said something funny like, "I waited until the helicopter took off and then called everyone long distance and told them to rush into the White House. The coast was clear." She paused for a moment and added, "Of course, he knew. You don't just have a meeting in the White House without informing the staff and the president." It was history. We definitely made history.

I think this meeting meant a lot to the whole community. It meant that we had been recognized by the highest institutional establishment of our country. And for gay people who were looking for signs, for symbols, for recognition, for anything along those lines that would make their lives valid, it was a wonderful breakthrough. I was very proud for NGTF and I was very proud for our community.

There was solid follow-through on all of the issues we raised at the White House. We had meetings with the heads of all the departments that were involved in the specific issue areas. We also went to meeting after meeting with the Civil Rights Commission. They had us testify. Gay people had never done this before; it was groundbreaking. We made some changes and were able to implement a few things, but mostly we were raising consciousness by sitting down and telling these people what the problems were. Often, the people we met with didn't want to be there, but they knew that when Midge called from the White House they had better show up and listen to what we had to say.

THE SUPPORT from the White House was mild mannered. When Midge asked President Carter to appoint me to the International Women's Year commission, he said, "Well, does she have to use her title?" I was still with NGTF. Midge said, "Sir, that would be like asking you if you had to use yours." She went on to tell him the story about how I had switched my vote for him at the Democratic convention in New York and that I voted for him despite very heavy pressure not to. I had been on the Udall slate, so I was committed to voting for Udall on the first ballot, but I switched my vote to Carter in the next round. Midge told Carter this story, and he made the appointment.

Sometimes our gay community does not understand the political process and how you have to play it in order to get anywhere. Some people who do understand it simply hate it. I understand it and love it and I believe it's a way to make real progress. I knew in this case that Carter was going to win, and I wanted to be able to say that I had voted for him. Loyalty is very important when it comes to politics, and I knew that my vote for Carter would later facilitate access to the president on behalf of the gay community. Of course, I also really believed in the man; otherwise I would not have voted for him.

Anyway, the idea behind the International Women's Year commission was that it would set the feminist agenda. Forty-two women were appointed. There was one other gay woman besides me, but she was closeted. I had three supporters, and the closeted person was not one of them, as you can imagine.

The commission meetings were very painful because I was an outsider. They wouldn't accept me as a team player because the gay issue was always there, and they did not want to deal with it. My job was to make that issue visible and get the issue of sexual orientation on the feminist agenda. As much as I would have liked to have been part of the gang, I wasn't able to do that.

We brought up the issue of sexual orientation, and it got voted down by a big margin: It was absolutely out of the question. The women weren't clear as to the reason why. They didn't say, "We don't want it on the agenda because it's unpopular, and we risk losing support for other issues, like the Equal Rights Amendment. If we support this we'll all be looked at as a bunch of dykes." They didn't say it, but that was exactly the thought. Instead they said, "You know why we don't want this issue on the agenda." My answer was, "You know why it *should* be on the agenda."

Fortunately, I had recourse. The agenda was also being discussed at conferences in every state in the country. I hired someone, and between us we organized women in all fifty states. A great majority of the states, perhaps thirty-five, passed "sexual orientation" on a local level for the agenda. I said to the commission, "The states have spoken. There is no way that you cannot include sexual orientation on the commission's agenda."

So we got our issue onto the commission's agenda, but the worst was yet to come. Some of the states passed it as "lesbianism." Some passed it as "sexual orientation." We had twenty-six issues on the agenda, and I knew we were not going to get through the entire list, which was in alphabetical order. It would be very hard to handle all these emotional issues within a few days with these thousands and thousands of women delegates. So I said that we had to go for the issue of *lesbianism* because this was a feminist conference. But they knew exactly what I was doing.

The vote came in 39 to 3, to put it under "sexual orientation." I said, "Okay, now we have to campaign to keep the agenda moving." We had buttons made saying something to the effect, "Let Every Issue Be Heard." We got supporters, heterosexual as well as gay, to wear these buttons because there were lots of people who had issues at the bottom of the agenda and didn't want to get left off.

Finally, the conference took up sexual orientation. The resolution we wanted passed was that sexual orientation was a feminist issue, was part of the feminist agenda, and that we should work to eliminate discrimination of all types based on sexual orientation. There was a terrible floor fight, but I knew we were going to win. We had set up things like Betty Friedan apologizing for her past treatment of lesbians, and we had very good speakers. But there were also people who were totally opposed to us. Whole delegations turned their backs when the vote came up.

When our resolution passed, I had hundreds of lesbians in the back balcony and on the floor release these huge bunches of helium-filled balloons all over the place. Hundreds of balloons went flying up to the top of the hall, and everybody in the back of the hall shouted, "Thank you, sisters! Thank you, sisters!" We were all very happy. We had reason to be: This was the first time that sexual orientation, or lesbianism, had officially been made part of the feminist agenda. That was a fifty-state organizational campaign that lasted over a year and a half. God, it was exciting!

I think that one thing our enemies will never understand, that they just don't seem to get, is that the harder they try to push us back into the closet, the more outpouring there's going to be. They just don't

Jean O'Leary at the 1988
Democratic Convention,
where she served as a
Dukakis whip. (*Courtesy Jean
O'Leary*)

understand the cause-and-effect principle. By trying to repress us, they really bring out the militancy in us and make for a lot more visible gay people.

In the end, some issues from the conference received attention and were worked on, but sexual orientation was not one of them. The proceedings of the conference and all the issues that were taken up were compiled in a book. The issue of sexual orientation was simply brushed over. The woman who was writing that book, I just hated her. I tried everything: I cajoled; I threatened; I said, "Look, we should be included! We've got to have more coverage! There is so much that happened around this issue!" But, no, it was treated very lightly. To anyone reading the book, we were invisible. That's what I've been fighting against all my life: invisibility.

The Jock
David Kopay

WHEN DAVID KOPAY, *a thirty-three-year-old former National Football League running back, publicly acknowledged his homosexuality in 1975, he was national news. Kopay was the first professional American athlete to come out of the closet and one of the only public figures to come out during the 1970s. Before Kopay, the most prominent public person to come out was Dr. Howard Brown, the former New York City chief health officer. In 1973, when Dr. Brown announced he was gay in an address to six hundred physicians at a symposium on human sexuality, he made the front page of the New York Times. Public disclosure of homosexuality by prominent people at that time was unheard of.*

David Kopay was the all-American athlete, the antithesis of the public's image of homosexuals. A cocaptain of the University of Washington's 1964 Rose Bowl team, Kopay played professional football for ten years for the San Francisco Forty-Niners, the Detroit Lions, the Washington Redskins, the New Orleans Saints, and the Green Bay Packers.

Fresh from a workout at the gym, Kopay made clear that all he really wanted to do in life was play football and later, coach. Today, he sells linoleum at his uncle's store in Hollywood, California.

I never really thought much about a profession. Everybody said I should be a lawyer or a doctor. But I wasn't very good at science and math, so I transferred to political science and history. I was so into playing football—that was my main concern.

When you're a borderline athlete—in terms of pro talent—the way I was, you had to be really focused. I think it's almost scary how focused I was. Everybody told me, "You'll never, ever make it." But I thought I would be drafted fairly high because of what teams had been telling me ever since 1964, when I was captain of the Rose Bowl team that played Illinois. But I wound up not being drafted at all, and signed as a free agent with the San Francisco Forty-Niners. I was lucky enough not to get injured when I went to training camp and made it onto the team.

The money wasn't big at all, but I wanted to play football. I absolutely loved playing football. You had to love it to try to stick around for ten years and be cut five or six times. I had to make the team almost every year I played in pro football except one year when I was traded from the Forty-Niners to the Detroit Lions. They were really looking for good things from me, but I wound up having a very average season. I hurt my knee in training camp and had to have it drained before the game on Friday and then after the game on Monday. I did that the entire year, which was really insane. Getting your knee drained is very painful. But when I was healthy and playing, I absolutely loved it. Things were very simple out on the football field. If someone took a shot at you, you could take a shot at them. If you were angry, you could get relief. It was very simple.

I knew from an early age that I was a very intense person and that I had a temper. But my temper wasn't out of control because I always used to think about it. I didn't wind up in many fights as a kid because I was very big to begin with. I looked like I would tear someone's head off, so mostly, people backed off. But I wasn't a bully.

I always knew I was a bit different, but I kept it kind of quiet. I didn't think of myself as queer. In fact I couldn't even say that word for years and years. Perry Young* got me to use that word. He was always using it, and finally I thought, *Yeah, that's kind of fun.* Then I'd refer to myself as a queer football player: "This is one queer they're not going to intimidate. You better know what you're talking about when you want to talk to me." I was overcompensating in a way, even though I don't know if I was consciously doing that. I think a lot of athletes overcompensate with toughness and aggressiveness.

WHEN I thought about the future, I assumed I'd be able to get a job in coaching because I was a player-coach my last few years playing. I was always working behind the scenes with the young ballplayers, coaching them. But I wasn't getting any interviews. There were all kinds of rumors about me being gay—you know, bullshit stuff. All those rumors about how gay men are into sex constantly, how they can't control themselves in the locker room. The whole bullshit that you're one of those people who lurks in the bathrooms at the park, who's after young boys. Sometimes bringing it all up and talking about it pisses me off. That kind of talk really bothered me and made me angry—that's one of the reasons I spoke out. I wanted to speak out and say, "Hey, listen, I don't lurk and I don't go after young boys." Maybe young men, but that's a different story.

*Kopay's coauthor on his best-selling autobiography, *The Dave Kopay Story.*

By the time I spoke out, I really had nothing left to lose. It felt like I didn't have a choice—I just had to do it. Then one morning in 1975 I saw an article in the *Washington Star* about homosexual athletes and why they had everything to lose. There was an interview in the article with Jerry Smith.* I knew it was Jerry, even though they didn't use his name. Jerry talked about how everything in football was apple pie and ice cream as long as you didn't tell the truth, as long as you lied. As I was reading his interview I was thinking, *Hey, wait a minute, let's get this straight. You take it this far, why don't you set the record straight and say what you are and who you are?*

I was very disappointed because Jerry and I had talked for a number of years about doing a book together, about speaking out. And when I saw that article and didn't see him score, I was angry. I was at a time and place in my own coming out where I felt that if I was going to survive, I had to speak out. It was do that or maybe go crazy.

So I called Lynn Rosellini, who was the reporter for the article that quoted Jerry Smith. Lynn was doing an entire series on gay athletes. I felt that she would be fair and honest with me because I knew her father when he was governor of the State of Washington. Her father used to travel with the team. So I called Lynn and said, "I'm David Kopay." And she said, "Oh, Dave, we met many times a long time ago." I said, "I'd like to meet with you." She asked, "Are you sure?" I said, "I'm sure."

I think Lynn was stunned. She was also very thankful to have a professional athlete who was willing to go public because it gave her series some credibility. But see, I didn't have the $150,000 or $200,000 beer commercial to lose. I didn't have a huge income. I didn't have any of that. I was doing it out of desperation. I felt that this was something I could do. I didn't feel like any big hero or any big courageous dude or any of that stuff. I felt, *Dammit! I can do something here and I know it's important because I wish I had that kind of person to read about when I was younger.*

Everybody said there was going to be a terrible backlash against me when Lynn's article was published. But there wasn't a backlash against me personally: There was a backlash against all the television shows and radio stations that I went on. And the newspapers. The *Washington Star* said they had never received more negative mail for anything they'd ever done—hundreds of horrible hate letters. Only two or three were addressed to me directly; the rest were addressed to the *Washington Star* editor and Lynn Rosellini for doing the series

---

*Jerry Smith was a Washington Redskins tight end from 1965 to 1977. He died of complications from AIDS in 1986.

on gay athletes. The letters said things like, "It doesn't belong on the sports page as a model for our young boys and girls." "How could the *Washington Star* run an article like this?" I got letters that said, "I hope you never get a coaching job. Yours in Christ. Love. . . ." Just horrible things.

I never did get a coaching job. I was really quite frightened because I didn't know what I was going to do. No one would hire me to be a coach, I think, because of the image problem. They didn't think I could fill the role of the coach as guardian of the morals of the young students—the father figure. I also knew that I probably wouldn't get that really good sales-rep job that a lot of the other guys got. I had to make a spot for myself somehow, so I wound up working with Perry Young for a year on my book, *The Dave Kopay Story*.

I think we knew we were doing something good. The book was chosen by the American Library Association in 1977 as a recommended book for all students, and it was on the *New York Times* best-seller list. So we did something good.

A lot of kids still write. They say that the book meant so much to them. They remember that it changed them a lot or made a difference. I've had people come by the store where I work and introduce themselves. One guy, who was changing careers to be an athletic trainer for the love of being around the sport, told me that my book gave him the courage to do what he wanted to do. Those are great strokes. I can take a lot with strokes like that.

Because of the book I was able to speak at a number of universities. I wasn't able to make a real living at it. It kind of filled the void a little bit until I wrote a letter to my uncle asking him for a job in his store.

The movie rights were sold a number of times, but nobody's ever done it. I think the NFL maybe had something to do with discouraging anyone from doing a film version of the book. In all these years I haven't heard a word from anybody in the NFL. Here I've been asked to speak in front of the American Bar Association. I was asked to go to San Francisco and be the keynote speaker at the American Association of Pediatricians to talk to doctors and at least try to give them a glimpse of somebody who they might be able to relate to. I've done a lot of creditable things toward improving the mental health of our society, yet the NFL still acts as if I don't exist, which pisses me off.

The NFL has hired a number of ex-drug addicts, for example, to counsel the ballplayers. Well, maybe instead of hiring the ex-drug addicts and alcoholics to talk to the guys about drugs and alcohol, they should get into hiring someone who understands a few of the reasons why some of the guys get into the drugs and booze so much.

Maybe the guys do it to tame that flame of desperation that we have in us.

I still want to coach. If I had the opportunity to coach at the major college or professional level, I'd jump at it. If I had the opportunity to go someplace like Stanford, even today, even though I'm making a good living and I'm pretty comfortable, I would probably do it. I've even fantasized that maybe Stanford or Cal would be two schools that could deal with me. But then I think, *No, I'm going to be forty-seven years old. Some of the head coaches are thirty-five.* So, maybe I don't want to do that. But then again, maybe I would do it. Age has never bothered me much before. I would love to do it, but I don't think it's going to happen.

The Good Sailor

Vernon E. "Copy" Berg III

WITH ITS uncompromising position that gay men and women are not fit to serve in the armed forces, the U.S. military became a target of gay rights activism beginning in 1964, when a handful of protesters picketed the Whitehall Induction Center in New York City, demanding that homosexuals be allowed to enlist.

During the short era of gay liberation, however, activists retreated from the fight for equal treatment by the military. The armed forces and service in them had simply become anathema to most gay activists, who, like so many young American men and women, opposed U.S. involvement in Vietnam. As far as most gay activists were concerned, it made no sense to seek equal treatment from an institution they sought to destroy.

Nonetheless, by the early 1970s a handful of homosexual service people decided to challenge their ruinous dishonorable discharges. One of these cases attracted the attention of Congressman Ed Koch—later the mayor of New York—who, in 1972, called on the Department of Defense to alter its policy on dishonorable discharges for homosexuals. Calling the Pentagon's policy "cruelly out of date," he suggested giving homosexuals honorable discharges instead.

In 1975, a twenty-four-year-old Annapolis graduate and navy officer, Copy Berg, found himself at the center of a national controversy when he filed suit against the navy to keep his job. Copy wasn't interested in merely upgrading a dishonorable discharge; he wanted to save his military career.

A professional artist, Copy Berg now works in Manhattan's SoHo district in a studio he shares with a fellow artist who, like him, was forced out of the military because of his homosexuality. Copy still has the bearing—and the haircut—of a career naval officer. Handsome, articulate, and self-confident, he came across as exactly the kind of individual the U.S. Navy would, under other circumstances, seek to attract, retain, and honor.

Growing up, nobody ever discussed gays. My father, who was a navy chaplain, had purchased a set of books on sex, which he kept in his bookcase. We could all see them, but we weren't supposed to touch them. Of course, we read them while he was gone. One book was on sexually deviant behavior. It contained case studies and interviews with people who had been in therapy, including a lot of gay people and transvestites. I'm sure that made me somewhat aware of what I was doing with my best friend.

In hindsight, I realize that my best friend was my lover. He and I did things at school together, we were in Boy Scouts together, we went everywhere together. That also meant sharing a sleeping bag and having sex. At the time, my impression was that a homosexual was someone who wanted to be a woman, a cross-dresser. To me what we were doing was just play. So my friend and I had sex, lots of it, for almost four years, but we never talked about it.

At the same time I was involved with my best friend, the two of us also dated women. We would double-date and drop the girls off and go home and have sex. Our relationship continued all the way through high school, until my senior year when I got mononucleosis, which knocked me out of school for six months. That ended the relationship with my friend because by the time I came back to school, I was very focused on graduating and getting to Annapolis. I went off to boot camp, in June 1969. Then I spent a year at the Naval Academy Preparatory School in Maryland.

EVEN THOUGH this was 1969, and there were changes going on throughout society, I wasn't really touched by them. I was living in a military environment. All my friends were military juniors. Their parents were career military people. We were very removed from what was going on in the rest of society. Prior to 1968 or 1969, none of us had ever even heard of marijuana. Drugs, as well as peace demonstrations, were considered part of the fringe.

I was clearly not part of the fringe. I always had a crew cut. I was student body president in my high school. I traveled and spoke on behalf of all kinds of groups. I held office in the Boy Scouts and traveled for them.

My first encounters with antiwar demonstrators happened after I entered the U.S. Naval Academy and was traveling with the academy glee club. We would do as many as three states in two weeks, five concerts a day, mostly in high schools, because we were recruiting people to come to Annapolis. That was the primary function of the glee club. Wherever we performed, we were met by demonstrators. They would walk up to us and ask us how many babies we'd burned. It was a very surreal experience because none of us had ever seen combat. None of us had ever been to Vietnam.

At the academy, we were told not to wear our uniforms off base.

This was a complete reversal of policy, but the situation warranted it because we were subject to violence, especially in urban areas like New York, Washington, Philadelphia, and Detroit. Vietnam was very unpopular, and if you walked down the streets in uniform, you were subject to abuse.

After graduating from Annapolis, I was sent to Italy with NATO forces as an assistant chief of staff to Vice Admiral Frederick C. Turner on the Sixth Fleet staff for public relations. Shortly after I got to Italy, in June or July of 1975, I was called in by the Naval Investigative Service officer on the ship. I didn't think anything of it because this guy was a friend of mine. I had worked with him on cases involving security clearances; I thought he wanted to talk to me about one of my men. Two men from NIS were there, and they said, "We're here to talk about your homosexuality." I said, "What homosexuality?" And they proceeded with a good cop–bad cop routine. One guy screams at you and then he leaves the room, and the other guy says, "He's in a bad mood. If you'll cooperate things will get better."

At the same time they were questioning me, they had Lawrence Gibson, the man with whom I was having a relationship, in another room. Lawrence was a civilian employed by the navy to teach English as a second language to the Filipino stewards. The NIS officers would go from room to room and say, "Mr. Gibson has just said this; do you deny it?" Then they would take what I said and go back to him and say, "Mr. Berg has just said this; do you deny it?"

It turned out that, at first, they didn't know I was actually involved in a relationship—my name was simply on a list of suspected homosexuals at the academy. It seems that the investigation somehow started while we were still at Annapolis. The NIS maintained that they had a confidential informant. This person, who is still an active informant, is protected, so they've taken the name off all the records, including the documents we were able to obtain under the Freedom of Information Act.

The list of suspected homosexuals they confronted me with included professors, students, and officers at Annapolis, most of whom I didn't know. These NIS investigators wanted to believe that I knew all these people and that I was guilty of colluding with them. They believed that there was this wonderful underground network of homosexuals and that we all talked to each other and we all fucked. I was mortified by the implications of this. I had never been confronted by these kinds of tactics before. I was pretty buffaloed by all this so I gave them a confession. I said that yes, I was gay, and I had had sex with people in high school. I didn't give them names—I just said that I had had sex with other men. I also insisted that the statement include the fact that I had had sex with women, and I itemized those experiences, too. I decided the only way to establish credibility was to assert what was true and deny the rest.

In the process of getting my confession, they used my friend Lawrence against me. Lawrence was summarily dismissed and sent back to the United States. Before this happened, I had handled my relationship with Lawrence in the same way I handled my relationship in high school. It wasn't something you talked about. It wasn't something you exposed. It also wasn't something I was ashamed of. I was happy in the relationship, but we were as highly closeted as we could be because I knew that if you got caught, you got thrown out of the navy.

People had been thrown off the ship for being gay before my encounter with the NIS. I remember two guys who were caught in the act. Within twenty-four hours everybody on the ship knew it. The next day, during business hours and in a very visible way, these two guys were told to pack all their stuff and leave the ship. Then they walked off the gang plank and down the pier to a police van that took them away. Everybody who could, went and looked. The navy may have been confidential in how they handled the records, but they were not the least bit confidential about how they put somebody over the side of a ship and sent them home. They really sent them off in great disgrace, with high drama and fanfare.

AFTER MY confession I was greatly relieved. I was practically ecstatic, for two reasons. For one thing, there had been a cloud hanging over me because of the possibility of this happening. And once it happened, I thought, *Great, it's over!* The other thing was, the life I was leading on the ship was pretty miserable. I was working sixteen- or seventeen-hour workdays, and then we'd go to sea, and I'd work even longer hours. I was an assistant chief of staff, responsible for a lot of things. It was a rigorous, unpleasant life-style. There were no frills, no real benefits to the job, so I was just as glad to be rid of it.

Now one of the greatest ironies of this whole thing—and one that came back to haunt the navy later in the U.S. Court of Appeals—was that after I had been confronted and subsequently resigned, I asked to be taken off the ship to avoid embarrassment to the command. Of course, I was thinking only of the admiral. The command denied the request. They said, "No, you can't leave the ship. You must stay here and work." The reason was, my immediate superior commander was due for vacation, and he wanted his two weeks. So he left the ship, and I assumed full responsibility for my department for the first time ever, and I maintained that position for two weeks while the ship went on deployment. If I was such a threat, if I wasn't competent, if I wasn't doing my job, why did they promote me after I resigned to this position I had never held before? It was indefensible.

About a month after my boss returned, the navy sent me back to the United States for processing. So I came back and reported to Norfolk. I was immediately subjected to very blatant surveillance. They followed me around. They parked a van right outside my window. It was not at all like the movies—you knew the guy was there; you knew the phone was tapped, and you knew they were following you. What they expected to find, I don't know, because I had already said that I was gay. You would think that that would have been enough.

Nothing happened for six months. They didn't process me; they didn't discharge me. I was trying to do job interviews. I was trying to think of what I wanted to do next, but nothing happened. I didn't get paid either because my service records were stolen, along with all my luggage, in Italy when I was on my way back home. I was very lucky that two people in the Norfolk area from the gay community took good care of me.

As the months passed I knew something was wrong. What I didn't know was that Leonard Matlovich, an enlisted man in the air force, had already filed suit to challenge his discharge for being gay. Because Matlovich had filed suit, the Pentagon was terrified. The Pentagon didn't know what to do because nobody had ever filed suit against the military over this issue before.

During those six months, I read about Matlovich in the newspaper and went and talked to his attorneys in Newport News, which was just across the river. These were the first people who actually said, "Your career is worth fighting for. Your reputation is good. You're going to get a dishonorable discharge if you don't fight it, and your service is worth an honorable discharge." So I got my own attorney.

During the same six months, I went to a gay-lesbian conference at Columbia University in New York City. I went to a workshop where I stood up and made a little speech about what was happening to me. Afterward, Bill Thom, an attorney with a new gay legal organization called Lambda Legal Defense and Education Fund, came over and gave me his card and said we should talk. I was one of the first cases Lambda Legal ever took. They didn't even have an office yet. Bill also introduced me to the people at the American Civil Liberties Union [ACLU], which decided to cosponsor the case.

The point of my challenge was to block my discharge entirely. This was to take place at an administrative hearing. Normally, what happens at an administrative hearing is that you stand up and say why you don't want to be discharged. And they say, "That's very nice, but we're going to discharge you anyway." The hearing is over, and you go home. But in my case that didn't happen. The whole thing blew up in this incredibly bizarre way. There was a whole press pool there; they even set up a press room. They had a battery of some five attorneys against me. Representatives from the Pentagon came and sat through all the hearings. And, of course, they were still following me and I assumed they were tapping my phone. They were more paranoid than I was. Their overreaction was overwhelming. None of us knew quite what to do.

You have to remember that I was a very young man, so I wasn't really prepared for all of this. What did come easily for me, though, were press interviews. Because of my glee-club touring experience and my position in public relations with the Sixth Fleet, I knew how to do interviews and handle the press. I knew everybody responsible for newspaper contacts all over the East Coast of the United States and all over Europe, and they all knew me on a first-name basis. I was fairly well prepared for the press. That was one of the ironies of the whole thing.

I gave lots of interviews. I came to realize that there wasn't anything I wasn't willing to discuss. That, in itself, was probably the greatest shock of the whole case, that I would stand up and discuss my sexual history and the ethical and religious aspects of it. This was shocking because when my case started, the social climate was so bad that you couldn't even say the word homosexual in public. Reporters who asked me about it and the military officers who were trying the case would choke on the word, which was always said with a cough and never in full voice. Reporters were so afraid of the subject that they certainly were not going to ask me anything that I hadn't thought about. After these interviews, a lot of reporters would say to me, "You're just terrific. You're great. It's all those other people I don't understand." That was a long time ago.

In preparation for the administrative hearing, the ACLU sent me to Johns Hopkins University to be interviewed by Dr. John Money and his staff, so they could present an expert witness who had met and evaluated me. John is a human sexuality expert. At Johns Hopkins, they put me through the Minnesota Multiphasic Personality Inventory test, which asks whether you'd rather be a forest ranger or an artist or a truck driver. They gave me the ink-blot test. I was just terrified; I thought for sure there was something wrong with me. I knew that psychiatrists were serious business, and if anybody was ever going to discover something wrong with me, this would be it.

After all of the testing, I went in to meet John Money himself. We had a conversation that lasted for about three hours and then we went out to dinner. We were fast friends. What I didn't realize was that the whole conversation was the interview: John based his evaluation on the time we spent talking. He later testified that I was very stable and that the number of orgasms I had had with each sex—which at that point had been about 50–50, men to women—qualified me as a true bisexual.

Before the hearing started, John said something interesting to me: "Remember when you get down there, it doesn't matter what they do. Every affidavit you submit is one foot farther out the door. You're going to be discharged. The only thing that matters is what you write about it after it's over."

The whole thing was so bizarre because although it was supposed to be an administrative hearing, it had been blown up into a trial with a prosecutor. They spent plenty of time grilling me on the stand, and remember, this was not a court-martial. It was not a trial, so I had no rights. There were no protections. It was a kangaroo court. They could do anything they wanted, and they did.

In the middle of all this, one commanding officer was reported to have said that I should have my ring finger cut off because I was still wearing my Annapolis ring. There were death threats. The Ku Klux Klan was involved. Matlovich also had terrible troubles because he was so highly visible. He had a lot of threats, including one where people threatened to cut his balls off and stuff them in his mouth. So he had FBI protection the whole time.

One morning I came out of the apartment where I was staying and found that somebody had messed with the hood of my car. Another morning I discovered that somebody had stolen the wheels off the car and disconnected the distributor cap. I don't even remember all the things that happened. On the other hand, I would be at lunch and some guy would walk up and say, "USNA Class of '63. Good job! Go get 'em!" So there was encouragement, too, but that was very secretive. They would come shake my hand, but then they were gone. I didn't hear their names, and I didn't see them again.

By the end of the second week, things had become a disaster. Carrington Bogan, the lead attorney from Lambda Legal who was handling my case, had a laid-back style. He was a very nice person, but he was so laid back about it that it almost looked like he wasn't trying, although I'm sure he was. I had four lawyers—an air force lawyer, a navy-appointed lawyer, an ACLU lawyer, and Bogan—and a legal assistant. The navy lawyer told me that he was deeply religious and that because I was an unrepentant sinner, he didn't think he could represent me fairly.

All of these lawyers came in at the last minute, and they were all trying to put together a defense, yet none of them really knew what had gone on. So I wrote my own briefs and told the lawyers what to say. Despite this, we were still in a position where I would take the stand to testify, and the lawyers would ask me questions we hadn't discussed in advance. So they didn't know how I would respond. It was a real circus.

Another example of how crazy things were during the two-week hearing was when the admiral in charge of the base went on television, of all things, and said to a reporter that there was no way that any homosexual would ever be retained while he was in command. It was a prejudicial statement if I'd ever heard one. If I had been his press aide, that never would have happened. You just don't say that to the press. So there were grounds for dismissing the whole thing. There were grounds for appeal. Everybody who could do something wrong on the military's part had done something wrong. And that sort of thing happened every day of the hearing.

The press covered every aspect of the hearing. They printed everything I said. They printed everything the navy said. It was front-page news in the local community. The Associated Press wire carried every story. Then *Time* magazine and the *New York Times* came in, which was a big shock because I thought it was really a local story. Because of all the publicity, I got lots of mail. Most of it was very sad. People would write and say, "I have nobody I can talk to. I think I'm the only one in the whole world. My life is miserable. I can't tell my parents." I heard stories from people in the military who had been arrested, thrown in the brig, and beaten. Horrible, horrible stories about what other people had suffered. I even got one letter that was addressed to "The Gay Ensign, Norfolk, Virginia," and it was delivered to my home!

THE NAVY produced one witness to testify against me. His name was Laurent Crofwell. They brought Crofwell over from Italy, and he was supposed to testify that I made a pass at him—not that sex took place, not that I had hurt him, not that there was any assault, but that I had made a pass, which, in fact, I did not. This testimony was supposed to blow my case out of the water, especially after Vice Admiral William T. Mack came from the Naval Academy to testify that I should be retained, and John Money testified that I was psychologically stable, and lots of other witnesses testified that I was this great guy and great officer.

Well, the old Greek maxim is, One witness is no witness, and that was exactly true here. Crofwell testified, and all he could say were good things about me: how popular I was on the ship, how helpful I had been to him as an individual, how I took an interest in people, how effective I had been on the staff, and lots of things. Crofwell also testified under oath that I'd made a pass at him, so it was a wash. He didn't blow my case out of the water. After his testimony, Crofwell was dumped. The prosecutor and the whole staff walked off and left him standing at the court building with no way to get home.

My father also testified at my hearing. The experience destroyed him. My parents didn't know anything about the fact I was gay until the hearing started. I had been dating women and had almost gotten married while I was in Annapolis, so they didn't think anything was unusual or wrong. I had gone off to Italy as the great Annapolis graduate. I was a big success.

The only thing I told my parents after I handed in my resignation was, "I'm being sent back to the United States." Then I said, "I'm being processed for discharge." Finally, I said it was because I had been accused of being a homosexual, and I was going to fight it. And they said, "Fine. Fight it." But they thought I was going to defend myself against false allegations. I finally told them what was really going on. I was frightened. It was not easy, and I never would have told my parents about my sexuality if I hadn't had to tell them. I knew it would be a great disappointment and that it was not something to be proud of. But *Time* magazine was there covering the story, so I didn't have much choice. There was no way to hide it.

At any rate, my father flew down for the hearing because I told him I wanted him there, and I wanted him there in uniform. He was still a navy chaplain, and at the time he was a commander. He had just come back from Vietnam. He showed up in uniform and sat there for the whole two weeks of the hearing just watching. He listened to the interviews and to all the conversations with the lawyers. He heard everything, and some of it was not exactly pleasant.

At the end of the two weeks, when I asked my father to testify, he said he wanted to. Nobody knew what he would say, but I decided it just didn't matter. He was my father; he was a career military officer, and I thought he should take the stand.

What my father said was about as revolutionary as anything anybody could have said. He was incredibly supportive. He testified that he thought that my sense of personal honor was higher than his own. And that the reason I was in trouble was because I had been asked a

Ensign Copy Berg with his father, Commander Vernon Berg, in front of the hearing building at the Naval Air Station in Norfolk, Virginia, January 1976.

question and told the truth. He said he didn't think I should be punished for having told the truth. He then went on to say that he knew of undetected homosexuals who served as openly gay combat marines. The prosecutor was nonplussed. He couldn't believe it. He said, "And there was no discrimination?" My father said, "No, of course not. Quite the contrary. Those people lived together in fox-holes and fought side by side. If these people thought there was discrimination, they would band together to protect the guy who was being discriminated against." Then he said, "Who cares who you sleep with? It's not a factor."

There was wonderful testimony where my father said, "If I hold a man in my arms and kiss him on the forehead because he's dying, does that make me gay? How are we going to define this? Am I never allowed to show affection to another human being?" Then he went on to say that he knew of undetected homosexuals serving in the ranks of commander, captain, and rear admiral and that my accusers had better be careful who they criticized because their bosses might be gay. That testimony made the front page of nearly every paper in the country.

The sad part of this story is that my father was severely criticized and severely punished by his navy-chaplain colleagues, especially the admiral-level chaplains at the Pentagon. They criticized him for what they thought was a betrayal of professional trust. They felt that people had confessed to him as a clergyman and that he had betrayed that trust by saying in public that he knew of people who were gay. My father blew up. He said, "I didn't betray a professional trust! I only testified about people who had made passes at me!"

To the day my father died he was furious about what the church did to him. The navy chaplains and the national Presbyterian church structure—he was a Presbyterian minister—all turned their backs on him. They ostracized him. They wouldn't talk to him or return his phone calls. Then he got cancer from the Agent Orange he'd been exposed to in Vietnam. He was retired—theoretically, for the cancer—but he had already been passed over for promotion. In the military, when you're passed over, your career is over.

So he retired and went down to the Outer Banks of North Carolina, where he opened a guide service for duck hunters and carved ducks until the day he died. He just turned his back on the whole thing. He said that the only place he felt comfortable was on the marsh in a boat with his dog and a gun. He would go out all day, every day, and sit there all by himself. For the longest time we were really afraid that he would end it all out there on the marsh, especially when the cancer was so bad. I really expected that, but I couldn't have been more wrong. He hated the idea of dying even worse than all the rest of it.

This was clearly a case of the sins of the son visiting the father. My father died an absolutely broken man. He came back from Vietnam very bitter to begin with. I didn't know it at the time; he never talked about Vietnam. It was only shortly before he died, long after the hearing was over, that he revealed that he felt that the church had failed him, that the military had failed him, and that virtually all of his friends had failed him. I was furious. I still am.

THE CIRCUS finally ended in January of 1976. For another six months I was required to go into work every day and just sit there. In June I was finally discharged—it was a dishonorable discharge—and I came to New York just in time for the big bicentennial celebration. It wasn't until I got to New York that I found out what a dishonorable discharge meant. I couldn't get veterans' benefits. I couldn't get unemployment, food stamps, assistance, or anything. Why they included food stamps is beyond me.

Nonetheless I was happy to be in New York after Virginia, which had been a very bad experience. The press coverage in Virginia was so saturated that I was recognized almost everywhere I went. I had teenagers throwing things at me from their cars. People screamed at me on the streets, "Get lost, faggot!" It's a very conservative area with a lot of Bible beaters who beat the Bible but don't read it. I was the small-town-boy-made-bad. Don't forget that the high school where I was student-body president was in Virginia Beach, and the hearing took place in Norfolk. It's all one big metropolitan area. I knew I couldn't stay in Virginia. I couldn't even get a job there.

When I first came to New York, I went to art school and at the same time tried to get a job in advertising. I thought it was something I could do. I met a lot of creative gay people in advertising, and they passed me around from interview to interview. They all said that they had read about my case in the *New York Times* and they wanted me to tell them all about it. But every single one of them sent me away. Their reasoning was, "It's okay with me if you're gay, but we could never send you out to talk to clients. We might lose an account." I found the hypocrisy and the duplicity I encountered in New York to be more exasperating than what I had encountered in the military. It shocked me. I came to New York for my salvation, thinking it was the only place on the face of the Earth where I could work and survive, only to find out that they were more closeted than I had been in the military. I finally got a job through the Pratt Institute after I graduated from there with my design degree. I was hired by a Pratt graduate. By this time I knew better than to say anything about my history.

My DISCHARGE wasn't the end of my case. It was combined with the Matlovich case and taken before the U.S. Court of Appeals. The cases were merged as a kind of class-action suit during the Jimmy Carter White House. The legal team was talking with the White House, specifically with Midge Costanza and Marilyn Haft, and they were dealing with the Pentagon. They were putting pressure on the Pentagon to alter its policy of giving homosexuals dishonorable discharges, and the Pentagon changed its policy, which flabbergasted me. I still can't believe the Pentagon did it. They changed the policy to state that if you were discharged for reasons of homosexuality, you would get an honorable discharge, which they'd never done before. They went even further and made the policy retroactive, so that any person who had ever been discharged for reasons of homosexuality could have their discharge upgraded to honorable.

Ultimately, the U.S. Court of Appeals said that homosexuality per se was not enough of a reason to justify my discharge and that the Pentagon had to discharge me on other grounds. At this point, the case went back to the Pentagon for them to resubmit, which is when they offered the deal of upgraded discharges. By this time Carter had just lost to Ronald Reagan, and things didn't look very promising for us. The lawsuit had gone about as far as we thought it could go, and the upgraded discharge was about as good a policy change as we could have expected. The court could not have done better than that for us. We decided that that was as much law as we could make, so we settled out of court. Both Matlovich and I got cash settlements and signed a piece of paper saying that we would never try to reenlist.

DURING THE five years from the hearing until the out-of-court settlement, I was not treated very well by most of the gay activists I came in contact with. Most of them were also antiwar activists and felt I had no business being in the military to begin with. When I first moved to New York, I used to get a phone call once a year for about four years. Somebody would call me and say, "The Christopher Street Liberation Day gay pride parade committee has decided that you are not to be invited to the parade." And I thought, *What are they talking about? I didn't ask to go.* It turned out that for about four years running, there was a big fight within the committee. Some people thought I should be nominated as grand marshal, and others thought that I shouldn't be there at all. The people who thought that I shouldn't be there always won. So some guy would call me up and say, "There was this big fight, and you lost."

In the late seventies I worked on a book about my experience called *Get Off My Ship*, which Lawrence Gibson wrote. I did a book tour, appeared a lot on television, and spoke to a lot of gay groups. In most cases I found the groups at that time very petty. They were jealous of success on the part of other groups and individuals, so if you aligned yourself with one gay group, the others wouldn't talk to you. Then you had the lesbians fighting with the gay men, and the black gays fighting with the white gays.

Quite frankly, since that time, nobody has ever asked me to even speak. I volunteered a number of times, and they just didn't call me back. Now that I'm successful enough in my own life, I'm solicited by gay rights organizations for contributions. So it's come full circle.

Today I'm sort of a military adviser, in that people come to me from the military for guidance and advice. They call me because I'm a name that military people know. I always do what I can to help. I feel like an underground railroad.

I think the military will ultimately lose this battle over excluding homosexuals. The very best thing that could happen is that one day somebody will quietly say, "We are no longer pursuing a policy of discharging gays." You just stop throwing people out. But they're afraid of the public relations impact on their recruiting, that if they're perceived as a "haven for homosexuals," then mothers and fathers will not allow their sons and daughters to enlist. Well, they're the ones who control that image. They could very quietly stop the processing for discharges, and their problem would essentially evaporate. I think that's the way the change should happen, but it won't. They're going to fight this every inch of the way, and they're going to fall just like the Communist governments did. The sand is going to give out from underneath them, and the courts are going to clobber them, and the media's going to clobber them. They're going to have the very public relations disaster they're trying to avoid.

I JUST went to my fifteen-year reunion at Annapolis in October [1989]. It was the first time I had gone back for an official function. I had a great time; it was wonderful. Everybody was happy to see me—almost everybody, except four big guys who were in my class, football types, who I did not know. There were two moments over the weekend when I walked past these guys and heard them say something to the effect, "You know who's here? Copy Berg, ha, ha, ha. Can you believe it?" I walked past the same four guys at dinner that night when I was in the company of a classmate's wife, a very beautiful young woman. The look of shock on their faces was so profound that I wished I had a camera. I thought, *Great! That's perfect!* They knew I wasn't embarrassed to be there, that I had nothing to hide. They also knew that everybody else there was completely comfortable with me.

I thought the funniest comment of the whole evening was when one person said to me after I told him that I was living in New York, "Oh, you didn't stay in the navy?" He must never have read a newspaper in his life.

The Iconoclast

Nancy Walker

THROUGHOUT THE 1970s, *people who depended solely on the mainstream media to inform themselves about what was going on in the world would hardly have been aware of the gay rights movement. With a few notable exceptions, the television networks, daily newspapers, and newsmagazines avoided gay issues. To keep up, gay people increasingly turned to gay newspapers that were published independently or by gay organizations. One such newspaper, the weekly* Gay Community News, *which began publication in Boston in 1973, tried to fill the role of the national gay newspaper of record. By the mid-1970s, it had a weekly readership of approximately eight thousand people across the country.*

In 1976 Nancy Walker, a forty-one-year-old Jewish woman originally from New York City, began volunteering at GCN. It was an instant generation gap and culture clash. Yet somehow, Nancy went on to become the newspaper's only columnist and a moderate voice in a paper that prided itself on its Radical Left politics.

Nancy; Penny, her partner of nearly three decades; and their dog, Christopher Robin, share a cavernous old house in a residential neighborhood just outside Boston. Nancy looked tired, but recalling her years at GCN brought her to life. She spoke emphatically and with great drama, evoking the formidable presence she must have brought to the offices of the Gay Community News.

The war years—World War II—really shaped my view of the world. I was terrified throughout the whole war because I had a warped perception—maybe not so warped—of what was going on with Jews in Europe. I was sure that if we lost, I was going to get cooked. To this day, when I hear a siren similar to the air-raid sirens we had during the war, I get very upset.

This is part of the reason why I love this country so much. When I later met Jewish people in Canada, one woman said to me, "You know, you are so aggressively Jewish. Here, you keep your mouth shut." I thought, *What an awful way to live.* There are all these god-damned closets all over the world. I have to be closeted about being

Jewish? I'm sorry, but I've got enough trouble. There's nowhere else in the world but in America that Jews are open about being Jewish and are proud of it.

GROWING UP, I really felt at odds with the world, but I didn't know why. I always felt peculiar. For one thing, I was at odds with my family. I wasn't what they wanted. My mother was a perfect lady. When she had a little girl, she thought, "Oh, a little me!" Well, I wasn't at all like her. She wanted to dress me in pretty little pink dresses. But I wanted to climb trees. I would put worms in my pockets. I was going to do what I wanted, so there was a lot of fighting. I would defy my parents, and they would beat the shit out of me. I always remained who I was and never felt guilty for anything. I didn't even feel guilty for telling my mother I hated her.

Even though I felt different, I didn't think I was gay because I really liked boys. Strangely enough, all the men I ever had a crush on as a kid turned out to be gay. I was so crazy about one of my teachers in seventh and eighth grade. He looked just like Errol Flynn. I mooned over him. He was annoyed because I got the best marks in the class, and I was a girl. Of course, he liked the boys better, but I didn't know that. Then when I was in high school, we had an exchange-teacher program. I had a Belgian for French class. I loved him, too. It turned out that he and the teacher who looked like Errol Flynn were lovers. Go know! Actually, at that time I had no idea what a gay man was, not until somebody introduced me to one when I was living in Canada many years later. I had never even thought about the possibility before. My reaction when I finally met this gay man was, "Oh boy, there are gay men in the world! Isn't that funny?" I still really have the need for male companionship. Interesting, isn't it? Even my dog is a boy.

In high school it was beginning to get to me. I was beginning to wonder what these conflicting feelings were all about. We had to do a term paper in our senior year, and I narrowed my choices to three topics. I only remember two of them: homosexuality and rabbits. The teacher said, "Rabbits!" So I learned a lot about rabbits. I went to the library and looked up homosexuals anyway. What I found was just horrifying.

At college I met a fellow whom I married. He was gentile, born in Massachusetts, a perfect gentleman. He wouldn't say "shit" if he had a mouthful of it. I don't know what he wanted with me. I never did understand. I kept saying, "Go find some nice shiksa. What do you want with me? I'm going to ruin your life." But I married him.

I fell in love with a girl for the first time in 1955, after I was already married. I met Valerie in 1954 at a convention of the National Conference of Christians and Jews at the Roosevelt Hotel in New York City. Valerie was a Hunter College student from the Bronx. She was blond, very dynamic. We talked all the time and became friends. At first I had no idea what was going on because I'm very slow to figure these things out. But she was the first person I really, really loved. Eventually, when I knew that what I felt for Valerie wasn't a silly little crush, I realized I was gay. There was no question about it. It wasn't that I didn't like men. I had no sexual problems with men, but the overwhelming emotional involvement for me was with this young woman. My relationship with Valerie was never sexual, just emotional. A couple of years later, when she got married and moved to California, I thought that the world had come to an end.

The minute I knew I was in love with Valerie, I went to Jeff, my husband, told him about my feelings for her, and said, "You want a divorce?" And he said, "No, you'll outgrow it." Well, I never did outgrow it, and eight years after I met Valerie, I met Penny. That was 1962. By this time my husband was the assistant technical director of the Playhouse, at Hofstra College, where I had gone to school. Penny was a drama student. It was like déjà vu, although Penny and Valerie are totally different physically. Penny was tall and had black hair. She had this dreadful haircut, and she was gawky. She was still a kid, a freshman. All her clothes were wrong. But like Valerie, she had an extraordinary speaking voice, and she would say the same damned things Valerie said.

We fell in love. Oh God, did we ever! And I thought, *How can this be happening a second time in my life? I can't lose it again because I'll go nuts.* I was sure Penny had this man who was interested in her and I thought, *Oh, my God, she's going to get involved with him, and I'd better prepare myself because this is not going to work.* But she said, "I love you." And I said, "You're crazy! You don't know what you're talking about! This is not what your mother had in mind." She kept looking at me, smiling, and saying, "I love you." I told her, "I don't believe it. It's puppy love. You'll get over it." This went on for quite some time, long after we were involved in a relationship. When she was twenty-five she said, "Do you believe me now?" I said, "I'll believe you when you're thirty." She finally got old enough, and I figured she really meant it. You see, I wasn't sure that the bubble wasn't going to burst, that she wasn't going to disappear on me. It was too good to be true. But all these years later, we still love each other.

* * *

WHEN PENNY and I met, we didn't know anything about gay liberation and gay organizations. This was 1962. Who knew from gay liberation? We were together nine years before we got involved in anything. It wasn't that we needed someone to tell us it was OK to be gay. Neither of us felt the least bit guilty or bad about being gay. But we had no gay friends. We were living in Toronto, where Penny had been in graduate school for a couple of years already, when we finally got brave enough to say, "We're going to do something about this." So we were on vacation in New York during the summer of 1971 and we saw a listing in the *Village Voice* of organizations and meetings. That's how we found out about the Firehouse of the Gay Activists Alliance and the Daughters of Bilitis.

Even though we thought we were big shots, it took us a long time to get the guts to go to a DOB meeting. We kept finding excuses, but finally we went to a meeting. We looked around the room and saw people who looked just like our grandmothers. I said, "What the hell, is this what we were afraid of?" That was the beginning. We went back to Canada and saw a notice in a little newspaper that talked about a homophile organization, CHAT—Community Homophile Association of Toronto. That was 1971, when we first got involved. Penny wound up as the program chairman, and I was the vice president for a couple of years.

CHAT was an umbrella group for everything, including counseling, legal work, and social events. It was early in the movement in Canada—they're always behind America. They already had legal advantages in Canada because they had a consenting-adult law, but they didn't have the social advantages. Homosexuality was still terribly condemned. People were conservative in Toronto. So, of course, the Americans who were there took over a large part of the gay movement, and the Canadians resented us for that. We were constantly embattled and embittered, but it was exhilarating because for once we were with our own people, both men and women.

CHAT was politically correct, and Penny and I weren't, which really made us the radicals—we were so different from what we were surrounded by. I remember the women didn't want anybody to be a hostess, and Penny would always try to round up a tray of cookies when there was a meeting. They thought that was terrible. But if no one is supposed to do that, who's going to pass the goddamned cookies?

Another time at a meeting we had broken up into small discussion groups of ten or twelve people. We were talking, and somebody said to me, "You can't talk! You can't use proper English because that's part of the Establishment!" I said, "What should we do, sit here and grunt? What goes on?" It got to be so dreadful—no matter what you did, it was wrong. So I have always been politically incorrect. I want to be humanly correct, not politically correct. And kindness has to come into it somewhere, too.

People in Canada came to CHAT for mostly personal reasons. They really needed to work on their own self-images. These people were really devastated. They had religious convictions, and everything told them that they were abominations. We had a lot of very unhappy, disturbed people. One of our big functions was maintaining a twenty-four-hour, seven-day-a-week hot line, which I managed. We had call forwarding, so we had it in our house. As soon as we left for Boston, they cut the hot line back to normal daytime hours and an answering machine, which is not what people need. I still think that tape recorder is a dreadful thing.

WE LEFT Toronto for Boston in 1975. Penny had gotten a job teaching at Northeastern University. Before we left, we wrote to Lois Johnson at DOB in Boston, which Lois still runs to this day. It's the only functioning DOB left in the country. Lois and her lover Sheri wrote back to us and said, "When you come to Boston, contact us." When we got to Boston, we walked to their place through Chinatown and through the most dangerous parts of Roxbury. We didn't know where the hell we were.

We arrived at their house at nine o'clock at night in the midst of a domestic quarrel. Sheri said, "You walked here? Are you crazy?" So she started telling us what we should and shouldn't do from that day on. She's still telling us. We've been friends with them ever since. They were wonderful to us. They said, "Stay here. Use our house as a base of operations." They didn't know us. And here they exposed their home and their precious cats to two total strangers. They were always taking people in and helping them.

We soon found our own place. One day I walked to the little convenience store across the street, and lo and behold, there was a gay newspaper for sale, the *Gay Community News*. In Canada I tried so hard to get hold of any gay publication I could, so I could find out what was going on in the world. There was one little sleazy bookstore in Toronto that carried a few gay papers. You had to be willing to go into what was labeled and known to the public as a filthy bookstore. I'd go in, but Miss Priss Penny wouldn't. In Boston it was out in the open. We didn't have to do sleazy things to be gay.

In May of 1976 I went to the *Gay Community News*, which is published here in Boston, to help out as a proofreader. GCN is a national gay newspaper, the only gay national weekly that's been published continuously since the early 1970s. I decided to volunteer at GCN because I wanted to do something in the gay community. They were always running ads that they needed help on Thursday nights, which was layout night, so I volunteered. I don't know what I expected, but the place was unbelievable. It was up a long, steep flight of stairs, and at the top, you came into this big open space that was a mess. There were some scruffy-looking, very radical people. Any kind of dress you can imagine, they wore. It was a real mixed bag, everything from the typical straight man, with short hair, to cross-dressers. This one young man, who I hope is still alive, was wearing a pair of very short shorts and sandals. He had his legs crossed and was bouncing his feet up and down. He had glitter nail polish on his toe nails. I thought, *How am I going to deal with this guy?* But I came to love him very much. He cross-dressed and did outrageous things. The pressure is really on people like that. I think it takes tremendous courage, a kind of physical courage that I haven't got. I'm not about to go and wear a man's suit and jump up and down. That's not for me.

The real radicals, like the cross-dressers—the people others point fingers at—are the ones who spearhead a movement. They get the attention. They've done something. We can disapprove, but without them, we don't get anywhere. We can come along in our suits and ties and our dresses and be very proper afterwards and get the legislation we want, but that's after they stick their necks out and get beaten up.

GCN was absolutely nonprofit, and plenty of people volunteered their time. They had to work very hard to get materials. They never had any money. Our typesetter, David Stryker, another man now dead from AIDS, carried us for as many years as we went without our own typesetting equipment. If he had charged anything like the normal rates, the paper would have dissolved. He gave the typesetting away, and he did that for every gay publication in town.

David and I saw eye to eye politically, and we saw eye to eye on language. So when he saw things in articles that weren't correct, he'd fix them. The kids had a fit. I said, "David is right. If you don't want him to change something, put a note on it: 'David, I know this is wrong, but I'm doing it for a reason.' Otherwise he's going to do as I would do and correct it."

GCN called itself a collective, which meant there were no bosses. We had endless meetings to make tiny decisions. Like over the subtitle of the newspaper. It used to be called the *Gay Community News, The Gay Weekly*. Then it became *The Gay and Lesbian Weekly*. I said, "Why don't you call it *The Gay Communist Weekly* and be done with it!" We had endless, horrible meetings on the goddamned subtitle that nobody was going to notice anyway! Yet every Thursday night, and sometimes into Friday morning, we laid out that fucking paper. We went through whatever we had to, to get that paper out. When arsonists burned the place down once, we just moved over to a place in Cambridge. We never missed a week, except for two weeks during the year when everyone took vacations.

I WOULD say at least 90 percent of the people at any one time at GCN were thoroughly radical—and then some of the rest were mostly radical. *Radical* in those days meant denouncing the government, hating the country. Those were the kind of people to whom I'd say, "Go! Go live in Russia! See how long you last!" There was never any logic to their positions. OK, so the country is bad. Fix it! Tell me a solution! But they would say, "Tear it down!" I said, "Don't you guys realize that if there was genuine anarchy, we'd be the first to go? What's the matter with you? If there's no law to protect us, they'll shoot us down in the streets." Nobody understood that logic. My friends at GCN thought I was the world's worst conformist, but my whole life I was never a conformist.

The people at GCN would demonstrate. They would zap. They found fault with everything. They called themselves progressives, but you know, it translates as *Red*—and I don't even dislike communism as a philosophy. But I disliked these people's behavior. Theoretically, we shared a common goal: We wanted gay liberation. But what did that mean? Did it mean equal rights? That's all I ever wanted. On the other hand, some of them wanted to be able to fuck in the parks. Well, that's wonderful, but if they did, I wouldn't take my children to the parks, either. I didn't think that group sex was terrific. I didn't think that we had the right to do that. How far is sexual freedom supposed to go? Are you allowed to have intercourse on the street corner because you feel like doing it? How does that make you different from a dog? What happens to civilization when people lose all their socialization and have sex when, where, and with whom they please? We have to have a little bit of self-control, a little discipline. I'm sorry, but I'm not interested in sexual freedom. I'm interested in being able to live.

As much as I disliked GCN politically, it had one policy that was wonderful, the ad policy. They did not use ads that exploited human beings, like the *Advocate*, so it was very hard to survive financially. I said to them once, "Great, publish GCN this way, and let's also have a filthy rag that takes any kind of garbage to make money." I was kidding, but they were horrified at everything I said.

Another thing that horrified them was what I said over the issue of black people. GCN had to be politically correct, which meant that you had to have black people. And I said, "You want to go into the street and drag them in here by the hair?" I said, "All you have to do to be politically right is to say you are welcome. Goddamit! We don't have to go out there and solicit!" Somehow or other, whatever it was about GCN, it didn't attract the black movement. They were working out other problems at the time. I think GCN didn't respect the fact that gay black people had a lot of other issues to deal with before dealing with their homosexuality and coming in to work at what they must have seen as a predominantly white gay paper. People at GCN were very anxious about it, and we had many conversations about how to attract black people.

I was unpopular for another thing that I truly believe, that we should deal with gay issues and not try to spread ourselves all over the world. Like that Rainbow Coalition stuff. When I was fighting for gay civil rights, I didn't want to get into women, blacks, or South America. I wanted to deal with gay issues. They thought I was wrong, but that's how I felt.

One time we had this big blowup over someone who burned a Bible at a Gay Pride Day rally. It almost tore the newspaper apart. A fellow named Charlie Shively, who was terribly, terribly radical, tore up his Harvard degree and burned the Bible. Later we found out that he did not actually destroy his diploma—it was a photocopy. That was the kind of shit I couldn't stand. But anyway, even before I knew this, I was livid. Not that burning the Bible offends me—I'm not at all religious. I just didn't think that burning the Bible when every camera in the city was focused on you was such a good thing. Why constantly offend the very people whose votes and friendship you need to get what you supposedly want? We don't have to kiss asses; I think that's undignified. But you have to deal with these people in a way that makes sense.

I went back to the office, and I think smoke was coming out of my typewriter. I wrote a "Speaking Out" column and said that I thought that burning the Bible was the most deathly thing he could have done. I don't remember what else I said, but it was quite clear that I was angry. After reading my column, the news editor said to me, "They're going to call you a Nazi for denouncing Charlie." I said, "I don't give a shit what they call me, just publish it." And what was so nice about them was that they published it.

There was a big debate over whether the paper should make an editorial statement about what happened at the rally. The whole office was split. We almost threw typewriters at each other over what the statement should be because there were two diametrically opposed opinions. One was to say, "Right on Charlie!" The other was to say, "Ring his fucking neck!"

After a couple of hours of this debate, we stopped and looked at each other and said, "No, we're not going to make a statement. That is the only way we can save this paper." So there was no editorial statement. The rest of us went crazy and wrote whatever we thought.

WE DIDN'T get along with each other at all, even people of the same political persuasions, but you could be yourself at GCN. We knew we were among our own. It was safe, like getting to home plate. You know, it's like a Jewish family: You may not get along, but you know that this is your place, and the rest of it out there is the diaspora, where it's not your place. The rest of the world was the enemy, somehow. GCN was a sanctuary. That's how I felt. It may not sound like it, but I just loved to be there.

When I wrote the "Speaking Out" column about Charlie, I didn't yet have my own regular column. I was just another writer, a person who worked there. Everybody had the right to say whatever the hell he or she thought in a letter or a Speaking Out column. But finally I got a regular place where I could write and other people could read it. All my life I said, "I've got these great ideas and I would like somebody to know about them." There were no other columnists at GCN. They had only one, and I was it. They never had another one, and they said they were never going to have another one, because they hated me. The thing that bothered them the most, and they told me this, was that my column, "Odyssey of a Unicorn," was the single-most-popular thing in the paper. It drove them crazy. They didn't want a star at GCN. I wasn't trying to be a star, though—it just happened. But everybody was supposed to be on the same level. GCN was the great leveler.

They were heavy, heavy at GCN. Very serious stuff. I was the only one there who was happy, and every once in a while I made happy noises in my column. I was also very critical of my colleagues in my column. For all these reasons they tried to keep me from writing what I wanted to write about. They used to have meetings and tell me what I could write and what I couldn't write.

Most of the time I wrote about us, Penny and me. It was sort of like the *Perils of Pauline*, personal essays, or whatever happened during that week. It was not exactly a one-to-one relationship with the truth. Some of it was exaggerated for humor. One of my favorite columns was the one about "A" people and "Z" people always getting together. I squeeze the toothpaste from the bottom of the tube very carefully. Penny just goes shoosh!

I got a lot of positive feedback, as well as avalanches of hate mail, over the columns where I expressed a real opinion. I think the largest avalanche was over the man-boy love column. It was already a major issue when we were in Toronto. Then when we came here, it was NAMBLA—the North American Man/Boy Love Association. I thought it was terrible. I thought it was bad news. We were still fighting for our civil rights, and they were doing things that were going to horrify the nice, straight middle class without whose support we couldn't get anywhere. Society doesn't like us to begin with. They're frightened of us. And now if we start fooling with the kids, that's going to give them just the material they need to keep us in chains forever. I said, "This is the fuel they need to kill us."

Everybody, every group, every individual, does things they don't want published. That's how I felt about this issue. I would rather have kept it quiet, swept under the carpet. Let us get our rights first and then go crazy, if you have to go crazy, but don't do it publicly. You see, we needed to be perfect. That's what happens when you're a minority struggling for your rights. You've got to be good. It doesn't mean it's right. It's not fair. But you've got to be good. You've got to do things better and be perfectly moral, otherwise you don't have a chance. Maybe I'm wrong, but that's how I think. Sometimes you think something is really evil, really destructive. I just had the gut feeling that man-boy love, in addition to the political aspect, was awful.

After the big blowup over the man-boy column, the next one I wrote was about bananas. I wrote about how Penny and I would buy a certain number of bananas, and when we got down to the last one, Penny wouldn't eat it because she wanted me to have it and I wouldn't eat it because I wanted her to have it. So the banana got blacker and blacker and more disgusting and finally got thrown out. I managed to stretch that out for a number of pages. It was a very funny article. And I ended it with, "Mother has just sent us some grapefruit." After that, and for quite some time, I would find bananas on my doorknob at GCN. People left me bananas all over the place. They were hysterical.

I WAS at GCN from 1976 to 1984. During that time, it changed its typeface and the way it looked, but I don't think it changed its basic philosophy. Finally, I just got really tired of the hassle. Everything was a big battle. I had no freedom. I had to constantly fight to get them to put the column in. They would always tell me they didn't have the

Nancy Walker *(left)* with Barbara Gittings in Boston in 1979. *(© Penelope S. Tzougros)*

space, that they couldn't run the column when they were supposed to. I was working full time, and it just got to be too much. Another publication in Boston, *Bay Windows*, wanted me to write for them, so I quit GCN and started writing for *Bay Windows*. GCN hated me for going over to the enemy. We couldn't live in the same town.

The day I left GCN, nobody said good-bye, except for one woman. Chris was very kind and gave me a long-stem rose. Nobody else even spoke to me. But I wasn't there for them—I was there for my readers. Today I miss my readers. Some of them were very dear. I keep thinking that by quitting GCN, I may have denied them the voice that they needed to hear. I would get letters saying, "Somebody finally said what I believe." I don't know who else is writing the kind of stuff I wrote.

I was more comfortable at *Bay Windows*, for a while. It really didn't pretend to be a newspaper. It was a social rag with a lot of columnists and personal-interest stuff. I knew I didn't have a mission there. There was no illusion of doing anything meaningful. At GCN you could feel like you were some kind of hero. At *Bay Windows* you were a writer with an audience, and that was nice, but it wasn't a heroic act of any kind. Then we had an editor who screwed up my columns once too often, and I just had enough. I finally said, "The hell with it!"

I do want to put in a plug for GCN. After all the personal battles, I think it is a great thing. Not because it was the first gay weekly paper, but because of the courage those people had. They provided something that was desperately needed. In those days, gay news wasn't covered in the mainstream press. We needed to let people know what was going on, and we needed contact with each other. There were still gay people who didn't know there was anybody else in the world like them, so we had a tremendous sense of mission at GCN. So even though we may not have loved each other, we loved the newspaper and we protected it. If anything was holy, it was GCN. GCN got the word out. It took years before we got more than thirty seconds on the news even during Gay Pride Week or the rallies. And all during that time, GCN was there.

The Insider
Charles Brydon

IN 1977, when Anita Bryant, pop singer and orange-juice spokeswoman, began her campaign to repeal the newly won gay rights ordinance in Dade County, Florida, Charlie Brydon wasn't concerned. A politically well-connected, accomplished businessman, Charlie founded and ran Seattle's Dorian Group, a thriving downtown gay professional organization that sponsored regular luncheons and dinners. He and many other gay men and women had worked for years to give Seattle's gay community a significant voice in the political life of the city. But as Bryant's successful crusade against gay rights laws went national, Charlie realized he would have to call on every one of his political connections to help save his city's antidiscrimination ordinance.

Forging political connections and building professional coalitions was nothing new to Charlie Brydon. Through the Dorian Group, he had already formed a genial relationship with Seattle's mayor, Wes Ulman. "The mayor was facing a recall effort," Charlie explained, "and he knew that in cities elsewhere in the country gay people were emerging as a political force. He wanted to tap into that community in Seattle, and I was probably a comfortable person for him to talk to as opposed to those who were constantly engaging in confrontation. He needed me, and I needed him."

Charlie, a Vietnam veteran, is a lifelong Democrat, and a self-described "political animal." His partner, David, thinks he looks more like an archconservative. To the more radical gay activists in Seattle during the 1970s, Charlie Brydon was far worse than that: an Uncle Tom who was in bed, figuratively, with every heterosexual political leader and power broker in Seattle, from the mayor to the Catholic archbishop. "To the radical gays," said Charlie, "I suspect I was a worse enemy than the heterosexual public at large. They wanted a them-versus-us presentation of the gay rights issue. And here I was, a businessman who had ready access to the mayor and members of the City Council. Plus, I didn't immediately cast the police department as villains."

Charlie Brydon's involvement in the struggle for gay equal rights led him to serve in the late 1970s as co-executive director of the National Gay and Lesbian Task Force. Today, trim and fit in middle age, he runs his own insurance business in Seattle.

'Ready when you are, Anita'

Charlie Brydon on the cover of *Seattle Weekly* (July 29–July 5, 1977). (*Courtesy* Seattle Weekly)

We never thought Anita Bryant would be a problem for us. You know how there's this attitude easterners have toward westerners? Well, it works both ways. At one of the Dorian dinners we raised a couple of thousand dollars for the effort to stop the Dade County repeal, but people here didn't think that Anita Bryant was a threat to us. Our thinking at the time was, "Here in Seattle we're way beyond that. It couldn't happen here because the environment is so different."

Then things started to get a little uncomfortable as Bryant's campaign spread across the country and gay rights ordinance after gay rights ordinance was successfully repealed. When it happened in St. Paul, people in Seattle started to get concerned. There are a lot of connections between Minneapolis–St. Paul and Seattle. For one thing, both are big Scandinavian towns.

When it started to look as if we were going to have a problem here—in late June 1977—the *Seattle Weekly* newspaper put me on its front page. It was a full-page picture of me with the heading, "Ready When You Are, Anita." I raised hell with the editor, because I never even said that, and he put it in quotes! What a provocative thing to do.

When this cop here in Seattle filed the petitions to gather signatures to put the repeal initiative on the ballot, I never thought he would get enough signatures. But just in case, we immediately formed a very quiet group to begin planning. Most of the people in this group were the political brains of the city. Their advice was, "Don't do anything to give this signature drive media attention." That immediately put me at odds with the radicals. They wanted to focus attention on us. And, I suspect, they wanted to try to create the feeling that you were a bad person if you signed the petitions.

Probably the darkest day of my life was when I heard on the news that the petitions had been filed and they contained more than an adequate number of signatures to place this thing on the ballot. I just didn't know what we would do. We had seen a chain of defeats around the country. Why would it be any different here?

WHEN I got over the initial shock, I saw how much better positioned we were in Seattle in terms of our relationship with the mainstream. At that point, thanks to the Dorian Group, as well as other groups and individuals, the gay community had been visible in Seattle in a positive way. To many thoughtful people, including those in the church hierarchy, who had already dealt with us and gotten through their homophobia, we were not much of a threat. It also helped that the two police officers who were the primary advocates for Initiative 13 were as bumbling as they could possibly have been. One of them managed to shoot a black kid going over a fence in a chase about two months before the vote, which took the black community off the political fence.

Perhaps most important, we realized that we had to define the issue in such a way that the larger community would want to support our efforts. We started by making a trip to St. Paul in March of 1978. The repeal in St. Paul had taken place the year before, and this was the first time since then that the people who fought the repeal got together. For them it was a very difficult and emotional thing to have to bring up their defeat again, but for us it was very useful.

By the time we got back to Seattle, it was clear to me that we needed a different approach from the one used in Florida or St. Paul. They took the civil rights and "Gay is good" and "We should be approved because we're good people" line. Obviously, that was just a flop.

Fortunately for us, we had some significant help in framing the issue. At the same time we were contending with our initiative, California was dealing with Proposition 6, the Briggs initiative—a proposed statewide law that would have forbidden gay teachers from working in the public schools. A lot of great political talent was suddenly focused on "How do we articulate the issue in such a way as to make it understandable and supportable by the majority of voters?" That's what politics is all about. What we came up with was the "Right-to-privacy" line. We said that sexual orientation applied not only to gay people, but to heterosexuals and bisexuals as well. And that we needed to keep the government and your employer out of your bedroom. The right-to-privacy line is something that everyone can put themselves into. So *we* defined the issue, and we defined it early.

We had a wonderful campaign poster. It showed a huge keyhole with an eye peering through it. And our television ads showed people living in a fishbowl with people peering in at them. That got the message across.

Now there were those in the gay community who tried to define the issue in terms of our differences. "This is what makes us unique. This is what makes us special." I think those things have to be said within the gay community, but when you start to define your issue in terms of the public at large, you have to define it in such a way that people can feel that what you're trying to accomplish is right and that it's something they want to be a part of. That's the only way you'll win.

When election night came around, our group, Citizens to Retain Fair Employment, had the biggest hall in town. Of course, ours was not the only group fighting Initiative 13. There was SCAT, the Seattle Committee Against Thirteen. There was WAT, Women Against Thirteen. And then there was a fourth organization, in which a lot of the radical and younger gay people got involved. We spent a fair amount of energy preventing war between the organizations.

As the early returns came in and showed there was going to be an overwhelming defeat of Initiative 13, people just jammed our hall. We had the media attention, so everybody ended up coming downtown, trying to get in. It was fantastic!

Ironically, that was the same hall where we had our kickoff campaign to defeat 13. Practically no one had come to that, which was really scary at the time. I suspect that nobody thought these repeal campaigns could be defeated. No one had defeated them before. By winning, we demonstrated that when an antigay measure is brought up on a municipal level, you don't have to run and hide and assume that you're just going to get your tail whooped.

Nationally, our win was overshadowed by the win on Proposition 6 in California, as it should have been. That was an incredible achievement: a statewide ballot issue coming through as well as it did in a state with such a diverse population. It was just a magnificent achievement. But we relished the fact that we won up here in Seattle by a greater percentage of votes than they did in California.

AFTER THE success on Initiative 13 and after having worked on the Dorian Group for several years, I felt I needed to back away from all I had been involved in. I've always believed that you can't make a career out of being an activist. You need to get on with life. I had also reached a point in my business career where I had accomplished what I set out to do. I was forty, single, and not sure where I was going next. I just knew I was ready for a change. At this time I was offered the job of co-executive director of the National Gay Task Force [NGTF] in New York City. Now it's called the National Gay and Lesbian Task Force [NGLTF].

I'd been on the board of the Task Force since 1975, so I knew the organization very well. When I was first asked to join the board, my sense was that Bruce Voeller, the co-executive director at the time, was really trying to reach beyond the New York City base of the organization, which was this fairly radical core group. I think he was trying to season it with some more politically and geographically diverse points of view.

I have a very vivid impression of the first board meeting I attended. Here I was coming to a national organization, and I thought, *This will be an impressive and serious-minded group.* But it was like a trip back into the sixties counterculture era. We met in a loft, and everybody sat on the floor. By and large, people involved in the movement at that time were not your mainstream persons. They were individuals who did not have to worry about risking their careers to do this kind of work because they didn't have professional careers. They were different from me in their approach and their views.

There was a lot of this touchy-feely sort of thing at this board meeting. We'd break up into small groups and have discussions. Very utopian kinds of ideas or solutions to problems would be expressed. Now, I'm not a utopian person and I'm not an idealist. I'm a pragmatist. So you can imagine how out of it I felt.

I came away with mixed feelings. It was very uplifting, on the one hand, because I had a chance to talk with people from around the country. But it was also disturbing to go into this strange setting and hear these unrealistic, usually ideologically skewed, points of view expressed. It just wasn't what I expected. I expected to offer my perspective from the Northwest and to get some practical ideas to take back with me.

Perhaps what struck me most strongly was that I had thought the

NGTF board would be representative of the gay community nationally. But they weren't. I didn't know how this group could represent gay people because they were too small a slice of a very big pie.

WHEN I was hired by NGTF to be co-executive director, it was fairly controversial. They didn't quite know what to make of me because I was not your typical activist. On the other hand, they couldn't deny that we had won the battle against Initiative 13 in Seattle—and we had won big.

I thought long and hard before taking the job. I had lots of reservations, particularly the unwieldiness of the organization, its financial poverty, and its small membership. I didn't see how it would be possible to have much impact with only seven thousand members. And given the power of the closet, I wasn't certain how much we could increase that number. NGTF was tiny in relation to the size of the gay community nationally.

The financial poverty of NGTF was staggering. Hell, they paid the staff poverty wages. These people were living in dreadful conditions. I took the job at a totally impossible salary. I think they were paying me around $17,000. Admittedly, this was 1979, but that salary was still terrible for New York City. But more important, if I was getting $17,000, the other staff people were getting, in some cases, less than $10,000. I will say that one of my accomplishments was to get the salaries to near-market levels. That had a big impact on self-esteem.

When I took the job, I wanted to work along the same lines as the two previous co-executive directors, Bruce Voeller and Jean O'Leary. They had had a number of successes in dealing with the federal government. I thought there was some opportunity there—for example, working with the Justice Department to change immigration laws that discriminated against gays. I was also very keen on NGTF being a truly national organization because, despite its name, NGTF was really just another New York City organization. That meant pulling NGTF out of New York City issues, which didn't go over very well with the NGTF staff.

In addition to improving staff compensation and professionalizing the staff, I felt we needed to do more to help local gay organizations around the country. To raise money and address the financial problems, I really wanted to take advantage of these new gay mailing lists that had become available as a result of all these antirepeal campaigns around the country. With the lists we would finally have someone to mail our fund-raising letters to.

But getting anything done proved to be impossible. What hap-

pened was that after I was hired, the board set out to find someone
to fill the other co-executive director position. They were looking for
a contrasting person, a woman, who would be as different from me as
they could find. Well, this was a formula for disaster. Lucia Valeska
was the board's choice. She came from outside New York City. As
soon as she got comfortable in her job, she began to assert herself, and
everything was a battle. It was just one unending battle; it was paralysis. We tried negotiations. We tried everything.

The ideological reason behind having male-female co-executive directors was that since women and men are equal and have equal roles
in the movement, they should have equal visibility. But there are a
couple of problems with this reasoning. First, historically, women
were not visible in the gay rights movement, so this arrangement was
a way to sort of force that equality. My instinct would have been to
encourage women to participate, not to allocate a specific number of
slots. The second—and bigger—problem was that by having coexecu-
tives, you couldn't get anything accomplished. For running an organization day to day, dual responsibility was a formula for frustration.
And the fact that Lucia and I didn't see eye to eye on anything only
compounded the frustration.

Everything fell apart toward the end. Nothing could be resolved.
Anything that I did was subject to suspicion if Lucia had not been
there to participate in the decision. Eventually, what it came down to
was that Lucia wanted to be there for every single decision. And she
wanted to *make* the decisions. It just wore me out. All that energy
could have been directed into something positive and constructive,
but it got soaked up by internal battles, by process. I hate process!

Ultimately I was eased out. The board favored Lucia's side in all
these disputes, so I was excluded. Despite all that, I think I was willing
to be forgiving about what had happened and just chalk it up to
experience. But not after the send-off I got. I'll never forget that
evening when they accepted my resignation. Dick, the male cochair of
the NGTF board, and I met for dinner on a Saturday evening at a
restaurant in the Village. His lover was there, along with a few other
people. We had a pleasant dinner. We paid the check and we were
standing there about to say our good-byes when Dick said, "Oh, yes,
I almost forgot," and he hands me this paper bag, which had an
inexpensive plaque in it with an engraved message thanking me for my
time at NGTF. I thought, *These people are absolutely fucked up if this is
the best they can do.*

I wasn't angry at Dick personally. He's a nice fellow, well meaning.
My rage was really at the organization and its collective notion of
what was an appropriate way to deal with someone who had not only

served the organization as a staff member, but who had been on the board for years and years. It just seemed to me like a shabby way to deal with anybody. And it's not just NGTF. We as a movement do not know how to treat the people who expend considerable time and energy and give something of their lives to work for what needs to be done. Now, whether you agree with them or whether you like their approach, we've got to find a better way to treat those who make a contribution.

It's not just that people aren't acknowledged for the work they've done or for the personal sacrifices they've made. By pushing them aside, we're also losing their collective experience. If we didn't lose that experience, there would be a lot less reinventing of the wheel. A tragic example is what happened in Tacoma in the November 1989 election, where antigay forces successfully repealed the sexual-orientation provisions of Tacoma's human rights ordinance. Did those people who were fighting the repeal approach any of us who were involved on the successful side up here in Seattle in 1978? I'm not aware of it; I know that I was never asked. In Tacoma, they seemed to make all the wrong moves. While they lost by a fairly narrow margin, they still lost, and it wasn't necessary.

I THINK the biggest failure of NGTF during my tenure was its complete surprise at the Reagan victory and its inability to formulate a response to the Reagan administration. But there wasn't much I could do—at that point I was losing my influence and ability to control things. Ironically, the Reagan administration had more gay people on the White House staff than the Carter administration had.

I think the reason NGTF was paralyzed in dealing with the new administration was because of the ideological bent of most of the key people on the board and on the staff. The board and staff just couldn't see communicating with Ronald Reagan. It was a tremendous opportunity missed. I feel very sad about that. We could have done some important things. But the Left couldn't see the Right doing anything positive for gays. They couldn't even see talking to them. So who lost? Gay people lost.

I accept a lot of responsibility for the total lack of communication between the radicals and myself, both in Seattle and at NGTF. I was just not capable of dealing with them. They tended to be strong advocates of the poor and oppressed, but they were not talking about me. They didn't speak for me. Some people are able to balance competing ideological forces and maintain good rapport on all sides, but I just instinctively rejected the radicals. I wouldn't have acknowledged this a few years ago, but now that I've been away from it for a long time, it's easier to see where my strengths and weaknesses were. I just didn't have the personality or disposition to do it.

I GOT a letter last year from some current NGLTF person, asking all the former board members and staff members to come back for this dinner and how it would be so wonderful, and it just triggered me. I sent her a blistering reply and I made it clear that it was not her I was attacking, but I said that this organization has got a long way to go before I'd be willing to come back for a reunion. The Task Force was such an awful experience that I've really shut down that whole chapter of my life. I don't even like talking about it.

A Boy from Boise

Morris Foote

THE STRUGGLE for personal dignity and gay rights was not confined to big cities. By the late 1970s, it had reached places like Boise, Idaho, a city better known for its infamous 1955 "homosexual panic" than for its tolerance of gay men and women.

The Boise scandal began in October 1955, following the arrest of two men on morals charges and the false claim by a Boise probation officer that "about 100 boys" were involved in a "homosexual ring." According to journalist John Gerassi, whose 1966 book, The Boys of Boise: Furor, Vice and Folly in an American City, chronicles the scandal, the police questioned nearly fifteen hundred Boise citizens and gathered the names of hundreds of suspected homosexuals by the time the investigation ran its course the following year. All told, sixteen men were arrested on charges ranging from "lewd and lascivious conduct with minor children under the age of sixteen" to "infamous crimes against nature." Of the sixteen, ten went to jail, including several whose only crime had been to engage in sex with another consenting adult male.

World War II veteran Morris Foote was born in Caldwell, Idaho, in 1925 and went to high school in Middleton, about twenty miles from Boise. During the 1950s, he worked in Boise at the capitol building as an elevator operator. When he had time, he went to downtown bars in search of sex with men. The outbreak of the "homosexual panic" frightened Morris, though he was not arrested.

Like many gay men, Morris fled Boise for fear of being caught up in the scandal. He went home to Middleton and didn't return to Boise until 1978, when he found his way to a local gay discussion group and into the gay rights movement.

Today, Morris Foote lives in an old trailer just down the road from the house where he grew up. Since his mother died several years ago, he has cared for his younger brother, who has severe cerebral palsy. Morris Foote is a quiet man who has done his best to stay out of trouble. He asked that the conversation about "anything gay" take place in the privacy of his trailer, rather than at the café next door, where he and his brother frequently have lunch and dinner.

BACK IN high school, I was very active. Helped put out the newspaper. Done a lot of typing. Writing. No sports. I loved basketball, but I was afraid the kids would tease me because I'm a hairy man. I have more hair on my body than on my head. I didn't care to wear those little shorts.

Growing up I didn't know what I was. I was latent. No crushes. But I always went around with boys. Growing up, that's customary for boys to go with boys in high school, as friends. I went with a boy from about seventh grade all through high school and college. We owned a car together and property. Just before graduating from college, why, he took me aside and told me what I was. I didn't know. Billy explained what a gay homosexual was. He said I was one. I had just taken abnormal psychology, the study of those things. In the psychology book there was only about a paragraph on homosexuality, and it said that about 3 percent of the population had it. I still have that book right here on my desk.

So after Billy explained it, I got interested and started going into Boise to find boyfriends because Billy went off and got married to a woman. I've missed him all my life. One of the saddest things in my life was last year when I went to his funeral. They had a private interment, but they notified me. They wanted me to be present. Yes, he was interred in Middleton. He wanted to be buried next to his mother.

ONCE I knew what I was, I started going into Boise, where I took out my latency. Main Street was skid row. Across the street from where the Egyptian Theater is was bar after bar after bar. The rumor was that there were only two bars where homosexuals usually hung out, but I was never sure, because when you went in them they looked just the same as straight bars. Homosexual activity could take place in almost any bar down there, but always in the rest rooms. You'd go into some of the bars, and there was very plentiful homosexual activity in the rest rooms. Open. It was too open. They were just asking for trouble. You wouldn't recognize Main Street now, though. Urban renewal has cut out all the buildings where those bars were except for the Idanha Hotel. The Idanha used to have a bar down in the basement.

We wouldn't have sex with anyone except at the bar. You see, what you did was, you went to the bathroom and took a leak and then someone would come up to you and say, "Would you like to have it?" Afterwards you'd go back to the bar and you'd never see the guy

again. You wouldn't know where the guy went to. You didn't know
their names and you didn't tell them yours. It was all private. What
business was it of anyone else's if it was all private? But, again, looking
back on it, it was too open to have it in a bar. Today, that wouldn't
be allowed, even in a gay bar.

I had no idea that there was anything wrong with what I was doing.
Absolutely not, not until 1955, when the Boise newspaper, the *Idaho
Statesman*, put out an editorial that all homosexual activity must
cease, that it was a sin of society. It also said that there was a homosexual ring operating in Boise and it must be put down. I looked at that
and said to myself, *Is that act illegal?* I thought any time you had sex
in private no one would bother you as long as you were with another
adult. But here they had men in jail on felony warrants for doing it!

I was commuting into Boise for work every day, but after reading
that editorial I thought I better not go there anymore. I left town,
came back to Middleton, and worked on my father's farm. I had no
communication with anyone in Boise after that scandal got started. I
was afraid of getting caught up in it. I did know one of the men who
got arrested. He was mentioned in the book, *Boys of Boise*. He was a
shoe cobbler, but I never seen him afterwards. I didn't even know he
was one of them involved until I read the book.

For years I didn't go into Boise. I didn't want to go to the peniten-
tiary, like some of those men did. I don't know whether I could be
hauled into court today because I told you I had sex with someone
back then. I still don't know what the statute of limitations is. Do
you?

I DIDN'T learn about the gay community in Boise until 1978. I heard
about a gay bar on television. I guess they had been there a whole year
and were up for a license renewal. The city was denying seven bars
licenses, and they said one of them happened to be a gay bar. I didn't
know they had any in Boise. So I started going to Boise again. I was
a frequent customer thereafter. The bar wasn't like the old Idanha or
the Gas Light, where there wasn't any gay talk. This was strictly gay.
You knew what you were getting into.

As soon as I went in there, I met a man who invited me to the first
gay rap session. That's how I got interested in the movement, although I joined the rap group in the first place to socialize, to meet
other guys. We talked about movies, books, any television shows that
dealt with homosexuality. Then that gay rap group spun off into the
church, the Metropolitan Community Church, the gay church. I liked

Standing on the steps of Idaho's Capitol are Morris Foote *(front row, second from right)*, with board members of Your Family, Friends and Neighbors, the organization that sponsored Boise's first Gay and Lesbian Freedom Parade and Festival, held on Saturday, June 23, 1990. *Front row from left*: Rita Wood, Brian Bergquist, John Hummel, Morris Foote, and Gary Peters. *Back row*: Ann Dunkin, Robert Broadfoot, and Kelly Reister. *(© Troy Maben)*

evening worship service. Of course, being my sexuality, it was right nice to go to MCC.

Now I consider myself a part of the gay movement, but since I live so far out, I don't get into Boise very often. I did get in for a protest against Jerry Falwell. I think it was 1982. We were all meeting in Boise, Idaho, for a district convention of the MCC. Our district includes Alaska, Washington, Oregon, Idaho, northern California, and northern Nevada. Two days before the meeting was to start, the Reverend Falwell scheduled a rally on the steps of the state capitol. He was going to every state capital at that time. I think he was trying to organize his political party. A lot of us gays went to the Jerry Falwell Crusade. You always want to go to the opposition and see what they have to say. Falwell spoke so much against homosexuality.

When the MCC convention started, they voted to have a march to counteract what we heard a couple of days before from Jerry Falwell. We did that at eleven o'clock at night, so those that didn't want to be seen or didn't want to be on television wouldn't have to worry and no one would lose a job or anything over it. There was just a mass of humanity out there. They had put the word out at the gay bars. I think they had five then in Boise. Reverend Freda Smith, who was born in Pocatello and is one of the elders in the church, gave the most wonderful talk that night on the steps of the state capitol. She said that she was born and raised in Pocatello and she wished that someday MCC would be there. She said that the word was out that we are human beings, too, that we should have our rights.

I believe that we should have equal rights. Sexual acts among true consenting adults done in private should be legal. We need to change the laws where it's still illegal. That's why I plan to march in Boise's first gay pride march this spring [1990].

The Christian Educator

Carolyn Mobley

WHEN CAROLYN Mobley turned to the man next to her at the 1978 *Southern Baptist Convention in Atlanta and challenged him on an antigay remark, she realized that her career as a church educator could not continue indefinitely. So Carolyn was not surprised a few years later when she was fired after her sexuality had become public knowledge.*

Carolyn Mobley had wanted more than anything to become a Christian educator when she was growing up in central Florida. But she also knew from an early age that she was a lesbian and that being a lesbian was not compatible with the teachings of the Baptist church in which she was raised.

Upon leaving her church teaching job, Carolyn felt free to get involved in Atlanta's gay community. She worked on many projects, including the establishment of the African-American Lesbian/Gay Alliance (AALGA), for which she served as the first woman cochair.

Now in her early forties, Carolyn Mobley is an assistant pastor for the Metropolitan Community Church (MCC) of the Resurrection in Houston, Texas. MCC, a Christian church whose membership is primarily gay and lesbian, was founded in Los Angeles in 1968 by the Reverend Troy Perry. It now has more than 250 congregations in more than a dozen countries.

As an assistant pastor, Carolyn has been able to combine her love of the church with her commitment to the gay community and to gay and lesbian civil rights.

I grew up in a small central Florida town called Sanford. Sanford was a segregated town. I went to an all-black school. We shopped in the black neighborhood, in black grocery stores. When I was really small, in elementary school, I didn't ever think to question it. That was simply the way it was. To me, white people weren't real. They were only on TV, like cartoon characters.

I was about eleven or twelve when something happened to me that made me aware of racism in a very personal way. My mother was going to summer school in Tallahassee. She did that for many summers. Most of the time my brothers and sisters and I would stay with my mother's sister, Aunt Madgie, in Jacksonville. One summer, in

1959 or 1960, my cousin and I took the Greyhound bus from Jacksonville to Tallahassee, where we were going to spend a couple of weeks
with my mom.

When we got to the bus station in Tallahassee, my mother wasn't
there yet. So we looked around and saw a sign that said Waiting
Room. We went in. We had never been there before. We hadn't even
been on a bus before, so everything was new. We were sitting there
in the waiting room, and there were all these white people sitting
around looking at us. Then we noticed this cop walking up and down
in front of us, with his hand on his billy club. We didn't pay much
attention. My cousin went up to the counter to buy some candy. The
lady at the counter told her, "If you know what's good for your black
ass, you'll get the hell out of here." My sister jumped back and came
over and told me what happened. I couldn't believe it. Naturally, we
got scared.

We decided that we'd better leave the bus station. As we walked
back and forth in front, we saw this sign that said Colored Waiting
Room. And I said, "Well, I'll be damned! We was in the wrong
place!" We didn't have any money, but we decided to call a cab
because things were getting pretty heated. People thought we were
trying to make trouble. Just as we were about to get in the cab, my
mother drove up and blew the horn. We were glad to see her and get
out of there. That was the first time in my life that I was fixing to get
beat up because I was in the wrong place. It freaked me out.

I remember talking to my mom about it that night and crying. She
tried to tell us not to worry about it, that things were changing and
it wouldn't always be this way.

OUR CHURCH was a typical black Baptist church. It was fairly emotional in its expression. There was lots of good singing. The church
was the real social fabric of my life and community, and my whole
family was very active in it. My grandfather was a Baptist preacher.
All my teachers were in the church. It was the kind of community
where all the folk you looked up to or were taught to respect attended
church. Church was packed every Sunday. You just didn't think
about not going.

At the age of ten I became a Christian. In black Protestant churches,
kids, for the most part, aren't automatically taken in the church when
they're born. Unlike the Catholics, you have to make your own
decision and say, "Yes, I want to be baptized and I want to be a part
of the church." I remember deciding that whenever the judgment
came, I wanted to be counted on God's side. The only way to do that,

as I understood it, was to affirm my faith in Jesus Christ. That's what I did, and I was baptized at age ten.

It's been a firm faith for me. I've never wavered from it, even when I began to feel some tensions between my belonging to Christ and my being a lesbian.

EVEN BEFORE I started school, I had a fascination for older women. I used to have a recurring dream about a particular woman—I'm talking as early as the first grade! I would dream that she was going out on a date, and somehow during the date the man she was with would begin to attack her, or it was what I thought was an attack. She would seem to be struggling. And I would fly out of the sky like Super-woman and just beat the poor guy to a pulp. Then I'd take her away in my arms. I had that dream for years and years and years.

At school, in fifth and sixth grades, I didn't want to play house unless it was all girls and I got to be the daddy. Then it was fun. I was the typical tomboy.

I used to tell my mother, "I'm going to marry a girl when I grow up." When you're real small, you can get away with that talk, but by the time I got to be in fifth grade, I was told not to say such things anymore. One time, my older sister caught me kissing a little girl and ran and told my mom. We were just sitting on the side of the car, and I kissed her on the lips. We were friends. My mother sent for me. She said, "What were you doing?" I said, "Nothing." She didn't make anything of it. But then, at a later time, my sister told my mother that I was "funny," which meant "queer." My mother just slapped her and told her not ever to say that again. So I'm sure my mother knew the truth about me all along.

The older I got, the more conflict I felt about my feelings. It was a religious thing for me. I knew that what I was feeling was wrong according to the church. But I managed to use my convictions about being in the church to get out of dating boys. As a Baptist, I really wanted to be all that I thought God wanted me to be, which meant no drinking, no smoking, and no dancing. That reasoning worked well as an excuse for not going to the sock hops after the high school football games. Even in eighth grade, when we had a prom-type event, I didn't dance. There was a dinner, but after that I went out to sit in the car. My mother came and got me and made me go back inside. She said my behavior was very antisocial.

In high school, my mother gave up and didn't make me go to the proms, but she told me that she thought I should go. So I did, even though I didn't want to get all dressed up, put on the makeup, or dance with boys. I told the boy who took me that I didn't want to dance, that he could dance with other people. It was just trauma city for me, but I endured it.

You know, it wasn't that I didn't like to dance. I just didn't want to be held close by these guys. It just felt real awkward, very unnatural and uneasy. Later on, when I realized I could dance with women, I found out I loved dancing.

Besides going to the proms, I also dated, even though I didn't like it. I was praying God would change my feelings and take away my desire to be with females, to let me be more open to having a boy-friend. This boy walked me home from school most days and some-times he would come over on weekends, and we'd sit and watch TV. He would always end up wanting to neck and stuff. I would say, "Oh, no. I know God didn't want me to do this. It's one thing for me to sit here and watch TV with you, but no, no, no."

BY THE time I graduated high school, I had spent the night with one girl. We kissed in bed and I got really freaked out and thought, *Okay, that's as close as I come. All right Lord, never again.* So the very next year I went all the way to Abilene, Texas, to Hardin-Simmons University to get away from the pressure of this particular girl. Of course, I discovered that I couldn't get away from those pressures because they were internal.

Hardin-Simmons was a predominantly white, coed Baptist college. I chose a white school because I thought that would nip any interests in women in the bud. But I discovered that women are women, I don't care what color they are. I was falling in love with white women. That was really wild. I also thought that the strict rules would help me maintain my commitment. Girls could not wear pants on campus. There were curfews. There was no smoking on campus. No drinking. All these clean-cut American kids. I was the only black female in my freshman class. And I was one of only three black females on the whole campus after my second semester. There were about a thou-sand students in all.

Hardin-Simmons was a very positive experience. I'm sure there were some people who hated my guts and hated my presence. But there were more people, far more, who were ready to expand their horizons and be around people who were different. They were making a real serious commitment to be Christian, which meant understand-ing the inclusiveness of God's love and that they should emulate that by including everyone in their love, concern, and compassion.

People probably went out of their way to be kind to me. It was an attitude of, "Oh, boy, we've got to make up for all this shit that's happening in the world." Of course, King's assassination my fresh-man year changed things. For the first time people began to show some of the deeper racist attitudes that they had done a good job of hiding from me those initial months. I remember being in the bath-room brushing my teeth or standing in the shower and hearing other people talk about King's death. One time I overheard a girl who I was friends with—I thought—say, "Well, he had it coming. Maybe it's best anyway. He was nothing but an old Communist. He should have stopped doing all that stuff."

DR. KING's commitment to disobeying unjust laws had a profound impact on my thinking. I began to question the things that I was told to do: "Are they really right? Are they right if I'm told they're right by a person in a position of authority?" I began to realize that parents could steer you wrong. Teachers could steer you wrong. Preachers, God knows, could steer you wrong. They were all fallible human beings. That really changed my way of looking at myself and the world. And it certainly helped me reevaluate the message I was getting from the church about homosexuality. It made me examine more closely what scripture had to say about it.

As a college student, I continuously read scripture on my own. I especially reread Romans numerous times. I finally got the picture that God wasn't against homosexuals and that even Paul, who wrote that passage in Romans about homosexuality and was against homo-sexuals, was a human being subject to error, just like me. So I thought the man was wrong, period. What he was espousing was inaccurate, and it needed to be challenged. That was what Dr. King was about, challenging error wherever it was found.

With that understanding, I decided to live my own life. By the time I finished college, I was ready to become a sexually active adult. I began to come out to myself and I came out to my mom the very first year I was home after college. That was 1971. I had my first sexual experience shortly thereafter with a woman I had met in college.

WHEN I told my mother that I was a lesbian, she didn't say a whole lot. She kind of got teary eyed and then said, "Maybe you should see a psychiatrist." Then she said, "Maybe you ought to take birth con-trol pills. Then you'd feel freer to experiment with men and you might discover you're not this way after all." I said, "I really can't knock it until I've tried." I thought that maybe I owed it to her or the universe to try.

So I got on birth control pills and decided I would have sex with a man. I really thought that I would try this several times and see if it made a difference. I tried it once—with the boy who was my boyfriend throughout high school. Every summer when I came home he was constantly asking me to go to bed with him, and I never would. So I picked him and set up a time and spent the night with him at his apartment. It was like, this is a joke. I couldn't believe I was doing it. It was totally unsatisfying. I thought, *Well, so much for that. I don't think I need to do this again.* That was not a way to solve this "problem" at all.

I gave up on having sex with men and I got off the pill. I also began to reinterpret further that whole Romans scripture about giving up what was natural for something unnatural. A light went off in my head. Paul had a point. His argument about doing what was natural really did make sense, but you had to know what was natural for you. It was unnatural for me to screw a man, so I decided that I wouldn't do that again. The only natural thing was for me to do what I'd been feeling since day one in the world. Why would I try to change that? How foolish I'd been. I thought to myself, *Thank you, Paul. I got your message, brother. We're okay.*

When that light went on in my head, I knew it was from God, that it was my deliverance. God didn't deliver me from my sexuality. God delivered me from guilt and shame and gave me a sense of pride and wholeness that I really needed. My sexuality was a gift from God, and so is everyone's sexuality, no matter how it's oriented. It's a gift to be able to love.

FOR THE first two years after college, I worked as director of Christian education at a large black Baptist church in Orlando. Then I went on to Atlanta to go to seminary. I went to a black seminary deliberately because I had gone to a white college. I thought I needed some balance in my life, and I needed to reconnect to my home community. This was the 1972–73 school year.

Before I left Orlando to attend seminary, I had read about the Metropolitan Community Church, this new gay church that Troy Perry had started in California. It was a fairly negative article, but even negative press is good press when the right people read it. I was standing in the office of the Shiloh Baptist Church reading the article, thinking to myself, *If I ever get to California, I have to check this out. A gay church! What a neat idea.*

When I got to seminary in Atlanta, who should be in my entering class, but the assistant to the pastor at the local MCC. Jim was the only white man in the school, and he was the only openly gay man. He was wonderfully bold. No seminary—I don't care whether it's Catholic, Methodist, or black—wants an openly gay person. At first they were hesitant to admit him, but in the end they backed down, admitted him, and gave him a full scholarship. They really had no choice because how could they dare discriminate against him when we had been struggling to end discrimination against us?

When I met Jim, I thought, *Well, I'll be darned!* He invited me to visit his church, but I wasn't quite ready to go. I thought, *I have to think what I'm going to do about my career. Is this a good move?* Even though I didn't want to lead a double life, I was aware that if I wanted to work in a black church, I would have to keep this part of my life a secret. Nonetheless, by the time I graduated, Jim and I had come out to the whole school in a presentation we gave on pastoral care to gay and lesbian people.

Initially there were some people at school who came to me and said, "I know Jim made you say that. You're not really a lesbian, are you?" And I said, "Yes, I certainly am. I came out to him the first year I was here, and we've been friends all this time. I was a lesbian when I came here, so it's not anything he made me become or pulled me into by any stretch of the imagination." There were instructors who acknowledged that they thought it was a brave thing to do. They commended me and said they hoped things went well in the future.

During my senior year, I fell in love with a woman who was working at the same mission center I was. We were both doing student internships there. We started going to MCC services together. I wanted to go to a church where she could be with me and where both of us could feel comfortable. That wasn't happening at the black Baptist church because this was a white woman, so we went to MCC. We felt a little strange because MCC was just so different from anything we had experienced before. It was certainly very different from black Baptist churches.

The Atlanta MCC church had about seventy-five people or so, largely white male. There were two or three black men and maybe one or two other black women visiting from time to time. This was in the early years of that church's life. They had just bought a huge theater for their sanctuary and were in the process of renovating it themselves.

MCC had a tremendous impact on me because I was getting more and more comfortable with myself. It provided an oasis in the desert, a place where I could be whole for at least a few hours on Sunday and during the week. It was a place where I was totally accepted as a lesbian and a Christian. It was a nurturing, confidence-building time.

By the time I graduated from seminary, I was encouraged to get credentialed so I could become a minister in MCC. But my stronger calling was to serve the black community. I felt major tension between the two. I thought, *Why should I serve a white church, even though it was a gay church, when I feel such a commitment to the black community?* That was the whole reason I went to school in the first place: I just couldn't abandon this sense of belonging to a people. There was so much to be done in the black community.

I accepted a job doing Christian education. I was employed by the Southern Baptists, which is a predominantly white denomination, but the job they hired me to do put me in mission centers in the heart of low-income public-housing communities. There were four mission centers in Atlanta, and I had contact with all of them. I loved my job. Every day I worked with a class of children in a different center. Sometimes I would teach Bible study, and sometimes I would just do music with them.

IN THE beginning, no one asked me anything about my sexuality. But I find it very difficult to believe that they didn't at least suspect I was a lesbian when they hired me. I was interviewed by scads of people, including a psychiatrist, a social worker, the head of the department I was hired for, and the president of the board. They had me write my life story. They gave me a battery of psychological tests, which I figured had to show something. And the shrink who interviewed me after all those tests asked me point blank if I thought I would get married in the future. I told him no. And then he asked, "Are you hostile to marriage?" I said, "No, I think marriage is a wonderful institution for people who feel called to that, but I don't feel drawn to marriage." I just left it at that. He apparently left it at that, too, because the question wasn't raised again, and I got the job.

I really loved my work, but after a while, I began to get very tired of the homophobia of Southern Baptists. One time, in 1978, Anita Bryant was a guest in Atlanta at the Southern Baptist Convention. The Southern Baptists were always crazy about her for her outreach to families and children. But it freaked me out when she started campaigning to undermine the rights of gays and lesbians in this country. Naturally, at the convention, there were protests outside the World Congress Center where the convention was taking place.

I felt really, really torn about being connected with the Southern Baptists. As I went into the World Congress Center, I remember looking across the barricades at my friends and my lover, who were protesting. There were few people inside the hall who had any sympathy for the people outside. I couldn't stand hearing these negative comments from these old fat balding Southern Baptist preachers—comments like, "Why don't you just kill all these queers?" There was this one man sitting next to me in the hall who said some dumb-shit thing like that, and I just turned to him and I said, "If God wanted all these people dead, he could strike them dead right now. If God can allow them to do what they're doing, who are you to think that they don't have a right to do it?" I got up and moved because I was either about to throw up or hit him one.

That kind of tension might have led me to resign voluntarily in another year or two because the Southern Baptists were getting so homophobic. But it wasn't just that. There was the whole issue of women being ordained. I was just sick about all of it, but in the end, it wasn't really my decision because I was asked to leave.

One day in 1981 the directors of the Department of Christian Social Ministries at the Baptist Home Mission Board came to me and said that it had come to their attention that I might be a lesbian. I said, "How is that?" They told me that a student who had stayed with me had seen pictures and other things, including a poem, in my house that she said indicated I was a lesbian. This young woman had been our guest from a church in Mississippi. We had left her at home alone one afternoon, which probably wasn't smart, but you don't expect people to snoop around your house.

I just told them point blank that what this girl said made no sense whatsoever, that the poem she quoted was erotic in nature, not homosexual, and could as well apply to a man and a woman as to two men or two women. The pictures this girl saw in my photo album were of me and my roommate sitting on the hood of my car with my arms draped around her. There was nothing incriminating about that. Their biggest accusation was that I wrote checks to a gay church. I said, "I don't really know how she would know that, but if I do, it's my prerogative. As a matter of fact," I said, "I have a good friend who graduated seminary with me who is on the staff of a gay church here. And, yes, I have attended it. I've sung for them and I've gone there as a guest. I have also made contributions, but that's my prerogative."

So we went round and round for a little while, and following that initial investigation, they apologized. They said that what this young girl had told them bordered on slander, that she had no business prying into my checkbook, and that if I wanted to pursue it in the courts, they would back me up. That whole episode continues to strike me as eerie. I still wonder if that girl was sent to gather information.

A month and a half later, my immediate supervisor called me into his office and said that he had run into a mission director from Mississippi, who had apparently heard the whole story. Quite off the cuff, this man asked him, "What did y'all do with that homosexual missionary y'all had down there?" My immediate supervisor hadn't known about the investigation and said, "What homosexual missionary?" So the mission director from Mississippi told him the whole story. My boss felt he got caught with his pants down because he had never heard anything about it.

He came back and called me into his office and asked, "Are you a lesbian?" I said, "You don't really have a right to ask me that." He said, "If you can't tell us that you're not, we need your resignation." I said, "When do you want it?" It was clear that he had made up his mind, that there was no point in arguing with him. He said, "As soon as you can muster it." I said, "All right, as soon as we hire and train the new director, I will resign." I gave my resignation effective July 1, 1981. It was time. I was ready to get off that bandwagon.

AFTER MY resignation, I went to a seminary for a year in Decatur, Georgia, and then went to work for a courier company in Atlanta, which I continued to do for the next several years. During this time, I got involved as an AIDS volunteer and took part in protests against a local Baptist pastor who called AIDS "God's punishment for gays." For me, that was the beginning of a new kind of involvement in the gay community. I became more publicly active because I didn't have any job to keep me from it. In fact, when I went to work for the courier company, I let them know I was a lesbian from the start. I made a commitment to myself after I left the church job that I would not work anyplace where I couldn't be publicly gay.

As I became more involved in the broader white gay and lesbian community in Atlanta, there was always this question, "Where are black gays and lesbians?" Even though I was beginning to meet some, there was no visible organization of black gays and lesbians. I felt it was time to organize one.

The original inspiration for a black gay and lesbian organization came from the National Coalition of Black Lesbians and Gays. The NCBLG wanted us to organize a local chapter, so we could sponsor their national convention in Atlanta in 1986. That didn't work out, but we went ahead and formed our own local group, which became African-American Lesbian/Gay Alliance.

We had a lot of work to do. Besides the fact there was no dialogue between black gay men and black lesbians, we all wanted to overcome the sense of isolation that so many of us felt. We needed a place where we could talk about who we were and what we were about, to discuss basic issues like coming out to yourself and to your family. Until we formed our group, there was no organization to represent our concerns as black gays and lesbians in the city council, in gay pride march planning, or anywhere.

When we started meeting, we discovered that we had to deal with the very basic issue of gay identity. While the idea of a gay identity is well formed in the white gay and lesbian community, and has been for some time, that's not true in the black community. Many individual gays and lesbians in the black community still don't think of themselves as gay. They may be practicing homosexuals, but they're in denial about what they're doing. So they're not out to themselves as gay and lesbian persons, much less out to anybody else.

Building gay pride among black gays and lesbians was a challenge. We had to build this pride in ourselves. One of our mottoes was that we wanted to become as proud of our gayness as we were of our blackness. But even before that, we had to build our sense of black pride and black power. Once we'd done that, we had to turn around and say the same thing about ourselves as gay people. It was a dual struggle.

Most times people would give more attention to one identity over the other. For example, there are black gays and lesbians who are active in the broader gay and lesbian community who have never taken time to deal with their blackness. They've been so busy being gay that they don't identify with the black community at all. Talk about identity crisis! They don't know their history, and they don't want to know it. Many times it's because they've had some real negative experiences as a young person at the hands of black people who put them down for being queer. So they just say, "Well, fuck all you black people, I'll be a part of the queer nation and not be a part of the black nation!"

For some of us who got involved in AALGA, our motivation was clearly a matter of wanting to be whole. I wanted to be black and I wanted to really affirm that. But I wanted to be gay and really affirm that as well. AALGA gave me a sense of coming home. When we had our monthly meetings, here was a room full of black gays and lesbians in a black neighborhood, affirming that we were both gay and black, both of which were good.

One of the things we did in AALGA was to look at discrimination within the gay and lesbian community. We knew about discrimination in the broader society. But then we found the same thing in gay and lesbian organizations and gay and lesbian bars. A white lesbian group called Atlanta Lesbian Feminist Alliance went on a campaign to have people boycott certain bars because they were double-carding* black patrons and upping the cover charge for blacks. This practice was still going on in the mid-1980s.

LAST JANUARY 2 [1990], the pastor at the Metropolitan Community Church of the Resurrection in Houston called to ask me if I would apply for the position of assistant pastor. I had been working in a women's bookstore in Atlanta as a manager trainee and had already decided to quit my job. But I didn't know if I was ready to reenter the ministry professionally. I had never felt the call to pastor, but I thought I could handle the position of assistant pastor, especially since the position emphasized Christian education.

So I've chosen the ministry. I believe that the rest of my life will be devoted to this work, that this is the way I'll make my contribution. People come in and pour out their guts to me or cry in my arms because they've just been told they have AIDS or that they're HIV-positive. I also get lots of gay people who are struggling with the conflict that comes from believing that God is against them. They need to be reunited with God, to feel that God is on their side and not against them just because they are gay or lesbian. So this is where I need to be.

Activism will remain part of my work because in every town where there is an MCC, the local MCC pastor is involved in gay rights activism. Troy Perry, the founder of MCC, has set the example for us. He's been out there in the street from the beginning, sitting on capitol steps and doing hunger strikes and all kinds of things. While other MCC ministers don't have to do the very same thing, we do have to be available to the people and ready to lead.

In fact, this past spring I helped lead the first gay pride parade in Boise, Idaho. A young friend of mine who had recently moved there called me and said, "You wouldn't believe how backwards it is out here. We're starting this group called Your Family, Friends and Neighbors, and we're going to do a gay pride thing this year. It's going to be the first time they've ever done it. I want you to come help with the march." I said I would do it, and they flew me out.

I didn't know what to expect. My friend kept telling me, "I don't know if we'll have five people or a hundred." Well, they ended up

*Requiring two forms of photo identification.

Carolyn Mobley on the steps of Idaho's Capitol on Saturday, June 23, 1990, teaching marchers songs and chants prior to the start of Boise's first Gay and Lesbian Freedom Parade. (© *Troy Maben*)

having something like three hundred. It was quite a good showing for what I understand is an extremely homophobic town.

I got there on Friday. On Saturday there was a brunch and then the march from the capitol to the park. My task was to sing and lead chants as we marched, to keep the crowd revved up. One of the chants was, "Two, four, six, eight, God does not discriminate!" You know, the kinds of things that were real affirming of who we were as gays and lesbians. We were letting them know that we weren't going to put up with the shit anymore. We were standing up for our rights.

One of the other chants I used was, "Gay, straight, black, white, same struggle, same fight." That chant in particular rings true to me because gay people have the same essential struggles for human rights that black people do. Gay, straight, black, white, same struggle, same fight. We should want the same thing, which is equality for all of us.

The Fighting Irishman

A. Damien Martin

As THE gay rights movement developed during the 1970s, more and more organizations were formed by gay men and women, primarily in the major cities, to address a variety of needs. One of these organizations, the Institute for the Protection of Lesbian and Gay Youth—now called the Hetrick-Martin Institute—was founded specifically to help gay and lesbian young people in New York City. Damien Martin, a university professor, and his late life-partner Dr. Emery Hetrick, a psychiatrist, began organizing the group in 1979 after hearing about a gay teenager who had been ejected from a youth shelter after being raped and beaten there. Damien was infuriated, and he and Emery decided that something had to be done.

One of seven children, Damien and his siblings were placed in foster care in Philadelphia through the Catholic Children's Bureau in 1941, when Damien was eight years old. Today, Damien Martin lives alone in the Murray Hill neighborhood of Manhattan with his beloved cat, Radclyffe Hall, in an apartment he shared for more than a decade with Emery.

Growing up, I was a devout Catholic—in fact, I wanted to be a priest. But I was suffering tremendous turmoil because I was gay. How could I have these feelings and be Catholic? The fact that I was a real horny kid and was very sexually active just intensified the conflict. I was out there on the streets from the time I was twelve or thirteen years old. I would go out, commit the act, have terrible, terrible guilt, and go running to confession. I'd swear never to do it again, but five days later I would go running back to the streets. It was incredibly destructive for me.

That cycle ended at about age sixteen, when I finally stayed overnight with somebody. The next day was a Sunday, and I was going to go to mass. As I was laying there in bed with this man next to me, I started to think about what we had been taught in school concerning what that idiot Paul said about how if you pray long and hard enough, you can get enough grace to resist any temptation. I thought to myself, *I know I've been praying as hard as I can, but I'm not getting the grace to resist the temptation. If I'm already doomed to hell, why should I go through such agony with the church?* That broke my tie to the church. I stopped going to mass. I figured that since I was going to hell anyway, I would do whatever I wanted. So I got involved in some very self-destructive behavior, including drinking.

I was a street kid, basically, but I was one of those street kids who was able to maintain some sort of home base so he could stay in school. I had enough sense to know that the one hope for a kid like me was to get a high school education and further education after that. I was very lucky because a lot of nuns drummed that into me.

WHEN I graduated from high school, I went into the air force for six years, became a navigator, and flew in Korea, the Far East, and here in this country. I was sexually active the whole time I was in the service, but I was careful. This was the McCarthy period, and if you even associated with someone gay or were seen going near a gay place, you could be kicked out.

One time they had a big lecture about security. They talked about homosexuality and security risks. I said to myself, *Suppose somebody came up to you and said, "Betray the secrets of your country, or I will reveal you to be a faggot."* I asked myself what I would do in this situation. The answer was that I'd go to the FBI. I remember thinking that it would be terribly embarrassing and I'd hate it, but I wouldn't do anything like betray the secrets of my country. Looking back, it's so stupid that you even had to ask yourself a question like that. But we all accepted it back then.

When I think of the orgies that used to go on at air force bases, it's a wonder more people weren't caught. There was always this underground. People knew; there were certain codes. I very seldom did anything on the base. Most of the time I would go away to areas where people weren't likely to know me. I also had certain rules, like I would never approach somebody I was interested in. I would wait until somebody I was interested in approached me, which didn't always work because everyone was afraid. You have to understand that I was in the middle of some of the worst antigay purges the air force has ever known. I remember in about 1952 at Biloxi, Mississippi, there was a purge where people were committing suicide. The air force finally had to stop because people were turning people in just to get revenge for one thing or another. It's a little hard to comprehend the mentality of that time.

From the air force I went to Northwestern University. I worked part time at the library, where I used to read the *Mattachine Review* and *ONE*. They were locked in the pornography department. You had to have a key to get in, but I had access to the key because I worked there. I would feel a sort of guilty thrill reading those magazines because people were saying positive things about being gay. I was a little surprised. I remember reading in ONE that we were perfectly normal. I said to myself, *That's stupid!*

I think I had difficulty handling material like that because it was threatening. So much of your person gets tied up in the act of hiding that any effort made by people not hiding is seen as a threat. Like so many gay men of my generation, I developed two lives. I had a sexual life, which occurred in the bars and so forth, and I had another life with my straight friends. The issue of sexuality never came up, except that I would tell fag jokes just like everybody else.

THE FIRST time I met gay people where sex wasn't the basis of the relationship was when I joined a group in New York in 1960 to stop drinking. I'd been drinking very, very heavily since I was a teenager. This group was made up of about eighteen people—sixteen women and two men. All the women were lesbians. Through these women, many of whom are still friends, I started developing some interaction skills that were homosexually based, but not erotically based. I don't want to say these women were like mothers, but they were peers who were not peers, who sort of guided me. Meeting them was the important turning point for me.

At these meetings I was very open about being gay, but I was not at all involved in the gay movement during the 1960s. In fact, I was rather hostile to the few things I'd heard about. My feeling was, *Why cause trouble?*

The Stonewall riot in June 1969 provoked the same kind of feeling I'd had when I read the *Mattachine Review* and ONE in the library. I was thrilled, but a little fearful. I wasn't at the Stonewall that first night, but for some reason, on the second night, I had to go up Sixth Avenue in a cab. I passed right by where the old Women's House of Detention used to be, and there were these gay and lesbian people chanting. The police were out in force keeping the crowds back. I'll never forget the look on the cops' faces. They looked like someone who has just been bitten by a trusted pet, a look of astonishment and fear at that same time.

I finally got hooked into the movement around 1972. My ex-lover said, "You ought to go to Dignity." I said, "What's Dignity?" and he told me it was a group for gay Catholics. As far as I was concerned, the last thing in the world I needed was a bunch of Irish Catholics sitting around beating their breasts and saying, "Why did God make me like this?" So I said, "Forget it!" But he kept pushing, so I thought, *What the hell? I'll go. Maybe there'll be some cute Jesuits.* And there were!

I'll never forget walking into this room where they were having a business meeting. I was overwhelmed. It was the first time I had been in a room with a bunch of gay men where sex was not the issue. I immediately joined, but I kept saying, "I'm an atheist! It's just an ethnic identification, that's all."

Dignity was very good for me. For the first time I got involved in a gay rights activity, one in which people were really working together for a common goal. I ended up not agreeing with Dignity's goals. I was much more interested in political issues than in religion.

SOMETHING VERY important happened to me when I was a member of Dignity. It was right around the time of the vote on the New York City Gay Rights Bill in 1972. A majority of Dignity members decided they couldn't demonstrate in favor of the bill, but that they could pray for its passage. So they went to a Catholic church down near City Hall to pray. I got very snotty and said, "I don't believe in prayer, and I'm not going!" When they needed someone to bring some leaflets down to the church, though, I volunteered.

When I got to the church, everyone was praying outside on the steps, rather than inside. I just stood watching from across the street. One of the guys came over to get the flyers from me. He said that the pastor threw them out of the church and locked the doors when he found out what they were praying for, so they decided to have the vigil outside. He asked me to come over and I said that I couldn't. Thank God I had enough self-honesty to know that what was keeping me from going had nothing to do with the fact that I didn't believe in prayer. The truth was that I was scared to death to go across the street. I suddenly realized that although I thought I was out, it was absolutely not true. I was still just as afraid as that kid I was in high school.

I went home and got very depressed. I realized how afraid and closeted I still was even though I had been sneering at these people about their prayer vigil. As much as I pooh-poohed them, they were much braver than I was. I was a coward, and it was unjust to expect them to put their necks out for me. It was almost like I was committing a sin by not coming out. I felt very guilty, very depressed, and very ashamed.

To get out of the depression, I said to myself, *All right, the next time anybody asks me to participate in anything public, I'll do it!* Before long, I got a call from Ron Gold, from the National Gay Task Force [NGTF]. Ron told me that an antigay episode of "Marcus Welby,

M.D." was about to air on television. He asked me to spread the word that at a specific time people should call the television station carrying the show to tie up the phones for two days.

I had no problem calling the station. They were clever there because they said, "All the lines are busy. Leave your name and number, and we'll call you back." I got this sharp pain in my stomach remembering what I'd said to myself about being public the next time I had the opportunity. I gave my name and address. "And besides," I said, "here's my office number." I worked at the Veterans Administration at the time. The station called me back later at the office, and I raised all kinds of hell on the phone and felt marvelous! Wonderful! I remember not caring if something bad happened. I was ready to bust a few noses!

WHEN I met Emery Hetrick, I soon discovered we had different views about what it meant to be gay. We had met in 1974 at one of the meetings for people with alcohol problems. Very soon after we got involved—I think we had just had marvelous sex—I said, "Gee, isn't it great to be gay!" He started bouncing off the walls; he was enraged. "What do you mean? We're no different from anyone else! The only thing is we do something slightly different in bed! We're entirely like everyone else!" For once in my life, I didn't react with anger. I shrugged and said, "Well, you obviously need a consciousness-raising group if you think you're the same as everybody else." He didn't know what I was talking about, but when I explained to him what a consciousness-raising group was, he became intrigued. The next night he said, "Let's start one." So we did.

The CR group had a tremendous impact on Emery. He suddenly became aware of all the restrictions on his life and how different he really was. We formed other CR groups, stayed for about three weeks, left, and then let them start their own groups. We were like Johnny Appleseed. That first CR group was what really got Emery involved in gay rights. He had always been involved in social causes, setting up organizations of one kind or another, so he was no novice. He looked like such a part of the Establishment that he could say the most radical things and people would think it was the Daughters of the American Revolution talking. That's how he got things done.

About this time, after we had started several of the CR groups, we became involved in the National Gay Task Force. This was one of the few organizations around for people like Emery and me to get involved in. We were not into the left-wing radical political thing, and NGTF sort of appealed to middle-class squares like us. And even then, we only participated in a fund-raising capacity at first.

The level of our involvement changed after we went to a Task Force meeting and met Barbara Gittings. Barbara came over to us and said, "I'm glad you belong to the Task Force. What do you do?" And Emery said, "I'm a psychiatrist." Womp! She zeroed in on him. Well, you know, Barbara was very instrumental in the whole battle with the American Psychiatric Association [APA] over the listing of homosexuality as a mental illness. At the point we met her, she wanted to get psychiatrists themselves more involved in it. Well, she started working on Emery—the charm and everything else came through.

At the 1978 APA convention down in Atlanta, Barbara was going to do a booth with the theme, "Gay Love: Good Medicine." She wanted to have pictures of psychiatrists with their lovers as part of the display. So she asked Emery and me for a photo. After a little hemming and hawing, Emery said yes. Then she said, "Why don't you come down and be at the booth?" After more hesitation he agreed.

The experience was great for Emery. He called me from Atlanta and said, "You have to come down here!" It was the only time in my life I ever lied by calling in sick to cancel a class. I flew down to Georgia and found Emery transformed. He was standing there by the booth grabbing psychiatrists he knew were homophobic and saying, "Hi! Let's go look at the exhibit." He confronted them not with the fact that they were homophobic but with the truth about himself: "I'm gay. I'm open. I'm a psychiatrist. I'm as good as you are." After that, he just took off with the movement. He started the gay psychiatrists group here in New York. He got very involved with the national gay psychiatric group. Then he got involved in starting SAGE, Senior Action in a Gay Environment, a support and social organization for older gays and lesbians. He paid SAGE's expenses for one year, which I didn't find out about until afterwards. There was a little heavy breathing over that one.

SAGE WAS well on its way when we went to a political meeting where we heard about a fifteen-year-old boy who had been gang-raped and beaten up at one of the city's youth shelters. This boy was the one who was thrown out because he was gay—as if it was his fault. I went into one of my typical Irish hysterical snits and got very angry. Emery, who was much calmer and more focused, said, "Let's see what we can do about this." After helping start several different organizations, it wasn't surprising that Emery's approach was to see how we could organize to address this issue.

This was around 1979. We got together a group of about forty

National Gay Task Force exhibit at the 1978 American Psychiatric Association convention in Atlanta, Georgia. (© *Barbara Gittings*)

Damien Martin (*right*) and Emery Hetrick at the 1978 American Psychiatric Association convention, standing in front of the NGTF exhibit. (*Courtesy Damien Martin*)

people here at our apartment. Emery asked a lot of psychiatrists and social workers to come. Most of them agreed that there was a real need for an organization to address the problems of gay and lesbian youth. Of course, as usual, two out of the forty actually got involved.

We started meeting at a church and discussed where we were going to go with this. Before long a couple of people from NAMBLA, the North American Man/Boy Love Association, came around wanting to take part in the discussions. Our first reaction was, "No! Absolutely no!" Then we got talked into letting them come to the meetings.

They had come to about six meetings when we felt we had to face the issue of NAMBLA. We told them they couldn't stay, that we didn't want them involved. They couldn't quite believe it and kept saying, "We know you have to do that if you're going to get money, but we'll work with you secretly." We said, "We don't want to work secretly with you. We do not want anything to do with you!" As a result of excluding NAMBLA, we lost some people who had been working with us, including one man, who was not a member of NAMBLA, but felt the organization should be open to everyone. Then we lost our lawyer and a couple of other people who felt that Emery and I had not been strong enough in opposing NAMBLA from the beginning. This was our first major crisis.

By that time we were moving toward getting incorporated. We realized from the beginning that to do this we had to have credentials. This need was met, in part, by our professional titles. Emery was a psychiatrist. I was an associate professor of speech pathology and audiology at New York University. We had another psychiatrist and someone who was about to become a social worker. And so on.

At one particularly big meeting we decided on a name, The Institute for the Protection of Lesbian and Gay Youth. This was actually an awful name, but we had reasons for it, one of which was Anita Bryant's antigay Save Our Children campaign. Our argument always was, "Ours are the ones who need protection!" We wanted the name to say up front who we were and what we were about.

People started to hear about us and, unfortunately, called up and said, "I have this gay kid, and I don't know what to do with him. Can you help me?" We quickly made the decision not to get involved in anything we weren't prepared to handle at that time. We simply were not prepared to get involved in offering direct services. Some people were very upset about this decision, and a few even stopped coming to meetings. They said, "You're not doing anything! You're just talking!" And in a way they were right.

But, of course, we didn't just talk during that first year. When we heard of specific instances where government agencies were not providing the services they were supposed to provide for our kids, we would go out and ask what happened. We learned a lot from these interventions. We began to find many individual professionals out there, primarily straight professionals, who wanted to work with gay and lesbian kids. They didn't want to discriminate against them, but they were working under impossible circumstances. First of all, they had had no training to deal with gay kids, so they didn't understand a lot of the issues involved. They had to deal with hostile administrators who were afraid they'd lose their funding by trying to help these kids. They were afraid of community reactions. And they had to deal with the straight kids in the agency, who would react in all sorts of ways to the gay kids.

Meeting these professionals changed our understanding of what the problem was and what we were going to do about it. We could no longer view ourselves as knights and amazons on white horses going out to conquer discrimination, violence, and oppression. So rather than just checking out instances of discrimination or exploitation, we moved into a kind of educational, case-management mode, where we would help various agencies solve specific problems.

I remember the first agency we met with. It was a settlement house in Brooklyn that dealt primarily with black kids. They had a boy there who was sort of swish. He dropped out of high school because he got beaten up all the time. The teachers were not protecting him. This settlement house called us and said, "You've got to come! He's disrupting the whole agency." So we went and we listened. Everybody liked the kid. The disruption was a result of a disagreement between the staff. One group of professionals wanted to get him to macho it up a bit—they wanted to teach him how to box and to walk differently. Another group wanted to let him do what he wanted to do, which was to run the fashion show for the settlement house.

I wish we could have said this for most of the agencies we went to, but we found no real homophobia among those people. They really wanted to help this kid, but they were fighting among themselves because they disagreed about how to handle him. So we spent five or six sessions with the staff discussing issues related to homosexuality. We happened to agree with the staff people who wanted to let him do the fashion show, but at the same time we didn't dismiss what the others were saying. We spent time explaining why the macho approach didn't quite work. I'm a firm believer in teaching gay kids self-defense, but self-defense wasn't going to make him macho.

During this whole period, Emery kept saying, "We're going to have to move into direct social services." And I said, "Oh no we're not! It's going to eat us alive. It's going to take all our time." We were both right.

What eventually convinced me that we needed to provide direct services was the fact that we were getting more and more calls for help. People would call and say they had a fifteen year old and they didn't know what to do with him. Others would call to complain about how a particular agency was handling gay kids. Most of the complaints related to a group called Gay and Young. Gay and Young was supposedly a gay youth group, but it was run by a guy who was more interested in the kids than he should have been. It was complicated because everyone in the community was afraid of a scandal involving kids. Joyce Hunter, who was a social work student at that time, brought this situation to our attention. We tried to make some government officials aware of the problem, but they didn't want to touch it with a ten-foot pole.

The vice squad got involved. They came up to see us here in this living room. You could tell the police were wondering, "Who are these people, and what are they doing?" But pretty soon they were very open with us. One of the policemen finally got sort of irritated and said, "We don't know what to do with these kids. Do you people expect us to come up with solutions? We have no solutions to this. We already know that what we do doesn't work. Why don't you do something?"

EVEN THOUGH we were organized by this point and had a board of directors, we were still relatively unknown in the gay community, which proved to be a big problem in terms of funding. We couldn't offer direct social services or get a government contract because we didn't have an office. And we couldn't open an office because we didn't have the money.

About a year before the Gay and Young episode, which we resolved through some very careful political maneuvers, we had gone to this wealthy man in the community to see if we could get some money for a brochure. He said, "Look, you have no track record. Come back later when you've got one." It turns out that this man, who must remain anonymous, kept an eye on us in the year after we first approached him. He had contacts in the community. He was aware of our work solving the Gay and Young problem. And he knew that we had put on a major conference on gay and lesbian youth for social service professionals. He called us just after the conference and said, "I'd like to come down to see you. I want to give you a donation." It was Sunday night. I didn't want to meet with him because I wanted to go to the movies. But Emery told him to come on down. I yelled, "Why don't you put him off until tomorrow?" "No, no," Emery said, "it's money!"

The guy came down to our apartment. He was very casually dressed, wearing cowboy boots. He asked us what we'd do if we had a chance to get started. We told him our plans for an office. They were very limited plans at first. He asked how much we thought it would cost, and we told him. He said, "I can't do the whole thing." Then he said, "You know, here in New York you have to be so careful carrying money, so I always carry it in my boots." He reached in and took out twenty-five thousand dollars in checks! He said, "That's all I could squeeze into the boots. You'll get another twenty-five thousand dollars tomorrow." I almost shit! That was it. We had the money to open the office.

Now fifty thousand dollars sounds like a lot of money, but it really wasn't because what we started with was one room, an executive director, a social worker, and a secretary. Joyce Hunter had joined us as a volunteer, and I was working as a volunteer. Then Joyce graduated from school and she came on staff, so we had two social workers. By the time we got furniture and got the phones in, we really had just enough money for a few months' salary and rent. But the money gave us a start, allowing us to get contracts from the city's Youth Bureau and the Division for Youth. This was in November of 1983. I almost became a believer again. I had not had an urge to light candles like that since I was twelve years old.

THE KIDS get to you in different ways, but I always remember this one kid who came in after we had been in existence for about a year. We were still in the one room, where we did everything from administrative work to the support groups. This young man was fourteen years old. He came from a Hispanic family. His father brought him in. The father had gone to court to try to get the kid placed somewhere, not because he wanted to get rid of his kid, but because the kid had been identified as gay in his neighborhood and was constantly getting beaten up. The father was heartsick and didn't know what to do. He was actually willing to give up his kid for the kid's safety.

Joyce was doing the interview and then she sent the father off to get some coffee. She was talking to the boy by himself. He was a shy kid, a tiny little thing. He suddenly said to Joyce, "Are you gay?" And she said, "Yes." He said, "Is everybody here gay?" She said, "Well, not everybody, but most of us." And then I walked by, and he said, "Is he gay?" She said, "Yes." And he said, "That old man?" Now that's not the reason I remember the kid—I remember him because of the heartbreaking circumstances.

There was another case involving a young girl that got to me. As far as we knew, she didn't think of herself as a lesbian—or she hadn't identified as a lesbian yet. But she had a crush on her gym teacher and had sent her a note. I don't know what the gym teacher's problem was, but she took the note to the principal, who called in the parents and said, "We can't keep a child like this here. She could corrupt all the others. If you can't find any other place for her, put her in a school for the learning disabled." That's how we got her because one of the counselors at the school knew about us and brought her over. This kid just didn't know what had happened; she had no idea what she had done wrong. She was just being a teenager. The parents were ashamed. It was one of these horrendous things that came from ignorance. It was one of the times when I could understand violent revolutionaries. I really wanted to go out and just punch that principal right in the mouth. I am very much an Establishment person, but there does come a point, by golly, when you just don't take it anymore.

It's ironic that I got involved in starting this agency because I don't particularly like kids. One of the reasons I'm glad I'm on the administrative end of it is because kids get on my nerves. I probably never would have been a good father. I don't like the noise. I find kids silly. But they have a right to be noisy. They have a right to be silly. They have a right to be teenagers. And that's one of the things that's been denied to our kids. They're denied the right to be teenagers, to be pains in the ass without being beaten up or thrown out of school or thrown into the street.

At the Institute we give them the opportunity to be teenagers—and that includes disciplining them. We're very strict about certain things. For many of the kids who come here, this is the first place where they feel they don't have to hide. They think all the rules go by the wayside, that they can do anything they want. Part of what our kids have to learn is that freedom in one area does not mean anarchy in another. In some ways, I suppose I'm very much a traditionalist, and certainly my Catholic background comes through in this work. I remember one of the things the nuns used to say, that I believe very firmly, "For every right there's a corresponding responsibility." I hope it's one of the things we teach the kids at the Institute.

I think that the Institute is probably one of the most—if not *the* most—radical things that the movement has done. We took what was the most defective political charge against us, the biggest hate campaign, that we are a danger to children and to families, and we've turned it around. We've said, "No, that's not true. What *you* people are doing is a danger to children, and to *our* children in particular." But we often make the point that it's a danger to straight kids, too. You don't teach straight kids to hate without damaging them. What the Institute says is that gay and lesbian people are nurturing people who are just as interested in caring for kids as straight people.

I REMEMBER that first article in the early 1980s in the *New York Times* that talked about a group of gay men who had been diagnosed with what was then being called "the gay cancer." Our reaction was like that of a lot of people: "This is just something they're using to try and put us down." Besides, I didn't think you had to worry unless you were the kind who took drugs or had a thousand sexual partners a year. Emery, of course, approached it much more from a physician's point of view. He was interested in the characteristics of the disease.

It was a few years before we really began to think of AIDS as an issue for adolescents, probably in 1984, after we'd opened the Institute. We came to realize, from the information we were getting, that these kids were at risk.

So we became the first organization in the city to start a systematic education program on AIDS and HIV prevention for adolescents. We couldn't get anybody else interested. Nobody would admit that adolescents were at risk or that gay adolescents were at risk. That lack of interest, by the way, was prevalent in the gay community as well. We went to some of the AIDS organizations, and they just didn't want to face it. Part of their reasoning, I'm sure, was that they felt they had enough trouble without having to take on kids.

In 1984 AIDS also became a very personal concern of ours. We had just come back from a trip to Italy, when Emery started having night sweats. It was a terrifying time for him, although not for me. I still feel guilty about having felt that way. But any time Emery had any health problem, it was either complete denial or extreme hypochondria. If he had a scratch, that meant he had cancer and was going to die. So when the night sweats started, he began to panic. I just said, "It's your imagination." I really got irritated with him and wasn't all that supportive. That was my way of handling it.

This went on for about five months, into January of 1985. Emery developed a fever and was coughing and having trouble breathing. So he went to a physician, who told him he thought Emery had pneumocystis pneumonia. That meant he had AIDS. Emery called me when he got home. I'll never forget what he said. All along I had been saying, "Nothing's wrong. Nothing's wrong. Nothing's wrong." Emery was crying on the phone. He said, "Can you come right away?" Immediately I knew what it was. I dashed out and took a cab home. We sat here in this room and cried for four hours.

The next day they did a bronchoscopy and they didn't find any pneumocystis. I said, "Well that's it. You've got something wrong, but it's not AIDS. That's all there is to it." I told him that I wanted him to go to another doctor, one that was better known. And this new doctor said that he had no idea what was wrong with Emery.

Anyway, Emery was ill for the next year. He had tremendous fevers and difficulty breathing. We were going crazy not knowing what it was. Finally the doctors recommended open-lung surgery. I still remember, poor baby, Emery's respiration was so bad that the doctors had to be very careful how much anesthesia they gave him. He came out of it while they were still sewing him up. They brought him downstairs, and I could hear him screaming. I went flying down the hall ready to hit somebody. They were struggling to keep him from pulling out all the tubes. I climbed onto the stretcher with him to hold him down. He calmed down for a second and he looked at me and said, "I don't like it here. I want you and Radclyffe Hall to take me home." But we couldn't.

Even after the surgery the doctors didn't know what was wrong. They said, "All we know is, your lungs are turning to Styrofoam, and we don't know why." Because he was deteriorating so quickly, the doctors told us they had to treat his condition radically. If they didn't, they said he would be dead in six weeks. They gave him very high doses of steroids and a number of immunosuppressants that were really like miracle drugs. For about a month or two Emery was his old self again. He gained weight. He could walk. He could eat. But then he came down with the first of the opportunistic infections. The interesting thing was they still couldn't classify his illness as AIDS because they had just given him immunosuppressant drugs. But by this time the word didn't matter. He had it.

Emery was involved with the Institute clear up until the end. In fact, there's a picture of him on the table over there where he's sitting looking out. That was right before he went into the hospital for one of his illnesses. He used to come down, visit the staff, talk to them, and do things, although he couldn't do the trainings anymore.

From then on, it was a series of illnesses. He went steadily downhill. It'll be two years this coming February [1989] since he died.

THREE MONTHS before Emery died, I was diagnosed with AIDS. Poor baby, I remember he was upset on a number of levels when I got sick, but his major concern was, "Who's going to take care of you like you've taken care of me?" It was easy for me because he was so much sicker than I was that my illness sort of didn't have much reality.

I think the main reason I was able to handle it was because I truly expected to die very shortly and didn't mind that prospect for a number of reasons. Part of it is that without Emery, there really isn't a life. Emery was the first person in my life who I was able to trust completely—no reservations—and it's very difficult not to have that. The world seems like an unimportant place without him here. I'm not the type who would be silly and commit suicide or anything like that. It's just that things are so radically changed that life and the world are just not as good.

That old saying about "they become as one" has certain elements of truth. We were two very independent individuals who used to fight. We went our own ways in many ways, but we really became a unit. That unit no longer exists, so I feel very incomplete all the time. It's not just that I'm lonely, although I'm very, very lonely. It's just that I feel very incomplete. That's hard to take when you've felt complete. In fact, people have said to me, "Well, you must have been relieved when his suffering ended." I wasn't. Toward the end he was very sick, and I really had to take care of him. I feel privileged that I was there to do it. It was another level of our unity. But all the worst times during his illness were not so bad as not having him.

After Emery died, I got even more involved in the Institute with the idea of getting things ready for when I was going to leave. I wanted the organization to be strong enough that it could survive the loss of the two of us. This may sound corny, but I think the institution is much more important than any of us. Plus, by continuing to work at the Institute, I've felt as though I'm working with Emery. That's helped me with my grief. It was like I had not lost everything.

I MUST admit, I have difficulties. I usually just don't think about death anymore. But every once in a while it'll come to me in various ways. I was buying a suit recently and thought to myself, *What the hell are you buying a suit for, you'll probably be dead in six months?* And then I thought, *Well, so you'll be a well-dressed corpse.* I bought the suit.

The Protector

Joyce Hunter

JOYCE HUNTER *spent much of her free time during the 1970s counseling gay and lesbian students at Hunter College in New York City and speaking to college and high school classes on the subject of homosexuality. Joyce was not a professionally trained counselor, and she hadn't even finished high school. But by the time she went to work for the Hetrick-Martin Institute for Lesbian and Gay Youth in 1979, Joyce was well on her way to completing a master's degree in social work.*

Joyce was born in a home for unwed mothers on Staten Island in 1939, the daughter of a sixteen-year-old Orthodox Jewish mother and a black father. "My mother's family would have nothing to do with us," Joyce recalls. "To them, my mother was dead. They even sat shivah.* That was it, honey. It was over." Joyce lived with her parents until she was five, when her mother became seriously ill. She spent the next nine years in an orphanage.

Joyce Hunter lives in an apartment in Sunnyside, Queens, a working-class neighborhood a short subway ride away from midtown Manhattan. She looks like the tough New Yorker she is, and has the accent to match.

Growing up at the orphanage, I knew I was different, especially when I was around ten. But at that age you don't know what it is. I just didn't feel the same as everybody else. When they took us to the movies, I was crazy about the women. And I loved kissing girls. At the home, I had encounters with girls and sometimes even boys, but not sexual intercourse. It was mostly petting, but it didn't feel the same with boys as it felt with the girls. Until I was a teenager, I didn't know that there was anything wrong with what I felt for girls because we didn't really have anybody watching over us.

When I was fourteen, I left the orphanage and went to live with my mother and father in the Bronx in the Edenwald projects. It was a very different world. Growing up on the streets in the Bronx, you hear

*Shivah is the seven-day Jewish mourning period that immediately follows the death of a loved one.

everything. You get your introduction to words like *faggot* and *queer* and *lezzie*. To this day I don't even like abbreviations of the word lesbian. It irritates me like somebody scratching the blackboard.

On the streets it scared the hell out of me to be called any of those names. I thought somebody was going to come after me. I didn't look much different from the way I do now. I was kind of butchy looking, but I don't think they made the connection because, believe it or not, I was quiet. Then I went through a period where I was more than quiet; I wouldn't talk at all. That's when I tried to commit suicide.

I was a pretty unhappy kid. Once I left the orphanage and went to my parents' house, all I ever did was sit on the windowsill in my room and stare out. I was in a pretty violent situation. My father was very abusive. Also, I missed the kids at the orphanage. Of course, the other thing was feeling attracted to girls. I just thought it would be easier to be dead. I didn't see any future. I didn't see how things could get better.

That first time I tried killing myself, I tried to jump out the window in a neighbor's house. But before I could get out the window, my friend saw what I was doing. I don't remember the explanation I gave, but I bluffed my way out. It wasn't hard because they didn't want to believe what I was doing. The second time, I wasn't going to let anything stop me. I'll never forget that morning. I did things I never would have done ordinarily. I took a bath. (I usually took a shower at night.) I cleaned up my room immaculately. I went into the kitchen and got a knife. I had planned on cutting both my wrists and my throat. One of my brothers or sisters saw me take the knife into my room and told my mother. My mother was banging on the door as I was making the attempt. I stopped and let her in. She told my sister to get my coat and she took me to the hospital. I never went back home again.

When my mother took me to Jacobi Hospital, I didn't think they would lock me up. I thought they would send me back to the orphanage. I wanted to go back. But instead, they carted me off to a state hospital. I think there were questions about my sexuality. This was 1956 or 1957. When I got to the state hospital, I was fingerprinted. They hung numbers around my neck and took my picture. It was like a mug shot. I felt like I did something terrible—it was so dehumanizing. They kept me for a year.

When I got out of the state hospital, I was required to go to a therapist at Jacobi Hospital in the Bronx. That's when I started talking about my sexuality. The therapist said, "If you get married, your feelings for women will go away." So I got married. I was married one year when I fell in love with a woman. I had never experienced any kind of feeling like that, ever. Not with no guy. I knew those feelings were never going away. But it took me thirteen years to leave the marriage. So I continued to see her and other women while I was married. I had my two children during that time. I felt so terribly trapped.

Then one day, my former lover took me to a women's dance at the Firehouse in Greenwich Village. This was in 1971, and I was still married. It was an old fire station that had been taken over by a gay group. I'll never forget the moment I walked in. It was the first time I saw a group of women outside of a bar. For me it was like coming home. It was like, *Hey, this is it! This is who I am. This is where I belong.* I asked myself, *Why am I living this crazy life?*

I decided to come out after going to that dance. It was either kill myself or come out. Having kids kept me from killing myself. My marriage wasn't working, anyway, and we were in the process of breaking up. He didn't want to get divorced. He said, "You do your thing, and I'll do mine." He was already seeing another woman, and saw this arrangement as a way of keeping the family intact. I said, "You don't understand, I want a life." I had dreams of having a relationship someday and living happily ever after with somebody.

That dance didn't just get me out of the closet, I also got hooked into the movement. I started going to meetings where I learned about feminism. I didn't know nothing about feminism before then. I didn't know what it meant. I didn't know about the gay movement.

One of the things the movement did for me, especially in the early days, was give me a vehicle to express my anger. I was angry about everything. I had been denied my life. I had no adolescence. My childhood was robbed. I always say that when I come back in the next life, I want to come out of the closet at two and be able to enjoy who I am.

The movement gave me a vehicle not only to express my anger, but to be constructive as well. I was one of these people that would hand out leaflets. If they told me to go to Rockefeller Center and put up a table, I would do it. I would do anything I was told in those early days. I felt very brave. There was a lot of excitement in being part of the movement, of being part of something brand-new, something that was going to help people attain their civil rights.

At first I didn't join any particular group, but then my former lover, the same one who took me to the dance, got me involved with the Lesbian Rising Collective at Hunter College, where she was a student. This was a lesbian feminist organization that did conscious-ness-raising and provided support for students on campus. They asked me to be the organization's spokesperson, which none of the students wanted to be because they were all concerned about their careers. I wasn't a student, so I had nothing to risk. I agreed to do it.

We got active very quickly, and I was a very outspoken spokesperson. We put notices in the school newspaper to encourage young people to come to our group meetings. We created activities where lesbians, as well as gay men, could socialize. We helped my friend, Harold Pickett, start the Gay Men's Alliance at Hunter. Harold recently died of AIDS.

Sometimes we would meet at the gay table in the Hunter College cafeteria, which is where Mary Lefkarites, who taught at Hunter, found me. Mary asked me to speak to her human sexuality class. People like Mary need to be appreciated because it took a lot of guts in 1972 for a professor who wasn't tenured to come down to the gay table in the cafeteria looking for students to speak to her class. She also asked Harold.

So Harold and I walked into Mary's class. I was very nervous, but I felt very safe with Mary, who I knew was not going to let any of the students get out of line. We went in there and talked about who we were, with the intention of dispelling myths. People were extremely curious, but there was some hostility, most of it toward me from men. One man said, "Well, there's no way that women can make love with each other. They haven't got the parts." The women were curious about how my children responded to me being a lesbian. But for the most part, the students seemed to be much more fascinated with gay men. They asked, "How does it feel to be like a woman?" Over the years the questions got much more sophisticated—more on civil rights and more about custody cases.

Speaking at Hunter got me speaking engagements at other colleges and high schools. It was just something I felt I had to do. Even though it was uncomfortable at first, it was so important to dispel the myths about us. I also felt that if you went into a class of thirty, there had to be a couple of gay people in that class. My being there would let them know that there were other gay people, that they weren't alone, and that they were OK. You see, growing up, I didn't know what it meant to be gay. I had no idea. All I heard when I was growing up at the orphanage in Far Rockaway was really negative stuff: You were sick; you were a sinner. I didn't hear anything positive. I wanted to change that.

ONE OF the most important things I got involved in through the Lesbian Rising Collective was counseling. We were interested in counseling women on reproductive issues like birth control, abortion, and stuff like that. Word got around that there was a group of students in Room 245 who could give information on where to get birth control pills. People could come in for counseling and not have it put on their records. Eventually gay students started coming in, too, saying they wanted to talk to a counselor. Some of these gay people were bringing in gay high school students or kids they had picked up on the street. I would never say no to these kids because they had nobody else to talk to. They were very isolated and they were also dealing with coming-out issues. They said things like, "I'm afraid to tell this person." Or many times it was, "I wish I could meet people. Can you tell me how? Where can I go?" People don't want to be alone. Why should they be? So we decided to set up gay peer counseling.

DURING THE next few years, I continued the volunteer counseling at Hunter. At the same time, I worked as an apprentice chef at a restaurant on Fifth Avenue. But I had to give up my goal of becoming a chef after I got attacked coming back from my health club in Greenwich Village. I was walking with a friend beside Washington Square Park, and these three guys kept making nasty remarks to us. There was a woman with them, but she didn't say that much. We felt pretty safe at first because there was a fence separating us from them: They were in the park, and we were outside. But we came to a place in the fence where they could come out. They came up behind us and started kicking a tin can at me. By the time we got up to the north side of the park, they were kicking it pretty hard, and it was hitting me. So I turned around. I remember saying something like, "What's the matter here?" And the guy hit me. His first punch broke my nose. The other person hit me in the stomach. I couldn't stand up after that. I fell down. I was already a bloody mess, and then I got kicked in the back.

They were yelling antilesbian remarks: "Who do you think you are? You wanna' look like a man? We'll show you!" That kind of stuff. The woman with me, she had to fight off the other two. They took her glasses and flung them. Then they left. There was a guy on the street who hailed a cab and got us to the hospital.

The doctors were real concerned about internal injuries and didn't pay much attention to my face. They sent me home. The next morning I was disoriented and had to go back to the hospital. They found a hematoma practically right between my eyes. They had to operate. After I got out of the hospital, my back was really bothering me, and it was getting worse. I had to go back into the hospital for a month. When I got out, I was in so much pain that my doctor said that I couldn't work as a chef anymore. He told me to go to the Office of Vocational Rehabilitation, where they took all these tests and said, "You're college material; we'll send you to college." I didn't even have a high school diploma. So they sent me to New York University to take a college prep course and then the high school equivalency test. Boy, was I hungry for education.

It's funny, those guys in the park wanted to bust my face, which they half did. They crushed my nose. But their motive was not to make me this better activist or this person who would go on to make some real changes. No, I'm sure they wanted to put me six feet under. But instead, they sent an activist on her way. Some real good came of that. It changed my whole life.

My volunteer work became my career. I passed the high school equivalency test and then went to Hunter where I majored in health. I wanted to concentrate on health services and counseling. I went and talked to Mary Lefkarites, the professor who had asked me to talk to her class. I told her what I wanted to do, and she laughed because she never realized that I had been just a hang-around activist on campus before. She always thought I was a student.

Everything I did in school as a student was around gay issues or women's issues. I was able to incorporate my movement work into my school work. I wrote papers on it for sociology classes. I went to every meeting in the community as a representative from Hunter because I was curious. I was hungry for information. That's why I'm so well known here in New York. They remember me from the early days.

In 1979, I got involved in a project that brought together my education, my counseling work, and my movement work. I heard about an organization that Dr. Emery Hetrick and Damien Martin were starting, the Institute for the Protection of Lesbian and Gay Youth. You know how you get this feeling that you've met the right people at the right time? That's how I felt when I met both of them. I immediately took to them. Emery was such a wonderful, warm person—very caring. He was a man with vision, who really felt that we had to start protecting our youth. And he was so down to earth. He was my mentor in a lot of ways. Damien, too. I learned so much from both of them.

When we met, Damien asked me how long I had been working with kids. When I said, "All these years," he asked if I had any records or anything. I said, "I have these cards. I wrote down their age, sex, orientation, and the problem and resolution." He got very excited because the stuff I had was just the kind of information he and Emery needed at that stage of getting their organization started. I thought he was going to jump up and kiss me.

I joined Damien and Emery just a few months after they started their organization, but it was a few years before we opened our doors to the public. When we did, we thought the kids would dribble in. We thought we would have a chance to do long-term planning. From November 1983 to January 1984, I think we had about fifteen clients. The following year we had nearly three hundred clients, and since then, it's tripled and tripled again.

This number doesn't include our telephone counseling. Kids call from all around the country. They find out about us on television or read about us and call the hotline. I remember a twelve-year-old boy from the Bronx who would call me once a week just to talk and ask questions about being gay. He wanted to talk to another gay person. We'd also talk about a whole bunch of other things, like his schoolwork. Oh, I loved him and I was so curious about what he looked like, but he said, "My mother won't let me take the subway into the city until I'm thirteen, so I have to wait a year." Once he asked me, "Do you think I can meet other gay people?" And I said, "Sure, soon."

Finally, he came down to see us a year later. He was this cute little kid, a little on the chubby side. His family has since moved back to Puerto Rico, and now he writes to me. What a great kid! You know, I remember what it was like to be a teenager with nobody to talk to about this issue. This is one of the reasons I'm so committed to this work.

We get all kinds of kids. They run the gamut. Every race, class, socioeconomic group. Many families don't know their kids are coming to our agency, which is sad. A lot of these kids want to come out to their parents. They want to share who they are. But we don't encourage them to come out to their parents because you can't predict how a family is going to respond.

A good percentage of our kids are thrown out on the street by their parents. We had one young man who was a throwaway from Boston. He came from a close-knit Italian family. He thought that he could share his being gay with them. He did it as a sharing experience, not to slap them in the face. They threw him out of the house. He never went home. But he had us.

WE DIDN'T get a lot of attention from the gay or straight communities for the first couple of years. Then Steve Ashkinazy and I cofounded the Harvey Milk School for lesbian and gay kids, which is run here

Joyce Hunter in 1986 in her office at the Hetrick-Martin Institute talking with two students from the Harvey Milk High School. (© *JEB [Joan E. Biren])*

at the Institute. It's part of the Board of Education's alternative high school program for kids who are having trouble staying in mainstream schools. We opened the school on April 15, 1985. We sent out a press release to the gay community about the school with the hope that people in the community would help fund the program.

National Public Radio picked up the story. Then a reporter called us from the *New York Times*. Me and Steve talked to him; he talked to Damien. Nothing happened, so we forgot about it. We thought, "Oh well, if it gets in the paper, it'll probably be one little column in the third section of the paper under 'Family Life and Styles.'" Five or six weeks later, the article showed up on the front page! After the *Times* article we became hot. It was only then that the gay press came to us. It had to get validity from the heterosexual press first. We made front-page news around the world.

I think the reason the gay community has been reluctant to support us is because they have internalized that child-molesting myth. When I first started working with lesbian and gay teens, even I rationalized it. I said, "I'm a mother. I raised two children. It's not going to look like I'm after these kids or like I'm trying to recruit them for anything. I have a lover." I was concerned. I didn't want to be thrown out of Hunter. I don't think these feelings are always conscious, but we have to get that monkey off our backs because this work is vital. These young people are a part of our community. I believe very strongly that to be a community, you have to build for the future, and the future is our children.

My whole vision of this organization was to provide direct services for these lesbian and gay youth. To be advocates for them in other agencies. To go around training professionals to work with this population and to help other communities develop programs. And we're doing that. I've helped develop a group in Tulsa, Oklahoma. We helped start an organization in D.C. We're also working with a group in New Orleans, and I hope to do work in other countries soon.

YOU KNOW, I remember one time Steve Ashkinazy came to me in my office at the Institute. He said to me, "The kids are real quiet." I said, "Well, why don't you go back there and check out what's going on." So he went to the lounge area. Then he came back and said, "I want you to go back there and break it up." I said, "What's going on? Why don't you just break it up?" He said, "No, you have to see this to believe it." So I went back there. I never thought I would live to see something like this: A group of gay kids playing spin the bottle. I almost cried because I was so moved by it, remembering how hard it was for me. These kids weren't lonely. They weren't selling their butts on the street. They were laughing and having a good time. It was very affectionate, not heavy sex or anything. They were having fun. Seeing them, I realized that they were just like any other group of kids. If you left them alone, they were curious.

I said to the kids, "I want you to know that while I'm going to ask you to stop this game because you're in an agency, and it's really not the appropriate place to do this, there's nothing wrong with what you're doing." I made that very clear. And they all smiled and said, "All right." Nowhere in my wildest imagination did I think that a group of lesbian and gay kids could get together to do that.

The Conservative Congressman

Robert Bauman

IN SEPTEMBER 1980, *Republican Congressman Robert Bauman of Mary-land was working in his Capitol Hill office when two agents from the FBI arrived unexpectedly. The agents implied that unless Bauman pleaded* nolo contendere *to the misdemeanor charge of soliciting a prostitute, he would be charged with every felony and misdemeanor the FBI could throw at him. Robert Bauman, father of four and a proud conservative from the right wing of his party, was trapped. Even before he pleaded* nolo contendere, *his activities with male prostitutes were revealed in the press. A few weeks later, Bauman was voted out of office. It was a stunning end to a remarkable career and the beginning of a very painful period of self-discovery for Robert Bauman.*

A decade later, Bob Bauman is more than comfortable with his homosex-uality and his conservative politics. Which is not to say that his conservative friends are comfortable with his support of gay rights or that gay rights activists are comfortable with his conservative politics.

I was born in 1937 and was adopted at six weeks. I lived in Washing-ton for about seven years. Then my mother died. My father quickly remarried, and my stepmother decided that under the circumstances I should go to military school in Virginia. It was pretty much her decision to send me. She obviously thought it would be easier for them as newly married people to get along without this live-in eight year old. Besides, I was a rather headstrong and opinionated sort of child, and they thought the discipline would be good for me. In one sense, it was: It taught me to live on my own, to make my own bed, and to keep my life in some sort of order in an outward sense. To this day, I make my bed even if I don't have to.

The world of military school wasn't the worst life. You would wake up in the morning to a bugle. March to breakfast. March to class. March to lunch. March to gym. March to dinner. And lights out. If nothing else, you ate well.

What struck me most of all about this time in my life was the terrible feeling of homesickness. It was total debilitation. You couldn't do anything—you just felt isolated and alone and sad. Weeping a lot. Phone calls home. It was overwhelming, but you got over it eventually. Like everything else, you get over it or you succumb to it and go to a nuthouse. I decided to get over it, and I decided that if no one wanted me, then I would show the world. I would do it on my own. Of course, I took the whole experience of being sent away as a rejection. So now I didn't need anybody. And for the next thirty-five years, I followed that pattern to a T.

There was a lot of homosexual activity at military school. Generally, the rule was that it was all right to engage in these activities as long as you didn't initiate them. I'm not sure how it ever happened if someone else always had to be the initiator. Another unwritten rule was that it was acceptable to do these things, but if you appeared to want to do them too much, were too eager, or you enjoyed them excessively, then you were queer.

I enjoyed the closeness of another human being, the warmth of the embrace. The act of sex itself was certainly pleasing momentarily, but it was the closeness that appealed to me, which would probably fit together with the whole situation I found myself in, being away from home and the death of my mother. So human teddy bears were a nice thing to have around. I'm still a cuddler of sorts.

FROM A very early age, I had an acute interest in public affairs. A year or so before I went to military school, my aunt gave me a book called *Abraham Lincoln's World.* I read it cover to cover twice. Lincoln was so pleasing to me as a human being that I became a Republican right then and there and vowed that I would be a lawyer and that I would go into politics.

I was deeply emotionally involved in the presidential campaign in 1948. I was very much for Tom Dewey defeating Harry Truman because Dewey was a Republican. I was heartbroken when Truman won. In fact, I was so vocal in my classes about politics that the headmaster of the lower school came into my class the morning of the election and sought me out. This was a measure of my notoriety even in those days. It had been a very long count, and he wanted to tell me that Dewey had lost. The headmaster was a big Democrat. He was always one of my antagonists.

I was in military school for two full years and then went to West Virginia to live with my father and my stepmother. I don't think we were together a week before it was just total loggerheads. I decided that I had to get of there and started to look for a way out. It took me four years, but I finally got away. I went to Washington as a page when I was fifteen.

Like Fidel Castro, I got my job through the *New York Times*. I read an ad in the paper in December of 1952 that the Republicans, having taken over Congress, were firing all the patronage employees and replacing them with Republicans, including the pages. A light bulb went on. I already had an appointment with the dentist that day and had permission to leave school to go, but instead of going to the dentist, I called and arranged an appointment to see the local congressman. We were living in Easton, Maryland, by then, and our congressman lived in town. Easton is not a big town, only seven thousand or eight thousand people. Ted Miller was the kind of congressman you would see on the street and say, "Hi, Ted."

So I went to see Congressman Miller and told him I wanted to be a page. I told him a bit of what I had been doing. Ted was a very absentminded Phi Beta Kappa who had gone to Yale back in the days of World War I. He didn't know me well, but he called around and got good reports on all the work I had done. I had been involved locally in the 1952 Eisenhower versus Stevenson presidential campaign. I formed a group of kids who rode around town on their bikes, handed out stuff on the streets, and went door to door. I called the group Bikes for Ike. Miller said he'd see what he could do.

By this time, without knowing it, I was what came to be known as a traditionalist conservative. That view generally holds toward minimalist intervention of government in one's life—laissez-faire economics, an exultation of individual rights, generally. But there's also a strong vein in that traditionalist thinking that says the government does have the right and/or duty to impose certain moral principles upon people.

I WAS at school when I got the news. The Republican county chairman called the high school and had the principal come and find me. I got on the phone and he said, "It's come through, and you have a great responsibility to your state and to the county and to the Republican Party." I thought, *My God, what is this?* And then he said, "You've gotten the job, Bob, you're going to be a page." I remember going to one of my teachers, Mr. Zimmerman, who was an antagonistic Democrat, and telling him, "Mr. Zimmerman, I'm going to Congress! I mean, as a page!" He quoted that line for years afterwards.

I took office the day after Eisenhower did. I went to the Eisenhower inaugural as a congressman's guest. I remember being thoroughly overawed, particularly when we went through the receiving room.

There was Eisenhower and Mamie. The military guard standing next to me was announcing everybody: "Congressman so-and-so from Ohio." "Bob Bauman, page." Eisenhower, who was always a little bit befuddled, or at least appeared to be so, said, "You're a plebe? You don't look old enough to be a plebe." I said, "Oh, no, Mr. President, I'm just a page." And he said, "We're glad you could come, anyway."

The next day I raised my right hand and swore the oath and allegiance to the United States government against all enemies, foreign and domestic—the first of many times I did that—and I was a page. Not only had I escaped my domestic situation, but I was right where I wanted to be. I could walk thirty feet from the page bench out through the main door and stand where Abraham Lincoln had been a congressman.

I NEVER went home to live again. After serving as a page I went to Georgetown University's School of Foreign Service and then the law school there. In 1960 I got married to a woman with whom I had a great deal in common. We were both Roman Catholic. We were both very strong conservatives, politically. We were both active in the Nixon campaign. We both worked on the Hill. I met her when she was president of the Young Republicans at a Catholic girls' school in Washington. I was president of the Young Republicans at Georgetown University. We were making protest signs against Rockefeller or something when he was going to run against Nixon. We got engaged and courted throughout the 1960 election.

I remember going to a reception down on the Eastern Shore a month after Nixon lost. We walked in the door, and Bertha Adkins, who was a big Republican lady in those days, said, "Ah, here they are, the only Republican promises that were kept this election." We had only been married a month. We were very committed to a lot of different things and we loved each other strongly. It was just a match made in heaven.

IT WAS nearly twenty years later that my wife and priest confronted me. I was already a congressman by this time, drinking heavily, involved with hustlers, and in and out of gay bars. My wife had found some male magazines. That was not the first time; it was just the last straw. She knew something was wrong for a long time. It was a nightmare for her.

After they confronted me, I went to my good friend, Father John Harvey, and talked to him for three hours. Father Harvey officiated at our wedding and baptized several of our kids. He was the head of a seminary here in Washington. This was in 1980. I was forty-two years old. I had never told anybody the things I told him—ever, ever. In fact, he put on his stole at one point to hear confession. He said, "Should I consider this as a confession?" I said that I would appreciate that. When it was over, I felt as if a great burden had been lifted from me. He gave me absolution. Some months later he told me that it was one of the most painful sessions he had ever had.

I started going to a psychologist in February. I was going to deal with this problem I had about sexuality. I knew I had a problem, but I was convinced that I wasn't a homosexual. I also wasn't going to drink anymore. I stopped drinking on May 1, 1980. It was the last drink I ever had. For six months I went through a semieuphoria, thinking that I had gotten my life together. Carol and I were going to live happily ever after.

As far as I knew, this was purely a family matter. But at the time all this happened, in the winter of 1979–80, the FBI and a government task force were looking into the activities of a number of congressmen and senators, twelve or thirteen in all. I go through this step by step in the book I wrote later because it was so important to me to show that this was a political decision. No action was taken against any of the others on whom they had information. Some of them are still in Congress. But there were a number of reasons why they went after me, not the least of which was probably a certain dash of hypocrisy on my part—more than a dash.

There were also plenty of political reasons to get rid of me. The press called me the Watchdog of the House. I had been on the staff there for years as a page and as a legislative aide on the floor. I had left to go into the Maryland legislature, but came back to Washington in 1973, following a special election. It was as though a staffer who knew everything had suddenly been given the right to speak on the floor. I did know everything, and I used my knowledge of the rules to block all kinds of things the Democrats wanted, including pay raises. Tip O'Neill once said to me on the floor, "I personally resent the gentleman from Maryland." And I said, "Mr. Speaker, no higher honor could come to me." I was a prick, but I was effective in a gadfly sense. And then suddenly, this son of a bitch is discovered to be in and out of parking lots with hustlers, out at gay bars, and drunk besides. I was a natural target.

The Justice Department sent two FBI agents to my office in early September of 1980, a little less than eight weeks before the election, and informed me of all this shit that they had dredged up. They implied that I had the choice, according to U.S. Attorney Charles

Ruff, a Carter appointee, of pleading *nolo contendere* to a charge of solicitation for prostitution, a misdemeanor under the District of Columbia law, or of being charged with every felony and every other misdemeanor they could come up with, including white slavery.

At this point I became illogical: I really thought I could contain the situation. It was all thought of in political terms, in terms of the election—that was the most important thing. So the day after Congress went out of session, on October 3, I think it was, I pleaded *nolo*, and, of course, for the next two weeks it was front-page news all over—not just in the *Washington Post*, but all over the world.

At home it was like being in a bomb shelter. The mind has the capacity to withdraw at times of extreme stress—at least mine does. The mind denies the reality of the situation and says to itself, *This can't be happening to me. Don't worry about it. It will be worked out some way or another.* You just don't want to confront it. And eventually, of course, you have to, particularly if you're in the middle of an election campaign. So I sat in the house for four or five days. Carol and I talked about it. We had a meeting of all our political leaders. They all came to the house. They were all so glad to see I was still alive. The consensus without objection from forty or fifty leaders in my district was, run! "You look fine to us," they said. "Go out there and show them you're the same old Bob Bauman."

Ultimately I lost the election by less than two percentage points, about seven thousand or eight thousand votes. I got more votes in losing then I had gotten in winning with 65 percent of the vote two years before. It was a presidential year, so there was a big turnout.

The defeat was a relief in one sense. This whole experience was like having root canal every day, twenty-four hours a day. And then suddenly, it stopped. But the following February or March, my wife told me she wanted a separation. When that news broke, the press was so intrusive that we had to take the kids out of town for about a week. The reporters were going to the kids' school and trying to interview them—little kids—their teachers, and their friends. There were more television units on the streets of Easton than there were people. It was crazy; it was absolute madness. Eventually the attention turned elsewhere. The spotlight moved on.

ALL THROUGH this period I was thoroughly convinced that I wasn't gay. I wasn't a homosexual. I couldn't be a person like that. People wonder how I could have convinced myself of that, but from an early age it was a matter of building certain walls within my mind. Not only had the church told me about sin—and I assumed that anything like this was sinful—but I picked that up from my peers. Back then it was just ingrained, inculcated by the wink of the eye, the joke, the comment. A homosexual was less than a man. And a homosexual was something I was sure I wasn't, thank God! Somehow, over the years, I just did what was required of me as far as my emotions and sexual needs were concerned and, at the same time, I did what was required of me by my principles and the church. There was no way I could reconcile it.

Of course, the issue of homosexuality had come up while I was in Congress. I got a certain number of letters in the mail about that, but only a small number, because mine was a predominantly suburban and rural district where people, even the 10 percent who might have been, didn't put on paper that they were gay. The few letters that I got on the topic were generally supportive of gay rights and wanted me to support that view. I responded with a letter that I had one of my good legislative aides draft. It was a traditional and well-stated Catholic viewpoint of homosexuality—that I didn't condemn the individual, but I condemned the act; that I was sorry, but I couldn't support legislation that would enhance or give special status to what was essentially a perverse and a sinful activity, et cetera. To me, while gays weren't bad, they were, unfortunately, wrong. And, of course, all during this time I was engaging in the very same sinful activity.

Because of this religious view and my conservative politics, people perceived me to be antigay. I wasn't. I remember a reporter at the *New York Times* telling me a couple of years later, "We searched and we searched to find anything you ever said on gays. You never said anything." And I hadn't. Jimmy Breslin was wrong when he said in one of his columns, and this is a paraphrase, "He would stand on the floor of the House all day and rail against the faggots and then go out and suck cocks in the evening." He didn't quite use the language in the second part of that phrase, but he used the first part in his column. I did not rail against homosexuals. Publicly, I didn't say anything on the subject.

I don't think the fact that I didn't talk about gays was conscious. I think it was an unconscious unwillingness to address in public what I wouldn't address in private. I was doing the same thing in my own head as I was doing in public, avoiding the issue. Denial is a very, very strong emotion. Not only in alcoholism, but in other situations. I convinced myself that there was something wrong, but I just wasn't gay. That's how, at the time, I could say I was struggling against the twin compulsions of alcoholism and homosexuality. I believed what I was saying.

While I didn't say anything about gays, I did vote for antigay legislation three times in Congress. In one instance I cosponsored the Family Protection Act. I can't excuse myself on this one by saying that I didn't know there was government-sanctioned gay discrimination in the bill. Even if I had known about the discriminatory aspects of it, I still would have voted for the Family Protection Act because I wasn't gay then.

I wasn't gay until 1983. When people have heard me say that, they say, "What the hell are you talking about?" And I really mean it because it took almost three years of religious and psychiatric counseling for me to acknowledge that I was gay. What happened was, I received a piece of paper from the Catholic church that said that my marriage had been annulled. They didn't give reasons, but when I called the priest in charge of the diocese and asked him what the grounds were, he said, "Mistake of person." I called Father Harvey to ask him what it meant. After making some phone calls himself, he called me back and told me that there could have been no proper union in marriage because "Carol didn't realize that you were incapable of marriage, and neither did you. You may not have known or you may have known, but you were homosexual throughout this period. You could not have contracted a valid marriage." According to the church, I was a mistake. I didn't know who I was.

When I looked at this paper annulling my marriage, I said to myself, *What am I fighting this for?* You see, I had already fired one father because he'd told me, "You should consider the fact that you *are* gay." And I said, "Now, wait a minute! Aren't you a Catholic doctor? What are you telling me?" He finally said, "Maybe you'd better pick someone who can better handle this." So I looked at that annulment paper in 1983 and thought to myself, *If the church says I'm gay, if the holy Roman Catholic church, my church, says I'm gay, all right, fine, that's what I am.*

I thought about jumping off the Chesapeake Bay Bridge, which would have been a dramatic end and a newsworthy way to go. But I thought to myself, *The sons of bitches who have driven me to this— myself included—I'm not going to give these bastards the satisfaction! I'm going to stick around!* Just like I wasn't going to leave the Catholic church.

Along around 1983, after the annulment and after finally accepting that I was gay, Dan Bradley called me. During the Carter administration, Dan was the head of the Legal Services Corporation who had resigned and announced that he was gay. I had met him once briefly. After he quit, he went back and practiced law in Miami. He wanted to know if I would consider appearing before the annual meeting of the American Bar Association to speak in favor of gay rights. And I said, "Well, Dan, to tell you the honest truth, I've experienced enough discrimination in the last year or two trying to find employment that you caught me at a good time for you, maybe a bad time for me. Yes, I'll do it." So I did it.

At the American Bar Association meeting, I talked about the depth of feeling that most gay people, particularly men, undergo as a result of discrimination. Not just against their being gay, but what I've described as a rejection of their very constitution and being. Not only did parents and loved ones, the people who should have been the most understanding, reject you, but then the law enforced that rejection with a legal sanction for the discrimination.

After I spoke at the American Bar Association, "Good Morning America" called. Then I heard from the "Today" show. They all wanted me on. My God, a conservative faggot! The *Washington Post* did yet another feature.

That speech pissed off a lot of conservatives. Some of them said to me privately, "You've really done it now. It's one thing to be gay. It's another thing to get up and endorse gay rights." Even somebody like the late Terry Dolan, who was gay and the cofounder of NCPAC, the National Conservative Political Action Committee, said to me privately, "Bob, don't endorse gay rights. It's totally against the libertarian ethic and viewpoint. We don't need government laws on any civil rights. People should have the right to discriminate or not discriminate." And I said, "Yes, but Terry, that's all well and fine theoretically, but we both know what happens when there are no laws to protect you."

If I were back in Congress today, I would have no problem voting for civil rights laws in general, which I never did while I was there. That's because I think there's a separation between theory and practice. Theory is a good guide. Practice is what people live under.

Terry was the one who called me about forming a gay group for conservatives to counter the Jesse Helms and William Dannemeyer* types. Not really to counter Helms, but to oppose his views on homosexuality because I certainly agree with a lot of things that Jesse Helms believes in, but not in a lot of other things. Be that as it may, this was what the group was going to do. In 1985 we met at the Dupont Plaza Hotel and decided to start this group. Besides Terry Dolan and me, there was a guy from California who was very active

*A Republican congressman from Fullerton, California.

in Republican politics out there; Lenny Matlovich, the air force sergeant who fought his discharge in the mid-1970s; and two other people, who have to remain nameless. Terry thought Lenny would be an excellent spokesperson because he had the visibility from all of his activities, the lawsuit, and his *Time* magazine cover.

When Terry first approached me, I knew that he had once signed a fund-raising letter denouncing homosexuals as a threat to whatever, for one of the groups he was working with. It might have been NCPAC, his committee. But I put that conveniently aside in my head because here he was trying to form a group to support homosexuality—or at least gay conservatives. So I just didn't bring it up with him.

In his own conduct Terry was totally open about his sexuality. One time I was walking down Connecticut Avenue, and along came Terry with somebody who I thought I had already been introduced to by Terry. "That was last summer," he said. "This is Scott." Or Mark, or David, or whatever. So he was pretty open in one respect. But when people would ask him about it, as the *Washington Post* did at a press conference, he'd say, "When Ben Bradlee talks publicly about his sleeping with Sally Quinn, you can ask me questions about my private life." That was the kind of flip guy he was. He was a brilliant politician, but he obviously went through a lot of struggle, too. Not to excuse his homophobia.

The gay group for conservatives—Concerned Americans for Individual Rights (CAIR)—never got off the ground because we couldn't get any gay Republicans to openly come out and do anything about it. They wouldn't even write checks. They would give cash, so there was no traceable evidence. CAIR could fill a suburban Washington home for a cocktail party with nearly a hundred gay men who worked everywhere, from the White House to the offices of the most conservative Republican senators and congressmen, the Republican National Committee, and all parts of the Reagan administration. But they wouldn't publicly acknowledge their role in the group.

Terry's story is very sad, very pathetic. When the rumor went around that he had AIDS and then he died of AIDS, and the *Washington Post* reported it, Terry's family denied it vehemently. Then when they had the funeral, they had a memorial service before the mass and systematically excluded every one of his gay friends. Tony Dolan, Terry's brother, the White House Speech writer under Reagan, took out a two-page ad in the *Washington Times* to denounce the rumors about his brother. I was a target of the denunciation. Supposedly I was an organizer of the gay funeral service we had at Saint Matthew's. I was asked by Terry's lover to speak, and I did, but I wasn't an organizer. Terry's family was very, very uptight about the whole thing.

Lenny Matlovich also died of AIDS. The last time I saw him was when he came for the Gay Rights March on Washington in 1987. He stayed with me for a few days. The march organizers wouldn't let him speak on the Mall because he was a conservative Republican. They told Lenny to fuck off. Jesse Jackson could speak, and a few of the other crazies, but Lenny couldn't speak. He had AIDS—everybody knew that—but he couldn't speak because he was a Republican conservative. It offended me deeply because I saw how hurt he was. Lenny was an emotional guy, sometimes; at other times he was a very calculating politician. He was a scatterbrain, God bless him. But he was really hurt by that rejection, and he told me so.

I'VE HAD SO many prominent people in the movement say to me, "How can you be gay and conservative? It's impossible." Of course, they equate conservative with homophobia, with Jesse Helms. I understand that attitude, but they're wrong. A gay conservative is not a contradiction in terms any more than it is to be liberal and gay. But the overwhelming leadership of the gay movement is far left-liberal. I don't mean just average liberal, but far left, and they link gay rights and the legitimate concerns of the gay community, whether its AIDS research or privacy, with left-liberal concerns like whether the Sandinistas are good, bad, or indifferent. I just think there's enough difficulty in selling gay rights without freighting it with a lot of baggage. Gay rights is an awfully big platter to deal with on its own.

I don't think that the majority of gay people are left-liberal or radically left. I think that those who are the most visible are, and that's our fault for not coming out and having more courage to speak out. I think that the average—if there is such a thing—gay man or woman is in Chillicothe or in Chicago and is probably somewhat conservative in life-style, employment, and maybe even sexual practice. I know a lot of people who just live together quietly in small towns or even in cities. They don't go to marches and they don't join organizations. The liberal leadership would say they're not doing anything for the community and, therefore, that they should be condemned. But they're not antigay—they're just people who are living their lives and are as embarrassed as I am by things like Sister Boom, Boom.* As a

*In retirement since 1985, the character of Sister Boom, Boom was created by San Franciscan Jack Fertig in 1980. Sister Boom, Boom, who won twenty-three thousand votes in an unsuccessful 1982 race for city supervisor, was easily identified by her nun's habit, oversized-foam-rubber breasts, false eyelashes, and stiletto heels. Sister Boom, Boom, according to the San Francisco Chronicle, "brought national notoriety to the Sisters of Perpetual Indulgence," a group of men who dressed as nuns.

Catholic it just offended me to see the church ridiculed like that. But be that as it may, I'm a conservative, so naturally, what the hell do I know?

IN 1984 I was invited to lunch by a prominent conservative Republican senator who could have helped me immensely in getting a job with the government. The last ten years have not been kind to me economically. He invited me to lunch at the Senate dining room. The senator said, "I understand how things are, and I really think you should get back into government. It's a shame Reagan doesn't have your advice. But I want to ask you a question before I do anything. What do you think about homosexuality as a sin?" And I gave him the Catholic church's view about the nature of homosexuality and that it's not a sin. Although he's a fundamentalist Christian, he said, "I agree, but what do you think about homosexual conduct?" I said, "Well, Senator, to be honest with you, as someone who has known you a long time, I don't think that my kind of God would create a human being as He has created me or any other homosexual, and then tell them that for the rest of their lives they'll be denied any right to intimacy or love with someone to whom they're naturally attracted." He said, "Well, then, you don't believe it's sinful?" I said, "I think that's probably what I just said." He said, "Bob, I can't help you." I said, "I understand." I understand because I've been there. I don't like it, but I understand.

So I didn't get a job in government. I still practice law and do a little writing here and there. I have a client in Europe and one in Texas—nothing big or overwhelming. I'm certainly underemployed and frustrated to the extent that I have ability and I'm not using it. But I tried for a long time to work into Washington law firms. I tried to get into the government with the Reagan people, even again under Bush. And nothing has come of that.

I'm thinking about leaving Washington, but three of my four children still live here. I'm close to all of my kids. One daughter just got married, and she's finishing up at Georgetown Law. My youngest son is still in high school, about to go to the University of Virginia. My other daughter has just finished George Mason University. And I have a son at the University of Capetown. He got married last December [1988]. My daughter-in-law is classified as colored. I'd love to go to South Africa, but my son said they'd throw me out because down there I'd be considered a raving liberal.

Sale Juive

Paulette Goodman

IN 1980, *Paulette Goodman received a letter from her daughter's former boyfriend that changed her life. In it, he told Paulette about a relationship her daughter was having with a young woman, a relationship that was "more than a friendship." Paulette hoped her daughter was simply going through a phase. For months, she said nothing about the letter to anyone, including her husband.*

Paulette had spent most of her adult life raising two children, caring for her elderly mother, and looking after her husband. About a year after she learned that her daughter was a lesbian, she began to attend a local support group for parents and friends of gay people. Before long, she was hosting the meetings herself in her suburban home in Silver Spring, Maryland. Today, Paulette is president of the Federation of Parents and Friends of Lesbians and Gays (Parents FLAG, or P-FLAG), a support, education, and advocacy organization with more than eighty chapters around the country. She has become one of the most visible and effective advocates for the rights of lesbian and gay people.

Paulette Goodman was born in Paris in 1933, one of nine children. "We lived in a four-room apartment in a large low-income building on the outskirts of the city, where we were one of four Jewish families out of one hundred." During World War II, in occupied Paris, Paulette first learned what it meant to be different.

At school the kids called me a *sale Juive*, a "dirty Jew." Even my best friend did, yet she wouldn't let somebody else call me that. Today it's the same thing, only now they say "you queer" or "you faggot." You know how kids are.

We were made to wear the Star of David on our clothing because that was decreed by the Germans. It was also decreed that Jews weren't supposed to be in any public places. On Thursdays, which was the time for children to go to the movies, Jewish children were not allowed. So we would take off our Star of David and go, even though we knew that if we got caught, the whole family would have been wiped out.

We took even greater risks than going to the movies. I remember a terrible winter when we had no fuel, nothing. We had a cold flat with a wood or coal stove in our kitchen. So we stole coal from the Germans in this no-man's-land they occupied near where we lived. A group of us, maybe a dozen or more kids, would go in a band through this no-man's-land and find our way into the rail depot, Porte de la Chapelle. The older kids would go into the locomotives and steal the coal briquettes to take home for heat and cooking. My friend Jeanine and I—we were the two youngest—were assigned to look out and whistle if anybody came by. Now, the Germans went around with dogs. If they had heard any noise, they could have shot us on the spot. We would come back home from the depot with potato sacks filled with briquettes. The older kids carried the coal, and the younger children carried wood splinters from the bombed-out houses. To this day I don't know why our parents never questioned where we got the wood and coal. Perhaps because they were so desperate. For us, it was exciting and fun, but we took incredible chances. I would die if my kids had done anything like that.

Most Jews were deported from Paris. What saved us, I think, is that we stayed put. There were too many young children at home, and besides, we had no money. My father was an iron worker for the French national railroad, and because he was very much needed, he was given special working papers. He was a naturalized French citizen, which I think helped save the family, although that wasn't enough to save my sister, her husband, and my nephew.

My brother-in-law, who had a tailoring business at home, was born in Poland. He was not a French citizen. One day the Germans were rounding up what they called aliens, the non-French people, so the police and the gestapo went to my sister's home and took both my sister and her husband. The following morning, my aunt, who lived in their neighborhood, was supposed to go visit my sister. When she got to the apartment house, she found out what happened. She also found that my sister had left her child, André, with the superintendent. It turned out that my sister had somehow managed to give her son to the building superintendent before the gestapo and police came. She had begged, had pleaded for the super to take him. My sister knew that if they took her little boy, he, too, would be killed. We knew by that time what was happening to Jews.

For some reason, my aunt didn't bring my nephew back with her. She left him there and came to tell us what had happened. So my mother sent my sister, Gaby, who is five years older than I, to pick up André. She went to the building, found him, and started on her way home. Just after they left the apartment house, the gestapo came with the French police to pick up the child.

When the police questioned the superintendent, she said, "The child just left with his aunt." They followed my sister. As she was walking back to where we lived, they stopped her. They wanted her to get in the car with the child to go to the police headquarters, which was not in our district. My sister begged and cried. She said, "My mama is waiting for me. She knows I went to pick up my nephew. I have to go home and tell her." We didn't have telephones in those days. She couldn't just call. So they followed her to our apartment. She came up with the two French policemen. The gestapo stayed downstairs. The police said, "Madame Rozenberg, you will have to let this little boy go with us because his mother is asking for him." My mother replied, "If my daughter did not take the child yesterday, that means she doesn't want him to be there with her. I have brought up nine children and I can bring up a tenth. Please leave me my grandchild." This was her first grandchild. She made such a scene. She tore her hair out. She cried. We were there when this happened, so I remember everything. The police said, "Look, you better quiet down and you better let the child go because if you don't, those two gestapo downstairs will take you away with all the children."

She had no choice. They took my nephew and he was reunited with my sister. They spent several months in a camp right outside of Paris. We received a couple of letters from them. They threw the letters over the wall of the camp. We even sent some packages of food, whatever my mother could get hold of. Then they were sent to Auschwitz, and we never heard from them again.

So I know what it's like to be a minority and to be threatened with your life. I know what it's like to be in the closet. I know all too well.

As SOON as the war ended, my parents started making arrangements for us to leave. They felt that they never wanted us to go through such an experience again. Besides the issue of our safety, things were very bad financially after the war. Food was scarce; it was difficult to earn a living.

My parents left France for Montreal, Canada, with my youngest brother in 1949. We had family there. My older brother and I went to Montreal via New York, where I met my husband, Leo. I came back to the United States to marry Leo, waited three years to get my citizenship, and then brought my parents to the States, which is where they wanted to be in the first place.

* * *

WHEN I discovered that my daughter was involved with a young woman, I found myself in yet another closet. Shortly after we moved to Silver Spring in 1980, I received a letter from my daughter's former boyfriend. My daughter had dated this young man since she was fifteen and a half years old. We had met him at a monthly transcendental meditation course, and he became a friend of the family. He was seven years older than she was. He fell in love with my daughter, and they seemed to be compatible. They dated until her second year of college, which, I found out later, was when my daughter fell in love with a young woman. In his letter he told me about my daughter's new friend and that he thought it was more than a friendship.

I never breathed a word of this to my husband. I walk around the block for exercise. After I got the letter, I had all kinds of crazy thoughts on my walk. First, I thought, *It's a phase she's going through. She'll meet the right fellow, and things will be different.* I didn't know quite how to deal with it. I was afraid that someone would find out.

When my daughter came home from school on vacation, there were the same late-night long-distance telephone calls with this new friend that she had had with the young fellow. She was secretive when she wrote letters. I knew there was something going on, but I couldn't talk to her about it. Whenever she came home, we were both on edge. It was fine for the first couple of days, but then she would become anxious to go and be with the person she loved. But she never, ever said anything.

Finally, after nine months, I told Leo about what the young man had written. He said, "So what?" I was relieved.

Three months after I told Leo, my daughter came home for summer vacation. She asked her dad to go for a ride with her, and I realized what she was up to, that she was going to come out to him. When they came home, I was furious. I was so angry because I felt she didn't trust me. I was hurt. I'm her mother; I love her. I've always been crazy about her, yet for many years we had been on different planes. She was secretive. She was difficult as a teenager. She was undergoing all kinds of things, a good part of which was dealing with her sexuality. And she was angry at me for some reason.

So I confronted her, and we started to talk. She was crying. She said the only reason she didn't tell me was that she thought I'd never understand. She was afraid I wouldn't let her finish school. She went to Sarah Lawrence and thought we would yank her out of school, that we would cut her off. She had heard terrible stories from other kids.

Here I was, a devoted, loving parent, and my child was afraid to come to me. I think that's a terrible thing. And I was angry with her for not coming out to me, for thinking she couldn't trust me. Since I've been involved in Parents FLAG, I've spoken to a lot of kids on college campuses. We give Coming Out to Parents workshops. Many of the students say they're not ready to come out to their parents, that even if their parents confronted them, they would deny it because they're not ready. That helped me understand my child and the dynamics of what happened in our relationship.

My daughter went back to New York and she wrote us a beautiful letter saying that she was sorry that she didn't trust us, but she just didn't know. She also said that we could help the gay cause by supporting a couple of organizations with donations, which we did. And then I heard a public announcement on the radio, "If there's someone gay in your life and you have questions, you can call this number." So I called and talked to a man who was the first gay person I talked to. He was having meetings at his home, and I went. That was in 1981.

There were about three or four parents and a couple of gay men at this support group. I was very uptight, but we talked, and I found it very helpful. I kept going every month and I got hooked because I saw that I could help others. I was also voraciously reading everything that I could lay my hands on.

What helped me early on to understand my daughter was a panel discussion I went to at George Washington University. One of the mothers from the support group was on the panel, which was sponsored by a feminist group—not all lesbians, but feminists. They presented a slide show of the gay pride parade in New York. There was a group carrying a sign for the gay blind. There were the gay handicapped being pushed in wheelchairs. And there were the gay deaf. I realized that these people didn't choose to be gay. Why would they make their lives even more difficult? That really helped me to move from feelings of anger and blame to *this is a fact of life, and therefore whatever she is, that's fine. I've got to learn to live with it and know more about it.*

I also discovered the bigotry and hatred toward lesbians and gays. I went to hearings for a gay rights ordinance in Montgomery County, here in Maryland. At first I really had no opinion about it. But at the hearings I saw the nastiness, the bigotry. The Bible thumpers were saying things like, "Put them on an island and nuke them." They equated homosexuality with bestiality. On the one hand, these people would say that laws protecting gays in the workplace or in housing weren't needed, and on the other hand, they were saying such terrible things about gays. I really felt irked that people should be discriminated against. This never sat with me very well. I didn't see why my gay child should be considered less a person than my nongay child, so I testified in favor of adding sexual orientation as a protected class.

Gradually, I got more and more involved. I was holding meetings for parents at my home. I was answering a telephone help line. Then I went to New York to meet with people from Parents FLAG. Leo and I were both impressed by them and the organization. So we came home, and I convinced the other people in our group—there were six parents, including Leo, and two gay men—that we ought to become a chapter of Parents FLAG because they were doing wonderful work.

So in 1983 we became a chapter, and I became chapter president, which is not something I wanted. I'm a worker. I'm also a traditional person. I thought that a man should be president of our organization, but at the time Leo would not take on the job. There was another family involved, Fred and Arlene Boyer, who live in Berkeley now. I looked to Fred to be president, but he said, "We're going to be traveling to England and may be away for six months. I'll be vice president." So I was it. This was the one time I could not say no.

Despite being president of the Washington, D.C. chapter of P-FLAG, I was still very much in the closet. At the Parents FLAG convention in New York in 1983, parents were giving interviews for television. We had lived in New York; Leo is from New York. There was no way I was going to be interviewed and be seen on television. But I finally gave in and did an interview, but I insisted on using my initials. I just was not ready to be that public about being the parent of a gay child. I thought I would never be ready. But ready or not, the next year I came out with a bang.

In 1983, I went to my first Coming Out to Parents workshop, which was held in Philadelphia. I learned that the Philadelphia parents' group had sponsored a public ad campaign on the city buses to promote their organization. David, one of the gay men who was very involved with our Washington group, said, "We have to do this." He got information for me, but as president I had to make the calls to officials here in Maryland. I tried for several months to get through to the public transportation people in Montgomery County. I wrote letters, made telephone calls, and got no place. Finally, in January 1984, I reached the head public relations man at the public transportation department, and he put me in touch with the right officials. I felt just wonderful.

That afternoon, the phone rang. It was Bob Melton from the *Wash-*

ington Post. Bob Melton had just spoken with William Hanna, the antigay councilperson in Montgomery County. He told me that Mr. Hanna said, "If they're going to put ads on the buses to support the gay life-style, we can't let the taxpayers pay for that." Bob Melton wanted to know what it was we planned to put in the ads, and he wanted to know more about our parents' organization. I didn't quite know how to handle this. I was just devastated. It was like a ton of bricks fell on my head. How did Bob Melton find out, and how did Hanna find out?

I was frightened for two reasons. First of all I told the reporter that I did not want my name in the newspaper because I didn't want anyone finding out about me. He said, "I'm sorry Mrs. Goodman, but you testified publicly. Your name is in the public record." I had testified the year before in favor of adding sexual orientation to the county's human rights ordinance. Second, I didn't know what to say about the organization because we were so new. At the time there were just two dozen of us at most. I didn't know how much to say or how little. When Leo came home from work, I was just so upset and I had a headache. I told him the story, and he said, "Well, listen, don't worry about it. If you lose any friends over this, they're not your friends, anyway."

The *Washington Post* wasn't the end of the publicity. The next day the phone rang. It was a reporter from one of the local television news stations calling. He said, "Mrs. Goodman, we've just interviewed Mr. Hanna. Would you like to tell us your side of the story?" I said, "Yes, give me a couple of hours. I just got home. I have to unpack groceries, wash my hair, and have lunch." They were here in less than two hours. The reporter asked me what it was that we wanted to do. I said, "We just want to do a public-service ad campaign on the buses to tell people about our support organization for families of gay people." That evening, I was on the news at six o'clock.

It was very quiet after the broadcast. Then one of my neighbors two houses down called. She knew something was up. She said, "Paulette, are you all right?" I said, "Yes, Terry, I'm fine." She said, "Are you sure?" and I said, "Yes, everything's fine. But I'll tell you what, Terry, I've got something to tell you, and I'll try to make some time this week to see you."

Remember, we moved here in 1980, so Terry was a new friend. She didn't know my daughter. And I felt, first of all, it's nobody's business. I didn't want people who didn't know my daughter to pass judgment on my child, to label her right away. So I didn't talk about it. We used to have Parents FLAG meetings here at the house. The people in our group parked their cars on the street. Terry is from New

York originally and very nosy. She would ask me, "Oh, you're having a party?" The mornings after the meetings, I would always dread people coming to the door. The meetings usually went very late because people would linger on, and so I didn't have time to put away all the books and literature I had displayed on the piano and dining room table. If the doorbell rang, I would be absolutely beside myself. This is what it's like being in the closet.

When I told my friend Terry, she was very understanding. It turns out that she had a dear friend, almost like family, who had two gay sons. The reason I thought she wouldn't understand is that she is very religious. She's Catholic.

So I came out with a bang on the evening news. It was the best thing that ever happened to me because I was boiling inside; I was so stifled. My sense of justice is very strong, and I felt I wanted to speak out. Washington Parents FLAG was a new organization. I was the head of it. How could we reach out to people if I was not able to speak openly? So it was very liberating to be free to speak without fear, although I feared for a while that if people recognized me on the street or found out where I lived, they might throw a bomb at my house or something. You never know what kind of nuts are out there. I was fearful, but I realized that if I didn't conquer that fear, I just couldn't function. I decided I had to speak, that I'd have to take my chances, because it's better than to be afraid.

After I became liberated, I really found a great deal of satisfaction in speaking out. And I also found that because of my reasonableness, being a parent and having gray hair, that people listen to what I have to say and respect what I say. I was believable to a lot of people. I don't think there is a more powerful advocate than a parent. Some gay and lesbian people may be offended by this remark. They feel that they can speak for themselves. But I know from experience that parents who speak out on behalf of their children, no matter what situation it is, are very, very strong advocates. Any time parents take up a cause for their children, they will succeed.

Not every parent in our organization wants to be an advocate. There are those who feel that the sole purpose of the organization is to support other parents. This is certainly one of our aims. But we have various goals. One is to help families understand and accept their gay children with love and pride. Another goal is to help gay and lesbian people in their dealings with their families and the community, to help them come out. Still another is to educate ourselves and our communities on the nature of homosexuality, so we can change societal attitudes. Then we have to speak out and act whenever necessary to secure full human and civil rights for our gay loved ones. But as long as parents are self-centered and only worry about what their families or their friends are going to say about having a gay child, they are not tuned into what is going on in the world. When parents realize the injustices against their children, they start changing their minds and want to speak out.

IN 1987 at the Federation of Parents FLAG convention here in Washington, Elinor Lewallen was installed as the second president of the national group. Elinor was close to seventy, and after having been president-elect for a year and having given a lot of speeches and done a lot of traveling, she found that she just could not carry the load. She was exhausted. I was approached. Tom Sauerman, who was one of the vice presidents and a wonderful man, had most of the votes. People thought he was the best person, and so did I, but Tom could not take it on because it really is a full-time volunteer job. I had the time, so I agreed to be president-elect and was installed in Chicago in 1988.

The federation plays a very important role. The local chapters are the best providers of support services, and they have the opportunity to advocate locally for full human and civil rights. On the other hand, the federation can do what the chapters cannot do. The fact that the federation represents so many chapters, so many people, gives us strength to advocate on a national level with senators or representatives, churches, and so on. When an issue comes up, we can alert our regional directors, who are members of the board of the federation. And these people, in turn, will call on their regional chapters to get them activated.

But you want to know what I like doing best? I like the one-on-one work. I have found the most satisfaction in helping people, seeing the results, and getting the appreciation one on one or in the support groups. I have become a very good facilitator. I know that I'm a good advocate, too, and therefore I speak out. As president of the federation, my job is to speak out. And after all those years in the closet, I'm speaking out with a vengeance now.

I WOULD like us to go out of business one day because that would mean society has become accepting of all people and that we don't have to fight for our gay and lesbian children. That would be the best thing that could happen. Then I could have a vacation. I could go to Paris and visit my sisters.

I don't think that will happen soon, and I'm becoming impatient. I want to see things accomplished in my lifetime. This marks a change

Paulette and Leo Goodman in the lead car of the 1989 Washington, D.C., pride parade. Paulette was the parade's grand marshal. (© *Doug Hinkle, Washington Blade*)

from when I first started out because I used to think I would never live to see the changes that I hoped for. I just accepted that that was how it was going to be. Now, I don't want to wait. That's why I'm working so damn hard. And don't forget that I'm feisty. I'm gentle and I'm patient, but don't rub me the wrong way too long because there's a devil in me. I take after my mom. Not only was she feisty, but she lived to ninety-three!

The Hollywood Screenwriter

Barry Sandler

HOLLYWOOD FIRST *found itself the target of criticism from gay rights activists in 1970 at the premiere of* The Boys in the Band, *a film adaptation of an off-Broadway play. As described by film historian Vito Russo in his book,* The Celluloid Closet, *"the film presented a perfunctory compendium of easily acceptable [homosexual male] stereotypes who gather at a Manhattan birthday party and spend an evening savaging each other and their way of life." At the end of the movie, one of the relatively well-adjusted characters breaks down into sobs and says bitterly, "You show me a happy homosexual, and I'll show you a gay corpse."*

As objectionable as most gay activists found it, The Boys in the Band *was, in fact, an improvement over standard Hollywood fare of the 1960s, when gay men and lesbians first made their way onto the silver screen in the form of "pathological, predatory and dangerous villains and fools, but never heroes," according to Russo.*

Despite increasing pressure from gay rights organizations, Hollywood has been very slow to change. It took more than a decade after The Boys in the Band *for a major studio to release a movie that had something positive to say about homosexuality. In 1980, Barry Sandler, a young Hollywood screenwriter, began work on that film,* Making Love. *It told the story of a married man acknowledging and accepting his homosexuality. Sandler, who already had several motion pictures under his belt, including* The Kansas City Bomber, The Duchess and the Dirtwater Fox, *and* The Mirror Crack'd, *had decided he wanted to write something from personal experience. "Something personal" meant about the life of a gay man.*

I could have easily lived the life of Zack, the character in my movie who's gay and married. I was involved with a woman for a long time, and we were close to getting married. I wanted to marry very much. But there was something inside me screaming, "No, don't! This isn't you!"

If I had chosen that route, I know that, like the character in the film, I would have woken up one day—five, ten, or more years into the marriage—and said, "Why am I living this life? It's a fraud. It's not me." Or else, I would have gone to the back alleys and had very clandestine sex, betraying my wife, my family, myself, and made a lot of people very unhappy. My life would have ended up in shambles.

I DIDN'T have the burden of confronting my parents over being gay because I was seventeen when my father died and twenty-one when my mother died. As much as their deaths pained me, in a way it was a release. It allowed me to be as independent in my life as I wanted to. Nonetheless, I still repressed my sexuality. I didn't come out until I was twenty-three, in around 1973 or 1974. Until I came out, I always felt isolated from the group, like the outsider. Looking back, I can see that the isolation was part of my homosexuality. Even after you come to terms with your homosexuality, you still carry those wounds from childhood that made you feel inferior, that make you feel you were not as good as the heterosexual male.

Movies played an important role in how I saw myself. As a young kid growing up in Buffalo, New York, I saw really powerful negative images of gay people in the movies, and these images stayed with me. For example, in the early 1960s I went to see *Advise and Consent*, in which Don Murray plays a senator being blackmailed over a sexual involvement with a guy when he was in the army. There's a scene where he goes to New York to locate this old trick. He goes to this really wretched, disgusting bar, so grotesque, that for me, as a twelve year old, it was a horror show. It was like I was seeing creatures from a wax museum. So he finds the guy, but he runs from the bar because he's so repulsed by the place, races back to Washington, locks himself in his office, and kills himself.

They rarely showed a gay character in the movies, and when they did, he was so reprehensible that it was ingrained in my consciousness that this was a horrible thing to be. Is it any wonder that we grow up with this kind of negative self-perception? This negative image is what I hoped to reverse, hoped to make up for with my work, but that wasn't until later.

In the 1970s, before *Making Love*, I had done a number of big Hollywood-type films. I started while I was in college. I had about five or six films made up to that point: *The Loners*, *The Kansas City Bomber*, *Gable and Lombard*, *The Duchess and the Dirtwater Fox*, and *The Mirror Crack'd*. I also worked on a few other films that I didn't take credit for: *Evil Under the Sun*, *The Other Side of Midnight*, and one or two others. If you look at these movies, all of them are big, showy, glossy kinds of entertainment.

Around 1980 I was starting to reevaluate my life, my career, and where I wanted to go with my writing. I had been in therapy, I was around thirty, and I was clearly looking to make a shift in direction. I wanted to get more personal in my work. I really felt that I wanted to dig deeper and write from life experience. A close friend, Scott Berg, saw my need and desire to push myself to new limits and encouraged me.

My immediate reaction was to resist: I had all this angst that I couldn't do it. I didn't know if I could expose so much of myself on paper and ultimately on film. It was scary. And then there was the subject itself. This was to be the first mainstream Hollywood film to deal with the subject of homosexuality in a positive way, offering positive role models. It was to have an ending where the character came to terms with his homosexuality and was happier for it. The odds were so against that kind of movie being made. What Hollywood studio would want to make it?

At first I agreed to work with Scott on the story. I said that if we got to a point where I felt I could write a screenplay of the story, then I would do it. So we knocked out a story about a gay married man who realizes the fraud of his marriage and, through his relationship with another gay man, comes to terms with his homosexuality. Along the way he discovers his ability to live a full, rich, and gratifying life as a gay man.

I still resisted, right up to the point when I sat down and wrote the first page of the script, "Fade in. . . . " But once I made up my mind to do it, there was no stopping.

Despite my fears about getting a studio interested in the script, the development deal turned out to be easy. Sherry Lansing was the head of production at Twentieth Century-Fox. She thought there was potential here to make a very important film. She was very progressive and very daring. She has a pioneering spirit and saw the potential for a good film. But she responded as much to the heartbreaking romance of the male-female relationship as to the socially progressive aspect of making a positive statement about homosexuals.

Sherry had to go before the board of directors, who were not thrilled with the idea of this movie. They want you to do what's commercially feasible. And this was a big-risk movie because of the possibility of offending the great silent majority. Sherry fought for the movie, which was clearly a risky move on her part, and I applaud her for it. That took a lot of guts—and you don't find many studio heads with a lot of guts.

We chose Arthur Hiller to be the director. Again, this was someone who was not afraid to tackle this subject. We got together and cast the movie. It was a tough haul because a lot of actors just would not play a gay character. We approached a number of actors, including Dustin Hoffman, William Hurt, and Harrison Ford. None of them was interested.

It's very interesting that an actor like William Hurt would do *Kiss of the Spider Woman*, a movie where he played a gay character who was so clearly different from who he is. No one was ever going to mistake that character and William Hurt. You know that he doesn't walk around in drag all day. He was clearly an actor playing this flamboyant character. Whereas the two main characters in *Making Love* are recognizable as the guy next door. I think that a lot of actors had anxiety that the characters were perhaps too close to reality. Of course, not knowing William Hurt and not knowing what his thinking was, maybe he just liked the script of one movie better than the other.

We went through a lot of actors. Michael Ontkean was one of the first people we had talked to. He had originally turned it down, but we went back to him later and convinced him to do the picture. He played Zack, the married gay man. Harry Hamlin was one of my first choices for the man Zack falls for. I had seen him do a TV miniseries and thought that he had a raw energy and a real sexuality. And he's cute. Casting the role Kate Jackson played, Zack's wife, was no problem at all.

So we got the movie cast and went ahead and made the film. I was very involved. I was there every day. Hiller was very, very eager and determined to be as accurate as possible. Since no one on the picture other than me was openly gay, Hiller depended on me to make sure the beats were correct. I offered any advice I could in terms of the reality of what it was like to be gay and living in a gay world. In one scene, where Michael is looking for sex and drives down an alley that's a popular pickup spot, Hiller asked, as he got ready to shoot the scene, "Barry, are the guys standing the right way?"

Then there was one scene we shot in John Dukakis's apartment, and he had this poster on his wall of Bruce Lee. I didn't think it fit, so they found a different poster. John played the trick that Harry Hamlin picks up. He was an actor for awhile: real nice guy, straight, good actor. His father was governor of Massachusetts at the time. I remember talking to John at one point and saying, "Have you talked to your dad about playing the part? Does he know that you're doing this?" And he said, "Yes, he's very proud of me for doing it. He thinks it's terrific, and I have his full support." Which endeared Michael Dukakis to me for life. This was pretty gutsy for John, the son of a major political figure, to do his first movie playing this cute little trick. And then they go home and fuck, and you see them in bed saying, "Do you want to go out for a hamburger?"

Another time, I spent an afternoon graphically explaining to Arthur what we do—physically—and how far we could go in the film. He was very, very curious. Not in a prurient way, but just as a good director wanting to know all about the subject. Arthur is a real straight Jewish guy, married to the same woman for a hundred years, kids, and everything so far removed from the scene, that it was like he was doing a movie about aliens.

I took Arthur on a tour of the bars one night. We started at the Motherlode at Robertson and Santa Monica, which is a clean-cut preppy kind of bar. We progressed down Santa Monica Boulevard to the Spike, which is darker and seedier. We hit about a half-dozen bars and ended up at the One Way. The back room at the One Way had a lot of stuff going on. I took Arthur in there, and he was fascinated by that—just fascinated. Not threatened, not uncomfortable in any way, not turned on or titillated, but just fascinated from the sociological aspects, from the cultural aspects, and the physiological aspects of it. And probably by the sexual aspect, because it must have been so mind boggling to a straight man who's never seen it before.

Arthur and I also talked when he wanted to know about the courtship process, what two guys would do and how they would go about it—from talking, to making the first move, to what happens next. He wanted to get to the real primal truth of it all.

Harry Hamlin was also eager to get to the truth. Listen, any good actor is looking for the truth. So I took him to a gay bar. Harry wasn't a big star at the time—"L.A. Law" wasn't even a thought then. I walked into the bar with Harry. He was cool about it. I'm sure he was a little bit uncomfortable, but he's a good enough actor not to show it and wouldn't have revealed it to me. Guys hit on him. I can't believe he actually said, "I'm just here researching a movie." Yeah, sure. People asked about the movie. He was cool. He's a good guy.

Michael Ontkean didn't want to go to the bars. He felt his character was so uptight about the idea of walking into a bar in the first place that he wanted to use that. Michael approached acting from a different perspective. He was very concentrated and very focused and very studied and very intense. Harry was cooler, easier, more relaxed. He just got up and did it. Both of these guys were smart and eager to get it right.

WHEN WE shot the seduction scene, where Harry seduces Michael, both of the actors knew this was the day of reckoning, the moment of truth. They were real nervous about it. The shot where they kissed for the first time was scheduled for after lunch. Arthur Hiller is wonderful with actors. He's very paternal and very comforting and he knows the actor's psychology, and he saw how nervous they were. We expected it. Around eleven o'clock in the morning he said, "Let's run through it. Let's practice it." And they said, "Do we have to?"

Well, this screen kiss was going to be recorded in screen history, for posterity. The whole crew was very cool. If you've ever seen a movie crew, they're all these kind of redneck guys from the Valley. I never heard any gay put-downs. Whether they were on good behavior because they knew I was gay, I don't know.

They did the scene, and that broke the ice. The actors didn't know it, but Arthur had the cameras rolling during the rehearsal. Once he told them we had shot it, that the scene was done, they relaxed. The rest of the time was easy. There was no problem with the seduction scene, either, when they were undressing each other and rolling around in bed and all that.

We had plenty of discussions about how far that love scene would go, mostly in terms of getting the R rating. But there were commercial considerations, too. We didn't want to take it to the point where we would alienate a large part of the audience. We didn't want to cross that line. I don't think gays would have been upset if we took it further, but we were concerned that the straight audience might totally freeze up. I didn't want to lose that audience because I thought it was an important audience to get. I felt this film could be influential in making people understand that we're not a bunch of freaks and perverts or whatever.

For me, most importantly, I wanted gay people to see this film and be proud of who they were. I wanted them to see that they didn't have to live their lives in the shadows. I wanted them to be able to take their parents to see it and say, "Look at these two guys. They're smart, they're successful, they're happy, they're together, and they're gay. You can be gay, and you can be all that." I wanted my film to show that being gay didn't mean that you were the criminal or the degenerate that Hollywood had portrayed us as since the beginning of time. I really wanted to show that there were doctors and lawyers and teachers and policemen and accountants who were gay, too. I wanted to make this a breakthrough to mainstream heterosexual consciousness. I felt that by portraying these gay role models, I could do that.

THE PICTURE wrapped. We were doing postproduction on it, and the time came to publicize it. I had already done a lot of interviews about the movie while we were shooting. I did a major piece with Rex Reed for GQ [Gentleman's Quarterly] in which I was pretty open. I did a lot of stuff for the gay press. I just reached a point where I said, "Hey, if this film is going to have any credibility with gays and with the world, someone has got to step forward and say, 'It comes out of truth and it comes out of real-life experience. It comes from someone who knows the terrain.' " I just felt there was no choice.

This was when I was just starting to get political. I felt it was my opportunity to use my talent and skill and profession to make a larger point, to go for something more important than just selling a movie. I wanted to present a profile of someone who was openly gay, someone who was in a high-visibility field just talking about being gay and being very comfortable about it. In my television interviews I hoped people—gay and straight—would see someone who was a Hollywood screenwriter with a number of movie credits they were familiar with, who was not a part of the gay movement, so they could say to themselves, "Hey, if this guy isn't hiding it, maybe there's nothing to hide. Maybe it's not the grotesque thing we've been led to believe. Maybe it's not something terrible."

Twentieth Century-Fox sent me all over the country doing national and local talk shows. I also did a lot of radio call-in shows. You know, I had some anxiety about doing this, because there are a lot of crazy people out there. You never know who you're going to run up against or who's a real homophobic lunatic who might have a gun. But I never encountered it—I never had an antigay call. The one time I had any problem was in Atlanta when I did this call-in show. I was talking very openly about being gay, and someone called in and said to me, "You goddamned dirty Jews! You think you can do anything!" I was just taken aback because the question of my being Jewish had never entered my sphere of thinking.

FINALLY, THE time came for the first significant screening of the movie before a gay audience. This was before the official opening. It was in New York, a Broadway house, for about five hundred gay people. I was very nervous. These were my peers; these were gay people who were going to be the ultimate judges. It was a great experience for me. They laughed in the right places. They were spellbound in the right places. There was a gasp at the kiss and at the sex scene. And there was applause several times throughout the film. I remember one point where Michael says, "This is who I am. This is what I am, and I'm not going to change it. And you've got to accept it." And there was applause. And applause at the end.

Vito Russo, the film historian, was there. He had his tape machine on and was taking comments afterwards. I remember the feeling I had.

It was, "I think these people are shocked at what they saw. I think they can't believe that they've actually seen a film from a major Hollywood studio that says this." Whatever artistic quibbles they may have had that day were totally overwhelmed by the fact that they were seeing the first movie that told them it's OK to be who they are. There's nothing wrong with it, and you're as good as anybody else. We as gay people needed to hear that. And hearing it to the tune of a $12 million major motion picture from Twentieth Century-Fox was real important.

I was in Florida when the movie opened in February of 1982. I had been on the road doing publicity for the film and stopped in Miami where I had some family. We drove to a movie theater in Coconut Grove. I was told that there would be a lot of gay people in the audience because a lot of gay people lived in the area. There were about eight of us in the car—aunts, uncles, cousins. We pull up to this theater, and there was a huge line around the block. It was for the 7:00 P.M. movie, which was already sold out. So we bought tickets for the nine o'clock show and went for a bite to eat.

We came back for the next show, and I was going down the line and all I was seeing were straight couples. I wondered why the movie would be sold out to a 90 percent heterosexual audience. I thought, *Do they have any idea what this movie is about?*

It was a big theater. There were about eight hundred people in the audience. The lights went down. The movie was progressing, and at the point where the guys touch each other for the first time, there were titters from the audience. I thought, *This doesn't bode well.* Sure enough, when they started undressing, you would think someone yelled, "Fire!" in the audience. There was absolute pandemonium. The audience reacted with such hostility and turned so ugly toward the movie, it became unbearable, and I had to leave the theater. They became an angry mob. People were leaving; they just couldn't deal with two men showing affection toward one another. This situation played itself out all over the country.

I RECEIVED maybe five thousand letters. Fox said this was unprecedented in terms of a response to a movie, but I didn't think it was surprising. I knew this movie was going to provoke a lot of mail, primarily from gay people. It was great. They wrote, "You really changed my life." "You helped me accept who I am." "I told my parents." "I took my parents to see this movie." "I've seen it twenty times." "It's given me confidence." "You must have been in my life when you were writing it." This is the kind of response a writer

dreams of. I've gotten responses to other movies where people have
said, "I love this movie, it's great," which is always great to hear. But
when somebody writes to say that you've changed his life—every
writer lives for that.

The greatest satisfaction was the mail I got from young gay men in
the closet, who, after seeing this movie, felt more secure and were
willing to accept their homosexuality. This, to me, was the real audience this film was meant for, although I could hardly justify that to
Fox.

Along with the positive reaction from gays, there was some negative reaction from gays, too. When you make the first mainstream
Hollywood movie to deal with this subject, every gay person out there
is going to relate it to their own lives and experience. It's got to
measure up to their perception of their lives and who they are. One
movie can't do that. And obviously, the film prettified the lives of
these people. It made it look like everybody was attractive and
wealthy and smart. Most gay people don't look like Michael Ontkean
and Harry Hamlin. So people complained that it didn't reflect the real
gay world, that I was "Hollywoodizing" the story. It was a choice that
I wouldn't necessarily have made if I were directing the film, but I
wasn't. I think I would have downscaled it a bit. But no matter what
we would have done, when you're the first, you're going to find as
many detractors as supporters, which, indeed, we did.

Fox thought this film was going to go through the roof. I said, "No,
it's not, because no matter how you cut it, no matter how pretty the
actors are, and no matter how touching the ending is, it's still condon-
ing homosexuality, which is anathema in this society." I told them
that it might do well, but it was going to disturb a lot of people, repel
a lot of people, upset a lot of people, and be embraced by a lot of
people, both straight and gay. I knew that that was what we were up
against. After all was said and done, *Making Love* did OK. Not great,
but OK. It covered its costs and made some money. But I knew that
if the film didn't make a hundred million dollars, they were going to
write it off as a commercial disappointment. The fact that it did as well
as it did surprised me.

WHEN I came out very publicly after *Making Love* and went on the
"Today" show and "20/20" and spoke very forthrightly about being
gay, people said, "You're jeopardizing your career. It could hurt you
professionally." My response was, "This is what I am. This is who I
am, and I feel an obligation to acknowledge this." Looking back to the
years after the picture came out, I'm sure it did hurt me profession-

ally. I'm sure there were people who didn't want to work with me after that.

This is a very homophobic town. Forget the fact that it's liberal and forget the fact they are wildly supportive of Democratic candidates. And it's a town full of gay people, who are sometimes the most homophobic for fear of their own exposure. So it wasn't a surprise to me that after doing *Making Love*, I wasn't getting a lot of offers. But then I was never out there as a writer for hire. I like to write my own stuff; I'm a self-generator. And I don't have enormous materialistic needs. I live very comfortably, and I've had enough money to do that.

I don't regret having done this for one minute—not one minute. I'm glad I did it because it meant something. It served a purpose other than what it did for my own ego, which wasn't the motivation, anyway. If it did, indeed, hurt me, it doesn't matter.

NOT TOO long ago, about five years after *Making Love* came out, I remember reading an article on gays and something to do with AIDS in *Time* magazine. *Time* hadn't been overly kind in its initial review of the film. They weren't merciless, but they weren't kind. And in this article they were talking about the real milestone gay films in American history and listed *The Boys in the Band*, *La Cage Aux Folles*, and *Making Love*. And I remember thinking, *See, we did go down in history after all that.*

Since *Making Love*, there have been some very good positive images from smaller independent movies—*Parting Glances*, *My Beautiful Laundrette*. There are a handful of them. But from mainstream Hollywood it's tough. I had thought at the time we were doing the picture that if we progressed in a positive direction in terms of depiction of gay characters for the screen, we could reach the point some day in the not-too-distant future where they could make a movie like *Lethal Weapon*, and the Mel Gibson character would just happen to be gay and not say anything about it. You didn't have to show him having sex. Just establish the fact he's gay and then just do the picture, so subconsciously it becomes ingrained in people's awareness that being gay is not like being a leper, that we're a very important, active part of society. But it looks like it's going to be a long time before that happens, and that's too bad.

The "Sissy" from Mississippi

Greg Brock

GREG BROCK doesn't like the limelight. For most of his career as a journalist, he has been content to work in the background. But as a self-described "sissy boy" growing up in a small Mississippi town in the 1960s, blending into the background was never easy. And as Greg discovered at the Washington Post and San Francisco Examiner, simply being himself made him a very public role model and trailblazer in a profession where, even today, openly gay people are rare.

Greg's convictions and his determination to live outside the closet were tested and strengthened by two "gay-bashing" incidents he experienced in the early 1980s, while he was a reporter at the Charlotte Observer in Charlotte, North Carolina. Sitting in his modern office in downtown San Francisco, the first openly gay assistant managing editor of the San Francisco Examiner still finds it extremely difficult to recall those experiences. At five feet four inches tall, Greg Brock must have seemed like an easy target.

Greg grew up in Crystal Springs, Mississippi. He was a junior in high school when the Stonewall riot erupted in New York City.

I heard nothing about Stonewall. Crystal Springs is so isolated, they have to pipe in the sunshine. It's a town of about 4,500 people, about twenty miles south of Jackson. There was one school, grades one through twelve, all black, and one school, grades one through twelve, all white. My graduating class was about seventy kids. Normally it would have been around fifty kids, but in my senior year, 1970 to 1971, my high school was desegregated. Our county was the last one in Mississippi to be desegregated. So, my school became predominantly black. My parents pulled my little sister out of public school and sent her to a private white academy that sprang up overnight. They said, "We're going to let Greg stay. He's a senior, and all the whites are going to stay for their senior year." I thought it was great. I had a lot of black friends.

I was editor of the yearbook, and I was a reporter for the local paper covering the school. I wrote columns that got my dad's business boycotted—he had a car dealership body shop—because I wrote in a positive way about ball games and activities at the school. People in that town wanted desegregation to be divisive. They wanted fights. They wanted it to blow sky high because the "niggers" had taken over their high school and were wearing *their* school colors. Literally, there were generations in that town that had gone to that school.

We did the yearbook for both high schools that year—my high school, which was now 65 percent black, and the other high school, which was all black. The yearbook staff was all white, except for two tokens, who were added hurriedly. I made sure that there were lots and lots of campus scenes with blacks. Needless to say, I was the black sheep of my family in that town.

I was also the sissy boy in Crystal Springs. I didn't know I was gay. I mean, I knew I was gay, but I didn't know what to do about it. I was a sissy boy from the word go. In fact, on my birth certificate I was marked as a girl—still is to this day. I never had it changed because I thought it would get me out of the draft. That was always the running joke at family reunions. That's the one thing my dad always said, "Well, it took him years to figure out otherwise."

A sissy boy, for those who don't know, hangs around with girls all the time. I played with dolls. I took baton lessons. I was a mama's boy. I was effeminate. As a child I had huge blue eyes. I was very soft and very pretty—a pretty, pretty little boy. I also didn't do anything the other boys my age did. I didn't like to fish. I didn't like to hunt. This one time my dad took me to deer camp, a place that he and all of his buddies belonged to. There was this old house. About thirty men go and they have bunks. They have two black women who cook them meals. And they go out in the woods and kill deer. I may have been ten or eleven. I didn't have a gun; I wasn't going to kill a deer. It was just awful—it was disastrous.

At school, I was made fun of. The kids mimicked the way I walked, the way I talked. I was petrified. I'd go home and cry myself to sleep a lot of nights. But somehow, I managed to be a student leader. I held student body office. I got a lot of awards. I was elected to things because I was good at getting elected. Still, I was the sissy boy.

For my father, being a sissy boy meant that I wasn't normal. I wouldn't grow up to have a wife and 2.7 children and give them grandkids. I wouldn't carry on the family name. I'm the last Brock boy in our line. Thirty-four years after I was born, they finally got another boy in our line, but it's my sister's child, so he has the wrong last name. They gave him Brock as a first name.

I don't come from the happiest of families. Huge white antebellum home, columns all the way around it. In the context of that town, we were probably upper middle class. We had money, though we didn't have the old family name, which was really what counted there. Mother, father, three children. Nice car. We went to church every week. We did everything you were supposed to do. Except under that roof there was little love and no interaction. I had two sisters, younger and older. All of us are seven years apart. So that left you with no rapport with your siblings. My dad was a very masculine, very blue-collar type; he wanted me to play football and do all these things, but instead, I was the classic disappointment. We had no relationship whatsoever. I was nineteen years old the first time I ever sat down and talked to him.

So I just withdrew from the family. I turned inward. And I latched onto student activities—that's what validated me. When I finished high school, I left for the University of Mississippi in Oxford.

AFTER I graduated from college in May of 1975, I went home to visit before leaving for a newspaper job in Florida. My parents were going through a divorce. I went by my dad's body shop as I was leaving town. He got out his wallet and gave me some money. I was telling him about the job, and he asked, "Well, Son, how much are they going to be paying you?" "Well, $135 a week," I said. He said, "That's fine son, but you could stay here and work down at the plant and make more money than that." In his defense, he was all for my career choice if that's what I wanted, but he didn't understand it in the least.

So I left, first to a couple of different newspapers in Florida, then to the *Charlotte Observer* in Charlotte, North Carolina. My doctor in Charlotte, when I came out to him, asked me if I had ever discussed being gay with my family. And I said, "No." He said, "That's proba-bly appropriate." But you pay a price for that: You live a lie; you don't live a life. I was with a wonderful man for five and a half years. We had a wonderful life. But you can't share it with your family, so you end up talking about the weather a lot when you call home or they call you. They knew about Randy—he lived with me—but he was always referred to by Mother as "that boy from Charlotte." Over the years it just became easier to not deal with it, to avoid sharing that part of my life.

So I got to Charlotte and there were a lot of gay people at the newspaper. I met my lover there, who was not out at that time. Charlotte was hardly the fast lane, but we did good things. And on a personal level, my time in Charlotte was important. I came to terms with my sexuality, and I came out at the paper. I was also the victim of two gay bashings, both of which had a big impact on the way I live my life.

The first bashing was in March of 1981. By then I was out at the paper. My lover was working late that night. I got off early and went down to the corner gay bar, the Brass Rail, which was just a block and a half from the paper, to have a beer and wait for him. He ended up going straight home from work. We weren't living together at that point, so I left to go home. I got in my car, pulled out into the street, and stopped at the stoplight. This black Trans Am pulled up beside me. You can tell when someone's watching, so I kind of glanced over. There were these two little redneck types, hunky, but rednecks all the same, with their six-pack of beer. So I just kind of glanced over and looked back at the light. It changed, and I went on down the street. They got behind me, right on my bumper. So I looked up. I caught the next red light, which was right in front of the building where the *Observer* is located. They pulled up beside me again, taunting, pointing. I didn't look at them. I went on, but they got on my bumper again and then pulled up beside me.

I was annoyed at that point and also concerned. I was only blocks from my house, and I didn't want them to know where I lived. So I just kept driving out this street, which goes from being the heart of downtown Charlotte to being a warehouse district. They kept riding on my tail and kept pulling up beside me. Then I got scared. So I thought, *I'm going back to the newspaper* because you could drive right up under the building, and there were guards there. So I took the next left, and it was a dead-end street out in the warehouse district. My heart stopped. I looked up, and they were turning in behind me. I thought I was going to go around the block and head back into the city. So I started doing a three-corner turn, and they saw that I was blocked in. They sped right up, blocked my car, and got out. I had the doors locked at this point.

It could have been a water pistol, but one of them had a gun. He said, "Get out, you faggot," and all this kind of stuff. So I got out. I was in shock; I was in slow motion; I didn't know what I was doing. They were drunk. One of them, the smaller one, was calling me a faggot. "Get your ass off the streets, faggot. We saw you coming out of the queer bar." He hit me a few times, slamming me up against the car and knocking me around the face. I didn't hit back or anything. I was scared to—I thought he was going to blow my brains out.

It didn't take much to knock me to the ground. He was bigger than me and muscular, and I had never really been in a fight or anything. It's awful to get hit. He had on boots, and when I fell down he kicked me in the shoulder, and it snapped off the end of my collar bone. They just kind of laughed and kicked me once more. "You faggot! Stay off the streets!" Then they left. I sat there on the ground stunned. I got up and got in my car. I remember starting to put my car into drive and feeling excruciating pain. I had to reach through with my left hand and put it into gear. I went home; I didn't know what to do. I was in a brace for six weeks. It didn't mend, so I had to have surgery. It was awful.

My lover was just blown away, just mortified, as were the people at the paper. I went in the next day and told them. The editor had just come to Charlotte from Florida—a real family man, but a liberal, fortunately. He turned white when I told him what happened. He wrote a column about it in the Sunday newspaper that was just wonderful. He changed my name to Jeff to protect me from harassment. And he told the story blow-by-blow about this young man who sits over here in the newsroom. "This is what he does for a living and he's very good at it. . . . And I just wanted to tell you this story that happened in our fair city this last week." And he went all the way through it, never saying I'm gay, and talked about how I was pulled out of my car and beaten. And then he said, "But there's one other fact to this story, Jeff is gay." He went on and talked about that and just ended by saying that Charlotte, North Carolina, deserves better and can do better. We got a lot of reaction from that column, a lot of good letters. Plus some Baptist preachers wrote in and said that I got what I deserved.

Well, you would think I would be careful after that. But when people hear this other story, they think I had lost my mind. This was a year or so later. I lived in a restored house right off the downtown in a little turn-of-the-century neighborhood. Our house was set right up on the sidewalk with a picket fence. People came strolling through there on Sunday afternoons and evenings looking at homes.

I was sitting out on my porch in my rocking chair, and these two young men walked up—not unusual, just walking by. "Hi, how are you tonight?" You spoke to everybody there. It was early Friday evening. And they said, "Sir, I wonder if you could help us." They said they had come into the neighborhood, and their car had broken down. They were from some little town in North Carolina, and one of them needed to call his dad. They were very nicely dressed. I said, "Sure, I don't mind helping you out. Come in, there's a phone in the hallway." So I sat down and talked to one of them. The other went to make the call. He came back in. He said that the phone was busy. They started chatting, just talking, asking about the neighborhood. He said, "Do you mind if I use the phone again?" This went on for fifteen or twenty minutes, and the line was always busy.

Finally, they were kind of apologetic. He said, "I'm really sorry. I don't know what he's doing on the phone, but I really need to talk to him." And I told him he was welcome to try again, but I said, "I need to do some errands. I'm glad to help you out, but I don't have a lot more time." When I said that, the bigger one, probably the older one, just grabbed me and slammed me up against the wall in my dining room. He said something like, "You little faggot, we'll make as many phone calls as we want to!" I was just stunned. I couldn't believe it.

So this was all planned. They weren't looking for a specific person, I guess—they just happened to stumble upon me, and I seemed like the right one. They wanted money. They were wanting to rob somebody, and this was the perfect neighborhood to do it in. But then after they got in and realized I was a fag, that made it that much better.

You think that out in your car is bad enough, but in my own home, that's a real violation. So one of the guys, the bigger of the two, kind of knocked me around a little bit. I said, "Man, what do you want? What's up here?" He needed a little bail money. I had seven dollars in my wallet. And he said, "Well you better be figuring out where to get more money real fast, you little faggot, or you're gonna get it!" Having gone through the other incident, I knew that all I wanted was out, away from them. I would have given them whatever money they wanted. I said, "My bank is right around the corner. I can go get you some cash there." I was hoping I would see somebody, a policeman, or something.

He drove over to the bank in my car. I was thinking I was going to go to the teller machine and shag ass. They could have my car; I didn't care. But he went with me, of course. A policeman started coming down the street, and the guy said, "I wouldn't advise you to say or do anything right now." I was so petrified at this point that I didn't say anything. I just got the money, $150, and gave it to him. I said, "Okay, there you go." And he said, "Come back over here to the car." He told me to get in the car and then got in the driver's seat. I said, "Look, I gave you the money and I've helped you out, and that's all I can do." And he said, "Why don't we take a little ride, you faggot?" So they drove me through the backwoods of North Carolina until about four-thirty the next morning. I really thought that was it. He said he was going to kill me.

When they got back to the area of the state or the town where they knew people, they stopped at some houses. The young one would stay in the car with me. He was really nice. He kept telling the other guy, "Man, this has gotten out of hand. Let's just get out of here!" I kept begging him, "Please let me out of here, please let me out of here." He said, "I can't now." This other guy went in and got a bottle of whisky from some house and started getting really drunk. He drove down these roads at one hundred miles an hour in my car. Periodically he slapped me. He had me sitting between them. We stopped by another house and he said, "Hey, man, I want you to meet somebody who really likes faggots." So he went in and brought out this guy, a Hell's Angel, who got in the back seat of my car. It was a two-door car. They were joyriding, raising hell, talking about their faggot. The young guy got really quiet. They were just cutting up, passing the whisky bottle around. I was sitting in the middle hanging on for dear life. So finally we got to this place where there were some trailers. The driver went in and left the car door open. So I said to this young kid, "I really have got to piss like crazy. Do you mind if I stand by the door and take a leak?" He said, "Okay, but stand right there."

I knew if I ever got out of that car, they could have it. They could have anything. So I stepped out very slowly and even went to the point of pulling my zipper down and spreading my legs. I was too scared to piss. I turned and just shagged ass. Twenty-five yards away I fell down, and one of them was screaming—I think it was the Hell's Angel—"Hey, come back here! Come back here!" I got up and kept running, went down this embankment, and fell into this creek. I came back up and there were these railroad tracks. I didn't know where I was. I saw houses out in the distance and fields. I started running toward a house that had a light on in it. I finally got there, but the guy wouldn't let me in. He was an older man; I woke him up. But he called the police and they came and got me. I called the editors of the paper, who drove up to wherever the fuck I was and took me home. Now I'm just totally petrified. I wouldn't let my own mother in my house to use my telephone.

I don't talk about this incident a lot. I'm not as emotional about it as I used to be, and I don't dwell on it. I try not to think about it. But, clearly, the fact that I'm open, that I live my life out of the closet, that I live my life, period, has to stem from these experiences. Because you get very angry. And then you turn anger into courage. It would be easy enough to go into seclusion, to try to blend into the background so that nobody would ever notice you again. But they do notice. There are people out there looking for us. I'm convinced. They don't have anything else to do with their lives. And the fact is, I'm not going to blend into the walls. You just get tired and say, "I'm not going to take this anymore." But I'm also more careful now.

FROM THE *Charlotte Observer*, I went to work for the *Washington Post*. I made up my mind that I wasn't going to go in the closet and pretend. Professionally, I'm dubious about being an activist or being out. So I look at this as a personal statement, not so much professional. I'm

a journalist. That means I don't march in parades. I don't donate to
political causes, either straight or gay. But I guess when you do what
I've done, when you've been openly gay at the newspapers where I've
worked, that's a political statement whether or not you want it to be.

Later, when I was offered a job at the *San Francisco Examiner*, my
boss at the *Washington Post*, Milton Coleman, who is black, tried to
get me to stay. He's the assistant managing editor for the "Metro"
section. He said, "Greg, are you prepared to go out there and be *the*
Gay Editor in a gay city?" He had carried the burden of being *the*
Black Editor in a black city. It can be a lose-lose situation because you
can't please people.

Coming to San Francisco, I didn't think it would make much
difference that there was someone who was openly gay working at the
San Francisco Examiner. There are lots of gay people here. But ironically, a lot of them are not out of the closet. I just never hid it, so my
being here became a big deal to the gay community, particularly when
I got promoted to assistant managing editor. As assistant managing
editor, I'm number three here in the newsroom. I have a lot of
influence. I'm in charge of page one.

JUST AFTER I was promoted to assistant managing editor, I was on
"The Oprah Winfrey Show" for the first Coming Out Day, which
was October 11, 1988. That's when I discovered that as open as I was
professionally, I still had a long way to go personally. What happened
was, Jean O'Leary from the National Gay Rights Advocates [NGRA],
the group that was planning Coming Out Day, called me. They were
looking for names of people to give to the producers at "Oprah."
They had seen an article about my promotion in the *San Francisco
Sentinel*, one of the city's gay papers. I was probably one of the few
openly gay managers of a metropolitan newspaper in the country.

When the "Oprah" producer called, I said, "My God, I've been
out for years! I came out in 1978–79 at the *Charlotte Observer*. Everybody in the world knows I'm gay if they want to know it." Then the
producer asked, "What about your family?" And I said, "Gulp!" I
had never told my family because when you're gay and grow up in
Crystal Springs, you just simply leave and you don't have to deal with
it. I said, "Let me call you back."

It didn't take me long—about a day—to call back. I said to the
person at NGRA, "Give them my name." All NGRA was doing was
submitting my name. But I knew I was going to make it on the show
because my dad and Oprah are both from Kosciusko, Mississippi.

On the day before the Coming Out Day show, I got a call from the

"Oprah" producer. "Well, we'd like you to fly up tonight and do the show in the morning. But the deal is, you call your parents and tell them before you come on the show. And would you ask them if they would consent to a telephone hookup?"

I'd never felt so alone. I was in Washington, D.C., staying at the apartment of some friends who were out of town. When I hung up and realized what I was about to do—there's just no way to describe it. I was thirty-five years old, but I was scared. My knees were shaking. I was a grown man. I was about to call my dad, and I started thinking about what he was doing. It was a Monday afternoon. He's semiretired and he has his business kind of next to his house now. He gardens a lot. I had this mental image of his little house out in the country. In Mississippi, some things don't change. You go out and check the mailbox every day. When you get a letter from far away or a long-distance phone call, it's really a big deal. What was rushing through my mind was not so much what he was going to say or how he was going to take it, but just what I was about to do to his little world out there. I've lived there; I know what it's like when you get the phone call that someone's died. That's what I was about to do to him. I was about to, on a Monday afternoon in October 1988, shatter his life.

At some point, though, you begin to take up for yourself. While on some level I was about to destroy my dad's life, I myself had not had a life in thirty-five years. So I called. My stepmother picked up the phone. I asked to speak to Daddy, and she said, "Well, we're out in the garden. Let me get him." Then I said, "You stay on the phone, too." Dad got on the phone, and I said, "There's something I wanted to tell y'all, and I had been wanting to do this for a long time, and it's just never been appropriate." My voice started breaking, and my stepmother said, "Well, honey, that's all right, what is it?" I said, "I guess the best way to say it is the good news is, I'm going to be on 'The Oprah Winfrey Show' tomorrow." And she said, "Oh, that's wonderful, that's wonderful! I'll have to watch it." And I said, "Well, the bad news is, I'm not sure you're going to want to invite the neighbors over." They laughed, and that kind of broke the ice a little, and I got my voice back.

"The reason I'm going to be on 'The Oprah Winfrey Show' is the type of show she's doing. Since I've been out in San Francisco, I've moved into the public eye a little bit. More than I would like to be. There's been a feature story written about me. A lot of people know me there now. There's a reason for that. But I can't mail you these articles, even though I'd like to. I'd like to share them with you. I would like to think that this would be in the same vein as when I was at Ole Miss and I got awards, and you always got the newspaper clippings and you put them in the scrapbook. But my fear is that you wouldn't put these clippings in your scrapbook. And the reason is because for years now, at the newspapers where I've worked, I am gay and I am very open about it, but I've never told y'all."

I can't remember their precise reactions, but I remember my dad saying that he had prayed a lot that his suspicions were wrong. And then we went on to talk, and it was kind of teary. But he really opened up and he talked a great deal. I was stunned, because my dad is a man of few words. And I told him, "I've just lived a lie for so long. One thing I've been thinking here before I picked up the phone, I was trying to think what lie I told you when I was the victim of a gay bashing in Charlotte and my collarbone was broken. I had to go have surgery and all this kind of stuff." I wouldn't let them come up to see about me or anything like that. They were very concerned. I missed my tenth high school reunion because of the surgery, and I didn't want to have to explain it. I told him I was robbed or something. And he even said that if the "Oprah" people called him, he would talk to them on the telephone, which stunned me. The "Oprah" people didn't call because they ended up choosing my mother.

I had expected my father to hang up on me, to tell me not to come home again. But they said that they loved me and that they wanted me to come home to visit. That made it easier calling my mother, but I couldn't reach her. I was already in Chicago at the hotel before I finally got a hold of her. Her reaction was just the opposite of what I expected. When I told her, I thought she would start crying and fall on the floor. She was pretty low key about it and went into the typical Mississippi thing, just like people say about blacks, "Well, you know, I've got black friends, too." In this case, she said, "Well, Son, there are these two lesbians who come into the store all the time, and they're just as nice as they can be." And, of course, she said that this was my choice. And I said, "Well, it's not exactly a choice, but let's save that part of the conversation for later." She also said she'd talk to the "Oprah" people.

So the next morning they picked me up at the hotel in the little limousine. I was totally out of it by then. I was tired and starving to death. It was a friendly, mostly gay audience, hand picked by gay rights people. Oprah started by saying, "It's National Coming Out Day. People's lives today will be changed. They're about to tell people. . . ." So people in the audience started popping up at microphones and said, "Hi, Mom. Hi, Dad. There's something I've been wanting to tell you. I'm gay." "Hi, Cousin Sid. You've made me really uncomfortable at these family reunions, and I just wanted you to know I'm gay." It was great.

After the commercial Oprah came back for the second segment and introduced the panel. She took us one by one, and we did our individual stories. When she started talking to me, she really got into the southern routine, which made me more comfortable. Then she said, "We have Greg's mother, Mrs. Sharpe, on the phone." My mother's very southern, very country. Oprah said, "Mrs. Sharpe, are you there?" And she said, "Yes, I am."

I should have thought about what they were going to do with the cameras during this part of the interview. I should have guessed that they would be on me or Oprah because my mother was on the telephone being piped into the studio. But I didn't know where the cameras were. Oprah said, "Well, Mrs. Sharpe, what have you been thinking since Greg called you last night?" "Well," she said, "I haven't gotten a wink o' sleep all night." And I thought, *Oh my God! What have I gotten myself into?* I could hear how distraught she was. She had sounded pretty cool about it the night before, but she had obviously been in shock. She had called my little sister and my plumber brother-in-law, and I was sure they had been up all night just in a tizzy. They live for these things in the South. Crisis is what gets a southern family from one day to the next.

Sure enough, she was wound up. So I made this face—not knowing the camera was on me—that said *Oh, my God!* Oprah went on to ask her, "What did Greg say when he called you? Did he ask you about your gardening or how the weather was, or did he just lay it on you that he was gay?" And she said, "Well, he just laid it on me." They talked back and forth for awhile. My mother told Oprah that she never suspected. I made this horrendous face. It made my dad really mad that she said that. Hell, she had gotten me to take baton lessons at age five! Then she talked about her dad and how he had married late in life and she thought with my career that I would eventually get around to finding the right person and settling down. And Oprah said, "You mean, the right *woman.*" She said, "Yes, the right woman." She ended by saying, "But the bottom line is that he's my flesh and blood and my only son, and I love him." And the audience just burst out into applause.

So I came back to San Francisco, and on Thursday my mother called me. She said, "Well, your sister said you were going to call me this weekend, but I wanted to call and tell you that it's been a rough week, Son, and I haven't been anywhere in a long time, so John is going to take me down to New Orleans just to get away." John is my stepfather. I said, "Well that's good, y'all should go. Enjoy yourselves. Get some rest. I'll talk to you when you get back."

Saturday morning my answering machine had a hysterical message on it from my little sister that my stepfather had dropped dead of a heart attack in New Orleans. I immediately picked up the phone and called my ex-lover, who I still talk to every day. I said, "My stepfather just dropped dead with a heart attack, and I know it's going to be my fault." Sure enough, there was that discussion in the family. "Well, Greg just broke his mama's heart. Watching Greg's mama with a broken heart, John just couldn't stand the strain. He just keeled over with a heart attack." No matter that my stepfather had one lung, one kidney, and had already had four heart attacks.

By the time they got my stepfather's body back to Mississippi, his mother had died. So they had a double funeral. In the South, the only thing better than a double wedding is a double funeral. They love those things. They had matching caskets, and you viewed them side by side. I have a great book in me when they all die.

I didn't go back for that. No way! I decided that my absence would be best. I had caused enough stir that week. Although, I would have loved to have known what that little town was saying. They were in quite a stir. All the old ladies were calling each other. "Well, I always knew it," they said. "I just always knew he was queer."

THE "OPRAH" show didn't just change my life, it *started* my life on a lot of levels. I'd been living a lie, not being myself, not being open, carrying this tremendous burden around: It was a burden lifted, and now it was theirs. I sent my parents the book *Now That You Know.* My feeling was, "Let them deal with it." The psychologist on the show made a really good point that the parents who were hearing that day for the first time would also go through the same process that we had gone through years ago in coming to grips with our own selves. I remember how tortured I was in Charlotte. I didn't want to acknowledge it. I didn't even want to deal with it.

I think part of why I went on "Oprah" was revenge—not so much at my parents, but at that town. For picking on me, for making fun of me, for making my life miserable. For teaching me that gay was wrong, that I couldn't live my life. I bought into it for years and years and years. I shut down my life. I didn't live my life or share it. But I sure showed them.

I DIDN'T think the show would have any kind of impact, although the point was to make some sort of statement. But I didn't think there would be anything beyond the show itself. I never thought I would get home from Chicago and find messages from around the country on my answering machine. "Hello, this is Boston calling. We saw you on 'The Oprah Winfrey Show.' Thank you for doing that." "This is Atlanta calling." No names. Just cities.

That first week home in San Francisco, a friend called and said, "Come to the Midnight Sun for my thirtieth birthday." I said, "Fine, where is it?" I had heard of it—it's a gay bar—but I had never been. So I went in and I was talking to all these friends, and this cute young blond boy kept walking by and looking at me. It became distracting after a while. Finally, the boy walked up to me—he was very young and shy—and said, "May I ask you a question?" And then it hit me. I said, "Yes, you certainly may, but I think I know what the question is." And he said, "Were you on 'The Oprah Winfrey Show' on Tuesday?" And I said, "Yes, I was." And he turned around to his friend who was with him and he said, "It's him! It's him!" So they both came over.

The kid had been sick the day of the show and was at home watching television. He watched "Oprah" and taped it. I think he told me he was eighteen or nineteen. He had moved to San Francisco three weeks before from a little town in Iowa. He said he had watched the tape three times and that nothing had ever made such an impression on him. He told me that one reason he moved out here to San Francisco was to get away from his family. But watching me and listening to my mother, he decided that he was going to come out to his family. Even if they disowned him or he never heard from them, because he didn't want to spend as many years as I had shutting down his life and living a lie. And you just won't ever know what that did to me. It was wonderful. I never expected that—I knew it was all worth it then.

One of the things that being on "Oprah" helped convince me of was that coming out is key to the movement and to our lives. I don't think it will solve all of our problems or answer all the questions, but I just think it's a major part of the solution.

At the time I was on "Oprah," we were already working on a project at the *Examiner*, a sixteen-part series called "Gay in America." It was very special, unlike anything I'll ever have the opportunity to work on during the rest of my career.

I had lunch one day with a consultant from outside the paper, and we got to talking. He said, "What are you going to do on Stonewall?" This was fourteen or fifteen months before the twentieth anniversary of the riot. I said, "It hasn't been discussed, but I'm sure we'll do something. We should." He said, "I have an idea. I'd like to see a TV station, a newspaper, or maybe a book and pool the resources and really do a look at gay America." That was a great idea. So I brought it back; wrote a memo; and talked to Larry Kramer, the executive editor, and Frank McCulloch, the managing editor. We decided we didn't want to get involved with the other media, but that we would do it ourselves, that if any newspaper in America was going to do it, we would. The *Chronicle** wasn't going to do it. So we started to work, and I guess I guided it in a management sort of way. It had its own editor, Carol Ness, who brought it to life. She shaped the stories and the assignments. I did some editing on the series, but mostly I got the paper to commit to it and somehow got us to stick to that commitment when the going got rough. And it got very rough.

After we got the series launched, Frank McCulloch said he wanted me to be the senior management type on it. I said that I wasn't sure I should do that, or that I wanted to do that. But despite my misgivings, we decided that I had to do it. So I was made senior editor for the project. This could have been a series about Asians, and I would have played the same role in it, but because it was gay and because I'm gay, it became known in-house as Brock's pet project, the gay history project. Because people thought that way, the series was really poohpoohed. People fought it tooth and nail, both at some reporting levels and at the senior management level.

The issue of me being gay at the *Examiner* and its impact on my work had come up long before this series. I just became known as the gay editor. It was said out in the newsroom that if you wanted your story on page one, "Write something about gays, and Brock will take it and put it on page one." The managing editor and I run page one very closely on an edition-to-edition basis. He has a gay son. So we came under tremendous criticism, behind our backs for the most part. Unfortunately, no one has ever come in to talk to me directly about it.

So you've got that issue, the homophobia. Plus there was just some good old office politics. And then they also just didn't understand what we were trying to do. They kept calling it the gay history project. We weren't trying to write a history piece or an anniversary piece. It also wasn't the standard newspaper series. I explained, "If you're going to do a series right, take it to a higher level of reporting, of writing, of everything. For instance, if we write about coming out, let's don't go out and interview fifteen more people about what it's

*San Francisco's other daily newspaper.

like to come out in 1989 and write a fifty-five-inch story and put it in the paper. That's what we do every Sunday. That's good daily journalism. But that's not what we're after. If we write something about coming out, find a young man or a young woman and spend the next nine months with them and track them and live with them and see what it's like. Tell that story." They actually did that specific story. That was the "Bobby" story, which was always near and dear to my heart.

I didn't let the criticism stop the project. I just moved ahead and said, "Fuck the criticism!" I played my asshole role and caused some heartache. I stepped on a lot of toes, and maybe I shouldn't have. For example, early on, we told an in-house team to come up with a story plan. They proposed probably thirty story ideas, and twenty-seven of them had AIDS in them. I had to say, "This isn't it; this isn't what we're looking for." So we killed that and started over.

I didn't know until the end, almost right up to publication, how remarkable this project was. I knew the stories were good; I knew the scope of it. But it wasn't until about ten days before the series was starting, when Carol Ness and I walked over to the paper's photo studio to watch them do the series cover photo, that I realized it. Carol and I were so swamped and tired by that point—I had worked for forty-eight consecutive days or something like that—that we weren't even going to walk over there. But she said, "Let's just go see what the crowd is like." The crowd at the studio was mostly people in the stories and friends they brought. They had come to the studio to sit for photos for the cover sheet for the series. When we walked in and I saw all those people, the whole series came to life, and I just got chill-bumps. All of us in that studio knew it was going to work. I always believed in the series, but I wasn't sure I believed that we could pull it off as well as we did.

This June [1989] I started my fifteenth year in daily newspapers. If I stay in this racket—I guess I've got thirty more years to go—I won't ever work on anything like the "Gay in America" series again. Which is sad in some ways. But then you have to remember that some journalists don't ever get the chance to do the "one." There will be better things. I'm going back to the *Washington Post*. I'm taking several steps down to go there, but I'm going back to settle down and get in line. I'm sure there will be Pulitzer Prize stories there that I'll get to read or work on or be associated with. Maybe they'll bring down another president in the next thirty years. But there was something about this one, just the fact that nobody else would do it, that it was so controversial inside the paper, that it was my life. And that I did it professionally without being biased. Ethically, it was a major challenge. It's the best thing I've ever worked on in newspapers.

WE GOT lots of calls from various people, asking, "Now why did you do this?" "What was the motive behind this?" "What was in this for y'all?" Frank McCulloch summed it up. He said, "Well, it's simply good journalism." And it was true. I think even the doubters at the *Examiner* came one by one to my office or to Frank's and said, "You know, I really didn't think we should do this. I thought we had written everything in the world we could write about gays in this city. I didn't think you could sustain it for that long." Coming from cynical journalists, that was high praise.

We were really shocked by the response. I took probably three hundred phone calls over the course of four weeks, overwhelmingly positive. Of course, I took some real crazies, too.

The letters ran not quite three-to-one positive. We probably had 225 of them. And that's stunning because people who like something they read in the newspaper don't sit down and tell you that in writing. They'll call sometimes, but usually they don't even do that. So almost all the feedback we get here is negative. And you should have seen the negative letters. Some of those people writing in, my God, there's a long way to go!

I've saved two letters from all that were sent. One is from a seventeen-year-old girl from Oakland, California. She wrote:

> I was dismayed and saddened upon seeing that most of the readers who responded positively to your "Gay in America" series were gay themselves. I am amazed daily at "straight" people's ignorance about gays and gay issues. I used to watch such late night shows as the "Arsenio Hall Show," etc., but was turned off when I saw Arsenio's comical portrayal of an effeminate gay man, thus exemplifying the recent gay rights parade in Los Angeles. Gays are not silly people who are here to be made fun of. They are normal people like you and me who deserve the respect of society, not its ignorant hatred. I am a 17-year-old girl and I am not gay. I look forward to the day when everybody, not just straights, will be able to live in peace. It is a sad commentary on society that we cannot do so already.

That was worth the forty-eight-days' work and the heartache, the in-house turmoil over taking up so much space in the newspaper, the office politics, and the struggles with the business types who wanted to quantify this, wanted us to justify the cost of newsprint. They wanted to know, "What are we going to get out of this?" They didn't understand.

THE BEST thing I can say about my having been here at the *Examiner* is that for the next openly gay person who comes here, it doesn't have to be a big issue. And the path may be a little bit easier or smoother for gay people who work here who want to come out.

My being open in this newsroom has forced people to meet it head on and deal with it. When that *Sentinel* article was published about me, some people cut it out and posted it on the bulletin boards around here. There were people standing around making homophobic remarks, little fag jokes. It got back to me. But I don't think that's going to happen here much anymore. Oh, they can say it as much as they want to, but it's not considered particularly cool here to do that anymore.

Our survey in the "Gay in America" series showed that the more people get to know gays, the less problem they have with it. And I think that's probably the case here at the *Examiner*. Some people here were just ill informed, misinformed, not experienced. They now see me as a human being. That doesn't mean that some people aren't homophobic. I think there are people in the newsroom who hate me personally and professionally because I'm gay even more now than when I first got here. But at least now they know a gay person real well.

PART FIVE
1 9 8 1 – 1 9 9 0

AIDS and Beyond

THE EMERGENCE *of a perplexing disease afflicting gay men in Los Angeles, New York, and San Francisco first hit the pages of the mainstream press in 1981. As word spread, it was greeted with denial and disbelief by organized gay and lesbian communities in these cities. Some viewed the story as a setup, an organized campaign supported and promoted by the media to defame gay people and strip them of their hard-won rights. They feared that publicity about AIDS would stop gay rights efforts cold. Others argued that lobbying for gay rights legislation didn't matter if everyone was dead.*

AIDS was not a media fabrication. On the contrary, the media were, with tragically few exceptions, grossly irresponsible in their failure to warn the public adequately of a growing health disaster that, by the end of 1990, had taken the lives of more than one hundred thousand people in the United States, the majority of them gay men.

As the number of deaths soared, gay and lesbian rights organizations redirected their energies. New organizations joined existing ones to provide care for the sick and dying, conduct AIDS-education programs, lobby local and federal governments for increased funding for AIDS research, pressure medical researchers and drug companies to become more aggressive in their search for treatments and a cure, and fight discrimination against people with AIDS and those infected with HIV. Many thousands of gay people who had never participated in gay rights efforts were motivated to join the fight against AIDS.

AIDS threw many longstanding issues of discrimination against gay and lesbian people into sharp focus as those afflicted with AIDS were fired from jobs, evicted from their homes, and denied health insurance. There was no shortage of horror stories regarding lovers denied access to hospital emergency rooms, families challenging wills, and surviving partners losing custody of their deceased lovers' children.

AIDS *put gay people in the news almost daily, whether through prece-dent-setting discrimination cases or the revelation that a celebrity had died from the disease. Rumors that had circulated for years about such famous people as actor Rock Hudson, attorney Roy Cohn, and entertainer Liberace were confirmed as one after another died from AIDS. Willing or unwilling, AIDS forced celebrities and tens of thousands of other gay men out of the closet and into the public eye.*

While AIDS dominated the gay agenda for much of the decade, the struggle for gay and lesbian equal rights continued to yield gains—despite the Supreme Court's failure to rule against state sodomy laws in the cele-brated 1986 Hardwick case. More than fifty openly gay and lesbian people were elected and reelected to public office, including two Massachusetts congressmen. The first openly gay and lesbian judges were appointed to the bench. Almost every religious denomination in the country addressed the explosive issue of sexuality—several ordained openly lesbian and gay clergy—and an increasing number of religious leaders expressed support for the blessing of same-sex relationships. By the end of 1990, more than one hundred cities and counties and four states had passed laws protecting the rights of gay people, and several municipalities passed domestic-partnership laws that extended limited, but symbolically important, rights to same-sex couples. During this time, several gay and lesbian organizations trans-formed themselves into sophisticated lobbying and service organizations with thousands of members, paid staff, and seven-figure budgets. And in all walks of life, more and more gay men and women courageously stepped out from behind the closet door.

By the late 1980s, as the fight against AIDS became institutionalized, new and existing groups returned to classic issues, including same-sex mar-riage or its legal equivalent, antigay violence, and the status of gay men and women in the military. Many young people who had been at the forefront of AIDS advocacy reinvigorated the gay rights movement with confronta-tional—and controversial—tactics. Joining gay rights groups with names like Queer Nation and Queer Action, they shouted their demands in the streets, churches, city halls, and suburban shopping malls.

To veteran gay and lesbian activists, this latest generation was often reminiscent of the youthful and militant gay liberationists of the late 1960s and early 1970s. (Indeed, many veteran activists had been gay liberationists.) Like their counterparts of a generation ago, the Queer Nationalists are hell-bent on eliminating discrimination and forcing American society to accept gay and lesbian people as full and equal citizens. Whether American society—or the gay rights movement—is ready for them, Queer Nationalists have announced loud and clear: "We're Here! We're Queer! Get Used to It."

The Film Historian

Vito Russo

FROM THE time he was a teenager, Vito Russo loved the movies, and whenever he could, escaped to the world of the silver screen. He loved movies so much that in the early 1970s he studied film history and made it his career.

Vito came to believe that the overwhelmingly negative portrayal of gay men and women in film had a tremendous impact in shaping the public's antigay attitudes. By shining a light on Hollywood's long antigay history with his highly acclaimed 1981 book, The Celluloid Closet, Vito hoped to provoke discussion and encourage change.

Born in 1946, and raised in New York's East Harlem, Vito Russo is the classic New Yorker, from his broad accent and animated gestures to his fighting spirit. His passionate involvement in gay rights activism has spanned nearly two decades, from the early days of gay liberation to the fight against AIDS.

The first time I saw a movie with a gay theme was in 1962 at the Capitol Theater in Passaic, New Jersey. It was Advise and Consent, directed by Otto Preminger. At the end of the movie, Don Murray slit his own throat with a straight razor. I was horrified. He committed suicide only because he was accused of being gay! He had had one homosexual experience in the army in Honolulu and was being blackmailed. That movie impressed upon me that homosexuality was something so terrible that you committed suicide. I came home on the bus after seeing it, in shock. I had seen a character whom I identified with—I knew what I was—and this is what happened to him.

A few months later I saw a film called Victim at the Paris theater in New York. The Paris was an art house. It was the only theater showing Victim because it was the first film in the history of the movies to use the word homosexual on a soundtrack. The Motion Picture Production Code would not allow it to be released in mainstream theaters unless the word was cut. The producers refused to cut the word, so they opened it at the Paris.

I got exactly the opposite impression from Victim as I got from

Advise and Consent. Victim was a film about a homosexual hero. Here was the same story, a man being blackmailed for being homosexual, where the guy didn't slit his throat. Instead, he tracked down the blackmailers and cooperated with the police and put them in jail, all to challenge the existing laws against homosexual behavior. That was considered very shocking and very daring and very avant-garde. It was the first time I had heard anybody on the screen say that maybe it was okay to be gay.

By the time I saw these two movies, I already knew I was gay. See, I grew up in Manhattan at 120th Street between First and Second avenues. Growing up in a city like New York, I was sophisticated about the fact that there were other gay people. I never thought I was the only homosexual in the world because you had to be blind not to see that there were other gay people in New York. From the time I was eleven or twelve, I would get on the subway and go to the Museum of Natural History, the Bronx Zoo, or anywhere. I saw gay people all the time.

There were also gay people in my neighborhood. Nobody talked about it, but you could tell they were queer. I knew that that was what I had in common with them. And it wasn't like I didn't know any gay kids in high school. We knew that we shared this, and we talked about it.

When I was a sophomore in high school, my family moved to New Jersey. There were drag queens in town who used to have parties, and my friends and I would sneak off and go to them. I met a whole group of loud, very out-front queens, who ran around in towns like Paterson, Lodi, Hasbrouck Heights, and Hackensack. I remember once when they picked me up one night to go to the beach. I thought we were going to go to Seaside Heights and stay over. By then I must have been a junior or senior in high school. We got on the Long Island Expressway, and I said, "We're not going to Jersey?" And one of the guys said, "No, Mary, we're going to Fire Island!" I had never heard of Fire Island.

We arrived on Fire Island with no place to stay. We met some guy who was staying in the hotel in Cherry Grove who let us use his room. It was a total revelation to me that there was this gay community out there.

Even with all my Catholic religious education—I went to Catholic grammar school and high school—and with all the stuff in the movies telling me that homosexuality was wrong, for some reason I instinctively knew they were full of shit. I knew that if something could be so natural to who I was, then it had to be okay. I also knew that my only real choice was whether to express it openly. But I kept my mouth shut, otherwise the kids at high school would have beaten me up for it.

BY THE mid-1960s, I was already aware that there were gay people active in organizations who maintained the position that homosexuality was not wrong. I picked up magazines like ONE and I got the sense that there were people out there in places like Chicago who were making a case for gay people, saying that they shouldn't be persecuted. I always thought it was sort of odd and fanciful, but I never really related it to my life or my needs, probably because I was too scared and young to be militant in any way.

When I was in college at Fairleigh Dickinson University in Rutherford, New Jersey, I was on the student lecture committee. I invited Dick Leitsch of the Mattachine Society in New York to come and speak. That must have been 1967 or 1968. A professor of mine who knew I was gay said to me, "I'm warning you, if you push this thing, some day they'll shoot you in the streets. You're making a mistake." I invited Dick anyway, but that was the extent of my political involvement until after Stonewall.

I REMEMBER the night of the Stonewall riot very clearly because earlier in the day I had been to Judy Garland's funeral. Judy Garland was laid out at Frank Campbell's Funeral Home on Madison Avenue. The day before the funeral thousands of people had waited in the street to view the body. They were lined up all the way down Eighty-First Street and on Fifth Avenue by Central Park. They kept the funeral home open around the clock, and more than twenty thousand people filed through. It was a spectacle to behold.

I was in a foul mood that night because of the funeral. On my way home from work, I was walking west on Christopher Street toward Seventh Avenue, and there was this huge thing going on outside the Stonewall. I knew it was a raid the minute I saw it. I'd been in raids before, in Jersey and here. The police raided the bars all the time. I didn't see a lot of the hysteria that's been described in the press because I got there too late. But people were still out on the sidewalks yelling at the police.

I went to the little triangular park across the street and sat in a tree on a branch. I watched what was going on, but I didn't want to get involved. People were still throwing things, whatever they could find, mostly garbage. Then somebody came along and spray painted a message to the community on the front of Stonewall that this was our neighborhood, and we weren't going to let them take it away from us, that everybody should calm down and go home. But that's not the way it worked out because there were constant confrontations for the next two nights. The police made arrests and beat people. There was a lot of violence.

I was completely unaware that the riots had started an activist movement. I didn't come to realize this until nearly a year later, after the raid of another bar, the Snake Pit, which was a hideous, dark little hole in the basement of a five-story tenement building. It was an illegal after-hours bar where bartenders and waiters went after work. You had to knock on the door to get in. It was packed all the time.

The night of the Snake Pit raid, the police arrested more than 160 customers, which was pretty unusual, because by this time the police didn't usually arrest customers. Among those arrested was a twenty-three-year-old Argentinean national named Diego Vinales who was here on a visa. He was afraid that if it came out that he was gay he would be deported. So he jumped from a second-floor window of the police station to try to escape and landed on a spiked fence. They had to bring in acetylene torches to cut the fence around him, and he was brought to St. Vincent's Hospital—with the fence still in him—in critical condition. He was at the edge of death for days.

This is when I started hearing about organized activism. You see, one night when I was walking up Seventh Avenue, there was a candle-light vigil for Diego in front of St. Vincent's Hospital. It had been organized by the Gay Liberation Front and the Gay Activists Alliance. GLF was a radical activist organization, and GAA was a newly emerging group that was militant but nonviolent and more mainstream than GLF. As I walked by, I was handed a leaflet, which said, "No matter how you look at it Diego Vinales was pushed." That's when I put two and two together. I realized that, in fact, he was pushed from that window: He was pushed by society. I realized that if he didn't have to be so scared of being deported, he wouldn't have jumped. So for the first time, the organized response reached me on a gut level.

It was the following Thursday when I went to my first Gay Activists Alliance meeting. I felt like I should do something, or at least find out what they were talking about. I quickly got heavily involved in GAA. Because I was in graduate school at New York University getting a master's degree in film, I got involved in running the movie night at the Firehouse, which was the GAA community center. Every Thursday or Friday night, we did a film series. People came and watched movies, but we didn't let it go at that. We had filmmakers come in to participate in discussions. We also instituted a videotape committee at GAA, which videotaped all our demonstrations and our zaps.

At the same time I was doing all this, I was working at the film department at the Museum of Modern Art. The museum was a great place to work because for the first time I met interesting, intelligent, dynamic people who loved movies and didn't care if you were gay. Being gay was just perfectly OK. One day, the head of the film department at the museum said to me, "You're so involved with gay activism and since you love movies so much, it's just a natural extension that you should be the one to explore this subject." In 1973 I started doing research for a book about the history of the ways in which lesbians and gay men had been portrayed on the screen, especially in mainstream movies.

Researching the book was actually how I made the connection between my political activism and movies. I came to believe that our negative image was at the root of homophobia. People were being taught things about us as gay people that simply weren't true, and they were being taught these things by the mass media, by movies. If I could address this issue, I felt that would be my contribution to the gay rights movement. That was what I could do to help.

RESEARCHING THE book was not easy. For a couple of reasons it was very difficult to talk to people in Hollywood. First, they were too busy, and there was nothing in it for them. And then there was the subject matter, and that scared away virtually all the actors. Maybe one or two very secure heterosexual actors were willing to comment on the record about playing a homosexual role. One person I did get to talk to was Don Murray, who played the senator accused of being gay who committed suicide in *Advise and Consent*. Murray was delightful, absolutely charming. But while I couldn't get to stars, I got a good response from screenwriters and a few directors.

The book was rejected by eighteen publishers. Even the gay people in the publishing houses said, "Who cares? There's not a market for this book." I was astonished that gay people could not see the potential market, given the connection between gay men and the movies. And couldn't they see how this book would cross over to film freaks? But I guess I should have expected that kind of reaction because, for the most part, these people were in the closet and were frightened of the issue.

Then my friend Homer Dickens at Harper & Row got involved. He was a customer in the restaurant where I worked. He showed Harper & Row how there was a market for this book, and they published it in 1981.

In the years after *The Celluloid Closet* was published, I slowly began to hear what people in Hollywood thought of the book. For instance, I didn't know that Rock Hudson had read my book and agreed with it until I read an interview published after his death. He said, "Vito Russo is right. Movies are antigay. They were always antigay and they're always going to be antigay because people in this town are homophobic."

I WONDER—and I have no way of knowing—whether or not the book did any good in terms of its actual impact on movies because most mainstream Hollywood films are still virulently homophobic. It may have affected the way some directors or writers decided to write a gay character into a film because there have been some positive gay char- acters. And it may have raised the consciousness of the community as a whole about the issue, but I think there were other factors.

One significant factor was the increasingly vocal objections from gay people about what Hollywood was producing. There are two significant instances I can think of, although the first one didn't have much of an impact. That was in 1970, when *The Boys in the Band* opened. People were protesting the fact that this film once again categorized gay men as intrinsically self-hating and, furthermore, that the homosexuality of the characters was the reason for their unhappi- ness. That was probably the first time gay people protested against a Hollywood movie.

It wasn't until 1979, when *Cruising* was being filmed in New York, that protests by gays had an impact on Hollywood producers. *Cruis- ing* was about how a New York City policeman assigned to capture a psychotic killer of gay men becomes aware of his own homosexuality and begins murdering gays himself. I was more or less an observer of the whole thing because I was doing a piece for *New York* magazine on Billy Friedkin, the movie's director. Friedkin had also been the direc- tor for *The Boys in the Band*.

The protests were touched off by a column in the *Village Voice* by Arthur Bell, an openly gay writer, who had read an early draft of the screenplay and found it tremendously offensive. Bell's column was a call to arms. Essentially, it said, "Friedkin is going to be filming this movie in Greenwich Village. This is our neighborhood. This is the ghetto. I advise gay people to tell him to fuck off and not allow him to film. Do anything you can do to stop this."

There was no plan; it was truly a spontaneous community action. By this time there was no longer a Gay Activists Alliance. People just did whatever they wanted to do. For the entire six to eight weeks of the shooting, it got to be like a guerrilla warfare game. The production company would try to keep the location of the shooting for the next day secret, and somebody would find out, and there would be a mob there. There were a lot of arrests at certain points because the more radical members of the gay community would literally sabotage the movie. People used wire cutters to cut cables from the trucks on the streets so they'd lose sound. A couple of times that sort of tactic worked because they had to halt the shooting. Protesters also blew whistles during critical scenes on the street, so they had to reshoot them. That sort of thing cost the producers bundles of money.

In retrospect, it was totally disorganized and not the way to run that kind of a protest. This was very different from the early 1970s, when everything was voted on. There was no organization anymore to corral people and make them responsible to a code, an ethic.

What needs to be said about all such protests, and this one in particular, is that the gay community has never spoken with one voice. Many people have the impression that the gay community has an opinion. And the truth is, that there are all sorts of ideologies in the gay community, from liberal to conservative. So there were many different voices around the issue of Cruising. There were people who believed in working within the system and were quietly lobbying the filmmakers and the city government. At the other end of the spectrum, there were the street activists, who didn't give a shit about negotiations or the system. They just wanted to get Friedkin off their streets and were willing to do everything they could to disrupt the filming.

There was also a political and ideological split in the gay community about whether or not it was valuable or necessary to show the leather and sado-masochism aspect of the community on screen, which is what Friedkin was portraying in this movie. There were middle-of-the-road gays who found this kind of thing horrifying. This is something else that I don't think a lot of people realize. Just because you're gay doesn't mean you're necessarily acquainted with the more far-out aspects of sexuality, especially in the 1970s. There were a lot of gay men, and certainly lesbians, in this country who would have been deeply shocked by the sex bars in New York. You get the impression from reading the media that we all knew about this. But I think there were only small groups of people in places like New York who knew about and practiced sadomasochism and orgies and parties at these bars. So suddenly the issue became, "Do we want to present this to the world as the way gay people are?" The public was not going to distinguish between one group of gay people and another.

So that became a battle between the activists and the leather men because the extras in *Cruising* were mostly people who were picked up in the West Village, who were patrons of the leather bars. The gay activists were saying, "How could you betray your own community by appearing in this film? Do you realize what that's going to say?"

Nonetheless, I think it was the first time that an organized protest had an effect on the powers in Hollywood because they realized that through protests like this, they could waste a lot of money. And it taught them to be more sensitive to the issues.

That was the beginning of a heightened sensitivity around Hollywood. For a few years movie producers thought twice before they would put something into a movie that was destructive to gays. One studio, Twentieth Century-Fox, even released a very positive, although very dull movie, about a man who leaves his wife for another man. *Making Love* was the first film in which a gay couple was permitted a happy ending. Here were two sane, handsome leading men, who took off their clothes and went to bed with each other. Nobody killed himself. So for a fifteen-year-old kid today, unlike my experience in the 1960s, his first exposure to gay characters on the screen was Michael Ontkean and Harry Hamlin. Now that's a great step forward. The young gay male population could see this movie and say, "At the very least I'm not sick and I don't have to kill myself."

But then AIDS came along and threw a monkey wrench into that progress. With AIDS, everything changed. Never before in the history of the movies, even in the worst periods of film history, have screenwriters felt so comfortable being antigay. There is hardly a popular entertainment film that opens today that doesn't have some sort of antigay reference in it in some way or another. So when you're a politicized gay person and you love the movies, you spend your life sitting through movies waiting for the shoe to drop. I sit there and I'm enjoying a movie and then suddenly somebody says, "Faggot," and I think, *Oh, shit, why did they have to do that?* I can name a score of films in the last six months or a year, where this is the case. I'm talking about the use of the word *faggot* or a fag joke or a gay reference that's offensive. All of the brat-pack movies—*St. Elmo's Fire, Pretty in Pink, The Breakfast Club*—had offensive antihomosexual dialogue. And all of Eddie Murphy's concert movies. In *Punchline* there's this twelve-year-old girl who tells a cocksucker joke. Was it necessary to put that word in the mouth of a twelve year old so that kids could think it was OK to say that?

MY FRIENDS and I knew about AIDS well before most people in the country became aware of it because of politics and because of where we lived. We were among those who knew the first people to get sick in 1979. At the time, though, we didn't know what was going on.

I had met a guy named Nick through a group of people on Fire Island. Like me, Nick was a collector of films. He had a print of *Some Like It Hot*, which I used to borrow occasionally for parties. We would share movies to show in the community house in the Pines at Fire Island on weekends. In 1979 Nick got very sick. I remember his lover calling Larry Kramer* and saying, "Larry, I'm at the end of my rope with whatever this disease is that Nick has, but if we don't do something, Nick is going to die." Larry said, "Oh, how silly. This is ridiculous. He's not going to die." But none of the doctors Nick went to could figure out what he had. In the end, we were told that Nick died of cat-scratch fever, which simply does not kill people. It was just not possible. I said to Larry, "There's something going on here. There's more to this than what we're seeing because nobody dies of cat-scratch fever." But the fact of the matter was that Nick had no immune system, so he did die of cat-scratch fever.

The turning point for me was when my boyfriend, Jeffrey, got sick. We had lived together for five years. It was a very difficult, emotional period. It's hard for me even now, though it will be three years on March 6 [1989] since Jeffrey died. He was thirty. It's hard to believe that it's been that long because I was diagnosed while Jeffrey was still alive. That's a very difficult, emotional thing to come to terms with because first of all, when you get a diagnosis, you think that you're going to die right away. Then when you survive for a long period of time—it's been almost four years since I've been diagnosed now—you don't know quite how to relate to the world. People who were healthy when I was diagnosed are dead now. People I left things to in my will have died. It's very confusing.

The last time I saw Jeff he was in a drawer at the morgue. They took me to the morgue at the hospital and opened up the drawer and showed him to me. I spent a few minutes with him and held his hand and said goodbye. It was very painful. I miss him terribly. He's been gone almost three years now, and I'm still sick and I'm very lonely. It's hard to live alone and be sick alone.

All this has gotten me involved in a whole new phase of activism. I was one of the people, along with Larry Kramer, and Vivian Shapiro, and Tim Sweeney, and a couple others who founded ACT UP—AIDS Coalition to Unleash Power. This is a new kind of activism. It's a coalition that we were never able to achieve in the 1970s. Back then the ideal and the dream were that gay people would come

*A New York City writer. His interview appears next.

together with other oppressed groups like blacks and Asians and women to form a coalition. That didn't happen because we had too many differences. Lesbians were fighting with gay men, the black community didn't want to admit there was a gay population in their community, and blah, blah, blah. Now AIDS has brought us together in ways that we could not have foreseen. ACT UP is composed of gay people and straight people, women and men, black and white. And all these people have one thing in common: They want to put an end to the AIDS crisis by any means possible.

The first meeting of ACT UP was really not called as a meeting. Larry Kramer was speaking at the Lesbian and Gay Community Services Center in the Village on one of their Tuesday Writers' Nights. He said, "Turn on the lights. I have things to say." Instead of reading from his work, which is what he was supposed to do, he made a passionate and articulate plea that something needed to be done, that people needed to form some kind of a community organization to deal with the AIDS crisis. The group decided there would be weekly meetings and later they chose the name ACT UP.

I was at the community center that Tuesday evening and later I went to an organizing meeting. The concept grew and grew and grew. Now there are usually two or three hundred people there every week. It's been very effective. It's because of pressure by ACT UP that the public and the medical establishment have become aware how dissatisfied people are with the process of approving new drugs for AIDS treatment.

The AIDS crisis has illuminated the issues of homophobia that we talked about in the seventies. All of those issues that we claimed existed—discrimination in jobs, discrimination in housing, hatred for gay people on a very basic level because we're different—have been made more palpable by the AIDS crisis. I don't think that there's new bigotry or new homophobia. I think this is the same homophobia, but AIDS has given people permission to say it out loud. We're seeing that, in fact, we were right. We said that people were discriminated against because they were gay. AIDS has proved it.

Because of AIDS and this discrimination, gay people who under any other circumstances would never, ever have gotten involved in gay politics have gotten involved in ACT UP and in the politics around AIDS. These are people who have been touched by it personally. They lost a lover. They lost a friend. They got AIDS themselves. AIDS has hit people on such a personal emotional level that even basically conservative gay people have been brought out of the closet and into the battle. Most of these people had been safe in the past, they were never going to get touched by homophobia. They had

money, position, insulation, nice apartments, good friends—all that
stuff that upper middle-class and upper-class gay men always wanted
and had. And now a disease has shattered all that because they've
realized that no matter how much money they have, they can't save
their friends or themselves. So you have more gay men, wealthy gay
men, closeted gay men, coming out and giving money to AIDS organizations or to ACT UP because they feel in their hearts that they want
to do something.

In Hollywood, while there's still a lot of homophobia, and maybe
even more homophobia than ever before, there's now a network of
people working hard to fight this disease. You wouldn't have seen the
people in this network fighting homophobia twenty years ago. Elizabeth Taylor is not going to get involved in gay rights, but she got
involved in AIDS. She had a lot of gay men friends who died. So
AIDS has been a catalyst for people to become more involved. This
has made others more aware of gay life and of gay people than they
ever were before. So maybe something good is going to come out of
this.

IT'S DIFFICULT to say what my future role in ACT UP will be because
at this point my priority is my survival and my health. Very often I
have to take long breaks from ACT UP because it's emotionally and
physically exhausting for a person with AIDS to go out there in the
streets at seven o'clock in the morning in the freezing cold to block
traffic. You get sick from it.

After I gave a talk at the Food and Drug Administration, I was good
for shit for a week. As a rule, people with AIDS don't have an
enormous amount of energy. And it changes from day to day. You
can be perfectly fine one day, feeling like a million bucks and getting
on busses and running around New York doing all your errands. The
next day you can sleep eighteen hours and not be able to leave the
house.

In ideal terms, in the future there won't be an ACT UP for me to
be involved in. It's similar to a gay liberation organization in the sense
that what gay liberation should want to do is put itself out of business.
It should want to see the day when people are not hateful and homophobic and the word *faggot* does not appear anywhere, and there is no
fag bashing and there's no discrimination, a day when people can live
their lives openly. It's the same thing with ACT UP. You're hoping
to put yourself out of business. You're hoping for an end to the
disease, so we can all go home.

I don't think there's a gay politician or anyone who's in the gay rights movement who doesn't really just want to lead a normal life. I don't want to be out on the streets screaming and sitting in traffic. Nobody wants that. Maybe there are a few professional political activists who like that sort of activity, but most of us do it because we have to, not because we want to. I want to enjoy my life, to have dinner with my friends, and spend time going to the theater and the movies.

I feel like my role right now is to be one of the people who survives this disease. I would like that very much, obviously—nobody wants to die. But also I want to be around to kick their asses after it's over. There's an old Phil Ochs song called "When I'm Gone." The lyrics are:

> There's no place in this world where I'll belong, when I'm gone. And I won't know the right from the wrong, when I'm gone. And you won't find me singin' on this song, when I'm gone. So I guess I'll have to do it while I'm here!

Later in the song it says something like:

> Can't say who's to praise or who's to blame when I'm gone. And I won't be laughing at the lies, when I'm gone. And the sands will be shifting from my sight, when I'm gone. So I guess I'll have to do it while I'm here.

I want to be here when it's over to say who's to praise or who's to blame. I want to say I lived through it, to have witnessed it. It's very important to me to tell the world what happened so that people will realize what we all went through. Because these are brave, courageous, beautiful people who are dying. It's a shame that the world is just throwing them in a garbage heap the way it has. They've lied about what they died from, altered their obituaries, and not wanted to pay attention to their struggle. And there are some of us who are determined that the story is going to be told well in the end.

I DON'T think I could have chosen to live my life in any other way but as an openly gay person. There are certain things that you suffer for by being openly gay. For instance, if I had wanted it, I don't think I could ever be a television movie critic. When you make your decision to be an openly gay person there are certain things you give up. I don't see that as honorable or courageous. I didn't do it for altruistic reasons, like I'm going to be some sort of martyr or hero. I did it because it was the only thing I wanted to do. I didn't really have a choice. It's not like I said, "Now I'm going to be courageous." This is the way my life worked out, and I'm pleased with it.

I think it was Pedro Almodóvar, an openly gay Spanish director from Madrid, who said, "What is the point of having a life if you didn't say something or do something that was going to survive after you're gone?" That's been my whole life, to leave my book and the other things I've written behind me. That's the reason I'm here. I know that after I'm dead my book is going to be on a shelf someplace and that some sixteen-year-old kid who's going to be a gay activist will read my work and carry the ball from there. That'll happen. It happened with me. Harry Hay passed the ball to Mattachine, and Mattachine passed the ball to us. We've already started passing it on. There are young people in ACT UP who don't remember the *Cruising* demonstrations because they were kids. Now they're teenagers. They'll be here to fight over the more radical issues, like whether gay people have the right to adopt children, get married, teach in the public schools, and be open about being gay. And they'll be fighting those battles long after you and I are gone.

The Unwanted Messenger

Larry Kramer

WHEN THE New York Times *published an article in the summer of 1981 about forty-one gay men who had been diagnosed with a rare form of cancer, New York writer Larry Kramer got scared. The medical profiles of these men resembled his own, and Larry knew instinctively that something needed to be done. Within six months, he and a small group of men in New York City founded the Gay Men's Health Crisis—GMHC—an organization Larry hoped would spread the news to gay men everywhere that they had to "stop having sex, or stop having it unsafely." On the heels of the hedonistic 1970s, in a city where many gay men considered sexual freedom a birthright, Larry's message was viewed as the ranting of a self-loathing, puritanical, middle-aged hysteric.*

Larry Kramer was already a well-known and controversial figure in New York's gay community as a result of his 1978 novel, Faggots—*his blunt, less-than-flattering account of gay life in New York in the mid-1970s. Larry has also enjoyed success in other media, especially writing and producing the film version of D. H. Lawrence's* Women in Love. *The 1969 movie earned Larry an Oscar nomination, and the movie's star, Glenda Jackson, won an Oscar for best actress.*

Since the start of the AIDS crisis, Larry Kramer has had a reputation as a passionate AIDS activist with high expectations and a very short fuse. His tirades have offended many people along the way and have periodically made him a pariah in the activist gay community.

During the 1980s, Larry wrote two plays and one book about the AIDS crisis, and in 1987, he founded the AIDS Coalition to Unleash Power, ACT UP, an AIDS advocacy and direct-action organization with more than one hundred chapters around the world.

Now in his mid-fifties, and himself HIV-positive, Larry continues to attend ACT UP meetings. "For me it's my social life and support group. It's a very moving organization because there are so many of us, and we represent so many different points of view, yet we get along. We're all out there fighting together." Larry is working on a new play, The Furniture of Home, *as well as a new novel,* Search for My Heart No Longer, *which he said was Proustian in its ambitions and length. Larry said, "Just like*

Marcel, I will work on it until it's finished. And when it's finished, I will die."

I was eighteen when I went to Yale in 1953. It was awful. There was a gay bar called Pierelli's only two blocks from campus, but it was a million years away. Everybody at school knew about it, but it was not a place college students went. The students made fun of it. It was very dark and gray and smoky inside and filled with older men. I only went there once. Somebody picked me up, and we drove for what seemed like hours before we found a place that was quiet. We did it, and then he drove me back. We didn't say a word that whole time.

When I went to Yale, I thought I was the only gay person in the world. I tried to kill myself that first year at school because I was so lonely. I ate two hundred aspirin. I went to bed and got scared, and I called the campus police. They came and took me to the hospital and pumped my stomach. Then I fell asleep and woke up in a room with bars at the Grace New Haven Hospital. There was a very unpleasant hospital psychiatrist who said, "All right, Mr. Kramer, why did you do it?" And I said, "Go fuck yourself," or words to that effect. He said, "You're not going to be allowed out of this hospital until you tell us why you did it." He rubbed me the wrong way. And who really knew why I did it?

Ordinarily when you did something like trying to kill yourself, you were shipped off to go join the army and then you would come back to Yale when you had grown up. But my brother, who has always looked after me and who went to Yale before me, came and got me out of the hospital. He was friends with the dean of freshmen, who decided to let me stay if I went to the university psychiatrist.

Dr. Clement Fry, the psychiatrist I went to see, was like a professor. You saw him in his suite of rooms in the college, the kind you would expect a professor of English to have. He was in his sixties and had silver hair. He was a good-looking man and wore a tweed jacket. He wore his rep tie and his button-down shirt. You just knew that he cared more about Yale than he ever did about you.

The first time I went to Dr. Fry, I told him about this experience I had had meeting these two guys, Jim and Peter, during my freshman year. Somehow they had mercifully found each other and were living together. I was invited for tea. You know how awful freshman-year rooms are. Well, they had done their room over entirely. It was painted all black, and everything had been taken out except for a low mattress, which was also black. There was a perfect coffee table with a rose in a vase that was spotlighted. Mabel Mercer was playing on the phonograph. I explained all this to Dr. Fry, and his reaction was, "I wouldn't see those guys anymore if I were you." And that's what Yale was like, and that's what going to a psychiatrist was like in 1953.

I GOT out of Yale in 1957 and worked in New York from 1958 through 1961, when I went to London. I was a film executive, and during the 1960s, I traveled back and forth between London and New York, before settling back here in 1971.

Everybody knew there were gay organizations in New York during the 1970s, but until only recently—1982 or 1983—it was all tinged with an "us and them" kind of thing. You just didn't want to get involved. It was not chic; it was not something you could brag about with your friends. You would sneak off and do it. This is all in my play, *The Normal Heart,* where Ned says, "No one with half a brain gets involved with gay politics. It's filled with the great unwashed radicals of every counterculture." I can remember being at Fire Island in the 1970s, and when there was a news story on television about the gay pride parade, people would sit in front of the TV set and make fun of it. Guys marching down Fifth Avenue was a whole other world.

The whole gestalt of Fire Island was about beauty and looks and golden men. Gay political people were certainly not that. They were physically unattractive and they almost gloried in it. I was living with all the Fire Island clones and was participating in that life and struggling to stay thin and go to the gym every day and find love and all the things that the lead character in my novel, *Faggots,* was trying to do.

Faggots was a seminal experience for me. I didn't have any preconceived notions when I started work on the book in 1975. I knew I wanted to write about what it was like to be gay in New York in the mid-1970s. And I started out with one question: I wanted a lover. I wanted to be in love. Almost everybody I knew felt the same way. I think most people, at some level, wanted what I was looking for, whether they pooh-poohed it or said that we can't live like the straight people or whatever excuses they gave. The wish for love and companionship is a fundamental human need and longing. Why, then, did I see so few people having what they wanted? Why did I see so few men in love, in relationships that I thought were sustaining, nurturing, and admirable? Were they out there? They could very well have been there, and I just didn't know about it.

I researched *Faggots* quite carefully. I was already going to Fire Island, but I really wanted to see the gay world everywhere, from gay synagogues to the Mine Shaft, which was a place in the meat-packing district in Manhattan that I describe in the novel. The Mine Shaft was gross. When you walked in the front door, the first thing you saw was a pool table and a bar. If you went beyond that, through a tiny hall, you came into an enormous dark cavern where you could either participate in or watch men being sexually assaulted in one way or another. They were engaged in either relatively calm encounters, like getting their dick sucked, or they were being strung up on gallows or in stocks or in swings where they were getting fisted. There was much more of the latter than the former. The sexual activities were much more toward physical abuse than sheer pleasure, or at least, my definition of pleasure.

Downstairs were the places where people got pissed and shit on, bathtubs and showers. There would be a bathtub with some poor soul in it and there would be men all around him pissing on him. Then there were these long underground tunnels where more of the same went on. There were little rooms off the tunnel, and if you weren't careful, you would step in somebody's shit. On a Saturday night at three o'clock in the morning, the place would be packed. You couldn't move; the stench was awful. And because so many of the activities were so arcane, the participants were quite often drugged out of their minds to have the courage to partake in them or to cancel out the pain. It's not easy to get one or two fists up your asshole.

I was never fist-fucked—I didn't carry my research that far—but I certainly observed it. And I observed all the different organizations. I would go to groups, and I would go to parties, and I would go to dinners where I would get the conversation going. Everything was loaded. If you asked pointed questions, people got upset. For example, if I was talking to an S&M person and I questioned S&M, he got angry and would tell me that I didn't understand, that it was really another way of showing love and concern. There's a rationale for it all. To this day I find S&M exceedingly distasteful and I don't understand why it is such a big part of gay life in big cities and why it's been legitimized so. Another time, when I was with a group from the gay synagogue, they got very angry at me for saying things like, "The Jewish religion doesn't seem to want us, fellahs. Why spend so much time in a religion that clearly doesn't want you?"

THE TROUBLE started long before *Faggots* was published because people knew that I was writing a gay novel. The one thing that I was asked all the time was, "Are you writing a negative book? Are you going to make it positive? Are you going to give us a good image?" I began to think, *My God, people must really be very conflicted about the lives they're leading.* And that was true: I think people were guilty about all the promiscuity and all the partying. And even though there was a rationale for it, in that everybody else was doing it, and the peer pressure was such as to make it acceptable, I think people were self-conscious about it.

Faggots got these vicious, vitriolic reviews, particularly in the gay press. I think the main reason the book was so pummeled in the gay press was because, indeed, I did just what people were afraid of. I told the truth. When the outcry is so strong, you know you've touched a nerve. Methinks they doth protest too much. I don't think there was a good gay review anywhere. The straight press was divided: There were nasty reviews, and there were good ones and even a few great ones.

This is where I first started learning my lesson that these gay publications, these gay leaders, and these so-called spokespersons did not represent the community because the book was a best-seller. I started getting thousands of letters from people saying, "Thank you for telling it how it is." "I really agree with you." "I support you." I didn't get any negative mail. Not one letter! Not one, which was unlike the responses I got to things I did later on. On *Faggots*, it was all "thank you" mail.

Now I have even more evidence that gay leaders and the gay press don't represent the community because I've put out more work. I make a very good living supporting myself as a gay writer. My stuff sells. People go to see my plays—and that's despite the fact I've been vilified by the gay political establishment and the gay journalist establishment. The political spectrum has changed in recent years and is much livelier and more vital, but I still think there's this divergence between the actual gay world out there and the people who are part of the active political spectrum.

PEOPLE DIDN'T talk to me after *Faggots*—people literally crossed the street not to talk to me. My best friend stopped talking to me and still really doesn't. When I went to Fire Island for the first time after the book came out, I was shunned. Several times, the guys who ran the supermarket on Fire Island let it be known that I was not welcome. I was made to feel that way until *The Normal Heart* opened. With that play I somehow redeemed myself. *The Normal Heart* is about the early years of the AIDS epidemic and how we came to be in the mess we're in now. The guys at the supermarket said they really liked *The Normal Heart* and that I could then go back in the store.

The Oscar Wilde Bookshop, the gay bookstore on Christopher Street, wouldn't sell *Faggots* from the shelves. Craig Rodwell, who owned the store and was from the old days of the movement, sold it from underneath the counter. I went in there one day and said, "I would rather you didn't sell it at all than sell it that way." And he said, "Done."

The trouble didn't end with *Faggots* because I continued to write what I thought. I wrote an Op-ed piece for the *New York Times* when *Faggots* came out, in which I referred to the hearings on the gay rights bill that were going on at City Hall. I said that an awful lot of the opposition to the bill came from Jewish leaders and Jewish organizations. Well, the guys from the gay synagogue wouldn't leave me alone. "How dare you say that in the press?" I was invited to speak at the gay synagogue. When I went down there, though, they wouldn't let me speak. They heckled and booed me, just because I said in the *New York Times* that a New York City councilman and the Hassidim and Jewish leaders and Jewish organizations were against us. What had I done? I stated the truth.

WHILE I'VE done a lot of things that in retrospect can now be seen as activism, I didn't consider them activism at the time. There was only one thing that made me an activist, and that was AIDS. The motivation was fear. The *New York Times* published an article on July 3, 1981, with the headline, "Rare Cancer Seen in 41 Homosexuals." The article said that all the guys had the same history of having had all these sexual diseases: amoebas, hepatitis A and B, mononucleosis, syphilis, and gonorrhea. The late 1970s were the years of the amoebas—we forget that. Just as everybody talks about AIDS now, you couldn't go to a party in the late 1970s without everybody telling an amoeba story. When I saw that article in the *Times*, I was scared because I had had all those diseases. Also, the *Times* has a way of making you sit up and say, "Wow!"

A few weeks later I had a conversation with Dr. Friedman-Kien from New York University, who told me, in essence, "This is what's happening. You've got to stop fucking. You're someone well known in the gay community. You have to do something about it. Somebody's got to go out there and tell them." As a result of that conversation, Dr. Larry Mass, who had been writing about this new health problem in a local gay paper even before the *Times* wrote about it, and two other guys, now both dead, and I, invited everyone we knew to come to a meeting here at my apartment.

In this very room, in August 1981, eighty men sat down with Dr. Friedman-Kien, who told us in no uncertain terms exactly what was happening. There were a lot of nasty questions put to Dr. Friedman-

Kien at that meeting. There were a lot of people who said, "You're a born-again. How can you make all these assumptions on the basis of so few cases? How can you expect a whole community to stop fucking?" No virus had been discovered then. That didn't come for another couple of years, so people could say that he had no evidence on which to base his opinions.

My first big fight over AIDS was in 1981, when I made an appeal in the *Native** and was attacked by another writer. In my article there was a line that said, "We don't know what we did with whom, or what we took that might have caused all of this and we're perplexed, but we have to get it together and do something about it. One thing you can do is send checks to New York University." That was the only game in town at that time. It was an appeal for money. And this writer, who had once interviewed me, threw an old quote back at me where I had said, "I really don't expect to go to the barricades for the right to have sex in the subways." The fact that I could say I wouldn't fight for the right to have sex in the subways meant I was an awful person and had no credibility when it came to talking about this health crisis.

That writer, like many others, took the position that sexual promiscuity was the one freedom we had and that we had to fight to maintain it—even if it killed us. And it did kill us, a lot of us. Oh, God, the battle over whether or not to close the baths became such a red herring because of this issue of sexual freedom. It took all our energy, and it took all our fighting. It shouldn't have been an issue, period! If you think about it rationally, can you imagine going to the barricades for the right to go to a whorehouse? I'm painting it at its most bleak because the baths certainly weren't the equivalent of a straight whorehouse. I understand why we went to bathhouses. I understand the great hungers people had—myself included—and how easy it was to go when you just couldn't take it anymore and you were so hungry that you needed the intimacy of another person. I understand all that. But didn't we see that we should have been fighting for the right to get married or fighting for the right to be noble and live outside in the world instead of fighting for the right to find our love in these tawdry little places? Were the baths the be-all and end-all of what being gay meant? I think that the baths represented the worst in all areas of what we were all about. Bartering our bodies, using them as things: It's all about what you look like, not who you are. It was all about fighting for the wrong rights.

*A gay weekly newspaper in New York City.

* * *

OUT OF the August 1981 meeting we eventually put together Gay Men's Health Crisis. We officially organized the group in January 1982. During the first two years of GMHC, of watching it grow, of watching guys and women respond to the call, I never felt so useful in my life. And it was a terrific high to go around and make speeches. It was gratifying; you saw results. One day you had twenty volunteers, and the next year you had six hundred or whatever. Everybody felt very committed, and there was a passion about really doing something. But GMHC didn't turn out to be what I expected. I thought I was working along with others to help set up an organization that would fight to make the system accountable, to spread information about what was happening, and to pass the word that we really had to stop having sex or having it unsafely. That was what I thought was happening. But I was in a dream because GMHC was not that at all. Very quickly the organization was taken over by the social workers. To quote a line from my play, *The Normal Heart*, "I thought I was starting with a bunch of Ralph Naders and Green Berets, and right in front of my eyes as soon as anyone had to take a stand on a political issue and fight, everybody became a nurse's aide."

It wasn't so much that these people did or did not believe what was happening. It was that they didn't think it was GMHC's or anybody's position to tell anybody else how to live their lives and that people had to make up their own minds. It's like people know that smoking causes cancer, and it's their decision as to whether or not they smoke. So a lot of valuable time was lost.

I eventually quit GMHC because I knew they wanted me out. I was too difficult and too opinionated. I was petulant. I failed in my role as a leader. I blame myself. I am very cognizant of the fact that I did not have the skills to deal with my adversaries and still be friends. To accomplish all of what we needed to do early on in the AIDS crisis was possible, and I think it was a tragedy that I—that we—were all very naive. We were all very inexperienced in the actual politics of having to deal with each other. God, if there is a God, did not give the gay community a leader when the gay community needed a leader. I feel very strongly that I failed in that role. In the end, sometimes, when I'm really hard on myself, I'll say, "OK, stop it Larry, stop blaming yourself. Where the fuck was everybody else in all this?" I don't know where the fuck they are. I've written about it endlessly. There are 24 million gay people out there, and the biggest gay organization has no more than 15,000 to 25,000 gay people on a mailing list. We have surprisingly few rights and surprisingly little power for the numbers that we represent. I get in a lot of trouble with people for saying this.

The reality is that most people—in this city, anyway—just want to be successful and do their work and live their lives and have a modicum of enjoyment. That's all most people want to do. They don't want to get involved; they don't want to make waves. Part of me says that I know all of that, but everybody's had somebody close who has died, who they really loved or were close to. I just don't understand why people can't make that connection to fight for that memory, to contribute so that it won't happen to another friend.

I'M HIV-positive myself. So now it's come home to me that my days may be numbered. That has made me real sad and then angry. Part of me just wants to be alone. But I find myself going back to ACT UP meetings, which I had not done in a long time because I had gotten fed up with it. Their fighting takes me out of my negativity. Being touched by the positivism helps me.

I don't want to give the wrong impression. If I've been critical and am critical, it's only because I think we are very special people and capable of so much more. I had words with an agent of mine the other day who said, "Now, now, Larry. Let's not you and I have a fight. You're known to be a bad boy, and we haven't had any trouble. Let's not start it now." And I said to him, "I don't ask of anybody else what I don't ask of myself." And that's true. I guess I don't have much tolerance for sloppiness and bad work by those who are capable of more.

I think being a gay man—even today with AIDS—is a wonderful thing. I love being gay, and it's taken me a long time to say that because I'm of a different generation. I was born in 1935. I'm the generation that was sent off to shrinks because shrinks then thought they could change you, and you were expected to change. It took me a long time and a lot of shrinks to come to terms with my homosexuality. Now, having come to terms with it and liking it, having to face AIDS is almost like a bum rap. Nevertheless, I think we are very lucky. We have great freedoms that other people don't have. For most of us, we don't have certain responsibilities. We don't have to raise children. We don't have to support a wife. We have great freedom of choice. If we don't like our jobs or what we're doing, we have the time and quite often the wherewithal to go and try something else. But with this freedom comes a certain responsibility—a responsibility to put more into the world, to be upstanding in a dignified way for what you represent.

Maybe I shouldn't expect so much, but I expect a lot from everyone. I'm also disappointed in straight people. I'm furious with the
straight world—I don't know what to do about that. There's a long
essay at the end of this new book of mine where I talk about this
anger, about the fact that I can't bear to be with my straight friends
who don't give a shit that we're all dying. And yet, what am I expecting them to do? I guess it's part of being angry at ourselves for what
we haven't done. You get angry at other people for not doing what
you should be doing yourselves. But it does seem that the liberal
straight world, where most of my friends are, has done exceedingly
little to help us in this fight. We have certainly helped them in many
fights. Perhaps I haven't said that loudly enough. Maybe I'll write an
Op-ed piece, "Why I Hate Straight People," by Larry Kramer. . . .

I LOVE going back to Yale now. This is my real yardstick of how far
we've come, even though I'm always yelling about how we've not
come far enough. I go back to Yale every year, and there's a dance
held for well over one thousand gay men and women. It's held across
the campus from where I tried to kill myself because I thought I was
the only one.

The Storekeepers
Neil Woodward and Dan Otero

IN THE late 1970s Neil Woodward, a librarian at the University of Denver, was very pleased that his local bookstore stocked a couple of hundred books written specifically for a gay and lesbian audience. Then he went to San Francisco, where he discovered there were bookstores that had thousands of gay books to choose from.

Neil returned to Denver inspired to open a similar bookstore of his own. In 1982 Neil and his business partners opened Category Six, Denver's first gay and lesbian bookstore, with about a thousand titles. "There were more books, perhaps four thousand," he recalls, "but we couldn't afford them all. We still can't afford to carry all the books of interest that are available, but of the twenty thousand titles of interest to gay and lesbian readers, we probably carry half that number over the course of a year." The name of the store is based on the famous Kinsey scale of human sexuality, in which six represents exclusive homosexuality.

After six months in business, Neil bought out his original working partner, freeing her to open a women's bookstore down the street. Neil now runs Category Six with his lover, Dan Otero. A Vietnam veteran, Dan had been a commercial airline pilot for thirteen years before he came to work at the store full time in 1983. The two men live together with their dogs, Woofer and Nacho, above Category Six, which is now located on the first floor of a white clapboard house in a residential area not far from downtown.

Neil:

Shortly after we met in 1980, Dan and I went on an ultraromantic vacation together driving down the coast of California. It was spectacular. It was a dream come true. When we got to San Francisco, we walked into a bookstore in the Castro neighborhood and saw whole walls of gay books. This was not even a gay bookstore! Back in Denver, we were all very proud of one of our local bookstores because they had a fine collection of gay books. They must have had five shelves.

Dan:

We didn't have a whole hell of a lot of money, but we were even poorer when we walked out of that bookstore in San Francisco.

Neil:

That's when it hit me over the head that, my God, these people at this local bookstore, who we thought were our friends and were doing us this wonderful service by providing us with five shelves of gay literature, had been doing us a disservice because they were only providing the top of the line. I had thought that that was all there was. How could you know unless you were confronted with the reality of it, like I was in San Francisco?

I came back to Denver knowing that I wanted to open a gay and lesbian bookstore. What I had in mind was a store that represented writings by, about, and for gay men and lesbians, in an inclusive sense, not an exclusive sense. The store would represent many sexualities. We would not be involved in censoring material or deciding what was appropriate or politically correct for Denver's gay people to read. Our thinking was that everybody was an adult and could make his or her own selections.

We also had an ideological commitment to gay liberation. What I mean by that is that gay people have a culture, which includes a body of literature. Gay people are entitled to have access to that culture, to that body of literature, but they don't have it. The only way they're going to have it is if somebody takes the risk financially, if somebody makes the effort to open a bookstore. I decided that I could do that.

Neil:

I had a friend at the University of Denver, and he and I planned to open up the bookstore together, but a family crisis came up, and he had to move to Florida. That kind of pulled the rug out from under that plan. So I got a job at the Denver County Jail as a librarian for the inmates. While I was there, a woman who lived here in Denver put a notice in one of the gay papers that she was looking for a business partner to open Denver's first gay and lesbian bookstore. Her name was Sue. I called her up, we talked, and in February of 1982, we got going on it. After a long search for a space to rent, we opened Category Six on Gay Pride Day in June 1982.

Dan:

Sue and Neil went to a number of places looking for a location for the store, and they got yelled at, spit at.

Neil:

It was vicious. "There's not going to be any gay-lesbian nothing in my building! Get out of here!" I was shocked; I had no idea there was that kind of hatred. Our motives were so pure, and we were so innocent. My thinking was, *Everybody thinks that gay books are pornography. Well, they're not. We're going to bring the nonpornographic books to Denver and show people what gay culture is really about. People will just love to have this here because it's not pornography.* Hell, no, they'd rather have pornography.

When we started looking for a place to rent, it wasn't just one or two rejections. It was one after the other. We finally found a place on East Colfax. Our accountant had told us to avoid it because it's the longest commercial-retail strip in the United States, and any business that located there was going to be lost. So we stayed away from East Colfax for a long time, but we were more or less forced there by the fact that no one else would consider our proposition.

It turns out that the people who rented to us did it because they had just rented a store two doors down to a radical Christian group, called Jesus on Main Street. We found out later that the owners thought it would be amusing to have us just two doors away from the Christians. Well, we were not the best of neighbors.

Dan:

One particular day this fellow was banging on the window, yelling, "You'll all go to hell!" We had a bunch of people in the store, and the tension just rose. And then some other guy threw open the front door.

Neil:

He came breezing into the store and said, "That's recommendation enough for me!" Everybody burst out laughing.

It was pretty awful for the two years we were on East Colfax. The people from Jesus on Main Street were pathetic. They would hand out little comic book antihomosexual tracts. They would also come into the store in pairs and walk around and pull out books, stuff them with the comic books, and then put the books back on the shelves. Every night we'd go pull books off the shelves and fan them out and let the comic books fall to the floor.

The most interesting thing about some of these people was that sometimes they would come back to Category Six on their own—in the morning before Jesus on Main Street opened or in the evening after it closed—and buy a copy of *The Joy of Gay Sex* or something. We may have represented demons and Satan and all that to these people, but some of them were evidently pretty infatuated with the idea of demons and Satan.

Neil:

We had a captive audience from the beginning. There hadn't been anything like this in Denver before. Before we opened the store, there wasn't even a gay space in Denver that was really comfortable for gay men and lesbians to be in together, except for the Gay and Lesbian Community Center, which was a social service agency. A lot of people had no cause to go there—they didn't need social services. But they did need books and women's music, which was very, very important and still is because it's such an integral part of lesbian culture.

All kinds of people have come into the store over the years, including some memorable clients. One day, I got a call from a state trooper that Dottie Lamm, the governor's wife, would be by shortly. This was when Richard Lamm was still in office. It turned out she was doing a column on Parents and Friends of Lesbians and Gays, Parents FLAG, for one of Denver's daily newspapers, and was looking for a particular piece of information to back up one of her assertions. So she needed to come and do a little bit of research in our shop, which she did. She wrote the column, and everything went real well. So when people have said to us that they couldn't afford to be seen in Category Six books, or said, "What would people think?" my response has often been, "Well, Dottie Lamm was in, and she didn't care if people thought that she was a lesbian." I admired her greatly for it. She made a public statement by walking in, and that made it OK for other people to come in.

Dan:

Then there was the woman who said, "My husband just found out that our two children are gay, and I don't want him to kill my babies! Do you have anything he can read?"

Neil:

First of all, it was nine o'clock on a weekend morning. We weren't really open, but this woman was standing outside our front door in a pink housecoat and pink curlers. She was banging on the door with her fist, tears streaming down her face. So I went to the door and unlocked it, and she pushed in and said, "You've got to help me! You've got to help me! I've got to get a book for my husband! He just found out that two of my babies are gay!" I said, "We have books that can help you, they're right over here. Why don't you come with me." Then she said, "Oh, I don't know what I'm going to do! I don't know what I'm going to do! It's not just two of my babies that are gay. I have five kids. I went to see my oldest daughter, and she said, 'Oh, Mother, how can you be so naive? They're *all* gay, all four of them! I'm the only straight one in the family!'" She started wailing again. Well, this woman's husband was a devout Roman Catholic, could not accept homosexuality, and was going to murder her babies with a gun. She couldn't let this happen. So she needed a book to give to him. So I showed her *Now That You Know* and a couple of books on Catholics and homosexuality. Then she decided that she needed two of each title because she was afraid that her husband might rip the books to shreds, and then she wouldn't have anything to read herself. So she got a set for him and a set for herself.

Then she went to pay for them. By this time, there was a stack of books on the counter. She pulled out a credit card, which had her husband's name on it. And I thought, *Oh, wonderful, when he gets done shooting the babies, he's going to come and shoot us!*

We also gave her the Parents FLAG phone number and sent her on her way. We never heard another word.

Dan:

In 1982, one of our friends came in and gave us a sign to put on the desk. "The Psychiatrist Is In, Five Cents." Boy, is the psychiatrist in these days. Holy shit!

Neil:

I wish I had five cents for every time someone came in seeking counsel or advice or support. I don't know if we have more people coming in here looking for that kind of help than other bookstores do, but ours is certainly focused on our issues.

Dan:

Those issues have changed drastically over the years. Now we have parents coming in, tears streaming down their faces, because they've found out their son is gay, but only after they've found out that he has AIDS. So it's a double whammy. We've had this happen numerous times. They're trying to understand AIDS, and then they're trying to understand gay at the same time. Some of these people are coming in from Nebraska or Bum-fuck, Egypt. They've never heard *gay*, or if they have heard it, it's nothing but abomination and all this kind of crap that they get from their fucked-up churches. They come here because they've been referred by Parents FLAG. They come looking for any information they can find. The mother in curlers has turned into the mother in mourning.

We have much more information for people today than when the store opened. I can say, "All right, let me point you to a couple of things that might help you," whether it's accepting your son as gay or your daughter as lesbian, or this is what the Catholics have to say and this is a rebuttal to what the Catholics say, or this is what the Episcopalians have to say. The only ones that are still fucked-up beyond comprehension are the Mormons. However, we just heard of a book today about a Mormon bishop coming out of the closet, and that may help. But my point is that there is so much available now and much more coming out that we can offer more as booksellers and as psychiatrists than we could in 1982.

It's changed so fast. When Neil and I went to our first American Booksellers Association convention, we walked through hundreds and hundreds of booths for the different publishing houses. We would say, "We specialize in gay and lesbian books," and the first response was, "Well, we don't have anything for you, snicker, snicker." But things have changed, and every year the changes are more and more evident. Instead of snickering, the publishers now say, "Well, this is what we've got for you. You've got to look at this."

Neil:

I think we play a pivotal role in Denver's gay rights movement. Sometimes I feel like we're at the center of the storm because we deal in information. A lot goes through our small bookstore. Everything gay related that happens in the media gets attention here. We've become a clearinghouse for news. Every morning Dan and I dutifully get up and read both papers and cut out everything that applies and pin it on the bulletin board for the day. We're always real current on everything. And if we should miss something, people will come in and bring it to our attention.

Dan:

Just to give you an example. This past week, the state legislature was reconvened, and one of our customers came in and said, "Have you heard about Senate Bill Number 19?" And I said, "No, what is it?" She said, "It's being introduced by so-and-so and so-and-so." Both of these guys had been very antigay in last year's session. They were fighting over something to do with AIDS reportability. So I immediately started putting in calls to people who are gay lobbyists. I said, "Has anyone heard about this thing? What does it mean? What can they sneak in at the last minute?" That started a chain of telephone calls literally throughout the city to lobbyists and attorneys because nobody had heard about this bill. That way, people were able to at least monitor this bill and make sure that the legislature was not going to sneak in an antisodomy amendment at the last minute.

Neil:

We really facilitate communications and the flow of information.

Dan:

I think it's necessary for someone—some organization or institution, be it a bookstore or whatever—to assume this role, as far as the quote-unquote movement is concerned. I say that in quotes because you have to be careful when you talk about a gay movement. Personally I think there is no gay movement per se. In the same way that there is not a single gay community, there is not one gay movement. There are a bunch of communities and a bunch of movements, all headed toward the same thing: "Hey, just let me be me."

Neil:

There shouldn't be any need for Category Six books. On one level it's a sad, sad commentary that there has to be a separate gay bookstore. Why can't people go to any bookstore and go buy gay books? They should be able to. On the other hand, straight society is not going to preserve gay culture. So, we'll do it ourselves. We often talk to people who ask, "What would it take to set up one of these in my town?" We helped the people who opened People Like Us Books in Chicago. They talked to us extensively by telephone for several months before they opened. Just the other day a couple of fellahs from Texas came in and asked our advice on getting started. It can only increase.

Dan:

When we win the lottery, we'll open a new bookshop in a warm climate. Maybe Cuernavaca.

The Mixed Couple
Deborah L. Johnson and
Dr. Zandra Z. Rolón

BY THE early 1980s dozens of cities and counties across the country had passed laws protecting the rights of gay people in employment, housing, and public accommodations. Yet the passage of antidiscrimination laws was no guarantee that the public would comply or that, if challenged, these laws would be upheld in court. That's what Zandra Rolón and Deborah Johnson discovered in January 1983, when the two twenty-seven-year-old veterans of the gay and lesbian rights movement went out for what was supposed to be a romantic dinner at Papa Choux, a Los Angeles restaurant.

Zandra had reserved a table in the section of the restaurant designed specifically for romantic dining. When she and Deborah got there, they were, to their surprise and horror, denied service. Romantic dining at this restaurant, they discovered, was the exclusive privilege of heterosexual couples.

Deborah and Zandra ultimately decided to file a discrimination lawsuit. What started out as an intimate meal turned into a very public test of city and state civil rights laws—as well as a test of the strength of Deborah and Zandra's relationship.

Deborah and Zandra now live in northern California, where Deborah is a consultant for gay organizations across the country, and Zandra is a chiropractor in private practice.

Zandra:

Deborah calls my family a Mexican commune. Three quarters of the population in Brownsville, Texas, are relatives of mine. My mother and father got divorced when I was still a child. I'm the oldest, so I was my mother's right arm with everything. We're very, very good friends and always have been. We've always respected each other as women first. A lot of my feminism I know I've learned from her. I think she was a feminist before she even knew she was.

I got a grip on the fact that I was a little different when I was about ten, maybe twelve. I remember discovering a box underneath my mom's bed that had all these adult novels. Every time she left the house, I'd run to this box and read the books. The descriptions of the women were the parts I liked the most.

I always had crushes on girls at school. In high school I even had a lover. We didn't call ourselves *lovers*, but we messed around all the time. She had her boyfriend; I had my boyfriend—that was just what we did at slumber parties.

I tried to do what was expected of me and got married. I got caught up in the romance of being in a relationship. I liked everything that came with falling in love. I just happened to fall in love with somebody who happened to be a man. Besides, it wasn't kosher for me to be in tune—nor did I know that I could be in tune—with the fact that I was lesbian. It wasn't until later, when I was going through my divorce in my early twenties, that I realized I had a choice.

After my divorce I left Houston and eventually wound up in L.A., where I worked with battered women and children in a shelter. Then one day about eight months after I started working there, the women I worked with took me to a lesbian club. I saw wall-to-wall women and thought, *This is it! This is it! I'm in heaven!* The light went on: I decided to stop lying and came out.

It was pretty hard for my mom. She went through all the typical things. She cried and she got mad. "What did I do? How did I cause it? Was it because we didn't have a man around the house?" She didn't want me seeing my younger brother and sister. She really tried to alienate me from the family, but I banked on the fact that we had a good relationship. What turned her around was the fact that I waited her out.

Deborah:

Our families are very different. I grew up in L.A. in a very upper-middle-class bourgeois black household. We're one of these very well-rooted, extremely well-connected families. I lived a privileged life: A new car when I was sixteen, traveling in Europe, the whole bit. If there was such a thing as grooming the future leadership of America, that was the approach my parents took. They spent a lot of time with their kids.

Growing up was quite traumatic for me because I really thought that I was a little boy trapped inside of a little girl's body. I was supposed to be sweet and docile, but I was a jock. I wanted to grab the world by the balls! It just didn't make any sense to me. And I had sexual feelings very, very early, but boys were not an interest. When the other little girls were starting to get crushes on boys and were talking about weddings, I always knew I wanted to marry a girl—always, always, always.

When I was seven, I remember telling my parents that I was not going to marry a man and all the reasons why. By the time I was ten, I explained to them that I was in love with this little girl. My dad told me that it was just a phase, that I was going to outgrow it. My mother knew better; she had worked for years as a teacher with teenaged girls. My relationship with my parents has been in the toilet ever since then.

I started reading a lot of my father's medical books. He's a pharmacist. I read about wet dreams, and that's what I thought I was having. I didn't know what was going on. I just knew that I was fantasizing about women and girls, and then I'd get this stuff between my legs that looked kind of like what they said semen looked like. So I was scared. I thought that there was something really, really wrong here. I didn't know there was such a thing as lesbianism, women with women, so I just assumed that I would have to be a male if I wanted to be with women. It was very confusing.

It was when I read *The Children's Hour* in seventh grade that I learned about women with women. I was doing a scene with this woman who I had a serious crush on, and she got to the part where she explained how she really felt for her female coworker. It hit me like a ton of bricks. "No fucking shit! That's what this is!"

This was 1967 or 1968. So it was just about the time where you were starting to hear the *g* word and the *l* word. It was also a time of social turmoil, with the riots and rebellions. And I'm black, so beyond the gay issue, I was dealing with black pride and the issues of being black. It was a challenging time of looking at who I was and where I fit in.

Right as I was getting a sense of who I was, I started a relationship with a girl in Girl Scouts. I was about fourteen. We didn't have a real name for our relationship, but it felt right and it felt good. If my parents had had any doubt about my being a lesbian, they knew for sure when they walked in on us in the act.

In the years after that, my parents confiscated my mail and read it. They hired a private investigator. It was very, very serious. You see, this was before the consenting-adult laws were passed in California. The antisodomy laws were still on the books. My dad's attitude was, "We're pumping all this money into you, and you're throwing your life down the toilet." He believed that my sexuality would ruin my life because it was bad, evil, and criminal. He really thought I was sick, that there was something hormonally off. My mother was into her whole Satanic stuff, believing that the devil was after my soul. She's a Pentecostal Evangelist. So not only did I have to deal with my mother, I had to listen to the shit from the pulpit that was very condemning of gays.

My way of coping was to be an overachiever and to give my parents something to be proud of. My thinking was, OK, I'll live one life for you so you'll love me, but then, behind your back I'm going to sneak around and live the life I want to live. My plan was to infiltrate the system. That way, no one could get rid of me. I was in Girl Scouts all through high school. I was also student body president.

When I got to college—my parents insisted that I go to the University of Southern California [USC], which is where they met—I had my own Girl Scout troop. I was president of my mother's sorority and of the YWCA. It was a lot of women's stuff, but traditional women's stuff. In my other life I had a girlfriend. She lived in another city, so it was difficult for us to see each other a lot. But we kept up with correspondence—at least we did when the letters weren't confiscated.

At school I used to secretly read the *Lesbian Tide*, a lesbian feminist publication. It came in a brown envelope, and I'd hide it between my mattresses. I used to read it and think, *How could they be so dykey? How could they be playing baseball and have everybody know that they're out?* I was still very much into hiding then. But I eventually had the sense that I was getting a free ride, that there were a lot of people who were putting a lot of shit out on the line, and that I needed to stand up and be counted. I also did it for my life because I thought I was going to die if I didn't.

So in 1972 I started getting involved in gay activism and went to rap groups at the Gay and Lesbian Community Services Center in Los Angeles. Two years later, by the time I was eighteen, I was leading rap groups. I brought all of the political work that I had been doing in student government and civic things right into the gay movement. I got into the speakers' bureau early on and went to college campuses, church groups, community groups, and radio shows and talked about what it meant to be gay. I did that at my own school, as well. I helped train the campus psychological counselors on issues of homophobia. My therapist at school got me involved in that. She was the head of the counseling service at USC, and my saving grace.

I was one of the youngest people and one of the only blacks at the Gay and Lesbian Community Services Center. You can be sure that being black had an impact on how people dealt with me. I had the advantage of at least being educated on an undergraduate level. This was an advantage because I found there was a lot of academic bias within the gay and lesbian movement. The activists tended to be fairly well educated. If you split infinitives and couldn't write, your opinions were discounted. There are a lot of good grass-roots activists who are very bright people but who don't have college experience. I have watched time and time again for their opinions to be devalued or not to be taken seriously, particularly if they're people of color. I have encountered this attitude constantly. And there was just a lot of racism.

The racism took different forms in the gay community, but perhaps the most blatant kinds I encountered during those years were the exclusionary policies at the gay clubs, at places like Studio One. If you were black, you could only get in on a certain night. We used to call it "Plantation Night." We used to picket all the time. On the nights when blacks weren't welcome, which was most nights, they used the whole ID bullshit.

Zandra:

Certain people needed to show two or three picture IDs. How many people carry three picture IDs? They never said it was because you were black. But people of color would get carded heavily.

Deborah:

So if I went with a white friend, maybe I wouldn't make it in the door and they would. It made me beyond crazy. My feeling toward the discrimination was, *How fucking dare you? Who do you think you are?* You've got to realize that besides being lesbians, we're both women of color. You can't separate our lesbianism from our racial identities. So we're up against all kinds of stuff in the larger society. But when we came to the gay and lesbian community, we naively expected it to be more sensitive. Ironically, we found that the gay and lesbian community was much further behind than the straight community when it came to basic civil rights.

Zandra:

As an oppressed group, how can the lesbian and gay community oppress other people? How can you do that?

Deborah:

The clubs were the most blatant. Usually, it was more subtle. Part of the way racism displayed itself was in the lack of cultural sensitivities. If you want a certain kind of people to attend meetings or events, then you have to recruit. You've got to advertise. You have to solicit. You have to make the experience something they would want to be involved in. But what I kept getting over and over again was that people of color didn't matter and that we were somehow ancillary. And when black people showed up at meetings or social gatherings, they would get the cold shoulder. Nobody would ever talk to them. The insensitivities were really bad. And there were racial comments all the time.

Because I felt ostracized and because of my own need to socialize with other women of color, I started a big social-club network for black lesbians when I was twenty-one. We did social events for a number of years and had as many as six hundred women participating. I met Zandy at one of our events in June of 1980.

Zandra:

At the time we were with other women. I remember walking in and seeing her at the bar and thinking to myself, *Goddamn! Perfect!* Then I met her and realized, *I am going to get in trouble with this woman. Somehow, somewhere, I will definitely get in trouble with this woman.* It just so happened that Deborah's lover was a really good friend of my lover. So it turned out that we hung out with each other for that whole evening. After that evening, we would party together during the weekends—go to each other's houses for dinner.

Deborah:

Zandy and I were working together in the movement, too. Through this social group we started to become more political, and we started rap groups for black lesbians.

Zandra:

I was a spokesperson also. Whenever the occasion came up for gay people to speak on gay issues, I would always volunteer, whether that meant on radio talk shows, at colleges, in newspapers—anything and everything.

Well, the energy between the two of us was so strong that we could not be in the same room together. I would get too nervous, and she would get too nervous. The feeling was, "Let's not cross boundaries. We're in relationships." At that time I thought that she was happy in her relationship, and vice versa. Needless to say, we weren't, and two years after we met, we left our relationships to be with each other.

Deborah:

We'd been together as a couple for only about six months, when Zandy decided to take me out for a romantic dinner. This was Thursday night, January 13, 1983. We were both going to take off work the next day to honor Martin Luther King, Jr.'s, birthday, which was that Saturday. This was a year before his birthday was made a holiday.

Zandra:

Deborah had just gotten her review at work, and we were going out, in part, to celebrate.

Deborah:

I was working for Prudential in acquisitions and sales as a real estate investment manager. I went to work there after I finished my MBA at UCLA. January was my first six-month review, and it was a rave review.

Zandra:

A friend of mine, who happens to be straight, told me about this really nice French restaurant, called Papa Choux. She said the restaurant had these six private booths that were very romantic. I thought it would be just perfect. So I made the reservations and requested a booth. This was going to be a surprise to Deborah.

We got to the restaurant, and the waiter who seated us asked, "Are you sure you want a booth?" We insisted that yes, we did. So he showed us to a booth. It's the kind where you have to move the table out so you can get in. Right in front of the table was a little white sheer curtain that closed. The booths were set in a horseshoe, and in the middle of the horseshoe was a fountain. There was candlelight, and a violinist who came around. It was romantic.

We were taking our jackets off, and the waiter came back and took the table away and said, "You'll have to move. You can't sit here." He kept saying, "It's against the law to sit here." And we said, "What's against the law? What did we do?"

Deborah:

He went into all this bullshit about, "It's against the law to serve two men or two women in these booths." That's when we explained to

him that we had been activists for a very long time, and that was
bullshit. I told him, "If I can get a motel room with this woman, I
know I can eat with her."

Zandra:

Of course, at that point, everybody was looking out of their little
booths to see what was going on. We asked to see the manager.

Deborah:

We were not going to move.

Zandra:

The manager came over, or at least we thought we were talking to the
manager—we found out later that he was the maître d'. He kept giving
us the back-of-the-bus type of thing. "Well, you can sit over there,
and you can have free drinks, but you cannot sit here. You will not
be served here." He kept insisting that it was against the law.

Deborah:

It makes me crazy thinking about it. You have to remember that we
were there, in part, because of Martin Luther King's birthday. We
were going to take off the next day from work as this real show of
solidarity. And if there's anything that King had taught us, it was that
we could sit anywhere in the restaurant that we wanted to sit. This was
just bizarre. And now I was pissed because this guy was trying to use
the law against people he thought didn't know the law. That's what
they used to do in the South—deny you your rights by telling you
you're breaking the law.

Zandra:

The maître d' finally got off it and said, "It is the house policy to serve
only couples in these booths, and the manager is very, very adamant
about it."

Deborah:

We said, "A couple of what?" At one of the press conferences later
he said that it was for mixed couples. It's not hard to see that we're

a mixed couple. But he kept on and he made it quite plain that the owner was adamant that no two men and no two women were going to be served there. This went on for fifteen minutes. We weren't budging, and we were screaming at each other. He looked at us like, "You can rot. You can freeze your ass over in hell. We will serve you someplace else, but this section is for other kinds of people than you."

Zandra:

We left there fuming. We took the names of everyone on staff. I had never, ever blatantly been denied anything because of who I was, ever. I knew about the discrimination that went on. My grandfather was discriminated against in the same way that blacks were discriminated against. But never had it happened to me. I had never been told that I couldn't do something or have something or be somewhere because of who I was or because of the color of my skin. How dare you! How dare you! Besides this, they completely blew my romantic date!

Deborah:

Zandy had all these expectations about what this evening was going to be. I didn't have any expectations, and to me it was the same old shit. It was like, "OK, here's some more butt we've got to kick." Whereas, for her, that Latin embarrassment came out. Now, I don't know if you know much about Latinos. First off, we're "the family," the two of us. And these people fucked with the family. Latinos have an expectation of respect. When they don't get it, they're hurt and they're pissed. But black people don't have an expectation of respect, so when we get it, we're surprised.

Zandra:

We left the restaurant knowing that we had to do something. I didn't know what it was, but we had to do something.

Deborah:

We thought, *Shit, let's sue the motherfuckers!* We decided that we were going to talk to Gloria Allred, who is a famous civil rights attorney.

Zandra:

She's a hard-hitting feminist attorney . . .

Deborah:

. . . who wins her cases. You name it, she wins. Gloria is also a media queen—nobody works the media like this woman does. And her law firm is good. They are the best, and they're bad. People tremble when they know Gloria Allred is coming because she wins. And while she's not a lesbian, she has won some of the biggest gay rights cases.

Zandra:

She didn't know if we had a case until after she did some research. Then she told us that we did have a case, that there was a city ordinance that prohibited discrimination on the basis of sexual preference.

Deborah:

But the ordinance was untested. She told us up front, "It's a very gray area of the law here, but I think we have a chance. And what's more, this case offers the possibility of doing some very important public consciousness-raising concerning issues of discrimination." Having a public case was not our intention. My intention when I went to Gloria was just to get the restaurant to stop discriminating, that's all. Do whatever you've got to do, but we don't want this to go on anymore.

This is the point when I got scared. I was afraid of what kind of impact the publicity would have. Quite frankly, I was afraid for my job. I had just graduated. I worked damn hard to get my MBA. I worked in financial investments in the biggest insurance company in the world. I'm black, and I'm a lesbian. And now I was going to be an out lesbian bringing a public lawsuit? I knew I was putting it all on the line. That made my parents beyond nuts because they felt I was just making it—making good money. "Are you a fool? What's wrong with you?" But I decided to go ahead and do it.

Zandra:

I made her do it.

Deborah:

No, you didn't make me. But you made it quite plain: "Shit or get off the pot." I made the decision to do it because I was madly in love, and I am still madly in love. To me, that is still the bottom-line issue that people don't understand. As I explained to my mother, "Either this is a country where I can live openly with this woman and love her the way I want to, or it isn't. And if it's not, tell me now—I'll go to Canada; I'll go to Sweden."

As far as my job was concerned, my attitude began to change. I decided that I didn't want to be someplace that really didn't want me. As I told my mother, "If I'm going to get fired because I'm a lesbian, I'm going to get fired because I'm a lesbian whether I sue Papa Choux or not." In other words, if my being a lesbian was going to be an issue, there was going to come a point where I was going to bottom out at that company, and I would rather know now that they don't like lesbians than wait ten years after I've invested sweat and blood someplace where I'm not wanted.

Zandra:

What ended up happening was that we announced the lawsuit in front of the restaurant.

Deborah:

We had a whole picnic scene. They wouldn't let us eat inside the restaurant, so we were going to eat outside.

Zandra:

It was media galore.

When the restaurant found out that we were suing them, instead of saying, "OK, we'll change the policy. Here's a free dinner," they said, "Fuck you!" They put ads in the paper saying, "They can send us to jail. They can hang us by our thumbs. But we're not going to serve two men or two women."

Deborah:

They said things like, "This makes a mockery, a charade, out of true romantic dining." Quarter-page ads in the *L.A. Times!*

Zandra:

"Gloria Allred has gone too far in leading her own parade, but we will never serve two men or two women."

Very quickly our story was front page in the newspapers. Every time you turned on the news, there it was: "Lesbian couple sues restaurant. . . ." Then Deborah started chickening out because our story was everywhere.

Deborah:

I began taking my fears and frustrations out on our relationship. What Zandy said to me was, "I'm not the one you're fighting. And if you're going to fight me, fuck it, it's just not worth it." I was testy; I was nervous; my parents were on my ass. It was rough. Then there was the whole corporate thing—it was a lot of pressure. My face was being plastered all over the television news and all over the L.A. Times.

Media was nothing new to us—we had done media stuff before. But when we agreed to go along with Gloria, we had no idea how big this thing was going to be. So it got to a point where I had to decide if I was going to stay with it.

We hadn't been together that long, and when we got together, I was not in the best shape. Emotionally I was just a wreck. And it began to feel like everything I was working for was going down the tubes. When Zandy first came into my life, amazingly my father fully embraced her. I mean, the man never cared about anybody I was with, not even so much as a friend. With Zandy he said, "This is my daughter." He even told her that she was the answer to his prayers for me! God, I was surprised. Then the lawsuit hit in the news, and we got this message on our answering machine. He was furious, "If I hear anymore, ANYTHING, about this GODDAMN restaurant thing, I am THROUGH with BOTH OF YOU!" The next morning we got a whole page in the L.A. Times with our pictures and everything. I was scared. I was scared because my family relationship was going right down the tubes, and at work it was a chill. I was a coward—I was a pure coward.

Zandra:

They still talked to her at the office, but nobody would bring up the issue.

Deborah:

It was very strained. I would have to leave work to go to court. It was hard to go to court and come back. I always made sure that I clocked out on my vacation time.

My boss and I finally had a discussion about it. He was a young Jewish guy. He liked Zandy and me a lot. He let me know that it had gone all the way up to headquarters in Newark and that the attorneys had discussed what to do with me—what to do with this "problem." They had caught the story out there, too, because it was airing everywhere. He said that they weren't going to fuck with me. His words were, "If you would sue over a restaurant, imagine what you would do over your job. And they don't want Gloria Allred down there on the steps of our building." He said that I had insulated myself by being so bold.

Then the head honcho came down one day and called the entire office together for an impromptu meeting. He said, "There's a rumor going around here. . . ." And I thought, *Oh, holy Jesus!* I was scared to death. "There's a rumor around that says if you work here for so many years, you're automatically going to get rewarded and that this is the only way you can get promoted, by staying here long enough. But that's not true. It's performance that counts, and I'm here to congratulate Deborah Johnson." They gave me an early promotion—a year early!

The promotion was encouraging because at the time we were still losing our case in the courts.

Zandra:

We lost the first two rounds.

Deborah:

It was scary because we were losing ground that the gay rights movement had already won. I was afraid we were setting the movement backwards, but I knew in the end that we had to continue the battle because I felt that if I didn't do something, I was never going to be able to sleep.

When we first filed the case, we filed under two laws. One was the local city ordinance, which prohibited discrimination on the basis of sexual orientation in housing, employment, and public accommodations. We also filed under the California State Unruh Civil Rights Act, which prohibits discrimination on the basis of sex, creed, race, color, and nationality, but doesn't specifically say sexual orientation.

We went to court the first time for an injunction asking the restaurant not to discriminate anymore. The lower court said, "No, we're not going to do that because we think it's an important issue, and it should really go to trial. If we issue that injunction, the restaurant may be hurt and, furthermore, we're not so sure that you had any rights as lesbians because we think there is a double standard in society." In other words, the judge said that behavior that was OK for straight people in public was not necessarily OK for gay people and that the public might be offended by us.

So we went to court again, but this time for what's called a "motion of summary judgment," which is in lieu of a trial. It's basically, "Here are all the facts. Nobody disputes the facts. Give us a ruling." Papa Choux never disputed the facts. The management even produced Zandy's name in the reservation book. This second judge didn't want to touch it with a ten-foot pole either, so we went on to the state appellate court.

Zandra:

Every time we went to court, every time there was a ruling, there was major press coverage. We were in magazines and every single newspaper.

Deborah:

And the restaurant kept taking all these ads out against us. It just became this big media zoo.

The appellate court overturned the lower court decisions and said, "You cannot discriminate arbitrarily like that. It's class discrimination. You can't do that." The restaurant petitioned the state supreme court, which declined to hear the case. That meant the appellate court's ruling was going to stand. We had won. The lower court issued the injunction and the motion of summary of judgment. Papa Choux paid all the attorneys' fees, which were almost $30,000. They also paid us $250 apiece, which was their fine for breaking the local ordinance.

But rather than serve us and comply with the law, Papa Choux just closed the booths. They said, "Fuck you! We're not going to do it at all!" So they had a public wake, with the television cameras from the eleven o'clock news and the whole bit. They gave out free drinks and declared, "True romantic dining died on this day." It's kind of like what they did in Mississippi and Alabama. Instead of letting the black kids swim in the public pools, they just closed the pools.

Deborah:

Politically, the timing of the court's decision was incredible because we won the exact same day that the state law that would have banned discrimination in employment based upon sexual preference was vetoed by Governor Deukmejian. That was April 1984.

Zandra:

So within Los Angeles County we were protected by law, but in the state we weren't.

Deborah:

But through our case, we not only put teeth into the local ordinance, which had never been tested before, but on the state level, we became one more instance where the state civil rights act was applied to gays and lesbians. What the appellate court said was that the list that included sex, race, creed, et cetera was meant to be illustrative, not exhaustive, and that we were to be included. So we won under both the local gay rights ordinance and the state civil rights law. We became a precedent-setting case. The case is in the law books now, so for gay rights it's done a lot. They certified it for publication, which is very rare. Now other people can use our suit as precedent anywhere in California. And emotionally, winning was just such a matter of pride.

Zandra:

In the end, it turned out to be bigger than what we ever expected. We had no intention of being a test case, and we wound up being heroes to the gay community. The level of respect that came with all of that was incredible. I had never, ever been so out. There was no one I needed to come out to anymore. By bringing this case, we said, "This is who we are. This is our relationship. And we will sue the restaurant—we will sue anybody—if we don't get the respect that we want."

The case also solidified our relationship because the whole thing had been a question of "Are we a family or aren't we?" And it solidified our relationship not only for us, but within the community, with our friends, and with our family.

The relationship was always the number one thing. We were not willing to put our relationship on the line, but we were willing to put everything else on the line for our relationship.

The Bridge Builder

Kathleen Boatwright

INVARIABLY WEARING *a sensible Sears dress or skirt and jacket, Kathleen Boatwright doesn't look the part of a social activist, as she describes herself. But as vice president of the Western Region of Integrity, the gay and lesbian Episcopal ministry, Kathleen uses her conventional appearance, her status as a mother of four, her Christian roots, her knowledge of the scriptures, and her disarming personal warmth to wage a gentle battle for reform in the church she loves—and to change the hearts and minds of individuals within the church. According to Kathleen, "I see myself uniquely gifted to show people what we do to each other in ignorance."*

Kathleen Boatwright's very difficult and painful journey from fundamentalist Christian, director of the children's choir at her local church, and pillar of her community to Episcopal lesbian activist began one day in August 1984, when Jean, a veterinary student at Oregon State University, walked through the door of Kathleen's church in Corvallis, Oregon.

The first time I met Jean, she was having a nice conversation with my fifteen-year-old daughter at our church. I was very impressed by the mature way in which she spoke to my daughter. Then, during the service, I sat in the front row and watched Jean sing. I was so enamored by her presence that she stuck in my mind. But then she left town and was gone until January the following year.

Come January, I was sitting in church and I looked across the room, and there was Jean, carrying her guitar, walking down the aisle with such determination. I had this incredible lump in my throat, and I said to myself, *Jean's back.* After the service, and despite my difficulty talking to new people, I just had to ask Jean where she had been. I had to talk to her.

I found out that she was back in Corvallis for five months to finish her degree. She didn't have a place to live. So I said to her, "Don't worry, my parents have always wanted to take in a college student. You're redheaded like Dad. They'll love it!" I went and dragged my mother away from where she was talking and I said, "You remember Jean, she's looking for a place to stay. Why don't you and Dad take her in and board her?"

From early on my parents encouraged the friendship because they saw how much Jean meant to me. Meeting her brought me to life in a way they hadn't seen before. They knew that I used to cry for hours on end when I was a child because no girls liked me at school. My mother would come in and rub my leg or pat my hand. I was extremely intelligent and bright, but I had low self-esteem because I wasn't able to find friendship. So my parents encouraged Jean to invite me to lunch or to take me for a drive or go horseback riding. They felt that her friendship was really wonderful for me. They were glad I was happy. For a while.

My husband didn't pay much attention—at first. He was a state policeman and had always been nonparticipatory, both as a parent and a spouse.

After four months of being friends, of having this wonderful platonic relationship, Jean had to go away for a month for her externship. While she was away she met a fundamentalist couple. Well, Jean sent me a postcard and said, "Something's going on. I'm playing with fire. I can't handle it. I've got to talk to you." My heart wrenched. What was going on?

When we were finally able to meet and talk, Jean explained to me how she and this fundamentalist woman started sharing in an intimate way. My response was to put my arm through hers and say, "Don't worry. We'll get it fixed." Jean couldn't be homosexual because it was wrong. Besides, if she was homosexual, then she would be leaving my life. And I think on a deeper level, I didn't want Jean exploring these things with anyone but me.

AFTER HER externship, Jean wanted to be more sensual with me. Her attitude was, "Now I'm going to show *you*." She said, "I'll give you a back rub some night." So one night—after Bible study, no less—she was over at my house and said, "Why don't you lay down on the blanket on the floor and take off your blouse and bra and I'll rub your back?" And I was like, "Okaaay!" My husband was working all night, and this just seemed like a great setup. So this nice little Christian lady rubbed my back, and I said to myself, *Gee, this is it!*

All the little pieces, all the little feelings came together. Even comments my mother made to me over the years began to make sense. She'd say things like, "Don't cut your hair too short." "You can't wear tailored clothes." It was then that I also realized that the neighbors I had grown up with were a lesbian couple, even though I had never thought about that before. I recalled the feeling of walking through the Waldenbooks bookstore, looking at *The Joy of Lesbian Sex* and longing for that kind of intimacy. It all came upon me at that moment, and I felt a real willingness to release myself to this person in a way I had never done before. Then the phone rang. It was my son from Bible college. I thought, *Oh, God, saved by the bell! I don't know where this would have gone.*

By the end of the month, Jean was graduating, taking her national boards, and trying to figure out what to do about her feelings toward me and what to do about the fundamentalist woman. It was Pentecostal hysteria.

Now don't forget, at this time I still had a husband and four kids. I had a nineteen-year-old son at a conservative Bible college. I had a sixteen-year-old daughter in the evangelical Christian high school, of which I was a board member. Two children were in parochial day school. My father was the worship leader at church. And I was still very bound to my parents for emotional support. I was the favorite child. And my grandparents lived in town.

Well, shit, I was in way over my head. I was really painted into a corner because there wasn't a single place I could turn for even questioning. So I started looking to some Christian sources. Some of the advice was so incredible, like, "If you feel homosexual tendencies, you can't have the person you have those feelings for over to your house in the evening." "You can never let a member of the same sex sit on your bed while you're chatting." "Meet only in a public place." I thought this advice was ridiculous, but I also thought it was my only option because my spiritual nature was more important than my physical nature. Intellectually and emotionally, I was so hungry and so turned on that I didn't know what to do with my feelings.

At this point, people pull the trigger, turn to the bottle, take drugs, leave town. But I didn't do any of those things because I was madly in love. If I had pulled the trigger, I wouldn't have been able to express the part of me I had discovered. I had found someone, someone who shared the same sort of values I had.

Everything reached a crisis point. I acknowledged to myself and to Jean that I was a lesbian and that I loved her. By this time we had already been sexually active. My husband began to get suspicious that something was going on, and he and I went into counseling. Jean was leaving for a job in Colorado and told me that I couldn't go with her because she was a responsible woman and didn't want to destroy my family. And I still hadn't yet found the spiritual guidance that I needed.

I had to get away and do some soul-searching. I needed to figure out if there was any Christian support somewhere that said I could reconcile my love for Jean and my love for my faith. I didn't feel I could build a life of love if I rejected my faith. So I packed my bags and told my parents that I was leaving to go to stay with my great-aunt in Los Angeles for ten days. I told my husband, "I am going to get away and I'm going to think about a bunch of issues, and then I'm coming back."

For the first time in my entire life, at the age of thirty-six, I was by myself with my own agenda. I had left my husband, my children, my parents, my support structures; got in a car; and started driving to West Hollywood, where I knew there was a lesbian mayor and a gay community. So surely, I thought, there had to be a spiritual gay community.

In West Hollywood I found Evangelicals Together. It's not a church, just a storefront ministry to the gay community for people coming out of an evangelical Christian background. It's led by a former American Baptist minister who talked my language. He said to me, "In order to deal with your dilemma, you have to take a step back from your relationship with Jean. Lay her aside and ask yourself, *Who did God create me to be?*"

Through our sharing, and by looking from a different perspective at the gospel and what Jesus had to say, I could embrace the theology that said, "God knew me before I was born. He accepted me as I was made to be, uniquely and wholly." Ultimately, in an obedience to God, you answer that call to be all that He has created you to be. I felt firmly and wholly that what I had experienced with Jean was no demonic possession, was not Satan tempting me with sins of lust, but an intimacy and a love that was beautiful and was God given. So now I had to figure out how to deal with it.

When you're my age, you're either going to go back to the way it's always been—go for the security you've always known—or take a chance. I felt that for the love I felt for Jean I was willing to risk all. Of course, having Jean there, I was hedging my bet a bit. I was jumping off a cliff, but I was holding somebody's hand.

Jean flew down a few days later to join me in Los Angeles. She agreed to commit to me and I to her. The first Sunday after we affirmed our relationship, we worshiped at All Saints' Episcopal Church in Pasadena because I was told that the Episcopals had the framework of faith I loved, as well as an ability to use reason in light of tradition and scripture.

It was God answering the cry of my heart to send me to that worshiping place. Jean and I had never been to an Episcopal church before. We went into this beautiful place with the largest Episcopal congregation west of the Mississippi River. We sat in the fourth row. It was just this incredible Gothic wonderful place. It was All Saints' Day at All Saints' Church. They played the Mozart Requiem with a full choir and a chamber ensemble, and a female celebrant sang the liturgy. We held hands and wept and wept. We could go forward because in the Anglican tradition, the Eucharist is open for everyone. God extends himself. There are no outcasts in the Episcopal church.

WHEN I got back to town, I met with my husband at a counselor's office. I said, "Yes, you're right. I am gay and I'm going to ask for a divorce. I'm going to take this stand. I want to meet with my older children and my parents to talk about the decisions I've made." I felt at least I had a right to make my own decisions. I went to pick up my two youngest girls at my father's house. I went to open the door and I heard a flurry of activity, and the children saw me. "Oh, Mommy's home! Mommy's home!" And my dad stepped out on the front porch and pushed the children away and slammed the door. He took me forcibly by the arm and led me down the stairs and said, "You're never seeing your children again without a court order! Just go shack up with your girlfriend!" And he forced me down to the street.

It took going to court to see my two youngest children. They hadn't seen me for two weeks. They asked, "Mommy, Mommy, what's wrong?" I leaned over and whispered in their ears, "Mommy loves you." My husband wanted to know, "What are you telling the children?" I had only a minute with them, then went downstairs, and my husband told me that he wanted me to come back, that he would be my brother, not my husband.

I tell you, my whole world came down upon my ears. I wasn't allowed to see my children. I was denied access to my residence. The church had an open prayer meeting disclosing my relationship with Jean. They tried to get Jean fired from her job. And when that didn't work, they called Jean's parents, who then tried to have her committed or have me arrested. My family physically disinherited me and emotionally cut me off. My older daughter, upon the advice of her counselor-pastor, shook my hand and said, "Thank you for being my biological mother. I never want to have anything to do with you again." After that, whenever she saw me in town, she hid from me. I saw her lay flat on the asphalt in the grocery store parking lot so I wouldn't see her. People I'd known all my life avoided me like I had the plague. I was surprised that Jean didn't just say, "Hey, lady, I'm out of here!"

Fortunately, I wasn't entirely without support. I went to Parents and Friends of Lesbians and Gays and I met some wonderful loving, Christian, supportive parents and gay children who said, "You're not sick. You're not weird. Everybody's hysterical." They offered any

Kathleen Boatwright convening a meeting of Western Region
representatives at the 1989 Integrity National Convention. Terry Lewis,
acting secretary of the Western Region, is seated at right. (© *Loudene*
"Gil" Grady)

kind of assistance possible. Through their emotional support, I felt
like it was possible to survive the crush.

LIVING IN a small rural county in Oregon, I didn't know anything
about women's rights, let alone gay rights. So it's not surprising that
I bought into the lie that children of lesbians or gays are better off
living with the custodial heterosexual parent. I believed my husband
could provide a sense of normality that I could not. So I signed away
my custodial rights and became a secondary parent. After being the
primary-care parent for twenty devoted years, the judge only let me
see the children two days a week.

By then I'd had enough. So I packed one suitcase and a few things
in grocery sacks and left my family and children behind. Jean and I
just rode quietly out of town in the sunset to her job in Denver,
Colorado.

As you drive into Denver, you go over this big hill about fifteen
miles from town. We stopped at a phone booth and called the local
Parents FLAG president to ask if there was a supportive Episcopal
parish in town. She said, "Yes, go to this place, look up this person."

It was getting to be evening. It was clear, and we were going over the mountain. It was a whole new adventure. It was real closure to my past and a real opening toward my future. Still, the guiding force in my life was, "The church has the answers."

Jean and I called the church and found out when services were and asked if they had an Integrity chapter. Integrity is the Episcopal ministry to the gay and lesbian community. There was one, so two nights later we walked into our first Integrity meeting. There were twelve attractive men in their thirties and the rector. They were shocked to see two women because it's unusual for women to be in Integrity. The only thing dirtier than being a lesbian in a Christian community is being a Christian in the lesbian community because it brings in so many other issues besides sexual orientation, like women's issues and patriarchy and all that stuff.

Denver Integrity was an affirming congregation. We were out as a couple. We were healed of so many things through the unconditional love and acceptance of this parish of eighty people. The rector there encouraged me to become involved. Out of his own pocket he sent me to the first regional convention I went to, in 1987 in San Francisco. Now, I'm vice president of the Western Region for Integrity, and I'm on the national board of directors. I'm one of only maybe 125 women in Integrity's membership of about 1,500.

Integrity gives me a forum for the things I want to say, both as a lesbian woman and as a committed Christian. And because of my background and experience, I can speak to the church I love on a variety of issues that others cannot. I can say, "I call you into accountability. You are bastardizing children raised in nontraditional households. You're not affirming the people that love and guide them. You say you welcome us, but on the other hand you don't affirm us. You don't give us rites of passage and ritual and celebration like you do for heterosexual families."

The church needs to change. What we're asking for are equal *rites*. We're asking the church to bless same-sex unions. I'm asking for canonical changes that affirm my wholeness as a child of Christ who is at the same time in a loving committed relationship with a woman. We're also challenging the church to make statements asking the government to legitimize our relationships and give us the same sorts of tax breaks, pension benefits, et cetera. But most importantly, we need the church to get off the dime and start affirming gay and lesbian children's lives. I never want a girl to go through what I went through. I want to spare everybody right up front.

* * *

To GET my point across when I go out and talk to groups as a representative of Integrity, I personalize the issue. I personalize my political activism by speaking to people as a person, as Kathleen Boatwright. People don't need to hear dogma or doctrine or facts or theology. They need to meet people.

Here's a great example. For the first time, the women of Integrity got seated at Triennial, which is this gigantic group of very traditional women who have a convention every three years. It used to be that while the men were making the decisions, the women held their own convention. With women's issues having changed so dramatically in the Episcopal church, that's no longer true. Now that women are allowed to serve in the House of Deputies and can be ordained into the priesthood, we've become full team members in the canonical process.

Triennial was made for me. Everybody wears their Sears Roebuck dress. Everybody is a mom. Everybody lived like I had lived for twenty years. I know how to network and how to deal with those women. But I also have a new truth to tell them that will have an impact on their lives in very special ways. Gays and lesbians are 10 percent of the population. Everybody is personally affected by that issue, including these women at Triennial.

During the convention, I attended a seminar given by conservative Episcopals who said gays and lesbians have confused gender identity. Later, we had an open meeting in which we talked about human sexuality. But no one talked about sexuality. Instead, we only talked about information on biological reproduction. After about forty minutes of hearing these women drone on, I stood up in my Sears Roebuck dress and said, "OK ladies, put on your seat belts because you're going to take a trip into reality. You won't want to hear it, but I need to say it because you need to know what people's lives are really like."

I talked to them about my journey. I talked to them about the misnomers, about "confused gender identity." I was wearing this circle skirt and I said, "As you can see from my appearance," and I curtsied, "I do not have a 'confused gender identity.'" Everybody who had been really stiff started laughing—and they started listening. The key is that I take risks. I risk being vulnerable. I risk sharing the secrets of my heart. We already know what the straight people feel in their hearts. But no one talks about how the lesbian or gay person feels in his or her heart.

For the next hour and a half, people talked about where they really live. They talked about their pregnant teenagers or the suicide attempts in their families. All those gut-level issues. But you have to have someone lead you to that. That's me—because I'm safe. I've also learned that instead of having all the answers, that God calls me to listen to people's pain, and not to judge it.

This one woman told me that she had been driving by her daughter's house for eight years and that her husband had never let her stop because her daughter was a lesbian. "But," she said, "I'm going to go home and I'm going to see her. My daughter's name is also Kathleen." Then she started to cry. She had never even told the women from her church about what had happened to her daughter. It's like the living dead for many Christian families. They just have a child who is lost prematurely in so many senses of the word.

Inevitably, everywhere I go I hear about parents who have made ultimatums. This one mother said, "I've never told anybody, but I said to my son, 'I wish you were dead.' And by forcing him into the closet, I fulfilled that prophecy. Three years later, he was dead." Then there was a woman who said to me, "Kathleen, I'm questioning my sexuality at seventy. Could you send me some information?"

I think in my heart that I represent the hidden majority of lesbian women because many, many are married or have been married, have children, and have too much to risk—like I've risked and lost—to come out. And those women who are out, who are much more political and aggressive, have seen enough successes happen, enough bridges built by my approach, that they're beginning to respect the fact that I can go through doors they never can.

The first time I spoke publicly to the leadership of the women of the church, I spoke along with another lesbian. She was politically correct and a strong feminist. *Feminist* was always a dirty word for me, so I've had to overcome a lot of my own bias. I said to her, "Please, don't speak about politics. Don't brow beat these people. Stand up and say that you're a doctor, that you've never been in a committed relationship, that you're a feminist. Because I want to stand up and say, 'I've been a Blue Bird leader.' What that will say is that we represent the gamut of human experience, just like the heterosexual community. It's just our ability to develop intimate relationships with the same sex that makes us different."

People don't have to identify with my ideology. They identify with my person, and then the questions come from them. We don't have to tell them. They start asking us. People say to me, "What do you call your partner?" "You don't have any medical insurance?" To me that's the best sort of teaching process: answering questions rather than giving information.

*   *   *

MY HUSBAND remarried; he married the baby-sitter. At Easter of 1987, I got a call informing me that he had removed my ten-year-old daughter from his house, accusing her of using "inappropriate touch" with his new stepsons. He wanted to unload the difficult child. Then he used that child as a weapon to try and deny me visitation for the younger one. The end result was that I had one child and he had one child. I filed suit against him without any hope or prayer of winning back custody of my other child.

I went to a lesbian minister to ask her about finding a lawyer to handle my case, and she said to me, "The best attorney in this town is Hal Harding, but he's your husband's attorney. Maybe that will prove to be a blessing." So I had to find another attorney.

As part of the custody proceedings, Jean and I eventually met with my husband's attorney. He took depositions and asked Jean and me really heartfelt questions. Then he advised his client—my ex-husband—to go ahead and have a psychological evaluation. The court had not ordered it and, in fact, would not order it because there was no precedent in that county. But my former husband agreed to go to the psychologist of his choice. That psychologist, a woman, took the time and energy to interview every person involved and recommended to the court that Jean and I become custodial parents. We now have custody of both children, sole custody. It was indeed a blessing.

We just added Jean's ninety-one-year-old grandmother to our family. So we are all-American lesbians living here in Greenacres, Washington. We are Miss and Mrs. America living together. The thing that we need in our life now that our faith doesn't give us is a community of supportive women. We have yet to find that place.

NOT LONG ago, I went to the National Organization for Women lesbian rights agenda meeting and gave a workshop on spirituality for women, from the Christian perspective. And I took a deep breath in my Betty Crocker suit—if I ever write a book it's going to be *The Radicalization of Betty Crocker*—and thought, *I wonder what the Assemblies of God girls would say now? From their perspective, I'm walking into the total pit of hell, and I'm bringing the very gift that they should be giving.* Who would have believed it?

The Brave Alaskan

Sara Boesser

SARA BOESSER *said she had long planned to become a gay rights activist, though not until she was an "old fart." But the threat of AIDS and a rising tide of antigay sentiment rolling north from the lower forty-eight toward Sara's hometown of Juneau, Alaska's capital, accelerated her schedule. In 1985, while in her early thirties, Sara helped create an organization to cope with the anticipated arrival of AIDS. Sara's AIDS education and advocacy work have since developed into a high-profile role in the struggle for lesbian and gay equal rights in her hometown and state.*

Sara Boesser grew up in Juneau, today a city of about twenty-nine thousand, where the sun sets at 3:30 P.M. on winter afternoons. When she was growing up, television programs arrived by plane two weeks late. Even now, the only way to get in and out of Juneau is by air or water. Sara left Juneau in 1970 to attend the University of the Pacific in California. She remained in the lower forty-eight for the next dozen years, returning in 1982 with her partner, Carol Zimmerman.

Today, Sara and Carol live in a comfortable house a few miles from downtown Juneau, within earshot of a tumbling stream fed by the massive Mendenhall Glacier in the nearby valley. Sara is employed by the city and borough of Juneau as a building inspector.

The first time I heard the word *gay* was in 1967, when I was a junior in high school. I asked my friends what it meant. The description I got was of two women or two men who spent their lives together. I went home and took my dog for a walk, and I thought, *That's perfect. That's what I am!* I knew my parents weren't going to like it, but I was real excited to know I fit in somewhere. Before I knew what gay was, I always had a sense that I was an odd duck because I wasn't interested in dating boys. I have three younger sisters, and I was definitely out of step with their interest in boys.

Once I knew I was gay, I still didn't talk to anybody about it for a couple of years. I knew that it was a hush-hush subject just from the tone of that first conversation. So I started looking for books on homosexuality, but it took me until college to find one. The first book

I found was a collection of psychological studies of people who had tried to commit suicide because of their sexual orientation. I read it and thought, *I might be gay, but I'm definitely not like these people!*

That first year at college I sort of put out feelers for other women who were like me. I'd talk about unusual women, or women who liked women, but nobody ever responded in a way that made me feel comfortable enough to go further with the conversation. It wasn't until I was on an archaeological dig in Washington State that I met another lesbian. We were there the whole summer, and it was great to have somebody to be open with. It was a wonderful feeling.

WHEN I left Juneau for college, I made a commitment to myself that I wasn't going to move back home unless I came back with a partner. Even at that young age I thought it would be very lonely to live here as a lesbian because at the time I left, I didn't know there were any lesbians in Juneau. I finished up my degree in anthropology in Seattle, and because I hadn't yet met anyone to take back to Juneau, I stayed there.

During the years I was in Seattle, I got involved in some gay activism through the campaign to fight the repeal of the Seattle gay rights ordinance. That's when I found out about the Dorian Group, which was an organization for gay professional people. I was amazed that all these gay people came to the Dorian Group's monthly dinners in a public place and that traditional politicians would come to speak to us. But I stayed on the sidelines of Dorian and just soaked up information; I was a real loner.

During the twelve years I lived in Seattle, I often thought about how I might like to be involved in gay rights activism one day. In the mid-1970s, I was living with a woman in a tiny one-bedroom house near Seattle that had wood heat and cold running water. Life was not easy. Once, we were trying to build a fire in the wood stove and were talking about our aspirations. It was one of those conversations where you talk about what you think you were meant to do in this life. I said, "Someday, when I get to be an old fart, I'm going to be a gay rights activist." I guess the reason I said that was because I knew things needed to be changed. For example, I didn't like the fact that I had to lead a double life. I was raised to be an honest, outgoing individual, and I had come to this point in my life where I could not be myself with most people because I was gay. I was afraid that if I let people know I was gay, I would run the risk of losing friends, or I would have difficulty working with my colleagues. So I was more withdrawn and less sincere and less direct than I would like to have been. People still respected me and thought I was a good person, but in the back of my mind was the thought, *You may like me, but I'm also gay and you think you hate gays.* It made me furious that people could like me and hate gay people. It also made me furious that I was being quiet about it and knew that someday I would have to speak up.

SEVERAL YEARS later, in 1982, I came back to Juneau with my new partner, Carol. Within a short time, I was getting newsletters from all over the country and I was reading about a lot of gay men dying from this unknown disease. There were horror stories about how they were not only dying, but were also being abandoned by their families, losing their jobs, and losing their insurance. There was even fear that there would be legislation to quarantine homosexuals. With the coming of AIDS, I realized I couldn't postpone forever what was important to me because I might not get to be an old fart. I had to take my stand today because tomorrow might not be here.

Some people considered AIDS to be an issue for the men only, but from what I read it seemed that homosexual rights in general were at stake. It occurred to me that if the men lost their rights, I'd lose mine, as well—after all, the word *homosexual* includes me. But more than that, if these people were being discriminated against on the same grounds of who I was—a homosexual—then I needed to stand up with them. It just didn't seem right to stand by and let them take all the heat.

I don't remember exactly how the first meeting took place, but somebody put out a call in 1985 for lesbians to come meet with the friends and relatives of a gay man who was dying of AIDS. This was just an informal educational thing where a public health nurse came to talk about AIDS. After that, we met weekly to choose spots on a twenty-four-hour "companionship schedule" to take care of him in his home so he could stay out of the hospital. By the time I was called in, which was months later, he was extremely ill and clearly near death. I took some custard for him to eat. He slept most of the time, so I just played some music for him. And when he was awake, we couldn't communicate because he had lost the ability to talk and he couldn't see. It was heart wrenching. That was the only time I saw him because he died a short time later.

From these weekly meetings, we put together a new organization, SEAGLA, the Southeast Alaska Gay and Lesbian Alliance. It was primarily a social organization at the start, a way to network, to find each other. We had events where people could mix; it was the first opportunity for lesbians and gay men in Juneau to meet. Besides organizing social events, we also became interested in pursuing gay and lesbian equal rights laws here in Alaska, and we very quickly organized a group called Shanti to take care of people with AIDS. We used the Shanti organization in San Francisco as our model, but because people weren't getting sick in the numbers we anticipated, we ended up emphasizing education about prevention.

I became co-coordinator of Shanti and put together workshops for ministers and counselors. We got news articles together and figured out how to get money. Then we started getting calls from other cities and villages. We were a constant response team, and, at the same time, we had to keep our own volunteers organized and energized.

I was often invited to speak to different groups of people. My favorite group was the Soroptimists, a philanthropic women's group—businesswomen and churchwomen, the upstanding women of the greater Juneau community. The Soroptimists wanted an AIDS education talk during their lunch. One of our Shanti nurses, Kim, was going to speak with me, but she had to cancel at the last minute, so without having ever done this before, I had to do the safe-sex part of the talk. Here were these women eating their lunch, and I got going on how to use a condom! I was embarrassed, and they were embarrassed, and we all chuckled about it.

The Soroptimists didn't know that I was a lesbian. It seemed important to me to keep the lesbian-gay issue sort of subdued in Shanti, so we could get heterosexual people involved, too. It was important that our outreach be accepted by the greater community, that people didn't view us just as a gay and lesbian group or view our services as exclusively for gay men. We also got a lot of funding from the state, and I was concerned that if we were too openly gay or lesbian in our individual presentations that somebody might cut our funding. It was an awful feeling.

WHILE THE AIDS work was satisfying, I was still very interested in gay rights, and attending three different events in 1987 helped push me in that direction. One was the march on Washington in 1987, another was a National Organization for Women [NOW] Conference, and the third was the National Lesbian Rights Agenda Conference.

The march on Washington was an opportunity I couldn't miss. It was almost a year before the national elections, and it seemed like an important time to have a show of numbers if gay and lesbian rights were to get any kind of attention. So I bought a thousand-dollar round-trip ticket and went back east. When I got to Washington, it seemed like everybody there was lesbian or gay or supportive of lesbian and gay people. I'd never seen people just be themselves on public streets in daylight. Carol and I don't even walk in real close proximity here in Juneau. It's not that people were demonstrating their affection for one another. It was just the way people talked, their body language, the way they were so exuberant. People who didn't know each other talked openly about who they were and where they were from. You had the freedom to do whatever felt right to do. And isn't that something? To not have to be protective? You didn't have to have that sensor out that checks, "Am I safe here? Am I safe here?"

I'd never been so out. I'd never felt so safe. Then I went to the public wedding, which took place outside the IRS building along Constitution Avenue the day before the actual march. It was to protest the fact that the IRS and others don't recognize a partnership between two people of the same sex. I met up with two friends of mine from upstate New York, who wanted to go see the wedding. Instead of just watching, they ended up participating in the ceremony. They'd been together for eight years.

Nobody had expected such a large crowd at the wedding. I heard there were something like seven thousand people; about two thousand actually participated in the marriage ceremony. So more and more police came, and they made a broader and broader area for us. People were packed in the street, and it stopped traffic. There were sets of women in wedding dresses or tuxedos and the same with the men, tuxedos or wedding dresses. Actually I didn't see any men in wedding dresses, but there must have been.

The wedding ceremony was conducted by a woman. She said, "Now, for those of you who aren't getting married, move to the outside and join hands." The people who were going to marry moved in. All of us who had joined hands were told to raise our hands and just hold them in the air while she said some kind of prayer. The emotion and the sincerity were very unexpected. Tears were streaming down everybody's faces. It was like this circle of love. I think people might have expected more of a show, and it turned into something very real. There were people in wheelchairs getting married. It was great. Then at the end of the ceremony they released balloons, which soared up into the sky.

The next day I went to the march and joined the Alaska contingent. There were twenty-two of us, mostly from Anchorage, and a couple of people from Southeast, but I was the only one from Juneau. I had one camera with slide film and one camera with black-and-white film. I also had a tape recorder. I was trying to get all this stuff together so that when I went back to Juneau, I could make a slide show for SEAGLA.

Sara Boesser on the morning of October 11, 1987, prior to the start of the National March on Washington for Lesbian and Gay Rights. (*Courtesy of Sara Boesser*)

I think we stood in place for three hours before the Alaska group moved. We marched from the Ellipse to the Mall, where there were speakers. I kept winding my way forward toward the platform. Among those I heard was Eleanor Smeal, who was then president of NOW. I did a double take because I hadn't realized that NOW was supportive of lesbian and gay rights. So I thought, *My God, this is great! I'd better pay a little more attention to NOW.* Smeal's voice was blaring, and she said, "We've just been handed the official count of the number of marchers who are here today, and it's five hundred thousand!"

Jesse Jackson was also a speaker that day. I didn't actually hear him, but this was soon after he announced his bid for the presidency. I was shocked that he would take that kind of risk, addressing the marchers. All the presidential candidates were invited, but he was the only one who came. So that moved me a lot, that he would take that kind of risk for people who aren't part of the mainstream.

That experience—the wedding, the march, hearing the speakers— changed my life. I came back to Juneau and got involved in the Democratic party. I had been an independent, so I registered as a

Democrat for starters. Then I went to the Juneau Democratic caucus and got elected a delegate. I went to the Southeast caucus and got elected a delegate and went to the state convention. I voted every time for Jesse Jackson. I thought, *If he'll take that risk for me, I'll do that for him.* Jackson won in Alaska, and he spoke of us in his speech at the national convention.

NOT LONG after the march, I attended a NOW conference in Buffalo that helped me make some decisions about how involved I was going to be with AIDS work and how involved with gay rights. I went to a workshop on women and AIDS that was run by three women—an AIDS researcher, a doctor, and an educator—who questioned our involvement as women caring for men with AIDS. They said that as they looked around the country, they saw a lot of women—lesbian women, in particular—in the forefront of pulling together AIDS support programs and staffing them as nurses, social workers, and educators. They pointed out that these women, especially the lesbians, were probably the most free from male oppression in their work and in their social lives. These were women, they said, who could really change the world, who were already out there changing the world in lots of ways, yet they changed their lives to take care of men, which was the traditional role women have had throughout history.

After saying all this, these three women said, "We just think that people who are doing this should consider what they're doing with their lives." I sat there stunned because there I was co-coordinator of Shanti of Juneau. I had a good job where I was paid equally with men, and I had freedom. This workshop made me look at what I was doing. I came back from that conference with a question in my mind: *What do I really want to do to make this a better world?* I was already doing education with people about AIDS and about homophobia. But what I really wanted to do was get equal rights for everybody, with my main focus on gay and lesbian people. I decided that if I was holding myself back in any way in Shanti with the AIDS work, then I had to step out of Shanti and move forward on the track that I really cared about.

I had to agree with the sentiment that a lot of women have ended up taking care of men as part of this AIDS struggle. But I didn't feel resentful in the way that these women at the conference did. Well, I felt resentful when I first thought about it, but then I realized that AIDS gave me great courage and it made me realize that I could make a difference. We took individuals, brought them together, and built an organization. We got state grants. We let ourselves shine and earned respect from health and social services people and ministers.

And by working together as openly gay and lesbian people, we learned that we didn't have to live bound up in the closet as we do in "normal" society. I also gained incredible courage from getting up in public and talking about safe sex and talking about AIDS. I mean, if I can talk about AIDS on TV, I can probably say to somebody I know and care about, "I'm a lesbian."

Later, I went to the National Lesbian Rights Agenda Conference in San Diego. What I learned there inspired me to bring the fact that I'm a lesbian to all the activist work I do, whether its Democratic politics or Shanti. At the conference we came up with statements of what the lesbian rights issues are for the nineties. One of the issues that really hit home for me was that all of us as lesbians are activists in different issues that are important to us, like choice, child care, peace. The question was: Should we be involved in these issues, or should we get more involved in gay and lesbian organizations? What we concluded was that we should continue to be involved in our wide range of concerns, but we should include in our work the fact that we are also lesbian. So if I'm involved with a church group or in my peace-activist work, I should also make clear that I'm a lesbian. So we don't have to leave what we're already very committed to, but we have to bring that other piece of us, so it will have a ripple affect—so these groups will have to start incorporating that aspect of us into their organizations.

For me, all of this has meant continuing my involvement with Shanti, but stepping back from a central role in the organization. Now I'm on Shanti's Community Advisory Board as the "gay contact." It was a difficult shift because I knew that AIDS work had to be done. There had been a period of time when a lot of lesbians, myself included, felt that if we didn't do it, no one would, so it was the right thing to do. But after the NOW conference I realized there were other people who could do this work and that maybe my strength and my focus had to be with gay rights. That was, after all, what had gotten me involved in the first place.

So I've refocused most of my energy on the Committee for Equality, of which I'm president. The committee is a statewide organization, started in the summer of 1988, to send out press releases, talk to the press, and talk to legislators about the need for laws guaranteeing equal rights in Alaska for gays, lesbians, and bisexuals.

As president of the Committee for Equality, I decided to write something about National Coming Out Day for Alaska's mainline newspapers. Coming Out Day was set up to mark the first anniversary of the 1987 march on Washington. I wrote a guest editorial that ended up getting printed in the *Anchorage Daily News* and the *Juneau Empire*,

Juneau's only mainstream newspaper. I wrote that this was the anniversary of the march and that everyone could come out, not just gay and lesbian people, but people who know and love and support gay people. Everyone could say on this day, "I know and care about someone who is gay."

In that article I didn't state anywhere, "I'm a lesbian," but I did state in my bio that appeared along with the editorial that I was president of the Committee for Equality, a nonprofit group organized to work for and secure equal rights for gay, lesbian, and bisexual Alaskans. To me that was almost the equivalent of saying, "I'm a lesbian."

A couple of days after I sent the editorial off to the newspapers, I started having shortness of breath and super anxiety attacks, which I had never had in my life. Even though my heart and mind knew it was the right thing to do, I was afraid. I feared that people—even gay and lesbian people—would feel I was too hot to associate with in public. But bottom line, what I feared most was death. To me, society tells us that if we remain silent, if we keep our place, we can live. But if we cross the line and we're too visible, we might just die. I had crossed the line, and I thought I could be killed. It wasn't rational, but that's how I felt.

It was shocking to me that nothing bad happened; life never tasted so sweet. I was not asked to leave the sports teams I played on. I was not asked to leave my volunteer groups. I was not shunned. In fact, some people started talking to me more. People who had never said hello to me on the street started waving to me and do so until this day.

Up to the time my editorial was published, I had only told a couple of people at work that I was gay. My traditional way of coming out all my life had been to get to know someone well enough, long enough, for me to trust them and for me to feel that they cared about me enough to accept this added piece of information. Also, by getting to know people over time, I discovered that there were people who would not receive this information well because of their homophobia. So I had always been very selective over who I told. But it turned out there were no problems at work.

There was an architect I work with, a very good person who I respect highly, who I wasn't sure would react well to the news. He was in visiting the office shortly after my editorial was published and he said very seriously, "Sara, I read your article. It was very good, but there's something I have to tell you." I said, "What?" He said, "I don't know if you're going to understand this and I hope you can deal with it, but I'm heterosexual." And I said, "That's OK, some of my best friends are, and I'm glad you told me." We both laughed. It was great.

This was the beginning of my awareness that we isolate ourselves because we fear for our safety and end up having less rich lives as a result. Even as I tell you this years later, there's a part of me that's still not totally trusting. It takes only one crazy person. But I have lived a much better life since 1988. It's incredible how freeing it is not to have to lead a double life. Just by being myself, I feel better about myself, and I can give more to the organizations I work with and more to my job. I can be more direct with people without fear that they will discover my secret.

The other thing I've discovered is that I no longer resent other people who seem so free. Just like heterosexuals, I'm now free to touch or talk or use pronouns that identify who I am and the life I lead. I'm no longer wasting energy hiding. So I have a lot more fun, and people benefit from me.

TWO YEARS after my editorial was published, I testified here in Juneau in favor of a bill that was designed to protect several different groups, including gays and lesbians, from discrimination in city employment. For the first time I actually said in a very public way: "My name is Sara Boesser, and I'm a lesbian." The next day I was quoted in the Juneau newspaper and on the radio, and I was identified as a lesbian. Saying the word proved to be the most freeing in the end. It was the scariest line to cross, but I'm glad I did it because now there's no turning back.

The Radical Debutante

Ann Northrop

UNTIL 1987, *Ann Northrop's résumé reads like that of a journalist on her way to the top:* "ABC Sports," *Ms.* magazine, Ladies Home Journal, "Good Morning America," *and* "CBS Morning News." *The impressive list of national media ends with 1987 because it was in that year that the silver-haired, Vassar-educated Boston debutante abandoned her career.*

Ann Northrop jumped ship and became an educator on AIDS and homosexuality. Along the way, she also joined the ranks of the new wave of direct-action AIDS and gay rights activists. Today, Ann is an outspoken member of the AIDS Coalition to Unleash Power (ACT UP) and has been arrested twice while participating in public protests, including the much-publicized and controversial disruption of Sunday services at New York's St. Patrick's Cathedral in 1989. She's also an active member of Queer Nation, the highly visible and very vocal rights group that has spread to cities across the country. At forty-two, two decades older than the average Queer Nationalist, Ann is an energetic late bloomer who is determined to make up for lost time.

All through my teenage years I tried to convince myself, *These feelings will go away. They're not real, because I'm not one of those awful people. I can't be one of those weirdos, those Martians, those horrible disgusting perverts.* The image I had was of limp-wristed men and women who looked like truck drivers and wore motorcycle boots—unattractive, disgusting people, fairies and bull dykes. I said to myself, *That's not me. I'm a nice upper-middle-class blue-blooded Boston debutante.*

So I hid throughout my teenage years. I dated boys. I sometimes say I've dated half the men in the world twice, including people like Pete Coors, now president of Coors Beer. This amuses me. I actually went out with Pete for quite a while in high school. I went to high school in Denver with all the Coors girls and that kind of crowd.

As a teenager I didn't see any positive gay images. I wasn't able to find them. And they certainly weren't in my high school curriculum. But I remember getting excited by characters in books who were marginally alluded to as gay. I also went to Rock Hudson and Doris

Day movies and spent my time focusing on Doris, putting myself in Rock's place. I was thinking about kissing Doris, rather than kissing Rock.

I went to college at Vassar from 1966 through 1970 and continued to date men, but less frequently. I wasn't enjoying it. But I thought that maybe I had to wait for someone to come along who I could really like. It wasn't that I didn't know how I felt, because I knew perfectly well how I felt by then. And it wasn't as if I didn't know any gay people. There was an openly gay group of women in my dorm at Vassar, and they happened to be friends of mine. But I didn't feel comfortable being associated with these friends and I distanced myself from them. I certainly never talked to them or anyone else at Vassar about my feelings of attraction for women. I did not come out to anybody there, and I did not join the group. I just did not want to identify myself as a lesbian, which was a word I absolutely couldn't use because if I accepted that identification, then I had to accept being alone for the rest of my life. I thought that being gay meant that I would never, ever be able to have a relationship with any of the women I was actually attracted to because they were all straight. All those other gay people could go out and have fun, but for me being gay meant being alone.

I CAME out in 1976, when I was twenty-eight, which was when I first got involved with my lover, Linda, who I'm still with. Linda has two sons who live with us, whom I've helped raise. I did not feel comfortable talking to another soul in the entire world about my homosexuality until I met my lover and felt there was now one other person who cared enough about me not to hate me for who I was. I was very scared and very conservative.

Five years later, by the time I went to work as a free-lance writer for "Good Morning America" ["GMA"] at ABC television, I was completely open, and that got me in a lot of trouble. When I got to "GMA," they had an institution called Lesbian Hour, which was quite interesting to me. Lesbian Hour was at about four in the afternoon when people would take a break. We'd hang out at Joy Behar's desk and talk. Joy is now a famous comedienne, but at the time she was a secretary at "GMA." This gathering was called Lesbian Hour because it was all girls who gathered around to talk. But there wasn't a lesbian in sight until I announced myself.

I was still feeling very fresh in my relationship at the time. This is a period when you want to go out and tell the entire world, so I was very aggressive about it—I felt it was my turn. Everyone else in the world had had the opportunity to have relationships and celebrate and enjoy them. I had been alone essentially for twenty-eight years. I had been holding back for my entire life, and this was my first chance to have a relationship and celebrate it and wallow in it and enjoy it. I was extremely flagrant in ways that I'm a little embarrassed about now. Not that I regret any of it, nor do I think I was entirely inappropriate.

I remember taking my lover, Linda, to a staff party at the home of a writer who was then married to a minister. She couldn't bear me because I was much too flagrant in my outness. Linda and I were being very affectionate, necking in the living room with a lot of other people around. You know, if a straight couple—or a gay couple—did that at a party now, I would probably find it objectionable because I would find it unfriendly to the party. At this particular party, they would have been offended by any couple necking in the middle of the living room, but I think they were much more upset by the fact that it was a gay couple, rather than a straight couple. There were mean remarks made behind my back, several of which were reported to me.

I THINK if I had been cooler and less aggressive in my behavior, I probably would have had a somewhat easier time at "GMA." In fact, by the time I got to "CBS Morning News," I had gotten a lot of that out of my system. I think I had a very successful and happy time at CBS with my colleagues. My problems there had to do, for the most part, with a small group of my superiors with whom I had conflicts over editorial issues. I was not an easy employee for them because when I didn't like something, I said it. The last year I was there I went around screaming, "Intellectual bankruptcy!" at them.

One of the lovely things at CBS was how my colleagues dealt with my crush on Angie Dickinson, which was treated in the same way that any heterosexual crush would have been. I had a picture of Angie on my telephone, and I would talk aggressively about her as someone I found enormously attractive. And I would refer to the fact that I was attracted to older sleazy blondes, of which she was the epitome.

There came a day when Angie was booked in the entertainment unit for a posttape—she was going to be interviewed on tape following the regular broadcast. When that got put on the schedule and became known, virtually everyone on the entire staff called me up or came running to my office to say, "Ann, Ann, guess who's coming! Angie!" They were so excited for me. They were truly happy for me that I was going to have the experience of being able to meet this movie-star crush. I escorted Angie around the building for a couple of hours. I got to chat her up and had a great time. I loved her even more after spending time with her because she was fully as wonderful and humorous as I thought she would be.

ONE OF the people at CBS who was totally supportive and totally accepting was Diane Sawyer. Besides really taking to my stepson, Peter, who I would occasionally take to the studio with me on mornings when I had to meet with guests, Diane always regarded me as having a family. I remember one morning when Linda and I were home watching the "Morning News" in bed. Linda is a high school English teacher, and she must have had the day off. At the start of the second half of the show, at eight o'clock, there was Diane saying, "Call me Ahab. . . ." Linda gave me a sharp jab in the ribs with her elbow and said, "Call me Ahab? It's 'Call me Ishmael!' " And I said, "You're absolutely right." So I picked up the phone and called the control room at CBS and said, "Tell Blondie it's 'Call me Ishmael.' " I settled back. Sure enough, ten minutes later, Diane said, "You know, I misspoke myself a few minutes ago. It's not 'Call me Ahab,' it's 'Call me Ishmael.' "

Nine months later we threw a "Morning News" Christmas party in May, black-tie, two hundred people. Linda and I went. Diane was at the party and came toward me at one point. I started to introduce Linda to her, and Diane stuck out her hand and said, "Oh, you must be the one who corrected me when I said, 'Call me Ahab.' " We had not discussed this from the time I called the control room, but Diane never forgets. And she never forgets to ask me about my family whenever we talk. She's one of the few people I know, and certainly the only "star," who says, "How's Linda?" every time I talk to her. "How's Peter?" Diane could not be nicer about asking after them as my family.

GIVEN WHO I am and how completely out I was, I rose nicely through the ranks at CBS in ways that other people didn't. I would insist on referring to Linda as my spouse and equating my life with theirs and making it have equivalent status. Nonetheless, I was given a great deal of power and responsibility there. I was hired as an associate producer and promoted to producer and then to coordinating producer. I had a lot of authority. I think that speaks well for the place.

After five years I decided to leave CBS. I had never worked anywhere before for more than a year and a half. I was not happy, and the show was getting worse and worse, so I quit. I left CBS for unemployment. I wasn't worried because I had done well financially at CBS, I had a wife who worked and made a decent salary, and I had some trust in my ability to survive.

After CBS I made a very definite decision not to look for work. I wanted to reenter the world. I had been working on the late shift for a long time. I wanted to see my friends again, whom I hadn't seen for years, and my family. As part of the process of reentering the world, I also thought about what it was I liked to do in life, what it was that would make me happy on a day-to-day basis. I realized that what I really liked about television and CBS was teaching people things, conveying values, getting my point across. I liked when clerks at "Morning News" would come to me and say, "You gave me values. You gave me standards. You taught me how to do it right."

I started thinking in terms of being an educator and then I thought, *Aha! Maybe the line I've been saying as a joke for years is true.* When people asked me what I really wanted to do when I grew up, I would say, "I want to be a gym teacher, but I'm afraid of fulfilling the stereotype." After I left CBS I said to myself, *You know what? It's absolutely true!* I had always enjoyed teen sports more than anything else in my life, but I was desperately afraid of being the stereotypical little butch gym teacher.

So I decided that I was going to teach field hockey in a private girls' school, like Brearley, where one of my grandfathers was headmaster many years ago. I would teach elite, smart-alecky girls just like me, and no more fooling around with what anyone else thought I should be doing. I would probably divide my time between team sports and maybe a little nineteenth-century English literature on the side. A little field hockey, a little Jane Austen. They would learn values and teamwork and have a good time like I did when I was their age.

In the midst of exploring this option and talking to friends who had been involved in schools like Brearley, I had lunch one day with a friend of mine, Vivian Shapiro. Vivian is a lesbian who has been politically involved for quite a few years and who is somewhat prominent in the current movement. As I described my thoughts to her, she said, "What about the Harvey Milk High School* as a place to teach?" I thought, *Perfect! What a great idea! I can have all the teaching function I've wanted and I can have it in a gay context.* Vivian told me to call her friend, Joyce Hunter, at the Hetrick-Martin Institute.

When I met with Joyce, I showed her my résumé, which knocked

---

*The Harvey Milk High School is an alternative high school for lesbian and gay adolescents who need a safe place to continue their studies. The school is certified and staffed by the New York City Board of Education and is located at the Hetrick-Martin Institute for Lesbian and Gay Youth.

her out. She gave me a look that said, "What are you doing here?" So I described my little teaching dream. I had adjusted my thinking to the Harvey Milk School by then, but I still had grandiose dreams. I had said to myself, *I'll take all these gay boys and make them into the city champ softball team and destroy all the stereotypes of gay boys. This will be my great accomplishment.* I described all this to Joyce, and she just got hysterical. She thought I was the funniest thing that had ever walked through the door because, as she explained to me, the Harvey Milk High School was not some great Gothic structure with hundreds of kids. It was one room in the back with maybe fifteen cross-dressers. And they certainly didn't have a gym or anything approaching a sports program.

Joyce told me that the Harvey Milk High School was not appropriate for me. But she said, "We have a contract from the city Department of Health to go around and talk to community groups, parents' groups, the Board of Education, whatever, to advocate for AIDS education." She asked if I would be interested in that. And I said, "You want to pay me cash to do public speaking? Me, the big ham? Where do I sign up?" I didn't care that it was AIDS. I didn't care that it was a gay agency. The most important thing to me about that offer was that I was going to get paid to do public speaking.

It turned out that I loved the subject matter and have gotten deeply involved in it. The most ironic thing of all is that I found what I enjoyed most was direct AIDS education with kids. The most exciting experience was at one of my earlier appearances, in 1988. I had been asked to go in and do AIDS education with an alternative high school group at a drug rehabilitation facility in Brooklyn. I sat down in a circle with about twenty kids, boys and girls. We had been talking for a little while, when one kid sitting next to me said, "Well, you know, the way to get rid of AIDS is to kill all the queers." This was the first time I'd had something like that happen, and I turned to him and said spontaneously, "It's interesting you should say that because I'm one of those queers and I'm certainly not crazy about your language. What you're suggesting is not the answer, but let's talk about it." Everybody's jaw dropped to the ground, and we proceeded to have a two-and-a-half-hour nonstop conversation. One girl came out as having a lesbian mother. The kids talked about their gay friends and how they felt about them and the difficulties they had dealing with it. Two and a half hours nonstop! Kids do not sit and talk to grownups for two and a half hours nonstop.

Talking with that group of kids was one of the most exciting experiences I've ever had. It was thrilling. It was like they were in the middle of the Mojave Desert and someone offered them a canteen of water.

They were so thirsty for this information, for this conversation. It took them about five seconds to drop their misbehavior and to lean forward with curiosity and a desire to learn, and listen, and exchange information and opinions. I felt privileged to be with them, privileged to have that conversation, privileged that they would respect and trust me enough to have that conversation. I feel very warm toward kids. I think they're very intelligent, caring, sincere, and basically wonderful people who have had rotten things done to them and are therefore missocialized into a lot of rotten behavior.

I had not been hired to go talk about homosexuality to people. But that experience made me understand how that was possible and how important and valuable it was. So I went on to develop a curriculum for teaching people about homosexuality.

Now I go out to high school classes with a gay male partner in a nice little imitation of heterosexuality as a male-female couple. We have a set routine. We start the class by saying, "Okay, divide yourselves up into small groups of four or five. Make a list of every word you've ever heard having to do with homosexuality. Any curse word, anything nice, any phrase, any description." They make all these lists, and they laugh and giggle. It gives them permission to get all that out in the open. Then we say, "All right, call out the words." As they call them out, we write the words on the blackboard. My favorite phrase that I learned from the kids is *fudge packer*—we hear it all.

After making the list we say, "No one knows where sexual orientation comes from—straight, gay, bisexual, whatever you want to call it. But we do know that orientation, the ability to be attracted to whoever you're attracted to, is set either by birth or within the first couple of years of life. It is not something that happens to you later on. So, say you're nine, ten, eleven, twelve, and you're coming to a realization of your sexual feelings, and these words are all you've ever been taught?" Then we point to the blackboard and say, "These words are all any of us are ever taught about homosexuality. This is it. This is all we ever learn about the subject. So the fact that you think that gay people are disgusting is absolutely legitimate. I thought that, too."

I don't go into these classes and get defensive. I don't challenge the kids and I don't point fingers at them and put them in a position where they have to say, "No, I'm right, and you're wrong." I say, "I'm with you." I tell people that they're right to feel the way they do because they are products of their environment and the education they've had. I don't tell people they're crazy because they're not. Now, I also say to them, "We're all starting from the same point of information. We are all blameless because we've all been taught this and we were never given an alternative. So if we all hate gay people, that's fine, because that's all we've ever been taught. But now I'm going to give you a different point of view. If you still disagree with me after what I have to say, then I may hate you. Then I may get angry at you. But until then, we're all pals." They laugh when I say that to them.

I have found that these conversations are marvelously revolutionary. In forty or forty-five minutes in a public high school classroom, we can have a very meaningful exchange about our lives with twenty or thirty very misinformed lower-class kids. I think we change their lives by giving them an alternative point of view they've never had before. We're giving them the experience of finding out that we're human beings. For these kids, it's the first time that they've had a chance to really have a conversation about homosexuality with someone who's gay. A surprisingly great number of them announce that they have gay friends. That's different from twenty or thirty years ago, when I was their age. But I don't think they feel comfortable, as much as they may love their gay friends, talking to them about their gay lives or about their own feelings.

When these kids I've talked to get called faggot or are tempted to call someone else a faggot, when they hear these kinds of slurs, I want them to have an alternate point of view. I want them to stop and think and say, "Wait a minute, that isn't what I thought of her. She was a human being. So maybe these stereotypes aren't right."

I've heard stories that I've left waves in my wake all over the five boroughs of New York, not to mention everywhere else I've been, because I go in with what is, in fact, a radically different point of view, which is my own normalcy. Don't tolerate me as different. Accept me as part of the spectrum of normalcy. That turns out to be a radical point of view, but one that is very exciting to most people.

I think this kind of education is crucial. There was a poll taken by the governor's office that confirmed for me how important it is. The poll asked teenagers all over the state how they felt about members of different minority groups and whether they would be willing to live next door to a member of this or that group. There was a list of about a half a dozen. All the kids, no matter what group they came from were very willing, at levels of 90 to 98 percent, to live next door to members of any minority group except gay people. When the kids were asked whether they would be willing to live next door to gay people, the yes answers were in the 40 percent range. We are still regarded as weirdos from outer space. We're regarded as disgusting human beings who have made a choice to do something self-indulgent, disgusting, and sinful. We are not regarded as legitimate.

I see as my agenda the need to go out and attack the root of the problem, which is this feeling of disgust toward us. That's what I'm out to change, and that's why I see the conversations I have with teenagers as so important. I do it for those who are having feelings of same-sex attraction, to feel better about themselves, particularly at an age when they are tremendously isolated and at very high risk of suicide. And I do it for those who are not having feelings of same-sex attraction, to decrease their panic, loathing, and violence against those of us who are lesbian and gay. It's possible to create a better world with the generation that I think is open to this change, as opposed to those who are already in power, who are harder to reach.

I truly believe I can reach most people. I have some of my most enjoyable conversations with self-identified fag bashers on Staten Island. I really enjoy talking to people like that because I find that they're so open to it—they really are.

The problem I have is with religious fundamentalists—they are the most resistant. They're the ones who you can't get to with the kind of argument that I make because they accept as their guide a biblical injunction against homosexuality. Although we can very easily argue technically that the Bible does not condemn us, I don't try. When I get challenged by someone in an audience who says, "But the Bible says. . . ." I say, "Look, I know perfectly well that that's your point of view and I'm not going to affect it. That's fine. You're entitled to your views. But I have a different point of view, and while I could argue scripture with you, I'm not going to."

WHEN I first plunged into the AIDS-education work, I quickly became horrified by what I saw: AIDS education that was not getting done or was getting done very badly, news media lying about the epidemic and refusing to talk about the virus because they said the truth was too complicated, a federal government that would not look at things the way they were, and city and state governments that were not doing what they should. I was seeing the breakdown of the health-care system and racism and the old issues that I had been seeing for years and years and years.

At around this time, I became aware of an event about to happen. It was called the War Conference, and it took place in February of 1988 in Virginia, a little ways outside Washington. It was a weekend conference of about 220 lesbian and gay leaders—so-called—from across the nation. Because of my old journalistic instincts, I can't bear to miss important events if I can possibly help it, so I wangled an invitation.

The conference was a fascinating affair, but the most important thing for me happened on the last day at a plenary session. A couple of people got up and talked about ACT UP and the importance of people being on the front lines, being out in the streets and marching and demonstrating and protesting, not just doing this work professionally. I was a child of the sixties who had marched and demonstrated against the Vietnam War and for the rebirth of feminism. It really felt very nostalgic.

Almost in reaction to this emotional blackmail, I decided that I at least needed to check this out. I came back to New York and went to my first ACT UP meeting the next night. It was around the first of March 1988. I haven't left since. I was totally head over heels in love at first sight.

At ACT UP I found a great working democracy that was very positive and supportive of everybody. All the goals appealed to me. They included everything from finding a cure for AIDS to doing the right education, which meant telling the truth, being explicit, not pulling any punches, and supporting real protective health measures, as opposed to ineffective supposed moral standards. ACT UP was willing to confront all these things directly, to go out in the street and scream and yell. So that was the beginning of my activist work, which I did in addition to my professional work.

I started going to ACT UP meetings just at the very end of the organization's first year, just as all the excitement was building about the Wall Street II demonstration. Wall Street II was a protest to acknowledge the first anniversary of the founding of ACT UP/New York. The idea was to repeat a Wall Street demonstration that had taken place at the beginning, in March of 1987. ACT UP chose Wall Street because the business community is seen as having large responsibilities in this area. Businesses profiteer on AIDS drugs, and insurance companies won't cover people. It's all about money and companies being unwilling to spend what it takes to do a good job of taking care of people. Some ACT UP protests are targeted at specific issues or goals, but a lot of it is just screaming and yelling to say, "Pay attention! Don't ignore this! Do something!"

For Wall Street II we chose a busy location during the morning rush hour. We chose the morning on the assumption that people would be a lot less upset if they were interrupted on the way to work than on the way home, which I thought was a very clever approach.

We split up into what were known as "affinity" groups. One group would take to the street and sit down and all be arrested. Then as soon as they were cleared up, the next group would go in. That went on for awhile. About one hundred people were arrested. I was one of them. That was my first arrest ever. It was fabulous!

At one time, getting arrested seemed like the scariest thing in the world to me. But somehow, during the Wall Street II protest, sitting in the street just seemed to me to be a perfectly sensible thing to do. But I think the real key is that once I came to work in the community, six months earlier, it took away the last barriers in my life. Now I could be totally free and be who I was. It made all sorts of things possible that I was scared to do before. When I was working in the straight world, there always seemed to be the chance that I could ultimately be punished for being lesbian, and if I wasn't going to be punished directly, they would punish me for everything else I did. I always felt that I was in danger.

When I went to work in the lesbian and gay community, it was an enormously liberating experience—contrary, of course, to my assumption when I went to work there. I thought it was going to be a death, a dark cave from which I would never emerge. I thought I was limiting myself, cutting off possibilities. The irony was that I was, in fact, liberating myself completely, opening up my life in ways that I couldn't begin to imagine or anticipate. The proof of this was that I felt completely complacent about the idea of getting arrested, which was a complete departure from how I felt before. At any previous point in my life, I wouldn't have gone anywhere near a situation that could have resulted in my being arrested.

The police were fairly rough. They threw me onto a bus with about twenty or thirty others. The bus drove around for a while and finally ended up at a police precinct. We were all herded off and into cells, three in each cell. We went through about three or four hours of processing: Fingerprints. Polaroids. Being questioned. One of the things we'd been told at civil-disobedience training was to be prepared to spend several hours in jail. I had followed instructions and brought two peanut butter sandwiches and a book. I think that's some of the best advice I'd ever received in my life.

I PARTICIPATED in scores of demonstrations over the next couple of years, but I wasn't arrested again until the St. Patrick's Cathedral protest. (I am not someone who goes out and gets arrested routinely.) There were a number of reasons ACT UP chose St. Pat's as a target for a protest, but it was particularly significant for me because of AIDS education. The archdiocese in New York does everything it can to interfere with instruction about safe sex in the public schools. It is currently trying to stop any availability of condoms in public high schools. It's doing this in very nefarious ways. And Cardinal O'Connor, especially at that time, was telling the general public that monogamy would protect them from HIV infection and that condoms didn't work. As far as I was concerned, those were both major lies that were going to kill people. I thought it was important to alert the public to the fact that these were lies. And while people were certainly entitled to make their own decisions about their lives—and far be it from me to tell them what to do—I would not sit by silently while they were being lied to. So when the group decided to target St. Patrick's, it just made absolute perfect sense to me because it is an extremely important target in this epidemic.

There was a lot of publicity leading up to this protest, which was planned for the 10:15 A.M. mass on December 10, 1989. People were amazed at the turnout. It really took on a life of its own and became a huge, huge protest, far beyond anybody's expectations. People were so angry at Cardinal O'Connor and the archdiocese here that they came out in droves, even though it was extremely cold. There were five thousand demonstrators outside from ACT UP and Wham!, the Women's Health Action Mobilization. It was chaos in the streets.

Forty or fifty of us drifted into the church in little groups at about 9:10 A.M. We tried to get there early to make sure we could get seats. But then they cleared the church, for one of the few times in history, filled it with cops, took bomb-sniffing dogs inside, and made us wait outside while they searched everything. Then they opened up the doors and let us in again.

The entire broadcast and print media were there on a special platform built for them in the middle of the congregation. Normally the local press was there every Sunday to cover the cardinal's sermon, but because there had been so much advance publicity about the planned protest, there was ten times the normal press in there, including local and network television. Mayor Koch was there to defend the cardinal. The police commissioner was there to defend the cardinal. There were hundreds of cops, bomb-sniffing dogs, and several hundred seminarians who had been brought in as decoration for the front area. There were undercover cops as ushers everywhere. And then there were maybe three dozen of us who planned to do nothing more than just read a statement. The place was quite tense.

We had decided that we were going to wait until the cardinal was giving his sermon before we did anything. Our intention was not to interfere with any hymns or anything else, but simply to make a gesture of protest during his sermon. Every week he stands up in the church and during his sermon makes political statements about AIDS, abortion, homosexuality, and crime in the city. We believed we were entitled through our right of free speech to confront his political statements. Besides, by having the broadcast and print media in there on a regular basis, he had breached the limits of a religious service himself and was setting up a political event.

At any rate, the cardinal began his sermon, and we started doing our prearranged protest. Maybe twenty-five or thirty of us lay down in the middle aisle. Several clumps of people in various parts of the cathedral started to read a statement aloud. A few people handcuffed themselves to pews. They didn't say anything, but just sat there handcuffed. Then, as the cops started swarming all over the cathedral blowing whistles and the parishioners were trying to drown out the statements with loud singing, one particular guy decided that we were all being wimps and started screaming. Then some of our younger, newer members started yelling. The whole place got a little chaotic. The police just arrested us one by one and carried us out of the cathedral on big orange stretchers.

As the arrests were going on, the plan was for one group to go up and take Communion. And as Communion was offered to them, they would politely refuse and make some statement like, "I refuse Communion because the church murders women." One guy, who was dressed in a suit and tie, was handed the host and just spontaneously and very calmly crumpled it and dropped it to the ground. He was planning to refuse Communion, but rather than refuse it or give it back, he instinctively crumpled it and dropped it.

I was the last one carried out of the cathedral. The place was very quiet by then. There was some praying, some hymn singing. I had been silent throughout the entire time I was lying on the floor. I didn't make a sound or do anything other than reach out and take the hands of the people next to me in an attempt to keep them quiet. Later, at the trial, I had one of them testify on my behalf to the fact that I was silent on the floor, because a cop took the stand and said I'd been screaming while I was lying there.

After I was picked up and was being carried out on the stretcher, during the time that the cathedral was very quiet, I yelled in a resounding voice through the cathedral, "We're fighting for your lives, too! We're fighting for your lives, too!" and repeated that half a dozen times. Who plays this in the movie version is our next question. I'm hoping Elizabeth Taylor will play me, with Angie Dickinson posters all over her apartment.

THERE WAS a great deal of negative comment in the press and by politicians about the protest. Nonetheless, I think we succeeded in opening up the dialogue on issues that had never been legitimized before. Cardinal O'Connor still can't go around town without being challenged about his position on condoms and safe-sex education. Today I read in the *New York Times* about the Catholic church impeding AIDS prevention in Ireland. I don't think that's an article that would have been written without this demonstration. I think we knocked the ground out from under the Catholic church in this city, revealed that the emperor has no clothes, and made it possible to improve the AIDS-education curriculum in the schools and the availability of condoms. I think we have devalued the church's position on these issues and called them into question forever more. I truly think we did a magnificent thing.

We had our critics and still do. They believed that this protest was a bad thing to do, that it would make people hate gay people. But my favorite positive reaction was one I heard from the mother of Gabriel Rotello, the editor of *OutWeek*.* Shortly after the demo, Rotello's mother, who lives in Danbury, Connecticut, told him that she and her friends were amazed to see that gay people, who they had thought were weak and wimpy, were in fact strong and angry.

I don't care that people disagree with me. That's one thing about being forty-two years old. I don't care. There are many things in life that I am not sure about and maybe more and more as I grow older. But the things I am sure about I feel enormously confident of. I felt confident that my participation in this action was the right thing to do from the moment it was mentioned. I haven't had a moment's regret about it ever since. In fact, I have only one regret at this point in my life, and that's not having been able to date women in high school.

FROM THE time I first joined ACT UP, there has been tension over what is and is not AIDS-related activism. There are those within ACT UP who don't think it's appropriate to do anything under the aegis of ACT UP that isn't directly and intimately connected with AIDS, the illness. My definition of things that are AIDS related is virtually everything. I heard a guy get up at a meeting yesterday and say, "We should not be working on national health care. That is not an AIDS issue." Well, I couldn't disagree with him more. I think that is a bottom-line AIDS issue. And I think racism is a bottom-line AIDS issue. And I think homophobia is a bottom-line AIDS issue, and sexism and class issues and all of this. I think that we are not going to solve the AIDS epidemic unless we deal with these issues, and vice versa. I think they're all interrelated.

Repeatedly in ACT UP meetings someone would bring up some

---

*A former New York City–based weekly gay and lesbian magazine.

particular incident that seemed to be *only* lesbian and gay related and our need to do something about it. Someone would inevitably stand up and say, "What does this have to do with AIDS?" Well, as someone who does AIDS education professionally, as well as education about homosexuality that is regarded as AIDS education, I have very little patience with that question and the position it represents.

Just a little under a year ago, I got a call from a friend of mine in ACT UP. He and his lover and another guy were inviting people they knew to a meeting to discuss doing direct action around lesbian and gay issues, without having to justify everything as AIDS. It made immediate perfect sense to me. Do I go to six meetings a week? Yes, far too often. Do I need more? No, not at all. But this was just one more meeting, and I was interested, so I thought I'd check it out.

I arrived a little late and I walked into a room expecting to find a small group of maybe ten or fifteen people. In fact, there were at least fifty or sixty, arranged in a very large circle. At that first meeting there was a lot of argument back and forth about what the goals of this group should be, how fast the group should move, what its agenda should be, whether there were enough people of color in the room, and why there weren't. Not unlike ACT UP, it was to be an organization that existed to do direct action; to get out on the streets; to scream and yell; to do particular events, targeted at particular things. But unlike ACT UP, the main agenda, the main theme, was to be gay and lesbian rights.

From the very beginning there was a split between those who wanted the organization to function much like ACT UP, which had a fair amount of structure and process, versus those who wanted very little of that. By the third meeting everyone agreed on the process for deciding what direct action to take. We decided that everybody who had an idea for something they wanted to do would stand up and describe it. Then we would split up into groups, one for each direct-action idea. We would reassemble and describe the results of these little meetings and then each group would proceed with the actions. The organization as a whole did not have to approve a particular action. Actions would rise and fall, depending on people's interest in doing them.

A lot of little things took place at first, from making T-shirts to lesbian and gay couples going into a normally straight bar just to make their presence known.

My idea was to hang big banners on billboards with pro-lesbian and gay messages. So I found an empty billboard, eventually managed to measure it, and got a group together who painted a big sign. The slogan I wanted was, "Lesbians Have Always Run Everything," which

I want to see on billboards all across America. But I was out of town when they finally decided on "Fags and Dykes Bash Back." There was a lot of debate about the appropriateness of that slogan. While that was not a slogan I, myself, would have written, it was one that I was willing to support in the end.

They hung it on the billboard on top of Badlands, a gay bar at the end of Christopher Street, facing the West Side Highway. The sign stopped traffic on the West Side Highway.

THE BIGGEST question when this new group was organized was what to call it. At the first meeting one suggestion that everyone loved was that we give it a different name every week so the press would think there were a lot of new groups in town. But somehow we didn't seem able to stick with that idea. By the second or third meeting, people were calling the group Queer Nation. There was a great deal of debate about it. I was one of those who was against it at first. I got up and argued against it once or twice on the grounds that I didn't think it was going to be productive. I said that I didn't remember there being an organization called "The Nigger Panthers." I lost; I didn't feel hugely emotional about it. Within a month I was totally comfortable with it. I thought, *Aha. This is just another example of the need for acclimatization.*

The minute that news of this organization hit the West Coast, new Queer Nation groups immediately sprung up there. It was the most quickly replicated group on the face of the Earth, and one of the most immediately newsworthy. It hit all over, particularly when a little pipe bomb went off at a gay bar down in the Village, and Queer Nation immediately marched up Sixth Avenue carrying the "Fags and Dykes Bash Back" banner. That "Bash Back" image became very attractive to the press, so Queer Nation got publicized widely, quickly attracting a lot of new people, particularly young people, to the organization.

I'M OLDER than almost everyone in Queer Nation and most people in ACT UP, but you have to understand that having joined the community so recently and having experienced this new sense of liberation, I feel like an adolescent. I'm forty-two now. But I'm not the only older person, at least not in ACT UP. Early on I remember some guy getting up and identifying himself as having been the national secretary of SDS* twenty years ago.

*Students for a Democratic Society.

I joke about myself as the grandmother of ACT UP, but even though I'm operating with all these young people, I feel very comfortable about the fact that we're all peers. If I happen to be a little older and know some things and have seen some things they haven't, well, that's just my particular contribution. I do think I have a unique presence, given the combination of my age, my background, and my silver hair.

The Bishop

John Shelby Spong

FEW RELIGIOUS institutions made it through the 1980s without confronting or being forced to confront the issue of homosexuality. The divisive and heated debate ranged from the ordination of openly gay men and women to the blessing of same-sex relationships. The Right Reverend John Shelby Spong, the Episcopal bishop of Newark, New Jersey, emerged during this time as one of the most prominent and outspoken proponents of the full and complete acceptance of gay and lesbian people in the life of the church. This tall and charismatic native North Carolinian has been the Episcopal bishop of Newark, New Jersey, since 1976, where his diocese includes 130 parishes in northern New Jersey and more than 280 priests.

Bishop Spong's support for the ordination of gay people and the blessing of same-sex unions has been welcomed quietly in some quarters of the Episcopal church, although more often, his beliefs have been strongly condemned. But both the supporters and detractors of Bishop Spong acknowledge that the debate he has led within the Episcopal church will continue for years to come.

In 1988, Bishop Spong presented his views on homosexuality in his controversial book on human sexuality, Living in Sin? The book and the subsequent international publicity have earned Bishop Spong a place on the cutting edge of the gay and lesbian rights movement. For a man who dedicated himself to the causes of black civil rights and women's rights in decades past, the cutting edge seemed a perfectly logical place to be.

I was raised in the 1930s by a strict fundamentalist Presbyterian mother and an alcoholic father in a community where segregation was an unquestioned way of life. There was a common cultural assumption at that time that black people were inferior by nature and that white people were kind to them by giving them jobs as servants. But there was one incident when I was three or four years old that left me confused. I can almost remember it today as the first wedge where I began to separate from the value system of my parents.

One day I was out in the yard with my father, and we had two rather elderly black men doing some work. One of them said something to me, and I said, "Yes, Sir," to him. My father and mother were very strict people when it came to manners. I was taught as a very young child to always say, "Yes, Ma'am," and "No, Sir," to anybody who was my elder. That was drilled into me. It was like not eating peas with your knife. But when I said "Yes, Sir," to the black man, my father said, "You never say 'Sir' to a nigger," and he punished me. Even at that age my little mind said, *There's something wrong with this equation.* It didn't add up.

While that was a vivid experience, it wasn't until the civil rights movement that my consciousness was born. *Brown vs. Board of Education* was decided in 1954. I was the rector of a church in Tarboro in the eastern part of North Carolina by the time the first schools were desegregated in places like Greensboro, Raleigh, and Winston-Salem. There were maybe two black children in each school. It was tokenism—still, it created riots, and the cops had to usher the little black children through spitting, angry mobs. Well, little towns like Tarboro, which had 8,500 people at that time, half of them black, went through the same kind of thing. That was the first time I was a public person involved in conflict because I supported those black children's right to attend what had been an all-white grammar school in Tarboro and defended publicly their legal right to attend. I went into that school to make that point very clear. That had to be in 1959.

In my mind there was no question that I had to do it—it was obviously the right thing to do. But because of my stand, I got night-rider calls and was threatened. I didn't have a cross burned in my front yard, but that was only because I was warned that they were on the way and I was out in the front yard to meet them. I turned on the flood lights, and they weren't willing to do anything publicly, so they left. There were also people who had been my friends who wouldn't speak to me anymore. I was disinvited from my golf foursome. And there were people who came to church but would go out the side door because they refused to shake my hand at the front door.

We also had people calling up and threatening our children. They told me, "We'll have your children raped by the biggest, blackest nigger we can find." My children were six, three, and one at the time. I never felt like I was in any great physical danger, but we took precautions with the children. Tarboro was the kind of town where a six-year-old child could walk four blocks to school and back, which our daughter did frequently. But until everything calmed down, I walked my daughter to school in the morning, and somebody met her at school at the end of the day and walked her home.

* * *

THE CIVIL rights movement radicalized me in a real way. It forced me to raise issues of justice. That has been central to every issue in which I've been engaged. The women's movement also radicalized me, and it was also clear to me that the gay rights movement was overwhelmingly a justice issue.

My first awareness of gay people was in a very negative sense. I was writing a book in the early 1980s called *Into the Whirlwind.* A major section of that book was on the sexual revolution vis-à-vis women. In that section I used my research on homosexuality to demonstrate how gay people in the church had oppressed and stood against women achieving power and prestige. You see, historically, there have been an overwhelming number of homosexual male priests. This should come as no surprise: When you make celibacy a prerequisite for priesthood in a homophobic society, what you do is validate a well-respected profession for people who have no intention of marrying. In the church they can come live in closets that are very acceptable, like monasteries and rectories.

One of the ways these men protected themselves was to be violently antifemale. That is, they didn't want any female coming into their world to blow their cover. When the church began to invite women into positions of power, the places in the church that were the most violently antifemale were the extreme Catholic wing of the church and the Catholic wing of the Episcopal church. Roman Catholics require celibacy, and the Catholic wing of the Episcopal church values it highly.

So my first experience with gay males in the church was that they were part of the enemy that I had to push aside to allow women to stand with dignity in the life of the church. Now, I don't think all gay persons are antifemale, but I think that a significant number of those who were dedicated to something called "Mother Church" had adopted this stance.

As I worked on this book, I became aware that it might be interpreted by some people as antihomosexual. I was uncomfortable with the fact that while I was trying to free one group of people from oppression, I was adding to the oppression of another group of people. By the time I turned in the completed manuscript, I had removed what I thought was offensive and made very clear that I did not raise the issue of homosexuality to lay one more burden of oppression and guilt and blame on the homosexual population, which is so easy for society to dump on.

As I looked deeper into the issue of homosexuality during this time, I began to see things that were hidden from most people—namely, committed, life-giving, healthy gay and lesbian relationships.

I first saw this relationship in one priest in this diocese who sort of tested me over a period of years and finally shared his life with me. It would have been perfectly obvious if I'd opened my eyes, but heterosexual people have an incredible way of keeping blinders on and not seeing what they don't want to see. This priest lives in a heavily urbanized area with his lover. They have lived together for over twenty years. They happen to be related. As teenagers, their families thought it was just wonderful that they were such close friends.

This priest's congregation knows he's gay and that the man who shares his home is his spouse. This priest is very effective, in part because he can live honestly. He doesn't have to hide and slink around. He's not a crusader and he's not someone who wants to be identified and go out and make speeches. He just wants to live his life. I would call him one of my outstanding clergy today, one of my personally supportive people. So, he was the first step in my education.

There was also a time when I had to remove a gay priest, not because he was gay, but because his church was simply dying under his leadership. I discovered he was gay by visiting his home—the rectory—which was physically attached to the church. He shared his home with his lover. When I went to use the bathroom, which was in a semipublic area, I saw photographs of nude males on the walls and "His-and-His" towels hanging from the towel rack. This community was an Archie Bunker kind of town, a place where I could never have protected the priest. To me, this was all unwise, to say the least. I thought, *Dear God, I'll never be able to rescue this man once the realization that this is a gay couple dawns on the congregation.*

When I discovered this priest was gay, I had already been planning to remove him, but I postponed that action for a year because I didn't want it to be connected to my discovery. But finally I had no choice: Either I was going to have to try new leadership, or I was going to have to close the church. So I gave him notice. He's still absolutely convinced that I did this because he was gay.

This was for me, however, a learning experience. When I told this priest that I wouldn't allow a heterosexual couple to live in the rectory without marriage, he said, "But, Bishop, they can get married, and I can't." I guess that was the first time I realized that I was not comparing apples with apples and that that was an injustice. We have ways that we believe heterosexual people can live out their sexual orientation, and we call it moral—indeed, we honor it and bless it and support it. But there's no way a gay person can do that in this society. Our church and society do not support these relationships. And that's a radical injustice. My experience with this priest kept the wheels turning for me.

I had one other experience with a gay priest that was terribly rending and learning for me. This involved one of my very best priests in this diocese who I had assumed was gay, but we never talked about it. He lived with a man in the rectory, and they had been in two different churches and had moved together each time. He's a very effective priest, and my way of dealing with him was to not raise the issue unless someone forced me to raise the question either by constantly complaining or because the priest was in some way indiscreet.

It so happened that a gay man fell in love with this priest. This was the first time I had confronted that kind of emotion in a homosexual setting. This man began to pursue my priest in a very neurotic way. The priest told him many times that he wasn't interested in another relationship and that he had been in a relationship for fifteen years and was very happy with his partner. This guy went through a period of calling him excessively, and he even turned in a fire alarm on his church in the middle of the night so he could watch the priest come out of the house in his bathrobe as the fire trucks roared up.

The priest gave this man no encouragement. He asked him as nicely as he could to cease his bothersome attention. But this now-rejected suitor decided that if he couldn't have him, nobody was going to have him. So he wrote letters to many priests in our diocese. He wrote letters to the members of the congregation. He wrote letters to God knows who saying that sexual orgies were going on in the rectory between the priest and his friend. No one could have been more discreet than this priest. He and his partner had worked out their lives so that their social life was within one circle and the priest's professional life in the church was within another. He was very closeted.

All of a sudden the closet that he had built over the years was obliterated. And he had to deal with the fact that most of the clergy of his diocese and the members of his congregation now knew he was gay. He thought he'd be removed. I don't think he thought he'd be removed by me, but I think he thought his congregation would ask him to leave. He'd been there for several years.

So there was a meeting with this priest and his congregation during Holy Week. His vestry said to him, "Father"—they're very formal—"we've always suspected this about you. Now we know it. But we want you to know we love you and we don't want anybody here as our priest except you." The fortress that he had built to guard himself was no longer necessary. It was a great experience of redemption and resurrection for this man. All of a sudden he realized he didn't have to hide his life anymore. What has happened, though, is that the priest and his partner have gone back to exactly the same style of life they lived before he was forced out of the closet. I've invited them to dinner as a couple, and they will not come—they will not come even into safe settings. This man's professional life is lived out in the church. His social life is with his gay friends. The two do not mix.

In the process of watching that painful experience, I again became sensitive to and aware of the pressure that people have to live under when they have to be dishonest. From that point it was a matter of thinking this through. You see, I'm a cerebral person. My brain always converts my emotions. No matter how homophobic my early life and training and value system were, my brain finally converted, as indeed it did on the issue of race and on the women's issue. What I do then is I begin to think, talk, and write from the perspective of my brain and I allow my prejudices to be challenged. In the process I find I challenge a lot of other people's prejudices because I'm not that different from those other people.

As the bishop, I'm in two different churches every Sunday of my life, and part of my job is to educate people. So I began to preach on this subject. I got both positive and negative responses. The most negative response was from black West Indian people—they really are tied up in knots on that subject. But because my people know me and because they really like me, they are willing to listen to all of my strange, screwy ideas.

ONE WEEK I was preaching my sermon on homosexuality and prejudice at St. Elizabeth's church in Ridgewood, which is a very conservative, wealthy Episcopal congregation. After the service was over we had a coffee hour, and this man almost had to be restrained from coming up to me. I thought he was hostile—I've had a lot of that, so I'm sort of used to it. But that wasn't the case with this man, who introduced himself as Dr. Robert Lahita, associate professor of medicine at Cornell University Medical Center. He was a Roman Catholic, but he believed the Roman Catholic church was backward because, he said, all of its moral theology was based on nineteenth-century science that no scientist believes any longer. He has constantly apprised John Cardinal O'Connor of New York and other ecclesiastical leaders to whom he's had access, how dated Roman Catholic ethical theology has become because it doesn't take into consideration modern science.

By this time I was already working on my book, *Living in Sin?* in which I discuss homosexuality at length, and Robert said that he wanted to help me. He began to supply me with materials from work

he and others were doing at Cornell, materials that scientifically supported what I had begun to conclude: that homosexuality is a minority expression of the human sexual cycle—that it is not arrested
development, as Freud would say, or a result of a weak mother or
overbearing father or seductive policeman or schoolteacher or priest.
At some point it occurred to me that if we could take away all that
stuff, we'd take away all the guilt. No mother or father would then
blame the other for their gay son or lesbian daughter. And they might
be able to recognize the fact that their gay son or lesbian daughter was
a normal person. And if society would simply undergird that person
with some sort of normal acceptance, some of the aberrant behavior
that marks segments of the gay community wouldn't be necessary.

IT BECAME very clear to me—and I later wrote about this in my
book—that a critical part of the undergirding that we had to provide
to gay and lesbian people was the blessing of gay unions. We have to
bless gay unions because I think these relationships are holy, and what
a blessing does is announce publicly that this is a holy relationship.
In marriage, when two people are willing to say to the public, "I am
going to live in a relationship with this person in which we will be
mutually responsible for each other in every area of life," then the
public begins to relate to them as a couple. By relating to them as if
they belong to each other in some sense, we undergird a couple's
commitment.

I don't think there's a heterosexual marriage in this country that
would exist with the absence of support that we give to gay couples.
So the very fact that some gay people are able to forge lifetime
relationships is to me almost a miracle. When you understand what
pressure gay people live under—where the prejudice is enormous,
where the hostility is enormous, where in many circumstances they
can lose their jobs, be run out of their neighborhoods, and be physically abused—and they're still able to make commitments that are life
giving to each person, then I think we ought to take off our hats to
them and cheer. I think they've got something to teach the rest of us
about a holy relationship.

And when somebody says, "But you know that most gay relationships don't last a lifetime," my answer is, "Well, neither do most
marriages." And heterosexual marriages at least have the overwhelming support of society, including the church. The church is an important bearer of the value system of the society, whether people are
believing Christians or believing Jews or believing anything. The
church is still an institution that affirms certain values that are still

alive within our society. So for the church to bless gay unions is a very important symbol to me. In fact, I think it's *the* most important symbol if the church ever hopes to minister to gay people.

BECAUSE OF my writing, I've gotten letters from gay couples that say, "We want to come over and have you marry us." But I have to write them back and say that I believe the church ought to bless committed gay relationships, but it ought to be done by whoever the pastor of the church is where you worship. I say this because I believe that it's the social context that makes all the difference.

You see, the only people I marry today are those in my congregation, and by that I mean my clergy, my seminary students, or someone who is a very close personal friend. I have said to my gay priests, many of whom are in the closet, that I would want to relate to their unions in the same way I would want to relate to a heterosexual union. If they want to have a liturgy, a service, in which the holiness of their relationship is liturgically proclaimed in the company of people with whom they're comfortable, then I'm willing to do that for them. I have done it, and I don't want to say any more about it than that because I don't want somebody to try to figure out who they are and then blow their cover. It's really important to me that I protect their integrity.

My diocese has passed a resolution regarding gay unions. It's as mild a resolution as you can imagine, but it had its significance. The resolution simply says that if any priest of this diocese blesses a committed relationship of two people, then this diocese will protect and affirm that priest's right to do that. In effect, we declared every priest free from pressure from the church hierarchy. At least they've got to get through me to get to the priests who perform union ceremonies.

GETTING MY book *Living in Sin?* into print was something of an ordeal. The book came about when I was contacted by a young editor at Abingdon Press, the publishing arm of the United Methodist Church. In the letter he told me that he was aware of newspaper stories across the country regarding our diocese and quotations from me on the issue of homosexuality, the blessing of gay unions, and sexuality in general. He said that he was interested in having me write a book on this subject. I was interested in doing the book and had reams of material that I had prepared during a series of debates I had had with an ultraconservative bishop from Eau Claire, Wisconsin. I basically put all of my notes together and wrote the book between Easter and September 1, 1987.

The one thing I decided when I wrote *Living in Sin?* was that I would make specific recommendations. Anybody can discuss these issues, but what do you do about it? So I came up with various proposals: the idea of recognizing a commitment that young people make when they're not ready to get married, the idea of blessing a divorce, the idea of blessing a gay union, and so on.

That December, after handing in the manuscript, I met with all the top executives at Abingdon. I was wined and dined. They were really excited. They were planning big publicity, including a national media tour and extensive advertising. They clearly thought they had a winner. When I read some of the other titles in their catalog, I could understand why.

About the first of March 1988, a month before publication, they put ads in several publications, including a Methodist publication called the *Circuit Rider*. Then about a week before the publication date, I got a call from my editor. I assumed that he had good news for me, but he said, "Jack, I don't know quite how to tell you this, but we've canceled your book." I said, "You've done what?" He explained to me that they had gotten some very negative reactions from Methodist church circles about the ad they had run in *Circuit Rider*. He went on to say, "There's been a letter-writing and telegram campaign directed at our board, and the chairman of our board has simply come in and said we can't publish this book. The United Methodist Church is meeting in St. Louis sometime in April, and it's going to be a major issue. If we publish this book it's going to look like we're advocating a point of view."

Abingdon Press put out a press release, which I thought was derogatory to me. They were trying to cover themselves for what I thought was a cowardly decision. Among other things, the press release said the book was too provocative. I wrote the chairman of the board of trustees and told him that I thought he had mistreated me. He never wrote back. They had paid me five thousand dollars as an advance. It's not a great big advance, but it's five thousand dollars they'll never see again. I met my part of the contract. They did not.

Within forty-eight hours after that press release hit the trail, I had something like nine publishing houses calling me wanting to publish the book. Harper & Row was one of them, and I was delighted to go back to them. They had published my previous books.

Living in Sin? came out two months later, and from that point on, it was a mind-boggling experience. To me it was like running for president. I traveled about fifteen thousand miles in those two weeks.

I had interviews in airports. I had six media events a day. I had escorts. I rode in stretch limousines. I was interviewed by celebrities. Kathleen Sullivan was one of the first to interview me—and one of the loveliest, I might add. She told me, "I wish we had bishops like you in my church."

I've emerged now as a person who's doing a lot of college lectures. I started out at a great big college called Lynchburg College, in Lynchburg, Virginia. Some students from Jerry Falwell's Liberty University came over to heckle me, and, I'm told, Falwell himself preached against me that Sunday. I've gone on to speak at many universities, which I really love, because that gets my message outside the walls of my institution. If it remains a church book, it will have a very limited impact.

From the thousands of letters I've received, it's become obvious to me that I have gotten my message out. Overwhelmingly the negative mail comes from religious people. Overwhelmingly the positive mail comes from people who are either gay or have had a primary experience with gay people: parents, sisters, and spouses. A lot of the gay letters are anonymous, particularly the ones from Roman Catholic priests. They simply identify themselves, but say they can't risk signing their names even in a letter to a non–Roman Catholic bishop. I appreciate that. The letters are rending; they bring tears to your eyes. I've gotten letters from mothers and fathers of gay people who have said, "Your book has helped me love my child again, and I want to thank you for that."

MOST OF the hostility I've experienced because of my views has been expressed in the letters I've received. But there was an incident at my wife's funeral in Richmond, Virginia, where I was confronted in person by a very angry woman. In the Episcopal church, when you go into church, the custom is that you kneel and pray. We went in about ten minutes before the funeral to pray and to listen to the organist, who was a good friend of mine.

We came in the side door of the church and sat down in the front row. I was on the aisle next to the casket. My oldest daughter and her husband, my middle daughter and her husband, and my youngest daughter and her boyfriend were seated next to me. I knelt to say my opening prayer, and as I knelt, a woman of about seventy-five got up from a pew in the back of the church—I was told this later—walked down the aisle, pushed the casket aside, and took her walking cane and whacked me on the back. The only thing I can remember is her face, this snarling face. And she said, "You son of a bitch!" and walked out the side door. She walked past my pall bearers and said to them, "I've been wanting to tell that bastard what I think of him for years, and I finally got the opportunity!" With that she disappeared. I have no earthly idea who the lady was, none at all, but I assume that she was angry over the gay issue because that was the hot issue at the time.

When the service was over, everybody filed out. Because I have so many friends in Richmond and because I was the rector of that church for eight years, there were a lot of people who wanted to talk to me before we left for the cemetery. While I was talking with people, I saw the young man who had carried the cross and led the procession. He was in his early thirties. This was two o'clock on a Wednesday afternoon, which meant he had to get off work to provide this service at the church. I went up to him and said, "I'd like to thank you for taking the time to be here. It meant a great deal to me." He responded by saying, "Bishop Spong, you don't know me, but I know you. I'm a member of the Richmond chapter of Integrity." That's the organization for Episcopal gay and lesbian people. And he said, "We called the church and asked what we could do at the service. They said that they wanted to organize a choir and needed somebody to carry the cross." So four members of the Richmond chapter of Integrity— three members of the choir and this man carrying the cross—volunteered. Then he said, "We wanted to do something for the person who has done so much for us."

Well, that was exhilarating and saving. When I put those two stories together, they really typify the kind of response I get. My mail could be put in those two categories. About half my mail comes from people who are like that woman. The other letters are like the ones I get from somebody in Nevada or Montana who has seen an Associated Press wire story about me and sends me a six-page handwritten letter in which he reveals his entire life to me. These people don't know me from Adam; I'm a complete stranger to them. But because they've read a blurb in the newspaper that I believe that homosexual people are normal human beings, they're willing to take that risk and write me the history of their lives. The loneliness that this reveals is just incredible. It's as if they haven't had anybody to talk to for fifty years. And they probably haven't.

These letters say to me that these people have seen a little glimpse of acceptance and redemption in what I've said. And the words have come from someone called a bishop, who they identify with the heretofore rejecting religious establishment, with the power structure, and with God. But now my words come with grace to these gay and lesbian people. They are used to being condemned; they have come to expect rejection and hostility, which has been so killing. Now here is a voice that says, "Not only are you not condemned, but you are loved. And it's not just a bishop who loves you, but it's the God this bishop represents who loves you." That's a powerful lesson that cuts through a lot of garbage, and it's a healing lesson I can bring to people.

Now, you've got to remember that my homophobia was at one time as deep as anybody else's. But I know that there's something really wrong with the way we have treated gay and lesbian people historically. And I do believe that prejudice against gay people is going to go the way of witchcraft—soon, I hope. It's still around. Believe me—I know better than most that the anger is still around.

The Television Anchor

Tom Cassidy

AIDS HAS forced many secretly gay public figures—from politicians and athletes to entertainers and famous designers—out of the closet and into the public eye. Ironically, the disease that has claimed more than one hundred thousand people—most of them, gay men—has helped prove what gay and lesbian activists have long asserted, that many successful, prominent, well-loved Americans are also gay.

Tom Cassidy, business news anchor for Cable News Network and host of CNN's "Pinnacle" interview series, knew that he had to keep his homosexuality a secret. His career depended upon it. Tom had come a long way from the Boston projects where he grew up; he had achieved status, respect, and financial security and loved his work. He knew that there were no publicly gay men or women reporting the news on national television, and there was no reason for him to believe that he would be allowed to become the first in an industry that is so sensitive about its image with the viewing public. By the time Tom got to CNN, keeping his homosexuality hidden from his colleagues had become second nature.

Even after he was diagnosed with AIDS in July 1988, Tom did what was necessary to keep his personal life a secret. He had little doubt that having AIDS and being gay, if revealed, would destroy his career as a national television journalist. For a year and a half, Tom did his best to hide the truth from almost everyone he knew. Ultimately, he could not keep his illness a secret. But little did he know that the truth would make him an influential pioneer as the first national television journalist to come out of the closet about his AIDS diagnosis and homosexuality.

In person Tom Cassidy looks a little older than he does on television. His hair is thinning. His broad face is lined and a bit gaunt, the skin tight around his high and well-defined cheekbones. Yet, at forty-one, Tom still has the solid build of a college football player, a strong voice, and a boyish smile. As long as he was seated, except for an occasional deep cough, you wouldn't have known that Tom had had two close brushes with death since his AIDS diagnosis. It was only when he walked down the hall to his office that you could see the toll the disease had taken. He moved slowly, deliberately, occasionally lurching to one side or the other. Tom said that for the first time in his life he knew what it meant to be physically vulnerable.

I was raised a poor kid in a public housing project in Roslindale, which is a part of Boston. Ours was considered a fashionable housing project, although there was no grass anywhere to be seen. My mother always thought my flat feet were attributable to the lack of grass. They eventually put in grass when I was older, but only behind fences.

My mother and father split up when I was two and a half. My father was a profound alcoholic and probably an abuser of wives and children. I didn't see him again until I was eighteen, and then only for a day. My mother raised my sister and me. My sister is four and a half years older than I am.

I think I always knew I was different, which was probably reinforced by this interesting experience I had when I was six. One day the police were at my mother's door. Somehow they had found out that a group of us boys had been playing with this older kid, who was sixteen. He was playing with us sexually. What we did felt pretty good to me, but the way it was handled made it seem incredibly scandalous and dirty. It was very frightening for me because they took us all down to the courthouse where I was questioned about what happened. They eventually decided to put this older kid on probation. Because of society's strong reaction, even at that age, I was very reluctant to try anything like this again.

My family never talked about it. I'm sure my mother just wanted to contain the damage, which in a Catholic family meant not talking about it. It just went away, but everybody in the project knew about what had happened.

PLAYING FOOTBALL got me out of the projects. I was a good football player and a pretty smart kid. I went to the University of Massachusetts on a football scholarship and hated it. It was like a zoo. I was expected to be a football player *only*. They wanted me to be a phys. ed. major, and I wanted to be a liberal arts major. So I applied to this little place called Bowdoin College in Maine.

It was hard to get into Bowdoin. I was not up to the standards of the college. Dick Moll, the director of admissions, told me he thought it was sort of outrageous that I should think of going to Bowdoin, given my record. So I asked him who his boss was. He was intrigued by this very cocky eighteen-year-old kid. It was pretty clear to him that I had high ambitions and that I was trying to claw my way out of the ghetto. He thought it would be interesting for me *and* for Bowdoin

Tom Cassidy in 1967 as a freshman at the University of Massachusetts. *(Courtesy Lorraine Potts)*

if I were to go to school there. So he gave me some standards that I had to hit while I was still at U. Mass. I went to U. Mass. for a whole year. For me it became a prep school, the biggest prep school in the world. After a year at U. Mass., I transferred to Bowdoin and went there for a full four years.

In college I wasn't quite clicking with women—it was very forced. I was very shy. All these other kids were able to get these great-looking dates, but I wasn't forward enough to do that, partly because I didn't really want to. So I would end up having a date to go to the prom, but she was no great looker. Getting a date was important to me because I had all these friends who were straight, and I was trying to keep up with them.

My junior year, I went away to Mount Holyoke for a semester. I really tried one final time to get head over heels about women. I was one of twelve men on the Mount Holyoke campus, and the women were all over you. While it didn't feel great to me, I dated women, but I tended to notice the guys women dated more than I noticed the women.

When I went back to Bowdoin my senior year, it had become

crystal clear to me that I was in love with my roommate, Whit. Whit was straight. He was a very good athlete—he played football and hockey. I just told him what my feelings were, that I thought I was gay and that I had homosexual leanings to the point where I was lusting after him. With Whit I felt passion for the first time in my life. He was very understanding about it. He's a very secure person and wasn't threatened at all. He told his girlfriend. You know, when you're students you think in very open-minded ways. But it ultimately became a real frustration for me.

DURING THE years I was at Bowdoin, I was very aware of the gay rights movement because I realized I had a vested interest. Also, the civil rights movement was going on at the same time. A lot of my friends as a kid were black, so I was very sensitive to civil rights issues. With these two movements, there was a sense of liberation in the air, liberation for two groups I considered the good guys: black people and gays. The society seemed to be getting more tolerant. But I felt I was on the periphery of what was happening in the gay rights movement—the movement just didn't fit into my priorities at the time. I was busy doing other things. I was what they refer to as a Big Man on Campus, running a lot of things like fraternity houses and student organizations.

WHEN I graduated from Bowdoin, I went to Europe on my own. I had to get away from Whit, so I just left altogether and traveled for almost a year. That's really where I came out. Not in a heavy way—I think I probably went to bed with men four times the whole year in Europe. I remember meeting this American in London who was doing his Ph.D. at the British Museum. This was the first time I was involved in a cruising or pickup situation. I didn't know what to do. He was older, so he knew what he was doing. We went back to my place in London and proceeded to chase each other around. A pillow fell off the bed and landed on the heater and caught fire. Oh, it was very traumatic for me—very traumatic. You want to talk about interruptus—that was really frightening.

After Europe I moved here to New York and went to work for *Reader's Digest*. That was in 1973. In a lot of ways, I went to New York to come out, although I didn't plan on coming out at work. I thought that would be a liability. *Reader's Digest* was a very conservative company, which always made me feel a little uneasy, but they were wonderful to me. I worked on the publishing side, which I quickly realized was essentially the advertising business. I didn't like Madison Avenue—I thought they were a bunch of phonies—and really thought all the fun was being enjoyed on the editorial side. But I didn't know how to do it; I wasn't good enough. So I decided that I would go to both the graduate school of business and the graduate school of journalism at Columbia University.

When I graduated from Columbia, my choices for work in television news were Eugene, Oregon, or Butte, Montana. The investment bankers were lining up to hire me, but I couldn't get a good job in this stupid business. So off I went to a television station in Eugene, Oregon. Nine months later I went to San Francisco. And nine months after that I got a job in Chicago as business editor for Mutual Radio.

All during this time I was involved with somebody. I got involved in September of 1974 with John Woods. John was twelve years older than I was, a real jet-set New Yorker and a lot of fun. He really encouraged me with my career. We were very close, even while I was away working in other places. We talked all the time.

Right when I landed in Chicago, John, who in many ways would have been identified as my lover, took the wrong person home and was brutally murdered. He was massacred, just destroyed. I got the phone call about John on a Saturday morning. It was very hard. It happened about two months after my mother had died suddenly of a stroke. John had been very helpful to me during that period. It was a difficult time for me. I had lost the two most important people in my life.

What was very strange was that I couldn't tell a lot of people about losing John. I remember the general manager of the station in Chicago didn't want to let me go to the funeral because I had only gotten there three days before. He said, "You've just started here. It's not family." Of course, he didn't know who John was to me, but I told him that this was a very important person to me. I told him that he would have to trust my judgment, but he started to really contest my decision. So I said, "It's not negotiable," and I turned around and walked out.

I went to Duncan, Oklahoma, where John was to be buried. I sat right between his mother and his father. They knew who I was, although it was never discussed. They were wonderful people in a very simple Oklahoma sense.

The whole thing makes me sad, very sad. I couldn't grieve in any public way. I was in shock, and I couldn't talk to anybody about it except via telephone with friends here in New York. But everyone was so devastated by it, because it was such an awful murder, that it was hard to talk about it. I got involved in another relationship very quickly, one that I kind of forced. I met the person about two weeks after John was killed. That person became my second lover, and the relationship lasted about ten years.

I WAS in Chicago for about a year and a half before CNN contacted me. CNN got started in 1981 and nobody knew whether it was going to make it, so everyone was a little cautious. But I went for an interview and decided to make the switch to CNN as a newscaster and reporter for the business news department.

Staying in the closet at work was not hard at all. I've always felt like I had some sort of mechanism that let me separate work from play. And once you make a decision to separate the parts of your life, you get the habit down. I was very good at separating my lives—I had to be. Before I got sick, I was a rising star for CNN. I was very concerned about career growth. I didn't want to complicate my career by having people know.

First of all, I made a point of not socializing with people I worked with. I could be holier than thou with this "professionalism" business. Over the years people sometimes didn't understand my view on this, but that sort of professional behavior is rewarded in journalism.

I also never got involved with anybody I worked with. I was very wary. I would police myself diligently about ever being attracted to any of the kids who work here. You've got great-looking young men and women who come through here, so you couldn't help but notice. But I made a conscious decision not to work with those people. I would avoid them—I didn't want to be enticed. I never wanted to put myself in a situation where I could be accused of favoritism, particularly because I've always been in a powerful position here.

Outside of work I was more open. In the 1980s I remember going to a dinner for the Human Rights Campaign Fund.* Because I was an on-air person I had to think about that. It made me a little nervous to just think about going, but I was committed to not living in fear. HRCF was a very important group. They were the gay community's primary lobbying group. I contributed money, but I thought it was even more important both for the group and for me that I be seen there because I was a public person. I was willing to take the risk of asserting my public support for what HRCF was doing.

I knew that I was opening myself up to potential criticism. That

---

*A political action committee that represents issues of concern to the gay and lesbian community.

concerned me, but I wasn't afraid of being blackmailed as someone in my position would have been years ago. I also went to bars, and people would chat with me. They recognized me, but it was all very quiet and private.

I FIRST got the news that I tested positive for HIV on October 19, 1987, the day of the stock market crash. I was too busy reporting from the New York Stock Exchange to think about it. When I finally had time to think about it, I didn't know what being HIV-positive meant because I felt good. I was doing a lot of work. I was traveling two hundred thousand miles a year and being the attack-dog reporter in economics. I was going full speed. I had producers who were catching me as I bounced off the walls.

It was in the spring of 1988 when I first thought I might have AIDS. I came home from work one night and put on the soundtrack from *Out of Africa*. It's beautiful music. All the lights were out in my apartment, and I was looking out on my street. For some reason I was feeling very emotional and particularly sensitive, and I thought that I might have AIDS. I felt, *Something's happening. Something's happening.* I remember it making me very melancholic because in 1988 we didn't think there was anything that could be done. These were powerful emotions to deal with as I listened to this beautiful music. I remember thinking, *Well, gee, I'm going to have AIDS, and I'm going to die.*

In July I took a week's vacation and went out to Fire Island to shake this cold—or, at least, that's what I thought I had. I came back to work that Monday, and I still couldn't shake this damn cold. So I called my doctor, and he said I should come to see him that afternoon. He took a chest X-ray. He was very surprised: It was classic pneumocystis. He said, "Do you know what that means?" And I said, "AIDS?" My instinct was, *I have to go back to work!* It was my first day back from vacation. He said, "You are not allowed to go back to work. You are to go home and pack a bag and go to Mount Sinai hospital."

When I got home, I called the office and said that my doctor was putting me in the hospital and that I had pneumonia. I was very much in shock. I didn't know what it meant to have AIDS. Even though I was tuned into the AIDS situation, I didn't know anybody who had AIDS. But I knew it was real serious because once I was in the hospital I could see the doctors were really worried. And I felt terrible. Terrible! I was a jock and I had never felt terrible. I had always been a very able runner, for instance, and suddenly my lungs weren't right—that was a strange feeling. And I had never been in a hospital before—that was a very powerful experience.

I almost didn't make it. They had to take me through a regimen of treatments that I had more and more trouble handling because of the toxicity of the drugs. My fever went up to 106 degrees. In the middle of all this, I had to undergo this dreadful procedure called a bronchoscopy. No one took my temperature before we did the bronchoscopy and, as it turns out, it was about 105. I almost had a heart attack on the table. It was unbelievable. It was very traumatic.

When I came back from the bronchoscopy there was another transport guy waiting to take me to X-ray. I said, "I'm not going anywhere." But he didn't listen; he was dragging me off the side of the bed and putting me in the chair when I did this routine right out of *The Exorcist.* If my head could have spun around, it would have. This stream of blood and red stuff went shooting out of me. The attendant finally realized I was sick, and he left rubber. He just split.

I WAS scared; I wasn't prepared to die. It was such a shock. It was kind of rude; it really was—I wasn't ready. I hadn't said good-bye to anybody. It wasn't my time. I'm certainly not supposed to just suddenly die. And nobody knew where I was, almost no one knew what the situation was. My family didn't know; nobody here at CNN knew—they didn't even know I was gay, not really. It's amazing how people believe what they want to believe.

For a solid year and a half, I didn't tell anybody at work that I was sick. You just didn't tell anyone. I was trying to fight the best way I could. And in 1988, the world was not as compassionate or understanding of AIDS as it is now in 1990. I was afraid of what would happen if they knew. So my objective was to *contain* it because I thought I would pay a big price if I didn't. I was afraid I'd lose my job and my insurance. I could see that AIDS was very expensive. For these reasons, probably a maximum of six people in my life knew I was sick.

During that year and a half after I got out of the hospital, I was popping those AZT capsules and going to work every day and feeling wobbly. AZT was very useful, but it was a very heavy pill for me. Eventually I became so anemic from the AZT that I had to have nine transfusions. I would go and get the transfusions and then rush to work. This whole time I was on television, and the camera doesn't lie. I didn't look that bad—I looked quite different, but I didn't look that dreadful. Extra makeup helped. It's unbelievable what my capacity was to adapt to this. I eventually came off AZT because it was making me too anemic. I went on DDI instead.

Everything was going hunky-dory from January of this year [1990] until April. Then, on Easter Sunday, I was in Boston and I wasn't feeling right. It was my stomach. I had never had a problem before with my stomach. There had been some signs of discomfort, probably a couple of weeks earlier, but I have a very high pain threshold, which is a liability in this kind of situation.

While my sister was preparing this splendid meal for a late-afternoon family dinner, I just was not feeling great. So I got her to push the dinner up and eventually I left. My nephew took me to the airport. I was really hurting; I had to decide what to do. Should I let him drop me off and go to Mass. General? Or do I jump on the shuttle and get down to Mount Sinai? I jumped on the shuttle and came down to New York.

When I got to New York, I didn't go right to the hospital. I went to my house and called my doctor. It was a Sunday. He got back to me in fifteen minutes. I was laying down. I said, "Well, Ray, I'm feeling better." He said, "Maybe, but you're to meet me at Mount Sinai in twenty minutes."

As it turns out, my pancreas was six times the normal size. So they put a tube through my nose and down my throat. It was dreadful, just dreadful. The treatment for pancreatitis is essentially nothing. You can't eat or drink a thing, and your pancreas makes up its mind if it wants to live or die. I didn't realize how close I was to dying, but a couple of weeks after I got out of the hospital, two doctors said, "We really didn't think you were going to make it."

BEFORE I left for the Mount Sinai emergency room to meet my doctor, like a responsible reporter, I called the assignment desk and said I would not be in the next day. For some reason this message got lost. So on Monday they couldn't find me and they didn't know why. This had never happened in all the years I'd been at CNN. Throughout the day the level of worry really started to rise. They called the police. They called the FBI. They ended up calling morgues. Then they called my sister, who didn't know where I was. So she called my college roommate, Whit. He was one of the few people who knew I was sick. He remembered that when I was in the hospital the first time I was at Mount Sinai. So he called Mount Sinai.

By this time, I must tell you, there was a real brouhaha going on here at CNN. They thought I'd been murdered. The people in New York were communicating with the people in Atlanta—major worry.

Whit called me in the hospital, and I answered the phone. At that point I think they were giving me Demerol. Whit said, "Butch!" I used to be called Butch Cassidy when I was in college. I said, "Hi,

Whit, how are ya?" I was real casual. He started to tell me what was going on, and I thought, *Oh, no!* Then he told me that it was time to tell my sister what was going on and asked me what he should tell her. And I said, because I was hurting, "Tell her everything. Everything!" Up until then I had never discussed with her the fact that I was gay, much less the fact that I had AIDS. Whit said, "Are you sure?" I said, "Yes." He told her, and she called me twenty minutes later. She was great.

Then Whit had to tell CNN that they had found me at Mount Sinai. Then I was able to explain to them that I had called in the day before and talked to this woman on the assignment desk. They found the message in a computer file, but it was in the wrong one. At that point CNN still did not know that I had AIDS. They just knew that I had pancreatitis.

When I came back to work, which was a week after I got out of the hospital, I went right back on the air. I didn't look great, but I had looked worse. After I finished my first day back, my boss, Lou Dobbs, asked me to come into his office. Now, you have to understand that Lou Dobbs is one of the most important people in my life. He's clearly a brother figure, and so powerful that he could almost be a father figure. He's a western cowboy, a macho guy who was really a very good friend of mine. His wife, who I used to coanchor with in Oregon, is an excellent friend of mine. Our relationship was very intense; we used to fight a lot. I was afraid of what his reaction would be to both the fact I had AIDS and was gay.

So I went into his office and he said, "How are you doing?" And I said, trying to put the best foot forward, "Great! Great! It's great to be back!" He said, "How sick were you?" And I said, "Well, I was pretty sick." And he said, "How sick?" I said, "I was very sick." And he said, "*How* sick?" I said, "Well, I have AIDS." His eyes just sort of rolled back. But he totally surprised me—totally. I did not have any negative reaction from him. He said, "What do you want me to do? Do you want me to tell anybody or do you want me not to tell anybody?" I said, "I think you'd better tell everyone."

This was very much a feeling of relief for me. By this time I was tired: I was tired of living a lie about having AIDS and also about being gay. The two issues were so intertwined at that point. I was ready. For the last two years I had lived a very difficult and sheltered, and fabricated life where all I would do was come to work. Because of the AZT, I used to have to sneak home sometimes and lay down during the day when I had time off. I was living in a double closet. It was a nightmare.

By five o'clock that night Lou Dobbs had told all the managers here. They all came out of his office crying and wanted to hug me. Word was starting to spread; people were shocked. They had to do "Moneyline," which is the premier program we have. So Dobbs scheduled a meeting for the whole department after the program. It was conference-called to our other bureaus. And he told them. That night the news that I had AIDS was put in our CNN database. So it went to all twenty-two of our bureaus, a couple of thousand people.

I don't know what I expected to happen once everyone knew, but I feared rejection. First of all I thought people would freak because I had AIDS. I was afraid people would want to walk around the office wearing rubber gloves. But I came in the next day . . . and . . . there were flowers . . . and . . . there were cards . . . and a lot of messages.

People said they were sorry. They said I should hang in there and not give up. They hugged me; they were very supportive. Also, they all became little AIDS students. For many of them I was the first AIDS patient they had ever known personally. They were very upset—very upset. Newsrooms are like families. They were trying to deal with that upset and also they were trying to support me. And they watch me. Sometimes I'm wobbly on my feet, so every once in a while I may bounce off a column in the office or something, and they all run to help.

There was a lot of love. My life hasn't been the same since.

AFTER SEEING the impact that all of this had on the newsroom, I realized that, given my role as a television anchor, I could do some good beyond CNN. So when I had the opportunity to go public, I said yes.

There's a woman who sits across from me at CNN, Beverly Schuch. Her husband is Mike Taibbi, a reporter for WCBS television here in New York. Mike asked Beverly whether she thought I might consent to doing a story, and she told him that she had no idea, that it was up to him to call me. I didn't know Mike very well, but I knew him—he's a very serious reporter. When he said, "I want to meet with you," I knew that he didn't just want to tell me he was sorry—he would have said that on the phone. So I went to CBS, and Mike was very nervous about dealing with me. I was real cool, real cool. He made his pitch and said, "Would you agree to participate in a series that we want to do about AIDS through your eyes?" I said, "Sure." I didn't even blink. That kind of threw him because he thought he was going to have to sell me on it.

I didn't have to be sold because I wanted to do some good. I really wanted to make a political statement as a gay person, as well as an

AIDS patient. I didn't think I had anything to lose by trying it, and I thought I could make AIDS patients feel better. I could make the public understand that some of their TV newsmen are gay and sick. I'm one of the good guys. Everyone identified me as one of the good guys, and there are millions of people who have seen me on television. I wanted them to know that a favorite of theirs could get this disease—and, secondarily, that he happened to be gay.

I also thought that maybe I could help show people that AIDS is not just a gay problem. When gay people die of AIDS, the whole society is so much poorer because in a lot of ways, gay people are the spice of life in this country and in others. The straight world hasn't really thought about it. Life isn't as much fun in this country after losing eighty-five thousand creative, well-intentioned, funny, productive people in the prime of their lives. The straight world sort of knew it, but they really needed to have it mapped out right in their face. And I became a face. I am a face. I make my living essentially being a face. What I decided to do was to lend that face to AIDS.

THE EARLY CBS pieces were very powerful and very emotional. These were not normal local news stories. These pieces were very long. CBS was committed to it and very supportive, and they promoted it heavily. I left town and went on vacation when the stories ran. They landed with an amazing impact. When I came back, there were probably a hundred messages for me. You know the media—they steal from each other all the time. So *People* magazine suddenly wanted to do a piece, which they did. Then I got a call from "The Donahue Show."

Because of all the publicity, I've gotten three hundred letters from people I have never met before in my life. In addition, I've heard from everybody I have ever known, dating back to when I was five years old and living in the projects. My athletic director from Bowdoin, Sid Watson, wrote. I got another letter from the equipment manager, Donnie Orr, who's retired now. These are hard-boiled Mainers. They understand an economy of words—they don't say a lot, but when they say something, it's usually very meaningful. They just said they were real sorry. They were very loving. It didn't matter a bit to them that I was gay; they were much more upset by my being sick. Sid said that for so many years he had gotten such a kick out of being able to point to me on television and tell the kids at the college that that's what they should be. "You should grow up and be like him."

There's a whole other dimension to it now, but they're still proud of me. I can see that. But I also know that some people now have had to think about their disposition toward gay people because of what they've learned about me, and hopefully they've really been stretched.

MY WHOLE life is now so tenuous. AIDS breaks your life and any ambition you have. I don't dream anymore. I don't have ambition. And this was a guy who was very ambitious, whose whole life was made of dreams. It's hard to see the future when you think you may only have another year to live.

People don't realize how much it hurts when they declare that AIDS is a death sentence because a lot of AIDS patients are not willing to believe that they're really going to die from this thing. They're hoping that they won't. I don't want to die. I know I'm getting very good medical attention. But I also can see how little they can do as I slide. I'm actually on an upswing right now—I've even put on eight pounds. But I don't trust it. Your body is not your best friend the way it used to be. This body of mine now has a mind of its own, and I have to try to keep up with it.

But I'm hanging on. They're accommodating me here at CNN. I'm still able to do my job, and I could still be a very effective reporter. I have no dementia or cerebral problems, so I can still judge stories with the best of them. I don't move as well as I used to, and I don't look as good, but I'm still an asset. When it becomes bad enough, I'll know it's time to leave or to pull back. But for now, I'm working five days a week, eight hours a day. It's very important to me to keep a normal regimen because it reminds me I'm alive. You know, when you're a person like me, you define your life by what you do. This is my life.

IF NOT for AIDS, I don't think I would have come out right now, but it would have only been a matter of time. I just don't like secrets. Plus there's a part of you, when you have to live your life as a secret, that's angry. You're angry because you're forced to be closeted for practical reasons. It makes you feel a little bit like a second-class citizen.

I don't have any regrets about coming out. No regrets, which is a real amazement to me. I didn't think that people would be this accepting. But it's probably been made easier as a person with AIDS. I don't know if people would be as sympathetic and supportive as they have been if I didn't have AIDS. It's easy to feel sorry for the cripple. That's sort of a sarcastic way of putting it. I have genuinely been amazed at the acceptance.

Before AIDS, I was kind of living the American dream: the kid who climbs out of the ghetto and grows up to be on television. Even though my dream has turned into a nightmare, the dreams and the journey were wonderful, just great. Even though I may die from AIDS, I'm not real angry about it. This sounds very strange. I'm not soured; I'm not going to say the world is a dreadful place because of it, because it hasn't been. I got a bad break. Hopefully these bad breaks will go away soon. People won't get sick. And gay people should keep stretching, like I did, and understand that they can do almost anything they want with their lives—almost. When I was a kid, I really did want to grow up to be president of the United States. But I couldn't because I'm gay.

I think that maybe I've helped pave the way for kids who dream about having the kind of job I've had. I'm a respected news person. There are gay people in so many lines of work. I like being part of that in a very obvious way. I like the public knowing that now. It makes me feel free. It really does.

The Role Models

Cecelia Walthall and
Nancy Andrews

MORE AND more leaders in the gay and lesbian rights movement have come to recognize that the struggle for full equal rights depends more than ever on broad-based public support and that public opinion will be changed only through a one-on-one effort. Ever larger numbers of gay and lesbian people will need to come out of the closet and confide in their friends, families, and colleagues. To that end, coming out of the closet now even has its own annual holiday: National Coming Out Day, which has been celebrated every October 11 since 1988 with events and publicity campaigns in cities across the country.

Nancy Andrews, a photographer for the local newspaper in Fredericksburg, Virginia, and Cecelia Whitehall, a student at Mary Washington College in Fredericksburg, believe that being themselves is the best way they can contribute to achieving equal rights. By being open about their homosexuality and their relationship, they believe they will force people around them to confront their biases and the stereotypes on which those biases are built. They hope to deprive people of the excuse that they "don't know any gay people," and they want to show other gay people that they don't have to hide.

Cecelia and Nancy met in 1986 through friends. They share an attic apartment in an old house in downtown Fredericksburg, a historic town about an hour south of Washington, D.C. Nancy was born in 1963 and grew up in rural Virginia. Cecelia was born in 1965 and grew up in Richmond.

Cecelia:

We first got involved in gay rights at school through PAL—People for Alternative Lifestyles. We were going through the various metamorphoses of gay rights awakening. We were getting to the point where we felt the importance of gay civil rights action and we wanted some sort of group we could work in. Nance and I are both active, do-things people. And I don't think either of us was happy—and I don't think we're very happy now—with the status of gay rights, which is to say, they don't exist. For one thing, you don't have the right to live as an openly married couple would, which is what we consider our relationship. Ours is modeled along marriagelike lines.

Nancy:

We feel a lot of discrimination as a couple. We could join the Y, but we couldn't go in as a family. We would have to pay two individual fees.

Cecelia:

There are always threats of antigay violence.

Nancy:

Antigay laws are on the books. You can say, "Well, they're not enforced." But that's even worse because they're just there to pass moral judgment on you. And they can be enforced. Just look at the Hardwick* case.

Cecelia:

Then there's insurance.

Nancy:

Cecelia's a student. She's not working, but she can't go on my insurance policy at work as a spouse. I'm not yet ready to push those issues, but at one point I will be.

I've taken this all in stages. I've felt the need to get more involved with things now because I wasn't involved when I was a student at the

---

*On August 3, 1982, the police arrested Michael Hardwick, a twenty-nine-year-old Georgia man, in his own home for having oral sex with another man and charged him with sodomy. Under Georgia law, sodomy is a felony that is punishable by up to twenty years in prison. Hardwick challenged his arrest in a case that eventually landed in the U.S. Supreme Court. In a landmark decision on June 30, 1986, the Supreme Court ruled 5 to 4 that the Constitution does not protect homosexual relations between consenting adults, even in the privacy of their own homes. Therefore, individual states retained the right to outlaw private homosexual acts. The ruling was considered a major defeat for advocates of gay rights and is often compared to the notorious 1896 *Plessy vs. Ferguson* case, which enshrined the "separate but equal" rationale for racial segregation. Four years later, retired Justice Lewis F. Powell, Jr., who cast the deciding vote against Hardwick, said, "I think I probably made a mistake."

University of Virginia [UVA]. I was still discovering myself then. I wasn't even ready to show up at their Lesbian and Gay Student Union meetings.

I gradually came out to more and more people on the school newspaper where I was managing editor, but at that stage I was not ready to stand up and address a group of people and say, "Hello, my name is Nancy Andrews, and I am gay." That came later. But even without doing that so publicly, you can do that on an individual basis with your friends, with your roommate, with your parents, and co-workers.

Cecelia:

Every time you tell someone, not only are you having an impact on them, but they're going to relate some of that to their friends and family members.

Nancy:

I think it matters if you tell just one person. It's a grass-roots effort, like in any political campaign. If gays were visible, if everyone knew who was gay, people who can now legitimately say, "I don't know anyone who is gay" couldn't say that. I think that's part of the reason I went back to UVA to speak before a group of students. The other reason I went back was that I felt I really hadn't helped any gay people at UVA when I was there. And I have a strong love for the school.

Through our involvement with PAL we attended a statewide conference of gay student organizations. At the conference, the UVA students were talking about some of the things that had happened during Gay Awareness Week, which had taken place on campus just a few weeks before. When I was a student at UVA, one of the things they did during that week was "Jeans Day": You wore jeans if you were in favor of gay rights. Everybody just laughed at it because everybody wears jeans anyway. But for the most recent Jeans Day, there had been a concerted effort to encourage people to wear khaki pants to show they didn't support gay rights. Also during the week there was a public display of affection on the lawn to protest that as gay people you don't get to walk down the street and hold hands with your lover without getting stares or worse. When the gay students had this demonstration, about fifteen hundred other students stood around and yelled obscenities at them.

I was really ashamed that this had happened at my school. I thought it was time for me to make a contribution. I was trying to figure out what I could do. So I wrote a letter to this professor. I told her who I was and that I'd taken her class two years before. I also told her I was gay and that if she would like to have a former student who was gay come speak to the class, I wanted to offer my services.

It's a gut class called Problems in Personal Adjustment. It meets at night for two hours once a week. Each class has a topic—one's on death and dying, one's on divorce, one's on sexuality. The project for the class is to go see a counselor for three sessions and then write a paper about it. The teacher's thinking behind the assignment is that everyone has something they can talk about with a counselor. The counselors, who are all graduate students, also get people to talk to. So it works out well for everyone.

I took this class senior year. I went to a counselor, and she said, "Well, what did you want to talk to me about?" I said, "Well, I'm gay." She froze and slid over in her seat. Obviously, she hadn't gotten to this part in the textbook yet. She didn't know what to do. There were so many things that she could have said that would have helped me. She could have said, "Hey, that's not a problem." But she didn't. It was a horrible experience talking to her.

So then you had to write a paper about talking with your counselor and what you got out of it. I'm a great procrastinator and I never did papers on time, but I did this paper a week *early!* I turned it in, in a sealed manila envelope because I was paranoid. I didn't want anyone to know I was gay.

So I got the paper back and the teacher had written, "I'm sorry. It must have been a horrible experience for you. If you'd like to come to talk to me. . . ." I really liked this teacher, and that's who I wrote to.

Well, she accepted my offer to speak to her class. But before I did this, I felt I had to come out to my family. If someone in the class asked me, "Do your parents know about you being gay?" I wanted to be able to answer that they did. So I went and told my parents. They were very supportive. I was surprised. My mom has been the organist in her Southern Baptist church for twenty-five years. Mom's very financially and materially oriented. It's very important to her that her children do well financially. She wrote me this letter and asked very practical questions. Not "How do you feel?" questions, but "Are you aware that this will make life more difficult for you?" I was quite happy with my family's response. That following Christmas, Cecelia was given in-law status as far as the Christmas gifts went.

Cecelia:

The materialist in me rejoiced.

Nancy:

So I went to UVA, and it was scary. Gosh. I had the first three-fourths of my talk typed up. Being a procrastinator, I hadn't finished. It was a class of about two hundred. I knew from being in the class myself that they would sit in groups. Four or five people from a sorority or fraternity house would all take the class together. You'd be sitting among these friends, so it was a great situation for you to be able to crack jokes about gay people to impress your fellow fraternity brothers. I felt they'd be hostile. The teacher warned me that there was the possibility that there would be a hostile reaction.

In my speech I planned to identify myself. I could have just said my name, and they wouldn't have known who I was. But I knew that people would have seen my work. I've sold more than six thousand posters of a photograph I took of the Rotunda, which is a building on campus that's sort of like Mecca for the university. There's a lightning bolt in the photo coming down behind the Rotunda. People buy it and hang it up in their rooms. My goal in my talk was to show them that a gay person had touched their lives. I was banking on the fact that they'd seen the poster, liked it, and possibly purchased it, not knowing that it was done by a gay person.

I dressed as I would have to go to work. I wore khaki pants, a white shirt, and a black cardigan. I didn't want to wear a dress. I wanted to feel comfortable in what I was wearing. But I knew my appearance was important because these people might not have ever met another gay person. How I looked was going to be their visual image of a gay person.

Before I gave my talk, I met with the teacher to go over a few things. I asked her where she looked into the audience. I wanted to be a good speaker. I didn't want to be a bumbling fool because, again, that would be their lasting impression until the next gay person they met. She warned me that I'd hear everything. I'd hear people opening wrappers, tape recorders clicking on and off, books being shuffled, bubble-gum being popped. Well, I started speaking and you couldn't hear a sound. People leaned forward in their seats and were staring right at me.

In the first part I essentially said, "I took this class three years ago, when you were first-year students." And I told them how I could have touched their lives. I said, "If you walked down the lawn, you would have gone past my room. If you read the *Cavalier Daily*, you would have seen my work. If you'd gone through sorority rush, I would have met you and voted on you." At that point where I was identifying myself, I cried. I was telling them who I was. There were no tissues. But I had to make it through. I was confronting all my fears from when I had been a student. My worst fear had been for people to know I was gay. I was afraid that people would think negatively of me, that they would now not respect any of my accomplishments.

Cecelia was sitting near the teacher, who physically grabbed her to keep her from running up to console me.

Cecelia:

I wasn't going to console you. I was going to drag you off the stage.

Nancy:

But I must have gotten through to these people because they sat there and listened. I just told them about what it was like for me being gay and closeted at UVA. And then I cried the second time when I talked about the reaction of my best friend. It's upsetting, and it still upsets me, because we had been such good friends. When I told her about being gay, we became very distant. I explained to them how it was such a *Catch-22* kind of thing. I needed my friends most at that time, but I also feared my friends because I didn't know how they would react.

The teacher had scheduled it so that I could talk for as little as thirty minutes or as long as an hour or an hour and a half. With the question-and-answer time, we went an hour and forty-five minutes. It was amazing. They asked me questions as if I was the sole representative of all gay people. They asked me these broad opinion questions. There were also really stupid questions. I remember one was, "Is any prejudice against you warranted?" There were other questions like, "What do you think about gay people adopting?" "What do I do if my roommate is gay?"

Afterwards there was a great round of applause. Then people came up to me and spoke to me. They thanked me for coming. Someone came up from my sorority. I had thought that someone like that would have been really hostile because the sorority would get a bad name if people knew that gay people had lived in that house.

It was so scary, but it turned out to be the most exhilarating thing I've ever done. I hope I accomplished my goal, which was primarily to help the gay people in that class. I knew there were people like me sitting in that class. I wrote my speech to go to gay people who wondered if they were gay or were struggling with that, who were closeted. And I also wrote it to people who were somewhat open to the idea, who were liberal, but were prejudiced just because they never thought about it and who were probably doing prejudiced things because they never thought about it. Maybe they said things or listened to gay jokes and laughed. Now, after hearing my talk, maybe in the future when they hear one of those jokes, they will associate that gay joke with me or someone else and won't think it's quite as funny.

Cecelia:

While Nancy was talking, I was thinking about my situation at work one time. I was an assistant manager at a retail clothing store. We hired a lot of college freshmen to work there, people who in many cases have inherited all of the prejudices and bigotries of their parents. And they're not yet at the point where they're thinking for themselves. So you heard a lot of highly prejudicial comments. Like one time, when an obviously gay man walked into the store. One of my salespeople looked at him and after he walked by said something to him about being a faggot. I said, "Wait a minute. I don't like the way you said that. I don't like the way you said that at all. He may be a gay man, but that doesn't make him any less of a human being." And we got into this whole big discussion.

At that point I hadn't come out to this particular salesperson. I was just standing up and saying, "Wait a minute. Bigotry is bad. And adopting this attitude that you're so good in comparison to everyone else in the universe and that you can pass judgment on everyone else is wrong, and you should think that through."

So he stopped and thought about it, and when I came out to him later, he gave me a big hug and a kiss and he laughed, and said, "You know, you've had a big effect on me. You've really made me more liberal." He's a staunch Republican and comes from a very patriarchal Roman Catholic Italian family. They're very conservative. He went on to say, "Before, if someone had told me she was gay, I might not have liked them because of it, but you're a nice person and you're good to me and that's what counts. And the fact that you're gay, I don't care so much about those sorts of things anymore."

I'm getting goose bumps as I talk about this. It was really a beautiful thing for him to say. He was exposed to me, and he had positive experiences with me. We came to recognize one another's mutual inherent worth as human beings and members of the same planet. So then you tell him that you're gay and it doesn't really matter. It's okay.

Nancy:

We've both been reading a lot of books about gay issues. One was *The Men with the Pink Triangle* and another was *The Pink Triangle*. They're about the Holocaust and what happened to gays in Germany after Hitler came to power. After we read the books, we were walking through all these antique shops downtown looking for a desk. And we were in this military antiques store. I walked past the counters and they had all these little badges from the Civil War and World War II. We were just on our way out of the store, and I stopped abruptly because I saw these concentration-camp badges. There was a green triangle and a yellow Star of David. Here was physical evidence of the Holocaust in Fredericksburg. Green was for criminals.

Cecelia:

Red was for politicals. The yellow Star of David was for Jews.

Nancy:

The pink triangle was for gays. And so I looked at these things and I was like, "Gosh, I wonder if he has any. . . ." So I asked the man if he had a pink one, but he didn't.

Cecelia:

Then we saw a yellow Star of David with a pink triangle superimposed. That would have been worn by someone at the negative end of the popularity spectrum in the concentration camps, a gay Jew.

Nancy:

It was forty bucks. I think we would have bought it if it was over a hundred. It was something we were just drawn to.

Cecelia:

It was tangible. It was worn by someone suffering the worst persecution of anyone. When you read the stories of the concentration camps, they always gave the gays the worst tasks. Thousands of gays

Cecelia Walthall *(left)* and Nancy Andrews in 1987. *(Courtesy Nancy Andrews and Cecelia Walthall)*

died, but that's a part of history you just don't hear about. But we have to remember what happened, so it's not repeated. Because it can happen at any time.

Nancy:

Maybe it won't happen to such a degree, but look at the guy whose military career is ruined because he's gay.

Cecelia:

I get charged when I touch that badge. It was attached to someone who was abused and tortured and possibly gassed or hung or shot, or who knows what. It belonged to one real person.

Nancy:

Things like this badge serve a purpose. We're trying to figure out what we want to do with it. We want to frame it. Then when our friends come through—gay friends and straight friends—they'll come by and they'll look at it. And it will make them think for a moment about what it means. And every time someone thinks about prejudice, I think you're closer to solving the problem.

Oh, one more thing about that badge. We paid for it with a check from our joint account. It has both our names on it.

IN MEMORIAM

Vito Russo died on November 7, 1990,
of complications from AIDS.

Chuck Rowland died on December 27, 1990,
of prostate cancer.

Tom Cassidy died on May 26, 1991,
of complications from AIDS.

Morty Manford died on May 14, 1992,
of complications from AIDS.

A. Damien Martin died on August 15, 1991,
of complications from AIDS.

Shirley Willer died on December 31, 1991,
of heart failure.

Index